UNDERSTANDING LEGISLATION

Understanding Legislation provides a practical, accessible guide to interpreting both English and European legislation of all kinds. This book can be used as a first port of call for practitioners and students on all matters of statutory construction. It is designed to serve as a succinct and authoritative point of reference for questions concerning sources of legislation, the anatomy and structure of differing instruments and matters of interpretation. As well as considering how to read statutory language, and the key principles and presumptions that the courts will apply, the book addresses how other legislation and materials can influence the interpretive exercise and in what way. To this end, it discusses the interpretive significance of the different components of legislation, the various external aids to construction that may exist, and the role of international law, the European Convention on Human Rights (through the Human Rights Act 1998) and EU law in interpreting domestic law. While the primary focus is on English law, the treatment of EU and international law will also serve as concise freestanding guidance as to the sources of EU law, the construction of EU legislation and the construction of treaties.

Understanding Legislation

A Practical Guide to
Statutory Interpretation

David Lowe and Charlie Potter

With a Foreword by The Rt Hon Lord Neuberger of Abbotsbury,
former President of the UK Supreme Court

•HART•

OXFORD • LONDON • NEW YORK • NEW DELHI • SYDNEY

HART PUBLISHING

Bloomsbury Publishing Plc

Kemp House, Chawley Park, Cumnor Hill, Oxford, OX2 9PH, UK

HART PUBLISHING, the Hart/Stag logo, BLOOMSBURY and the Diana logo are
trademarks of Bloomsbury Publishing Plc

First published in Great Britain 2018

Reprinted 2018 (twice)

A catalogue record for this book is available from the British Library.

Library of Congress Cataloging-in-Publication data

Names: Lowe, David, (Lawyer), author. | Potter, Charlie, (Lawyer), author.

Title: Understanding legislation : a practical guide to statutory interpretation /
By David Lowe, Charlie Potter.

Description: Portland, Oregon : Hart Publishing, 2018. | Includes bibliographical
references and index.

Identifiers: LCCN 2018002511 (print) | LCCN 2018002813 (ebook) |
ISBN 9781782254324 (Epub) | ISBN 9781849466417 (hardback : alk. paper)

Subjects: LCSH: Legislation—Great Britain. | Law—Great Britain—Interpretation
and construction. | Legislation—Europe. | Law—Europe—Interpretation and construction.

Classification: LCC KD660 (ebook) | LCC KD660 .L69 2018 (print) | DDC 349.41—dc23

LC record available at https://lccn.loc.gov/2018002511

ISBN: HB: 978-1-84946-641-7
       ePDF: 978-1-50992-132-4
       ePub: 978-1-78225-432-4

Typeset by Compuscript Ltd, Shannon
Printed and bound in Great Britain by CPI UK (Group) Ltd, Croydon CR0 4YY

To find out more about our authors and books visit www.hartpublishing.co.uk.
Here you will find extracts, author information, details of forthcoming events
and the option to sign up for our newsletters.

For Carrie ('At last!'), and Nathan, our precious gift

—DL

For Mum and Dad, with all my love. Thank you for everything.

—CP

FOREWORD

It is particularly important in this country for lawyers, indeed for many non-lawyers, to understand legislation—both what it is and what it means. This is not merely because so much of our law is now contained in legislation. It is also because, unusually, the UK has no coherent written constitution (a distinction it shares with Israel and New Zealand) and it enjoys parliamentary sovereignty. This means that statutes, laws formally enacted by the Queen in Parliament, have a special, effectively inviolable, status.

It is also a particularly challenging time for those who want to understand legislation. Partly because of the increasingly complex and fast-moving character of modern life, socially and technologically, the sheer amount of legislation has grown exponentially over the past 50 years. The former Law Lord, Lord Steyn, suggested that there was 'an orgy of statutes'[1] in 2003, and the output of legislation has increased since then. And there is not only a problem with the sheer volume of legislation: again, reflecting modern life, many statutes are increasingly complex and are frequently amended.

And, of course, it is not merely statutes, primary legislation, which are increasingly substantial in volume and increasingly complex in content. The same is true of secondary legislation, in particular statutory instruments, which do not have the benefit of parliamentary scrutiny, redrafting and refining. In that connection, there is also the prospect of an increase in the use of statutory instruments pursuant to Henry VIII clauses in statutes. The former Lord Chief Justice, Lord Judge (echoing a less distinguished predecessor, Lord Hewart),[2] has rightly articulated fundamental concerns about these clauses:[3] they involve a serious democratic deficit because they authorise the unelected Executive to amend or add to statutes enacted by Parliament. Legislation which is partly in statutes and partly in statutory instruments also raises further room for complexity, as well as increasing the risk of errors on the part of both the drafting lawyer and the interpreting lawyer. There is something of a price to be paid by the Executive in that statutory instruments, unlike statutes, can be subject to judicial review, as recent decisions

---

[1] Johan Steyn, 'Dynamic Interpretation Amidst an Orgy of Statutes', The Brian Dickson Memorial Lecture, 2 October 2003, available at https://commonlaw.uottawa.ca/ottawa-law-review/sites/commonlaw.uottawa.ca.ottawa-law-review/files/11_35ottawalrev1632003-2004.pdf.

[2] Lord Hewart, *The New Despotism* (London, Ernest Benn, 1929).

[3] Lord Judge, 'Ceding Power to the Executive; the Resurrection of Henry VIII', lecture of 12 April 2016, available at https://www.kcl.ac.uk/law/newsevents/newsrecords/2015-16/Ceding-Power-to-the-Executive---Lord-Judge---130416.pdf.

of the Supreme Court[4] illustrate, but that of itself adds yet another potential for significant pitfalls in the way of anyone seeking to navigate his or her way through legislation.

The advent of the Human Rights Act 1998 with its requirement 'if possible' to interpret legislation so as to comply with the rights granted by the European Convention on Human Rights[5] is another snare for the unwary. Furthermore, as long as the UK is subject to EU law, there is the obligation on the courts to disregard legislative provisions which fail to comply with EU law. And if and when the UK withdraws from the EU, there will be many further challenges, including the increased use of Henry VIII clauses and the challenges of interpreting EU legislation transposed into UK legislation.[6]

A quarter of a century ago, in *Pepper v Hart*,[7] the Law Lords created another difficulty for those who have to interpret legislation. In that case it was decided that, provided the legislation concerned was 'ambiguous or obscure' or its 'literal meaning … leads to an absurdity', it could be interpreted by reference to what was said in Parliament provided that 'such material clearly discloses the mischief aimed at or the legislative intention lying behind the ambiguous or obscure words'.[8] Although that may seem dubious as a matter of principle, it all sounds pretty unobjectionable in practice. However, in my view, Lord Hoffmann accurately summarised the consequences in a later House of Lords case[9] when he said:

> Your Lordships' experience … suggests that such evidence will be produced in any case in which there is the remotest chance that it may be accepted and that even these cases will be only the tip of a mountain of discarded but expensive investigation. *Pepper v Hart* has also encouraged ministers and others to make statements in the hope of influencing the construction which the courts will give to a statute and it is possible that negotiating parties will be encouraged to improve the bundle of correspondence with similar statements.

I must confess that one of my regrets is that, during my five years as President of the Supreme Court, there was no opportunity to confront the question of whether we should reconsider that principle. When advising on an issue of statutory interpretation, a lawyer now almost always has to consider whether to trawl through Hansard to see if there is any relevant material, and in many such cases an adviser will conclude that such trawling must be done, if only for protective reasons. Having done the trawling, which can take a fair time and therefore involves significant costs to the client, it is difficult not to refer to the material in court,

---

[4] *R (Public Law Project) v Lord Chancellor* [2016] UKSC 39, [2016] AC 1531; and *R (UNISON) v Lord Chancellor* [2017] UKSC 51, [2017] 3 WLR 409.

[5] Human Rights Act 1998, s 3(1).

[6] See the European Union (Withdrawal) Bill (HC Bill No 5).

[7] *Pepper (Inspector of Taxes) v Hart* [1993] AC 593.

[8] ibid 634D–E (Lord Browne-Wilkinson).

[9] *Chartbrook Ltd v Persimmon Homes Ltd* [2009] UKHL 38, [2009] AC 1101 [39] (Lord Hoffmann), in the course of considering the analogous issue of whether evidence of pre-contractual negotiations should be admissible in construing a contract.

if the issue becomes litigious, so further costs, and also court time, are taken up. Yet the cases in which the material has made any difference to the outcome are very rare (if they exist at all), and indeed there are very few cases indeed where the material has even been admissible on the basis of the test laid down in *Pepper v Hart*. Bearing in mind the almost vanishingly few cases in which *Pepper v Hart* makes any difference, I would question whether the game is worth the candle. *Pepper v Hart* may be a classic case of hard cases making bad law, and Lord Mackay of Clashfern, who was the sole dissenter, may turn out to have the last laugh—but that is for others to decide.

More generally, statutory construction, like any exercise in documentary interpretation, has always involved considering both the language and the context. In my nearly 50 years as a practising lawyer and judge, my impression is that the various developments identified above have resulted in context playing a somewhat larger part and the actual language a somewhat smaller part than when I started in practice. Nonetheless, the words are where one has to start and, in my view, they remain the bedrock on which any questions of statutory interpretation must rest. The tussle between language and context will always lead to differences of opinion in some cases of documentary interpretation, but with statutes there can be additional issues of constitutional factors such as those considered by the House of Lords in the *Simms* case[10] and the Supreme Court in the *Evans* case.[11]

Statutory interpretation was always a demanding task. However, the combination of all the various developments which I have mentioned means that there is an ever-increasing premium on the skills and know-how required to navigate legislation and to understand and apply the correct principles in order to construe legislation.

In these circumstances, it is very valuable to have a new book on the topic, which seeks to take a practical, accessible approach. It will be of great value to practitioners, students, academics and judges—whatever their level of experience. As the authors rightly say, there are more comprehensive and detailed books on the subject of statutory interpretation, but this book is more concise and readable. The trouble for many legal practitioners, and indeed for many legal book writers, can be a failure to see the wood for the trees, and that is a particular risk when it comes to a subject as fissiparous as statutory interpretation. David Lowe and Charlie Potter are to be congratulated for having avoided that risk: they have written a crisp and engaging book, which covers this important topic in an informative and accessible way. They are also to be congratulated for finding the time to write this book bearing in mind their busy careers.

David Neuberger
The Rt Hon Lord Neuberger of Abbotsbury
London, 13 October 2017

---

[10] *R v Secretary of State for the Home Department ex p Simms* [2000] 2 AC 115 (HL).
[11] *R (Evans) v Attorney General* [2015] UKSC 21, [2015] 1 AC 1787.

AUTHORS

David Lowe MA (Cantab), BCL (Oxon). David is a barrister at Blackstone Chambers, Temple, London, specialising in commercial and public law.

Charlie Potter MA Hons (Cantab), Dip Law (City University). Charlie is a barrister who is a senior corporate communications adviser and Partner at Brunswick Group, co-leading the firm's global litigation practice. He is a former member of Blackstone Chambers, Temple, London.

CONTENTS

Foreword vii
Authors.. xi
Table of Cases xix
Table of Legislation xlvii
Introduction lvii

1. **Introduction to Domestic Legislation: Statutes and Subordinate Legislation**...1
   Primary Legislation: Acts of Parliament 2
   Types of Statutes..4
   Enactment of Statutes 5
   Pre-parliamentary and Parliamentary Materials.......................7
   Effect on Other Statutes...8
   Subordinate Legislation: Statutory Instruments.......................8
   Types of Statutory Instrument 9
   Enactment of SIs: Variable Parliamentary Control and Scrutiny 10
   Explanatory Notes and Memoranda 13

2. **Anatomy and Structure of Domestic Legislation**....................15
   Constituent Components of an Act 15
   Introductory Components 15
   Operative Components..17
   Organisation and Structure: Headings and Divisions............21
   Constituent Components of Statutory Instruments 22
   Introductory Components 22
   Operative Components..24
   Organisation and Structure: Headings and Divisions............25
   Signature and Explanatory Notes...25

3. **Core Principles and Approach** 27
   The Central Objective and Overall Approach 27
   Reading the Statutory Language..29
   Statutory Language as the Starting Point.................................29
   Rules of Interpretation...30
   Words are Presumptively Given their Ordinary or Natural Meaning..30
   The Presumption that Language is Used 'Correctly and Exactly'..........35

The Presumption that Statutory Language Must Mean Something......35
The Presumption that General Provisions Do Not Override Specific
    Provisions 37
Presumed Consistency of Meaning..38
The Presumption that Different Words Have Different Meanings........39
The Presumption that Legislation is 'Always Speaking'..........................39
The *Noscitur a Sociis* Principle...42
The *Ejusdem Generis* Principle 43
The *Expressio Unius* Principle..45
The Role of Context and Purpose 47
The Centrality of Context...47
The Importance of Purpose..49
Judicial Correction of Obvious Errors in Statutory Drafting....................51
Contextual Construction: The Presumption that Parliament Knows
    the Law and Endorses Certain Judicial Decisions 53
The Role of Subsequent Practice in Interpretation 56

4.   **General Presumptions as to the Intended Effect of Legislation** 59
The Presumption that Legislation Accords with 'Common Sense'............59
The Presumption of Reasonableness: Presumption against an Absurd,
    Irrational, Futile or Unreasonable Result..60
The Presumption that Penal Provisions Should be Strictly Construed.....62
The Presumption against Changes in the Common Law...........................64
The Presumption that Legislation is Not Contrary to Fundamental
    Rights or Basic Tenets of the Common Law: The Principle
    of Legality 65
    Necessary Implication..67
The Presumption of Fairness...68
    The Presumption of Notice 69
The Presumption of *Mens Rea* in Statutory Offences 70
The Presumption against the Exclusion of Judicial Review: Presumption
    that Ouster Clauses are to be Strictly Construed...................................72
    When Should a Provision be Interpreted as an Ouster Clause? 74
    Interpretation of Ouster Clauses..76
    Implied Limitations on the Availability of Judicial Review 78
The Presumption that Parliament Does Not Authorise a Tort 78
The Presumption that Legislation Does Not Bind the Crown..................79
The Presumption against Retrospectivity..79
    The Presumption that Legislation is Not Intended
    to be 'Retroactive'...81
    The Presumption that Legislation Does Not Interfere
    with Vested Rights...81
    The Presumption that Legislation Does Not Affect Pending
    Proceedings 82

The Presumption that Purely Procedural Changes Apply
  to All Actions 83
The Presumption of Compatibility or Conformity
  with International Law..84
Territoriality: Presumptions as to Extent and Application 84
  The Presumption against Extraterritorial Application 86
  The Presumption against Extraterritoriality in Statutory Criminal
    Offences 89
The Presumption of Regularity 91

5. **Interaction of Legislation** 93
    Amendment, Repeal and Consolidation 94
      Amendment...94
      Repeal...98
      Consolidation 101
    Construction by Reference to Other Legislation: General Rules 104
    Construction by Reference to Other Legislation: Specific Instances 106
      Express Reference 107
      Amendment and Consolidation...107
      Statutes *in Pari Materia*..107
      Using Parent Acts to Interpret Subordinate Legislation.......................112
      Using Subordinate Legislation to Interpret Parent Acts......................113

6. **Internal Aids to Interpretation** 117
    Interpretive Effect of Ancillary Components...............................117
      Ancillary Components in Acts..119
      Ancillary Components in Statutory Instruments....................121
      Structure, Format and Punctuation 122
    Interpretation Provisions..123
      Scope and Location of Interpretation Provisions....................123
      Language and Effect of Interpretation Provisions....................124
    Deeming Provisions 129
    Provisos and Savings 131

7. **External Aids to Interpretation**...135
    The Rationale for Recourse to External Aids...............................135
    Specific Kinds of External Aids and their Use..............................137
    Parliamentary Statements 137
      Hansard...137
      The Rule in *Pepper v Hart* 138
      Reference for Context and to Ascertain Mischief....................141
      Human Rights and EU Law Cases...142
      The Practicalities of Using Hansard......................................143
    Explanatory Notes 144
      Explanatory Notes to Acts...145
      Explanatory Notes to Statutory Instruments.........................147

Explanatory Memoranda 149
Pre-legislative Materials 150
Post-legislative Materials 152
General Principles for the Use of External Aids 153

8. The Interpretation Act 1978...157
Scope of Application of the 1978 Act.......................................157
Key Provisions 158

9. The Effect of International Law on Domestic Legislation.......................161
Sources of International Law..161
International Conventions or 'Treaties' 162
Customary International Law 165
General Principles of International Law................................168
Judicial Decisions and Academic Writings 168
Interpretation of Domestic Legislation in the Light of Treaties 169
The Presumption of Conformity 170
The Presumption of Compatibility......................................174
Contribution to Context...176
Interpretation of Treaties...176
The General Rule 177
Core Elements 178
Subsequent Agreement and Practice...................................180
Treaties as International Instruments 180
Supplementary Means of Interpretation 183
Interpretation of Domestic Legislation in the Light of Customary
International Law..185
The Presumption of Conformity 185
The Presumption of Compatibility......................................185
Contribution to Context..186

10. Impact of the Human Rights Act 1998: Sections 3 and 4 187
Section 3 187
The Interpretive Obligation in Section 3............................187
Scope of the Application of Section 3 189
Performing the Interpretive Obligation under Section 3................190
The Limits of Section 3...193
Section 4: Declarations of Incompatibility 195

11. Sources of EU Law and the Nature, Anatomy and Structure
of EU Legislation..199
History and Development of the EU Treaties...........................199
The Treaty Establishing the European Economic Community
1957 (TEC)...200
The Single European Act 1986 (SEA) 200
The Treaty on European Union 1992 (TEU)......................200

The Treaty of Amsterdam 1997 201
The Treaty of Nice 2001 201
The Treaty of Lisbon 2007 201
Practical Consequences of Treaty Revisions 201
Sources of EU Law 202
(1)(a) The Treaties 202
(1)(b) The Charter of Fundamental Rights...............................204
(1)(c) The General Principles of EU Law 205
(2) Relevant International Law 206
(3) EU Legislation 208
(4) Delegated Acts 210
(5) Implementing Acts..210
Framework Decisions 211
Legislative Procedure 211
The Anatomy and Structure of EU Legislation 213

12. **Interpretation of EU Law and its Effect on Domestic Legislation** 219
The Legal Basis for Application of EU Law in the UK 219
Section 2(1) of the ECA 1972: Effect Given Generally
    to 'Directly Enforceable' Provisions of EU Law.....................220
Section 2(2) of the ECA 1972: Power to Implement EU
    Law by Delegated Legislation 221
Section 2(4) of the ECA 1972: Primacy of Directly Enforceable
    EU Law Rules 222
Section 3 of the ECA 1972: Resolution of Questions
    of EU Law..223
The Effect of EU Law on Domestic Law: Duties of Disapplication
    and Conforming Interpretation 226
The Duty of Disapplication..227
The Duty of Conforming Interpretation 228
Interpretation of EU Law..234
Hierarchy of Norms 234
The General Principles of EU Law...235
General Rules of Interpretation of EU Instruments 237
External Aids to the Interpretation of EU Legislation: *Travaux*
    Préparatoires..242

13. **Research Tools and Works of Reference** 247
Finding Legislation and Related Commentaries and Materials...........247
Printed Sources 247
Electronic Sources: Free to Access..248
Electronic Sources: Subscription-Only Services..............................249
Finding the Meaning of Words and Phrases...250
Electronic Case Law and Commentary Searches 250
Printed Sources 251

14. Checklist: Practical Considerations..253
  Application of Legislation...253
  Relevance of Other Legislation and Aids to Interpretation 254
  Interpretive Considerations..255

Index 261

TABLE OF CASES

United Kingdom

9 Cornwall Crescent London Ltd v Kensington and Chelsea Royal London
    Borough Council [2005] EWCA Civ 324, [2006] 1 WLR 1186 ....3.24, 3.45
41–60 Albert Palace Mansions (Freehold) Ltd v Craftrule Ltd [2011] EWCA Civ 185,
    [2011] 1 WLR 2425 ....5.6
A v Secretary of State for the Home Department (No 2) [2005] UKHL 71,
    [2006] 2 AC 221 ....9.15
A Local Authority v A Mother and Child [2001] 1 Costs LR 136 (CA) 5.9
AB v JJB [2015] EWHC 192 (Fam) 12.6
Adan v Secretary of State for the Home Department [1999] 1 AC 293 (HL)..................9.49
Agassi v Robinson (Inspector of Taxes) [2006] UKHL 23, [2006] 1 WLR 1380 .....4.62, 4.63
Agnew v Länsförsäkringsbolagens AB [2001] 1 AC 223 (HL)...9.59
Ahmed v HM Treasury [2010] UKSC 2, [2010] 2 AC 534..................... 4.18, 4.19, 4.20, 5.11,
                                                      9.15, 10.11, 10.13
Air-India v Wiggins [1980] 1 WLR 815 (HL)..4.65
Aitken v Director of Public Prosecutions [2015] EWHC 1079 (Admin),
    [2016] 1 WLR 297 ....3.12, 4.8
AKJ v Commissioner of Police of the Metropolis [2013] EWCA Civ 1342,
    [2014] 1 WLR 285 ....4.17
Al-Jedda v Secretary of State for the Home Department [2013] UKSC 62,
    [2014] AC 253 ....13.4
Al-Saadoon v Secretary of State for Defence [2016] EWHC 773 (Admin),
    [2016] 1 WLR 3625 ....10.9
Al Sabah v Grupo Torras SA [2005] UKPC 1, [2005] 2 AC 333 ....4.57
Alcom Ltd v Colombia [1984] AC 580 (HL) 9.64, 9.65
Ali v Secretary of State for the Home Department [2016] UKSC 60,
    [2016] 1 WLR 4799 ....1.4
Ambatielos v Anton Jurgens Margarine Works [1923] AC 175 (HL) 3.36
Anisminic Ltd v Foreign Compensation Commission [1969] 2 AC 147 .... 4.31–4.39
Anyanwu v South Bank Student Union [2001] UKHL 14, [2001] 1 WLR 638 ....5.28
Arnold v Mayor, Aldermen and Burgesses of the Borough of Gravesend
    (1856) 2 Kay & J 574 ....6.34
Aspinalls Club Ltd v Revenue & Customs Commissioners [2013] EWCA Civ 1464,
    [2015] Ch 79 ....6.23
Assange v Swedish Prosecution Authorities [2012] UKSC 22,
    [2012] 2 AC 471 .... 3.22, 3.24, 9.27, 9.33, 9.36,
                                                   9.47, 9.54, 11.39, 12.22.2
Associated Minerals Consolidated Ltd v Wyong Shire Council
    [1975] AC 538 (PC) 5.16.7

Assuranceforeningen Gard Gjensidig v International Oil Pollution Compensation
  Fund [2014] EWHC 1394 (Comm), [2014] 2 Lloyd's Rep 219..................................9.28
Attorney General v Associated Newspapers Ltd [2011] EWHC 418 (Admin),
  [2011] 1 WLR 2097...14.21
Attorney General v Barker [2000] 1 FLR 759 (CA)..14.21
Attorney General v Lamplough (1878) 3 Ex D 214 (CA) 2.14
Attorney General v Prince Ernest Augustus of Hanover [1957]
  AC 436 (HL)...3.44, 3.44.3, 3.45, 5.25, 5.26, 5.35, 5.37,
                                                                              6.4.1, 6.4.3, 6.4.4, 6.5, 6.7
Attorney General v Ryan [1980] AC 718 (PC) 4.37.3
Attorney General v Times Newspapers Ltd [1992] 1 AC 191 (HL)...............................6.34
Attorney General's Reference (No 1 of 1988) [1989] AC 971 (HL) 3.16, 4.10
Attorney General's Reference (No 5 of 2002) [2004] UKHL 40,
  [2005] 1 AC 167 ....3.47, 3.48
Augean plc v Revenue & Customs Commissioners [2008] EWHC 2026 (Ch),
  [2009] Env LR 6 ....5.31
Austin v Southwark London Borough Council [2010] UKSC 28,
  [2011] 1 AC 355 ....14.20
Autologic Holdings plc v Inland Revenue Commissioners [2005] UKHL 54,
  [2006] 1 AC 118 ....12.8
AXA General Insurance Ltd v HM Advocate [2011] UKSC 46, [2012] 1 AC 868 ....4.18
B (A Minor) v Director of Public Prosecutions [2000] 2 AC 428 (HL)..........4.22, 4.27, 4.28
B v Secretary of State for Justice [2011] EWCA Civ 1608, [2012] 1 WLR 2043 ....4.20
B v Secretary of State for Work and Pensions [2005] EWCA Civ 929,
  [2005] 1 WLR 3796..3.55
Baker v Quantum Clothing Group Ltd [2011] UKSC 17, [2011] 1 WLR 1003.......3.26, 3.32
Bakewell Management Ltd v Brandwood [2004] UKHL 14, [2004] 2 AC 519.............3.38.1
Balamoody v United Kingdom Central Council for Nursing, Midwifery and
  Health Visiting [2001] EWCA Civ 2097, [2002] ICR 646...14.21
Bank Mellat v HM Treasury (No 2) [2013] UKSC 39, [2014] AC 700..............................3.42
Barclays Mercantile Business Finance Ltd v Mawson [2004] UKHL 51,
  [2005] 1 AC 684 xvii
Barnes v Jarvis [1953] 1 WLR 649 (QB)..4.2
Barras v Aberdeen Steam Trawling and Fishing Co Ltd [1933] AC 402 (HL)........3.53–3.55,
                                                                              3.57, 5.20, 5.38
Bates van Winkelhof v Clyde & Co LLP [2014] UKSC 32, [2014] 1 WLR 2047............10.22
BBC v Johns [1965] Ch 32 (CA) 4.41
BBC v Sugar [2009] UKHL 9, [2009] 1 WLR 430 ....3.14.3
BBC v Sugar (No 2) [2012] UKSC 4, [2012] 1 WLR 439..13.17
Belhaj v Straw [2017] UKSC 3, [2017] 2 WLR 456 ....9.15, 9.16
Bellinger v Bellinger [2003] UKHL 21, [2003] 2 AC 467...10.20
Benkharbouche v Embassy of Sudan [2015] EWCA Civ 33, [2016] QB 347...................11.20
Bentine v Bentine [2015] EWCA Civ 1168, [2016] Ch 489 ....3.55, 5.20, 5.21, 5.23
Beswick v Beswick [1968] AC 58 (HL) 3.3, 5.21
Bilta (UK) Ltd (in liquidation) v Nazir [2015] UKSC 23, [2016] AC 1 ....4.62, 4.63
Birmingham City Council v Oakley [2001] 1 AC 617 (HL)............................3.26, 3.31, 3.33
Birmingham City Council v Walker [2007] UKHL 22, [2007] 2 AC 262 ....6.24
B-J (A Child) (Non-molestation Order: Power of Arrest), Re [2001] Fam 415 (CA)......3.40

Black-Clawson International Ltd v Papierwerke Waldof Aschaffenberg AG
    [1975] AC 591 (HL).. 3.3, 3.46, 4.13, 6.5, 7.5, 9.59
Blackland Park Exploration Ltd v Environment Agency [2003] EWCA Civ 1795,
    [2004] Env LR 33 ....12.53
Blackwood v Birmingham and Solihull Mental Health NHS Foundation Trust
    [2016] EWCA Civ 607, [2016] ICR 903..12.27
Blain, ex parte (1879) 12 Ch D 522 (CA) 4.60, 4.62
Bloomsbury International Ltd v Department for Environment, Food and
    Rural Affairs [2011] UKSC 25, [2011] 1 WLR 1546 .... 3.9, 3.45, 3.59, 3.60,
                                                                                                                          5.6, 5.7, 5.42
Boake Allen Ltd v Revenue & Customs Commissioners [2007] UKHL 25,
    [2007] 1 WLR 1386...9.25, 9.32
Boaler, Re [1915] 1 KB 21 (CA) 6.6
Boddington v British Transport Police [1999] 2 AC 143 (HL).......................4.32, 4.35, 4.70
Bogdanic v Secretary of State for the Home Department [2014]
    EWHC 2872 (QB)..3.51, 4.8, 4.9, 4.11, 4.12, 7.4, 7.5
Boss Holdings Ltd v Grosvenor West End Properties [2008] UKHL 5,
    [2008] 1 WLR 289...5.6
Bourne v Norwich Crematorium Ltd [1967] 1 WLR 691 (Ch).......................................3.34
Boyce v The Queen [2004] UKPC 32, [2005] 1 AC 400...................................9.32, 9.34, 9.64
Bricom Holdings Ltd v Inland Revenue Commissioners [1997] STC 1179 (CA)............6.28
Bridge Trustees Ltd v Houldsworth [2011] UKSC 42, [2011] 1 WLR 1912 xx
British Airways plc v Williams [2012] UKSC 43, [2013] 1 All ER 443............................12.21
British Concrete Pipe Association's Agreement, Re [1983] ICR 215 (CA) 3.11
British Pregnancy Advisory Service v Secretary of State for Health [2011]
    EWHC 235 (Admin), [2012] 1 WLR 580 ....5.7, 5.43
Broadhurst v Tan [2016] EWCA Civ 94, [2016] 1 WLR 1928 ....7.37.1, 7.43.2
Brown v Bennett (No 2) [2002] 1 WLR 713 (Ch)..5.7, 5.26, 5.31
Brown v Innovatorone [2009] EWHC 1376 (Comm), [2010] 2 All ER
    (Comm) 80..6.12
Brown v Stott [2003] 1 AC 681 (PC) 9.42, 9.43
Brownsea Haven Properties Ltd v Poole Corp [1958] Ch 574 (CA)...................................3.36
Brutus v Cozens [1973] AC 854 ....3.14.3
BT Pension Schemes (Trustees of) v Clarke [2000] Pens LR 157 (CA) 3.38
Bulmer v Inland Revenue Commissioners [1967] Ch 145 (Ch) 6.8, 6.22
Cachia v Faluyi [2001] EWCA Civ 998, [2001] WLR 1966..10.19
Camille and Henry Dreyfus Foundation Inc v Inland Revenue Commissioners
    [1954] Ch 672 (CA); [1956] AC 39 (HL) 5.41
Campbell v Peter Gordon Joiners Ltd [2016] UKSC 38, [2016] AC 1513 ....3.52
Campbell College, Belfast (Governors) v Commissioner of Valuation for
    Northern Ireland [1964] 1 WLR 912 (HL)...3.31, 3.60
Canada Southern Railway Co v International Bridge Co (1883)
    8 App Cas 723 (PC) 5.31.2
Canadian National Railways v Canada Steamship Lines Ltd [1945] AC 204 (PC) 3.36
Canterbury City Council v Colley [1993] AC 401 (HL)..4.7, 5.21
Cape Brandy Syndicate v Inland Revenue Commissioners [1921]
    2 KB 403 (CA)..5.40, 5.41
Cawley v Secretary of State for the Environment (1990) 60 P&CR 492 (QB).................6.12

Century National Merchant Bank and Trust Co Ltd v Davies [1998] AC 628 (PC) 4.32
Chartbrook Ltd v Persimmon Homes Ltd [2009] UKHL 38, [2009] AC 1101.................. viii
Chief Adjudication Officer v Foster [1993] AC 754 (HL)....................................5.31.1, 5.35
Chief Constable of Cumbria v Wright [2006] EWHC 3574 (Admin),
    [2007] 1 WLR 1407..7.42
Chiron Corp v Murex Diagnostics Ltd (No 8) [1995] All ER (EC) 88 (CA) 12.13
Christian Institute v Lord Advocate [2016] UKSC 51, [2016] HRLR 19 ....3.45
Churchwardens and Overseers of West Ham v Fourth City Mutual Building
    Society [1892] 1 QB 654 (QB) 5.16.1
Clark v In Focus Asset Management and Tax Solutions Ltd [2014] EWCA Civ 118,
    [2014] 1 WLR 2502...3.46
Clark (Inspector of Taxes) v Oceanic Contractors Inc [1983] 2 AC 130 (HL) 4.60, 4.62
CMA CGM SA v Classic Shipping Co Ltd [2004] EWCA Civ 114, [2004]
    1 All ER (Comm) 865 ....9.24, 9.44, 9.45, 9.60
Colquhoun v Brooks (1888) 21 QBD 52 (CA)...3.41
Coltman v Bibby Tankers Ltd [1988] AC 276 (HL) 6.19.1, 6.19.2, 6.20.2, 6.20.3
Connolly v Director of Public Prosecutions [2007] EWHC 237 (Admin),
    [2008] 1 WLR 276..10.19
Consorzio del Prosciutto di Parma v Asda Stores Ltd [1998] 2 CMLR 215 (ChD);
    [2001] UKHL 7, [2001] 1 CMLR 43 ....12.4
Cooke v MGN Ltd [2014] EWHC 2831 (QB), [2015] 1 WLR 895...............................7.38.4
Corocraft Ltd v Pan American Airways Inc [1969] 1 QB 616 (CA) 9.28, 9.45, 9.54
Cotton v Secretary of State for Works and Pensions [2009] EWCA Civ 1333.................3.24
Council for Civil Service Unions v Minister for the Civil Service
    [1985] AC 374 (HL)..1.7
Coventry and Solihull Waste Disposal Co Ltd v Russell [1999] 1 WLR 2093 (HL) 7.29,
                                                                                                 7.34.3, 7.43.2
Cox v Army Council [1963] AC 48 (HL)..4.65
Cox v Ergo Versicherung AG [2014] UKSC 22, [2014] AC 1379....................4.59, 4.60, 4.63
Cramas Properties Ltd v Connaught Fur Trimmings Ltd [1965] 1 WLR 892 (HL) 4.3
Cream Holdings Ltd v Banerjee [2004] UKHL 44, [2005] 1 AC 253 ....14.21
Cretu v Local Court of Suceava, Romania [2016] EWHC 353 (Admin),
    [2016] 1 WLR 3344...11.39
Cusack v Harrow London Borough Council [2013] UKSC 40,
    [2013] 1 WLR 2022...3.10, 3.12, 3.21
Customs & Excise Commissioners v Viva Gas Appliances Ltd [1983]
    1 WLR 1445 (HL) 3.35
Customs & Excise Commissioners v Zielinski Baker & Partners Ltd [2004] UKHL 7,
    [2004] 1 WLR 707..3.44.1
Dar Al Arkan Real Estate Development Co v Al Refai [2014] EWCA Civ 715,
    [2015] 1 WLR 135..4.63
David T Morrison & Co Ltd v ICL Plastics Ltd [2014] UKSC 48,
    [2014] SLT 791 ....3.3, 3.5, 3.9, 3.13, 3.20
DCC Holdings (UK) Ltd v Revenue & Customs Commissioners [2010] UKSC 58,
    [2011] 1 WLR 44..6.27
Dean v Wiesengrund [1955] 2 QB 120 (CA)..3.41
Debt Collect London Ltd v SK Slavia Praha-Fotbal AS [2010] EWCA Civ 1250,
    [2011] 1 WLR 866...12.53, 12.55

Deep Vein Thrombosis and Air Travel Group Litigation, Re [2005] UKHL 72,
    [2006] 1 AC 495 ....9.44
Deposit Protection Board v Barclays Bank plc [1994] 2 AC 367 (HL).................5.47, 5.48.2
Digital Satellite Warranty Cover Ltd, Re [2011] EWHC 122 (Ch), [2011] Bus LR 981;
    [2011] EWCA Civ 1413, [2012] Bus LR 990; [2013] UKSC 7, [2013] 1 WLR 605......4.11,
                                                                        12.23.2, 12.42, 12.46
Dilworth v Commissioner of Stamps [1899] AC 99 (PC) 6.20.2
Dingmar v Dingmar [2006] EWCA Civ 942, [2007] Ch 109.....................................4.6, 6.15
Director of Assets Recovery Agency v Green [2005] EWHC 3168 (Admin) 7.31
Director of Legal Aid Casework v Briggs [2017] EWCA Civ 1169 ....3.9, 3.13, 7.29
Director of Public Prosecutions v Bull [1995] QB 88 (CA)..7.38.4
Director of Public Prosecutions v Ottewell [1970] AC 642 (HL).....................................4.10
Director of Public Prosecutions v Schildkamp [1971] AC 1 (HL).....................2.19.1, 3.44,
                                                                        6.7–6.9, 6.13, 6.15
Director of Public Prosecutions v Vivier [1991] 4 All ER 18 (QB) 3.39
Director of the Serious Fraud Office v O'Brien [2014] UKSC 18, [2014] AC 1246 ....6.14
DMWSHNZ Ltd v Revenue & Customs Commissioners [2015] EWCA Civ 1036 ....3.20
Dorset County Council v House [2010] EWCA Crim 2270, [2011] 1 WLR 727 ....3.2
Dunnachie v Kingston upon Hull City Council [2004] UKHL 36, [2005] 1 AC 226.......3.29
Duport Steels Ltd v Sirs [1980] 1 WLR 142 (HL) 3.3, 3.13
Dyson Ltd v Qualtex (UK) Ltd [2006] EWCA Civ 166, [2006] RPC 31 ....7.38.1, 7.43.2
Ealing London Borough Council v Race Relations Board [1972]
    AC 342 (HL)...3.44.3, 6.20.4, 6.32, 6.35
Earl of Antrim's Petition [1967] 1 AC 691 (HL) 5.16.3
Easyair Ltd v Opal Telecom Ltd [2009] EWHC 339 (Ch)..14.21
Ecuador v Occidental Exploration and Production Co [2005] EWCA Civ 1116,
    [2006] QB 432..9.9
Edwards v Kumarasamy [2016] UKSC 40, [2016] AC 1334 ....3.11
Edwards & Walkden (Norfolk) Ltd v City of London [2012] EWHC 2527 (Ch).............3.17
Effort Shipping Co Ltd v Linden Management SA (The Giannis NK)
    [1998] AC 605 (HL)...7.43.2, 9.44, 9.58, 9.60, 12.54
EK (Ivory Coast) v Secretary of State for the Home Department [2014]
    EWCA Civ 1517 ....4.25
Elkins v Cartlidge [1947] 1 All ER 829 (KB) 3.39
Ellerman Lines v Murray [1931] AC 126 (HL)..9.28
EN (Serbia) v Secretary of State for the Home Department [2009]
    EWCA Civ 630, [2010] QB 633 ....3.40, 3.42, 9.10, 9.27
Energy Solutions (EU) Ltd v Nuclear Decommissioning Authority [2017]
    UKSC 34, [2017] 1 WLR 1373 ....12.26
Entick v Carrington (1765) 19 State Tr 1029...4.20
Epping Forest District Council v Essex Rendering Ltd [1983] 1 WLR 158 (HL).............5.24
ESS Production Ltd v Sully [2005] EWCA Civ 554, [2005] BCC 435 ....4.9, 4.12
Evans v Amicus Healthcare Ltd [2004] EWCA Civ 727, [2005] Fam 1 ....7.5
F Hoffmann-La Roche & Co AG v Secretary of State for Trade and Industry
    [1975] AC 295 (HL)..4.70
Farley v Secretary of State for Work and Pensions (No 2) [2006] UKHL 31,
    [2006] 1 WLR 181..4.34
Farrell v Alexander [1977] AC 59 (HL) 3.53, 5.17, 5.18, 5.20–5.22.2,
                                                                        5.24, 5.26, 5.37

Feakins v Department for Environment, Food and Rural Affairs [2005]
    EWCA Civ 1513, [2006] Env LR 44 ....14.20
Federal Steam Navigation Co Ltd v Department of Trade and Industry [1974]
    1 WLR 505 (HL) 14.17
Feest v South West Strategic Health Authority [2015] EWCA Civ 708,
    [2016] QB 503 ....9.42, 9.52
Fendoch Investment Trust Co v Inland Revenue Commissioners
    [1945] 2 All ER 140 (HL) 5.33, 5.35, 5.37
Finch v Inland Revenue Commissioners [1985] Ch 1 (CA)...5.40
Fitzpatrick v Sterling Housing Association Ltd [2001] 1 AC 27 (HL) 3.28, 3.31
Fleming v Revenue & Customs Commissioners [2008] UKHL 2,
    [2008] 1 WLR 195..12.8, 12.15, 12.19, 12.20.1
Flood v Times Newspapers Ltd (No 2) [2017] UKSC 33, [2017] 1 WLR 1415 ....4.42
Flora v Wakom (Heathrow) Ltd [2006] EWCA Civ 1103, [2007] 1 WLR 482.................7.29
Forde & McHugh Ltd v Revenue & Customs Commissioners [2014] UKSC 14,
    [2014] 1 WLR 810..5.47
Fortis Bank SA/NV v Indian Overseas Bank [2011] EWCA Civ 58,
    [2012] Bus LR 141 ....9.60
Fothergill v Monarch Airlines Ltd [1981] AC 251 (HL) 7.38.4, 9.24, 9.38, 9.39,
                                                                            9.50, 9.52, 9.54, 9.56, 9.59, 9.60
G1 v Secretary of State for the Home Department [2012] EWCA Civ 867,
    [2013] QB 1008..9.18
G (Adoption: Unmarried Couple), Re [2008] UKHL 38, [2009] 1 AC 173...........1.20, 10.25
G (Children), Re [2012] EWCA Civ 1233, [2013] 1 FLR 677 ....3.31
Gallagher v Church of Jesus Christ of Latter-Day Saints [2008] UKHL 56,
    [2008] 1 WLR 1852..3.53, 3.54
Galloway v Galloway [1956] AC 299...3.55
Gammon (Hong Kong) Ltd v Attorney General of Hong Kong [1985] AC 1 (PC) 4.27,
                                                                                        4.28, 4.30.1, 4.30.3
Gard Marine and Energy Ltd v China National Chartering Co Ltd
    [2017] UKSC 35, [2017] 1 WLR 1793 ....9.24, 9.44, 9.45, 9.60
George Wimpey & Co Ld v British Overseas Airways Corp
    [1955] AC 169 (HL)..4.13
Ghaidan v Godin-Mendoza [2004] UKHL 30, [2004] 2 AC 557.................10.5–10.5.2, 10.7,
                                                                            10.10, 10.12, 10.13, 10.15,
                                                                            10.17–10.21, 10.26–12.28
Gingi v Secretary of State for Work and Pensions [2001] EWCA Civ 1685,
    [2002] 1 CMLR 20 ....12.25
Globespan Airways Ltd, Re [2012] EWCA Civ 1159, [2013] 1 WLR 1122.................3.7, 3.25
Goluchowski v District Court in Elblag, Poland [2016] UKSC 36,
    [2016] 1 WLR 2665..11.39
Goodes v East Sussex County Council [2000] 1 WLR 1356 (HL)....................................5.24
Gopaul v Baksh [2012] UKPC 1...7.12, 7.43.2
Goulandris Bros Ltd v B Goldman & Sons Ltd [1958] 1 QB 74 (QB) 6.30
Gow v Grant [2012] UKSC 29, 2012 SLT 829...7.17
Grays Timber Products Ltd v Revenue & Customs Commissioners [2010] UKSC 4,
    [2010] 1 WLR 497...7.42, 13.3

Green Lane Products Ltd v PMS International Group Ltd [2008] EWCA Civ 358,
[2008] Bus LR 1468 ....12.54
Greene v Associated Newspapers Ltd [2004] EWCA Civ 1462, [2005] QB 972 ....4.13
Greenweb Ltd v Wandsworth London Borough Council [2008] EWCA Civ 910,
[2009] 1 WLR 612...3.13, 4.7, 14.15
Grey v Inland Revenue Commissioners [1960] AC 1 (HL) 5.21
H v Lord Advocate [2012] UKSC 24, [2013] 1 AC 41...5.16.2, 5.16.3
H (Minors), Re [1998] AC 72 (HL) 9.50
Haile v Waltham Forest London Borough Council [2015] UKSC 34,
[2015] AC 1471 ....3.24, 3.54
Hamnett v Essex County Council [2017] EWCA Civ 6, [2017] 1 WLR 1155...................5.14
Hanlon v Law Society [1981] AC 124 (HL)..5.45–5.48.2, 6.15
Harb v Aziz [2015] EWCA Civ 481, [2016] Ch 308 ....9.63, 9.65
Harrison v Cornwall County Council (1991) 90 LGR 81 (CA) 6.20.1
Henry Boot Construction (UK) Ltd v Malmaison Hotel (Manchester) Ltd
[2001] QB 388 (CA) 5.16–5.16.2, 5.16.5
Heydon's Case (1584) 3 Co Rep 7, 76 ER 637...3.46
Higgs v Minister of National Security [2000] 2 AC 228 (PC) 9.8, 9.9, 9.32
Higham v Horton [2004] EWCA Civ 941, [2004] 3 All ER 852 ....3.11
Hill v William Hill (Park Lane) Ltd [1949] AC 530 (HL)...3.18, 3.19
Hillsdown Holdings plc v Pensions Ombudsman [1997] 1 All ER 862 (QB) 7.15
HJ (Iran) v Secretary of State for the Home Department [2010] UKSC 31,
[2011] 1 AC 596 ....9.45
HM Treasury v Ahmed, *see* Ahmed v HM Treasury
Holt & Co v Collyer (1881) 16 Ch D 718 (Ch)..3.15
Hone v Going Places Leisure Travel Ltd [2001] EWCA Civ 947 ....7.12
Hotak v Southwark London Borough Council [2015] UKSC 30, [2016] AC 811...........3.13,
3.54–3.56
Hounslow London Borough Council v Powell [2011] UKSC 8,
[2011] 2 AC 186 ....10.19, 13.3
Howe v Motor Insurers' Bureau (No 1) [2016] EWHC 640 (QB),
[2016] 1 WLR 2707...12.26
Hunte v Trinidad and Tobago [2015] UKPC 33..6.4.2
I v Director of Public Prosecutions [2001] UKHL 10, [2002] 1 AC 285.........................7.38.3
Imperial Chemical Industries plc v Colmer (No 2) [1999]
1 WLR 2035 (HL) 12.8, 12.20.2
Inco Europe Ltd v First Choice Distribution [1999] 1 WLR 270 (CA);
[2000] 1 WLR 586 (HL) 3.47, 3.49–3.51, 5.5
India v India Steamship Co Ltd (No 2) [1998] AC 878 (HL)...9.37
Inland Revenue Commissioners v Butterley [1955] Ch 453 (CA);
[1957] AC 32 (HL)..5.41
Inland Revenue Commissioners v Dowdall, O'Mahoney & Co Ltd
[1952] AC 401 (HL)...5.3.2
Inland Revenue Commissioners v Hinchy [1960] AC 748 (HL)..................................4.3, 4.7
Inland Revenue Commissioners v Joiner [1975] 1 WLR 1701 (HL).......................5.17, 5.21
Inland Revenue Commissioners v McGuckian [1997] 1 WLR 991 (HL) 3.45, 3.47
Inland Revenue Commissioners v Parker [1966] AC 141 (HL) 6.19.2, 6.20.2, 6.22

Inter Lotto (UK) Ltd v Camelot Group plc [2003] EWCA Civ 1132,
 [2003] 4 All ER 575 ....6.33, 6.35
Investment Trust Companies v Revenue & Customs Commissioners [2017] UKSC 29,
 [2017] 2 WLR 1200 ....4.15
Isle of Anglesey County Council v Welsh Ministers [2009] EWCA Civ 94,
 [2010] QB 163 ....3.31, 3.59, 3.60
Ivey v Genting Casinos UK Ltd [2016] EWCA Civ 1093, [2017] 1 WLR 679 ....7.23
Jackson v Attorney General [2005] UKHL 56, [2006] 1 AC 262 ....7.12, 7.17
James Buchanan & Co Ltd v Babco Forwarding & Shipping (UK) Ltd
 [1978] AC 141 (HL) 9.10, 9.12, 9.24, 9.28, 9.49,
                                                                                                                  9.50, 9.53, 9.54
Januzi v Secretary of State for the Home Department [2006] UKHL 5,
 [2006] 2 AC 426 .... 9.43–9.45
Jennings v Kelly [1940] AC 206 (HL) 6.32, 6.35
JH Rayner (Mincing Lane) Ltd v Department of Trade and Industry
 [1990] 2 AC 418 (HL) 9.8, 9.9, 9.23, 9.24
Jindal Iron and Steel Co Ltd v Islamic Solidarity Shipping Co Jordan Inc
 [2005] UKHL 49, [2005] 1 WLR 1363 ....9.60
John Mander Pension Trustees Ltd v Revenue & Customs Commissioners
 [2015] UKSC 56, [2015] 1 WLR 3857 ....5.7, 5.31.3
Johnson v Moreton [1980] AC 37 (HL) 5.22.2
Johnston Publishing (North) Ltd v Revenue & Customs Commissioners
 [2008] EWCA Civ 858, [2009] 1 WLR 1349 ....3.20
Jones v Tower Boot Co Ltd [1997] 2 All ER 406 (CA) 3.15
K (A Child), Re [2014] UKSC 29, [2014] AC 1401 ....9.51
Karpavicius v The Queen [2002] UKPC 59, [2003] 1 WLR 169 ....3.47, 3.48
Kennedy v Information Commissioner [2011] EWCA Civ 367, [2012] 1 WLR 3524,
 [2012] EWCA Civ 317, [2012] 1 WLR 3524; [2014] UKSC 20,
 [2015] AC 455 .... 5.3.2, 5.27, 6.16, 7.17, 10.12
Kensington International Ltd v Congo [2007] EWHC 1632 (Comm);
 [2007] EWCA Civ 1128, [2008] 1 WLR 1144 ....4.52
King v Director of Serious Fraud Office [2009] UKHL 17, [2009] 1 WLR 718 ....4.59
Kirkness v John Hudson & Co Ltd [1955] AC 696 (HL) 3.11, 5.3.2, 5.29, 5.39, 5.40
Knowles v Liverpool City Council [1993] 1 WLR 1428 (HL) 13.12
Kupeli v Atlasjet Havacilik Anonim Sirketi [2017] EWCA Civ 1037,
 [2017] 4 Costs LO 517 ....12.54
Laws v Society of Lloyd's [2003] EWCA Civ 1887 ....4.45
Lawson v Serco Ltd [2006] UKHL 3, [2006] 1 All ER 823 .... 3.14.3, 4.55, 4.59, 4.60,
                                                                                                                  4.62, 4.63, 4.64
Legal Services Commission v Loomba [2012] EWHC 29 (QB),
 [2012] 1 WLR 2461 ....5.46, 5.47, 5.48.1, 5.48.2
Lehman Bros International (Europe) v CRC Credit Fund Ltd [2012] UKSC 6,
 [2012] 3 All ER 1 ....12.16
Lehman Bros International (Europe), Re (No 4) [2017] UKSC 38,
 [2017] 2 WLR 1497 ....3.9, 3.50, 4.2
Letang v Cooper [1965] 1 QB 232 (CA) 3.35
Litster v Forth Dry Dock & Engineering Co Ltd [1990]
 1 AC 546 (HL) 12.15, 12.28, 12.29

Littlewood v George Wimpey & Co Ltd [1953] 2 QB 501 (CA) 3.22
Littlewoods Mail Order Stores Ltd v Inland Revenue Commissioners
  [1961] Ch 597 (CA) 5.33, 5.36
Liversidge v Anderson [1942] AC 206 (HL) xvii
Lloyd v McMahon [1987] AC 625 (HL) 4.24
Lloyds and Scottish Finance Ltd v Modern Cars and Caravans (Kingston) Ltd
  [1966] 1 QB 764 (QB) 6.30
Lock v British Gas Trading Ltd [2016] EWCA Civ 983, [2017]
  1 CMLR 25 ....12.23.1, 12.27, 12.28
L'Office Cherifien des Phosphates v Yamashita-Shinnihon Steamship
  Co Ltd [1994] 1 AC 486 (HL) 4.43, 4.44, 4.50, 4.53
Lo-Line Electric Motors Ltd, Re [1988] Ch 477 (Ch) 4.11
London Corp v Cusack-Smith [1955] AC 337 (HL) 3.53
London Transport Executive v Betts [1959] AC 213 (HL) 3.34
Lowsley v Forbes [1999] 1 AC 329 (HL) 3.53, 3.54
M v Secretary of State for Justice [2017] EWCA Civ 194, [2017] 1 WLR 4681 ....4.21
M v Secretary of State for Work and Pensions [2004] EWCA Civ 1343,
  [2006] QB 380; [2006] UKHL 11, [2006] 2 AC 91 ....6.18
Mac Fisheries (Wholesale & Retail) Ltd v Coventry Corp [1957]
  1 WLR 1066 (QB) 5.44
MacDonald v Dextra Accessories Ltd [2005] UKHL 47, [2005] 4 All ER 107 ....6.23
MacLeod v Gold Harp Properties Ltd [2014] EWCA Civ 1084,
  [2015] 1 WLR 1249 ....2.16
MacManaway, Re [1951] AC 161 (PC) 5.41, 5.43
MacNiven v Westmoreland Investments Ltd [2003] 1 AC 311 xvii
Macris v Financial Conduct Authority [2017] UKSC 19, [2017] 1 WLR 1095 ....3.45
Magmatic Ltd v PMS International Group plc [2016] UKSC 12,
  [2016] 4 All ER 1027 ....12.13.2, 12.13.3
Majorstake Ltd v Curtis [2008] UKHL 10, [2008] 1 AC 787 ....3.11, 3.44, 4.2
Manchester City Council v Pinnock [2010] UKSC 45, [2011] 2 AC 104 ....10.19
Manchester Ship Canal Co Ltd v United Utilities Water plc [2014] UKSC 40,
  [2014] 1 WLR 2576 ....4.40, 4.50, 6.5
Mangin v Inland Revenue Commissioners [1971] AC 739 (PC) 4.3
Manuel v Attorney General [1983] Ch 77 (CA) 6.5
Mason v Bolton's Library Ltd [1913] 1 KB 83 (CA) 3.15
Masri v Consolidated Contractors International (UK) Ltd (No 2)
  [2008] EWCA Civ 303, [2009] QB 450 ....4.62
Masri v Consolidated Contractors International (UK) Ltd (No 4)
  [2008] EWCA Civ 876, [2010] 1 AC 90; [2009] UKHL 43,
  [2010] 1 AC 90 ....4.59, 4.60, 4.62, 4.63
Massey v Boulden [2002] EWCA Civ 1634, [2003] 1 WLR 1792 ....3.38.1, 3.38.2
Matthew v Trinidad and Tobago [2004] UKPC 33, [2005] 1 AC 433 ....6.4.2, 6.7
Maunsell v Olins [1975] AC 373 (HL) 3.7, 3.10–3.13, 3.15, 3.45,
                                                                                                    5.21, 5.24, 13.16
McCartan Turkington Breen v Times Newspapers Ltd [2001] 2 AC 277 (HL) 3.26
McCarthy & Stone (Developments) Ltd v Richmond upon Thames London
  Borough Council [1992] 2 AC 48 (HL) 5.28
McCaughey, Re [2011] UKSC 20, [2012] 1 AC 725 ....10.9

McDonald v McDonald [2016] UKSC 28, [2017] AC 273 .... 10.16, 10.19, 10.20
McDonald v National Grid Electricity Transmission plc [2014] UKSC 53,
    [2015] AC 1128 .... 3.41, 6.10, 6.32
McDonald v Newton [2017] UKSC 52, 2017 SLT 87 .... 7.34.1
McDonnell v Congregation of Christian Brothers Trustees [2003] UKHL 63,
    [2004] 1 AC 1101 .... 7.12, 7.14.1
McE v Prison Service of Northern Ireland [2009] UKHL 15,
    [2009] 1 AC 908 .... 5.16.5, 5.16.7
McEldowney v Forde [1971] AC 632 (HL) 4.68
McKerr, Re [2004] UKHL 12, [2004] 1 WLR 807 .... 10.9
McKiernon v Secretary of State for Social Security (1989–90) 2 Admin
    LR 133 (CA) 5.10
McMonagle v Westminster City Council [1990] 2 AC 716 (HL) 3.18, 3.19
McTier v Secretary of State for Education [2017] EWHC 212 (Admin) 4.50
Melluish (Inspector of Taxes) v BMI (No 3) Ltd [1996] AC 454 (HL) 7.10, 7.12, 7.22
Melville Dundas Ltd v George Wimpey (UK) Ltd [2007] UKHL 18,
    [2007] 1 WLR 1136 .... 7.38.1
Memco Engineering Ltd, Re [1986] Ch 86 (Ch) 6.30
Milk Supplies Ltd v Department for the Environment, Food and Rural Affairs
    [2010] EWCA Civ 19, [2010] 2 CMLR 40 .... 12.33.2
Ministry of Justice, Lithuania v Bucnys [2013] UKSC 71, [2014] AC 480 .... 7.12
Mirga v Secretary of State for Work and Pensions [2016] UKSC 1,
    [2016] 1 WLR 481 .... 12.13.2
Mitsui Sumitomo Insurance Co (Europe) Ltd v Mayor's Office for Policing
    and Crime [2014] EWCA Civ 682, [2015] QB 180; [2016] UKSC 18,
    [2016] AC 1488 .... 5.25, 5.46, 5.47, 5.48.1
Mohammed v Ministry of Defence [2014] EWHC 1369 (QB);
    [2015] EWCA Civ 843, [2016] 2 WLR 247; [2017] UKSC 1,
    [2017] 2 WLR 287 .... 6.32, 9.9, 9.13, 9.14
Morris v Beardmore [1981] AC 446 (HL) 4.40
Morris v KLM Royal Dutch Airlines [2002] 2 AC 628 .... 9.42, 9.52
Moyna v Secretary of State for Work and Pensions [2003] UKHL 44,
    [2003] 1 WLR 1929 .... 3.14.3
MS (Palestinian Territories) v Secretary of State for the Home Department
    [2010] UKSC 25, [2010] 1 WLR 1639 .... 5.47, 5.48.2
MS (Uganda) v Secretary of State for the Home Department [2014] EWCA Civ 50,
    [2014] 1 WLR 2766; [2016] UKSC 33, [2016] 1 WLR 2615 .... 3.41, 7.30
Mutua v Foreign and Commonwealth Office [2011] EWHC 1913 (QB) 9.2
National Assistance Board v Wilkinson [1952] 2 QB 648 (QB) 4.13
National Dock Labour Board v John Bland & Co Ltd [1972] AC 222 (HL) 6.20.2
National Grid Co plc v Mayes [2001] UKHL 20, [2001] 1 WLR 864 .... 3.41
New Plymouth Borough Council v Taranaki Electric-Power Board
    [1933] AC 680 (PC) 3.16
NML Capital Ltd v Argentina [2011] UKSC 31, [2011] 2 AC 495 .... 3.26
Norman v Cheshire Fire & Rescue Service [2011] EWHC 3305 (QB) 5.33
Nova Productions Ltd v Mazooma Games Ltd [2007] EWCA Civ 219,
    [2007] Bus LR 1032 .... 12.54
Nwogbe v Nwogbe [2000] 2 FLR 744 (CA) 5.16.2

Oakley Inc v Animal Ltd [2005] EWCA Civ 1191, [2006] Ch 337 ....5.11, 12.4

Odelola v Secretary of State for the Home Department [2009] UKHL 25,
[2009] 1 WLR 1230...1.4, 4.50

Office of Communications v Floe Telecom [2009] EWCA Civ 47,
[2009] Bus LR 1116 ....1.4

Office of Communications v Information Commissioner [2010] UKSC 3,
[2010] Env LR 20 ....12.13.3

Office of Fair Trading v Abbey National [2009] UKSC 6, [2010] 1 AC 696 ....12.51, 12.53

Office of Fair Trading v Lloyds TSB Bank plc [2007] UKHL 48,
[2008] 1 AC 316 ....4.60, 4.63

Office of Government Commerce v Information Commissioner
[2008] EWHC 774 (Admin), [2010] QB 98 ....7.12

Office of the King's Prosecutor, Brussels v Cando Armas [2005] UKHL 67,
[2006] 2 AC 1 ....9.33

Omar Parks Ltd v Elkington [1992] 1 WLR 1270 (CA)...3.20

Ormond Investment Co Ltd v Betts [1928] AC 143 (HL) 5.39, 5.40, 5.41

Owners of Cargo Lately Laden on Board the MV Erkowit v Owners of the
Eschersheim (The Eschersheim) [1976] 1 WLR 430 ....9.23

Owners of the 'Anangel Horizon' v Owners of the 'Forest Duke' (CA, 2 July 1997) 6.30

Oxfordshire County Council v Oxford City Council [2006] UKHL 25,
[2006] 2 AC 674 ....6.24

Oyarce v Cheshire County Council [2008] EWCA Civ 434, [2008] 4 All ER 907 ....5.28

Padfield v Minister of Agriculture, Fisheries and Food [1968] AC 997 (HL)................14.14

Palm Developments Ltd v Secretary of State for Communities and Local
Government [2009] EWHC 220 (Admin), [2009] 2 P&CR 16 ....5.31.3

Palmer v Southend-on-Sea Borough Council [1984] 1 WLR 1129 (CA).......................14.21

Paramount Airways Ltd, Re [1993] Ch 223 (CA)..4.63, 4.64

Parkwood Leisure Ltd v Alemo-Herron [2011] UKSC 26,
[2011] 4 All ER 800...12.23.1, 12.26

Parliamentary Privilege Act 1770, Re [1958] AC 331 (PC)...5.16.3

Peart v Stewart [1983] 2 AC 109 (HL) 3.34, 4.33.3

Pennine Raceway Ltd v Kirklees Metropolitan Borough Council
[1983] QB 382 (CA) 5.25, 5.26, 5.37

Pepper (Inspector of Taxes) v Hart [1993] AC 593 (HL) ....viii–ix, xx, 7.3, 7.8,
7.10–7.17, 7.19, 7.21, 7.30.2,
7.34, 7.34.3, 7.34.4, 7.37.1,
7.38, 7.38.3, 7.43.2, 7.43.3.1

Phillips v News Group Newspapers [2012] UKSC 28, [2013] 1 AC 1...............6.19.2, 6.20.1,
6.22, 6.23

Phillips v Parnaby [1934] 2 KB 299 (KB) 5.31.2, 5.36

Pickstone v Freemans plc [1989] AC 66 (HL) 7.11, 7.33, 7.34.1, 12.15,
12.28, 12.29

Pinner v Everett [1969] 1 WLR 1266 (HL)..3.11

PNPF Trust Co Ltd v Taylor [2010] EWHC 1573 (Ch), [2010] Pens LR 261 ....7.29, 7.38.1

Polydor Ltd v Harlequin Record Shops Ltd [1980] 1 CMLR 669 (Ch);
[1980] 2 CMLR 413 (CA)..6.28

Pomiechowski v District Court of Legnica, Poland [2012] UKSC 20,
[2012] 1 WLR 1604..10.19

Poplar Housing and Regeneration Community Association Ltd v Donoghue [2001]
  EWCA Civ 595, [2002] QB 48 ....10.12
Post Office v Estuary Radio Ltd [1968] 2 QB 740 ....9.23
Practice Direction (Sup Ct: Hansard Extracts) [1995] 1 WLR 192 ....7.23
Presidential Insurance Co Ltd v Resha St Hill [2012] UKPC 33 ....7.17
Prestcold (Central) Ltd v Minister of Labour [1969] 1 WLR 89 (CA) 6.20.4
Principal Reporter v K [2010] UKSC 56, [2011] 1 WLR 18 ....10.19
Professional Contractors Group Ltd v Inland Revenue Commissioners
  [2001] EWCA Civ 1945, [2002] 1 CMLR 46 ....12.12
Professional Standards Authority v Health and Care Professions Council
  [2017] EWCA Civ 319 ....1.4
PW & Co v Milton Gate Investments Ltd [2003] EWHC 1994 (Ch), [2004] Ch 142 ......10.9
Pyx Granite Co Ltd v Ministry of Housing and Local Government
  [1960] AC 260 ....4.20, 4.32
Qader v Esure Services Ltd [2016] EWCA Civ 1109, [2017] 1 WLR 1924 ....3.49
Quazi v Quazi [1980] AC 744 (HL) 3.37, 3.38.1, 3.38.3, 3.39
Quebec Railway, Light, Heat and Power Co Ltd v Vandry
  [1920] AC 662 (PC) 3.18
R v A (No 2) [2001] UKHL 25, [2002] 1 AC 45 ....7.30.1, 10.11, 10.13, 10.19
R v Allen [1985] AC 1029 (HL) 4.8
R v Archer [2007] EWCA Crim 536, [2007] 2 Cr App R (S) 71 ....4.2
R v Asfaw [2008] UKHL 31, [2008] 1 AC 1061 ....9.10, 9.28, 9.35
R v Barnet London Borough Council, ex parte Shah [1983] 2 AC 309 (HL) 3.11, 5.27,
                                                                                    5.29, 13.12, 13.17
R v Bedwellty Justices, ex parte Williams [1997] AC 225 (HL) 4.36
R v Bentham [2005] UKHL 18, [2005] 1 WLR 1057 ....3.13, 3.48
R v Bloxham [1983] 1 AC 109 (HL) 4.11
R v Bow Street Magistrate, ex parte Pinochet (No 3) [2000] 1 AC 147 (HL) 9.15, 9.63
R v Bowden [2001] QB 88 (CA) 3.11
R v Bristol Justices, ex parte E [1999] 1 WLR 390 (QB) 4.8
R v Brown (Northern Ireland) [2013] UKSC 43, [2013] 4 All ER 860 ....4.27, 5.3.1,
                                                                                    5.5, 5.6
R v Budimir [2010] EWCA Crim 1486, [2011] QB 744 ....4.68, 4.69, 12.8, 12.33.3
R v C [2007] EWCA Crim 2581, [2008] 1 WLR 966 ....4.5
R v Cain [1985] AC 46 (HL) 4.33
R v Central Criminal Court, ex parte Francis & Francis [1989] AC 346 (HL) 3.16
R v Chambers [2008] EWCA Crim 2467 xx
R v Chard [1984] AC 279 (HL) 3.53, 3.54, 3.55
R v Choudary [2016] EWCA Crim 1436, [2017] 3 All ER 459 ....3.36
R v Clarke [2008] UKHL 8, [2008] 1 WLR 338 ....3.29
R v Commission for Racial Equality, ex parte Hillingdon London Borough Council
  [1982] AC 779 (HL) 4.23
R v Cornwall County Council, ex parte Huntington [1992] 3 All ER 566 (QB);
  [1994] 1 All ER 694 (CA) 4.35
R v Criminal Injuries Compensation Board, ex parte Lain [1967] 2 QB 864 (QB) 1.7
R v Cripps, ex parte Muldoon [1984] QB 68 ....4.33.2
R v Customs & Excise Commissioners, ex parte EMU Tabac Sarl [1997]
  Eu LR 153 (CA) 12.39

R v Customs & Excise Commissioners, ex parte Nissan (UK)
(CA, 19 November 1987)..5.26
R v D [2011] EWCA Crim 2082, [2012] 1 All ER 1108.......................................3.51
R v Director of Serious Fraud Office, ex parte Smith [1993] AC 1 (HL)..............5.16.6
R v Docherty [2016] UKSC 62, [2017] 1 WLR 181..4.42
R v Dowds [2012] EWCA Crim 281, [2012] 1 WLR 2576.....................................4.12
R v Emmett [1998] AC 773 (HL)...4.33
R v Evans [2005] EWCA Crim 1302, [2005] 1 WLR 1435...................................3.14.3
R v G [2003] UKHL 50, [2004] 1 AC 1034.........................3.26, 3.52, 5.3, 5.25
R v G [2009] UKHL 13, [2010] 1 AC 43..14.20
R v Galvin [1987] QB 862 (CA)...6.5, 6.6
R v H [2007] UKHL 7, [2007] 2 AC 270.....................................3.14.3, 5.3.2
R v Heron [1982] 1 WLR 451 (HL) 5.17, 5.17.2, 5.22, 5.22.1, 5.24
R v International Stock Exchange, ex parte Else (1982) Ltd [1993]
QB 534 (CA) 12.12
R v Ireland [1998] AC 147 (HL).........................3.26, 3.28, 3.30, 3.31
R v J [2004] UKHL 42, [2005] 1 AC 562...3.21
R v Jones [2006] UKHL 16, [2007] 1 AC 136..............9.16, 9.17, 9.17.2, 9.19.2
R v K [2001] UKHL 41, [2002] 1 AC 462..4.27
R v Kansal (No 2) [2001] UKHL 62, [2002] 2 AC 69...10.9
R v Kelly [2000] QB 198 (CA)..3.11
R v Keyn (1876) 2 Ex D 63...9.19.2
R v Lambert [2001] UKHL 37, [2002] 2 AC 545...............9.27, 9.37, 10.5.2, 10.9, 10.19
R v Lang [2005] EWCA Crim 2864, [2006] 1 WLR 2509 ....3.52, 14.21
R v Legal Aid Board, ex parte Bruce [1992] 1 WLR 694 (HL)...............................4.2
R v Lewes Crown Court, ex parte Hill (1991) 93 Cr App R 60 (QB) 3.45
R v Liverpool City Council, ex parte Baby Products Association
(2000) 2 LGLR 689 (QB) 3.21
R v London County Council [1893] 2 QB 454 (CA) 1.8, 1.8.1
R v Lord Chancellor, ex parte Lightfoot [2000] QB 597 (CA) 5.45
R v Lord President of the Privy Council, ex parte Page
[1993] AC 682 (HL)..4.33.3, 4.33.4, 4.36
R v Loxdale (1758) 1 Burr 445, 97 ER 394.....................................5.32, 5.33
R v Lyons [2002] UKHL 44, [2003] 1 AC 976 ....9.12, 9.17.3, 9.19.1, 9.20,
9.27, 9.32, 9.34, 9.64
R v Medical Appeal Tribunal, ex parte Gilmore [1957] 1 QB 574 (CA) 4.31, 4.37.1
R v Meeking [2012] EWCA Crim 641, [2012] 1 WLR 3349 ....13.4
R v Monopolies and Mergers Commission, ex parte South Yorkshire
Transport Ltd [1993] 1 WLR 23 (HL) 3.14.2, 14.21
R v Montila [2004] UKHL 50, [2004] 1 WLR 3141 ....3.43, 6.3, 6.8, 6.14,
7.29, 7.34.3, 7.43.1
R v Muhamed [2002] EWCA Crim 1856, [2003] QB 1031 ....4.28, 4.30.2, 4.30.3
R v North West Suffolk (Mildenhall) Magistrates' Court, ex parte
Forest Heath District Council [1998] Env LR 9 (CA)................................14.21
R v Okedare (No 2) [2014] EWCA Crim 1173, [2014] 1 WLR 4088 ....6.9
R v Rimmington [2005] UKHL 63, [2006] 1 AC 459 ....7.14.2
R v Rogers [2014] EWCA Crim 1680, [2015] 1 WLR 1017 ....4.66
R v Sanghera (Rashpal) [2001] 1 Cr App R 20...1.4

R v Secretary of State for Health, ex parte Hammersmith and Fulham London
  Borough Council (1999) 31 HLR 475 (CA) 4.5
R v Secretary of State for Social Security, ex parte Britnell [1991] 1 WLR 198 (HL).......5.10
R v Secretary of State for Social Security, ex parte Joint Council for the Welfare
  of Immigrants [1997] 1 WLR 275 (CA) 5.10
R v Secretary of State for the Environment, Transport and the Regions,
  ex parte Spath Holme Ltd [2001] 2 AC 349 (HL) 3.2, 3.3, 3.10, 3.11, 3.45,
                                          3.46, 5.10, 5.20, 5.21, 5.22.2, 5.24,
                                          6.1, 6.4.3, 6.5, 7.1, 7.3, 7.4, 7.6, 7.12,
                                          7.13, 7.22, 7.29, 7.34.1, 7.38, 7.43.1,
                                          7.43.3.1, 7.43.3.2, 7.43.4
R v Secretary of State for the Home Department, ex parte Adan
  [2001] 2 AC 477 (HL).. 9.38, 9.39, 9.50, 9.52
R v Secretary of State for the Home Department, ex parte Brind
  [1991] AC 696 (HL)..9.35
R v Secretary of State for the Home Department, ex parte Fayed
  [1998] 1 WLR 763 (CA) 4.37.3
R v Secretary of State for the Home Department, ex parte H [1995] QB 43 (CA) 5.25
R v Secretary of State for the Home Department, ex parte Leech
  [1994] QB 198 (CA) 4.18
R v Secretary of State for the Home Department, ex parte Mehari
  [1994] QB 474 (QB) 5.48.2
R v Secretary of State for the Home Department, ex parte Naughton
  [1997] 1 WLR 118 (QB) 4.2
R v Secretary of State for the Home Department, ex parte Pierson
  [1998] AC 539 (HL)..4.17–4.19, 4.23
R v Secretary of State for the Home Department, ex parte Saleem
  [2001] 1 WLR 443 (CA) 4.19
R v Secretary of State for the Home Department, ex parte Simms
  [2000] 2 AC 115 (HL).. ix, 4.17, 4.19, 4.23, 4.31
R v Secretary of State for Transport, ex parte Factortame Ltd (No 1)
  [1990] 2 AC 85 (HL).. 7.38.3, 12.4, 12.8, 12.15
R v Sissen [2001] 1 WLR 902 (CA)..4.67
R v Smith (Wallace Duncan) (No 4) [2004] EWCA Crim 631, [2004] QB 1418 ....4.66
R v Soneji [2005] UKHL 49, [2006] 1 AC 340...5.24
R v Stephens [2007] EWCA Crim 1249, [2007] 2 Cr App R 26......................................14.21
R v T [2008] EWCA Crim 815, [2009] 1 AC 1310; [2009] UKHL 20,
  [2009] 1 AC 1310 .... 3.46, 7.1, 7.14.2, 7.16, 7.38.1
R v Tearse [1945] KB 1 (CA) 3.23
R v Thames Metropolitan Stipendiary Magistrate, ex parte Horgan
  [1998] QB 719 (QB) 5.29
R v Tilley [2009] EWCA Crim 1426, [2010] 1 WLR 605 ....7.14.2
R v Titterton [1895] 2 QB 61...5.37
R v Unah [2011] EWCA Crim 1837, [2012] 1 WLR 545 ....13.12
R v Uxbridge Justices, ex parte Webb [1994] 2 CMLR 288..3.39
R v Waya [2012] UKSC 51, [2013] 1 AC 294...10.19
R v Wheatley [1979] 1 WLR 144 (CA).......................................5.31.1, 5.31.3, 5.35, 6.20.2
R v Wicks [1998] AC 92 (HL) 4.70

R v Wood [2000] 1 WLR 1687 (CA) 13.16

R v Z (Attorney General for Northern Ireland's Reference) [2005] UKHL 35,
[2005] 2 AC 645 .... 3.13, 3.44, 3.45, 3.47, 7.29

R (on the application of A) v Director of Establishments of the Security
Service [2009] UKSC 12, [2010] 2 AC 1 .... 4.32, 4.34, 4.38, 5.48.2

R (on the application of Adams) v Secretary of State for Justice [2011] UKSC 18,
[2012] 1 AC 48 ....4.54, 9.23, 9.25, 9.26, 9.33, 9.54, 9.55

R (on the application of Al-Fawwaz) v Governor of Brixton Prison
[2001] UKHL 69, [2002] 1 AC 556 ....9.27, 9.29

R (on the application of Al-Haq) v Secretary of State for Foreign and
Commonwealth Affairs [2009] EWHC 1910 (Admin)..9.16, 9.17

R (on the application of Al-Saadoon) v Secretary of State for Defence
[2009] EWCA Civ 7, [2010] QB 486..9.16

R (on the application of Al-Saadoon) v Secretary of State for Defence
[2016] EWCA Civ 811, [2017] 2 WLR 219..4.20

R (on the application of Al-Skeini) v Secretary of State for Defence [2007] UKHL 26,
[2008] 1 AC 153 .... 4.55, 4.57, 4.60, 4.61, 4.63

R (on the application of Alvi) v Secretary of State for the Home Department
[2012] UKSC 33, [2012] 1 WLR 2208 ....1.4

R (on the application of Amicus) v Secretary of State for Trade and Industry
[2004] EWHC 860 (Admin), [2007] ICR 1176..7.21

R (on the application of Anderson) v Secretary of State for the Home Department
[2002] UKHL 46, [2003] 1 AC 837 ....10.20, 10.30

R (on the application of Andrews) v Secretary of State for Environment,
Food and Rural Affairs [2015] EWCA Civ 669, [2016] 3 All ER 1022 ....3.17, 3.46

R (on the application of Anufrijeva) v Secretary of State for the Home Department
[2003] UKHL 36, [2004] 1 AC 604 ....4.23, 4.25, 4.26

R (on the application of Archway Sheet Metal Works Josif Family Trustees)
v Secretary of State for Communities and Local Government [2015]
EWHC 794 (Admin)..4.69

R (on the application of Bancoult) v Secretary of State for Foreign and
Commonwealth Affairs (No 2) [2008] UKHL 61, [2009] 1 AC 453 ....1.7

R (on the application of Bancoult) v Secretary of State for Foreign and Commonwealth
Affairs (No 3) [2014] EWCA Civ 708, [2014] 1 WLR 2921..9.45

R (on the application of Barclay) v Lord Chancellor (No 2) [2014] UKSC 54,
[2015] AC 276 ....4.57

R (on the application of Best) v Chief Land Registrar [2015] EWCA Civ 17,
[2016] QB 23..7.38.2, 7.40

R (on the application of Black) v Secretary of State for Justice [2016]
EWCA Civ 125, [2016] QB 1060; [2017] UKSC 81, [2018] 2 WLR 123 ....3.42, 4.21,
4.22, 4.41

R (on the application of Bourgass) v Secretary of State for Justice [2015] UKSC 54,
[2016] AC 384 ....3.41

R (on the application of Bradley) v Secretary of State for Work and Pensions
[2008] EWCA Civ 36, [2009] QB 114..7.17

R (on the application of British Telecommunications plc) v Secretary of State for
Culture, Olympics, Media and Sport [2012] EWCA Civ 232,
[2012] Bus LR 1766 ....12.55

R (on the application of Brown) v Secretary of State for the Home Department
[2015] UKSC 8, [2015] 1 WLR 1060 .... 5.3.2, 5.5, 5.6, 7.12, 7.15
R (on the application of Buckinghamshire County Council) v Kingston upon
Thames Royal London Borough Council [2011] EWCA Civ 457,
[2012] PTSR 854 ....14.20
R (on the application of Buckinghamshire County Council) v Secretary of State
for Transport [2014] UKSC 3, [2014] 1 WLR 324 .... 1.10.3, 5.16.3, 7.21, 9.24, 12.2,
12.8, 12.11, 12.13.2, 12.13.3,
12.33.2, 12.37, 12.44, 12.53, 12.55
R (on the application of Buddington) v Secretary of State for the Home Department
[2006] EWCA Civ 280, [2006] 2 Cr App R (S) 109 3,49
R (on the application of Carson) v Secretary of State for Work and Pensions [2002]
EWHC 978 (Admin); [2003] EWCA Civ 797, [2003] 3 All ER 577;
[2005] UKHL 37, [2006] 1 AC 173 ....4.58, 9.37
R (on the application of Cart) v Upper Tribunal [2009] EWHC 3052 (Admin),
[2011] QB 120; [2011] UKSC 28, [2012] 1 AC 663 ....4.31, 4.33–4.33.3, 4.34,
4.36, 4.37.4, 4.39
R (on the application of Chester) v Secretary of State for Justice [2013] UKSC 63,
[2014] AC 271 ....10.28, 12.20.3
R (on the application of Child Poverty Action Group) v Secretary of State for
Work and Pensions [2010] UKSC 54, [2011] 2 AC 15................................4.15, 4.21, 4.27
R (on the application of Condron) v Merthyr Tydfil County Borough Council
[2010] EWCA Civ 534, [2010] 3 CMLR 32 ....12.38, 12.40
R (on the application of Confederation of Passenger Transport UK) v
Humber Bridge Board [2003] EWCA Civ 842, [2004] QB 310............. 3.49, 7.34.2, 7.34.4,
7.39, 7.43.2
R (on the application of Corner House Research) v Director of the Serious Fraud
Office [2008] EWHC 714 (Admin), [2009] 1 AC 756; [2008] UKHL 60,
[2009] 1 AC 756 ....9.44
R (on the application of Countryside Alliance) v Attorney General
[2007] UKHL 52, [2008] 1 AC 719 ....12.13.3
R (on the application of D) v Secretary of State for Work and Pensions
[2010] EWCA Civ 18, [2010] 1 WLR 1782 .... 3.13, 7.29, 7.34.3, 7.35, 7.37.2,
7.43.2, 7.43.3.1, 7.43.4
R (on the application of Daly) v Secretary of State for the Home Department
[2001] UKHL 26, [2001] 2 AC 532 ....4.18
R (on the application of Data Broadcasting International Ltd) v Office of
Communications [2010] EWHC 1243 (Admin) 1.4
R (on the application of Eastenders Cash & Carry plc) v Revenue & Customs
Commissioners [2014] UKSC 34, [2015] AC 1101..7.26, 7.38.4
R (on the application of Edison First Power Ltd) v Central Valuation Officer
[2003] UKHL 20, [2003] 4 All ER 209..4.3, 4.5
R (on the application of English Bridge Union Ltd) v English Sports Council
[2015] EWHC 2875 (Admin), [2016] 1 WLR 957 .... 1.7, 5.5, 7.39, 7.40
R (on the application of European Roma Rights) v Prague Immigration Officer
[2004] UKHL 55, [2005] 2 AC 1 .... 9.10, 9.13, 9.14, 9.18, 9.19.2,
9.27, 9.45, 9.46

R (on the application of Evans) v Attorney General [2015] UKSC 21,
[2015] 1 AC 1787 ....ix, 4.31, 4.32, 7.16
R (on the application of Forge Care Homes Ltd) v Cardiff and Vale University
Health Board [2017] UKSC 56, [2017] PTSR 1140 ....3.52, 14.20
R (on the application of France) v Kensington and Chelsea Royal London
Borough Council [2017] EWCA Civ 429, [2017] 1 WLR 3206 ....3.42
R (on the application of Freedom and Justice Party) v Secretary of State for
Foreign and Commonwealth Affairs [2016] EWHC 2010 (Admin)..................9.16, 9.17.2
R (on the application of Friends of the Earth) v Secretary of State for Energy
and Climate Change [2009] EWCA Civ 810, [2010] Env LR 11 ....14.21
R (on the application of G) v Immigration Appeal Tribunal [2004]
EWCA Civ 1731, [2005] 1 WLR 1445 ....4.31, 4.32
R (on the application of G) v Westminster City Council [2004] EWCA Civ 45,
[2004] 1 WLR 1113..3.11
R (on the application of GC) v Commissioner of Police of the Metropolis
[2011] UKSC 21, [2011] 1 WLR 1230 .... 10.5, 10.7, 13.3, 14.14
R (on the application of George) v Secretary of State for the Home Department
[2014] UKSC 28, [2014] 1 WLR 1831 ....5.33, 5.35, 5.42
R (on the application of Ghai) v Newcastle City Council [2010] EWCA Civ 59,
[2011] QB 591..3.14.2, 3.15, 13.11
R (on the application of Gibraltar Betting & Gaming Association Ltd) v Revenue &
Customs Commissioners [2015] EWHC 1863 (Admin) (QB) 12.12, 12.20.1
R (on the application of Gibraltar Betting & Gaming Association Ltd) v Secretary
of State for Culture, Media and Sport [2014] EWHC 3236 (Admin),
[2015] 1 CMLR 28 ....12.20.1
R (on the application of Gibson) v Secretary of State for Justice
[2015] EWCA Civ 1148, [2017] 1 WLR 1115...3.47
R (on the application of Godmanchester Town Council) v Secretary of State for the
Environment, Food and Rural Affairs [2007] UKHL 28, [2008] 1 AC 221 ....6.30, 6.32
R (on the application of H) v Inland Revenue Commissioners [2002]
EWHC 2164 (Admin)...7.15
R (on the application of Harrison) v Secretary of State for Health [2009]
EWHC 3086 (Admin)...3.22, 3.34
R (on the application of Haw) v Secretary of State for the Home Department
[2006] EWCA Civ 532, [2006] QB 780 .... 3.45, 3.48, 4.8, 4.10, 4.11
R (on the application of Hillingdon) v Secretary of State for Transport
[2017] EWHC 121 (Admin), [2017] 1 WLR 2166 ....4.34, 4.35, 7.12
R (on the application of Hillsden) v Epping Forest District Council
[2015] EWHC 98 (Admin)...3.55
R (on the application of Howard League for Penal Reform) v Lord Chancellor
[2017] EWCA Civ 244, [2017] 4 WLR 92...4.25
R (on the application of H-S) v Secretary of State for Justice [2017] EWHC
1948 (Admin)..7.13, 7.17
R (on the application of Hurst) v London Northern District Coroner [2007]
UKHL 13, [2007] 2 AC 189 .... 10.9, 10.10, 12.25, 12.27
R (on the application of Hussein) v Secretary of State for Defence [2014]
EWCA Civ 1087 ....9.44

R (on the application of IDT Card Services Ireland Ltd) v Revenue & Customs
Commissioners [2006] EWCA Civ 29 .... 11.32, 12.16, 12.22.2, 12.23.1,
12.27–12.29, 12.38, 12.43
R (on the application of Infant and Dietetic Foods Association Ltd) v Secretary
of State for Health [2008] EWHC 575 (Admin), [2009] Eu LR 1 .... 12.53–12.55
R (on the application of Ingenious Media Holdings plc) v Revenue & Customs
Commissioners [2016] UKSC 54, [2016] 1 WLR 4164 ....4.17, 4.19
R (on the application of Innovia Cellophane Ltd) v Infrastructure Planning
Commission [2011] EWHC 2883 (Admin), [2012] PTSR 1132 ....5.31
R (on the application of Jackson) v Attorney General [2005] UKHL 56,
[2006] 1 AC 262 ....1.5, 1.6, 1.14, 3.40, 4.31, 5.3.2,
5.16.3, 6.7, 6.20.3, 6.20.4
R (on the application of Jaspers (Treburley) Ltd) v Food Standards Agency
[2013] EWHC 1788 (Admin) 12.4
R (on the application of Jones) v First-tier Tribunal [2013] UKSC 19,
[2013] 2 AC 48 ....3.14.3
R (on the application of Junttan Oy) v Bristol Magistrates' Court [2003] UKHL 55,
[2004] 2 All ER 555 ....4.11, 4.12
R (on the application of Kaziu) v Secretary of State for the Home Department
[2015] EWCA 1195, [2016] 1 WLR 673 ....5.3.2, 5.6
R (on the application of Kelly) v Secretary of State for Justice [2008] EWCA Civ 177,
[2009] QB 204 .... xx, 3.13, 3.47, 3.48, 3.50, 3.51
R (on the application of Keyu) v Secretary of State for Foreign and
Commonwealth Affairs [2015] UKSC 69, [2016] AC 1355 .... 9.16, 9.17, 9.17.1, 10.9
R (on the application of Khatun) v Newham London Borough Council
[2004] EWCA Civ 55, [2005] QB 37 .... 1.4, 12.35, 12.51, 12.53
R (on the application of L) v West London Mental Health NHS Trust
[2014] EWCA Civ 47, [2014] 1 WLR 3103 ....4.25
R (on the application of Lumsdon) v Legal Services Board [2015] UKSC 41,
[2016] AC 697 ....12.33.4
R (on the application of Marchiori) v Environment Agency [2002] EWCA Civ 3,
[2002] Eu LR 225 ....12.52, 12.53
R (on the application of Miller) v Secretary of State for Exiting the European
Union [2016] EWHC 2768 (Admin), [2017] 2 WLR 583; [2017] UKSC 5,
[2017] 2 WLR 583 .... 1.5, 1.7, 1.19, 4.19, 4.31–4.39, 5.27,
5.31, 5.39, 6.5, 9.8, 9.9,
11.15, 12.2, 12.4, 12.6
R (on the application of Minton Morrill Solicitors) v Lord Chancellor
[2017] EWHC 612 (Admin), [2017] HRLR 5 ....7.12, 7.16, 9.27
R (on the application of Mohamed) v Secretary of State for Foreign and
Commonwealth Affairs (No 1) [2008] EWHC 2048 (Admin),
[2009] 1 WLR 2579 ....9.15
R (on the application of Morgan Grenfell & Co Ltd) v Special Commissioner
of Income Tax [2002] UKHL 21, [2003] 1 AC 563 ....4.17, 4.20, 4.21
R (on the application of Mullen) v Secretary of State for the Home Department
[2004] UKHL 18, [2005] 1 AC 1 .... 9.11, 9.25, 9.26, 9.28, 9.33
R (on the application of Munir) v Secretary of State for the Home Department
[2012] UKSC 32, [2012] 1 WLR 2192 ....1.4

R (on the application of Munjaz) v Mersey Care NHS Trust [2005] UKHL 58,
[2006] 2 AC 148 ....1.4

R (on the application of N) v Lewisham London Borough Council
[2014] UKSC 62, [2015] AC 1259............................... 3.53, 3.54, 3.56, 3.59, 3.60

R (on the application of N) v London Borough of Barking and Dagenham
Independent Appeal Panel [2009] EWCA Civ 108, [2009] ELR 268.........................3.22

R (on the application of National Aids Trust) v National Health Service
Commissioning Board (NHS England) [2016] EWCA Civ 1100,
[2017] 1 WLR 1477...5.46

R (on the application of Newby Foods Ltd) v Food Standards Agency
[2017] EWCA Civ 400 ....12.10

R (on the application of Newhaven Port & Properties Ltd) v East Sussex County
Council [2015] UKSC 7, [2015] AC 1547...3.54

R (on the application of Nicklinson) v Ministry of Justice [2014] UKSC 38,
[2015] AC 657 .... 10.20, 10.27, 10.28, 10.30

R (on the application of Noone) v Governor of Drake Hall Prison [2010] UKSC 30,
[2010] 1 WLR 1743...3.47, 3.49

R (on the application of O'Byrne) v Secretary of State for the Environment,
Transport and the Regions [2001] EWCA Civ 499, [2002] HLR 30;
[2002] UKHL 45, [2002] 1 WLR 3250.....................3.11, 5.15, 5.16.1, 5.16.4

R (on the application of Parekh) v Upper Tribunal [2013] EWCA Civ 679,
[2013] CP Rep 38...4.52

R (on the application of Pepushi) v Crown Prosecution Service [2004]
EWHC 798 (Admin)...9.28, 9.30, 9.35

R (on the application of Plantagenet Alliance Ltd) v Secretary of State for
Justice [2014] EWHC 1662 (Admin), [2015] 3 All ER 261 ....4.23

R (on the application of Privacy International) v Investigatory Powers Tribunal
[2017] EWHC 114 (Admin); [2017] EWCA Civ 1868, [2018] HRLR 3 ....4.38

R (on the application of Public and Commercial Services Union) v Minister
for the Civil Service [2010] EWHC 1027 (Admin), [2011] 3 All ER 54.....................7.26

R (on the application of Public Law Project) v Lord Chancellor [2015]
EWCA Civ 1193, [2016] AC 153; [2016] UKSC 39, [2016] AC 1531 ....viii, 1.20, 1.23,
4.19, 5.9, 5.10, 7.14, 10.25, 10.30

R (on the application of Quintavalle) v Secretary of State for Health
[2003] UKHL 13, [2003] 2 AC 687 .... xvii, 3.2, 3.9, 3.26, 3.32,
3.33, 3.44, 3.45, 6.5

R (on the application of Ramsden) v Secretary of State for the Home Department
[2006] EWHC 3502 (Admin), [2007] Prison LR 220 ....3.41

R (on the application of Revenue & Customs Commissioners) v Liverpool Coroner
[2014] EWHC 1586 (Admin), [2015] QB 481 ....4.41

R (on the application of Revenue & Customs Commissioners) v Machell
[2005] EWHC 2593 (Admin), [2006] 1 WLR 609 ....4.37.1

R (on the application of Richards) v Pembrokeshire County Council [2004]
EWCA Civ 1000 ....4.35

R (on the application of Roberts) v Parole Board [2005] UKHL 45,
[2005] 2 AC 738 ....4.23

R (on the application of Rottman) v Commissioner of Police of the Metropolis
[2002] UKHL 20, [2002] 2 AC 692 ....4.13, 4.16, 4.65

R (on the application of S) v Chief Constable of South Yorkshire Police
[2004] UKHL 39, [2004] 1 WLR 2196..7.29
R (on the application of Satu) v London Borough of Hackney [2002]
EWCA Civ 1843 ....2.14
R (on the application of Sisangia) v Director of Legal Aid Casework [2016]
EWCA Civ 24, [2016] 1 WLR 1373... 6.20.1, 6.20.2, 6.20.4, 6.23,
7.38.1, 7.43.2
R (on the application of Sivasubramaniam) v Wandsworth County Court
[2002] EWCA Civ 1738, [2003] 1 WLR 475..4.31, 4.39
R (on the application of SRM Global Master Fund LP) v HM Treasury
Commissioners [2009] EWCA Civ 788, [2010] BCC 558..6.26
R (on the application of ST) v Secretary of State for the Home Department
[2012] UKSC 12, [2012] 2 AC 135... 6.26, 9.18, 9.42, 9.43,
9.46, 9.48, 9.51
R (on the application of T) v Chief Constable for Greater Manchester
[2014] UKSC 35, [2015] AC 49..10.25
R (on the application of Telefonica O2 Europe plc) v Office of Communications
[2007] EWHC 3018 (Admin)..12.14
R (on the application of Thames Water Utilities Ltd) v Bromley Magistrates' Court
(No 2) [2013] EWHC 472 (Admin), [2013] 1 WLR 3641 .... 4.30.1, 4.30.2, 4.30.4
R (on the application of Thames Water Utilities Ltd) v Water Services Regulation
Authority [2010] EWHC 3331 (Admin), [2011] PTSR 857; [2012] EWCA Civ 218,
[2012] PTSR 1147...3.23
R (on the application of ToTel Ltd) v First-tier Tribunal (Tax Chamber)
[2012] EWCA Civ 1401, [2013] QB 860 ....5.10
R (on the application of Tummond) v Reading County Court [2014]
EWHC 1039 (Admin)...4.39
R (on the application of UNISON) v Lord Chancellor [2017] UKSC 51,
[2017] 3 WLR 409..viii, 4.18, 4.31–4.39, 5.10
R (on the application of UNISON) v Monitor [2009] EWHC 3221 (Admin),
[2010] PTSR 1827...3.14.3
R (on the application of W) v Lambeth London Borough Council [2002]
EWCA Civ 613, [2002] 2 All ER 901 ....5.3.2
R (on the application of W) v Secretary of State for Health [2015] EWCA Civ 1034,
[2016] 1 WLR 698...3.21
R (on the application of West) v Parole Board [2005] UKHL 1, [2005] 1 WLR 350 ....3.42
R (on the application of Western Sahara Campaign UK) v Revenue & Customs
Commissioners [2015] EWHC 2898 (Admin)..11.24
R (on the application of Westminster City Council) v National Asylum Support
Service [2002] UKHL 38, [2002] 1 WLR 2956........................... 3.43, 7.3, 7.12, 7.26, 7.27,
7.29, 7.30.2, 7.31, 7.34, 7.34.3,
7.41, 7.43.1, 7.43.3.1, 7.43.4
R (on the application of Whiston) v Secretary of State for Justice [2014] UKSC 39,
[2015] AC 176 ....3.42
R (on the application of Wilkinson) v Inland Revenue Commissioners
[2005] UKHL 30, [2005] 1 WLR 1718..8.8, 10.11, 10.20
R (on the application of Woolas) v Parliamentary Election Court [2010]
EWHC 3169 (Admin), [2012] QB 1 ....3.53, 4.33.2

R (on the application of Wright) v Secretary of State for Health [2009] UKHL 3,
[2009] 1 AC 739 ....10.20
R (on the application of Yam) v Central Criminal Court [2015] UKSC 76,
[2016] AC 771 ....4.20
R (on the application of ZA (Nigeria)) v Secretary of State for the Home Department
[2010] EWCA Civ 926, [2011] QB 722 ....5.16.2
R (on the application of Zagorski) v Secretary of State for Business, Innovation
and Skills [2011] HRLR 140 ....11.18
R (on the application of ZO (Somalia) v Secretary of State for the Home
Department [2010] UKSC 36, [2010] 1 WLR 1948 ....12.12
R (on the application of ZYN) v Walsall Metropolitan Borough Council
[2014] EWHC 1918 (Admin), [2015] 1 All ER 165 .... 3.27, 3.29, 3.31, 3.33,
5.27, 5.29, 5.41, 5.42
Racal Communications Ltd, Re [1981] AC 374 (HL) 4.33, 4.33.1, 4.36
Raymond v Honey [1983] 1 AC 1 (HL)..5.44
Recovery of Medical Costs for Asbestos Diseases (Wales) Bill, Re [2015] UKSC 3,
[2015] AC 1016 ....7.11, 7.19, 7.20
Revenue & Customs Commissioners v Aimia Coalition Loyalty UK Ltd
[2013] UKSC 15, [2013] 2 All ER 719; [2013] UKSC 42 ....12.10
Revenue & Customs Commissioners v Anson [2015] UKSC 44, [2015]
4 All ER 288..9.44, 9.45
Revenue & Customs Commissioners v Cotter [2012] EWCA Civ 81,
[2012] STC 745; [2013] UKSC 69, [2013] 1 WLR 3514 ....3.24
RFC 2012 plc v Advocate General for Scotland [2017] UKSC 45,
[2017] 1 WLR 2767..3.14.2, 13.11
Rhondda Waste Disposal Ltd, Re [2001] Ch 57 (CA) 3.38
Rhys-Harper v Relaxion Group plc [2003] UKHL 33, [2003] 4 All ER 1113 ....5.28
River Wear Commissioners v Adamson (1877) 2 App Cas 743...7.3
Riverstone Meat Co Pty Ltd v Lancashire Shipping Co Ltd [1961] AC 807 (HL)............9.44
Robinson v Secretary of State for Northern Ireland [2002] UKHL 32 ....7.12, 7.16
Rowstock Ltd v Jessemey [2014] EWCA Civ 185, [2014] 1 WLR 3615.......6.14, 12.27, 12.28
Royal College of Nursing of the United Kingdom v Department of Health
and Social Security [1981] AC 800 (HL) 3.32
Rugby Football Union v Consolidated Information Services Ltd
(formerly Viagogo Ltd) (in liquidation) [2012] UKSC 55,
[2012] 1 WLR 3333..11.18
Ryanair Ltd v Revenue & Customs Commissioners [2014] EWCA Civ 410............3.18, 3.19
S (A Minor), Re [1998] AC 750 (HL) 9.44, 9.45
S (Care Order: Implementation of Care Plan), Re [2002] UKHL 10,
[2002] 2 AC 291 .... 10.5.1, 10.8, 10.18, 10.20, 10.21
Sabha v Attoeney General of Trinidad and Tobago [2009] UKPC 17................................1.7
Salomon v Customs & Excise Commissioners [1967] 2 QB 116 (CA) 4.54, 9.11, 9.23,
9.25, 9.28, 9.33–9.35, 9.64
Samick Lines Co Ltd v Owners of the Antonis P Lemos [1985] AC 711 (HL).................9.26
Sanneh v Secretary of State for Work and Pensions [2015] EWCA Civ 49,
[2016] QB 455..12.53
Sarrio SA v Kuwait Investment Authority [1999] 1 AC 32 (HL)......................................9.50
Seal v Chief Constable of South Wales Police [2007] UKHL 31, [2007] 1 WLR 1910 ....3.9

Secretary of State for Defence v Guardian Newspapers Ltd [1985] AC 339 (HL).........6.20.2
Secretary of State for Defence v Nicholas [2015] EWCA Civ 53,
    [2015] 1 WLR 2116...10.28
Secretary of State for Defence v Spencer [2003] EWCA Civ 784,
    [2003] 1 WLR 2701..3.18
Secretary of State for Energy and Climate Change v Friends of the Earth
    [2012] EWCA Civ 28, [2012] Env LR 25 ....4.46, 4.47
Secretary of State for Social Security v Tunnicliffe [1991] 2 All ER 712 (CA)..................4.43
Secretary of State for the Environment, ex parte Ostler [1977] QB 122 (CA) 4.35
Sema Group Pension Scheme (Trustees of) v Inland Revenue Commissioners
    [2002] EWCA Civ 1857, [2003] Pens LR 29 ....6.19.2, 6.22
Sepet v Secretary of State for the Home Department [2003] UKHL 15,
    [2003] 1 WLR 856...9.45
Serious Organised Crime Agency v Perry [2012] UKSC 35, [2013] 1 AC 182 ....4.65, 9.64
SerVaas Inc v Rafidain Bank [2010] EWHC 3287 (Ch); [2011] EWCA Civ 1256,
    [2012] 1 All ER (Comm) 527; [2012] UKSC 40, [2013] 1 AC 595...............................9.23
Shahid v Scottish Ministers [2015] UKSC 58, [2016] AC 429............................3.13, 3.48, 4.7
Shamoon v Chief Constable of the Royal Ulster Constabulary [2003] UKHL 11,
    [2003] 2 All ER 26..3.34
Shanks v Unilever plc [2010] EWCA Civ 1283, [2011] RPC 12 ....6.28
Sheldon v RHM Outhwaite (Underwriting Agencies) Ltd [1996] AC 102 (HL)...........5.22.1
Sheldrake v Director of Public Prosecutions [2004] UKHL 43,
    [2005] 1 AC 264 .... 10.11, 10.15, 10.19, 10.20, 10.26
Sidhu v British Airways plc [1997] AC 430...9.24
SJ & J Monk (a firm) v Newbigin [2017] UKSC 56, [2017] 1 WLR 851 ....7.17
Smith v East Elloe Rural District Council [1956] AC 736 (HL)......................4.35, 4.68, 4.69
Smith v Smith [2006] UKHL 35, [2006] 1 WLR 2024 ....xvii, 3.6
Smith International Inc v Specialised Petroleum Services Group Ltd
    [2005] EWCA Civ 1357, [2006] 1 WLR 252...5.16
Société Eram Shipping Co Ltd v Cie Internationale de Navigation [2003] UKHL 30,
    [2004] 1 AC 260 ....4.60
Solar Century Holdings Ltd v Secretary of State for Energy and Climate Change
    [2014] EWHC 3677 (Admin).. 3.13, 7.12, 7.17, 7.29, 7.43.4
Spillers Ltd v Cardiff (Borough) Assessment Committee [1931] 2 KB 21 (KB) 3.16
St John's College School Cambridge v Secretary of State for Social Security
    [2001] ELR 103 (QB)..6.20.2
Stamp Duties Commissioner v Atwill [1973] AC 558 (PC) 6.31, 6.32
Stephens v Cuckfield Rural District Council [1960] 2 QB 373 (CA) 3.14.2
Stock v Frank Jones (Tipton) Ltd [1978] 1 WLR 231 (HL)...............................3.11, 3.13, 4.7
Stott v Thomas Cook Tour Operators Ltd [2014] UKSC 15, [2014] AC 1347 ....9.15
Suffolk Mental Health Partnership NHS Trust v Hurst [2009] EWCA Civ 309,
    [2009] ICR 10..3.24
Sweet v Parsley [1970] AC 132 (HL)... 4.8, 4.27, 4.28, 4.30.1
Swift v Robertson [2014] UKSC 50, [2014] 1 WLR 3438 ....3.46, 12.23.1, 12.28
Taylor v Provan [1975] AC 194 (HL)..6.32
Test Claimants in the FII Group Litigation v Revenue & Customs Commissioners
    [2010] EWCA Civ 103; [2012] UKSC 19, [2012] 2 AC 337 .... 12.13.3, 12.22.2, 12.23.1,
                                                            12.23.2, 12.27, 12.29

Thet v Director of Public Prosecutions [2006] EWHC 2701 (Admin),
[2007] 1 WLR 2022..7.14.2
Thoburn v Sunderland City Council [2002] EWHC 195 (Admin),
[2003] QB 151... 5.9, 5.15, 5.16.1, 5.16.3, 12.2, 12.8
Thomas v Bridgend County Borough Council [2011] EWCA Civ 862,
[2012] QB 512..10.18
Thomas v Marshall (Inspector of Taxes) [1953] AC 543 (HL).............................6.19.2, 6.22
Thompson v Dibdin [1912] AC 533 (HL)..6.30, 6.32
Thorn v Mayor and Commonalty of London (1876) 1 App Cas 120 (HL)..................6.20.4
Tillmanns & Co v SS Knutsford Ltd [1908] 2 KB 385 (CA).........................3.36, 3.37, 3.38.2
T-Mobile (UK) Ltd v Office of Communications [2008] EWCA Civ 1373,
[2009] 1 WLR 1565..12.54
Trendtex Trading Corp v Central Bank of Nigeria [1977] QB 529 (CA)........................9.16
Trinity Mirror plc v Customs & Excise Commissioners [2001] EWCA Civ 65,
[2001] 2 CMLR 33 ....12.12
Tuck & Sons v Priester (1887) 19 QBD 629 (CA) 4.9
Tucker (A Bankrupt), Re [1990] Ch 148 (CA) 4.63
Twentieth Century Fox Film Corp v British Telecommunications plc
[2011] EWHC 2714 (Ch), [2012] Bus LR 1461..12.23.1, 12.34
United States v Nolan [2015] UKSC 63, [2016] AC 463 .... 11.20, 12.6, 12.26, 12.28
Unwin v Hanson [1891] 2 QB 115 (CA) 3.15
Vibixa Ltd v Komori UK Ltd [2006] EWCA Civ 536, [2006] 1 WLR 2472............2.31, 6.11
Vidal-Hall v Google Inc [2015] EWCA Civ 311, [2016] QB 1003................................12.29
Vinos v Marks & Spencer plc [2001] 3 All ER 784 (CA).....................................3.21, 5.16.5
Vodafone 2 v Revenue & Customs Commissioners [2009] EWCA Civ 446,
[2010] Ch 77 ....12.27, 12.28
W Devis & Sons Ltd v Atkins [1977] AC 931 (HL)..5.40
Wainwright v Home Office [2001] EWCA Civ 2081, [2002] QB 1334 ....4.48, 10.9
Walker v Centaur Clothes Group Ltd [2000] 1 WLR 799 (HL) 3.20
Walker v Hemmant [1943] KB 604...5.16.7
Walker v Innospec Ltd [2017] UKSC 47...4.42
Walker v Leeds City Council [1978] AC 403 (HL)...5.31
Wandsworth London Borough Council v Winder [1985] AC 461 (HL) 4.32
Wathan v Neath and Port Talbot County Borough Council [2002]
EWHC 1634 (Admin)...6.18
Watkinson v Hollington [1944] KB 16 (CA)..6.5
Webb v Emo Air Cargo Ltd [1993] 1 WLR 49 (HL) 12.23.1
Welham v Director of Public Prosecutions [1961] AC 103 (HL)....................................3.52
West Midland Baptist (Trust) Association Inc v Birmingham Corp
[1970] AC 874 (HL)..5.3.2
Western Bank Ltd v Schindler [1977] Ch 1 (CA)..3.51
Whiteman v Sadler [1910] AC 514...3.40
Whitsbury Farm and Stud Ltd v Hemens (Valuation Officer)
[1988] AC 601 (HL)...6.20.2, 6.20.3, 6.22
Wickland (Holdings) Ltd v Telchadder [2014] UKSC 57, [2014] 1 WLR 4004................5.25
Wildtree Hotels Ltd v Harrow London Borough Council [2001] 2 AC 1 (HL) 3.57

Wilkinson v Secretary of State for Work and Pensions [2009] EWCA Civ 1111,
 [2009] Pens LR 369 ....3.50
Williams v Central Bank of Nigeria [2014] UKSC 10, [2014] AC 1189...................3.5, 3.13,
 7.4, 7.15, 7.17, 7.29, 7.38.3,
 7.43.1, 7.43.2, 7.43.3.1
Wilson v First County Trust Ltd (No 2) [2003] UKHL 40,
 [2004] 1 AC 816 .... 4.42, 4.43, 4.45, 4.47–4.53, 6.5,
 7.12, 7.14, 7.19, 7.20, 7.38, 7.41, 7.43.1,
 7.43.3.1, 9.27, 10.5.1, 10.8, 10.9, 10.24
Wilson, Re [1985] AC 750 (HL) 8.10
Wirral Metropolitan Borough Council v Salisbury Independent Living
 [2012] EWCA Civ 84, [2012] PTSR 1221 ....3.40
Wood v Gossage [1921] P 194 (CA) 5.29
Woodley v Woodley (No 2) [1994] 1 WLR 1167 (CA) 4.8
Wright v Hale (1860) 6 H&N 227, 158 ER 94 ....4.52
Wyre Forest District Council v Secretary of State for the Environment
 [1990] 2 AC 357 (HL)...6.16
Yarl's Wood Immigration Ltd v Bedfordshire Police Authority [2009]
 EWCA Civ 1110, [2010] QB 698 ....3.13
Yates v Starkey [1951] Ch 465 (CA)..6.22
Yemshaw v Hounslow London Borough Council [2011] UKSC 3,
 [2011] 1 WLR 433...3.30, 7.42
Yew Bon Tew v Kenderaan Bas Mara [1983] 1 AC 553 (PC) 4.53
Zainal bin Hashim v Malaysia [1980] AC 734 (PC)...4.51

European Union

Adeneler v Ellinikos Organismos Galaktos (Case C-212/04) [2006] ECR I-6057.........11.32,
 12.22.2, 12.23.3, 12.23.4, 12.27
Akzo Nobel Chemicals Ltd v Commission of the European Communities
 (Case C-550/07P) [2010] ECR I-8301 ....12.33.1, 12.33.2
Albert Ruckdeschel & Co v Hauptzollamt Hamburg-St Annen (Joined Cases 117/76
 and 16/77) [1977] ECR 1753...12.33.1
Alemo-Herron v Parkwood Leisure Ltd (Case C-426/11) [2014] 1 CMLR 21...............12.26
Allonby v Accrington & Rossendale College (Case C-256/01)
 [2004] ECR I-873..12.40, 12.41
Arcaro (Case C-168/95) [1996] ECR I-4705 ....12.24
Association de mediation sociale v Union locale des syndicats CGT
 (Case C-176/12) [2014] ICR 411 ....11.20
Atlanta Fruchthandelsgesellschaft mbH v Bundesamt für Ernährung und
 Forstwirtschaft (Case C-465/93) [1995] ECR I-3761 ....11.15
Audiolux SA v Groupe Bruxelles Lambert SA (Case C-101/08)
 [2009] ECR I-9823...11.22
Banks v Théâtre Royal de la Monnaie (Case C-178/97) [2000]
 ECR I-2005...12.51, 12.53, 12.55
Belgium v Commission of the European Communities (Case C-110/03)
 [2005] ECR I-2801...12.33.2, 12.45

Berlioz Investment Fund SA v Directeur de l'administration des contributions
directes (Case C-682/15) [2018] 1 CMLR 1 ....12.33.3, 12.33.5
Bowden v Tuffnells Parcels Express Ltd (Case C-133/00)
[2001] ECR I-7031 .... 12.51, 12.53, 12.55
Budějovický Budvar, národní podnik v Anheuser-Busch Inc (Case C-482/09)
[2011] ECR I-8701 .... 12.35, 12.46, 12.47
Caronna (Case C-7/11) (CJEU, 28 June 2012) 12.24
Carp v Ecorad (Case C-80/06) [2007] ECR I-4473 ....11.34
Casa Fleischhandels-GmbH v Bundesanstalt für landwirtschaftliche Marktordnung
(BALM) (Case 215/88) [1989] ECR 2789...12.47
Centre d'Exportation du Livre Francais (CELF) v Societe Internationale de Diffusion
et d'Edition (SIDE) (Case C-199/06) [2008] ECR I-469 ....11.15
Centrosteel Srl v Adipol GmbH (Case C-456/98) [2000] ECR I-6007 ....12.24
Chakroun v Minister van Buitenlandse Zaken (Case C-578/08)
[2010] ECR I-1839...12.53
CILFIT Srl v Ministero della Sanità (Case 283/81) [1982] ECR 3415...........12.13.1, 12.13.3,
12.35–12.37, 12.40, 12.42
Cipra v Bezirkshauptmannschaft Mistelbach (Case C-439/01) [2003] ECR I-745........12.12
Commission of the European Communities v Germany (Case 107/84)
[1985] ECR 2655...12.44
Commission of the European Communities v Germany (Case C-361/88)
[1991] ECR I-2567..12.33.2
Commission of the European Communities v Germany (Case C-61/94)
[1996] ECR I-3989..11.27, 12.31
Commission of the European Communities v Greece (Case C-210/91)
[1992] ECR I-6735..12.33.4
Commission of the European Communities v Greece (Case C-216/98)
[2000] ECR I-8921..12.55
Commission of the European Communities v Italy (Case C-120/88)
[1991] ECR I-621..12.33.2
Commission of the European Communities v Portugal (Case C-55/02)
[2004] ECR I-9387..12.48
Commission of the European Communities v United Kingdom (Case 128/78)
[1979] ECR I-419..11.29
Consorzio del Prosciutto di Parma v Asda Stores Ltd (Case C-108/01)
[2003] ECR I-5121, [2003] 2 CMLR 31........................... 11.16, 11.29, 12.4, 12.5, 12.33.2
Coöperatieve Vereniging De Verenigde Bloemenveilingen Aalsmeer BA
(VBA) v Florimex BV (Case C-265/97P) [2000] ECR I-2061 ....11.50
Deckmyn v Vandersteen (Case C-201/13) [2014] Bus LR 1368 ....12.40
Defrenne v SA Belge de Navigation Aerienne (SABENA) (Case 43/75)
[1976] ECR 455..11.15
Deutsches Milch-Kontor GmbH v Hauptzollamt Hamburg-Jonas
(Case C-136/04) [2005] ECR I-10095 ....12.47
Develop Dr Eisbein GmbH & Co v Hauptzollamt Stuttgart-West
(Case C-35/93) [1994] ECR I-2655 ....12.49
Duff v Minister for Agriculture and Food (Case C-63/93) [1996] ECR I-569 ....12.33.2
EasyCar (UK) Ltd v Office of Fair Trading (Case C-336/03) [2005] ECR I-1947.........12.41

ED & F Man Sugar Ltd v Hauptzollamt Hamburg-Jonas (Case C-274/04)
[2006] ECR I-3269 ....12.33.2
Farkas v Nemzeti Adó- és Vámhivatal Dél-alfödi Regionális Adó Főigazgatósága
(Case C-564/15) (CJEU, 26 April 2017) 12.33.3
Foto-Frost v Hauptzollamt Lübeck-Ost (Case 314/85) [1987] ECR 4199 ....11.15
France v Commission of the European Communities (Joined Cases C-68/94
and C-30/95) [1998] ECR I-1375 ....12.54
Fratelli Variola SpA v Amministrazione italiana delle Finanze (Case 34/73)
[1973] ECR 981 ....11.29, 12.6
Gassmayr v Bundesminister für Wissenschaft und Forschung (Case C-194/08)
[2010] ECR I-6281 ....11.16, 12.5
Gaston Schul Douane-expediteur BV v Minister van Landbouw, Natuur en
Voedsclkwaliteit (Case C-461/03) [2005] ECR I-10513 ....12.14
Germany v Commission of the European Economic Community (Case 24/62)
[1963] ECR 63 ....11.48, 11.50
Grad v Finanzamt Traunstein (Case 9/70) [1970] ECR 825 ....11.34
Halifax plc v Customs & Excise Commissioners (Case C-255/02)
[2006] ECR I-1609 ....12.33.2
Impact v Minister for Agriculture and Food (Case C-268/06) [2008]
ECR I-2483 ....12.33.3
Kadi v Council of the European Union; Al Barakaat International Foundation
v Council of the European Union (Joined Cases C-402/05P & C-415/05P)
[2008] ECR I-6351 ....11.13, 11.23, 11.25
Karl Könecke GmbH & Co KG v Bundesanstalt fur Landwirtschafthche
Marktordnung (BALM) (Case 117/83) [1984] ECR 3291 ....12.33.2
Kolpinghuis Nijmegen (Case 80/86) [1987] ECR 3969 ....12.24
Kommunikationsbehorde Austria (KommAustria) v Osterreichischer Rundfunk
(ORF) (Case C-195/06) [2007] ECR I-8817 ....12.40
Koschniske v Raad van Arbeid (Case 9/79) [1979] ECR 2717 ....12.36
Kücückdevici v Swedex GmbH & Co KG (Case C-555/07)
[2010] ECR I-365 ....11.20, 11.23
Kuusijärvi v Riksförsäkringsverket (Case C-275/96)
[1998] ECR I-3419 ....12.51, 12.53, 12.55
Land de Sarre v Ministre de L'Industrie (Case 187/87) [1988] ECR 5013 ....12.43
Leonard Knubben Speditions GmbH v Hauptzollamt Mannheim
(Case C-143/96) [1997] ECR I-7039 ....12.49
Leonesio v Ministero dell'Agricoltura e Foreste (Case 93/71) [1972] ECR 287 ....11.29
Lyckeskog (Case C-99/00) [2002] ECR I-4839 ....12.13
Margetts and Addenbrooke v Cuddy (Case 143/86) [1988] ECR 625 ....12.49
Marleasing SA v La Comercial Internacional de Alimentacion SA (Case C-106/89)
[1990] ECR I-4135 ....9.23, 10.10, 11.32, 12.21, 12.22, 12.22.2,
12.23.1–12.23.4, 12.27, 12.29
Milk Marketing Board of England and Wales v Cricket St Thomas Estate
(Case C-372/88) [1990] ECR I-1345 ....12.35, 12.36
Moccia Irme SpA v Commission of the European Communities (Case C-280/99)
[2001] ECR I-4717 ....12.47
Morson and Jhanjan v Netherlands (Joined Cases 35–36/82) [1982] ECR 3723 ....12.20.2

Murphy v Bord Telecom Eireann (Case 157/86) [1988] ECR 673 ....12.23.3
Nijemeisland v Minister van Landbouw, NatuurenVoedselkwaliteit
  (Case C-170/08) [2009] ECR I-5127 ....12.33.4
Omega Spielhallen v Bonn (Case C-36/02) [2004] ECR I-9609 ....11.23, 12.33.5
Parti Ecologiste 'Les Verts' v European Parliament (Case 294/83)
  [1986] ECR 1339...11.14, 11.15
Pfeiffer v Deutsches Rotes Kreuz, Kreisverband Waldshut eV
  (Joined Cases C-397–403/01) [2004] ECR I-8835.............................12.21, 12.22, 12.23.1
Pupino (Case C-105/03) [2005] ECR I-5285 ....11.39
R v Customs & Excise Commissioners, ex parte EMU Tabac Sarl (Case C-296/95)
  [1997] Eu LR 153 (CA); [1998] ECR I-1605 ....12.33.2, 12.36
R v Intertanko (Case C-308/06) [2008] ECR I-4057...11.25, 12.31
R (on the application of Air Transport Association of America) v Secretary of State
  for Energy and Climate Change (Case C-366/10) [2011] ECR I-13755.........11.25, 11.26
R (on the application of Gibraltar Betting & Gaming Association Ltd) v Revenue &
  Customs Commissioners (Case C-591/15) [2018] 1 CMLR 13 ....12.20.2
R (on the application of International Air Transport Association (IATA))
  v Department of Transport (Case C-344/04) [2006] ECR I-403 ....11.15, 12.11,
                                                                                                                        12.12, 12.14
Rauh v Hauptzollamt Nürnberg-Fürth (Case C-314/89) [1991] ECR I-1647 ....12.31
Revenue & Customs Commissioners v AXA UK plc (Case C-175/09)
  [2010] ECR I-10701...12.41
Revenue & Customs Commissioners v Rank Group plc (Joined Cases C-259/10 &
  C-260/10) [2011] ECR I-10947..12.33.1
Rijksdienst voor Pensioenen v Engelbrecht (Case C-262/97) [2000] ECR I-7321 ......12.23.2
Rottmann v Freistaat Bayern (Case C-135/08) [2010] ECR I-1449 ....9.18
Schmidberger v Austria (Case C-112/00) [2003] ECR I-5659.......................................11.23
Schrems v Data Protection Commissioner (Case C-362/14) [2016] QB 257.....11.14, 11.23,
                                                                                                                        12.31
Sociedad General de Autores y Editores de España (SGAE) v Rafael Hoteles SL
  (Case C-306/05) [2006] ECR I-11519 ....11.27, 12.34
Spain v Commission of the European Communities (Case C-197/13P)
  (CJEU, 4 September 2014) 12.42
Unibet (London) Ltd v Justitiekanslern (Case C-432/05) [2007] ECR I-2271...........12.33.3
United Kingdom v Commission of the European Communities (Case C-209/96)
  [1998] ECR I-5655...12.33.2
Van der Weerd v Minister van Landbouw, Natuur en Voedselkwaliteit
  (Joined Cases C-222–225/05) [2007] ECR I-4233...12.33.3
Van Gend en Loos v Nederlandse Administratie der Belastingen (Case 26/62)
  [1963] ECR 1...11.15
Van Munster v Rijksdienst voor Pensioenen (Case C-165/91)
  [1994] ECR I-4661..12.23.2
Vodafone Ltd v Secretary of State for Business, Enterprise and Regulatory Reform
  (Case C-58/08) [2010] ECR I-4999 ....12.33.4
Von Colson v Land Nordrhein-Westfalen (Case 14/83) [1984] ECR 1891......12.22, 12.23.3,
                                                                                                                        12.23.4
Williams v Court of Auditors (Case 134/84) [1985] ECR 2225 ....12.33.1

International

Chorzow Factory Case (1928), Merits, PCIJ Series A, No 17, 47 ....9.18
Effect of Awards of Compensation Made by the United Nations Administrative
    Tribunal, Advisory Opinion, ICJ Rep 1954 (13 July), 47, 53 ....9.18
North Sea Continental Shelf (Federal Republic of Germany/Denmark; Federal
    Republic of Germany/Netherlands), Judgment, ICJ Rep 1969 (20 February) 9.14

United States

Cabell v Markham (1945) 148 F 2d 737 xvii

TABLE OF LEGISLATION

United Kingdom

Access to Justice Act 1999
  s 55..5.16
Acts of Parliament (Expiration) Act 1808..2.13
Antarctic Act 1994
  s 23..9.27
Antarctic Act 2013
  s 13..6.17.2
Anti-social Behaviour, Crime and Policing Act 2014
  s 184..2.18.2
  s 185..2.18.4
Arbitration Act 1996
  s 69(8)..5.16
Armed Forces Act 2016
  s 14..5.14
Asbestos Industry Regulations 1931, SR & O 1931/1140....................................6.10, 6.32
Banking (Special Provisions) Act 2008
  s 5(4)..6.26
Bankruptcy Act 1914
  s 25(1)..4.63
Bill of Rights 1689
  Art 9... 7.11, 7.12, 7.20, 7.21, 12.8
Bribery Act 2010...2.4
  s 20..2.4
British Nationality Act 1981
  s 6..5.3.2
  s 40A..5.3.2
Broadcasting Act 1996
  s 114(2)(c)..14.21
Carriage by Air Act 1961..9.24
  s 1(1), (2)..9.24
  Sch 1, Pts I, II..9.24
Charities Act 2011
  s 248(2)..6.20.5
Children Act 1989
  s 105(1)..6.19.4
Church of England Assembly (Powers) Act 1919
  s 4..1.7

Civil Authorities (Special Powers) Act (Northern Ireland) 1922
  s 1(3)..4.68
Civil Procedure Act 1997
  ss 2, 3..1.22.3
  s 4..5.9
Civil Procedure Rules 1998, SI 1998/3132 ....1.22.3
  r 6.26..6.26
  r 24.2(2)(a)..14.21
Communications Act 2003
  s 151..6.17.2
Companies Act 1985
  s 731(2)..5.29
Companies Act 2006
  Pt 3 (ss 17–38)..2.19.3
  s 497(2)..2.20
Compulsory Purchase Act 1965
  s 10(2)..3.57
Consolidation of Enactments (Procedure) Act 1949
  ss 1, 2..5.17.2
Constitutional Reform and Governance Act 2010
  Pt 2 (ss 20–25)..9.8
Consumer Credit Act 1974 ....10.9
  s 75(1)..4.63
Contempt of Court Act 1981
  s 2(2)..14.21
Contracts (Applicable Law) Act 1990
  s 3(3)..9.59
Corporation Tax Act 2009
  s 133N(4), (5)..1.25.2
Criminal Damage Act 1971
  s 1..3.52
Criminal Justice Act 1991 ....5.25
Criminal Justice Act 2003
  ss 225(1), 226(1) 14.21
Criminal Law Act 1977
  s 9(2)..9.22
Crown Proceedings Act 1947
  s 2(1)..6.32
Defamation Act 2013
  s 10(2)..6.17.3, 6.19.4
Digital Economy Act 2010..5.3
  s 45..5.14
  Sch 2..5.14
Disability Discrimination Act 1995..5.28
Domestic Violence, Crime and Victims Act 2004
  s 5..14.21
Education Act 1962..13.12
Education Act 1980..13.12

Electronic Commerce (EC Directive) Regulations 2002, SI 2002/2013 ....11.30
Employment Rights Act 1996
   s 94(1)...3.14.3
   s 244(1)...4.55, 4.57
   s 244(2)...4.57
Environmental Information Regulations 2004, SI 2004/3391 ....2.31
Environmental Protection Act 1990
   s 33(1)(a)..4.30.4
Equality Act 2010 ....5.18
   s 20...2.15
   s 31(10)..2.14, 2.15
   s 66(1)..6.26
   s 150...2.15
   s 211(2)..2.15
   s 214...2.15
   Sch 3..2.15
   Sch 19..2.15
   Sch 27..2.15
   Sch 28..2.15
European Communities Act 1972 .... 5.1, 6.5, 9.1, 11.5, 11.15, 12.2
   s 1..9.10
   s 1(2).. 11.5–11.10
   s 2... 9.10, 11.5, 12.8, 12.22.2
   s 2(1)..11.15, 12.3–12.6, 12.15
   s 2(1)(a)...12.6
   s 2(2).. 1.22.1, 2.31, 5.11, 11.30, 12.6, 12.7
   s 2(2)(a), (b)...12.6, 12.7
   s 2(4)... 12.4, 12.7, 12.8, 12.19, 12.20.2
   s 3...12.9–12.14, 12.30
   s 3(1)..9.19.1, 12.9, 12.11
   Sch 1, Pt I..11.5
   Sch 1, Pt II, para 1 ....12.6, 12.9
   Sch 2, para 1 ....12.7
European Communities (Amendment) Act 1986
   s 1...11.6, 11.8
   s 1(1)..11.7, 11.9
   s 2..11.10
European Union Act 2011
   s 2..9.8
   s 18...12.4
European Union (Withdrawal) Bill viii
Explosive Substances Act 1883 ....5.31.1
Explosives Act 1875 ....5.31.1
Extradition Act 2003
   Pt 1...9.33
Fair Trading Act 1973
   s 64(3)..14.21
Finance Act 2003 ....13.3

Financial Services and Markets Act 2000 (Regulated Activities) Order 2001,
  SI 2001/544
  Sch 1 ....4.11
Forestry Act 1967 ....5.31.3
Forgery Act 1913 ....3.52
Fraud Act 2006
  s 13 ....4.52
Freedom of Information Act 2000 ....2.4
  Pt I (ss 1–20) 2.20
  s 1 ....2.20
  s 11(1), (2) 14.21
  Pt II (ss 21–44) 2.20
  Pt IV (ss 50–56) 2.20
  s 50(2)(c) 14.21
  Pt V (ss 57–61) 2.20
  s 84 ....6.17.1
Gaming Act 1968 ....5.31
General Dental Council (Constitution) Order 2009, SI 2009/1808 ....1.22.2
Highways Act 1980 ....3.21, 5.17.3
  s 31(1) 6.30, 6.32
Housing Act 1996
  s 117(1) 3.30
  s 175 ....3.24
  s 182 ....1.4
  s 191 ....3.24
Human Fertilisation and Embryology Act 1990 ....6.5
Human Rights Act 1998 .... xxii, 1.20, 2.15, 2.32, 4.17, 4.57, 5.1,
                        5.16.3, 6.5, 7.11, 7.18, 7.19, 9.1, 9.27,
                        10.1, 10.9, 10.23, 10.25, 14.5, 14.6
  s 1 ....10.4
  s 2(1) 9.19.1
  s 3 ....2.32, 4.19, 7.18, 8.8, 10.2, 10.3, 10.5, 10.5.1,
                        10.5.2, 10.7, 10.9–10.14, 10.16, 10.18–10.24,
                        10.26, 10.28, 12.25, 12.27, 14.5
  s 3(1) .... viii, 10.4, 10.5, 10.6, 10.8, 10.9
  s 3(2)(a) 10.8
  s 3(2)(b), (c) 10.6
  s 4 ....7.18, 10.3, 10.5.2, 10.23–10.30, 14.5
  s 4(1), (2), (3), (4) 10.25
  s 4(5) 10.23
  s 4(6) 10.29
  s 6 ....4.63, 10.25, 13.3
  s 6(1) 4.55, 10.25
  s 6(2) 10.25
  s 10 ....1.6, 1.25.4, 10.29
  s 12(3) 14.21
  s 21(1)(d), (e), (f)(i) 1.7
  s 22 ....9.37

s 22(1)..10.6, 10.25
s 22(4)..10.9
s 22(6)..4.55
Sch 1..2.15
Sch 2..1.25.4, 10.29
Humber Bridge Act 2013..1.10.2, 2.10
Hunting Act 2004..2.11
Hypnotism Act 1952..2.7
Identity Cards Act 2006
   s 25(5)...13.12
Immigration Act 1971
   s 3(2)...1.4
   s 11(1)...6.26
Immigration and Asylum Act 1999
   s 31...9.28
   s 31(2)...9.28
Immigration (Notices) Regulations 2003, SI 2003/658..............................5.47
Inquiries Act 2005
   s 18(3)...2.4
Insolvency Act 1986..4.30.2, 5.45
   ss 1–251...2.19.3
   s 213..4.63
   s 217..4.9
   s 238(2)..4.63
   ss 411, 412...1.22.3
   Sch B1...2.15
Insolvency (England and Wales) Rules 2016, SI 2016/1024........................1.22.3
Interpretation Act 1889..8.2
Interpretation Act 1978..xxii, 5.1, 8.1–8.13, 14.7
   ss 1–3..8.4
   s 1...2.13
   s 3...1.8
   s 4...1.22.4, 8.6
   s 4(a)...2.9
   s 4(b)...2.9, 8.4, 8.6
   s 5...5.31.1, 8.7
   s 6...8.8
   s 11...5.44, 8.9
   s 12(1)...8.10
   s 14...5.8, 8.11
   ss 15–17..5.13, 8.12
   s 16(1)...6.33
   s 17(2)(a)...5.19
   s 20...8.13
   s 20(2)...5.4
   s 20A...8.3, 8.13
   s 21...1.8.2, 1.19
   s 21(1)...1.4, 8.3, 8.4

s 22 ....8.3
s 23 ....8.4
s 25(1) 8.2
s 26 ....2.9, 8.2
Sch 1 ....5.31.1, 8.7
Sch 2, Pt I 8.3
Sch 2, Pt II 8.4
Sch 3 ....8.2
Justice and Security Act 2013 ....2.2
Law of Property Act 1925 ....10.9
Laying of Documents before Parliament (Interpretation) Act 1948
s 1(1) 1.25.1
Legal Aid, Sentencing and Punishment of Offenders Act 2012
s 9(1) 2.14, 2.15
s 32 ....2.18.2
s 41 ....2.18.3
s 43 ....2.18.2, 4.41
Sch 1 ....2.15
Limitation Act 1980
s 38(1) 6.18
s 38(2) 6.26
Local Government Act 1972 ....3.21
Magistrates' Courts Act 1980
s 127 ....5.29
Magistrates' Courts (Forfeiture of Political Donations) Rules 2003, SI 2003/1645 ....2.22
Maritime Conventions Act 1911
ss 1(1), 2, 3(1) 6.30
Mental Health Act 1983 ....5.25
s 118 ....1.4
Merchant Shipping Act 1995
s 224 ....9.10
Sch 11, Pt I 9.10
Ministers of the Crown Act 1975
ss 1, 2 ....1.22.2
Misrepresentation Act 1967
s 5 ....6.33
Nationality, Immigration and Asylum Act 2002
s 82 ....5.47
s 82(2)(h) 5.47
Northern Rock plc Compensation Scheme Order 2008, SI 2008/718 ....6.26
Official Secrets Act 1911 ....6.6
Oil in Navigable Waters Act 1955
s 1(1) 14.17
Parliament Act 1911 ....1.14, 2.11
s 1 ....1.14
s 1(2) 1.11
s 2 ....1.14

s 2(1)..3.40
s 5...3.40
Parliament Act 1949...1.14
Poisons Act 1972
  s 14(2)..4.57
Police and Criminal Evidence Act 1984...1.4, 4.65
Public Health Act 1961...5.31
Public Health (Control of Disease) Act 1984
  s 74..6.20.5
Race Relations Act 1976..5.28
Registered Homes Act 1984..6.20.1
Regulation of Investigatory Powers Act 2000
  s 18...2.17
  s 67(8)...4.38
  s 81(5)...6.19.3
Rent Act 1977
  Sch 1...3.28
Scotland Act 1998...5.16.3
Secretary of State for Business, Innovation and Skills Order 2009, SI 2009/2748.........1.22.2
Senior Courts Act 1981...7.38.3
  s 72..6.20.1
  s 72(5)...6.20.1
Sex Discrimination Act 1975..5.28
Single European Act 1986..11.6
Social Security Act 1975...5.31.1
Social Security Act 1986
  s 22...5.31.1
State Immunity Act 1978..9.64, 9.65
  s 20..9.63
Statutory Instruments Act 1946...1.22, 7.32
  s 1(1)..1.22
  s 4(1)..1.25.1
  ss 5, 6..1.25.2
  s 11..1.24
Suicide Act 1961
  s 2(1)..10.20
Supply and Appropriation (Anticipation and Adjustments) Act 2016.........................2.9
Supreme Court Act 1981
  s 31..7.38.3
Taxation of Chargeable Gains Act 1992
  s 80...6.26
Taxes Management Act 1970...3.24, 4.20
  s 118(2)..6.26
Terrorism Act 2000...13.12
Town and Country Planning Act 1990...5.31.3
Trade Marks Act 1994...6.35
  s 2(2)...6.33, 6.35

United Nations Act 1946
  s 1...1.22.2
  s 1(1)...4.18, 5.11
Vagrancy Act 1824
  s 5..2.19.1
Video Recordings Act 2010
  s 1..5.17.1
  s 1(a)...5.14
War Damage Act 1965
  s 1..4.48
Water Industry Act 1991 ....6.5

European Union

Charter of Fundamental Rights 11.14, 11.17–11.21
  Art 47 ....11.20, 12.33.3
  Art 51(1)...11.18
  Art 52(1)...11.21
  Art 52(5)...11.20
Directive 77/388/EEC (Sixth Directive)
  Art 13...12.41
Directive 2000/31/EC (Directive on electronic commerce)..............................11.30
European Convention on Human Rights........................... xxii, 9.1, 9.5, 9.27, 10.2
  Arts 2–12 ....10.4
  Art 2..10.9
  Art 6..4.38
  Art 6(1)...12.33.3
  Art 8...10.19, 10.20
  Art 10...10.19
  Art 13...9.27, 9.37, 12.33.3
  Art 14..10.4
  Arts 16–18 ....10.4
  Art 41
  First Protocol
    Arts 1–3 ....10.4
    Art 1..10.19
  Thirteenth Protocol, Art 1 ....10.4
Regulation 593/2008 (EC) (Rome I)...11.45–11.48, 11.51
Treaty Establishing the European Economic Community 1957 (TEC).........11.5, 11.10
  Art 119...11.15
  Art 202...11.37
Treaty of Amsterdam 1997 ....11.8
Treaty of Lisbon 2007 ....11.10, 11.13, 11.39
  Protocol on Transitional Provisions, Art 9 ....11.38
  Art 1(2)..11.10
Treaty of Nice 2001 ....11.9
Treaty on European Union 1992 (TEU) 11.7, 11.10
  Art 2...11.22

Art 3(5)..11.24
Art 4(3)..12.22.2
Art 6(1)..11.17, 11.18
Art 6(3)..11.22, 11.23
Art 16..11.43
Art 34..11.38
Treaty on the Functioning of the European Union (TFEU)..11.10
Art 1(2)..11.14
Art 56..11.23
Art 207..11.24
Art 216(1), (2)..11.24
Art 218..11.24
Art 249..12.22.1
Art 267... 12.11–12.13
Art 288..11.28, 11.29, 12.4
Art 290..11.35
Art 290(3)..11.35
Art 291..11.36
Art 291(4)..11.36
Art 294..11.42, 11.43
Art 294(15)..11.43
Art 296..11.48

International

Charter of the United Nations...9.5
Convention for the Protection of Human Rights and Fundamental Freedoms................9.5
Convention on the Conservation of Antarctic Marine Living Resources
Art XXIV 9.27
Convention relating to the Status of Refugees 1951.......................................9.10, 9.27, 9.35
Art 31..9.28
Statute of the International Court of Justice
Art 38(1)...9.2, 9.19.1
Art 59..9.2
Vienna Convention on the Law of Treaties 9.6, 9.39
Art 2(1)(d)..9.7
Arts 11–16 ....9.6
Art 11..9.6
Arts 12–16 ....9.6
Arts 19–23 ....9.7
Art 31..9.39, 9.40, 9.58, 9.60
Art 31(1)...9.41
Art 31(3)(a)...9.47
Art 31(3)(b)...9.44, 9.47
Art 31(3)(c)...9.44
Art 31(2)...9.44
Art 32..9.39, 9.44, 9.57, 9.58, 9.60
Art 32(a), (b)..9.58

Art 33 ....9.55
Art 53 ....9.15
Art 64 ....9.15

New Zealand

Misuse of Drugs Act 1975
  s 6(2A)(c) 3.47

INTRODUCTION

In a judicial utopia every statute or statutory instrument would be expressed with such clarity and would cover every contingency so effectively that interpretation would be straightforward and the only task of the courts would be to apply their terms. Utopia has not yet arrived, however, and judges facing the interpretation of ambiguous or obscure provisions must use the well-worn tools of statutory construction to arrive at a result.[1]

[I]t is one of the surest indexes of a mature and developed jurisprudence not to make a fortress out of the dictionary; but to remember that statutes always have some purpose or object to accomplish, whose sympathetic and imaginative discovery is the surest guide to their meaning.[2]

'When I use a word,' Humpty Dumpty said in rather a scornful tone, 'it means just what I choose it to mean, neither more nor less.'

'The question is,' said Alice, 'whether you can make words mean so many different things.'[3]

The idea for this book was born of a realisation that dawned on two barristers very early in their practice at the Bar, namely that the ability to interpret (or 'construe')[4] legislation properly is a vital skill which all lawyers need to master from the start of their careers, rather than just developing it 'on the go'. It is also one based on core principles which can be distilled in a clearly accessible and *practical* way. Few academic legal courses focus extensively on how to interpret and apply the various forms of legislation as part of their students' training in substantive law.

---

[1] *Smith v Smith* [2006] UKHL 35, [2006] 1 WLR 2024 [79] (Lord Carswell).

[2] Statement by the distinguished US judge Learned Hand J in *Cabell v Markham* (1945) 148 F 2d 737, 739, cited with approval in *R (Quintavalle) v Secretary of State for Health* [2003] UKHL 13, [2003] 2 AC 687 [21] (Lord Steyn).

[3] Lewis Carroll, *Through the Looking-Glass*, cited (without approval) in *Liversidge v Anderson* [1942] AC 206 (HL) 215 (Lord Atkin, dissenting).

[4] The terms 'interpretation' and 'construction' tend to be used by the courts interchangeably and without meaningful distinction: see, eg, *Barclays Mercantile Business Finance Ltd v Mawson* [2004] UKHL 51, [2005] 1 AC 684 [32] (Lord Nicholls), in a speech to which all members of the Judicial Committee hearing the case had contributed: 'the question is always whether the relevant provision of the statute, upon its true *construction*, applies to the facts as found. As Lord Nicholls of Birkenhead said in *MacNiven v Westmoreland Investments Ltd* [2003] 1 AC 311, 320, para 8: "The paramount question always is one of *interpretation* of the particular statutory provision and its application to the facts of the case"' (emphasis added). The terms are likewise used interchangeably in this book. See further Oliver Jones, *Bennion on Statutory Interpretation*, 6th edn (London, LexisNexis, 2013) section 1, 3, which also adopts the practice of using these terms without distinction.

This is striking given that statutes and subordinate legislation are, in the words of Professor Sir Rupert Cross, 'the most abundant source of legal rules in the United Kingdom'.[5] Introductory student textbooks on 'legal method' and learning the law have historically approached the subject in outline only, sometimes by way of commentary focused on those old chestnuts the 'literal', 'golden' and 'mischief' rules, and often with only limited coverage of the specific principles which modern courts most often cite (and apply) in construing legislation today. Furthermore, established practitioners' texts—for all their qualities—do not always necessarily provide the easiest, most digestible route into the subject or the quickest point of reference.

What is Statutory Interpretation and Why is it so Important?

As the distinguished Law Lord Lord Wilberforce once observed: 'the interpretation of legislation is just part of the process of being a good lawyer; a multi-faceted thing, calling for many varied talents'.[6]

The first talent that Lord Wilberforce may well have had in mind is the simple ability to read legislation, to understand its various forms and interrelationships, and to master its structure and anatomy. Another is the talent to identify the purpose and scope of particular enactments in their surrounding legislative context. Then there is the art of determining the intended meaning expressed in the particular language of specific provisions, so as to ascertain how they most properly and suitably apply to a given set of circumstances.

Why are these talents so important for lawyers? The reason is simple: there is now virtually no field of legal expertise which remains untouched by the long arm of legislative provision enacted by Parliament and government ministers, let alone the legislative bodies of the European Union (EU)—the supranational legal order of which (in its various forms) the UK has been a member for over four decades, but which it has now voted to leave by referendum in June 2016. Whether you practise criminal, commercial, company, competition, employment, family, immigration, property or any other area of the law, you need to be at least familiar with the established interpretive rules of the road when negotiating the various statutory gyratories built across your legal landscape.

The proliferation of legislation in these areas and beyond has entailed a constant and continuing process of legislative amendment, repeal, consolidation and

---

[5] Rupert Cross, John Bell and George Engle, *Cross: Statutory Interpretation*, 3rd edn (Oxford, Oxford University Press, 1995).

[6] HL Deb 9 March 1981, vol 418, col 73.

expansion. This process is not, of course, confined to (primary) Acts of Parliament: it also applies to a dizzying array of (secondary) rules and regulations which are made under their 'parent' statutes.

Between 2000 and 2016, Parliament passed (on average) 34 UK public general Acts per year. In the decade before that (1990 to 1999), the number was 54.[7] But the average number of UK statutory instruments enacted each year between 1990 and 2016 was over 3,100.[8] The output of EU legislation has also been prodigious: more than 2,000 basic and amending acts of various kinds were enacted in each year from 2000 to 2016.[9] The government itself has estimated that, at the point of negotiating the UK's withdrawal from the EU, there are more than 12,000 EU regulations in force and there have been about 7,900 statutory instruments that have implemented EU legislation.[10]

There are a number of reasons for such sustained legislative activity. No doubt one factor is the substantial evolution of complex regulatory regimes (administered and enforced by various independent statutory bodies[11] or EU agencies[12] established specifically for that purpose) and the increased number of statutory tribunals set up to exercise specialist adjudicatory functions.[13] More regulation and more tribunals mean more rules and procedures are required to ensure their effectiveness. Another reason is the continued development of European law and, in particular, the UK's implementation into domestic legislation of obligations and frameworks enacted in new EU Directives. Now that the UK has voted to leave the EU (and has given formal notice of its intention to leave under the relevant treaty), complex legislative change is required to fully effect that process of withdrawal and make long-term provision for the UK's future relationship with the legal order of the EU.[14]

The reforming zeal of incoming domestic governments also inevitably results in legislative change, both to put their policy agendas into effect and to respond to rapid developments across society—in globalised financial markets, health, science, communications, the environment, transport, technology, education and crime. Such developments constantly throw up some aspect of existing

---

[7] See the annual totals of UK public general Acts by year at www.legislation.gov.uk/ukpga.

[8] See the annual totals of UK statutory instruments in Vyara Apostolova, House of Commons Library Briefing Paper CBP 7438, 21 April 2017, 'Acts and Statutory Instruments: The Volume of UK Legislation 1950 to 2016', 7, Table 1b.

[9] See, eg, eur-lex.europa.eu/statistics/2016/legislative-acts-statistics.html for the figures for 2016. Figures for other years can be viewed by selecting those other years in the dropdown menu on this page.

[10] Department for Exiting the European Union, *Legislating for the United Kingdom's Withdrawal from the European Union*, updated 15 May 2017, para 2.6.

[11] Such as, eg, the regulatory jurisdiction of the Office of Communications (OFCOM) or the Office of Gas and Electricity Markets (OFGEM).

[12] Such as, eg, the European Medicines Agency.

[13] See, eg, the various chambers of the First-tier Tribunal and the Upper Tribunal within the structure of the Tribunals Service: www.justice.gov.uk/about/hmcts/index.htm.

[14] We do not seek in this book to speculate on possible future developments in this area. Our treatment of EU law and its impact on the interpretation of domestic law is based on the law as in force at the time of writing (while the UK remains a Member State of the EU).

legislation which is not operating properly, has not kept pace with events or is not being applied in the way that the government would like. So some legislative change is introduced to solve perceived problems as and when they arise.

The result is that provisions are enacted which, to put it mildly, are not always clear in their application or their relationship with other enactments. As Lord Griffiths commented in *Pepper v Hart*: 'The ever increasing volume of legislation must inevitably result in ambiguities of statutory language which are not perceived at the time the legislation is enacted.'[15] Moreover, the profusion of legislation means statutory law can be practically difficult to access, with the applicable law on many subjects often having to be located in a complicated 'patchwork of primary and secondary legislation'.[16] It is far from uncommon for the courts themselves to express frustration at the complexity of the legislation that they are required to interpret and apply.[17] It is therefore the job of lawyers (and ultimately the courts) to make sense of Parliament's intention as it is expressed in its often labyrinthine enactments, and the voluminous delegated legislation made thereunder, by interpreting pieces of legislation and working out how they should apply—or should arguably apply—to a given set of facts and circumstances.

The Purpose of this Book

In that context, this 'Practical Guide' aims to be an accessible point of reference and to serve as an introduction to the key materials and concepts in relation to statutory interpretation—both for qualified legal practitioners and for students of the law in general. There are, of course, already a number of well-established and highly regarded practitioners' texts on the principles of statutory interpretation to which the courts are commonly referred in legal proceedings (and to which we refer from time to time in this book, principally where the courts themselves have done so). One is the weighty *Bennion on Statutory Interpretation*, 6th edn (2013),[18] something of a practitioner's bible. Others are *Craies on*

---

[15] *Pepper v Hart* [1993] AC 593 (HL) 617E (Lord Griffiths).

[16] *R v Chambers* [2008] EWCA Crim 2467 [64]–[72] (Toulson LJ).

[17] See, eg, *R (Kelly) v Secretary of State for Justice* [2008] EWCA Civ 177, [2009] QB 204 [30] (Laws LJ): 'These appeals have required us to conduct an examination of interlocking statutory provisions, an exercise of no little complexity ... it is I think much to be regretted that so intricate a process is required in order to ascertain definitively the competing rights of state and prisoner as regards release on licence'; and *Bridge Trustees Ltd v Houldsworth* [2011] UKSC 42, [2011] 1 WLR 1912 [79] (Lord Walker), expressing 'considerable sympathy' with a call for clarity in legislation governing pension schemes, which he thought would be felt by 'many others who have to grapple with the complexities of the primary and secondary legislation relating to occupational pension schemes'.

[18] Jones (n 4). The much-respected author Francis Bennion sadly died on 28 January 2015 while this work was in progress.

Legislation, 11th edn (2016)[19] and the more slender volume, *Cross: Statutory Interpretation*, 3rd edn (1995).[20]

This guide is not intended to be a substitute for those scholarly texts. It does not set out to provide any historical analysis of statutory interpretation as an academic subject, nor does it provide detailed insight into the parliamentary and governmental processes that bring legislation into being. Still less does it seek to provide the same level of detailed discussion on the constant flow of judicial decisions which keeps the law in this area in flux. Its purpose is to provide a distillation of the basics as a 'way in' to the subject, which may be supplemented by the weight of learning which is to be found within the pages of more learned or comprehensive volumes. At the same time, it provides a reference manual for those practitioners in need of a 'quick principle' with an authority to support it, and a signpost to the key cases they may need to consider.

Structure and Approach

This guide begins by identifying the key types of domestic legislation which apply in the UK, explaining in outline the process of their enactment and their key components. Chapter 1 considers the different types of domestic legislation and how they are made. Chapter 2 discusses the 'anatomy and structure' of statutes and statutory instruments, naming and explaining the workings of their constituent parts.

Having laid these essential foundations, we turn to address the key principles and presumptions cited and applied by the courts of England and Wales in their construction of domestic legislation today. Our approach throughout has been to make reference so far as possible to up-to-date case law of the highest authority in order to give confidence that the principles we identify are ones with modern currency which can readily be cited and applied. We begin in Chapter 3 by setting out the core principles of domestic statutory interpretation, focused on how the courts will seek to read statutory language in its context. Chapter 4 sets out a number of the most commonly applied 'presumptions' that the courts apply as to the *effect* of legislation. Chapter 5 gives guidance on what we have called the 'interaction of legislation', that is, the ways in which one piece of legislation can affect the form, content, application or interpretation of another.

With the courts' core approach established, we then consider some of the essential tools and contextual factors that can help in exercises of statutory construction. Thus, in Chapter 6, we discuss 'internal aids to construction'—those features and parts of a piece of domestic legislation which may give particular assistance in interpreting the remainder of that piece of legislation. In Chapter 7, we look at

[19] Daniel Greenberg, *Craies on Legislation*, 11th edn (London, Sweet & Maxwell, 2016).
[20] Cross, Bell and Engle (n 5).

'external aids to construction'—documents found outside of the four corners of the legislation itself to which the courts may permit reference to help determine the meaning of that legislation. Chapter 8 discusses the particular role of the Interpretation Act 1978 in interpreting other legislation.

Chapters 9 to 12 discuss the way international law can affect the meaning and application of domestic legislation. In Chapter 9, we provide an overview of how, in general terms, rules of international law affect the interpretation of domestic legislation. Chapters 10 to 12 focus on the impact of two specific aspects of international law on questions of domestic statutory interpretation, namely the European Convention on Human Rights and EU law. Chapter 10 addresses the former by discussing the effect that the Human Rights Act 1998 has on the interpretation and application of UK legislation. Chapters 11 and 12 address the latter, with Chapter 11 discussing the sources, nature, anatomy and structure of EU law, while Chapter 12 explains how EU law affects the interpretation and application of domestic legislation, as well as how the courts interpret EU law itself.

We then conclude in Chapters 13 and 14 with some practical matters designed to assist with interpreting legislation. Accordingly, Chapter 13 provides a brief overview of some of the main written and electronic resources that allow access to legislation or which may help in its interpretation. And finally, Chapter 14 contains a practical checklist of useful 'pointers' and questions to bear in mind at the outset when construing statutory provisions, drawing together key parts of the learning in the rest of the book and identifying some further points that may arise.

No guide—especially one designed with accessibility as its core aim—can be comprehensive. But we trust that, at the very least, this guide will assist its readers in ascertaining what is meant by the phrase 'the letter and spirit of the law'.

We have endeavoured to state the law so that it is up-to-date as at 1 September 2017 (although we have been able to include some later developments).

A Word of Thanks

Finally, we would like to thank all those who have helped us in preparing this book by considering or assisting with drafts, or offering suggestions and insights, as well as all those who have encouraged us in our efforts. Special thanks are due to Adrienne Anderson and Jonathan Lowe for their hard work helping get our drafts into shape. We are grateful generally for the support, assistance and inspiration provided by our friends and colleagues in Blackstone Chambers, and we owe particular thanks to those who reviewed drafts of parts of this work: Kieron Beal QC, Sam Grodzinski QC, Ravi Mehta and Jason Pobjoy. All errors, of course, remain our own. We would also like to thank Hart Publishing for their patience with us and their belief in this idea.

More than anyone, however, we would like thank our wives and families for their support and sacrifices which have made this book possible.

1

Introduction to Domestic Legislation: Statutes and Subordinate Legislation

1.1 The starting point is to understand the basic *types* of domestic legislation which may require interpretation in a given case, so as to appreciate the differences in their legislative status and know how they interrelate.[1]

1.2 The most fundamental distinction to make is between *statutes* (primary 'Acts of Parliament') and *subordinate legislation* (or 'secondary' or 'delegated' legislation), in its various forms, of which the most common is the *statutory instrument*. Subordinate legislation is made under the authority of primary legislation.

1.3 The same approach to interpretation generally applies to both types of legislation, except to the limited extent that the differing natures of these instruments call for a distinction in approach. Where such a distinction applies, it is addressed in the course of this book.

1.4 Both primary and secondary legislation (the subject matter of this book) are to be further distinguished from other kinds of instruments—such as certain rules,[2]

---

[1] The phrase 'domestic legislation' is used to refer to legislation made by UK authorities (Parliament or others with legislative power) applicable in (at least) England. It is used in distinction to EU legislation (made by the institutions of the EU).

[2] See, eg, the Immigration Rules 'laid down' by the Home Secretary, which are required to be laid before Parliament under s 3(2) of the Immigration Act 1971. Although they create legal rights, the House of Lords held them to be 'not subordinate legislation' or 'made ... under [an] Act' for the purposes of s 21(1) of the Interpretation Act 1978: see *Odelola v Secretary of State for the Home Department* [2009] UKHL 25, [2009] 1 WLR 1230 [6] (Lord Hoffmann), [45]–[47] (Lord Neuberger). Note, however, that this finding was said to have been obiter in *R (Munir) v Secretary of State for the Home Department* [2012] UKSC 32, [2012] 1 WLR 2192 [34]-[40] (Lord Dyson). Nevertheless, it appears to have been widely accepted: see, eg, *R (Alvi) v Secretary of State for the Home Department* [2012] UKSC 33, [2012] 1 WLR 2208 [33] (Lord Hope), specifically reaffirming Lord Hoffmann's statement that the Immigration Rules are 'not subordinate legislation'; and *Ali v Secretary of State for the Home Department* [2016] UKSC 60, [2016] 1 WLR 4799 [17] (Lord Reed): 'The Rules are not law.'

statutory licences,[3] statutory codes[4] and guidance[5]—which, although mandated or contemplated by, and issued pursuant to, statutory provisions, and having some form of legal effect or relevance, have a more nebulous quasi-legislative status. Note that the name given to the relevant instrument is not determinative of the nature of its quasi-legislative status or legal effect.[6]

Primary Legislation: Acts of Parliament

1.5   Statutes, or 'Acts of Parliament', are *primary* legislation, as they do not depend on any other legislation for their status as law.[7] They constitute the highest, or

---

[3] See, eg, *R (Data Broadcasting International Ltd) v Office of Communications* [2010] EWHC 1243 (Admin) [88] (Cranston J), where it was held that licences granted by Ofcom pursuant to statutory powers given to them by Parliament were not contracts, but rather 'public law instruments'. See also *Office of Communications v Floe Telecom* [2009] EWCA Civ 47, [2009] Bus LR 1116 [102] (Mummery LJ): 'the licence is neither domestic law made to implement the EC directive, nor is it any other kind of "law" in the generally understood sense of general rules laid down either in the form of legislation or of case law'.

[4] See, eg, *R (Munjaz) v Mersey Care NHS Trust* [2005] UKHL 58, [2006] 2 AC 148 [21] (Lord Bingham), referring to a Code of Practice prepared and issued by the Health Secretary under s 118 of the Mental Health Act 1983 (in relation to the admission and treatment of patients) which was required to be laid before Parliament, and observing that 'the Code does not have the binding effect which a statutory provision or a statutory instrument would have. It is what it purports to be, guidance and not instruction' albeit guidance that 'should be given great weight' and is 'much more than mere advice', such that a departure from it would require 'cogent reasons'. Lord Steyn referred to the Code as 'a very special type of soft law' (at [38]). Lord Hope stated: 'Statutory guidance of this kind is less than a direction. But it is more than something to which those to whom it is addressed must "have regard to"' (at [68]). See further *R v Sanghera (Rashpal)* [2001] 1 Cr App R 20 [6] (Lord Woolf CJ), referring to a Code of Practice relating to the search of premises by police officers: 'The Code has statutory backing under the Police and Criminal Evidence Act 1984. However, it remains a code and it does not have the status of subordinate legislation.'

[5] See, eg, *R (Khatun) v Newham London Borough Council* [2004] EWCA Civ 55, [2005] QB 37 [47] (Laws LJ), referring to statutory guidance issued under s 182 of the Housing Act 1996 in relation to homelessness: 'Although the guidance is provided for by statute and housing authorities are obliged by section 182 of the 1996 Act to have regard to it, it is not a source of law.' And see, eg, *Professional Standards Authority v Health and Care Professions Council* [2017] EWCA Civ 319 [26]–[27] (Lindblom LJ), finding that the Indicative Sanctions Policy issued by the respondent Council 'is not akin to the code of practice considered in *Munjaz*' (as discussed in n 4 above), as it had 'no specific statutory provenance and status'.

[6] See, eg, *Alvi* (n 2) [99]–[106] (Lord Dyson), holding that certain parts of a Code of Practice were 'just guidance', while others constituted 'rules within the meaning of section 3(2)' of the Immigration Act 1971.

[7] *R (Miller) v Secretary of State for Exiting the European Union* [2017] UKSC 5, [2017] 2 WLR 583 [43] (Joint majority judgment): 'Parliamentary sovereignty is a fundamental principle of the UK constitution ... Parliament, or more precisely the Crown in Parliament, lays down the law through statutes—or primary legislation as it is also known'; *R (Jackson) v Attorney General* [2005] UKHL 56, [2006] 1 AC 262 [9] (Lord Bingham): 'The bedrock of the British constitution is ... the supremacy of the Crown in Parliament'; and [24]: 'The meaning of the expression "Act of Parliament" is not doubtful, ambiguous or obscure. It is as clear and well understood as any expression in the lexicon of the law. It is used, and used only, to denote primary legislation.'

supreme, source of domestic law, taking precedence over all forms of secondary legislation and the exercise of legal powers deriving from the Royal prerogative.[8]

1.6   Statutes may be enacted to introduce completely new laws or to effect some change in existing laws. They are brought into being upon their formal enactment by the UK's sovereign legislature, the 'Crown in Parliament'. In the ordinary course, this will require an Act to be formally passed by both Houses of Parliament (the House of Commons and the House of Lords) and to be granted Royal Assent by the reigning monarch.[9]

1.7   There exist certain other forms of legal instrument which are 'primary' in nature, in that they do not derive their legal effect from other legal instruments, but instead from the Royal prerogative. These include certain Orders in Council[10] and Royal Charters.[11] However, the long-established limits on the scope of prerogative powers mean that such instruments cannot nowadays be used in relation to the UK to exercise any power which is truly legislative in nature[12] (although prerogative Orders in Council may be used to legislate for

---

[8] See the discussion in the previous note, and *Miller* (n 7) [48] (Joint majority judgment): 'consistently with Parliamentary sovereignty, a prerogative power however well-established may be curtailed or abrogated by statute ... The statutory curtailment or abrogation may be by express words or, as has been more common, by necessary implication'.

[9] See the exposition in *Jackson* (n 7) [9] (Lord Bingham). Exceptionally, Acts may be made without the consent of the House of Lords: see below at paragraph 1.14. Further, amendments may be made to Acts of Parliament by those given authority to do so by an Act of Parliament (eg, under s 10 of the Human Rights Act 1998).

[10] Some Orders in Council are made under the prerogative, while others are made by powers granted by statute. An example of the former is the order of 14 June 2017 amending the Charter of the Society of Biology. For an example of the latter, see n 40 below. Note that prerogative Orders in Council are designated as primary legislation for the purposes of the Human Rights Act 1998 by s 21(1)(f)(i) of that Act.

[11] With regard to the nature and interpretation of Royal Charters, see *R (English Bridge Union Ltd) v English Sports Council* [2015] EWHC 2875 (Admin) [32]–[33] (Dove J).

[12] As explained in *Miller* (n 7) at [41]–[44] (Joint majority judgment), the Crown historically had legislative powers in its own right as part of the Royal prerogative, but this power has been curtailed such that: 'The legislative power of the Crown is today exercisable only through Parliament ... Parliament, or more precisely the Crown in Parliament, lays down the law through statutes—or primary legislation as it is also known—and not in any other way.' This has been 'firmly established' since the end of the seventeenth century. The majority continued at [50]: 'it is a fundamental principle of the UK constitution that, unless primary legislation permits it, the Royal prerogative does not enable ministers to change statute law or common law' and explained at [52]–[53] the non-legislative ways in which the exercise of the prerogative can nonetheless have very significant legal effects. Accordingly, the occasional description by the courts of certain prerogative powers or prerogative instruments as being 'legislative' appear to be inapt or inaccurate characterisations: see, eg, *R v Criminal Injuries Compensation Board ex p Lain* [1967] 2 QB 864 (QB) 886 (Diplock LJ), referring to 'the narrow field still left to the prerogative legislative power (for example, declaration of war or blockade)'; *Council for Civil Service Unions v Minister for the Civil Service* [1985] AC 374 (HL) 399C–E (Lord Fraser), describing the Civil Service Order in Council 1982 as 'primary legislation'; and *Sabha v AG of Trinidad and Tobago* [2009] UKPC 17 [22] (Lord Hope): 'The Prerogative in its original form enabled the Sovereign to do all manner of acts, including that of legislating. Although much restricted, that power survives to the present day' (although this may have related to the particular 'constitutional and colonial background' in question, and see at [38]–[39] the distinction drawn between the power to legislate, and the power to make 'law' in a wider sense).

certain overseas territories).[13] Accordingly, at least in relation to the UK and for practical purposes, the terms 'primary legislation', 'Act of Parliament' and 'statute' may be used interchangeably (and they are throughout the remainder of this book).[14]

Types of Statutes

1.8   There are two main types of Act of Parliament:[15]

1.8.1   *'Public General Acts'*: these are the most common form of primary legislation and are the main focus of this book. A general Act is one that 'prima facie ... applies to the whole community', not only certain persons or places[16] (subject, of course, to specific principles as to the territorial 'extent' and 'application' of UK legislation, as to which see Chapter 4.55–4.67).

1.8.2   *'Local Acts and Personal Acts'*:[17] these affect a particular area, person or body.[18] They are much less common and, due to their limited application and service of particular interests, are generally of much less public importance than public general Acts. Personal Acts were known as 'private Acts' prior to 1948.[19]

---

[13] See the discussion in *R (Bancoult) v Secretary of State for Foreign and Commonwealth Affairs (No 2)* [2008] UKHL 61, [2009] 1 AC 453 [31]–[35] (Lord Hoffmann).

[14] For completeness, Measures of the Church of England are sometimes described as primary legislation (and are so designated for the purposes of the Human Rights Act 1998 by s 21(1)(d) and (e) of that Act). However, they are not truly primary in nature, given that they derive their ultimate authority as legislation from s 4 of the Church of England Assembly (Powers) Act 1919, which gives them 'the force and effect of an Act of Parliament'. In any event, they are extremely few in number and their significance is limited to the Church of England.

[15] See the discussion in *R v London County Council* [1893] 2 QB 454 (CA) 462 (Bowen LJ), stating that the key distinction is between 'general Acts and local and personal' rather than between 'public' and 'private' Acts, 'because, of course, a local and personal Act may be public without losing its character of local and personal'. Indeed, 'public' Acts are simply those Acts of which judicial notice is to be taken (ie, those of which parties before a court do not need, as a matter of evidence, to prove the existence or status). Section 3 of the Interpretation Act 1978 provides: 'Every Act is a public Act to be judicially noticed as such, unless the contrary is expressly provided by the Act.' For a fuller discussion of the distinction between public general Acts and local and personal/private Acts, see Daniel Greenberg, *Craies on Legislation*, 11th edn (London, Sweet & Maxwell, 2016) at paras 1.4.1 and 1.4.5–1.4.8, 24–30; and Oliver Jones, *Bennion on Statutory Interpretation*, 6th edn (London, LexisNexis, 2013) at section 28, 153–56.

[16] *London County Council* (n 15) 462 (Bowen LJ).

[17] The definition of an 'Act' in s 21 of the Interpretation Act 1978 expressly includes 'a local and personal or private Act'.

[18] See *Halsbury's Laws of England*, 5th edn, vol 96 (London, LexisNexis, 2012) paras 626–27.

[19] See www.legislation.gov.uk/changes/chron-tables/private for a chronological listing of all private or personal Acts; and www.legislation.gov.uk/changes/chron-tables/private/intro for an explanation of the history of the publication of such Acts. The term 'private Act' is also sometimes used to mean an Act that is not public, or an Act that began life in Parliament as a private Bill. Given this ambiguity, we avoid the phrase in this book.

Enactment of Statutes

1.9 Statutes start life as 'Bills' introduced to Parliament, in the form of a draft Act of Parliament that it is proposed should be enacted to make new law and/or to consolidate, amend or repeal existing law. The function of Bills has been described in the following terms:

> [A] Bill is not there to inform, to explain, to entertain or to perform any of the other usual functions of literature. A Bill's sole reason for existence is to change the law. The resulting Act *is* the law. A consequence of this unique function is that a Bill cannot set about communicating with the reader in the same way that other forms of writing do. It cannot use the same range of tools. In particular, it cannot repeat important points simply to emphasise their importance or safely explain itself by restating a proposition in different words. To do so would risk creating doubts and ambiguities that would fuel litigation. As a result, legislation speaks in a monotone and its language is compressed.[20]

1.10 *Types of Bills*: there are three types of Bills. A Bill's type will determine the parliamentary procedure to be adopted to consider its passage:[21]

1.10.1 *Public Bills* propose law of general application and of general public interest and will become public general Acts of Parliament if passed. They may be introduced to Parliament by government ministers ('Government Bills') or other members of the House of Commons or the House of Lords ('Private Members' Bills').

1.10.2 *Private Bills* propose laws to confer particular powers or benefits on individuals or organisations (for example, companies and local authorities) that go beyond, or depart from, existing law of general application.[22] They are introduced to Parliament following a petition by the person or persons who wish to see the Bill become law. The applicable parliamentary procedure gives opportunity for persons particularly affected by the Bill to petition against it.

1.10.3 *Hybrid Bills*, like public Bills, are of general application and public interest but, like private Bills, they affect certain persons particularly.[23] Given this 'hybrid' nature, the parliamentary procedure adopted for their consideration incorporates elements of the procedures used for both public and private Bills.[24]

---

[20] An Extract from a Note from First Parliamentary Counsel to the Select Committee on the Modernisation of the House of Commons: *Second Report*, HC 389 (3 December 1997), Appendix, p 2, Annex A, para 35, cited in *Jackson* (n 7) [76] (Lord Steyn).

[21] Note that a *private* Bill will, unless it states otherwise, become a *public* Act upon enactment: see n 15 above (and see also n 19 regarding the ambiguity of the term 'private Act').

[22] For an example, see the Humber Bridge Act 2013, a local Act (and a public Act) that began as a private Bill.

[23] They are used, for example, to legislate for major infrastructure projects such as the Channel Tunnel and Crossrail.

[24] The procedure was discussed in *R (Buckinghamshire County Council) v Secretary of State for Transport* [2014] UKSC 3, [2014] 1 WLR 324 [57]–[58] (Lord Reed).

1.11   All Bills are presented for debate and scrutiny by Parliament and may be introduced in either House (that is, Commons or Lords)—save that Money Bills are always introduced in the Commons.[25] They are then subject to formal 'reading', 'Committee' and 'Report' stages in the first House, before passing to the second House to go through the same stages.

1.12   The five principal stages that a Bill must go through in each House in turn before being granted Royal Assent are as follows:[26]

(1)   *First Reading*: the formal announcement that the Bill has been presented. This is a formality to introduce the Bill to the House, following which the Bill is printed. There is no debate at this stage.
(2)   *Second Reading*: the first opportunity for debate, focusing on the general principles and purpose of the Bill.
(3)   *Committee Stage*: the stage at which in-depth, line-by-line scrutiny of the Bill is carried out. In the House of Commons, this stage is usually done by a Public Bill Committee of between 16 and 50 MPs appointed specifically to consider the relevant Bill.[27] The Committee can hear evidence from experts and interest groups if the Bill starts in the House of Commons. In the House of Lords, the Committee stage normally happens in the Lords Chamber and any Member can participate. If the Bill is amended, it is reprinted for the Report stage.
(4)   *Report Stage*: the Bill returns to the floor of the whole House, giving an opportunity for all Members to consider (further) amendments to the Bill.
(5)   *Third Reading*: the final chance for the House to debate the contents of a Bill. In the Commons, it usually follows immediately after the conclusion of the Report stage debate, and no amendments can be made. In the Lords, this stage allows for a Bill to be tidied up, with limited further amendment permitted.

1.13   If the second House considering the Bill amends it from the version approved in the first, the Bill must be sent back to the first House for consideration of those amendments. A Bill may go back and forth between each House

---

[25] 'Money Bill' is defined in s 1(2) of the Parliament Act 1911.

[26] For a fuller explanation of the various stages of the parliamentary process, see the 'Passage of a Bill' section of the Parliament.uk website at www.parliament.uk/about/how/laws/passage-bill. Note that, since 22 October 2015, there has been the potential for an additional procedure to apply to the passage of certain Bills, known as 'English votes for English laws'. This procedure gives power to Members of Parliament from England, or England and Wales (as the case may be), to withhold consent from legislation judged by the Speaker to affect only England, or England and Wales (as the case may be), and which relates to issues falling within devolved legislative competence. We do not consider this procedure in any detail in this book, but for a fuller explanation, see www.parliament.uk/about/how/laws/bills/public/english-votes-for-english-laws.

[27] www.parliament.uk/about/how/committees/general.

(in what is known as 'ping pong') until both Houses reach agreement. This process can be lengthy and complicated. When agreement is reached, the Bill awaits the constitutional formality of Royal Assent, which, when granted, will make it an Act.

1.14 Exceptionally, if the House of Lords refuses to pass a Money Bill for over a month or rejects in two successive parliamentary sessions[28] almost any other public Bill passed by the Commons in those two sessions, the Bill can be passed and receive Royal Assent without the consent of the House of Lords under the procedures of the Parliament Act 1911 (as amended by the Parliament Act 1949).[29] Statutes properly passed under the Parliament Act 1911 (as amended) are primary Acts of Parliament and not a species of subordinate legislation.[30]

Pre-parliamentary and Parliamentary Materials

1.15 The pre-legislative and legislative processes of consulting on, preparing, debating and scrutinising Bills will often generate an array of pre-parliamentary and parliamentary materials, many of which can prove useful in interpreting the legislation ultimately passed (as considered in more detail in Chapter 7).

1.16 Of particular use in elucidating the meaning of an Act are *Hansard* (the 'Official Report' of Parliamentary debates) and *Explanatory Notes* which since 1999 have been published alongside legislation. These resources and their role in statutory interpretation are discussed at Chapter 7.8–7.24 and 7.25–7.31 respectively.

1.17 Pre-parliamentary materials, generated prior to the introduction of a Bill to Parliament, may also help shed light on an Act's meaning, in particular by elucidating its context and intended purpose (as discussed at Chapter 7.38–7.41). Of particular relevance are:

1.17.1 '*Green Papers*': initial consultation documents published by government, designed to inspire discussion on the potential need for legislation whilst proposals are still at a formative stage.

---

[28] Parliamentary sessions are usually, but not always, annual.

[29] Money Bills are dealt with in section 1. Section 2 makes provision for the circumstances in which, subject to certain exceptions, provisos and procedural safeguards, 'any Public Bill' can be enacted without the consent of the House of Lords.

[30] *Jackson* (n 7) [24] (Lord Bingham): 'The 1911 Act did, of course, effect an important constitutional change, but the change lay not in authorising a new form of sub-primary parliamentary legislation but in creating a new way of enacting primary legislation'; [64] (Lord Nicholls): 'To describe an Act of Parliament made by this procedure as "delegated" or "subordinate" legislation, with all the connotations attendant on those expressions, would be an absurd and confusing mischaracterisation'; [94]–[95] (Lord Steyn); [111] (Lord Hope); [173] (Lord Carswell); and [187] (Lord Brown).

1.17.2 '*White Papers*': finalised policy statements setting out detailed proposals for legislation to be put before Parliament. They are often accompanied by a statement in the House of Commons from the Secretary of State in charge of the government department sponsoring the proposals.

1.17.3 Reports by the Law Commission or advisory committees—sometimes reports of these kinds will have acted as the impetus for the enactment of a piece of legislation.

Effect on Other Statutes

1.18 Acts may have the effect of *amending, repealing* and/or *consolidating* (either partially or wholly) other statutes previously enacted by Parliament. Indeed, sometimes the sole or principal purpose of an enactment will be to alter the substance or form of existing legislation. When any of these actions are effected by legislation, transitional provisions or savings will often be enacted at the same time to remove anomalous or unfair effects arising out of the changes being made. The interaction between different pieces of legislation, including by way of amendment, repeal and consolidation, are discussed in detail in Chapter 5.

Subordinate Legislation: Statutory Instruments[31]

1.19 All legislation applying in the UK must be made either by Act of Parliament or pursuant to authority granted by an Act of Parliament.[32] In practice, the vast majority of legislative instruments enacted are not primary legislation in the form of Acts of Parliament, but are 'subordinate'[33] or 'secondary' or 'delegated' legislation, so called because they are made (ultimately) under powers granted by a statute (known as an enabling, empowering or 'parent' Act of Parliament).

1.20 The nature of subordinate legislation means that, unlike an Act of the sovereign Parliament, it can be invalid or ultra vires where its substance goes beyond

---

[31] See generally, House of Commons Briefing Paper Number 06509: *Statutory Instruments* (15 December 2016), available at http://researchbriefings.files.parliament.uk/documents/SN06509/SN06509.pdf; and House of Commons Information Office, *Factsheet L7 on Statutory Instruments*, available at http://www.parliament.uk/documents/commons-information-office/l07.pdf.

[32] Certain instruments made under the Royal prerogative are sometimes referred to as legislation, but following *Miller* (n 7) they are best viewed as not truly legislative in nature: see paragraph 1.7 above.

[33] 'Subordinate legislation' is a term adopted and defined by s 21 of the Interpretation Act 1978 and 'means Orders in Council, orders, rules, regulations, schemes, warrants, byelaws and other instruments made or to be made under any Act'.

what is permitted by the parent enactment,[34] or the wider law (such as under the Human Rights Act 1998),[35] or where it is not passed in accordance with a required procedure.[36] It can therefore be important to know by what power subordinate legislation has (purportedly) been enacted in order to determine its validity. Statutory instruments will ordinarily state on their face—in the 'preamble'—the particular provisions of primary legislation under which they have been enacted: see Chapter 2.31–2.32.

1.21 Like primary legislation, subordinate legislation can be used to amend (or repeal) other subordinate or primary legislation, but only where power to do this is given by its parent Act. This is discussed further in Chapter 5.8–5.11.

Types of Statutory Instrument

1.22 By far the most common form of subordinate legislation is the *statutory instrument* (SI), which will be our focus in this book.[37] Common examples of SIs are as follows:

1.22.1 *Regulations*: these are a particularly common method of making legislation, and new regulations are constantly brought into force. As well as making new law under a host of domestic parent statutes, regulations are also the ordinary method used to 'transpose' or 'implement' EU Directives into English law pursuant to the powers under s 2(2) of the European Communities Act 1972.[38]

1.22.2 *Orders in Council*: these are issued by Her Majesty, 'by and with the advice of Her Privy Council'. In practice, the 'Privy Council' in this context means the government of the day.[39] They tend to be used for addressing matters to which UK government regulations are less well suited, such as interdepartmental or international matters. For example, Orders in Council are used to reorganise

---

[34] *Public Law Project v Lord Chancellor* [2016] UKSC 39, [2016] AC 1531 [23] (Lord Neuberger): 'Subordinate legislation will be held by a court to be invalid if it has an effect, or is made for a purpose, which is ultra vires, that is, outside the scope of the statutory power pursuant to which it was purportedly made.'

[35] See, eg, *Re G (Adoption: Unmarried Couple)* [2008] UKHL 38, [2009] 1 AC 173 [3] (Lord Hoffmann), [46] (Lord Hope); and see further the discussion at Chapter 10.25, especially at n 61 to that paragraph.

[36] But note that it is presumed that any requisite steps were taken and that legislation is valid, unless and until the contrary is proven: see Chapter 4.68–4.70.

[37] It has been said that the term 'statutory instrument' is not, technically speaking, a *kind* of delegated legislation, but rather a formal *method* of making such legislation (by virtue of the Statutory Instruments Act 1946): see Greenberg, *Craies on Legislation* (2016) (n 15), para 3.1.4, 123–24. However, the term is commonly used, and is used here, to refer to the legislation itself since s 1(1) of the Statutory Instrument Act 1946 expressly states that any subordinate legislation made under particular powers identified by that Act 'shall be known as a "statutory instrument"'.

[38] As to which see further Chapter 12.7, especially at n 13 to that paragraph.

[39] Available at http://privycouncil.independent.gov.uk/privy-council.

government departments[40] and for giving effect to resolutions of the United Nations Security Council in the UK or other territories governed by Her Majesty.[41] There are also (more rarely) '*Orders of Council*', which are a form of legislation made where the relevant power is conferred directly on the Privy Council itself rather than Her Majesty in Council.[42]

1.22.3   *Rules*: these are often used for making provision in relation to certain types of proceedings, procedures or regulatory regimes.[43]

1.22.4   *Commencement Orders*: commencement Orders (or commencement regulations, as the case may be) are designed to bring into force the whole or part of an Act, where the power to do this has been delegated to a minister.[44]

Enactment of SIs: Variable Parliamentary Control and Scrutiny

1.23   The extent to which SIs are subject to parliamentary scrutiny and control varies depending on the requirements set out in the parent statute.[45] There is no firm correlation between the content of the SI being passed and the intensity of the procedure that the parent Act will require to be applied,[46] although in general the more 'substantial and important' a measure, the higher the degree of control Parliament will normally reserve to itself.[47] However, even those subject to the more exacting procedures 'are not subject to the same legislative scrutiny as bills'.[48]

---

[40]   See, eg, the Secretary of State for Business, Innovation and Skills Order 2009, SI 2009/2748, transferring to the new Secretary of State for Business, Innovation and Skills the functions of two existing Secretaries of State (pursuant to powers under ss 1 and 2 of the Ministers of the Crown Act 1975).

[41]   Under s 1 of the United Nations Act 1946.

[42]   Orders of Council are often used for regulating professional bodies: see, eg, the General Dental Council (Constitution) Order 2009, SI 2009/1808.

[43]   See, eg, the Insolvency (England and Wales) Rules 2016, SI 2016/1024 (made under ss 411 and 412 of the Insolvency Act 1986); and the Civil Procedure Rules 1998, SI 1998/3132 (made under ss 2 and 3 of the Civil Procedure Act 1997).

[44]   If no such delegation is made, an Act will come into force either on the date it specifies or the day it receives Royal Assent: Interpretation Act 1978, s 4.

[45]   For more information generally about the making of statutory instruments, see the publications cited in n 31 above.

[46]   Malcolm Jack (ed), *Erskine May: Parliamentary Practice*, 24th edn (London, LexisNexis Butterworths, 2011) 671.

[47]   ibid 673–78,

[48]   *Public Law Project* (n 34) [22] (Lord Neuberger): 'Although they can be said to have been approved by Parliament, draft statutory instruments, even those subject to the affirmative resolution procedure, are not subject to the same legislative scrutiny as bills.' It should also be noted that, in practice, extremely few SIs are rejected by Parliament; see the discussion of this issue by the former Lord Chief Justice, Lord Judge, in his lecture of 12 April 2016 at www.kcl.ac.uk/law/newsevents/newsrecords/2015-16/Ceding-Power-to-the-Executive---Lord-Judge---130416.pdf, 10-11, stating that, since 1950, only 17 out of around 170,000 SIs have been rejected by one or other House of Parliament.

1.24 For some SIs, no parliamentary involvement is required.[49] They can simply be 'made' upon a draft being signed into law by the person with statutory authority to do so, which is usually the Secretary of State for the relevant government department that will have drafted the SI.[50] The SI will become law either when it is made or on a date specified in the SI.

1.25 The level of parliamentary participation in the legislative process usually takes one of four forms (considered below in increasing order of intensity):

1.25.1 *Laying before Parliament*:[51] some SIs must be 'laid' before Parliament after being made. Where this is required, the SI should not be made so as to come into operation before being laid unless this is 'essential'.[52] What 'laying' means precisely is determined by the rules of parliamentary procedure in force at the relevant time.[53]

1.25.2 *Negative Resolution Procedure*:[54] some statutes will require that Parliament be given an opportunity to vote against an SI made under its provisions. This is the most common form of parliamentary control. After it is made, the SI must be laid before Parliament, and it will be annulled if within 40 days either House passes a motion (known as a 'prayer') requiring this.[55] In some cases, a slight variation is prescribed, under which the SI is laid in *draft*, and if either House resolves within 40 days that it should not be made,[56] no further action can then be taken on the SI.[57] Note that only the House of Commons will be granted the power of control in the case of financial instruments.[58] It is very rare indeed for Parliament to vote against an SI.

1.25.3 *Affirmative Resolution Procedure*:[59] this procedure requires one or both Houses of Parliament (as the case may be) positively to approve an SI for it to become (or remain) law. As a result, it is generally deployed where much greater scrutiny is considered appropriate. This may take three forms, depending on the terms of the parent Act:

(1)   the Act may require the SI to be laid in draft and not made unless approved by Parliament;

---

[49] This is often the case for uncontroversial items such as Commencement Orders: Jack, *Erskine May* (n 46) 671.

[50] Statutory Instruments Act 1946, s 11.

[51] For more information on the laying of instruments before Parliament, see Jack, *Erskine May* (n 46) 673–75.

[52] Statutory Instruments Act 1946, s 4(1).

[53] Laying of Documents before Parliament (Interpretation) Act 1948, s 1(1).

[54] For more information on the negative resolution procedure, see Jack, *Erskine May* (n 46) 678.

[55] Statutory Instruments Act 1946, s 5.

[56] Or should not be presented to Her Majesty, in the case of an Order in Council.

[57] Statutory Instruments Act 1946, s 6.

[58] See, eg, Corporation Tax Act 2009, s 133N(4) and (5).

[59] For more information on the affirmative resolution procedure, see Jack, *Erskine May* (n 46) 675–77.

(2)   the Act may allow an SI to be made, but not allow it to come into force until approved by Parliament;[60]

(3)   the Act may allow an SI to be made and to come into force, but to cease to have effect after a certain date unless, by then, it has been approved by Parliament.

1.25.4   *Super-Affirmative Procedure:*[61] some statutes exceptionally require a procedure even more exacting than the affirmative resolution procedure, for example, where the SI in question permits the amendment of primary legislation.[62] This procedure ordinarily requires a draft of the SI to be laid before Parliament to allow a period of time (usually 60 days) for Parliament to comment or propose amendments. After this time, a draft SI (either with or without amendments to reflect Parliament's input) can then be laid for approval in the same way as under the affirmative procedure. Sometimes the parent Act will permit an SI to be made in urgent cases and then be subject to annulment if not approved by Parliament pursuant to some variant affirmative or super-affirmative procedure.

1.26   Save in very exceptional cases where this is expressly provided for, the various procedures do not give Parliament the opportunity to amend the draft legislation, only giving it a power ultimately to accept or reject it in the form proposed by the delegate of the power.

1.27   *Parliamentary committees*: various special Parliamentary committees have been established with circumscribed roles in scrutinising SIs:

1.27.1   The *Joint Committee on Statutory Instruments* (JCSI)[63] is responsible for scrutinising almost all SIs or draft SIs (as well as other instruments) to determine whether to draw them to the 'special attention' of both Houses of Parliament by way of a report (which will include its reasons for its decision).[64] It may do so where one of eight specified grounds applies, which relate to matters such as drafting quality, procedural delays, unpermitted retrospectivity, whether there is power to make the SI and the like, or 'on any other ground which does not impinge on its merits or on the policy behind it'. The full remit and procedures of the JCSI (including the eight grounds) are set out in House of Commons Standing Order 151.[65]

---

[60] In practice this procedure is seldom used: see ibid 676.

[61] For more information on the super-affirmative procedure, see ibid 677–78.

[62] See, eg, Human Rights Act 1998, s 10 and sch 2.

[63] Further information regarding the JCSI is available at www.parliament.uk/jcsi.

[64] Reports of the JCSI are available at www.parliament.uk/business/committees/committees-a-z/joint-select/statutory-instruments/publications.

[65] Available at www.publications.parliament.uk/pa/cm200102/cmstords/27519.htm.

1.27.2 The Commons *Select Committee on Statutory Instruments* (SCSI)[66] has exactly the same remit as the JCSI, but in relation specifically to those SIs (and other instruments) which statute requires be laid before only the House of Commons and not the House of Lords. It is accordingly empowered to draw any relevant SI to the special attention of the Commons alone. The SCSI is also established by House of Commons Standing Order 151.[67]

1.27.3 The Lords *Secondary Legislation Scrutiny Committee* (SLSC)[68] has the broad remit of considering almost all SIs and draft SIs (as well as other instruments) laid before each House of Parliament, and deciding whether to draw them to the 'special attention' of the House of Lords by way of a report.[69] An SI may be drawn to the Lords' attention on specified grounds relating to its merits— such as its legal or political importance, inappropriateness in view of changed circumstances or inadequacy in meeting its policy objective—and the Committee can also consider any 'other general matters relating to the effective scrutiny of secondary legislation and arising from the performance of its functions', unless that matter is within the JCSI's remit.[70]

Explanatory Notes and Memoranda

1.28 The published draft of an SI will include an '*Explanatory Note*' which explains its scope and purpose, although it is not part of the legislation itself. In addition, in more recent times an SI will normally be accompanied by an '*Explanatory Memorandum*' during its passage through Parliament. Explanatory Memoranda are designed to explain the policy objective and implications of the measure, and are available to the public.

1.29 Further discussion regarding Explanatory Notes and Memoranda, and how they can be used to assist in the interpretation of an SI, can be found at Chapter 7.32–7.37.

---

[66] Further information regarding the SCSI is available at www.parliament.uk/scsi.

[67] At para 10 of the Standing Order.

[68] See www.parliament.uk/business/committees/committees-a-z/lords-select/secondary-legislation-scrutiny-committee. From its establishment on 17 December 2003 to the beginning of the 2012–13 parliamentary session, the Committee was known as the Merits of Statutory Instruments Committee.

[69] Reports of the SLSC are available at www.parliament.uk/business/committees/committees-a-z/lords-select/secondary-legislation-scrutiny-committee/publications. The SLSC's terms of reference can be found at www.parliament.uk/business/committees/committees-a-z/lords-select/secondary-legislation-scrutiny-committee/role/tofref.

[70] See the terms of reference, available online at the address cited in the previous note.

2

Anatomy and Structure
of Domestic Legislation

2.1 Interpreting legislation properly requires a good understanding of its anatomy and structure. In this chapter we consider the various constituent components of Acts and statutory instruments (SIs), as well as the way they are organised and structured through the use of headings and divisions.

Constituent Components of an Act

Introductory Components

2.2 Acts of Parliament have common and recognisable constituent elements at their outset. Below is set out part of the Justice and Security Act 2013 as an example of the typical introductory text included within Acts of Parliament.[1] The word 'Preamble' has been added in parenthesis for illustrative purposes to show where one would have been placed if it had been included. The numbers in superscript have been added to identify the various components, which are then described in the following paragraphs by reference to those numbers:

[1]**Elizabeth II**   [3]**c.20**

[Royal Coat of Arms]

[2]**Justice and Security Act 2013**

[3]2013 CHAPTER 18

[4]An Act to provide for oversight of the Security Service, the Secret Intelligence Service, the Government Communications Headquarters and other activities relating to intelligence or security matters; to make provision about closed material procedure in relation to certain civil proceedings; to prevent the making of certain court orders for the disclosure of sensitive information; and for connected purposes.   [5][25th April 2013]

---

[1] Note that, in a published copy of the Act, this introductory text will follow any contents page that is included as part of the publication.

[⁶*PREAMBLE*]

⁷BE IT ENACTED by the Queen's most Excellent Majesty, by and with the advice and consent of the Lords Spiritual and Temporal, and Commons, in this present Parliament assembled, and by the authority of the same, as follows:—

2.3 *Name of the monarch and Royal Coat of Arms (1)*: the very start of an Act bears the name of the reigning monarch at the time it was passed, along with the Royal Coat of Arms to signify Royal Assent.

2.4 *Short title (2)*: this is followed by the '*short title*' of the Act (for example, the 'Justice and Security Act 2013' or the 'Bribery Act 2010'), which allows the Act to be easily identified and is expressly conferred on the Act by a provision in its main body, generally in the final section.[2] Acts will often refer to other Acts by their short title.[3]

2.5 *Year and chapter number (3)*: the next item is the calendar year in which the Act was passed, which appears along with the 'chapter number' of the Act.

2.6 Each Act is given a unique chapter number which denotes the order in which each Act is passed in a given year. For example, '2010 Chapter 23' for the Bribery Act 2010 means that the Act was the twenty-third public general Act passed in 2010. Local Acts are given a separate sequence of chapter numbers, denoted by Roman rather than Arabic numerals, while personal Acts receive *italicised* Roman numerals.[4] The chapter number also features at the top right of the printed page containing the introductory text, next to the monarch's name.

2.7 Before 1 January 1963, in giving the year and chapter number, Acts would refer to the regnal year of the reigning monarch or monarchs during the parliamentary session in which the Act was passed rather than the calendar year. For example, the Hypnotism Act 1952 states in its heading '15 & 16 Geo. 6 & 1 Eliz. 2' to indicate it was passed during the parliamentary session taking place during the fifteenth and sixteenth years of the reign of George VI and the first year of the reign of Elizabeth II. At that time, chapter numbers indicated the order of an Act's

---

[2] See, eg, s 20 of the Bribery Act 2010, headed 'Short title', which states: 'This Act may be cited as the Bribery Act 2010.' Sections conferring short titles were introduced in the 1840s, but were not always used in the decades that followed (as they are routinely today). Acts without such sections have been given short titles by subsequent legislation passed specifically for this purpose. For further explanation, see the Law Commission and Scottish Law Commission, *Statute Law Reform: Fifteenth Report Draft Statute Law (Repeals) Bill* (March 1995), at Appendix 2, 76–78, which can be found at: www.bailii.org/ew/other/EWLC/1995/233.pdf.

[3] See, eg, s 18(3) of the Inquiries Act 2005, referring to a section of 'the Freedom of Information Act 2000 (c. 36)'.

[4] As to the distinction between public general Acts and local and personal Acts, see Chapter 1.8.

passage during a particular parliamentary session rather than during a particular calendar year.

2.8 *Long title (4)*: there is then a '*long title*' which serves as a very general description of the purposes of the Act, as in the example above.

2.9 *Royal Assent/Commencement (5)*: the date provided below the 'long title' is the date on which the Act received *Royal Assent*. If no provision is made for the commencement of an Act (or certain of its provisions), the Act (or those provisions, as the case may be) will come into force at the beginning of the day on which the Act receives Royal Assent.[5] However, many Acts contain 'commencement' provisions, which may provide for the Act (or some of its provisions) to come into force on a certain date or by further order (that is, by way of secondary legislation).[6]

2.10 *Preamble (6)*: some Acts may have a '*preamble*' immediately after their long title (though the example cited does not). This is rare nowadays for public general Acts,[7] but they are routinely found in local Acts.[8] They will usually set out background facts or intentions which set the scene for the Act in question.

2.11 *Enacting formula (7)*: after the long title and date of Royal Assent, there then appears the 'enacting formula', which is a standard form of words indicating that the Act has been through the formal legislative procedure in both Houses of Parliament: see the final paragraph in the above example. (Note that there is a different form of wording used for local Acts,[9] and where an Act is passed without the approval of the House of Lords under the Parliament Act 1911.)[10]

Operative Components

2.12 What may be termed the '*operative components*' of an Act are those components that are intended to operate directly as law in themselves. Other components (such as the introductory components and headings) may be described as 'ancillary components', since their principal effect is to describe or contextualise the operative components or to serve some formal function. They may influence the law's content, but only incidentally.

---

[5] Pursuant to s 4(b) of the Interpretation Act 1978.

[6] Pursuant to ibid s 4(a). For an example of an Act making provision for its commencement, see s 26 of the Interpretation Act 1978: 'This Act shall come into force on 1st January 1979.'

[7] For a recent example of an Act with a preamble, see the Supply and Appropriation (Anticipation and Adjustments) Act 2016.

[8] See, eg, the Humber Bridge Act 2013.

[9] For an example, see the previous note. As to local Acts generally, see the reference in n 4 above.

[10] See, eg, the Hunting Act 2004.

2.13   *Sections*: the fundamental operative component of a statute is the '*section*' (often abbreviated to 's', plural 'ss').[11] Sections are denoted by sequential Arabic numerals. Where a section has subdivisions, these are named and denoted as follows:[12]

	1st Subdivision	**2nd Subdivision**	**3rd Subdivision**
Name	Subsection	Paragraph	Subparagraph
Format	Arabic numerals in brackets	Lower case letters in brackets	Lower case Roman numerals in brackets
Example	s 1(1)	s 1(1)(a)	s 1(1)(a)(i)

2.14   *Schedules*: the other main operative component of an Act is the '*schedule*' (often abbreviated to 'sch'). Although as a matter of structure, schedules follow the sections contained in the main body of the Act and are usually expressly given effect by a section,[13] they are in no way subordinate to any of an Act's sections. Sections and schedules alike must be construed in the light of the Act as a whole to determine their true meaning. As the Court of Appeal has stated: 'Whether provisions in a statute go into a schedule or into a section or sections in the main body of an Act is often a matter of drafting preference, with no significance in terms of legislative force.'[14]

2.15   In practice, schedules often contain lists or detailed sets of provisions which are too unwieldy for inclusion in the main parts of the Act and may be more conveniently set out together in a schedule to the Act. Schedules commonly set out, for example: (i) a list of persons to whom or situations to which other provisions are intended to apply;[15] (ii) a set of exceptions to a particular provision;[16] (iii) a list of provisions to be repealed or revoked;[17] (iv) an index of terms defined

---

[11] See s 1 of the Interpretation Act 1978, which provides: 'Every section of an Act takes effect as a substantive enactment without introductory words.' Strictly, an Act need not be divided into sections, and historically this was not always done (see, eg, the Acts of Parliament (Expiration) Act 1808). However, dividing an Act into sections is the invariable modern practice.

[12] Before enactment, the main numbered divisions of a Bill are referred to as 'clauses' rather than 'sections', with their subdivisions otherwise being referred to as set out in the table set out at paragraph 2.13.

[13] For two different forms of this, see, eg, Equality Act 2010, s 31(10); and Legal Aid, Sentencing and Punishment of Offenders Act 2012 (LASPO), s 9(1).

[14] *R (Satu) v London Borough of Hackney* [2002] EWCA Civ 1843 [18]–[19] (Keene LJ), citing *Attorney General v Lamplough* (1878) 3 Ex D 214 (CA) 229 (Brett LJ): 'The schedule is as much a part of the statute, and is as much an enactment as any other part.'

[15] See, eg, sch 19 to the Equality Act 2010, which defines who is a 'public authority' for the purposes of s 150; and sch 1 to LASPO (n 13), which defines what are 'civil legal services' for the purposes of s 9(1) of that Act.

[16] See, eg, sch 3 to the Equality Act 2010 (given effect by s 31(10)), setting out exceptions to what qualifies as 'services' or 'public functions' under s 29.

[17] See, eg, Equality Act 2010, sch 27 (given effect by s 211(2)).

in various parts of an Act;[18] (v) a self-contained framework of rules to govern a particular area;[19] (vi) the text of all or part of a relevant instrument, such as a treaty which is to be incorporated into or given effect in English law to the extent set out in the Act.[20]

2.16 A schedule may take the form of a table or a list, or may be set out like the provisions of a section. An item in a list or table is referred to as an 'entry'. Where schedules are set out like sections, their numbered subdivisions are known as 'paragraphs' (abbreviated to 'para'). Further subdivisions are known as 'subparagraphs' and then 'heads' or sometimes 'paragraphs'.[21] The notation of paragraphs and their subdivisions takes the same format as for sections, as described in the table set out at paragraph 2.13 above.[22]

2.17 *Indication of amendments*: where an amendment is made to insert a new section, schedule or subdivision into, before or after an existing sequential series of provisions in an Act, the new provision will generally be denoted as follows:[23]

2.17.1 If a new provision is to appear *between sequential provisions* in a series, it will be denoted using the number or letter of the existing provision after which it is to appear, followed by a further letter, and further provisions will then run in a new alphabetical sequence. So section 1A would appear between sections 1 and 2, and sections 1B, 1C, 1D etc would then follow 1A, still preceding section 2; new paragraphs between (a) and (b) would be (aa), (ab) etc, and new subparagraphs between (i) and (ii) would be (ia), (ib) etc. Further alphabetical sequences of letters can be used for further amendments to be inserted within an existing series where required so that, for example, sections 1AA, 1AB etc would appear between sections 1A and 1B.

2.17.2 If a new provision is to appear *before the first provision* in a series, it will be denoted by the number or letter of that first provision, preceded by a new letter, with further new provisions following in a new alphabetical sequence.

---

[18] See, eg, Equality Act 2010, sch 28 (given effect by s 214).

[19] See, eg, Insolvency Act 1986, sch B1 (given effect by s 8), which governs company administrations.

[20] See, eg, sch 1 to the Human Rights Act 1998, which sets out certain Articles of the European Convention on Human Rights which are to be given effect as set out elsewhere in the Act. On the Human Rights Act 1998, see further Chapter 10; on legislation incorporating and giving effect to treaties, see further Chapter 9.10–9.12 and 9.20–9.37.

[21] See, eg, *MacLeod v Gold Harp Properties Ltd* [2014] EWCA Civ 1084, [2015] 1 WLR 1249 [21] (Underhill LJ), referring to paragraphs, subparagraphs and heads.

[22] So a paragraph with three levels of subdivision might take the following form: para 1(1)(a)(i).

[23] As to the notation of amended provisions, see further the Drafting Guidance issued by the Office of the Parliamentary Counsel in June 2017 at para 6.4, 41–42, which can be found at https://www.gov.uk/government/publications/drafting-bills-for-parliament. For an example of a heavily amended provision showing the way amendments are denoted in practice, see s 18 of the Regulation of Investigatory Powers Act 2000.

The new letters will begin with 'A' when preceding an Arabic number (so sections or schedules A1, B1, C1 etc will precede section 1 or sch 1); 'a' when preceding a Roman numeral (so paragraph (ai) will precede paragraph (i)); and 'Z' or 'z' when preceding an upper or lower-case letter respectively (so sections 1(2)(za), 1(2)(zb) etc will precede section 1(2)(a)). If further provisions are to be added ahead of ones already beginning with a Z, then multiple Zs can be used. Thus, paragraphs 1(1)(zza), 1(1)(zzb) etc will precede paragraph 1(1)(za).

2.17.3 Note that the guidance in the previous subparagraph means that where provisions are inserted *between existing series*, preceding letters will be used to allow for this. Thus, if provisions are to be inserted between sections 1 and 1A, they will be denoted as 1ZA, 1ZB etc rather than 1AA, 1AB etc; likewise, provisions inserted between section 1A and 1AA will be denoted as 1AZA, 1AZB etc.

2.17.4 A provision inserted *after the final provision* in an existing series will be denoted by numbers or letters so as to continue the existing sequence.

2.18 *Introductory/miscellaneous/supplemental/general/final provisions*: often an Act (or one of its divisions or schedules) will contain one or more important provisions designed to inform the scope, application or interpretation of the remainder of the Act (or division or schedule). They are often conveniently grouped together towards the beginning of the relevant Act, division or schedule (as the case may be) under a group heading such as 'Introductory', or towards the end under group headings such as 'Miscellaneous', 'Supplemental', 'General' or 'Final'. Examples include:

2.18.1 *Interpretation provisions*: defining, in whole or in part, the meaning of key words or phrases within a statute.[24]

2.18.2 *Scope-defining provisions*: for example, savings qualifying what might otherwise be the effect of an Act's provisions,[25] or provisions defining the subject matter,[26] persons[27] or territory[28] to which an Act does or does not apply.

2.18.3 *Provisions concerning delegated powers*: provisions detailing the scope of powers granted by the Act to make delegated legislation or the applicable parliamentary procedure.[29]

---

[24] As to the interpretation of such sections, see Chapter 6.19–6.24.
[25] See further (including as to the interpretation of savings) Chapter 6.29 and 6.33–6.35.
[26] See, eg, s 32 of LASPO (n 13), providing that, in general, legal aid is not to be provided for cases relating to foreign law.
[27] See, eg, ibid s 43: 'This Part binds the Crown.'
[28] See, eg, Anti-social Behaviour, Crime and Policing Act 2014, s 184.
[29] See, eg, LASPO (n 13), s 41.

2.18.4 *Commencement provisions*: detailing when specified provisions come into force or providing for how they are to be brought into force.[30]

Organisation and Structure: Headings and Divisions

2.19 *Headings and divisions*: a statute's headings, although ancillary rather than operative components (see paragraph 2.12 above), are designed to assist in the comprehension of the statute. Among other things, they serve to demarcate the way an Act is structured and divided up.[31] The key headings and divisions used in Acts are as follows:

2.19.1 *Section headings*: sections of Acts have their own headings, which appear together with the section number.[32] These 'indicate the main subject with which the section deals'.[33]

2.19.2 *Group headings*: groups of sections are sometimes set out under an italicised heading identifying their function or subject matter. These are sometimes called 'cross-headings'.[34]

2.19.3 *Chapters, Parts and Groups of Parts*: some longer statutes are internally divided into '*Parts*', which in turn may be internally divided into '*Chapters*'.[35] The Parts in particularly lengthy statutes may be clustered together into '*Groups of Parts*'.[36] Each of these divisions may have its own heading.

2.20 Understanding an Act's structure can be important for a number of reasons. Often an Act will make reference to particular elements of its structure for the purposes of definitions or the applicability of certain of its provisions.[37] It may also be that different divisions of an Act may be brought into force at different times. In some cases, particularly where an Act provides a complete code for how a particular area of law is to work, it is only possible to navigate an Act's provisions successfully if one has a proper grasp of its structure (which can often helpfully be gleaned from its table of contents).[38]

[30] See, eg, Anti-social Behaviour, Crime and Policing Act 2014, s 185.
[31] For the use of headings and structure as aids to construction, see Chapter 6.8–6.9 and 6.14 respectively.
[32] Prior to 2001, each section would have a side note in the margin instead. See, eg, the side note to s 5 of the Vagrancy Act 1824: 'Who shall be deemed incorrigible rogues.' See further Chapter 6.8, especially at n 19.
[33] *DPP v Schildkamp* [1971] AC 1 (HL) 10F (Lord Reid).
[34] ibid 10E–F.
[35] See, eg, ss 17–38 of the Companies Act 2006, which together make up Part 3 of the Act. Part 3 is headed 'A COMPANY'S CONSTITUTION' and is divided into four Chapters, each with its own heading, with various group headings used as well.
[36] See, eg, ss 1–251 of the Insolvency Act 1986, which make up the first Group of Parts.
[37] See, eg, Companies Act 2006, s 497(2).
[38] See, eg, Freedom of Information Act 2000. Section 1, in Part 1, makes provision for a '[g]eneral right of access to information held by public authorities', which is further circumscribed by other

Constituent Components of Statutory Instruments[39]

Introductory Components

2.21   The introductory components of an SI are more variable than for Acts, given that there are different types of SIs,[40] and given the variety of purposes for which they are made, the powers and procedures by which they are made, and the timing of their coming into force. Nevertheless, an example of the heading from a typical instrument will assist in describing certain components commonly found in SIs.

2.22   The text below is taken directly from the Magistrates' Courts (Forfeiture of Political Donations) Rules 2003, with numbering added in superscript to identify the various components which are then described in the following paragraphs. The word 'CONTENTS' has been inserted in parenthesis in the extract below for illustrative purposes to show where a table of contents would have been placed if one had been included (as is the case with some SIs):

---

[1]STATUTORY INSTRUMENTS

---

[2]2003 No. 1645 [3](L. 28)

[4]MAGISTRATES' COURTS, ENGLAND AND WALES

[5]PROCEDURE

[6]The Magistrates' Courts (Forfeiture of Political Donations) Rules 2003

[7]Made	22nd June 2003
Laid before Parliament	27th June 2003
Coming into force	24th July 2003

[[8]*CONTENTS*]

[9]The Lord Chancellor, in exercise of the powers conferred upon him by sections 144 and 145(1)(g) of the Magistrates' Courts Act 1980 ... and section 60(1) of the Political

---

provisions in that Part and the 'exemptions' in Part II. The right given by s 1 is made effective in practice by Parts IV and V, which provide respectively for 'Enforcement' by the Information Commissioner and 'Appeals' to the First-tier Tribunal.

[39]   For a detailed guide to the current formatting of statutory instruments, see *Statutory Instrument Practice*, 4th edn (London, Her Majesty's Stationery Office, 2006), which is updated from time to time by circulars.

[40]   See Chapter 1.22.

Parties, Elections and Referendums Act 2000 ..., after consultation with the Rule Committee appointed under section 144, makes the following Rules:

2.23   *SI heading (1)*: the heading 'Statutory instruments' in tramlines denotes that the legislation in question belongs to the SI series of instruments rather than another series of instruments prepared in similar format (for example, Ministerial Orders).

2.24   *Serial number (2)*: every SI has a unique serial number or 'SI number', which (like the year and chapter number of an Act) indicates the year in which the SI was made and its place in sequence among SIs made that year. SIs may be cited using their serial number, in this case as 'SI 2003/1645'.

2.25   *Subsidiary serial number (3)*: some SIs have one or more further serial numbers, which indicates the SI's place in the annual sequence of a particular kind of instrument. 'L' denotes the 'legal series' of instruments, which covers procedural matters in the English courts. 'C' denotes the annual series of commencement Orders. 'S' and 'NI' respectively denote instruments relating to Scotland and Northern Ireland, while 'W' denotes instruments made by the Welsh Assembly.

2.26   *Subject heading (4)*: every SI will have a subject heading which will state the broad legislative or administrative area with which the SI deals. This is used to classify instruments in the annual publication of SIs by Her Majesty's Stationery Office. Sometimes an SI may have more than one subject heading, the second of which will appear directly below the first in the same format. Where appropriate, the subject heading will contain a suffix after a comma indicating the part of the UK to which it applies (as in the example SI above).

2.27   *Subject subheading (5)*: some SIs will contain a subheading below the main subject heading or headings (in a smaller font) giving a further description of the SI's subject matter.

2.28   *SI title (6)*: this is the unique name of the SI by which it may be cited, essentially equivalent to an Act's short title. It should give an indication of the subject matter of the SI.

2.29   *Relevant dates (7)*: an SI will state in its introduction the date on which it was made. It will usually also state the date on which it was laid before Parliament and the date on which it comes into force. However, varying formats may be used to give the relevant legislative history of the SI where, for example, an SI is not laid before Parliament or where the commencement provision is non-existent or more complex.

2.30   *Table of contents (8)*: some SIs, for ease of comprehension, will contain a table of contents for its operative provisions. This will appear between the relevant dates and the preamble and words of enactment.

2.31   *Preamble and words of enactment (9)*: the final paragraph in the above example is what is commonly referred to as the '*preamble*'. But it may be more accurate to say that the paragraph contains both the preamble and formal '*words of enactment*', which perform the role of the 'enacting formula' in an Act, stating that what follows is intended to be law. Preambles are 'not intended to change the law but merely to recite the authority to make the instrument and any step (such as consultation) which the maker of the instrument must undertake before making the instrument'.[41] The authority to make the instrument will be the provisions of the legislation that give power to make the SI, and these provisions will usually be specified expressly in the preamble (as in the example above). Where an SI implements an EU Directive, the enabling power specified will be section 2(2) of the European Communities Act 1972.[42] Knowing the enabling power used may be important in interpreting the legislation—for example, because of the presumption set out in s 11 of the Interpretation Act 1978 that terms in subordinate legislation are to be given the same meaning as in the primary legislation under which they are made.[43]

2.32   An SI's preamble may (perhaps in addition to specific references to one or more empowering provisions in a parent enactment) contain *general* enabling words that do not refer to any particular empowering provisions. These words 'will not be interpreted as including [a particular] enabling power simply because the maker of the statutory instrument could have used that power'.[44] However, in appropriate cases general enabling words may by implication be taken to refer to a particular enabling power. Whether this is the case 'is to be assessed objectively from the terms of the instrument and other matters relevant to the interpretation of the instrument'.[45] Such an interpretation may (depending on the circumstances) be appropriate where, for example, the 'statutory instrument would otherwise fail or it is clear from the operative provisions of the statutory instrument that the maker of the statutory instrument must have intended to use an unspecified enabling power', or where a conforming or compatible interpretation is required by EU law or section 3 of the Human Rights Act 1998 respectively.[46]

Operative Components

2.33   As with Acts, the introductory components of SIs are ancillary rather than operative components. It is the operative components which serve to create law

---

[41] *Vibixa Ltd v Komori UK Ltd* [2006] EWCA Civ 536, [2006] 1 WLR 2472 [18] (Arden LJ, giving the judgment of the Court).

[42] See, eg, Environmental Information Regulations 2004, SI 2004/3391.

[43] *Vibixa* (n 41) [22] (Arden LJ, giving the judgment of the Court).

[44] ibid [17] (Arden LJ, giving the judgment of the Court).

[45] ibid [23] (Arden LJ, giving the judgment of the Court).

[46] ibid [24] (Arden LJ, giving the judgment of the Court). See generally Chapters 12 and 10 below in relation to the interpretive duties that apply respectively in relation to EU law and under the Human Rights Act 1998.

in themselves (see paragraph 2.12 above). The name of the principal, operative provisions in an SI varies according to the type of instrument in question: (i) regulations contain '*regulations*'; (ii) rules contain '*rules*'; (iii) Orders (whether commencement Orders, Orders in Council or Orders of Council) contain '*articles*'. These provisions are denoted using sequential Arabic numerals like sections in Acts.

2.34 Subdivisions of rules, regulations or articles are called 'paragraphs', whose subdivisions are in turn called subparagraphs. Their format follows the table set out at paragraph 2.13 above.

2.35 Like Acts, SIs may contain schedules. These may take many forms, but their provisions will be named and numbered in the same way as schedules to Acts (as discussed at paragraph 2.16 above).[47] Again like Acts, they routinely feature provisions as to citation, commencement, extent of application, interpretation and the like (see paragraph 2.18 above).

Organisation and Structure: Headings and Divisions

2.36 Save for the differences in the introductory components (discussed above), and the inclusion of a signature and Explanatory Notes (both discussed below), the structure of SIs is similar to that of Acts insofar as they feature individual provision headings and, where appropriate, italicised subheadings for groups of provisions, and 'Parts' and 'Sections' (as opposed to 'Chapters') with appropriate headings.

Signature and Explanatory Notes

2.37 At the end of an SI will be found the signature of the person (usually a minister) authorising the making of the instrument, along with a statement of their position and the date of the signature. This is an ancillary rather than operative component, but is an important formal feature and demonstrates the provenance of the SI.

2.38 An 'Explanatory Note' is usually attached at the end of an SI (with Acts, Explanatory Notes are published separately), providing a short commentary on the SI's provisions. However, it is not part of the SI itself, as will be stated at the beginning of the Explanatory Note.[48]

---

[47] Where provisions are added into an SI by amendment, they will, where appropriate, usually be denoted in the same format as for Acts: see paragraph 2.17 above.

[48] As to Explanatory Notes to SIs and their use as aids to construction, see Chapter 7.32–7.34.

3

Core Principles and Approach

3.1   This chapter starts with the central objective of statutory interpretation and the overall approach to be taken to issues of construction. From there it moves on to discuss how to read statutory language, and the role in statutory interpretation of context, purpose and subsequent practice.

The Central Objective and Overall Approach

3.2   The central and guiding mission of statutory interpretation is to determine the objective intention of the legislator as expressed in the language of the legislation, read in its context.[1] In the words of Lord Bingham, in line with many similar formulations of this doctrine: 'the overriding aim of the court must always be to give effect to the intention of Parliament as expressed in the words used'.[2]

3.3   Determining the so-called 'intention of Parliament' is not 'merely an exercise in linguistics'.[3] It also does not entail a search for the meaning of legislation detached from its language, nor does it involve a historical inquiry into the subjective thoughts of those making up that body at any given time.[4] The nature and

---

[1] See, eg, *R (Quintavalle) v Secretary of State for Health* [2003] UKHL 13, [2003] 2 AC 687 [38] (Lord Millett): 'In construing a statute the task of the court is to ascertain the intention of Parliament as expressed in the words it has chosen. The Parliamentary intention is to be derived from the terms of the Act as a whole read in its context. Once it has been ascertained, the court must give effect to it so far as the legislative text permits.' See also, eg, *Dorset County Council v House* [2010] EWCA Crim 2270, [2011] 1 WLR 727 [28] (Hickinbottom J), stating that courts must 'construe the intention of Parliament (or an authority to which Parliament has delegated its legislative function) through the legislative words used, reading the instrument as a whole and in its context'.

[2] *R v Secretary of State for the Environment, Transport and the Regions ex p Spath Holme Ltd* [2001] 2 AC 349 (HL) 388D (Lord Bingham).

[3] *David T Morrison & Co Ltd v ICL Plastics Ltd* [2014] UKSC 48, [2014] SLT 791 [48] (Lord Neuberger).

[4] See, eg, *Duport Steels Ltd v Sirs* [1980] 1 WLR 142 (HL) 157C–D (Lord Diplock): 'the role of the judiciary is confined to ascertaining from the words that Parliament has approved as expressing its intention what that intention was, and to giving effect to it'; *Beswick v Beswick* [1968] AC 58 (HL) 73G (Lord Reid): 'In construing any Act of Parliament we are seeking the intention of Parliament and it is quite true that we must deduce that intention from the words of the Act.'

significance of the concept of the 'intention of Parliament' as employed in exercises of statutory interpretation were explained by Lord Nicholls as follows:[5]

> Statutory interpretation is an exercise which requires the court to identify the meaning borne by the words in question in the particular context. The task of the court is often said to be to ascertain the intention of Parliament expressed in the language under consideration. This is correct and may be helpful, as long as it is remembered that the 'intention of Parliament' is an objective concept, not subjective. The phrase is a shorthand reference to the intention which the court reasonably imputes to Parliament in respect of the language used. It is not the subjective intention of the minister or other persons who promoted the legislation. Nor is it the subjective intention of the draftsman, or of individual members or even of a majority of individual members of either House. These individuals will often have widely varying intentions. Their understanding of the legislation and the words used may be impressively complete or woefully inadequate. Thus, when courts say that such-and-such a meaning 'cannot be what Parliament intended', they are saying only that the words under consideration cannot reasonably be taken as used by Parliament with that meaning. As Lord Reid said in *Black-Clawson International Ltd v Papierwerke Waldof Aschaffenberg AG* [1975] AC 591, 613: 'We often say that we are looking for the intention of Parliament, but that is not quite accurate. We are seeking the meaning of the words which Parliament has used.'

3.4   Practically speaking, the task of statutory interpretation requires a court to consider the language of the legislation together with all the relevant interpretive factors and, in the light of those, reach a view as to how the legislator intended the enactment in question to apply to the situation before it.

3.5   The *language* of the statute will always be central to the task of construction and will provide the best starting point in this endeavour; it is never 'merely one item' to be considered.[6] However, as the natural meaning of the words 'is seldom, if ever, the only factor to take into account',[7] it will then be necessary to consider the legislation's *context* (including any admissible external aids to construction) and apparent purpose, along with any applicable presumptions as to parliamentary intention and any other relevant legislation that may affect how it is to be interpreted.

3.6   While there are guidelines as to what factors can influence statutory meaning in what circumstances, there is no strict formula that prescribes the process by which each is to be considered, and there are no hard-and-fast rules as to the weight to be accorded to a particular factor in any given case. However, the courts have devised many principles and presumptions which can helpfully be brought to bear as 'well-worn tools of statutory construction'.[8]

---

[5] *Spath Holme* (n 2) 396F–397A.
[6] *Williams v Central Bank of Nigeria* [2014] UKSC 10, [2014] AC 1189 [72] (Lord Neuberger), as cited more fully at n 24 below. As to statutory language as the appropriate starting point, see paragraph 3.9 below.
[7] *David T Morrison* (n 3) [48] (Lord Neuberger); and see paragraph 3.11 below.
[8] *Smith v Smith* [2006] UKHL 35, [2006] 1 WLR 2024 [79] (Lord Carswell).

3.7   Where the statutory language and all the relevant interpretive factors point the same way, the meaning will be clear and can be straightforwardly applied. Otherwise, where there is conflict, the court will have to weigh up the indications from the text and those factors to reach its conclusion.[9] The extent to which the meaning of the statutory language will be influenced by any or all of the relevant interpretive factors will be a matter of judgement in the light of all the circumstances, aided so far as is appropriate by the presumptions and principles of construction which the courts have laid down.[10]

3.8   Both this chapter and the two that follow address the core aspects of how the courts go about ascertaining the intention of Parliament (or the maker of delegated legislation) in a given case. This chapter focuses on questions of language, context and purpose, while the next looks at the array of presumptions applied by the courts as to the intended effect of legislation. Chapter 5 then discusses how one piece of legislation can affect the content, form, effect or interpretation of another.

Reading the Statutory Language

Statutory Language as the Starting Point

3.9   Generally, the appropriate starting point is to consider the particular wording of the provisions that require interpretation.[11] Ultimately, whatever other

[9] For an instructive example of the way in which the courts will consider a very wide range of factors in reaching an overall conclusion on a question of construction, see *Re Globespan Airways Ltd* [2012] EWCA Civ 1159, [2013] 1 WLR 1122. Having extensively surveyed the practical and statutory context within which the provisions under consideration operated, Arden LJ (with whom Lord Neuberger MR and Moses LJ agreed) took account of: the natural meaning of the statutory words ([42]–[43]); the use of different words to denote different concepts ([42]); the statutory purpose of a provision ('where the wording permits') ([44]–[45] and [60]); the policy behind other legislation in the field of company law ([46]); the practical realities of carrying out the statutory function to which the provisions under construction related ([47]–[48]); the level of any 'practical difficulty' entailed by applying the natural meaning of words ([49]); whether certain provisions are intended to provide a 'complete code' ([59]); and the implications which can be derived from Parliament's not having adopted a different course ([62]).

[10] In *Maunsell v Olins* [1975] AC 373 (HL), Lord Reid discussed the proper approach to using so-called 'rules of construction', particularly where these point in different directions. This can be seen as of general application to the way in which all factors relevant to the statutory interpretation exercise must be weighed and balanced and considered along with the statutory language. See at 382E–F: 'rules of construction … are not rules in the ordinary sense of having some binding force. They are our servants, not our masters. They are aids to construction, presumptions or pointers. Not infrequently one "rule" points in one direction, another in a different direction. In each case we must look at all relevant circumstances and decide as a matter of judgment what weight to attach to any particular "rule"'.

[11] *Seal v Chief Constable of South Wales Police* [2007] UKHL 31, [2007] 1 WLR 1910 [5] (Lord Bingham): 'In construing any statutory provision the starting point must always be the language of the provision itself.' See also *David T Morrison* (n 3) [48] (Lord Neuberger): 'the natural meaning of an expression or a provision is as good a place as any (and very often the best place) to start'; and

factors may indicate, the court must be satisfied that those words can and ought to be given the interpretation it concludes is correct.[12]

Rules of Interpretation

3.10 In interpreting statutory language, the courts employ various so-called 'rules', 'maxims', 'principles', 'canons' or 'presumptions'. A number of these are discussed immediately below. They are valuable tools, even if they point in different directions from one another, but they must always be seen as 'guidelines rather than railway lines, as servants rather than masters'; they 'exist to illuminate and help, but not to constrain or inhibit'.[13] In every case, all relevant factors must be taken into account.

Words are Presumptively Given their Ordinary or Natural Meaning

3.11 Words or phrases should be given their 'natural' or 'ordinary' meaning in the general context of the legislation in question[14] (including in particular

Director of Legal Aid Casework v Briggs [2017] EWCA Civ 1169 [77] (King LJ): 'it is undoubtedly the case that the wording of the statute is the starting point and will often also be the finishing point'. But compare *Bloomsbury International Ltd v Department for Environment, Food and Rural Affairs* [2011] UKSC 25, [2011] 1 WLR 1546 [10] (Lord Mance), suggesting that 'identifying the legislative purpose and scheme' may be the best starting point, since these 'represent the context in which individual words are to be understood'.

[12] See *Quintavalle* (n 1), as cited in that note; and see also *Re Lehman Brothers International (Europe) (No 4)* [2017] UKSC 38, [2017] 2 WLR 1497 [123] (Lord Neuberger): 'when it comes to deciding the meaning of a legislative provision, judges are primarily concerned with arriving at a coherent interpretation, which, while taking into account commerciality and reasonableness, pays proper regard to the language of the provision interpreted in its context'. Note that, in rare cases, the courts will be able to correct obvious drafting errors in the legislation, where Parliament's intention is clear: see paragraphs 3.49–3.51 below.

[13] See *Cusack v Harrow London Borough Council* [2013] UKSC 40, [2013] 1 WLR 2022 [57]–[60] (Lord Neuberger): 'In my view, canons of construction have a valuable part to play in interpretation, provided they are treated as guidelines rather than railway lines, as servants rather than masters. If invoked properly, they represent a very good example of the value of precedent ... Of course there will be many cases, where different canons will point to different answers, but that does not call their value into question. Provided that it is remembered that the canons exist to illuminate and help, but not to constrain or inhibit, they remain of real value.' See also the passage in *Maunsell* (n 10) cited in that note; and *Spath Holme* (n 2) 397B (Lord Nicholls): 'In identifying the meaning of the words used, the courts employ accepted principles of interpretation as useful guides.'

[14] See *Spath Holme* (n 2) 397B (Lord Nicholls): 'an appropriate starting point is that language is to be taken to bear its ordinary meaning in the general context of the statute'; *Pinner v Everett* [1969] 1 WLR 1266 (HL) 1273C–D (Lord Reid): 'In determining the meaning of any word or phrase in a statute the first question to ask always is what is the natural or ordinary meaning of that word of [*sic*] phrase in its context in the statute?'; *Maunsell* (n 10) 382F (Lord Reid): 'I fully accept that a word should be given its ordinary meaning unless there is sufficient reason to give it in the particular case a secondary or limited meaning'; and at 391F (Lord Simon and Lord Diplock, dissenting): 'statutory

its purpose),[15] unless they are defined in the statute,[16] or unless the context, or the consequence of such a construction, indicates otherwise.[17] Many of the principles of construction cited below can be considered simply as aspects of this principle, since their purpose is to help give each 'word the natural meaning that it bears having regard to its context'.[18]

3.12   The principle 'that words are prima facie to be given their ordinary meaning' is sometimes known as the 'golden rule'.[19] This term is not adopted in this book as: (i) various common formulations of the so-called golden rule do not account for the role of context and purpose;[20] (ii) the term appears to be less

---

language must always be given presumptively the most natural and ordinary meaning which is appropriate in the circumstances'; *Majorstake Ltd v Curtis* [2008] UKHL 10, [2008] 1 AC 787 [44] (Lord Carswell): 'That ordinary meaning must be governed by the context of the statute in which it is found, for it does not have any universally applicable meaning as a matter of general usage'; *Re British Concrete Pipe Association's Agreement* [1983] ICR 215 (CA) 217E (Sir John Donaldson MR): 'the prima facie rule is that words have their ordinary meaning'. For examples of cases discussing the natural and ordinary meaning of particular terms, see, eg, *R v Barnet London Borough Council ex p Shah* [1983] 2 AC 309 (HL) on the meaning of 'ordinarily resident'; *R v Kelly* [2000] QB 198 (CA) on the ordinary meaning of 'exceptional'; and *R v Bowden* [2001] QB 88 (CA) on the natural and ordinary meaning of 'to make'.

[15]   See below at paragraphs 3.43–3.48.

[16]   See, eg, *R v Bowden* (n 14) 95E (Otton LJ): 'There is no definition section. Accordingly the words "to make" must be given their natural and ordinary meaning.' See also *Higham v Horton* [2004] EWCA Civ 941, [2004] 3 All ER 852 [15] (Peter Gibson LJ): 'The terms "member" and "membership" are not defined and accordingly they must be given their ordinary meaning in the context in which they are used', and see also at [28] (Jonathan Parker LJ) to similar effect.

[17]   *Edwards v Kumarasamy* [2016] UKSC 40, [2016] AC 1334 [17] (Lord Neuberger): 'Unless the natural meaning of the words of a statutory provision produces a nonsensical result, or a result which is inconsistent with the intention of the legislation concerned, as gathered from admissible material, the words must be given their ordinary meaning. (I should perhaps add that in many cases, particularly when the words are read in their context, they can have more than one ordinary meaning, and it is then for the court to decide which of those meanings is correct)'; *Kirkness v John Hudson & Co Ltd* [1955] AC 696 (HL) 729 (Lord Reid): 'it is only permissible to give to a word some meaning other than its ordinary meaning if the context so requires', cited by Lord Rodger in *R (O'Byrne) v Secretary of State for the Environment, Transport and the Regions* [2002] UKHL 45, [2002] 1 WLR 3250 at [74] before considering contextual factors pointing in different directions; *R (G) v Westminster City Council* [2004] EWCA Civ 45, [2004] 1 WLR 1113 [42] (Lord Phillips MR): 'In the absence of any case precedent, or any extrinsic aid to construction, we shall seek to give section 19 a meaning that accords with the natural meaning of the language used and makes sense, having regard to the overall scheme of the legislation.' As to the relevance of the consequences of giving words their natural meaning, see, eg, *Stock v Frank Jones (Tipton) Ltd* [1978] 1 WLR 231 (HL) 235G–H (Lord Simon), referring to the so-called 'golden rule' of construction that 'you are to apply statutory words and phrases according to their natural and ordinary meaning without addition or subtraction, unless that meaning produces injustice, absurdity, anomaly or contradiction, in which case you may modify the natural and ordinary meaning so as to obviate such injustice etc. but no further'. Lord Simon then made clear that these exceptions did not permit words to be given a construction they were not capable of bearing: see at 236E–H.

[18]   *R (G)* (n 17) [42] (Lord Phillips MR), citing the *ejusdem generis* principle in this regard (as to which, see paragraphs 3.36–3.39 below).

[19]   *Cusack* (n 13) [60] (Lord Neuberger).

[20]   See the citation from *Stock* at n 17 above. After setting out this formulation of the golden rule, Lord Simon then stated that a reference to understanding the words in their context ought to be included in it, and went on (at 236B–H) to affirm the importance of using the statutory purpose in deciding between possible meanings (though there is no scope for this in the formulation cited).

frequently used by the courts in recent times;[21] and (iii) the term has not always been consistently applied to denote the same principle.[22]

3.13   Where there is no ambiguity in the language being interpreted, the ordinary meaning is also sometimes termed the 'plain meaning'. Although on occasion the courts use strong language to say that if a 'plain meaning' is to be found it must be applied,[23] this should be seen as emphasising the primacy of the clear meaning of the text in the enactment at hand, rather than precluding all recourse to genuinely relevant context and other interpretive factors to inform the meaning of the statute.[24]

3.14   It is worthwhile noting at this stage some practical matters as to how the courts approach questions of the ordinary meaning of words and phrases:

3.14.1   First, the courts frequently have recourse to dictionaries to assist in interpreting words or phrases. See Chapter 13.17.

3.14.2   Second, the courts will be cautious not to take the generally 'inappropriate' course of laying down definitions of words or phrases where Parliament

---

[21] Although for a recent example see *Aitken v Director of Public Prosecutions* [2015] EWHC 1079 (Admin), [2016] 1 WLR 297 [38] (Bean LJ), taking as his 'starting point … the primary rule of statutory construction: the so-called "golden rule", that statutory words should be given their ordinary and natural meaning'. As to this principle, see generally the various citations at n 14 above.

[22] See *Maunsell* (n 10) 390H–391A (Lord Simon and Lord Diplock, dissenting), using the term to refer to a principle about when technical meanings or ordinary meanings apply.

[23] See, eg, *Shahid v Scottish Ministers* [2015] UKSC 58, [2016] AC 429 [20]–[21] (Lord Reed), stating: 'No amount of purposive interpretation can however entitle the court to disregard the plain and unambiguous terms of the legislation … The only principle of statutory interpretation which might enable the plain meaning of legislation to be circumvented is that it can be given a strained interpretation where that is necessary to avoid absurd or perverse consequences', although he acknowledged that 'even greater violence can be done to statutory language where it is plain that there has been a drafting mistake' (as to which, see paragraphs 3.49–3.51 below); *Duport Steels* (n 4) 157C–D (Lord Diplock): 'Where the meaning of the statutory words is plain and unambiguous it is not for the judges to invent fancied ambiguities as an excuse for failing to give effect to its plain meaning because they themselves consider that the consequences of doing so would be inexpedient, or even unjust or immoral'; *Stock* (n 17) 234G–235F (Viscount Dilhorne), 237D–F (Lord Simon), 238F–239E (Lord Scarman), all holding that unambiguous language should not give way merely to 'anomaly', as opposed to something more severe. These speeches in *Stock* were cited and applied as authoritative by the Court of Appeal in *Greenweb Ltd v Wandsworth London Borough Council* [2008] EWCA Civ 910, [2009] 1 WLR 612 [28]–[32] (Stanley Burnton LJ). See also *R v Bentham* [2005] UKHL 18, [2005] 1 WLR 1057 [10] (Lord Bingham), rejecting a purposive construction where that would create a criminal offence: 'Rules of statutory construction have a valuable role when the meaning of a statutory provision is doubtful, but none where, as here, the meaning is plain.' See further *Yarl's Wood Immigration Ltd v Bedfordshire Police Authority* [2009] EWCA Civ 1110, [2010] QB 698 [67]–[69] (Rix LJ), applying a historical formulation of the 'golden rule' and considering therefore that the plain meaning should be applied where there was no 'obscurity' about that meaning, it produced 'no overbearing inconsistency, absurdity or inconvenience', and the court was not dealing with 'detailed and complex statutory provisions'. See also *R (D) v Secretary of State for Work and Pensions* [2010] EWCA Civ 18, [2010] 1 WLR 1782 [47] (Carnwath LJ), discussing and endorsing the so-called plain meaning rule.

[24] See *Williams* (n 6) [72] (Lord Neuberger), considering the meaning of the text being considered in that case to be unambiguous and stating: 'When interpreting a statute, the court's function is to

has not done so,[25] especially where faced with 'ordinary words ... in common and general use'[26] or words that are 'inherently imprecise'.[27] This may be different where 'the context requires that some special or particular meaning should be placed upon' the statutory words in question, in which case further exposition may be appropriate.[28] Otherwise, the courts must limit themselves to applying the language of the statute itself to reach appropriate conclusions in the instant case. This means that previous decisions about the meaning of particular words as applied to particular facts should be viewed as such.[29] It also means that parties will generally be well advised to frame issues involving statutory construction in terms that are case-specific rather than more abstract.[30]

---

determine the meaning of the words used in the statute. The fact that context and mischief are factors which must be taken into account does not mean that, when performing its interpretive role, the court can take a free-wheeling view of the intention of Parliament looking at all admissible material, and treating the wording of the statute as merely one item. Context and mischief do not represent a licence to judges to ignore the plain meaning of the words that Parliament has used.' The cases cited in nn 14 and 17 above, and the fact that the natural meaning only 'presumptively' governs the meaning of statutory language (see the passage from the dissenting speech of Lord Simon and Lord Diplock in *Maunsell* (n 10) cited in n 14 above), further show that context and other factors should always be considered, although particularly strong weight ought to be given to a clear meaning apparent from the statutory language. See also *R (Kelly) v Secretary of State for Justice* [2008] EWCA Civ 177, [2009] QB 204 [24] (Laws LJ), stating that one cannot take literally statements that statutory words capable of only one meaning must be given that meaning, on the basis that this 'proves too much', does not recognise the 'growing acceptance of purposive constructions' and would prevent the correction of mistaken wording on the basis of such constructions (as to which see paragraphs 3.49–3.51 below); *Hotak v Southwark London Borough Council* [2015] UKSC 30, [2016] AC 811 [59] (Lord Neuberger): 'I have been anxious to emphasise the primacy of the statutory words'; the passage in *David T Morrison* (n 3) cited in the text to n 7; and *R v Z (Attorney General for Northern Ireland's Reference)* [2005] UKHL 35, [2005] 2 AC 645 [49] (Lord Carswell). This paragraph in *R v Z* was cited in *Solar Century Holdings Ltd v Secretary of State for Energy and Climate Change* [2014] EWHC 3677 (Admin) [52] (Green J), stating: 'if there is a collision between a literal interpretation of an enactment and the contextual material with the consequence that the literal interpretation "is manifestly contrary to the intention which one may readily impute to Parliament, when having regard to the historical context and the mischief ...", then the enactment should be construed in the light of the purpose as evident from the historical context and mischief'. This passage in *Solar Century* was in turn cited with approval in *Briggs* (n 11) [82] (King LJ), and see generally at [77]–[83] on the importance of context and purpose in interpretation, stating at [83]: 'the court, having taken proper cognisance of the precise wording found in the words of the statute, is thereafter entitled and indeed, where a dispute has arisen, must move on to consider the purpose of the disputed section'.

[25] See *R (Ghai) v Newcastle City Council* [2010] EWCA Civ 59, [2011] QB 591 [33] (Lord Neuberger MR), stating that 'in general' to do so was 'inappropriate' and 'would virtually be a judicial encroachment onto the legislative function'.

[26] *Stephens v Cuckfield Rural District Council* [1960] 2 QB 373 (CA) 382–83 (Upjohn LJ).

[27] See *R v Monopolies and Mergers Commission ex p South Yorkshire Transport Ltd* [1993] 1 WLR 23 (HL) 29C–D (Lord Mustill), considering the meaning of the word 'substantial': 'The courts have repeatedly warned against the dangers of taking an inherently imprecise word, and by redefining it thrusting on it a spurious degree of precision.'

[28] *Stephens* (n 26) 382 (Upjohn LJ).

[29] See, eg, *South Yorkshire Transport* (n 27) 29C (Lord Mustill), discussing the limited import of a previous decision. See also *RFC 2012 plc v Advocate General for Scotland* [2017] UKSC 45, [2017] 1 WLR 2767 [11] (Lord Hodge): 'the courts at the highest level have repeatedly warned of the need to focus on the words of the statute and not on judicial glosses, which may clarify or illustrate in a particular case but do not replace the statutory words'.

[30] *Ghai* (n 25) [33] (Lord Neuberger MR).

3.14.3   Third, questions of the proper construction of a statute are questions of law, including questions as to 'whether a word or phrase is being used in its ordinary sense or in a special sense'.[31] However, where a term is used in its ordinary sense, the courts often treat (to an extent) the application of that term to particular facts as a question of fact.[32] This means that appellate courts will therefore generally be slow to interfere with decisions on such issues by first instance judges.[33] This approach does not mean, however, that the courts will be similarly hesitant to interfere with an administrative decision where the decision maker has made a genuine error of interpretation rather than application.[34]

3.15   *Technical meanings*: if an enactment deals with a particular technical, professional or scientific context or area of expertise, and a particular term has (or is capable of having) a specific technical meaning in that context, this may suggest that the term in question is intended to bear that technical meaning rather than its ordinary or natural meaning. Presumptively, the subject matter of the enactment may give a strong indication, but the court must consider the overall context, and the enactment as a whole, to determine whether or not the technical or ordinary meaning is intended to apply.[35]

---

[31]   *R v Evans* [2005] EWCA Crim 1302, [2005] 1 WLR 1435 [15] (Dyson LJ), citing *Moyna v Secretary of State for Work and Pensions* [2003] UKHL 44, [2003] 1 WLR 1929 [23]–[25] (Lord Hoffmann) and *Brutus v Cozens* [1973] AC 854, 861–62 (Lord Reid).

[32]   *Moyna* (n 31) [21]–[27] (Lord Hoffmann), considering *Brutus* (n 31) 861 (Lord Reid). However, the distinction between questions of interpretation and application to specific facts 'is not … clear cut': *BBC v Sugar* [2009] UKHL 9, [2009] 1 WLR 430 [69] (Lady Hale). See also *R v H* [2007] UKHL 7, [2007] 2 AC 270 [107] (Lord Mance): 'The proper construction of a statute is a question of law. But a ruling as to the application of a statute to particular facts belongs to a complex category'; *Lawson v Serco Ltd* [2006] UKHL 3, [2006] 1 All ER 823 [34] (Lord Hoffmann): 'Whether one characterizes this as a question of fact depends, as I pointed out in *Moyna* … upon whether as a matter of policy one thinks that it is a decision which an appellate body with jurisdiction limited to errors of law should be able to review'; and the discussion of *Moyna* and *Lawson* in *R (Jones) v First-tier Tribunal* [2013] UKSC 19, [2013] 2 AC 48 [43]–[47] (Lord Carnwath). See also the citations in the following note.

[33]   *Moyna* (n 31) [25] (Lord Hoffmann): 'What this means in practice is that an appellate court with jurisdiction to entertain appeals only on questions of law will not hear an appeal against such a decision unless it falls outside the bounds of reasonable judgment'; but ultimately, as Lord Hoffmann stated at [27]: 'the degree to which an appellate court will be willing to substitute its own judgment for that of the tribunal will vary with the nature of the question'. See also *Lawson* (n 32) [34] (Lord Hoffmann), as cited in that note, and finding that 'the question of whether, on given facts, a case falls within the territorial scope of section 94(1) [of the Employment Right Act 1996] should be treated as a question of law' (to ensure appeals could be made), but 'is a question of degree on which the decision of the primary fact-finder is entitled to considerable respect'.

[34]   *R (UNISON) v Monitor* [2009] EWHC 3221 (Admin), [2010] PTSR 1827 [60] (Cranston J).

[35]   See *Unwin v Hanson* [1891] 2 QB 115 (CA) 119 (Lord Esher MR), distinguishing between Acts dealing with 'matters affecting everybody generally', where the ordinary meaning will apply, and Acts 'passed with reference to a particular trade, business or transaction', where any words with a meaning known and understood by 'everybody conversant with that trade, business, or transaction' will be given that meaning, even if different from the ordinary meaning; *Maunsell* (n 10) 391B–C (Lord Simon and Lord Diplock, dissenting), stating that words will 'presumptively bear' a technical meaning 'in statutes dealing with technical matters'; *Jones v Tower Boot Co Ltd* [1997] 2 All ER 406 (CA) 413F (Waite LJ): 'words in a statute are to be given their normal meaning according to general use in the English language unless the context indicates that such words have to be given a special or technical meaning as a

The Presumption that Language is Used 'Correctly and Exactly'

3.16 It is generally to be presumed that the legislator has used legislative language 'correctly and exactly, and not loosely and inexactly', with a heavy burden on those who would contend otherwise in a given case.[36] Since it is assumed that the choice of language is careful and intentional, it should also be presumed (a fortiori) that the legislator has not made a mistake in its drafting.[37]

3.17 This is the case at least for modern statutes enacted since the late nineteenth century. It should be recognised that Acts drafted prior to 'the creation of the Office of Parliamentary Counsel in 1869 (the office of dedicated statutory drafters now available to the Government)' cannot be expected to have been 'drafted with the precision and clarity which has come to be expected of statutory drafting since then'.[38] In considering questions of the interpretation of older statutes, this presumption and the following presumptions regarding the meaning of statutory language should be viewed in the light of this historical reality.

The Presumption that Statutory Language Must Mean Something

3.18 Allied to the previous presumption is another 'presumption that every word in a statute must be given some effective meaning',[39] otherwise known as the

---

term of art'; *Ghai* (n 25) [22] (Lord Neuberger MR): 'where ... the word is one which is used in ordinary language and has no established special legal or technical meaning, and is not defined in the ... Act ... one can usefully take as a starting point the word's ordinary meaning'; *Holt & Co v Collyer* (1881) 16 Ch D 718 (Ch) 720–21 (Fry J), accepting that technical words should be given a technical meaning, but where a word has both a common meaning and a secondary, technical meaning, it should be given the latter construction only where this can be shown to be appropriate 'from the instrument itself or from the circumstances of the case'; *Mason v Bolton's Library Ltd* [1913] 1 KB 83 (CA) 90 (Farwell LJ): 'It is a stringent rule of construction that in construing an Act of Parliament or a deed containing technical words those words must be given their technical meaning.'

[36] See *Spillers Ltd v Cardiff (Borough) Assessment Committee* [1931] 2 KB 21 (KB) 43 (Lord Hewart CJ), continuing: 'Upon those who assert that that rule has been broken the burden of establishing their proposition lies heavily. And they can discharge it only by pointing to something in the context which goes to show that the loose and inexact meaning must be preferred.' This passage was cited with approval and applied in *New Plymouth Borough Council v Taranaki Electric-Power Board* [1933] AC 680 (PC) 682 (Lord Macmillan). See also *R v Central Criminal Court ex p Francis & Francis* [1989] AC 346 (HL) 388G–389C (Lord Oliver, dissenting), citing and applying this passage, doubting that Parliament's choice of two different words was 'unintentional'; and *Attorney General's Reference (No 1 of 1988)* [1989] AC 971 (HL) 993H–994G (Lord Lowry), citing this passage and stating that it was not intended to preclude a finding that words bore a 'secondary but correct and acceptable meaning'.

[37] As to the courts' power to correct obvious drafting errors, see paragraphs 3.49–3.51 below.

[38] *Edwards & Walkden (Norfolk) Ltd v City of London* [2012] EWHC 2527 (Ch) [24] (Sales J), applied in *R (Andrews) v Secretary of State for Environment, Food and Rural Affairs* [2015] EWCA Civ 669, [2016] 3 All ER 1022 [30] and [54] (Lord Dyson MR, giving the judgment of the Court).

[39] *McMonagle v Westminster City Council* [1990] 2 AC 716 (HL) 726D–F (Lord Bridge): 'The presumption that every word in a statute must be given some effective meaning is a strong one, but the courts have on occasion been driven to disregard particular words or phrases when, by giving effect

presumption against 'surplusage'.[40] Parliament is assumed to have put each word there for a reason,[41] and each word should therefore be taken to add *something* to the meaning that an enactment would have in its absence, 'unless there is good reason to the contrary'.[42]

3.19   The presumption is 'a strong one',[43] and statutory words should generally only be disregarded and effectively 'deleted' in 'extreme cases', such as where 'to give the relevant words their natural (or any possible) meaning would fatally undermine the obvious purpose of the legislation',[44] or would render the operation of the statute 'insensible' or 'absurd',[45] or would offend against some other important principle of construction (such as the presumption against retrospective effect).[46]

3.20   The courts may also decline to follow the presumption where it is reasonable to conclude in a particular case that a word, phrase or provision has been included merely for the avoidance of doubt,[47] and especially where the relevant

---

to them, the operation of the statute would be rendered insensible, absurd or ineffective to achieve its evident purpose.' See also *Secretary of State for Defence v Spencer* [2003] EWCA Civ 784, [2003] 1 WLR 2701 [29] (Peter Gibson LJ): 'It is elementary that one must seek to give meaning to every word used in a statute.'

[40] See *Ryanair Ltd v Commissioners for HM Revenue & Customs* [2014] EWCA Civ 410 [38] Patten LJ: 'The general rule is that the court will seek to ascertain the intention of the legislature from the totality of the words used. Surplusage is not lightly to be assumed.'

[41] *Quebec Railway, Light, Heat and Power Co Ltd v Vandry* [1920] AC 662 (PC) 676 (Lord Sumner): 'effect must be given, if possible, to all the words used for the Legislature is deemed not to waste its words or to say anything in vain'.

[42] *Hill v William Hill (Park Lane) Ltd* [1949] AC 530 (HL) 546–47 (Viscount Simon): 'When the legislature enacts a particular phrase in a statute the presumption is that it is saying something which has not been said immediately before. The rule that a meaning should, if possible, be given to every word in the statute implies that, unless there is good reason to the contrary, the words add something which would not be there if the words were left out.'

[43] *McMonagle* (n 39), in the passage cited in that note. But see the cases cited at n 47 below.

[44] *Ryanair* (n 40) [38] (Patten LJ), citing *McMonagle* (n 39).

[45] *McMonagle* (n 39), in the passage cited in that note.

[46] See *Hill* (n 42) 547 (Viscount Simon). As to the presumption against retrospectivity, see Chapter 4.42–4.53.

[47] See *Walker v Centaur Clothes Group Ltd* [2000] 1 WLR 799 (HL) 805D–E (Lord Hoffmann): 'I seldom think that an argument from redundancy carries great weight, even in a Finance Act. It is not unusual for Parliament to say expressly what the courts would have inferred anyway.' This was cited and applied in *DMWSHNZ Ltd v Commissioners for HM Revenue & Customs* [2015] EWCA Civ 1036 [38] (Lewison LJ): 'That case was concerned with an argument that one sub-section of a taxing statute would be redundant if another sub-section of the same section was interpreted in a particular way. The argument from redundancy carries even less weight when what is in issue is a different section and, moreover, one introduced by amendment.' To similar effect to *Walker*, see *Omar Parks Ltd v Elkington* [1992] 1 WLR 1270 (CA) 1273H (Nourse LJ): 'An emphasis of the obvious, unnecessary to a judge who has had the benefit of argument, may yet be welcome to a busy practitioner who has not.' See *Johnston Publishing (North) Ltd v Revenue & Customs Commissioners* [2008] EWCA Civ 858, [2009] 1 WLR 1349, where these dicta from *Walker* and *Omar Parks* were cited, but the majority nevertheless affirmed the importance of seeking to avoid redundancy if possible: see at [23] (Sir John Chadwick); [46] (Tuckey LJ), saying this was the case even though 'surplusage is not unusual in tax statutes'; but compare [37]–[42] (Toulson LJ, dissenting), emphasising that tax statutes 'are seldom models of succinctness'.

words would otherwise have to be given 'unnatural meanings simply to avoid them being surplusage'.[48] This entails the less drastic conclusion that a matter has been repeated, clarified or expanded upon for some reason, rather than the more extreme finding that words must be disregarded altogether.

The Presumption that General Provisions Do Not Override Specific Provisions

3.21   As a general rule, where there is a potential for conflict between two legislative provisions, then it is presumed that the provision which addresses a particular situation more specifically will apply to that specific situation and that the more general provision will not. In other words, 'general words do not derogate from specific words', so that '[w]here there is an unqualified specific provision, a general provision is not to be taken to override that specific provision'.[49] This presumption will apply with particular force where it is clear that applying the general provision would defeat or circumvent the parliamentary intention behind making the more specific provision, or would deprive it of any real effect.[50] However, in certain cases it may not be appropriate to characterise one of two provisions as general and another as specific, such that one does not apply in a particular instance; they may be 'simply different provisions concerned with overlapping aims and overlapping applications'.[51]

---

[48] See *David T Morrison* (n 3) [49] (Lord Neuberger): 'Cautious drafters of statutes and contracts often include protective or qualifying words which are not strictly necessary, and it would hinder clarity and certainty in the law, and seriously risk subverting the parliamentary or contractual intention, if judges started giving such expressions unnatural meanings simply to avoid them being surplusage.' See also to similar effect at [23] (Lord Reed), but compare [88] (Lord Hodge, dissenting), giving greater weight to the principle against surplusage.

[49] See *Vinos v Marks & Spencer plc* [2001] 3 All ER 784 (CA) [27] (Peter Gibson LJ), in the context of two powers to extend time in the CPR; and at [20] (May LJ). This principle is sometimes known by the Latin expression 'generalia specialibus non derogant'.

[50] See *R v Liverpool City Council ex p Baby Products Association* (2000) 2 LGLR 689 (QB) 178E–F (Lord Bingham CJ), considering powers under two different Acts: 'A power conferred in very general terms plainly cannot be relied on to defeat the intention of clear and particular statutory provisions'— in that case a detailed statutory code, containing various procedural safeguards, governing the enforcement of consumer protection legislation, which would have been undermined by the use of a local authority's general powers to publish information under the Local Government Act 1972. This statement was applied in *R (W) v Secretary of State for Health* [2015] EWCA Civ 1034, [2016] 1 WLR 698 [57] (Lord Dyson MR, giving the judgment of the Court). See also to similar effect *R v J* [2004] UKHL 42, [2005] 1 AC 562, holding that where Parliament had laid down a time limit for the prosecution of a particular offence, and that time limit had expired, Parliament could not have intended that a prosecution could then be brought on the same facts for another overlapping offence carrying the same penalty. See at [18] (Lord Bingham), noting that any other construction would deprive the time limit of 'any meaningful effect whatever', [37] (Lord Steyn), [48] (Lord Clyde) and [64] (Lord Rodger).

[51] See *Cusack* (n 13) [61] (Lord Neuberger), in the context of two powers in the Highways Act 1980.

Presumed Consistency of Meaning

3.22   It is presumed that, since legislative instruments are to be read as a whole, words and phrases are intended to have a consistent meaning throughout a single instrument.[52] This presumption applies with even greater force to multiple instances of the same word or phrase in a single sentence or provision, or in neighbouring provisions.[53]

3.23   In practice, this means that if one instance of a word or phrase in an enactment is not straightforward to interpret, it may assist first to determine the meaning of the same word or phrase as it occurs elsewhere in the enactment in a context that makes its meaning clearer. This can then be read across to the more opaque instance.[54]

3.24   However, although this presumption is a 'powerful' aid to construction, it is not an 'immutable rule'.[55] It will not apply where the legislation expressly provides for the word to bear different meanings in different contexts,[56] where its application would frustrate the purpose of the legislation,[57] or where this is otherwise clear from 'the nature of the word or phrase in question and the contexts in which it appears in the instrument'.[58]

---

[52] See *Assange v Swedish Prosecution Authorities* [2012] UKSC 22, [2012] 2 AC 471 [75] (Lord Phillips): 'When considering the meaning of a word or phrase that is used more than once in the same instrument one starts with a presumption that it bears the same meaning wherever it appears' (this statement was made in the context of interpreting an EU Framework Decision, but it is clear that it is of general application). See also *R (N) v London Borough of Barking and Dagenham Independent Appeal Panel* [2009] EWCA Civ 108, [2009] ELR 268 [46] (Toulson LJ): 'there is a strong presumption that where the same formula is used in different parts of the same Act it is intended to bear the same meaning'.

[53] *Littlewood v George Wimpey & Co Ltd* [1953] 2 QB 501 (CA) 518 (Denning LJ, dissenting): 'It is a well-settled rule of construction that the same word occurring in the same document should, prima facie, be given the same meaning whenever it occurs. All the more so in the same sentence'. See also *R (Harrison) v Secretary of State for Health* [2009] EWHC 3086 (Admin) [44] (Silber J): 'where a word, like services, has no one settled meaning, it must take its colour from the context in which it is found and a fundamental aspect of that context is the use given to that word in other neighbouring provisions of the same Act'. He then cited the statement of Toulson LJ in *R (N)* (n 52) cited in that note, stating: 'That presumption must become even stronger when the same word is used in the same section.'

[54] See *R (Thames Water Utilities Ltd) v Water Services Regulation Authority* [2010] EWHC 3331 (Admin), [2011] PTSR 857 [17]–[18] (Mitting J), citing with approval Francis Bennion, *Bennion on Statutory Interpretation*, 5th edn (London, LexisNexis 2008) 1160. The relevant passage in Oliver Jones, *Bennion on Statutory Interpretation*, 6th edn (London, LexisNexis 2013) is at section 355, 1034. This decision was affirmed on appeal, without addressing this principle: [2012] EWCA Civ 218, [2012] PTSR 1147. For another example of this method of interpretation (albeit in combination with other principles of interpretation), see *R v Tearse* [1945] KB 1 (CA) 6 (Wrottesley J).

[55] *Cotton v Secretary of State for Works and Pensions* [2009] EWCA Civ 1333 [37] and [39] (Goldring LJ). See also *Assange* (n 52) [75] (Lord Phillips), stating that it 'is not ... an irrebuttable presumption'.

[56] *Suffolk Mental Health Partnership NHS Trust v Hurst* [2009] EWCA Civ 309, [2009] ICR 1011 [65] (Wall LJ).

[57] *Cotton* (n 55) [37] (Goldring LJ).

[58] *Assange* (n 52) [75] (Lord Phillips); [150] (Lord Dyson), agreeing with Lord Phillips on this point; and see also *9 Cornwall Crescent London Ltd v Kensington and Chelsea Royal London Borough Council*

The Presumption that Different Words Have Different Meanings

3.25 Since it is presumed that the legislator will repeat words if it wishes to convey the same meaning in multiple places, it can conversely be presumed that where the legislator has used different words, it intends them to bear different meanings.[59]

The Presumption that Legislation is 'Always Speaking'

3.26 Legislative language should normally be interpreted and applied as understood in the light of *current* circumstances, rather than being limited in its effect by reference to how the enactment would have been *historically* interpreted and applied at the date of enactment. This is known as the presumption that legislation is 'always speaking'.[60] Strictly, the always speaking principle does not involve the *meaning* of the statutory language changing over time (although in substance this

---

[2005] EWCA Civ 324, [2006] 1 WLR 1186 [31] (Auld LJ): 'As a general rule the same expression used in different parts of the same Act should be construed in the same way unless the Act, expressly or by reference to the different contexts in which the expression appears, otherwise requires.' Each of these cases provides an example of the presumption not being applied (in the case of *Assange*, this was in the context of interpreting an EU Framework Decision, but it is instructive more generally). For a further example, see *Haile v Waltham Forest London Borough Council* [2015] UKSC 34, [2015] AC 1471 [21] (Lord Reed), finding that the phrase 'continue to occupy' in ss 175 and 191 of the Housing Act 1996 could not 'be interpreted in an identical manner in both contexts', but that the 'symmetry' between the two sections meant it could be inferred that those words were 'intended to be interpreted so as to enable the provisions to operate harmoniously together'. The potential for multiple interpretations of a word within an enactment was also recognised in, eg, *HM Revenue & Customs Commissioners v Cotter* [2013] UKSC 69, [2013] 1 WLR 3514, where the Supreme Court held that the word 'return' bore a particular meaning in the context of certain sections of the Taxes Management Act 1970, while acknowledging that it 'may have a wider meaning in other contexts within the 1970 Act': see at [25] (Lord Hodge). The Supreme Court overturned the Court of Appeal's decision, [2012] EWCA Civ 81, [2012] STC 745, which had held at [28] (Arden LJ): 'Where a word is used more than once in the same set of statutory provisions, it bears the same meaning unless it is clear it cannot do so' (although the Supreme Court did not comment on this statement of principle).

[59] See, eg, *Globespan* (n 9) [42] (Arden LJ): 'Paragraph 83(4) uses two different concepts: receipt and registration. Since different words are used, it must be assumed that different events are referred to.'

[60] See, eg, *McCartan Turkington Breen v Times Newspapers Ltd* [2001] 2 AC 277 (HL) 296A–C (Lord Steyn): 'Unless they reveal a contrary intention all statutes are to be interpreted as "always speaking statutes" … courts must interpret and apply a statute to the world as it exists today' and 'in the light of the legal system as it exists today'; citing the statement and explanation of this principle in *R v Ireland* [1998] AC 147 (HL) 158D–G (Lord Steyn). See also *NML Capital Ltd v Republic of Argentina* [2011] UKSC 31, [2011] 2 AC 495 [142] (Lord Clarke): 'unless a contrary intention appears, an enactment is intended to develop in meaning with developing circumstances and should be given what Bennion calls an updating construction to allow for changes since the Act was initially framed', citing Bennion, *Statutory Interpretation* (2008) (n 54) at section 288, 890; and *Baker v Quantum Clothing Group Ltd* [2011] UKSC 17, [2011] 1 WLR 1003 [173] (Lord Kerr, dissenting), likewise citing with approval the 'principled way of addressing the question' found in Bennion, *Statutory Interpretation* (2008), at section 288, 890. For the relevant passage in Jones, *Statutory Interpretation* (2013) (n 54), see section 288, 797 (and more generally 797–815).

may appear to be its effect)—it is only the 'context or application' of the legislation that changes.[61]

3.27 The principle applies because Parliament is ordinarily taken to desire that its legislation, which will usually apply indefinitely, should remain relevant in the face of developments in society, technology, knowledge and the world in general. To apply it assuming that 'the world had remained static since the legislation was enacted ... would usually be perverse and would defeat the purpose of the legislation'.[62]

3.28 However, while 'statutes will generally be found to be of the "always speaking" variety',[63] there is also a 'relatively rare category of cases where Parliament intended the language to be fixed at the time when the original Act was passed', with the result that the legislation is of unchanging effect as time passes.[64]

3.29 Accordingly, it will often be necessary to decide whether to apply the 'updating approach' to statutory interpretation, treating a statute as always speaking, or the 'historical approach', fixing its meaning at the time of enactment.[65] However, this will not be necessary where the choice of approach would make no difference to the outcome in a particular case.[66]

3.30 When a difference in approach would lead to a difference in outcome, 'it is a matter of interpretation whether a court must search for the historical or original meaning of a statute or whether it is free to apply the current meaning of the statute to present day conditions'.[67] Broadly, '[t]he essential question ... is whether an updated meaning is consistent with the statutory purpose'.[68]

---

[61] See *R v G* [2003] UKHL 50, [2004] 1 AC 1034 [29] (Lord Bingham): 'Since a statute is always speaking, the context or application of a statutory expression may change over time, but the meaning of the expression itself cannot change. So the starting point is to ascertain what Parliament meant by "reckless" in 1971.' See also *Quintavalle* (n 1) [9] (Lord Bingham); and *Birmingham City Council v Oakley* [2001] 1 AC 617 (HL) 631E–632F (Lord Hoffmann), citing *R v Ireland* (n 60) 158–59 (Lord Steyn).

[62] *R (ZYN) v Walsall Metropolitan Borough Council* [2014] EWHC 1918 (Admin), [2015] 1 All ER 165 [45] (Leggatt J), and see generally the discussion at [39]–[51].

[63] *R v Ireland* (n 60) 158G (Lord Steyn).

[64] See *Fitzpatrick v Sterling Housing Association Ltd* [2001] 1 AC 27 (HL) 49H–50A (Lord Clyde) in relation to whether same-sex partners could come within the scope of the term 'family' in sch 1 to the Rent Act 1977 (finding that they could).

[65] These are the terms adopted in *ZYN* (n 62), eg, at [42] (Leggatt J).

[66] See, eg, *R v Clarke* [2008] UKHL 8, [2008] 1 WLR 338 [18] (Lord Bingham): 'The "always speaking" principle has no application. The answer to the question now is the same as should have been given then.' See also *Dunnachie v Kingston upon Hull City Council* [2004] UKHL 36, [2005] 1 AC 226 [17] (Lord Steyn): 'It is not a case in which the ambulatory consequences of the always speaking canon of construction has any role to play. Nothing that happened since 1971 could justify giving to the statutory formula a meaning it did not originally bear.'

[67] *R v Ireland* (n 60) 158F–G (Lord Steyn).

[68] *Yemshaw v Hounslow London Borough Council* [2011] UKSC 3, [2011] 1 WLR 433 [27] (Lady Hale), and see generally in her judgment at [25]–[28] in relation to the meaning of the term 'violence' in s 117(1) of the Housing Act 1996.

3.31 More specifically, the courts have given guidance that the use of general language may support applying the updating approach,[69] and in particular that 'when a statute employs a concept which may change in content with advancing knowledge, technology, or social standards, it should be interpreted as it would be currently understood'.[70] By contrast, an historical interpretation 'may sometimes' be appropriate for less common pieces of legislation 'dealing with a particular grievance or problem', as opposed to the more common sort of legislation which is 'usually intended to operate for many years'.[71] Further, given that the 'always speaking' presumption derives in part from the practice of parliamentary draftsmen since the late nineteenth century,[72] historical interpretations may more often be appropriate when interpreting 'very old statutes where indeed the language itself may have had a rather different meaning in those days'.[73]

3.32 When applying an updating approach, the appropriate course in practice is to ascertain the intention of the legislature at the date of enactment, but then to ask whether particular situations, in view of changed circumstances which were not or could not have been directly contemplated by Parliament, nevertheless 'fall within the Parliamentary intention' given the purpose or policy of the legislation. However, this does not mean that the courts are permitted to go beyond the legislation itself and guess at what Parliament might have done had it considered the present situation. In the words of Lord Wilberforce:

> In interpreting an Act of Parliament it is proper, and indeed necessary, to have regard to the state of affairs existing, and known by Parliament to be existing, at the time. It is a fair presumption that Parliament's policy or intention is directed to that state of affairs. Leaving aside cases of omission by inadvertence, this being not such a case, when a new state of affairs, or a fresh set of facts bearing on policy, comes into existence, the courts have to consider whether they fall within the Parliamentary intention. They may be held to do so, if they fall within the same genus of facts as those to which the expressed policy has been formulated. They may also be held to do so if there can be detected a clear purpose in the legislation which can only be fulfilled if the extension is made. How liberally

---

[69] See *ZYN* (n 62) [46] (Leggatt J): 'The generality of language used by the legislature may also support the implication that it was intended to accommodate change.'

[70] *Oakley* (n 61) 631F–G (Lord Hoffmann). See also, eg, *Re G (Children)* [2012] EWCA Civ 1233, [2013] 1 FLR 677 [33] (Munby LJ) in the context of children's 'welfare'.

[71] *R v Ireland* (n 60) 158E–G (Lord Steyn).

[72] ibid.

[73] *Campbell College, Belfast (Governors) v Commissioner of Valuation for Northern Ireland* [1964] 1 WLR 912 (HL) 941 (Lord Upjohn). This decision was cited with approval in *Fitzpatrick* (n 64) 49H–50A (Lord Clyde), stating (in agreement with Lord Upjohn): 'The rule of contemporary exposition should be applied only in relation to very old statutes.' Note, however, the doubts expressed about the correctness of Lord Upjohn's dictum in *Isle of Anglesey County Council v Welsh Ministers* [2009] EWCA Civ 94, [2010] QB 163 [40]–[43] (Carnwath LJ), who acknowledged that there are 'various conflicting strands of authority' on this point. However, Carnwath LJ's comments were not made in the context of discussing the 'always speaking' principle, but rather in the context of discussing the role of subsequent practice in interpretation (see paragraphs 3.58–3.60 below, and in particular the discussion at n 151).

these principles may be applied must depend upon the nature of the enactment, and the strictness or otherwise of the words in which it has been expressed. The courts should be less willing to extend expressed meanings if it is clear that the Act in question was designed to be restrictive or circumscribed in its operation rather than liberal or permissive. They will be much less willing to do so where the subject matter is different in kind or dimension from that for which the legislation was passed. In any event there is one course which the courts cannot take, under the law of this country; they cannot fill gaps; they cannot by asking the question 'What would Parliament have done in this current case—not being one in contemplation—if the facts had been before it?' attempt themselves to supply the answer, if the answer is not to be found in the terms of the Act itself.[74]

3.33   Thus, it may be appropriate to apply a concept in accordance with the way the understanding of that concept has developed over time, but one cannot 'construe the language of an old statute to mean something conceptually different from what the contemporary evidence shows that Parliament must have intended'.[75]

The *Noscitur a Sociis* Principle

3.34   The principle that a word or phrase 'is known by its associates' (to translate from its Latin epithet *noscitur a sociis*) requires that statutory words should be construed in the light of associated wording in the statute.[76] This is a recognition that a term's immediate context is of particular importance to its proper interpretation.[77]

3.35   As always, there are limits on the extent to which context, even such immediate context, can influence the meaning of legislative language, especially so as to

[74] *Royal College of Nursing of the United Kingdom v Department of Health and Social Security* [1981] AC 800 (HL) 822B–F. Although this passage comes from a dissenting speech, it has been subsequently upheld as authoritative at the highest level: see, eg, *Quintavalle* (n 1) [10] (Lord Bingham) and [24] (Lord Steyn). See also *Baker* (n 60) [175] (Lord Kerr, dissenting), calling it the 'clearest exposition' of the principle.

[75] *Oakley* (n 61) 631E–632C (Lord Hoffmann). In terms of the idea that the content of a concept may change, Lord Hoffmann gave the following example: 'the concept of a vehicle has the same meaning today as it did in 1800, even though it includes methods of conveyance which would not have been imagined by a legislator of those days'; and see also the illustrations given in *Quintavalle* (n 1) [22] (Lord Steyn). See also *ZYN* (n 62) [48] (Leggatt J): 'The fact that the usage of a word has changed may well not be a matter which should result in the word being given its new meaning.'

[76] See *London Transport Executive v Betts* [1959] AC 213 (HL) 243 (Lord Denning, dissenting), regarding the construction of the word 'maintenance': 'Its meaning can be gleaned from its context. It is used in company with two associated words "housing" and "stables": and it is to be known by its associates. *Noscitur a sociis*.' For further examples of the principle being applied, see *Shamoon v Chief Constable of the Royal Ulster Constabulary* [2003] UKHL 11, [2003] 2 All ER 26 [34] (Lord Hope); and *Peart v Stewart* [1983] 2 AC 109 (HL) 117A–C (Lord Diplock).

[77] *Bourne v Norwich Crematorium Ltd* [1967] 1 WLR 691 (Ch) 696A–B (Stamp J): 'English words derive colour from those which surround them. Sentences are not mere collections of words to be taken out of the sentence, defined separately by reference to the dictionary or decided cases, and then put back again into the sentence with the meaning which one has assigned to them as separate words so as to give the sentence or phrase a meaning which as a sentence or phrase it cannot bear without distortion of the English language.' See also *Harrison* (n 53), as cited in that note.

permit a departure from its ordinary or natural meaning. The extent to which the principle is applicable or influential will depend on the circumstances, including the openness of the word or phrase in question to more than one meaning, how clear its association is with nearby words and whether a 'common characteristic' can be discerned in those other words.[78]

The *Ejusdem Generis* Principle

3.36 This is a specific instance of the *noscitur a sociis* principle. The *ejusdem generis* principle is that when general words follow other words that fall into a more specific 'category' or 'genus', the general words may be restricted by implication to matters 'of the same kind' as those other words (to translate from the Latin).[79] Although the rule is 'commonly' applied where a statute provides a list of items followed by the word 'other', it is not limited to such instances.[80] Note, however, that the principle does not apply where the wider words precede rather than follow the narrower words.[81]

---

[78] *Customs and Excise Commissioners v Viva Gas Appliances Ltd* [1983] 1 WLR 1445 (HL) 1450H (Lord Diplock): 'The maxim *noscitur a sociis* may be a useful aid to statutory interpretation, but the contexts in which it is applicable are limited. In the case of a word which is capable of bearing various shades of meaning, the fact that it is included in a list of words of greater precision in which some common characteristic can be discerned may enable one to say that the chameleon word takes its colour from those other words and of its possible meanings bears that which shares the characteristic that is common to the others.' In that case, Lord Diplock considered that no such common characteristic could be discerned. See also *Letang v Cooper* [1965] 1 QB 232 (CA) 247D–E (Diplock LJ): 'The maxim *noscitur a sociis* is always a treacherous one unless you know the *societas* to which the *socii* belong' (that is, the association to which the associates belong).

[79] See, eg, *Brownsea Haven Properties Ltd v Poole Corp* [1958] Ch 574 (CA) 597–98 (Lord Evershed MR), a statutory interpretation case citing with approval certain passages concerning the *ejusdem generis* rule from *Tillmanns & Co v SS Knutsford Ltd* [1908] 2 KB 385 (CA), a contractual interpretation case. In *Tillmanns*, the Court was considering the meaning of 'other cause' in the phrase 'in consequence of war, disturbance, or any other cause'. In *Brownsea*, Lord Evershed MR cited in particular the passage in *Tillmanns* at 403 (Farwell LJ): 'when there is a clear category followed by words which are not clear, unambiguous general words, it would violate a settled rule of construction to strike out and render unmeaning two words which were presumably inserted for the purpose of having some meaning' (ie, in that case the two words 'war' and 'disturbance'). See also *Tillmanns* at 408 (Kennedy LJ): 'The doctrine of "ejusdem generis" is that you treat general words which might under certain circumstances have a wider meaning as being restricted because, according to the true construction of the immediately preceding expression, you find it to designate things which may properly be described as belonging to the same genus.'

[80] *Brownsea* (n 79) 598 (Lord Evershed MR): 'I cannot find that the presence of that word has been regarded as essential to the application of the rule as it is, in my judgment, irrelevant to its principle.'

[81] See (in a contractual construction context) *Ambatielos v Anton Jurgens Margarine Works* [1923] AC 175 (HL) 183 (Viscount Cave LC): 'I know of no authority for applying that rule to … a case where … the whole clause is governed by the initial general words.' This was cited with approval and applied (in a statutory interpretation context) in *Canadian National Railways v Canada Steamship Lines Ltd* [1945] AC 204 (PC) 211 (Lord Macmillan): 'It is not a case to which the *ejusdem generis* rule applies, for the general words do not follow on an enumeration of particular instances but precede the particular instances.' See also *R v Choudary* [2016] EWCA Crim 1436, [2017] 3 All ER 459 [54] (Sharp LJ).

3.37   Two main justifications for the principle have been advanced: first, the presence of a discernible genus in the more specific words indicates an implied limitation in the draftsman's mind when using the general words;[82] and, second, to read the general words without such a limitation could render the presence of the more specific words redundant.[83]

3.38   Determining when the principle applies requires careful judgement in each case on the basis of the statutory language and purpose, and it should not 'exclude other matters which may help to indicate the legislative purpose' and which may in some cases provide greater assistance to this end.[84] In general terms, the principle will not apply where:

3.38.1   no genus can be discerned in the more specific words;[85]

3.38.2   the statutory language indicates that the general words are intended to be read very generally. This may be so where, for instance, words such as 'any other' or 'whatsoever' are used, although this is not conclusive;[86]

3.38.3   its application would be contrary to the statutory purpose.[87]

3.39   The House of Lords has held that in order to identify a genus in the more specific words, those words must contain at least two example 'species' from which it can be discerned.[88] Despite this limitation, in the context of a particular

---

[82]   *Quazi v Quazi* [1980] AC 744 (HL) 808A–B (Lord Diplock).

[83]   See the first citation from *Tillmanns* (n 79) set out in that note.

[84]   See *Re Rhondda Waste Disposal Ltd* [2001] Ch 57 (CA) [49] (Robert Walker LJ), also stating: 'The rule should not be applied in a mechanistic fashion, since (except in the simplest cases) the recognition of expressions as "sharing some common characteristics" may involve the exercise of judgment.' See also *Trustees of BT Pension Schemes v Clarke* [2000] Pens LR 157 (CA) [38] (Robert Walker LJ), referring to the rule as a 'rather blunt instrument' and preferring to base his conclusion on a question of statutory interpretation on 'a combination of contextual indications'.

[85]   See, eg, *Massey v Boulden* [2002] EWCA Civ 1634, [2003] 1 WLR 1792 [15], [17] (Simon Brown LJ) and [65] (Sedley LJ). *Massey* was disapproved in *Bakewell Management Ltd v Brandwood* [2004] UKHL 14, [2004] 2 AC 519, but not on the statutory construction point, which was not addressed. See also *Quazi* (n 82) 809H (Viscount Dilhorne): 'this rule does not apply for there is no genus'.

[86]   See, eg, *Massey* (n 85) [15] and [17] (Simon Brown LJ), holding the principle inapplicable to the words 'any common land, moorland, or land of any other description' (which had previously been 'land of whatsoever description'), but acknowledging that such wording was not necessarily determinative. Compare, eg, *Tillmanns* (n 79), where the principle was applied to the words 'war, disturbance or any other cause'.

[87]   See, eg, *Quazi* (n 82) 823H–824A (Lord Scarman): 'the *ejusdem generis* rule ... is, at best, a very secondary guide to the meaning of a statute. The all-important matter is to consider the purpose of the statute ... If the legislative purpose of a statute is such that a statutory series should be read *ejusdem generis*, so be it: the rule is helpful. But, if it is not, the rule is more likely to defeat than to fulfil the purpose of the statute. The rule, like many other rules of statutory interpretation, is a useful servant but a bad master'.

[88]   See *Quazi* (n 82) 808B–C (Lord Diplock), considering that the principle did not apply to the phrase 'judicial or other proceedings' so as to limit the 'other proceedings' to those of a judicial or

enactment it may nevertheless be appropriate to give general words a more limited reading on the basis of a single preceding 'expression of greater specificity', but this is not an application of the *ejusdem generis* rule as such.[89]

The *Expressio Unius* Principle

3.40   This principle is often referred to using the Latin maxim *expressio unius est exclusio alterius*, which translates as 'the expression of one thing is the exclusion of another'. It recognises that it is sometimes appropriate to infer from Parliament's express reference to something in legislation that something else is impliedly excluded.[90] It has two particular applications. The first is that provision for a matter in one context in a statute may impliedly exclude that matter's application in another context.[91] This is underpinned by a presumption that Parliament will adopt a consistent form of expression where it wishes to achieve consistent results. The second is that where a particular provision refers to certain items expressly, this may by implication exclude items that are not mentioned.[92] Conversely,

quasi-judicial character: 'unless the draftsman has indicated at very least two different species to which the enacting words apply there is no material on which to base an inference that there was some particular genus of proceedings to which alone his mind was directed when he used the word "other" which on the face of it would embrace all proceedings that were *not* judicial'. The treatment of this point in Jones, *Statutory Interpretation* (2013) (n 54) at section 381, 1111–1113 suggests that there *can* be a 'single genus describing term'. However, all but one of the cases cited in support of this pre-date *Quazi*. The one that does not—*Director of Public Prosecutions v Vivier* [1991] 4 All ER 18 (QB) 19–20 (Simon Brown J)—involved an application of an interpretation of a statute that was already 'well established' in authorities pre-dating *Quazi* (such as *Elkins v Cartlidge* [1947] 1 All ER 829 (KB)).

[89]   See *Quazi* (n 82) 808C–D (Lord Diplock), considering this could be appropriate 'if to give [the expression "other"] its wide prima facie meaning would lead to results that would be contrary to the manifest policy of the Act looked at as a whole, or would conflict with the evident purpose for which it was enacted'. For an example of this, see *R v Uxbridge Justices ex p Webb* [1994] 2 CMLR 288 [28] (Glidewell LJ), considering the power of HM Customs and Excise to forfeit 'any other thing mixed, packed or found' with a 'thing [that] has become liable to forfeiture' to be limited to 'things of a like kind'. Although Glidewell LJ referred to this as an application of the *ejusdem generis* rule, on the basis of *Quazi* (and perhaps in any event) it may be better seen as an application of an interpretation designed to give effect to the statutory purpose.

[90]   As stated in *EN (Serbia) v Secretary of State for the Home Department* [2009] EWCA Civ 630, [2010] QB 633 [79] (Stanley Burnton LJ), the principle is based 'on the assumption that what is expressly stated impliedly excludes what is not mentioned'.

[91]   See, eg, *Re B-J (A Child) (Non-molestation Order: Power of Arrest)* [2001] Fam 415 (CA) [38] (Hale LJ), with regard to the Family Law Act 1996: 'section 47(4) and (5) expressly give the court power to fix a shorter duration to powers of arrest attached to orders made without notice and then to extend it if appropriate. Where a statute clearly states a proposition in one context, it usually means to exclude its implication in another: "express enactment shuts the door to further implication" (*Whiteman v Sadler* [1910] AC 514) otherwise expressed in the maxim "expressio unius est exclusio alterius"'.

[92]   One example of this is where an interpretation provision sets out who or what falls within the ambit of a term or provision. See, eg, *Wirral Metropolitan Borough Council v Salisbury Independent Living* [2012] EWCA Civ 84, [2012] PTSR 1221 [23] (Hughes LJ): 'The principle of construction can be given the Latin tag "expressio unius exclusio alterius", but it is equally simply explained by the ordinary proposition that when a legislative provision sets out who or what is within the meaning of an expression, it ordinarily means that no one else or nothing else is. If it wishes to say that its provisions are

expressly to exclude something might by implication mean that something else is impliedly included (whether in that same provision or elsewhere in the statute)— *exclusio unius est inclusio alterius*.[93]

3.41   As ever, the strength of the presumption will depend on the context. It may have particular force, for example, when considering two provisions that 'appear in the same group of sections',[94] though even in that context it may be thought that applying the principle 'proves too much'.[95] By contrast, the principle is likely to have little application to 'patchwork provisions ... developed from different sources over the years'.[96] A key question will be whether there is another, better explanation for the contrasting inclusion and exclusion of certain matters, other than an intention to effect an implied exclusion. It may be, for example, that a particular matter has been expressly included solely for the avoidance of doubt.[97]

3.42   More generally, it has been said that the *expressio unius* principle is 'not a particularly strong rule' of interpretation.[98] Accordingly, it is likely to give way to

other than exhaustive, it usually says so' (then proceeding to describe terms that might be used to avoid being exhaustive). As to interpretation clauses using the word 'means', see Chapter 6.20.1.

[93]   See, eg, *R (Jackson) v Attorney General* [2005] UKHL 56, [2006] 1 AC 262 [138] (Lord Rodger), in relation to the Parliament Act 1911: 'The effect of sections 2(1) and 5 is therefore to exclude expressly from the scope of the term "Public Bill" any Money Bill, or any Bill containing a provision to extend the maximum duration of Parliament beyond five years or any Bill for confirming a Provisional Order. *Expressio unius exclusio alterius* or *exclusio unius inclusio alterius*. Since Parliament has expressly excluded these three types of Bill from the scope of section 2(1), in the absence of any indication to the contrary, I would read that provision as applying to a Public Bill to amend section 2(1) itself.' But note the caution expressed regarding the notion of an '*exclusio unius*' principle in the cases cited in Chapter 6, n 52.

[94]   *McDonald v National Grid Electricity Transmission plc* [2014] UKSC 53, [2015] AC 1128 [212] (Lord Reed, dissenting).

[95]   *R (Bourgass) v Secretary of State for Justice* [2015] UKSC 54, [2016] AC 384 [85]–[87] (Lord Reed).

[96]   See *R (Ramsden) v Secretary of State for the Home Department* [2006] EWHC 3502 (Admin), [2007] Prison LR 220 [31] (Toulson J), interpreting a statutory scheme regarding 'release and recall of prisoners on licence', and citing *National Grid Co plc v Mayes* [2001] UKHL 20, [2001] 1 WLR 864 [55] (Lord Hoffmann), who had remarked (in the context of interpreting a pension scheme) that *expressio unius* arguments 'are often perilous, especially when applied to a patchwork document'. Lord Hoffmann continued: 'The fact that a specific provision is made in one place may throw very little light on whether general words in another place include the power to do something similar.' See also more generally *MS (Uganda) v Secretary of State for the Home Department* [2016] UKSC 33, [2016] 1 WLR 2615 [28] (Lord Hughes): 'it is not ... safe to use a subsequently drafted section to construe a statutory provision which was written some years earlier. That is different from considering adjacent sections produced by the same author contemporaneously'.

[97]   See *Dean v Wiesengrund* [1955] 2 QB 120 (CA) 130–31 (Jenkins LJ): 'But this maxim is, after all, no more than an aid to construction, and has little, if any, weight where it is possible, as I think it is in the present case, to account for the "inclusio unius" on grounds other than an intention to effect the "exclusio alterius".' One of the explanations he cited for the express reference to one matter was that it might have been 'ex abundanti cautela desirable' to make that matter clear. He also cited with approval the statement of Lopes LJ in *Colquhoun v Brooks* (1888) 21 QBD 52 (CA) 65: 'The *exclusio* is often the result of inadvertence or accident, and the maxim ought not to be applied, when its application, having regard to the subject-matter to which it is to be applied, leads to inconsistency or injustice.'

[98]   *EN (Serbia)* (n 90) [79] (Stanley Burnton LJ). See also *R (Government of the Republic of France) v Kensington and Chelsea Royal London Borough Council* [2017] EWCA Civ 429, [2017] 1 WLR 3206 (Hickinbottom LJ), citing with approval the following passage from Rupert Cross, John Bell and

other, more powerful rules, such as the courts' duty to interpret legislation in conformity with EU law,[99] the presumption that legislation does not bind the Crown[100] and the presumption that legislation accords with the rules of natural justice.[101]

The Role of Context and Purpose

The Centrality of Context

3.43   Statutory wording can only be understood in its proper context, since 'language in all legal texts conveys meaning according to the circumstances in which it was used. It follows that the context must always be identified and considered before the process of construction or during it'.[102]

3.44   The word 'context' should be understood 'in its widest sense' as covering all of the many matters and materials capable of bearing on the meaning of the statutory language.[103] Many of these relate to the need to read a statute 'in the

---

George Engle, *Cross: Statutory Interpretation*, 3rd edn (Oxford, Oxford University Press, 1995), 140: 'it is doubtful whether the maxim does more than draw attention to a fairly obvious linguistic point, viz that in many contexts the mention of some matters warrants an inference that other cognate matters were intentionally excluded'.

[99] *EN (Serbia)* (n 90) [79]–[80] (Stanley Burnton LJ), following this duty to interpret a provision contrary to how the *expressio unius* principle would have indicated. As to this duty, see Chapter 12.21–12.29.

[100] *R (Black) v Secretary of State for Justice* [2016] EWCA Civ 125, [2016] QB 1060 [45] (Lord Dyson MR). As to this presumption, see Chapter 4.41.

[101] *R (West) v Parole Board* [2005] UKHL 1, [2005] 1 WLR 350 [29] (Lord Bingham): 'the maxim expressio unius exclusio alterius can seldom, if ever, be enough to exclude common law rules of natural justice', cited with approval in *Bank Mellat v HM Treasury (No 2)* [2013] UKSC 39, [2014] AC 700 [35] (Lord Sumption). The Supreme Court departed from *West* in *R (Whiston) v Secretary of State for Justice* [2014] UKSC 39, [2015] AC 176, but expressly only on another point: see at [41] (Lord Neuberger). As to this presumption, see Chapter 4.23–4.25.

[102] *R (Westminster City Council) v National Asylum Support Service* [2002] UKHL 38, [2002] 1 WLR 2956 [5] (Lord Steyn), continuing: 'It is therefore wrong to say that the court may only resort to evidence of the contextual scene where an ambiguity has arisen.' This part of Lord Steyn's speech was cited with approval in *R v Montila* [2004] UKHL 50, [2004] 1 WLR 3141 [35]–[36] (Lord Hope, giving the opinion of the Committee). As to the importance of context in construction, see further paragraph 3.13 and nn 14, 17 and 24 above, and paragraph 3.44 below (and the notes to that paragraph, including its subparagraphs).

[103] See *Attorney General v Prince Ernest Augustus of Hanover* [1957] AC 436 (HL) 461 (Viscount Simonds): 'For words, and particularly general words, cannot be read in isolation: their colour and content are derived from their context. So it is that I conceive it to be my right and duty to examine every word of a statute in its context, and I use "context" in its widest sense, which I have already indicated as including not only other enacting provisions of the same statute, but its preamble, the existing state of the law, other statutes in pari materia, and the mischief which I can, by those and other legitimate means, discern the statute was intended to remedy.' This passage was cited with approval in *Majorstake* (n 14) [44] (Lord Carswell) and *Director of Public Prosecutions v Schildkamp* [1971] AC 1 (HL) 23B–D (Lord Upjohn).

historical context of the situation which led to its enactment'.[104] The contextual factors relevant to construction of statutory language include the following:

3.44.1   The entirety of the piece of legislation in which the provision being construed is contained.[105]

3.44.2   This includes what can be termed 'internal aids to construction'. Within that term we include: (i) ancillary components of the legislation such as the preamble or section headings that can permissibly be referred to in the interpretive exercise; (ii) the legislation's punctuation, format and structure; (iii) interpretation provisions; (iv) deeming provisions; and (v) provisos and savings.[106]

3.44.3   The state of domestic law at the time of the enactment, both legislation and case law. Connected pieces of legislation may be of particular relevance.[107]

3.44.4   Judicial decisions on identical language used in earlier legislation in the same area of law that are taken to have been endorsed by Parliament.[108]

3.44.5   Rules of EU law[109] and international law[110] which have inspired the legislation in question.

3.44.6   What are often called 'external aids to construction', a variety of sources external to the enactment itself that can help elucidate the legislator's intention, such as records of parliamentary debates and pre-legislative materials that have led to legislation, for example, government Green Papers and White Papers, and Law Commission reports.[111]

3.44.7   The purpose of the legislation, as discussed immediately below.

---

[104] *Quintavalle* (n 1) [8] (Lord Bingham): 'Every statute other than a pure consolidating statute is, after all, enacted to make some change, or address some problem, or remove some blemish, or effect some improvement in the national life. The court's task, within the permissible bounds of interpretation, is to give effect to Parliament's purpose. So the controversial provisions should be read in the context of the statute as a whole, and the statute as a whole should be read in the historical context of the situation which led to its enactment.' See also, eg, *R v Z* (n 24) [37] (Lord Woolf CJ): 'the controversial provision ... has to be read not only in the context of the statute as a whole but in the context of the situation which led to its enactment', [17] (Lord Bingham) and [49] (Lord Carswell), all citing Lord Bingham's speech in *Quintavalle* with approval.
[105] See the previous two notes. See also, eg, *Customs and Excise Commissioners v Zielinski Baker and Partners Ltd* [2004] UKHL 7, [2004] 1 WLR 707 [38] (Lord Walker), referring to the 'universally acknowledged need to construe a statute as a whole' and to take a 'holistic approach' to interpreting legislation; and see at [39], where he explains how this may work in practice with 'a text of some complexity'.
[106] See Chapter 6.
[107] See *Prince Ernest Augustus* (n 103), as cited in that note, and *Ealing London Borough Council v Race Relations Board* [1972] AC 342 (HL) 361E–F (Lord Simon), stating that regard should be had to 'a conspectus of the entire relevant body of the law for the same purpose'. See further paragraph 3.52 below, and Chapter 5 generally, especially at 5.25 and 5.31–5.38.
[108] See paragraphs 3.53–3.56 below.
[109] See Chapter 12.
[110] See Chapter 9.
[111] See Chapter 7.

The Importance of Purpose

3.45   One particularly important aspect of the context in which legislative words must be construed is the *purpose* of the legislation, upon which the meaning of the words used will depend.[112] Almost all legislation is designed to rectify some problem or otherwise bring about some positive change, and the task of the court is to construe provisions, so far as possible, consistently with that purpose. That purpose is to be ascertained from the legislation itself and from a consideration of all of the relevant context.[113] In searching for the statutory purpose, it is important to note that legislation may have more than one purpose,[114] or that its purpose may be to strike a balance between important competing interests (in which case particular interpretive considerations may apply).[115]

---

[112]   See, eg, *Bloomsbury* (n 11) [10] (Lord Mance): 'In matters of statutory construction, the statutory purpose and the general scheme by which it is to be put into effect are of central importance. They represent the context in which individual words are to be understood.' He then stated that the 'legislative purpose and scheme' should be identified before trying to discern the natural meaning of individual words. See also *R (Haw) v Secretary of State for the Home Department* [2006] EWCA Civ 532, [2006] QB 780 [17] (Sir Anthony Clarke MR): 'Like all questions of construction, this question must be answered by considering the statutory language in its context, which of course includes the purpose of the Act. The search is for the meaning intended by Parliament. The language used by Parliament is of central importance but that does not mean that it must always be construed literally. The meaning of language always depends upon its particular context.'

[113]   See *Quintavalle* (n 1), as cited at n 104 above. See also *R v Z* (n 24) [17] (Lord Bingham): 'interpretation … is directed to a particular statute, enacted at a particular time, to address (almost invariably) a particular problem or mischief' (citing his own speech in *Quintavalle*); and *IRC v McGuckian* [1997] 1 WLR 991 (HL) 999D–E (Lord Steyn) referring to the 'modern emphasis … on a contextual approach designed to identify the purpose of a statute and to give effect to it'. See also *9 Cornwall Crescent* (n 58) [52] (Arden LJ): 'Courts will not speculate as to Parliament's purpose, though they may infer it from (for example) the indications provided in the legislation itself'; *Prince Ernest Augustus* (n 103), as cited in that note; and *Spath Holme* (n 2) 396E–F (Lord Nicholls), in the context of ascertaining the purpose of a statutory power: 'The purpose for which a power is conferred, and hence its ambit, may be stated expressly in the statute. Or it may be implicit. Then the purpose has to be inferred from the language used, read in its statutory context and having regard to any aid to interpretation which assists in the particular case. In either event, whether the purpose is stated expressly or has to be inferred, the exercise is one of statutory interpretation'; and at 397E–F (Lord Nicholls): 'In adopting a purposive approach to the interpretation of statutory language, courts seek to identify and give effect to the purpose of the legislation. To the extent that extraneous material assists in identifying the purpose of the legislation, it is a useful tool'; and see, eg, *Christian Institute v Lord Advocate* [2016] UKSC 51, [2016] HRLR 19 [1]–[15] (Lady Hale, Lord Reed and Lord Hodge).

[114]   See *Spath Holme* (n 2) 385E–G (Lord Bingham), citing *Maunsell* (n 10), stating: 'Lord Simon and Lord Diplock went on to warn against a simplistic approach to construction based on an assumption that the draftsman has sought to remedy one mischief only (or, in other words, that an Act has only one statutory objective).'

[115]   Specifically, in such a case 'the courts must try to avoid any interpretation which would distort the parliamentary scheme and so upset the intended balance': *R v Lewes Crown Court ex p Hill* (1991) 93 Cr App R 60 (QB) 65–66 (Bingham LJ). See also *Macris v Financial Conduct Authority* [2017] UKSC 19, [2017] 1 WLR 1095 [25] (Lord Neuberger), considering how the balance ought to be struck between competing considerations where this was not clear: 'Because there are powerful policy arguments pointing in opposite directions, it seems to me that it is justified, indeed requisite, to have particular regard to the wording of the relevant statutory provision.'

3.46 The principle that legislation should be interpreted with regard to the issue—or what has traditionally been called the 'mischief'—that it was designed to fix is of very long standing.[116] The courts have long referred to this so-called 'mischief rule' as an important guide to statutory construction[117] and it remains a legitimate aid to construction.[118] However, 'identifying the mischief the statute is intended to cure' is merely one aspect of the broader concept of 'adopting a purposive approach' to interpretation and the need 'to identify and give effect to the purpose of the legislation.'[119] As such, it will generally be preferable to refer to the need to give legislation a 'purposive construction' rather than the mischief rule. 'A purposive construction is one which eschews a narrow literal interpretation in favour of one which is consonant with the purpose of the relevant legislation.'[120]

3.47 In recent decades there has been a marked shift towards giving legislation a purposive rather than a literalist construction.[121] Recourse to this method of

[116] This is sometimes called the rule in *Heydon's Case* (1584) 3 Co Rep 7, 76 ER 637, an early decision in which the principle was laid down.

[117] As to the mischief rule, see *Black-Clawson International Ltd v Papierwerke Waldhof-Aschaffenburg AG* [1975] AC 591 (HL) 614B–C (Lord Reid): 'It has always been said to be important to consider the "mischief" which the Act was apparently intended to remedy. The word "mischief" is traditional. I would expand it in this way. In addition to reading the Act you look at the facts presumed to be known to Parliament when the Bill which became the Act in question was before it, and you consider whether there is disclosed some unsatisfactory state of affairs which Parliament can properly be supposed to have intended to remedy by the Act.'

[118] See, eg, *R v T* [2009] UKHL 20, [2009] 1 AC 1310 [35] (Lord Phillips): 'It is a legitimate aid to the interpretation of that section to look … at the mischief that section was designed to obviate', having considered the relevant mischief at [20]–[26].

[119] *Spath Holme* (n 2) 397E (Lord Nicholls). See also *Clark v In Focus Asset Management and Tax Solutions Ltd* [2014] EWCA Civ 118, [2014] 1 WLR 2502 [101] (Arden LJ), referring to 'the mischief rule, more commonly called today purposive interpretation, namely the principle that the court should interpret legislation so as to best achieve the purpose of Parliament'.

[120] *Swift v Robertson* [2014] UKSC 50, [2014] 1 WLR 3438 [31] (Lord Kerr). But note that in some cases (for example, where the presumption against a change in the common law applies, as to which see Chapter 4.13–4.16), a purposive construction may indicate that a narrower rather than a wider meaning should be given to the statutory language: see *Black-Clawson* (n 117) 614C–D (Lord Reid). See also *Andrews* (n 38) [33] (Lord Dyson MR): 'Even in relation to modern statutes, which are drafted by skilled specialist draftsmen and are assumed to be drafted with precision and consistency, the courts adopt a purposive (in preference to a literal) interpretation so as to give effect to what is taken to have been intended by Parliament. We use the phrase "purposive interpretation" as shorthand for an interpretation which reflects the intention of Parliament. The court presumes that Parliament does not intend to legislate so as to produce a result which (i) is inconsistent with the statutory purpose or (ii) makes no sense or is anomalous or illogical. A purposive interpretation is all the more appropriate in a statute which is couched in language which is less consistent and more imprecise than that generally found in modern statutes.'

[121] See *McGuckian* (n 113) 999D–E (Lord Steyn): 'During the last 30 years there has been a shift away from literalist to purposive methods of construction. Where there is no obvious meaning of a statutory provision the modern emphasis is on a contextual approach designed to identify the purpose of a statute and to give effect to it.' See also to similar effect *Karpavicius v The Queen* [2002] UKPC 59, [2003] 1 WLR 169 [15] (Lord Steyn): 'In a more literalist age it may have been said that the words of section 6(2A)(c) are capable of bearing either a wide and narrow meaning and that the fact that a criminal statute is involved requires the narrower interpretation to be adopted. Nowadays an approach concentrating on the purpose of the statutory provision is generally to be preferred.' This passage was cited with approval in *R v Z* (n 24) [49] (Lord Carswell). See also *Kelly* (n 24) [24] (Laws LJ): 'As the law has developed since 1975 we have seen a growing acceptance of purposive constructions.'

interpretation requires no particular justification, and it is clearly a powerful tool: in appropriate cases it has been used to justify giving statutory language an interpretation that involves 'linguistic difficulty',[122] and in rare cases it goes so far as to allow the correction of mistakenly drafted legislation (as discussed immediately below).[123]

3.48   That said, there is always a balancing exercise to perform between the relevant interpretive factors and principles,[124] and there are limits to how far a purposive approach can be used to strain the meaning of statutory language,[125] particularly in the context of criminal statutes.[126]

Judicial Correction of Obvious Errors in Statutory Drafting

3.49   Where it is clear that an enactment contains an obvious mistake in its drafting, the role of the courts in construing legislation may even extend, in a suitable

---

[122] *Attorney General's Reference (No 5 of 2002)* [2004] UKHL 40, [2005] 1 AC 167 [31] (Lord Steyn), noting the 'linguistic difficulty' entailed by a particular interpretation, but continuing: 'this point is decisively outweighed by a purposive interpretation of the statute. No explanation for resorting to purposive interpretation of a statute is necessary. One can confidently assume that Parliament intends its legislation to be interpreted not in the way of a black letter lawyer, but in a meaningful and purposive way giving effect to the basic objectives of the legislation'.

[123] The jurisdiction to correct errors in statutory drafting in appropriate cases may be seen as an instance of applying a purposive construction and there is, understandably, something of a grey area between what amounts to using a purposive construction to give a provision a strained meaning and what amounts to using one to correct an error in statutory drafting. See, eg, *R (Gibson) v Secretary of State for Justice* [2015] EWCA Civ 1148, [2017] 1 WLR 1115 [49]–[51] (Treacy LJ), seeing these as two alternative ways of reaching the same conclusion. See also *R (Noone) v Governor of Drake Hall Prison* [2010] UKSC 30, [2010] 1 WLR 1743 [74]–[75] (Lord Mance), supporting his conclusion by reference to both approaches; and *Kelly* (n 24) [24] (Laws LJ), as discussed in that note, and at [27], where he expressly referred to 'purposive construction' as 'including recourse to the Inco Europe Ltd case', the leading case on the jurisdiction to correct errors of statutory drafting, cited at n 127 below. See also the references to purpose in the formulation of the scope of that jurisdiction in that case, as cited at paragraph 3.50 below. But see *Shahid* (n 23) [20]–[21] (Lord Reed), which emphasises that the corrective jurisdiction goes beyond what is ordinarily possible through purposive construction.

[124] The balancing exercise is implicit in the citation from *Attorney General's Reference (No 5 of 2002)* (n 122) in that note. See also *Kelly* (n 24) [24] (Laws LJ): 'purposive constructions ... have their dangers; there is a price to be paid in the coin of legal certainty, and in a debasement, however marginal, of the constitutional truth that it is the legislature's will, found from the words of the Act, and not the executive's will, found from the promoter's intentions, that drives the meaning of statute law. A way often has to be found between an approach that is too lax and an approach that is too austere'.

[125] See *Shahid* (n 23), as cited in that note.

[126] See, eg, *Bentham* (n 23) [10] (Lord Bingham): 'Purposive construction cannot be relied on to create an offence which Parliament has not created', rejecting a construction of the offence of possessing an imitation firearm that would make it cover the case of a man with his hand in his pocket pretending he had a gun. However, a purposive approach can still be legitimate in the context of criminal statutes, and the extent to which such an approach is appropriate will always depend on the particular case: see, eg, *Kelly* (n 24) [27]–[28] (Laws LJ), citing *Haw* (n 112); and *Karpavicius* (n 121) [15]–[16]. See also the discussion at n 135 below.

case, to correcting that mistake by adding, omitting or substituting words[127] (or punctuation)[128] to bring the legislation into line with its intended purpose. This applies at least equally to secondary as well as primary legislation,[129] if not more so.[130]

3.50 However, this is 'a very limited jurisdiction',[131] with the corrective power 'confined to plain cases of drafting mistakes', in order to avoid 'the appearance of judicial legislation'.[132] This is in keeping with the general presumption that the legislator has expressed itself 'correctly and exactly, and not loosely and inexactly' in legislation, and (a fortiori) that it has not acted in error.[133] The courts must therefore 'exercise considerable caution before adding or omitting or substituting words' in an enactment, and before doing so 'must be abundantly sure of three matters':

> (1) the intended purpose of the statute or provision in question; (2) that by inadvertence the draftsman and Parliament failed to give effect to that purpose in the provision in question; and (3) the substance of the provision Parliament would have made, although not necessarily the precise words Parliament would have used, had the error in the Bill been noticed.[134]

---

[127] *Inco Europe Ltd v First Choice Distribution* [2000] 1 WLR 586 (HL) 592C–D (Lord Nicholls). On the facts of that case, Lord Nicholls was 'left in no doubt that, for once, the draftsman slipped up' in the drafting of an amendment to an Act, having regard to the legislative history of the relevant provisions, the purpose of the amendment and the overall evident intention of Parliament (see especially at 592A–B).

[128] See, eg, *R (Buddington) v Secretary of State for the Home Department* [2006] EWCA Civ 280, [2006] 2 Cr App R (S) 109 [26] (Sir Igor Judge P).

[129] *R (Confederation of Passenger Transport UK) v Humber Bridge Board* [2003] EWCA Civ 842, [2004] QB 310 [36] (Clarke LJ). In that case, by reference to *Inco* (n 127), the Court of Appeal rectified three Orders (confirmed by statutory instrument) authorising the levying of tolls on traffic crossing the Humber Bridge, which had erroneously failed to make provision for levying tolls on 'large buses'.

[130] See *Noone* (n 123) [75] (Lord Mance), considering the *Inco* jurisdiction 'the more readily applicable ... when this case concerns delegated legislation made by executive action ... and subject only to the limited opportunity for any parliamentary scrutiny involved in the negative resolution procedure'. But see *Qader v Esure Services Ltd* [2016] EWCA Civ 1109, [2017] 1 WLR 1924 [53] (Briggs LJ): 'It may be said that the interpretative jurisdiction to put right obvious drafting errors in a statute is fortified by the difficulties which typically face Parliament in doing so, in relation to primary legislation, in the light of its heavy workload', noting that it may be easier for errors in secondary legislation to be corrected. However, he also noted with regard to secondary legislation that 'it is almost invariably the case that corrections cannot be made with retrospective effect' by the legislator, underlining the importance of the *Inco* jurisdiction notwithstanding the relative ease with which correction could be effected through legislation.

[131] *Wilkinson v Secretary of State for Work and Pensions* [2009] EWCA Civ 1111, [2009] Pens LR 369 [19] (Patten LJ), citing *Inco* (n 127).

[132] *Inco* (n 127) 592E–F (Lord Nicholls); see also *Lehman Brothers* (n 12) [120] (Lord Neuberger).

[133] See the discussion of this principle at paragraphs 3.16–3.17 above.

[134] *Inco* (n 127) 592F–G (Lord Nicholls), continuing: 'The third of these conditions is of crucial importance. Otherwise any attempt to determine the meaning of the enactment would cross the boundary between construction and legislation.' See also *Kelly* (n 24) [18] (Laws LJ), emphasising the need for certainty in this context: 'Finding such a mistake of course requires us to exclude any other rational explanation for the omission.'

3.51 Further, 'even when these conditions are met', it will not be permissible to correct legislation where the required alteration in language is 'too far-reaching', for example, because it would be 'too big, or too much at variance with the language used by the legislature' or where 'strict interpretation of the statutory language' is required, as it may be with penal legislation.[135]

Contextual Construction: The Presumption that Parliament Knows the Law and Endorses Certain Judicial Decisions

3.52 In passing any enactment, Parliament is presumed to be aware of the state of the relevant pre-existing law and to legislate in the light of that knowledge.[136] This presumption extends to knowledge of past judicial decisions on the relevant area of law, including on the meaning of particular statutory terms, and these decisions can legitimately be considered in seeking to ascertain Parliament's intention.[137]

---

[135] *Inco* (n 127) 592H (Lord Nicholls), citing *Western Bank Ltd v Schindler* [1977] Ch 1 (CA) 18 (Scarman LJ), who discussed there the sometimes slender distinction between interpretation and legislation. As to the limits of the *Inco* jurisdiction in the criminal context, see *R v D* [2011] EWCA Crim 2082, [2012] 1 All ER 1108 [64]–[67] (Thomas LJ), contrasting the use of the *Inco* jurisdiction to alter 'the substance of a criminal offence' as opposed to 'curing an error relating to procedure and evidence' (but without deciding whether the former would always be impermissible). See also *Kelly* (n 24) [26]–[28] (Laws LJ), stating that the criminal law context did not preclude giving a provision a purposive construction in accordance with the *Inco* jurisdiction and that 'much depends upon the individual case'. He considered it appropriate to rectify secondary legislation with the effect of extending criminals' licence periods upon release on the basis that they had 'no prior settled rights of liberty' or 'to be released free of licence'. See also *Bogdanic v Secretary of State for the Home Department* [2014] EWHC 2872 (QB) [47]–[52] (Sales J), invoking the *Inco* jurisdiction in an 'exceptional' case 'notwithstanding the penal context'.

[136] See *R v G* (n 61) [46] Lord Steyn: 'Parliament must be presumed to have been aware of the relevant pre-existing law', and see generally at [46]–[50], applying this principle in determining the meaning of 'reckless' in s 1 of the Criminal Damage Act 1971; *Campbell v Peter Gordon Joiners Ltd* [2016] UKSC 38, [2016] AC 1513 [44] (Lady Hale, dissenting): 'Parliament is presumed to legislate in the knowledge of the current state of the law when it is doing so.' See further the discussion of this principle, and how existing legislation can be used as an aid to interpretation, in Chapter 5 generally, and especially at 5.25 and 5.31–5.38.

[137] See, eg, *R v Lang* [2005] EWCA Crim 2864, [2006] 1 WLR 2509 [8] (Rose LJ, giving the judgment of the Court): 'It is not clear whether Parliament … was intending to adopt this court's criteria … or was seeking to introduce a new, more restrictive criterion … On the basis that Parliament is presumed to know the law, we incline to the former view.' See also, eg, *Welham v Director of Public Prosecutions* [1961] AC 103 (HL) 123 (Lord Radcliffe), considering that in the absence of a definition of the phrase 'intent to defraud' in the Forgery Act 1913, which was an Act 'to consolidate, simplify, and amend the Law relating to Forgery', including the common law, that phrase 'must be understood in the light of any established legal interpretation that prevailed at the date of the passing of the Act'; and *R (Forge Care Homes Ltd) v Cardiff and Vale University Health Board* [2017] UKSC 56, [2017] PTSR 1140 [26] and [35] (Lady Hale), considering that, in passing a certain Act, Parliament 'must … have intended to depart from the position established' in a particular judicial decision.

3.53 Arising out of this presumption is a more specific presumption known as the '*Barras* principle'[138] that 'when Parliament uses a word or term, the meaning of which has been the subject of judicial ruling in the same or similar context, then it may be presumed that the word or term was intended to bear the same meaning'.[139] To put it another way, in these circumstances, 'the presumption is that Parliament has adopted the meaning given by the courts'.[140]

3.54 It has been emphasised that the *Barras* principle should not be applied as 'an inflexible rule of construction'[141] as it 'is a presumption, not a rule'.[142] It is not a 'powerful point of principle' and, before concluding that the presumption should be followed, it must be possible to discern, in all the circumstances, a sufficient endorsement by Parliament in its legislation of the relevant judicial decision or decisions.[143]

---

[138] Following the decision in *Barras v Aberdeen Steam Trawling and Fishing Co Ltd* [1933] AC 402 (HL).

[139] *Lowsley v Forbes* [1999] 1 AC 329 (HL) 340F–G (Lord Lloyd). For other general statements of the presumption, see *London Corporation v Cusack-Smith* [1955] AC 337 (HL) 361 (Lord Reid): 'Where Parliament has continued to use words of which the meaning has been settled by decisions of the court it is to be presumed that Parliament intends the words to continue to have that meaning'; *Gallagher v Church of Jesus Christ of Latter-Day Saints* [2008] UKHL 56, [2008] 1 WLR 1852 [10] (Lord Hoffmann) and [26] (Lord Hope), the latter citing Lord Reid's speech in *Cusack-Smith*; and *R (N) v Lewisham London Borough Council* [2014] UKSC 62, [2015] AC 1259 [53] (Lord Hodge): 'where Parliament re-enacts a statutory provision which has been the subject of authoritative judicial interpretation, the court will readily infer that Parliament intended the re-enacted provision to bear the meaning that case law had already established'. As to the importance of the words being used in 'the same or similar context', see *R v Chard* [1984] AC 279 (HL) 291G–H (Lord Diplock), stating that *Barras* concerned 'the role that judicial construction of particular words and phrases used in previous statutes may play in the interpretation of the same words in subsequent statutes *in pari materia*'; and see in a similar vein *Farrell v Alexander* [1977] AC 59 (HL) 89F–H (Lord Simon). However, most references by the courts to the *Barras* principle are not accompanied by a reference to the concept of statutes *in pari materia*, and it is not clear whether the legislation being considered must be *in pari materia* with the relevant earlier legislation before the principle can apply. As to statutes *in pari materia*, see Chapter 5.31.

[140] See *R (Woolas) v Parliamentary Election Court* [2010] EWHC 3169 (Admin), [2012] QB 1 [86] (Thomas LJ, giving the judgment of the Court), citing Bennion, *Statutory Interpretation* (2008) (n 54) at section 235, 711 (the equivalent passage in Jones, *Statutory Interpretation* (2013) (n 54) is at section 235, 661). There is a reference in the passage cited from Bennion to the concept of 'tacit legislation'— the idea that one can infer that Parliament endorses a judicial decision merely from its not having taken an opportunity to change the law following that decision. This concept now seems to have been emphatically rejected by the Supreme Court: see paragraph 3.56 below.

[141] *R v Chard* (n 139) 294G–295B (Lord Scarman); see also at 291G–292C (Lord Diplock).

[142] *Gallagher* (n 139) [26] (Lord Hope), and see also at [10] (Lord Hoffmann): 'there is no rigid rule'. See also *Lowsley* (n 139) 340G–H (Lord Lloyd): 'The rule, like other rules of construction, is not in any way conclusive. It is an aid: no more', although in that case he afforded the presumption 'great weight' because the 'suspect reasoning' in the relevant earlier case had been endorsed by a report of the Law Reform Committee that had inspired the legislation being interpreted.

[143] See *Hotak* (n 24) [60] (Lord Neuberger), giving a number of reasons why a 'substantial re-enactment' of a provision did not demonstrate that there had been parliamentary approval of a particular Court of Appeal decision considering that provision. He appears to have generally endorsed and applied his own dissenting judgment in *R (N)* (n 139) [143]–[148], where he had expressed strong views about the limitations of the *Barras* principle. It may therefore be that, as he said at *R (N)* [147]: 'before this court could invoke the Barras principle, it would almost always require something more than the mere re-enactment of a previous statutory provision which has been interpreted by the Court of Appeal', with (as he said at [144]) some 'additional factor' probably being required. The fact that

3.55 Accordingly, the principle may be entirely inapplicable (or, at least, its application may be inappropriate) where, for example, the later enactment is a consolidating Act;[144] the wording of the later provision has been significantly altered;[145] or the case law relied upon does not represent sufficiently weighty or settled authority on the construction of the relevant provision, such that Parliament should be taken as having endorsed it.[146]

3.56 Further, there is no scope for the principle to apply where Parliament has simply not amended a provision when it might have done so, even where it has amended other parts of the same piece of legislation.[147] Such inaction 'comes nowhere near an expression of Parliamentary approval' of a decision.[148]

there was only a single Court of Appeal decision in that case appears to have been a significant factor in not applying the *Barras* principle, since (as he said at [143]) 'Parliament must be taken to know not only that the Court of Appeal has decided as it has, but also that the House of Lords, or now the Supreme Court, could overrule the Court of Appeal'. Compare Lord Neuberger's concurring judgment in *Haile* (n 58) [75], given a week later, where he cited and applied the *Barras* principle as articulated in *R (N)* [53] (Lord Hodge) (set out at n 139 above) as a reason for following a previous decision of the House of Lords in relation to a re-enacted provision, despite his having been 'somewhat less enthusiastic about' the principle in *R (N)*. See also *R (Newhaven Port & Properties Ltd) v East Sussex County Council* [2015] UKSC 7, [2015] AC 1547 [18] (Lord Neuberger and Lord Hodge): 'Implied Parliamentary approval of a court's decision should not be lightly inferred.' In that case, the Supreme Court had refused permission to appeal on a point of construction previously considered by the House of Lords because Parliament had since replaced the legislation construed by the House of Lords with legislation that 'for the purposes of the point at issue was identically worded' to the earlier Act, in circumstances where: (i) the relevant Bill had been before Parliament at the time the House of Lords gave its decision; and (ii) the House of Lords expressly observed that Parliament could amend the Bill if it disagreed with the decision, but it did not do so.

[144] *R v Chard* (n 139) 292B–C (Lord Diplock), stating that *Barras* (n 138) is 'certainly no authority' for the proposition 'that reenactment of *ipsissima verba* of an existing statute in an Act that is passed for the purposes of consolidation only (which is subject to a special parliamentary procedure precluding debate upon the merits of any of the individual clauses) is capable of having any effect upon the construction of those words'; but see *Bentine v Bentine* [2015] EWCA Civ 1168, [2016] Ch 489 [43]–[44] (Sales LJ), suggesting that it may be appropriate to apply the *Barras* principle to the interpretation of a consolidation Act in some cases, although *Chard* does not appear to have been cited.

[145] *R v Chard* (n 139) 292C–E (Lord Diplock).

[146] ibid 295A–B (Lord Scarman), stating that the presumption applies 'in circumstances where the judicial interpretation was well settled and well recognised'. See also *B v Secretary of State for Work and Pensions* [2005] EWCA Civ 929, [2005] 1 WLR 3796 [35] (Sedley LJ): 'there are limits to the theory of legislative adoption, known as the Barras principle ... Lord Radcliffe in *Galloway v Galloway* [1956] AC 299, 320 was disposed to limit it to instances of "authoritative judicial interpretation over a period", and no authority in any event rates it higher than a presumption'; and [50]–[51] (Buxton LJ), considering that to reach the appropriate conclusion in that case it was not necessary to go as far as Lord Radcliffe, but that on the facts the judicial decisions relied on were not fully reasoned out on the relevant point, not at appellate level, and given over too short a time period to establish a settled practice. As such, they could not 'possibly qualify as encouraging, much less compelling, an interpretation that the words of the statute do not naturally bear'. Lord Radcliffe's speech in *Galloway* was cited with approval and applied in *R (Hillsden) v Epping Forest District Council* [2015] EWHC 98 (Admin) [35] (McCloskey J). See also *Hotak* (n 24) [60] (Lord Neuberger), as discussed at n 143 above.

[147] *Hotak* (n 24) [60] (Lord Neuberger), stating that his own and Lady Hale's statements in *R (N)* (n 139) (at [143]–[148] and [167]–[168] respectively) 'albeit in dissenting judgments, represent the law on this topic'.

[148] *R (N)* (n 139) [167] (Lady Hale, dissenting, but see previous note); and see at [81]–[85] (Lord Carnwath).

3.57   It is worth noting that, exceptionally, Parliament may even make express provision for a section in a statute to be construed as having an effect that a section of a previous statute had been construed as having, thereby removing any need for consideration of the *Barras* principle.[149]

The Role of Subsequent Practice in Interpretation

3.58   It is debatable whether and to what extent interpreting legislation by reference to how it has been understood or applied for a significant period of time—whether by private individuals and companies, public authorities or even in judicial decisions—is permissible. This is sometimes referred to as interpretation by reference to 'subsequent practice', 'settled understanding or practice' or the 'customary meaning' of legislation. It is also uncertain whether (assuming it is allowed) taking account of subsequent practice is an aspect of understanding legislation in context or is a separate interpretive principle.[150]

3.59   The view that subsequent practice can be taken into account has firm judicial supporters (although they have differed as to the principled basis for doing so),[151] and this view has been accepted obiter in a majority judgment of the Supreme Court.[152] At the same time, it presents serious issues of principle and other senior judges have expressed reservations about the existence or extent of

---

[149] See, eg, Compulsory Purchase Act 1965, s 10(2) (now repealed), described in *Wildtree Hotels Ltd v Harrow London Borough Council* [2001] 2 AC 1 (HL) 6F (Lord Hoffmann) as 'an unusual provision which suggests some anxiety on the part of the legislature to discourage the courts from taking a fresh look at the statutory language'.

[150] See the following note. We incline to the view that if this approach should be followed at all, it should be permissible only as an aspect of contextual construction rather than as a separate principle.

[151] See, eg, the discussion in *Anglesey* (n 73) [40]–[45] (Carnwath LJ) and the cases cited there, considering that recourse to subsequent practice was justified on the basis of 'common sense and the principle of legal certainty'; and see also [84] (Pill LJ), agreeing with Carnwath LJ on the use of 'later history' as an aid to interpretation in view of the particular 'statutory context'. In *Bloomsbury* (n 11) at [58]–[59], Lord Phillips considered Carnwath LJ's reasoning, stating that it 'has the air of pragmatism rather than principle', but at [60]–[61] he endorsed recourse to settled practice on the basis of the principle of 'contemporaneous exposition' being an aid to the interpretation of legislation in its context, since 'those affected by the statute when it comes into force are better placed to appreciate that context than those subject to it 30 years later'. Lord Carnwath then discussed recourse to subsequent practice again in *R (N)* (n 139) [89]–[98], stating that legal certainty was a principled and not purely pragmatic basis for relying on subsequent practice, and doubted that contemporaneous exposition provided sufficient justification for this approach, at least in cases such as *Anglesey* where '[t]he issue was not one of linguistic usage, but of application in practice'. See further the discussion in n 73 above concerning statements by the courts (in the context of the 'always speaking' principle) about the limited scope for reliance on contemporaneous exposition in statutory interpretation.

[152] *R (N)* (n 139) [53] (Lord Hodge), agreeing with the view expressed by Lord Carnwath in his concurring judgment.

any such rule, which 'could be said to be a breach of the fundamental duty of the court to give effect to the will of Parliament as expressed in the statute'.[153]

3.60   Insofar as such a customary meaning rule (of some form) is applicable at all to statutory construction, it has been said to give rise to a 'strong'[154] or 'powerful presumption that the meaning that has customarily been given to the phrase in issue is the correct one'.[155] Recourse to this principle of construction will only be 'available where there is ambiguity in a statutory provision'[156] and only where there has been a sufficiently settled understanding or practice, for a 'significant period' of time, which has not itself caused 'serious problems or injustice'.[157] It appears as though the force of the principle will depend on how much practical difficulty would be caused if the courts were to decide upon a different interpretation than the customary one.[158] The principle may also have particular force in 'relatively esoteric' areas of the law which are seldom considered by the courts, where a customary meaning may be of greater practical significance.[159]

---

[153] ibid [148]–[149] (Lord Neuberger) and [168] (Lady Hale), agreeing with Lord Neuberger's reservations.

[154] ibid [95] (Lord Carnwath).

[155] *Bloomsbury* (n 11) [58] (Lord Phillips).

[156] *R (N)* (n 139) [53] (Lord Hodge), citing Lord Carnwath's concurring judgment (in which see at [95]).

[157] ibid [95] (Lord Carnwath).

[158] *Bloomsbury* (n 11) [57]–[58] (Lord Phillips). See also *Campbell* (n 73) 930–31 (Viscount Radcliffe).

[159] *Anglesey* (n 73) [43] (Carnwath LJ).

4

General Presumptions as to the Intended Effect of Legislation

4.1 The previous chapter set out certain presumptions guiding the interpretation of statutory language (words and phrases). But there are also wider presumptions of legal policy (sometimes called 'rules' or 'principles') established at common law that relate to the *effect* of legislation. They are still only presumptions, so they will not govern the meaning of an enactment where it is clear that Parliament intended otherwise. The clarity of statutory language needed to displace these presumptions depends on the force it is appropriate to give the relevant presumption in any given case. This chapter addresses some of the more common presumptions as to the intended effect of legislation.

The Presumption that Legislation Accords with 'Common Sense'

4.2 An 'important canon of construction is to interpret legislation so far as possible to equate with common sense'.[1] However, common sense is only one factor: 'it is statutory interpretation rather than common sense which must at the end of the day prevail if the two do not coincide'.[2]

---

[1] *R v Secretary of State for the Home Department ex p Naughton* [1997] 1 WLR 118 (QB) 130G–H (Popplewell J), citing with approval *Barnes v Jarvis* [1953] 1 WLR 649 (QB) 652 (Lord Goddard CJ): 'A certain amount of common sense must be applied in construing statutes.' See also *Majorstake Ltd v Curtis* [2008] UKHL 10, [2008] 1 AC 787 [44] (Lord Carswell), referring to a letter by Thomas Jefferson in 1823: 'Laws are made for men of ordinary understanding, and should, therefore, be construed by the ordinary rules of common sense.' For a further example of the courts applying 'a common sense construction', see *R v Archer* [2007] EWCA Crim 536, [2007] 2 Cr App R (S) 71 [31] (Burton J).

[2] *R v Legal Aid Board ex p Bruce* [1992] 1 WLR 694 (HL) 699F (Lord Jauncey). See also *Re Lehman Brothers International (Europe) (No 4)* [2017] UKSC 38, [2017] 2 WLR 1497 [123] (Lord Neuberger): 'when it comes to deciding the meaning of a legislative provision, judges are primarily concerned with arriving at a coherent interpretation, which, while taking into account commerciality and reasonableness, pays proper regard to the language of the provision interpreted in its context'.

The Presumption of Reasonableness: Presumption against an Absurd, Irrational, Futile or Unreasonable Result

4.3   There is 'a presumption that Parliament intends to act reasonably' and so should be taken not to 'intend a statute to have consequences which are objectionable or undesirable; or absurd; or unworkable or impracticable; or merely inconvenient; or anomalous or illogical; or futile or pointless';[3] or 'unreasonable or irrational'.[4] Accordingly, in general terms, where there is a choice between two constructions of an enactment and one would lead to the aforementioned results, then the court should if possible favour the alternative construction, in the absence of 'very strong reasons' to the contrary.[5]

4.4   In practice, the question of whether the presumption should be applied to determine the appropriate construction of an enactment is often a nuanced one: the answer will depend in each case on how readily the enactment in question, read in context, lends itself to a reasonable construction and how strong the presumption of reasonableness is in the context of the enactment in question.

4.5   The strength of the presumption in a given case 'depends on the degree to which a particular construction produces an unreasonable result. The more unreasonable a result, the less likely it is that Parliament intended it'.[6] Note, however, that a degree of caution must be exercised before identifying an absurdity or anomaly and in evaluating its seriousness: it may be that, on closer analysis,

---

[3] *R (Edison First Power Ltd) v Central Valuation Officer* [2003] UKHL 20, [2003] 4 All ER 209 [116] (Lord Millett), stating that the more specific presumption against double taxation was a species of this 'wider genus'. He contrasted the presumption of reasonableness with 'a strong presumption which gives effect to a high constitutional norm, like the presumptions against the abrogation of the privilege against self-incrimination or legal professional privilege' (a number of such presumptions are considered below at paragraphs 4.17–4.39). See also *IRC v Hinchy* [1960] AC 748 (HL) 768 (Lord Reid): 'One is entitled and indeed bound to assume that Parliament intends to act reasonably, and therefore to prefer a reasonable interpretation of a statutory provision if there is any choice.'

[4] *Cramas Properties Ltd v Connaught Fur Trimmings Ltd* [1965] 1 WLR 892 (HL) 898B (Lord Reid).

[5] ibid 898B–C (Lord Reid). See also *Mangin v IRC* [1971] AC 739 (PC) 746E (Lord Donovan): 'the object of the construction of a statute being to ascertain the will of the legislature it may be presumed that neither injustice nor absurdity was intended. If therefore a literal interpretation would produce such a result, and the language admits of an interpretation which would avoid it, then such an interpretation may be adopted'.

[6] *Edison* (n 3) [117] (Lord Millett); see also at [25] (Lord Hoffmann): 'The strength of the presumption depends upon the degree to which the consequences are unreasonable, the general scheme of the legislation and the background against which it was enacted.'

the apparently undesirable result reflects the legislative purpose, or at least should not be considered so objectionable as it might first have appeared.[7]

4.6 Where there is a basis for applying the presumption in a given case, its force must be balanced against the force of any textual imperative in favour of the unreasonable interpretation, applying the principle that '[t]he more absurd or inconvenient the result, or the more obvious the failure of the Act to achieve its purpose ... the clearer the language must be if it is to prevail'.[8]

4.7 Ultimately, there will be very little room for reliance on seemingly unjust or absurd or anomalous results to avoid an undesirable construction where the wording of a statute is plain[9] and where applying the presumption of reasonableness would involve 'substantially rewriting' a statutory provision when there is no contextual warrant for doing so.[10] Where, having regard to all relevant context, the statutory language leaves no room for a reasonable interpretation, the question to be asked is whether 'the consequences of the application of the clear statutory words ... are ... so absurd that one can see that Parliament must have made a drafting mistake', which the courts may then be able to correct.[11]

---

[7] *R v C* [2007] EWCA Crim 2581, [2008] 1 WLR 966 [24] (Sir Igor Judge P): 'Before arriving at the conclusion that the legislative process has produced uncovenanted absurdities, as part of the interpretation process, the question whether such results can possibly have reflected the legislative purpose must be addressed. Different views may be held about what may or may not constitute an absurdity, and, if it does, the extent of the absurdity' (going on to state that the *Inco* jurisdiction to correct errors in drafting may sometimes be available, as to which see Chapter 3.49–3.51).

[8] *R v Secretary of State for Health ex p Hammersmith and Fulham London Borough Council* (1999) 31 HLR 475 (CA) 480 (Sir Christopher Staughton), having stated: 'In truth this would appear to be another instance where there is a question of degree, a sliding scale'. See also *Dingmar v Dingmar* [2006] EWCA Civ 942, [2007] Ch 109 [99] (Ward LJ), effectively framing the question as whether, reading the 'Act as a whole there is enough ambiguity for the court to override what may be a literal meaning when its result is to produce palpably absurd and self-evidently capricious consequences'. He concluded that in that case there was sufficient ambiguity, and consequently that '[a] construction of the Act must be favoured which eliminates the ambiguity and anomaly by allowing common sense and justice to prevail'.

[9] See *Stock v Frank Jones (Tipton) Ltd* [1978] 1 WLR 231 (HL) 234G–235F (Viscount Dilhorne), 237F–G (Lord Simon) and 238G–239E (Lord Scarman). These passages were cited and applied as authoritative in *Greenweb Ltd v Wandsworth London Borough Council* [2008] EWCA Civ 910, [2009] 1 WLR 612 [28]–[31] (Stanley Burnton LJ), discussing the very limited circumstances in which it is legitimate for courts to depart from the plain (ie, 'clear and unambiguous') meaning of a statute by reason of purportedly anomalous or absurd consequences. This was a case where there was no ambiguity, and nothing in the background and history of the Act in question, or any other contextual factor, to support the more reasonable construction: see at [25]. See also *Hinchy* (n 3) 767 (Lord Reid): 'the question is whether these words are capable of a more limited construction. If not, then we must apply them as they stand, however unreasonable or unjust the consequences, and however strongly we may suspect that this was not the real intention of Parliament'; and *Shahid v Scottish Ministers* [2015] UKSC 58, [2016] AC 429 [20]–[21] (Lord Reed). As to the scope for departing from 'plain' meanings, see further Chapter 3.13.

[10] See *Canterbury City Council v Colley* [1993] AC 401 (HL) 406B–G (Lord Oliver).

[11] *Greenweb* (n 9) [31] (Stanley Burnton LJ). As to the jurisdiction to correct obvious drafting errors, see Chapter 3.49–3.51.

The Presumption that Penal Provisions Should be Strictly Construed

4.8 'It is a principle of legal policy that a person should not be penalised except under clear law.'[12] Accordingly, it is presumed that provisions having penal effect should be 'strictly construed',[13] with any 'real doubt'[14] as to how to interpret such provisions to be resolved in the way 'most favourable to the accused'.[15] This is sometimes referred to as the principle or the 'rule against doubtful penalisation'.[16] The principle 'is a long-standing one, of recognised constitutional importance'.[17]

4.9 The principle is most often invoked in relation to statutory provisions imposing criminal liability, but it also applies in relation to the imposition of civil or regulatory penalties.[18]

4.10 Despite the apparent breadth and force with which the principle is sometimes stated, 'it only applies where after full inquiry and consideration one is left in real doubt. It is not enough that the provision is ambiguous in the sense that it is capable of having two meanings'. The broader construction should be given to a penal provision where the courts are 'satisfied' overall that the broader meaning is the one 'Parliament must have intended the words to convey'.[19]

---

[12] *R v Bristol Justices ex p E* [1999] 1 WLR 390 (QB) 397E (Simon Brown LJ); cited with approval in *R (Haw) v Secretary of State for the Home Department* [2006] EWCA Civ 532, [2006] QB 780 [27] (Sir Anthony Clarke MR), calling this 'the principle of doubtful penality'.

[13] *Woodley v Woodley (No 2)* [1994] 1 WLR 1167 (CA) 1180A–B (Simon Brown LJ, dissenting), referring to 'the well settled principle that penal statutes must be strictly construed, the presumption being in favour of the liberty of the subject whenever the statutory language admits of two reasonable constructions'.

[14] *Bristol Justices* (n 12) 397E (Simon Brown LJ); and see paragraph 4.10 below.

[15] *Sweet v Parsley* [1970] AC 132 (HL) 149E (Lord Reid): 'it is a universal principle that if a penal provision is reasonably capable of two interpretations, that interpretation which is most favourable to the accused must be adopted'; *R v Allen* [1985] AC 1029 (HL) 1034E–F (Lord Hailsham LC): 'any ambiguity must be resolved in favour of the subject and against the Crown'.

[16] See, eg, *Aitken v Director of Public Prosecutions* [2015] EWHC 1079 (Admin), [2016] 1 WLR 297 [67] (Warby J).

[17] *Bogdanic v Secretary of State for the Home Department* [2014] EWHC 2872 (QB) [47] (Sales J).

[18] See the applications of the principle in, eg, *Bogdanic* (n 17), especially at [49] (Sales J), in the context of a civil penalties regime; *Tuck & Sons v Priester* (1887) 19 QBD 629 (CA) 638 (Lord Esher MR) and 644–45 (Lindley LJ), in the context of penalties for copyright infringement; *ESS Production Ltd v Sully* [2005] EWCA Civ 554, [2005] BCC 435, in the context of a director's personal liability for company debts under s 217 of the Insolvency Act 1986, especially at [78] (Arden LJ): 'the principle against doubtful penalisation ... should be applied to the imposition of a civil liability as well as to the imposition of criminal liability'.

[19] *Director of Public Prosecutions v Ottewell* [1970] AC 642 (HL) 649D–F (Lord Reid). This was cited and applied in *Attorney General's Reference (No 1 of 1988)* [1989] AC 971 (HL) 991C–G (Lord Lowry). See also *Haw* (n 12) [28] (Sir Anthony Clarke MR): 'all depends upon the circumstances of the particular case, even if the case involves the construction of a statute which contains penal provisions'.

4.11   It is clear therefore that 'it is not an absolute principle … It is capable of being outweighed by other objective indications of legislative intention, albeit it is itself an indicator of great weight'.[20] In other words, the question whether there is 'in the relevant sense clear law' under which someone may be penalised 'depends … upon the true construction of the relevant statute', which must be 'construed in its context'.[21] Accordingly, the courts often find the principle to be outweighed by other factors.[22] In particular, they have declined to follow the principle where provisions have a clear statutory purpose as part of a regulatory regime that is designed for the protection of the public and is not 'fundamentally penal' in nature, despite having penal consequences.[23]

4.12   The willingness of the courts to rely on other interpretive factors to adopt broader interpretations of penal provisions in spite of the principle against doubtful penalisation led Lord Steyn to comment that the principle applies only 'rarely … as a rule of last resort … if all other grounds of determining legislative intent have failed'.[24] However, a number of recent decisions show that 'the principle of strict construction of penal statutes … is alive and well even if it may often give way to other canons of construction'.[25]

---

[20] *Bogdanic* (n 17) [48] (Sales J). Other factors may, of course, also support a narrow construction: see, eg, *R v Bloxham* [1983] 1 AC 109 (HL) 114E–F (Lord Bridge): 'here there are, in my opinion, more specific and weightier indications which point in the same direction as the general rule'.

[21] *Haw* (n 12) [27] (Sir Anthony Clarke MR).

[22] See, eg, *Haw* (n 12); *Bogdanic* (n 17).

[23] See, eg, *Re Lo-Line Electric Motors Ltd* [1988] Ch 477 (Ch) 486A–B and 489C–F (Sir Nicolas Browne-Wilkinson V-C), rejecting the need for a strict construction of the word 'director' in the context of the disqualification of directors, and approaching the issue on the 'normal basis' of statutory interpretation because 'the paramount purpose of disqualification is the protection of the public not punishment'; *Re Digital Satellite Warranty Cover Ltd* [2011] EWHC 122 (Ch), [2011] Bus LR 981 [60]–[62] (Warren J), acknowledging but declining to apply this presumption to determine the scope of sch 1 to the Financial Services and Markets Act 2000 (Regulated Activities) Order 2001 in view of the weight of other interpretive factors, since the Order was designed to implement a Directive and to protect the public—in particular consumers (this decision was upheld on appeal by the Court of Appeal ([2011] EWCA Civ 1413, [2012] Bus LR 990), and the Supreme Court ([2013] UKSC 7, [2013] 1 WLR 605), but this argument was not pursued on appeal); and *R (Junttan Oy) v Bristol Magistrates' Court* [2003] UKHL 55, [2004] 2 All ER 555 [84] (Lord Steyn), declining to apply the principle where there was 'at stake a cogent countervailing legal policy: the protection of health and safety at work is of overriding importance'.

[24] *Junttan Oy* (n 23) [84] (Lord Steyn).

[25] *R v Dowds* [2012] EWCA Crim 281, [2012] 1 WLR 2576 [37]–[38] (Hughes LJ), considering Lord Steyn's statement in *Junttan Oy* (as cited in the text to n 24); and see also the recognition of the principle's importance in *Bogdanic* (n 17) as cited in the text to nn 17 and 20 above (though neither case ultimately followed the principle). For a case where the principle was applied, see, eg, *ESS Production* (n 18).

The Presumption against Changes
in the Common Law

4.13 It is a 'well-established principle' that a statute is not to be taken as effecting a substantial change in the existing common law unless Parliament makes this clear, either 'by express provision or by clear implication'.[26]

4.14 Where legislation may override a fundamental common law rule or right (such as the right to legal professional privilege), the overlapping 'principle of legality' (discussed below) will apply to prevent the common law from being overridden other than by express provision or as a 'necessary implication' of the legislation in question.[27]

4.15 In other circumstances, the presumption against a change in the common law is less powerful, though still important. In such cases, the issue of 'whether the provisions of a statute have impliedly overridden or displaced the common law ... is a question of construction of the statute in question'.[28] Necessary implication is not required.[29]

4.16 Thus, where Parliament introduces a statutory scheme in an area where common law rights and remedies already exist, whether the common law rules are impliedly abrogated depends on whether, 'looked at as a whole, a common law remedy would be incompatible with the statutory scheme and therefore could not have been intended [to] coexist with it'. However, courts 'should not be too

---

[26] See *R (Rottman) v Commissioner of Police of the Metropolis* [2002] UKHL 20, [2002] 2 AC 692 [75] (Lord Hutton): 'It is a well-established principle that a rule of the common law is not extinguished by a statute unless the statute makes this clear by express provision or by clear implication.' See also *National Assistance Board v Wilkinson* [1952] 2 QB 648 (QB) 658–59 (Lord Goddard CJ): 'it may be presumed that the legislature does not intend to make a substantial alteration in the law beyond what it expressly declares', and at 661 (Devlin J): 'It is a well-established principle of construction that a statute is not to be taken as effecting a fundamental alteration in the general law unless it uses words that point unmistakably to that conclusion'; *George Wimpey & Co Ld v British Overseas Airways Corporation* [1955] AC 169 (HL) 191 (Lord Reid): 'if the arguments are fairly evenly balanced, that interpretation should be chosen which involves the least alteration of the existing law'; *Black–Clawson International Ltd v Papierwerke Waldhof-Aschaffenburg AG* [1975] AC 591 (HL) 614C–D (Lord Reid): 'in the absence of any clear indication to the contrary Parliament can be presumed not to have altered the common law further than was necessary to remedy the "mischief"'. See further the discussion in *Greene v Associated Newspapers Ltd* [2004] EWCA Civ 1462, [2005] QB 972 [61]–[66] (Brooke LJ).

[27] See the discussion of 'necessary implication' below at paragraphs 4.21–4.22.

[28] *R (Child Poverty Action Group) v Secretary of State for Work and Pensions* [2010] UKSC 54, [2011] 2 AC 15 ('*CPAG*') [27] (Dyson JSC), and see generally at [26]–[35] (Dyson JSC). This decision was cited in *Investment Trust Companies v Revenue and Customs Commissioners* [2017] UKSC 29, [2017] 2 WLR 1200 [86] (Lord Reed), making clear that: 'The fact that Parliament will not have had in mind a particular common law right ... when enacting a legislative scheme ... does not preclude the common law right being excluded by that scheme.'

[29] *CPAG* (n 28) [31] (Dyson JSC).

ready to find that a common law remedy has been displaced by a statutory one' by implication, in particular because Parliament can expressly state when this is intended.[30]

The Presumption that Legislation is Not Contrary to Fundamental Rights or Basic Tenets of the Common Law: The Principle of Legality

4.17   Since it is presumed that Parliament does not intend to legislate contrary to fundamental rights[31] or any other 'basic tenet of the common law',[32] it will not be taken to have done so unless it makes its intention to this effect very clear by 'express language or necessary implication'. General or ambiguous words will therefore be interpreted so as not to override fundamental rights or principles of similar import.[33] This rule of construction is often called '*the principle of legality*'.[34]

4.18   As one might expect, this presumption also places implied limitations on the scope of statutory powers. 'The principle of legality means not only that Parliament cannot itself override fundamental rights or the rule of law by general or ambiguous words, but also that it cannot confer on another body, by general or ambiguous words, the power to do so.'[35]

---

[30]   ibid [34] (Dyson JSC). See also *Rottman* (n 26) [75] (Lord Hutton), referring to the need for a 'clear' (rather than necessary) implication.

[31]   See, eg, *R v Secretary of State for the Home Department ex p Pierson* [1998] AC 539 (HL) 575C (Lord Browne-Wilkinson, dissenting): 'the presumption is against the impairment of such basic rights'.

[32]   See *R (Morgan Grenfell & Co Ltd) v Special Commissioner of Income Tax* [2002] UKHL 21, [2003] 1 AC 563 [44] (Lord Hobhouse), and see the cases there cited.

[33]   See the classic statement of the principle and the explanation of its basis in *R (Simms) v Secretary of State for the Home Department* [2000] 2 AC 115, 131E–G (Lord Hoffmann): 'Parliamentary sovereignty means that Parliament can, if it chooses, legislate contrary to fundamental principles of human rights. The Human Rights Act 1998 will not detract from this power. The constraints upon its exercise by Parliament are ultimately political, not legal. But the principle of legality means that Parliament must squarely confront what it is doing and accept the political cost. Fundamental rights cannot be overridden by general or ambiguous words. This is because there is too great a risk that the full implications of their unqualified meaning may have passed unnoticed in the democratic process. In the absence of express language or necessary implication to the contrary, the courts therefore presume that even the most general words were intended to be subject to the basic rights of the individual.' This passage was considered in *R (Ingenious Media Holdings plc) v Revenue and Customs Commissioners* [2016] UKSC 54, [2016] 1 WLR 4164 [19]–[20] (Lord Toulson), stating: 'Lord Hoffmann said that this presumption will apply "even" to the most general words, but I would say further that the more general the words, the harder it is likely to be to rebut the presumption.'

[34]   See *Simms* (n 33), as cited in that note. See also, eg, *AKJ v Commissioner of Police of the Metropolis* [2013] EWCA Civ 1342, [2014] 1 WLR 285 [23] (Lord Dyson MR), citing *Simms*: 'The principle of legality is that fundamental rights cannot be overridden by general or ambiguous statutory words.'

[35]   *AXA General Insurance Ltd v HM Advocate* [2011] UKSC 46, [2012] 1 AC 868 [152] (Lord Reed), citing with approval *Pierson* (n 31) 575D (Lord Browne-Wilkinson, dissenting): 'A power conferred by

4.19   The courts have variously expressed this presumption as being concerned with preventing basic rights from being *overridden*,[36] *abrogated*, *curtailed*,[37] *adversely affected*[38] or *interfered with*.[39] In practice, the courts apply the presumption in a way which recognises that 'the more fundamental the right interfered with, and the more drastic the interference', the clearer legislation will need to be before it will be read as authorising such interference.[40] However, although the principle of legality is a powerful presumption, ultimately it does not permit 'a court to disregard an unambiguous expression of Parliament's intention' and it

Parliament in general terms is not to be taken to authorise the doing of acts by the donee of the power which adversely affect the legal rights of the citizen or the basic principles on which the law of the United Kingdom is based unless the statute conferring the power makes it clear that such was the intention of Parliament.' This passage from *Pierson* was also cited with approval in *Ahmed v HM Treasury* [2010] UKSC 2, [2010] 2 AC 534 [46] (Lord Hope), in a case where the Supreme Court held that the Government's power to give effect to United Nations Security Council Resolutions under s 1(1) of the United Nations Act 1946 was impliedly limited by the principle of legality (see especially the discussion at [42]–[47] (Lord Hope)). See also *R (UNISON) v Lord Chancellor* [2017] UKSC 51, [2017] 3 WLR 409 [87]–[88] (Lord Reed), in the context of the right of access to justice (as to which see further nn 80 and 88 below), stating: 'even where primary legislation authorises the imposition of an intrusion on the right of access to justice, it is presumed to be subject to an implied limitation ... the degree of intrusion must not be greater than is justified by the objectives which the measure is intended to serve', citing *R v Secretary of State for the Home Department ex p Leech* [1994] QB 198 (CA) and *R (Daly) v Secretary of State for the Home Department* [2001] UKHL 26, [2001] 2 AC 532.

   [36]   See, eg, *Simms* (n 33) in the passage cited in that note.
   [37]   See, eg, *R (Public Law Project) v Secretary of State for Justice* [2015] EWCA Civ 1193, [2016] AC 1531 [29] (Laws LJ). This decision was overturned on appeal ([2016] UKSC 39, [2016] AC 1531), but without consideration of the principle of legality.
   [38]   See, eg, *Pierson* (n 31), in the passage cited at n 35.
   [39]   See, eg, *Ahmed* (n 35) [76] (Lord Hope).
   [40]   *R v Secretary of State for the Home Department ex p Saleem* [2001] 1 WLR 443 (CA) 458B–C (Hale LJ): 'the more fundamental the right interfered with, and the more drastic the interference, the more difficult it is to read a general rule or regulation making power as authorising that interference'; and see the passage in *Ingenious* (n 33) cited in that note. See also *Ahmed* (n 35) [45] (Lord Hope): 'The closer those measures come to affecting ... the basic rights of the individual, the more exacting this scrutiny must become.' Lord Hope found that, while more limited interferences with certain rights were authorised under the relevant statute, the interference in question was so 'great' and 'overwhelming' that it was not. See also, eg, at [154] (Lord Phillips) and [185] (Lord Rodger), referring respectively to the serious, and grave and direct impact of the relevant interference, such that Parliament could not be taken to have authorised it by its general words. See also the nuanced way in which the right to freedom of expression was defined in *Simms* (n 33) 127A–C (Lord Steyn). Lord Steyn held that a prisoner's right to communicate freely with journalists to help him challenge the safety of his convictions engaged the principle of legality, while other instances of freedom of expression would not, stating: 'The value of free speech in a particular case must be measured in specifics. Not all types of speech have an equal value.' See also the general statement of principle by the Divisional Court in *Miller v Secretary of State for Exiting the European Union* [2016] EWHC 2768 (Admin), [2017] 2 WLR 583 [83] (Judgment of the Court): 'the stronger the constitutional principle the stronger the presumption that Parliament did not intend to override it and the stronger the material required, in terms of express language or clear necessary implication, before the inference can properly be drawn that in fact it did so intend. Similarly, the stronger the constitutional principle, the more readily can it be inferred that words used by Parliament were intended to carry a meaning which reflects the principle'. The Supreme Court upheld this decision on appeal ([2017] UKSC 5, [2017] 2 WLR 583), but although the majority cited in their judgment (at [87] and [108]) the principle of legality as stated in *Simms*, they did not consider its relative force in different circumstances.

is not as powerful as the interpretive duty under section 3 of the Human Rights Act 1998.[41]

4.20 Examples of the fundamental rights and basic tenets of the common law which have been held to engage the principle of legality are the 'right to liberty of the person';[42] a person's 'right to peaceful enjoyment of his property';[43] the 'right of unimpeded access to a court';[44] the right to legal professional privilege;[45] the presumption of fairness;[46] the presumption of notice;[47] the presumption of *mens rea* in statutory offences;[48] and the presumption that executive decisions are subject to judicial oversight.[49] With regard to rights, it is important to note that the principle relates only to 'rights and obligations recognised at a domestic level' and not to those which are recognised solely as a matter of international law.[50]

Necessary Implication

4.21 As stated above, legislation must make clear any intention to override fundamental norms by express language or necessary implication. The concept of 'necessary implication' is intended to set a 'high hurdle'.[51] In the words of Lord Hobhouse:

> A necessary implication is not the same as a reasonable implication ... A *necessary* implication is one which necessarily follows from the express provisions of the statute construed in their context. It distinguishes between what it would have been sensible or

---

[41] *Ahmed* (n 35) [117] (Lord Phillips).
[42] *B v Secretary of State for Justice* [2011] EWCA Civ 1608, [2012] 1 WLR 2043 [53] (Arden LJ).
[43] *Ahmed* (n 35) [75] (Lord Hope), citing *Entick v Carrington* (1765) 19 State Tr 1029, 1066 (Lord Camden CJ).
[44] *Ahmed* (n 35) [75] (Lord Hope), citing *Pyx Granite Co Ltd v Ministry of Housing and Local Government* [1960] AC 260, 286 (Viscount Simonds).
[45] *Morgan Grenfell* (n 32), where a power under the Taxes Management Act 1970 to require disclosure of documents was interpreted as subject to an exclusion for documents protected by the fundamental right to legal professional privilege (in the absence of clear language or necessary implication to the contrary).
[46] Considered below at paragraphs 4.23–4.25.
[47] Considered below at paragraph 4.26.
[48] Considered below at paragraphs 4.27–4.30.
[49] Considered below at paragraphs 4.31–4.39.
[50] *R (Yam) v Central Criminal Court* [2015] UKSC 76, [2016] AC 771 [36] (Lord Mance). This was cited in *R (Al-Saadoon) v Secretary of State for Defence* [2016] EWCA Civ 811, [2017] 2 WLR 219 [199] (Lloyd Jones LJ), stating: 'the principle depends for its application on the fundamental rights in question already being part of domestic law ... It does not operate by reference to rights and duties between states on the international plane, nor can it transform such rights into domestic law'.
[51] *CPAG* (n 28) [31] (Dyson JSC). But see *R (Black) v Secretary of State for Justice* [2017] UKSC 81, [2018] 2 WLR 123 [37] (Lady Hale): 'It is neither necessary nor desirable to add further glosses to the test, or to characterise it by adjectives such as "strict". The question is whether, in the light of the words used, their context and the purpose of the legislation, Parliament must have' had the relevant intention.

reasonable for Parliament to have included or what Parliament would, if it had thought about it, probably have included and what it is clear that the express language of the statute shows that the statute must have included. A necessary implication is a matter of express language and logic not interpretation.[52]

4.22   In other words, a necessary implication must be 'compellingly clear' from a consideration of the statutory language, the nature and purpose of the enactment, and 'any other circumstances which may assist in determining what intention is properly to be attributed to Parliament'.[53]

The Presumption of Fairness

4.23   Statutory powers must generally be read as implicitly subject to a requirement that they be exercised in accordance with the basic principles of procedural fairness, or natural justice. This has been described as an instance of the principle of legality.[54] In the words of Lord Diplock:

> Where an Act of Parliament confers upon an administrative body functions which involve its making decisions that affect to their detriment the rights of other persons or curtail their liberty to do as they please, there is a presumption that Parliament intended that the administrative body should act fairly towards those persons who will be affected by their decision.[55]

---

[52] *Morgan Grenfell* (n 32) [45] (Lord Hobhouse). In *Black* (n 51) [36] (Lady Hale), it was stated that this reference to a necessary implication needing to follow from the language of the legislation construed in its context 'must be modified to include the purpose, as well as the context, of the legislation'. For an example of the legislative purpose being taken into account in this regard, see *M v Secretary of State for Justice* [2017] EWCA Civ 194, [2017] 1 WLR 4681 [51] (Judgment of the Court).

[53] *B (A Minor) v Director of Public Prosecutions* [2000] 2 AC 428 (HL) 464A–B (Lord Nicholls), in the context of the presumption of *mens rea* in criminal offences: '"Necessary implication" connotes an implication which is compellingly clear. Such an implication may be found in the language used, the nature of the offence, the mischief sought to be prevented and any other circumstances which may assist in determining what intention is properly to be attributed to Parliament when creating the offence.' And see generally the guidance in *Black* (n 51) [36]–[37] (Lady Hale).

[54] *R (Roberts) v Parole Board* [2005] UKHL 45, [2005] 2 AC 738 [25] (Lord Bingham, dissenting), citing *Simms* (n 33), and see at [77]–[78] (Lord Woolf CJ). As to the principle of legality, see paragraphs 4.17–4.22.

[55] *R v Commission for Racial Equality ex p Hillingdon London Borough Council* [1982] AC 779 (HL) 787F–G (Lord Diplock). This was cited with approval in *R (Anufrijeva) v Secretary of State for the Home Department* [2003] UKHL 36, [2004] 1 AC 604 [30] (Lord Steyn), stating: 'Fairness is the guiding principle of our public law.' See also *Pierson* (n 31) 574A–B (Lord Browne-Wilkinson, dissenting): 'Where wide powers of decision-making are conferred by statute, it is presumed that Parliament implicitly requires the decision to be made in accordance with the rules of natural justice: Bennion on Statutory Interpretation, p. 737. However widely the power is expressed in the statute, it does not authorise that power to be exercised otherwise than in accordance with fair procedures.' This passage was cited with approval in *Roberts* (n 54) in the passages cited in that note and *R (Plantagenet Alliance Ltd) v Secretary of State for Justice* [2014] EWHC 1662 (Admin), [2015] 3 All ER 261 [91] (Hallett LJ).

4.24 Accordingly, as Lord Bridge has stated, in order to give effect to this presumption:

> [I]t is well-established that when a statute has conferred on any body the power to make decisions affecting individuals, the courts will not only require the procedure prescribed by the statute to be followed, but will readily imply so much and no more to be introduced by way of additional procedural safeguards as will ensure the attainment of fairness.[56]

4.25 What fairness requires in a given case will depend on the context, and in particular 'the character of the decision-making body, the kind of decision it has to make and the statutory or other framework in which it operates'.[57] The legislative framework 'may limit what fairness requires in a particular case', as the duty of fairness will generally not require extra steps to be taken where this 'would frustrate the apparent purpose of the legislation'.[58] But the extent to which the legislative scheme will be taken to exclude or limit the demands of fairness will depend on the force of the aspect of fairness in question and the 'importance of what is at stake'.[59] In particular, the requirements of fairness may be more exacting in cases involving a person's 'liberty, livelihood, good name etc'.[60]

The Presumption of Notice

4.26 A specific aspect of the presumption of fairness is the strong 'presumption that notice of a decision must be given to the person adversely affected by it before it can have legal effect'.[61] This is not merely 'a technical rule'; it is 'an application

---

[56] *Lloyd v McMahon* [1987] AC 625 (HL) 703A–B (Lord Bridge).

[57] ibid 702H (Lord Bridge), considered in *R (L) v West London Mental Health NHS Trust* [2014] EWCA Civ 47, [2014] 1 WLR 3103 [74] (Beatson LJ). See also the list of relevant factors identified in *R (Howard League for Penal Reform)* [2017] EWCA Civ 244, [2017] 4 WLR 92 [39] (Beatson LJ, giving the judgment of the Court), after referring at [35] to 'the commonplace and longstanding orthodoxy ... that what is required is acutely sensitive to context'.

[58] *R (L)* (n 57) [77] (Beatson LJ). See also *EK (Ivory Coast) v Secretary of State for the Home Department* [2014] EWCA Civ 1517 [31] (Sales LJ): 'the general public law duty of fairness ... supplements the PBS regime, but ought not to be applied in such a manner as to undermine its intended mode of operation in a substantial way'.

[59] *EK* (n 58) [35]–[37] (Sales LJ). See also *Anufrijeva* (n 55) [31] (Lord Steyn), in relation to the general presumption that 'a decision takes effect only upon communication', relying, as part of his reasoning that Parliament had not legislated clearly enough to displace this presumption, upon the fact that the decision in question 'involves a fundamental right'.

[60] *EK* (n 58) [37] (Sales LJ). *EK* involved a statutory scheme designed to simplify immigration decisions. The Court of Appeal rejected an argument that fairness required the implication of an additional requirement on the Government to make certain inquiries of an applicant in certain circumstances, since to do so would undermine the intended simplicity of the statutory scheme, and because the interests of the applicants at stake bore less weight than those concerned in cases involving a person's 'liberty, livelihood, good name etc'. See generally at [24]–[42] (Sales LJ) and [59] (Briggs LJ).

[61] *Anufrijeva* (n 55) [43] (Lord Millett). See to similar effect at [26] (Lord Steyn).

of the right of access to justice', which 'is a fundamental and constitutional principle of our legal system'.[62] Accordingly, the presumption of notice can only be displaced by express enactment in sufficiently 'specific and unmistakable terms' that notice is not required, or if the relevant legislation requires this by 'necessary implication'.[63]

The Presumption of *Mens Rea* in Statutory Offences

4.27　Another aspect of the principle of legality is the presumption that in 'every statutory offence', 'a mental element, traditionally labelled mens rea, is an essential ingredient unless Parliament has indicated a contrary intention either expressly or by necessary implication'.[64] This arises from the presumption that Parliament does 'not intend to make criminals of persons who are in no way blameworthy in what they did'. Accordingly, the courts will presume that when legislation is silent as to the mental element of an offence, 'in order to give effect to the will of Parliament, [they] must read in words appropriate to require mens rea'.[65]

4.28　Although the presumption applies to all statutory offences, '[t]he more serious the offence, the greater is the weight to be attached to the presumption, because the more severe is the punishment and the graver the stigma which accompany a conviction'.[66] Thus, 'the presumption is particularly strong where the offence is "truly criminal" in character'.[67] By contrast, where the associated stigma and maximum sentence are more limited and an offence is not 'particularly serious', the court may conclude that the presumption should be given

---

[62]　ibid [26] (Lord Steyn).

[63]　ibid [31] (Lord Steyn). As to 'necessary implication' see above at paragraphs 4.21–4.22.

[64]　*B (A Minor)* (n 53) 460G (Lord Nicholls). Lord Steyn referred to this as the 'paradigm' of the principle of legality at 470F (as noted in *CPAG* (n 28) [30] (Dyson JSC)); and see *R v Brown* [2013] UKSC 43, [2013] 4 All ER 860 [26]–[27] (Lord Kerr), citing this passage with approval. See also the statement of the relevant principles in *Gammon (Hong Kong) Ltd v Attorney General of Hong Kong* [1985] AC 1 (PC) 14B–D (Lord Scarman): '(1) there is a presumption of law that mens rea is required before a person can be held guilty of a criminal offence; (2) the presumption is particularly strong where the offence is "truly criminal" in character; (3) the presumption applies to statutory offences, and can be displaced only if this is clearly or by necessary implication the effect of the statute; (4) the only situation in which the presumption can be displaced is where the statute is concerned with an issue of social concern, and public safety is such an issue; (5) even where a statute is concerned with such an issue, the presumption of mens rea stands unless it can also be shown that the creation of strict liability will be effective to promote the objects of the statute by encouraging greater vigilance to prevent the commission of the prohibited act'.

[65]　*Sweet* (n 15) 148G–H (Lord Reid), cited with approval in *B (A Minor)* (n 53) 470H–471E (Lord Steyn), and in *R v K* [2001] UKHL 41, [2002] 1 AC 462 [32] (Lord Steyn), calling the presumption 'a constitutional principle of general application'. Lord Steyn continued: 'The applicability of this presumption is not dependent on finding an ambiguity in the text. It operates to supplement the text.'

[66]　*B (A Minor)* (n 53) 464B–C (Lord Nicholls).

[67]　See Lord Scarman's second proposition in *Gammon* (n 64), as cited in that note.

'[s]ome weight', but 'can be readily displaced'.[68] The cases where the presumption is less strong will often involve offences that are not 'truly criminal' (sometimes termed 'quasi-criminal'), which are typically found in legislation of a more regulatory character aimed at addressing 'an issue of social concern',[69] and would include many 'offences under public health, licensing and industrial legislation'.[70]

4.29 Consequently, when considering if the presumption is displaced, the 'starting point' is to determine the seriousness of the offence and 'accordingly how much weight, if any, should be attached to the presumption'.[71] Although as part of this process it may often be helpful to distinguish between 'truly criminal' and 'quasi-criminal' offences, there is no clear line between the two, and deciding how to classify an offence is neither necessary nor sufficient in assessing its seriousness overall.[72]

4.30 Having assessed the strength of the presumption in the case of a particular offence, the court must then consider whether it is clear that Parliament intended for no *mens rea* to be required for that offence from the express language of the statute or (as will often be the relevant issue) by necessary implication.[73] Although this test may appear to impose a high hurdle in all cases, it must be understood in the context of judicial comments concerning the variability of the strength of the presumption. Thus, it may be considered sufficiently clear that the presumption has been displaced where purposive and contextual factors such as the quasi-criminal nature of the offence point towards this. In deciding whether the presumption is rebutted, the following matters should be considered:

4.30.1 *Nature of the offence*: the fact that an offence is 'concerned with an issue of social concern'[74] (such offences often being 'quasi-criminal') may point towards the presumption being rebutted, but is not sufficient in itself: 'the presumption

---

[68] *R v Muhamed* [2002] EWCA Crim 1856, [2003] QB 1031 [16] (Dyson LJ).

[69] See Lord Scarman's fourth proposition in *Gammon* (n 64), as cited in that note. For an example of the courts using the terms 'quasi-criminal' and 'truly criminal' see, eg, *Sweet* (n 15) 149G–H (Lord Reid), discussed in *Muhamed* (n 68) [13]–[14] (Dyson LJ).

[70] *Muhamed* (n 68) [12] (Dyson LJ).

[71] ibid [16] (Dyson LJ). The words 'if any' are somewhat difficult to reconcile with Dyson LJ's statement at [15] that the presumption prima facie applies to all offences which may lead to punishment in a criminal court, however minor, and with the numerous statements by the House of Lords and Privy Council cited at paragraph 4.27 (and the notes to that paragraph), which indicate that the presumption applies to all statutory offences. These words should probably be read as indicating that the weight to be given to the presumption will be extremely limited in some contexts.

[72] ibid [14]–[16] (Dyson LJ), who did not reach a firm conclusion on how to classify the offence in question, instead focusing more broadly on the question of how serious the offence was.

[73] ibid [17] (Dyson LJ), turning 'to consider whether the presumption has been displaced' as a matter of necessary implication. As for necessary implication, see paragraphs 4.21–4.22 above.

[74] See Lord Scarman's fourth proposition in *Gammon* (n 64), as cited in that note. What 'social concern' encompasses is not entirely clear: see *R (Thames Water Utilities Ltd) v Bromley Magistrates' Court (No 2)* [2013] EWHC 472 (Admin), [2013] 1 WLR 3641 [49] (Gross LJ), observing that most legislation is in some sense designed to deal with what might be termed issues of social concern. Some light is shed on the sort of legislation to which Lord Scarman was referring by looking at his citations

of *mens rea* stands unless it can also be shown that the creation of strict liability will be effective to promote the statutory purpose.[75]

4.30.2   Mens rea *provision elsewhere*: the fact that legislation expressly provides for a *mens rea* element for other offences, but not the offence in question, is a relevant factor, although again 'it is not sufficient by itself'.[76]

4.30.3   *Maximum sentence*: the maximum sentence for the offence may be relevant. Where it is low, it may indicate the offence is one of strict liability, particularly where it is lower than the maximum sentence available for other offences in the same legislation for which *mens rea* is specified.[77] The converse also holds, but an offence can be one of strict liability even though it carries a substantial maximum penalty.[78]

4.30.4   *Defences*: the availability of a defence may mitigate the effect of the absence of a *mens rea* requirement for an offence and thus make it more likely that the presumption can be rebutted.[79]

The Presumption against the Exclusion of Judicial Review: Presumption that Ouster Clauses are to be Strictly Construed[80]

4.31   Courts have an 'ingrained reluctance to countenance the statutory exclusion of judicial review' because of the fundamental constitutional importance of

in *Gammon* at 13F–14B and 16A–B from *Sweet* (n 15) 163E–G (Lord Diplock), namely legislation regulating spheres of activity in which citizens may choose to participate and which present potential dangers to the public, such that Parliament may consider quasi-criminal regulation would help ensure greater care is taken by those undertaking such activities. In *Gammon* itself, the context was regulation of the construction industry in the interests of public safety.

[75]   See Lord Scarman's fifth proposition in *Gammon* (n 64), as cited in that note.

[76]   *Muhamed* (n 68) [18] (Dyson LJ), in the context of the Insolvency Act 1986, which he considered created a 'clear and coherent regime' in which the majority of offences expressly required *mens rea*. See also *Thames Water* (n 74) [31]–[32] and [50] (Gross LJ). See generally Chapter 3.40–3.42 regarding the *expressio unius* principle of construction.

[77]   *Muhamed* (n 68) [19] (Dyson LJ).

[78]   See *Gammon* (n 64) 17F–H (Lord Scarman), considering that the fact the relevant offences carried 'severe penalties' (three years' imprisonment and a substantial fine) was 'formidable' but not decisive: 'there is nothing inconsistent with the purpose of the Ordinance in imposing severe penalties for offences of strict liability'.

[79]   See, eg, *Thames Water* (n 74), [33]–[34] and [50] (Gross LJ), considering that the existence of a defence of due diligence meant it was not 'draconian or unduly draconian' for the offence under s 33(1) (a) of the Environmental Protection Act 1990 of depositing controlled waste in or on any land without a licence to be one of strict liability.

[80]   See generally the discussion of so-called 'ouster clauses' (ie, provisions which purport to oust judicial supervision of executive action) in William Wade and Christopher Forsyth,

the supervisory jurisdiction of judicial review as 'a principal engine of the rule of law'.[81] Accordingly, provisions that purport to remove this jurisdiction, often called '*ouster clauses*' (or sometimes 'finality clauses'), are 'jealously scrutinised' by the courts.[82] Generally, it will only be where Parliament has made itself 'crystal clear' that it intends to remove the right to judicial review that it will be taken to have done so, otherwise it will be presumed that this was not its intention.[83] It must use 'the most clear and explicit words',[84] as any ambiguity will be construed in favour of preserving the availability judicial review,[85] and the supervisory jurisdiction

---

Administrative Law, 11th edn (Oxford, Oxford University Press, 2014) 608–19 (under the heading 'Protective and Preclusive (Ouster) Clauses'). See further Michael Fordham QC, *Judicial Review Handbook*, 6th edn (Oxford, Hart Publishing, 2012) ch 28. While our focus here is on the presumption against the restriction of judicial review, note that more generally there is 'a strong presumption that Parliament does not intend to preclude access to the ordinary courts for determination of disputes': see the judgment of the Divisional Court in *Miller* (n 40) at [83], citing *Anisminic Ltd v Foreign Compensation Commission* [1969] 2 AC 147; and see also *UNISON* (n 35) [66]–[85] (Lord Reed), discussing the 'constitutional right of access to the courts'. See further the cases cited in n 88 below.

[81]   *R (Cart) v Upper Tribunal* [2009] EWHC 3052 (Admin), [2011] QB 120 ('*Cart (QB)*') [34] (Laws LJ). He continued (at [39]) to explain that the rule of law also lies behind the High Court's supervisory jurisdiction by way of judicial review of decisions of other courts and tribunals because it 'requires that statute should be mediated by an authoritative and independent judicial source'. On appeal to the Supreme Court [2011] UKSC 28, [2012] 1 AC 663 ('*Cart (SC)*') (affirming the decisions of the courts below, but on different grounds), Lady Hale endorsed at [30] Laws LJ's statements of the importance of judicial review as a requirement of the rule of law. She then stated at [37]: 'the scope of judicial review is an artefact of the common law whose object is to maintain the rule of law—that is to ensure that, within the bounds of practical possibility, decisions are taken in accordance with the law, and in particular the law which Parliament has enacted, and not otherwise'. See also *R (G) v Immigration Appeal Tribunal* [2004] EWCA Civ 1731, [2005] 1 WLR 1445 [13] (Lord Phillips MR), stating that statutory appeal rights 'are additional to the right of the citizen, subject to the permission of the court, to seek judicial review by the High Court of administrative decisions. The common law power of the judges to review the legality of administrative action is a cornerstone of the rule of law in this country and one that the judges guard jealously. If Parliament attempts by legislation to remove that power, the rule of law is threatened. The courts will not readily accept that legislation achieves that end', citing *Anisminic* (n 80); and see *R (Evans) v Attorney General* [2015] UKSC 21, [2015] AC 1787 [52] (Lord Neuberger): 'it is also fundamental to the rule of law that decisions and actions of the executive are, subject to necessary well established exceptions (such as declarations of war), and jealously scrutinised statutory exceptions, reviewable by the court at the suit of an interested citizen'. The decision in *Evans* concerned not an ouster clause as such, but the analogous question of whether a provision could be read as empowering 'a member of the executive effectively to reverse, or overrule, a decision of a court or a judicial tribunal, simply because he does not agree with it': see at [58] (Lord Neuberger). The Supreme Court found that it did not, Lord Neuberger relying upon the principle of legality and stating that, for a provision to have that effect, Parliament would have to make its intention 'crystal clear' (see again at [58]).

[82]   *Evans* (n 81) [52] (Lord Neuberger), as cited more fully in that note.

[83]   ibid [56] (Lord Neuberger), citing the speech of Lady Hale in *R (Jackson) v Attorney General* [2005] UKHL 56, [2006] 1 AC 262, and the speech of Lord Hoffmann in *Simms* (n 33).

[84]   *R v Medical Appeal Tribunal ex p Gilmore* [1957] 1 QB 574 (CA) 583 (Denning LJ), cited with approval in, eg, *R (Sivasubramaniam) v Wandsworth County Court* [2002] EWCA Civ 1738, [2003] 1 WLR 475 [44] (Lord Phillips MR), and *Cart (QB)* (n 81) [31] (Laws LJ).

[85]   *Anisminic* (n 80) 170C–D (Lord Reid): 'It is a well established principle that a provision ousting the ordinary jurisdiction of the court must be construed strictly—meaning, I think, that, if such a provision is reasonably capable of having two meanings, that meaning shall be taken which preserves the ordinary jurisdiction of the court.'

cannot 'be removed by statutory *implication*'.[86] Accordingly, as illustrated by the examples given below at paragraph 4.37, the courts have often gone to great lengths to interpret ouster clauses extremely narrowly.

4.32   This fierce protection of judicial review is a particularly powerful instance of the principle of legality, whereby the courts presume that Parliament does not intend to legislate contrary to fundamental rights.[87] In this regard, the presumption against ouster clauses may be seen as a very important part of upholding the wider 'right of the citizen to have access to the courts' to ensure that executive power is exercised lawfully and to seek effective judicial redress in vindication of their rights.[88]

When Should a Provision be Interpreted as an Ouster Clause?

4.33   Limitations upon rights of *appeal* are not subjected to the same kind of scrutiny as ouster clauses (at least in the civil sphere).[89] Accordingly, the starting point in determining whether to interpret a provision in line with the principles of construction applicable to ouster clauses is to ascertain whether, apart from that

---

[86] *Sivasubramaniam* (n 84) [44] (Lord Phillips MR): 'The weight of authority makes it impossible to accept that the jurisdiction to subject a decision to judicial review can be removed by statutory *implication.*'

[87] As made clear by Lord Neuberger's citations in *Evans* (n 81) at [56]. As to the principle of legality generally, see above at paragraphs 4.17–4.22.

[88] See *R (G)* (n 81) [13] (Lord Phillips MR). See also the link drawn between the right to challenge executive action and the wider right of access to the courts in *Wandsworth London Borough Council v Winder* [1985] AC 461 (HL) 510A–C (Lord Fraser) and *Boddington v British Transport Police* [1999] 2 AC 143 (HL) 161C–F (Lord Irvine LC), both citing *Pyx* (n 44) 286 (Viscount Simonds): 'It is a principle not by any means to be whittled down that the subject's recourse to Her Majesty's courts for the determination of his rights is not to be excluded except by clear words.' As to this principle, see further the cases cited in n 80 above. For a discussion of the limits of the presumption against denying access to the courts, see *R (A) v Director of Establishments of the Security Service* [2009] UKSC 12, [2010] 2 AC 1 [21]–[22] (Lord Brown), considering that the principle did not apply as the same statute created both a new right and a remedy for its vindication in an alternative forum to the ordinary courts, so that there was no pre-existing right of action in the ordinary courts to take away; and *Century National Merchant Bank and Trust Co Ltd v Davies* [1998] AC 628 (PC) 637E (Lord Steyn), stating that express words or a necessary implication may show that Parliament intended another remedy to be exclusive (in that case, an appeal to the Court of Appeal with a strict time limit).

[89] See *Re Racal Communications Ltd* [1981] AC 374 (HL) 385A (Lord Diplock): 'the words of the statute "shall not be appealable" mean what they say'. His reasoning at 380A–B suggests that a more limited interpretation could only be given to these clear words if giving them their ordinary meaning led to 'results so manifestly absurd or unjust' that it could be concluded this was not Parliament's intention. That is not to say, however, that *judicial review* might not lie against a decision of an inferior court against whose decision there was no right of appeal (see below at paragraph 4.33.3). However, in the criminal context the courts have stated that '[t]here is a strong presumption that except by specific provision the legislature will not exclude a right of appeal as of right or with leave where such a right is ordinarily available', referring to the need for express words or necessary implication to displace the presumption—see *R v Emmett* [1998] AC 773 (HL) 781H–782B (Lord Steyn), citing *R v Cain* [1985] AC 46 (HL) 55G–56D (Lord Scarman).

provision, there would be, in principle, a right to *judicial review* to begin with in the relevant case.[90] In this regard:

4.33.1   Decisions 'by judges of the High Court acting in their capacity as such' are not amenable to judicial review, but only to an appeal, if one is available.[91] Decisions of the Court of Appeal and Supreme Court are similarly not subject to review.[92]

4.33.2   A limited number of other courts are also immune from judicial review because they have 'a status so closely equivalent to the High Court that the exercise of the power of judicial review by the High Court is for that reason inappropriate'.[93]

4.33.3   Generally, however, the supervisory jurisdiction of the High Court extends to redressing 'any error of law made by an administrative tribunal or inferior court in reaching its decision'.[94]

4.33.4   Exceptionally, the judicial review powers of the High Court may be limited where 'the applicable law' being applied by the decision maker 'is not the common law of England but a peculiar or domestic law of which the [decision maker] is the sole judge'.[95] In such cases, judicial review will only lie where the decision maker 'has acted outside his jurisdiction (in the narrow sense) or abused his powers or acted in breach of natural justice'.[96]

---

[90] It should be borne in mind that, in practice, where an adequate alternative remedy is available to challenge a decision, permission to bring a judicial review claim will not be granted: see, eg, *Cart (SC)* (n 81) [33] (Lady Hale), [71] (Lord Phillips). The availability of an effective alternative means of challenge may also affect whether a clause is truly an ouster: see paragraph 4.34 below.

[91] *Racal* (n 89) 384F–G (Lord Diplock).

[92] *Cart (QB)* (n 81) [71] (Laws LJ).

[93] ibid [71] (Laws LJ), citing *R v Cripps ex p Muldoon* [1984] QB 68, where Robert Goff LJ had cited as examples of such courts the Restrictive Practices Court and the Courts-Martial Appeal Court. Another example may be the Employment Appeal Tribunal: see the decisions cited and discussed in *Cart (QB)* at [61]–[63] (Laws LJ). Laws LJ stated that whether a court is so immune requires an examination of 'all the characteristics of the court in question' and principally whether it has unlimited jurisdiction, since courts 'of limited jurisdiction should generally be subject to judicial review': see at [70], and the discussion generally at [43]–[73]. In the Supreme Court, Lady Hale summarised and generally endorsed Laws LJ's analysis of this issue: see *Cart (SC)* (n 81) at [30]. For an application of these principles, see *R (Woolas) v Parliamentary Election Court* [2010] EWHC 3169 (Admin), [2012] QB 1, in particular at [54]–[58] (Thomas LJ), finding that the parliamentary election court was subject to judicial review.

[94] *R v Lord President of the Privy Council ex p Page* [1993] AC 682 (HL) 702B–C (Lord Browne-Wilkinson), but see the caveats discussed below at paragraphs 4.36 and 4.39 about the limited grounds on or circumstances in which this may be available in some cases. As to the general rule, see also the citations from *Cart (QB)* (n 81) and *Cart (SC)* (n 81) in the previous note. As to 'inferior courts', see *Peart v Stewart* [1983] 2 AC 109 (HL) 114H–115B (Lord Diplock), considering whether the County Court fell within the 'ordinary meaning' of this term, stating: 'It bears all the indicia of an inferior court of record. Its jurisdiction is limited. It is subject to the supervisory jurisdiction of the High Court.'

[95] *Page* (n 94) 700E (Lord Browne-Wilkinson), in the context of a university visitor. See also the reasoning at 702E–703A (Lord Browne-Wilkinson).

[96] ibid 704F–G (Lord Browne-Wilkinson).

4.34   The next question is to consider whether the relevant provision is truly an ouster. The courts' concern is not with provisions that seek to *allocate* jurisdiction to ensure the legality of decisions, only those that seek to *oust* it.[97] As such, even where a provision may appear on its face to limit the supervisory role of the courts, the courts will not treat it as an ouster clause where 'an effective means of challenging the validity of a [decision] is provided elsewhere'.[98]

4.35   Similarly, the courts do not treat as ouster clauses provisions which seek to *regulate* challenges to the legality of decisions, for example by imposing strict time limits.[99] Such provisions are sometimes known as 'preclusive clauses'.

Interpretation of Ouster Clauses

4.36   One caveat to the general principle requiring strict interpretation of ouster clauses is that the courts may more readily consider the judicial review jurisdiction to be limited with respect to the review of decisions of inferior courts of law. In such cases, it has been said that a provision stating that an inferior court's 'decision is to be "final and conclusive" or the like will confine the remedy to cases of abuse of power, acting outside jurisdiction in the narrow sense, or breach of natural justice'.[100]

---

[97] *Farley v Secretary of State for Work and Pensions (No 2)* [2006] UKHL 31, [2006] 1 WLR 1817 [16]–[18] and [24]–[25] (Lord Nicholls); *R (A)* (n 88) [23]–[24] (Lord Brown), applying *Farley*.

[98] *Farley* (n 97) [18] (Lord Nicholls), approved and applied in *R (A)* (n 88) [23]–[24] (Lord Brown). See also *Cart (QB)* (n 81) [40] (Laws LJ). See generally the helpful summary of cases where the courts will not consider clauses limiting rights of judicial review as 'true ouster clauses' in *R (Hillingdon) v Secretary of State for Transport* [2017] EWHC 121 (Admin), [2017] 1 WLR 2166 [40]–[48] (Cranston J).

[99] See *Smith v East Elloe Rural District Council* [1956] AC 736 (HL) and *Secretary of State for the Environment ex p Ostler* [1977] QB 122 (CA), discussed in *R v Cornwall County Council ex p Huntington* [1992] 3 All ER 566 (QB) and [1994] 1 All ER 694 (CA). *Huntingdon* was applied in *Hillingdon* (n 98) [40]–[48] (Cranston J). But see *R (Richards) v Pembrokeshire County Council* [2004] EWCA Civ 1000 [37] (Neuberger LJ), questioning the correctness of *Smith* and *Ostler*, but noting that the point was 'very probably not open in this court'. However, the courts will be slow to consider that a provision regulating challenges has the effect of precluding a defendant in criminal proceedings from challenging in those proceedings the legality of legislation under which he is prosecuted: see *Boddington* (n 88) 161F–162H (Lord Irvine LC), referring to the existence of a 'strong presumption' that Parliament intends that such a defence can be raised.

[100] *R v Bedwellty Justices ex p Williams* [1997] AC 225 (HL) 233E–G (Lord Cooke), citing *Page* (n 94). In *Page*, see in particular at 693C–E (Lord Griffiths) and 703D–G (Lord Browne-Wilkinson), both citing the decision in *Racal* (n 89). In *Racal*, see in particular in this regard at 383E–384D (Lord Diplock). However, it is questionable how far this principle, at least in relation to decisions of courts that do not act in effect as the 'alter ego' of the High Court, is reconcilable with Laws LJ's reasoning in *Cart (QB)* (n 81), in particular at [38]–[39] (which was generally endorsed on this issue by Lady Hale in *Cart (SC)* (n 81) at [30]). See also at [80], where Laws LJ considered the compatibility of his reasoning with this passage in *Racal*. As to the meaning of 'inferior courts', see n 94 above.

4.37   Otherwise, the courts will give a narrow construction to any words in ouster clauses that admit of ambiguity. The following have not sufficed to exclude judicial review:

4.37.1   Words such as 'final and conclusive', which have been held to mean only that there is no *appeal* against a decision and that it is binding as between the parties.[101]

4.37.2   A provision that a determination of a body 'shall not be called in question in any court of law'. It was held that, if made in error of law, a purported determination is a nullity and 'no determination at all'.[102]

4.37.3   Language providing that a 'decision ... shall not be subject to appeal or review in any court', on the basis of the same reasoning that, if made without jurisdiction, it is not a 'decision' at all.[103]

4.37.4   A deeming provision declaring the Upper Tribunal to be a 'superior court of record' (even assuming that being a 'superior court of record' would make a tribunal immune from judicial review, which it does not).[104]

4.38   By contrast, the following has been said to constitute 'an unambiguous ouster ... of any jurisdiction of the courts over' decisions of a certain tribunal: 'determinations, awards, orders and other decisions of the Tribunal (including decisions as to whether they have jurisdiction) shall not be subject to appeal or be liable to be questioned in any court'.[105]

---

[101] See, eg, *Gilmore* (n 84) 583 (Denning LJ): 'The word "final" is not enough. That only means "without appeal". It does not mean "without recourse to certiorari". It makes the decision final on the facts, but not final on the law'; *R (Revenue and Customs Commissioners) v Machell* [2005] EWHC 2593 (Admin), [2006] 1 WLR 609 [24] (Stanley Burnton J): 'the provision that a referee's determination is to be "final and conclusive" does not exclude judicial review. Provisions purporting to oust the review jurisdiction of the Courts are narrowly interpreted, although I doubt whether a narrow interpretation is necessary in this case. A decision is "final" if there is no appeal from it [citing *Gilmore*] ... "Conclusive" means no more than that the decision as made is binding as between the parties. There is no unambiguous exclusion of judicial review'.

[102] *Anisminic* (n 80), especially at 170D–F (Lord Reid).

[103] *Attorney General v Ryan* [1980] AC 718 (PC) 729H–730F (Lord Diplock), cited with approval in *R v Secretary of State for the Home Department ex p Fayed* [1998] 1 WLR 763 (CA) 771B–773C (Lord Woolf MR).

[104] See *Cart (QB)* (n 81) generally at [28]–[73] (Laws LJ), and especially at [32], [33], [68], [71] and [72].

[105] See *R (A)* (n 88) [23] (Lord Brown), referring to s 67(8) of the Regulation of Investigatory Powers Act 2000 regarding the Investigatory Powers Tribunal, although the provision was not under consideration in that case, and was apparently viewed as unobjectionable by the parties in any event on the basis that 'there is no constitutional (or article 6 [of the European Convention on Human Rights]) requirement for any right of appeal from an appropriate tribunal'. This conclusion was endorsed by the Divisional Court in *R (Privacy International) v Investigatory Powers Tribunal* [2017] EWHC 114 (Admin): see generally at [36]–[45] (Sir Brian Leveson P), recording his conclusion at [44], with

Implied Limitations on the Availability of Judicial Review

4.39   For the sake of completeness, one further point should be noted. Notwithstanding the above, the courts are willing to accept that, even in the absence of any form of ouster clause, the implications of a particular legislative scheme designed to regulate challenges to certain decisions may be such that the public interest is best served by the judicial review jurisdiction being exercised in respect of those decisions only in limited circumstances, to the extent required by the rule of law.[106]

The Presumption that Parliament Does Not Authorise a Tort

4.40   When Parliament authorises conduct which would otherwise constitute a tort against someone, it is permitting an interference with that person's rights. Accordingly, it is presumed that 'Parliament did not intend to authorise tortious conduct' in the absence of express language or necessary implication.[107]

Leggatt J concurring in the result at [62], but expressing 'reservations' about the conclusion reached (as to which see his judgment at [46]–[62]). The Divisional Court's decision was upheld on appeal: [2017] EWCA Civ 1868, [2018] HRLR 3.

[106] See *Cart (SC)* (n 81), where the Supreme Court held that the appropriate restriction on judicial review of unappealable decisions by the Upper Tribunal should be the test applied to second-tier appeals to the Court of Appeal. See, eg, at [89] (Lord Phillips): 'Where statute provides a structure under which a superior court or tribunal reviews decisions of an inferior court or tribunal, common law judicial review should be restricted so as to ensure, in the interest of making the best use of judicial resources, that this does not result in a duplication of judicial process that cannot be justified by the demands of the rule of law'; and to similar effect at [100] (Lord Brown): 'The rule of law is weakened, not strengthened, if a disproportionate part of the courts' resources is devoted to finding a very occasional grain of wheat on a threshing floor full of chaff.' See also *Sivasubramaniam* (n 84), where the Court of Appeal held that judicial review of refusals to grant permission to appeal by County Court judges should be allowed to proceed only in 'exceptional circumstances' (note that this is still applicable following *Cart (SC)*: see *R (Tummond) v Reading County Court* [2014] EWHC 1039 (Admin)).

[107] *Morris v Beardmore* [1981] AC 446 (HL) 455E–G (Lord Diplock), referring to the need for 'express language' to authorise such conduct; and 463D–F (Lord Scarman), referring to the need for 'express authorisation' or 'necessary implication'; *Manchester Ship Canal Co Ltd v United Utilities Water plc* [2014] UKSC 40, [2014] 1 WLR 2576 [2] (Lord Sumption): 'A statutory right to commit what would otherwise be a tort may of course be implied. But since this necessarily involves an interference with the rights of others, the test has always been restrictive. The implication must be more than convenient or reasonable. It must be necessary.'

The Presumption that Legislation
Does Not Bind the Crown

4.41 'There is a presumption that Acts of Parliament only bind the Crown by express words or necessary implication.'[108] For this reason, many Acts contain short provisions stating simply that the Act, or part of the Act, 'binds the Crown'.[109]

The Presumption against Retrospectivity

4.42 There is a 'general presumption that legislation is not intended to operate retrospectively. That presumption is based on concepts of fairness and legal certainty. These concepts require that accrued rights and the legal effect of past acts should not be altered by subsequent legislation'.[110]

4.43 Since legislation can be considered 'retrospective' in a variety of ways (as discussed below) and because the consequences of a retrospective interpretation will differ greatly depending upon the legislative context, the underpinning 'criterion of fairness' governs the strength of the presumption in every case where there is a 'suggested degree of retrospectivity'.[111] Accordingly, the courts have articulated the 'true principle' as being that:

> Parliament is presumed not to have intended to alter the law applicable to past events and transactions in a manner which is unfair to those concerned in them, unless a

---

[108] *Black* (n 51) [50] (Lady Hale), and see generally the discussion of the principle at [22]–[37], and its application to that case at [38]–[50]. The rationale for the presumption has been said to be that 'laws are made by rulers for subjects': see *BBC v Johns* [1965] Ch 32 (CA) 78F–G (Diplock LJ). Diplock LJ's treatment of the presumption in *BBC* was cited and discussed in *R (Revenue and Customs Commissioners) v Liverpool Coroner* [2014] EWHC 1586 (Admin), [2015] QB 481 [42] (Gross LJ, giving the judgment of the Court), as part of a wider discussion of the presumption at [38]–[46]. But see *Black* at [33]–[35], where Lady Hale urged Parliament to consider the merits of abolishing or reversing the presumption.

[109] See, eg, Legal Aid, Sentencing and Punishment of Offenders Act 2012, s 43: 'This Part binds the Crown.'

[110] See *Wilson v First County Trust Ltd (No 2)* [2003] UKHL 40, [2004] 1 AC 816 [98] (Lord Hope). See also at [153] (Lord Scott), stating that this presumption is 'part of a broader presumption that Parliament does not intend a statute to have an unfair or unjust effect'; and at [186] (Lord Rodger). See also the general statements of principle in *R v Docherty* [2016] UKSC 62, [2017] 1 WLR 181 [17] (Lord Hughes); *Walker v Innospec Ltd* [2017] UKSC 47 [22] (Lord Kerr); and *Flood v Times Newspapers Ltd (No 2)* [2017] UKSC 33, [2017] 1 WLR 1415 [53] (Lord Neuberger), stating that part of the 'rule of law' is a citizen's entitlement to rely on the 'assumption that the law will not be changed retroactively— ie in such a way as to undo retrospectively the law upon which they committed themselves'.

[111] *L'Office Cherifien des Phosphates v Yamashita-Shinnihon Steamship Co Ltd* [1994] 1 AC 486 (HL) 525F–H (Lord Mustill): 'Precisely how the single question of fairness will be answered in respect of a particular statute will depend on the interaction of several factors, each of them capable of varying from case to case. Thus, the degree to which the statute has retrospective effect is not a constant. Nor is

contrary intention appears. It is not simply a question of classifying an enactment as retrospective or not retrospective. Rather, it may well be a matter of degree—the greater the unfairness, the more it is to be expected that Parliament will make it clear if that is intended.[112]

4.44   The assessment of the strength of the presumption in every case has there-fore been said to involve 'a single indivisible question, to be answered largely as a matter of impression'.[113] However, the courts have also articulated a number of more specific presumptions to aid their analysis in this context. These more specific presumptions are designed to distinguish between the different kinds of 'retrospective' effects legislation may be considered to have. Thus (as discussed below), the courts have identified a presumption against *retroactive effect*, a presumption against *interference with vested rights* and a presumption that changes in the law do not affect *pending legal proceedings*. They have also drawn a distinc-tion between changes to the *substantive* law and changes to *procedural* law, with the latter being presumptively unproblematic.

4.45   Accordingly, Lord Rodger sought to encapsulate the single criterion of fairness, and these more specific presumptions, in a single test to be adopted in applying the broader presumption against retrospectivity: 'would the conse-quences of applying the statutory provision retroactively, or so as to affect vested rights or pending proceedings, be "so unfair" that Parliament could not have intended it to be applied in these ways?'[114]

4.46   Note that the presumption against retrospectivity applies not only to the construction of potentially retrospective legislation itself, but also to the 'construction of a statute delegating legislative powers', with such provisions

---

the value of the rights which the statute affects, or the extent to which that value is diminished or extin-guished by the retrospective effect of the statute. Again, the unfairness of adversely affecting the rights, and hence the degree of unlikelihood that this is what Parliament intended, will vary from case to case. So also will the clarity of the language used by Parliament, and the light shed on it by consideration of the circumstances in which the legislation was enacted. All these factors must be weighed together to provide a direct answer to the question whether the consequences of reading the statute with the suggested degree of retrospectivity are so unfair that the words used by Parliament cannot have been intended to mean what they might appear to say.' Lord Rodger described this approach as involving the application of 'a single criterion of fairness' to all provisions said to be retrospective: see *Wilson* (n 110) [200]. See also his speech at [186] as to the principle that the nature and severity of the retrospective effect of provisions will vary.

[112] *Secretary of State for Social Security v Tunnicliffe* [1991] 2 All ER 712 (CA) 724 (Staughton LJ), cited with approval in *Wilson* (n 110) at [19] (Lord Nicholls) and [200] (Lord Rodger), and also in *L'Office Cherifien* (n 111) 525D–F (Lord Mustill).

[113] *L'Office Cherifien* (n 111) 525H (Lord Mustill). Lord Mustill eschewed reliance upon any further presumptions (see especially at 525B–C).

[114] *Wilson* (n 110) [201] (Lord Rodger), continuing: 'In answering that question, a court would rightly have regard to the way the courts have applied the criterion of fairness when embodied in the various presumptions.' As to the various presumptions, see generally Lord Rodger's speech at [186]–[201] (helpfully summarised in *Laws v Society of Lloyd's* [2003] EWCA Civ 1887 [28] (Waller LJ)).

presumptively being read as not including a power to make retrospective legislation unless they make the inclusion of such a power 'clear'.[115]

The Presumption that Legislation is Not Intended to be 'Retroactive'

4.47   The courts have drawn a distinction between two types of provision which 'alter the existing rights and duties of those whom they affect'. First, there are what have been termed '*retroactive*' provisions. These are provisions 'which change the substantive law in relation to events in the past' and therefore 'actually affect the position before the legislation came into force'. Second, there are provisions which alter pre-existing rights and duties 'only prospectively, with effect from the date of commencement'.[116]

4.48   In relation to *retroactive* provisions, the courts have articulated a 'general presumption that legislation should not be treated as changing the substantive law in relation to events taking place prior to legislation coming into force'.[117] This is a 'powerful' presumption, 'so powerful indeed that any statutory provision, such as section 1 of the War Damage Act 1965, which is intended to apply in this way can be expected to say so expressly'. This is because of the obvious potential for such provisions to 'cause serious injustice'.[118]

The Presumption that Legislation Does Not Interfere with Vested Rights

4.49   In addition to the presumption against *retroactive* effect, there is also a 'similar but rather narrower presumption against interference with vested

---

[115] See *Secretary of State for Energy and Climate Change v Friends of the Earth* [2012] EWCA Civ 28, [2012] Env LR 25 [43] (Moses LJ), commenting that the presumption may even be stronger in the context of interpreting powers of delegation, citing Lord Woolf, Jeffrey Jowell and Andrew Le Sueur, *De Smith's Judicial Review*, 6th edn (London, Sweet & Maxwell, 2007) para 5-040.

[116] *Wilson* (n 110) [187]–[188] (Lord Rodger), and see generally his discussion of the distinction at [186]–[192]. Lord Rodger emphasised in this discussion that only the first type of provision is properly 'retrospective' in effect, albeit that this label has often been applied (somewhat inaptly) to the second type as well. Accordingly, throughout his speech Lord Rodger was careful to avoid calling the second type of provision 'retrospective'. Nevertheless, it is convenient to consider both types of provision together (as indeed Lord Rodger did and the courts often do), since it is clear from the discussion at paragraphs 4.43–4.45 above that the single criterion of fairness governs the interpretation of them both. Further, while the distinction may be of analytical assistance, in some cases it may be that a provision does 'not neatly fall into either category': see, eg, *Friends of the Earth* (n 115) [45] (Moses LJ).

[117] *Wainwright v Home Office* [2001] EWCA Civ 2081, [2002] QB 1334 [27] (Lord Woolf CJ), cited with approval in *Wilson* (n 110) [187] (Lord Rodger).

[118] *Wilson* (n 110) [187] (Lord Rodger). Section 1 of the War Damage Act 1965 abolished *existing* (as well as potential future) common law rights to receive compensation from the Crown in respect of certain damage to, or destruction of, property.

rights'.[119] Although this presumption does apply to retroactive provisions, it more commonly 'falls to be considered in relation to legislation which alters rights only for the future' (that is, the second type of provision identified at paragraph 4.47 above). It is weaker 'in practice' than the presumption against retroactive effect because 'it is more likely that Parliament intended to alter vested rights in this way than that it intended to make a retroactive change'.[120]

4.50   The narrower nature of the presumption is due to its application only to so-called 'vested rights': there is no 'general presumption that legislation does not alter the existing legal situation or existing rights', since the 'very purpose' of legislation is to change the existing law, often by 'altering existing rights for the future'.[121] The courts have not provided a clear definition of what constitutes a 'vested right', and hence when the presumption applies. Instead, applying circular reasoning, they 'have tended to attach the somewhat woolly label "vested" to those rights which they conclude should be protected from the effect of the new legislation'. As such, it is necessary to look to the principle of 'simple fairness' to determine whether the presumption is strong enough to overcome the otherwise apparent meaning of the statutory language.[122]

The Presumption that Legislation Does Not Affect Pending Proceedings

4.51   There is a 'further presumption, that legislation does not apply to actions which are pending at the time when it comes into force unless the language of the legislation compels the conclusion that Parliament intended that it should'. This 'narrower presumption' is 'a more limited version of the general presumption that

---

[119] *Wilson* (n 110) [19] (Lord Nicholls).

[120] ibid [194]–[195] (Lord Rodger).

[121] ibid [192] (Lord Rodger); and see at [98] (Lord Hope): 'the mere fact that a statute depends for its application in the future on events that have happened in the past does not offend against the presumption'. See also *McTier v Secretary of State for Education* [2017] EWHC 212 (Admin) [75] (Kerr J), contrasting the 'strong form' of retrospective effect 'where vested or accrued rights are retrospectively taken away' with 'a weak form involving only the application of an adjusted sanctions regime to conduct of the type which, in a broad sense, was already the subject of a similar though narrower sanctions regime at the time of the conduct complained of', and noting that '[t]he significance of the distinction between these two forms of retroactivity was emphasised' in *Wilson* at [98] (Lord Hope).

[122] *Wilson* (n 110) [196] (Lord Rodger), citing cases where attempts have been made 'without conspicuous success' to explain what is a 'vested right' and citing *L'Office Cherifien* (n 111) 525A (Lord Mustill) for the principle of 'simple fairness'. See also *Odelola v Secretary of State for the Home Department* [2009] UKHL 25, [2009] 1 WLR 1230 [31]–[33] (Lord Brown), discussing the 'difficulties inherent in the presumption itself' explored by Lord Rodger in *Wilson*, before applying the test of 'what simple fairness demands in the present context' by reference to Lord Mustill's speech in *L'Office Cherifien*; and *Manchester Ship Canal* (n 107) [56] (Lord Neuberger): 'the precise nature of a vested right is somewhat elusive', citing *Wilson* [196].

legislation is not intended to affect vested rights', and it similarly applies to all legislation, not just the retroactive kind. However, it will usually 'be that much harder to displace', '[s]ince the potential injustice of interfering with the rights of parties to actual proceedings is particularly obvious'.[123]

The Presumption that Purely Procedural Changes Apply to All Actions

4.52   The specific presumptions above apply to provisions which affect matters of *substantive* law, but not to provisions affecting matters of *procedure*. A litigant cannot generally be entitled to expect that no changes to matters of procedure (which are needed from time to time 'for the general benefit of litigants')[124] will occur during the course of proceedings in which he is engaged. Nor will such changes ordinarily be likely to cause any real injustice. Accordingly, it is presumed that a provision that deals with 'procedure only ... applies to all actions, whether commenced before or after the passing of the Act', unless the contrary intention is shown.[125] Evidential provisions are treated for these purposes as 'procedural', even in a penal context.[126]

4.53   Of course, in practice, 'the distinction between matters of substance and matters of pure procedure is ... not always ... easy to apply, especially in relation to legislation on limitation or prescription', where an apparently 'procedural' change may have more of an impact on a party's position than one that would be categorised as 'substantive'. As ever in this context, the 'single criterion of fairness' will need to be applied in each case.[127]

---

[123] *Wilson* (n 110) [198] (Lord Rodger), citing *Zainal bin Hashim v Government of Malaysia* [1980] AC 734 (PC) 742C–D (Viscount Dilhorne), who stated: 'for pending actions to be affected by retrospective legislation, the language of the enactment must be such that no other conclusion is possible than that that was the intention of the legislature'.

[124] *R (Parekh) v Upper Tribunal* [2013] EWCA Civ 679, [2013] CP Rep 38 [16] (Davis LJ).

[125] *Wright v Hale* (1860) 6 H&N 227, 232; 158 ER 94, 96 (Wilde B), cited with approval in *Wilson* (n 110) [199] (Lord Rodger). Lord Rodger's speech was applied in *Parekh* (n 124) [16] (Davis LJ), stating: 'The normal presumption ... is that procedural provisions take effect from the date that they come into effect and apply to current as well as to future proceedings. In effect, you conduct the proceedings according to the rules of conduct relating to the action for the time being in force.'

[126] See *Kensington International Ltd v Republic of Congo* [2007] EWHC 1632 (Comm) [74]–[80] (Gross J), holding that s 13 of the Fraud Act 2006, an evidential provision affecting the privilege against self-incrimination, applied to proceedings relating to conduct occurring prior to the section coming into force. This was upheld on appeal: [2007] EWCA Civ 1128, [2008] 1 WLR 1144 [68]–[72] (Moore-Bick LJ), [91] (May LJ, agreeing).

[127] *Wilson* (n 110) [200] (Lord Rodger). See also two of the cases cited in this paragraph by Lord Rodger: *L'Office Cherifien* (n 111) 527G–528C (Lord Mustill), doubting the appropriateness of a strict application of this distinction, and whether the rights he was considering could 'unequivocally' be categorised as substantive or procedural, and preferring, 'whilst keeping the distinction well in view ... to look to the practical value and nature of the rights presently involved as a step towards an assessment of the unfairness of taking them away after the event'; and

The Presumption of Compatibility or Conformity with International Law

4.54   International law does not of itself form part of English law. However, there is a 'presumption that Parliament does not intend to act in breach of international law'.[128] It is also presumed that where legislation is passed in order to give effect to international law, it should be given a meaning that conforms with the law to which it is intended to give effect.[129] These presumptions are discussed in detail at Chapter 9.22–9.36.

Territoriality: Presumptions as to Extent and Application[130]

4.55   When considering the geographical relevance of an enactment, it is important to take into account the distinction between the concepts of *extent* and *application*.[131] The *extent* of an enactment relates to the territories in which it

Yew Bon Tew v Kenderaan Bas Mara [1983] 1 AC 553 (PC) 558G–559A (Lord Brightman): 'these expressions "retrospective" and "procedural", though useful in a particular context, are equivocal and therefore can be misleading. A statute which is retrospective in relation to one aspect of a case (e.g., because it applies to a pre-statute cause of action) may at the same time be prospective in relation to another aspect of the same case (e.g., because it applies only to the post-statute commencement of proceedings to enforce that cause of action); and an Act which is procedural in one sense may in particular circumstances do far more than regulate the course of proceedings, because it may, on one interpretation, revive or destroy the cause of action itself'.

[128]   *Salomon v Commissioners of Customs and Excise* [1967] 2 QB 116 (CA) 143F–G (Diplock LJ), in the context of treaty obligations.

[129]   *R (Adams) v Secretary of State for Justice* [2011] UKSC 18, [2012] 1 AC 48 [14] (Lord Phillips), in the context of treaty obligations.

[130]   For a detailed treatment of this topic, see Oliver Jones, *Bennion on Statutory Interpretation*, 6th edn (London, LexisNexis, 2013), Part V 'Extent and Application of Acts', 305–69.

[131]   See *R (Al-Skeini) v Secretary of State for Defence* [2007] UKHL 26, [2008] 1 AC 153 [86] (Lady Hale): 'there is an important difference between *the legal system* to which any Act of Parliament extends and the *people* and *conduct* to which it applies', citing *Lawson v Serco Ltd* [2006] UKHL 3, [2006] 1 All ER 823 [1] (Lord Hoffmann): 'It is true that section 244(1) [of the Employment Rights Act 1996] says that the Act "extends" to England and Wales and Scotland ("Great Britain"). But that means only that it forms part of the law of Great Britain and does not form part of the law of any other territory (like Northern Ireland or the Channel Islands) for which Parliament could have legislated. It tells us nothing about the connection, if any, which an employee or his employment must have with Great Britain [for him to be an "employee" within the meaning of that Act].' Lady Hale continued in *Al-Skeini* at [87]: 'The Human Rights Act [1998] extends to England and Wales, Scotland and Northern Ireland: see section 22(6). But by itself this tells us nothing about the public authorities to which section 6(1) applies, or about the acts to which it applies, or about the people for whose benefit it applies.'

forms part of the law. The *application* of an enactment relates to the persons and matters which it seeks to regulate. Although application is not a purely territorial concept, it is the territorial aspects of the application of enactments which are considered here.

4.56 As ever, both the extent and application of an enactment are ultimately a matter of the construction of the particular enactment in question. However, certain presumptions apply to assist in this regard, as discussed below.

4.57 *Presumption as to extent*: unless the contrary intention is clear from the statute, it is presumed that Acts of the UK Parliament are intended to extend to the whole of the UK (that is, England, Scotland, Wales and Northern Ireland), but no further.[132] This follows from the primary role of Parliament, which is to act as the supreme legislative body for the whole of the UK, by whose population the members of the House of Commons are elected. It is therefore taken, in the ordinary course, to intend to make law for all of the UK's constituent territories,[133] though it will sometimes make clear that it intends to legislate only for certain territories[134] or not to legislate for certain of them.[135] Less frequently, Parliament will also seek to legislate (or, more usually, delegate power to legislate) for other territories for which it has the power to do so, but it will usually expressly state such an intention.[136]

---

[132] See *Al Sabah v Grupo Torras SA* [2005] UKPC 1, [2005] 2 AC 333 [13] (Lord Walker), referring to the 'long-standing practice, in construing statutes of the Westminster Parliament, of presuming that their intended territorial extent is limited to the United Kingdom, unless it is clear that a wider extent is intended'. He remarked that due to 'increasingly precise drafting techniques', the presumption 'appears to have become stronger over the years'.

[133] See *Al-Skeini* (n 131) [38] (Lord Rodger), citing 'the accepted rule of interpretation' as stated by Francis Bennion, *Bennion on Statutory Interpretation*, 4th edn (London, Butterworths, 2002) 282: 'Unless the contrary intention appears, Parliament is taken to intend an Act to extend to each territory of the United Kingdom but not to any territory outside the United Kingdom' (the equivalent passage in Jones, *Statutory Interpretation* (2013) (n 130) is at section 106, 314). Note the reference by Lord Rodger to the 'usual, slightly puzzling, practice' of specifically providing that legislation extends to Northern Ireland having been followed in the case of the Human Rights Act 1998—a puzzling practice because, in view of the presumption as to extent, this would be taken as read in any event.

[134] See, eg, Employment Rights Act 1996, s 244(1): 'Subject to the following provisions, this Act extends to England and Wales and Scotland but not to Northern Ireland', with s 244(2) stating that certain sections 'extend to England and Wales only'.

[135] See, eg, Poisons Act 1972, s 14(2): 'This Act shall not extend to Northern Ireland.'

[136] See, eg, in relation to the Channel Islands *R (Barclay) v Lord Chancellor (No 2)* [2014] UKSC 54, [2015] AC 276, [12] (Lady Hale): 'The United Kingdom Parliament has power to legislate for the islands, but Acts of Parliament do not extend to the Islands automatically, but only by express mention or necessary implication. The more common practice is for an Act of Parliament to give power to extend its application to the Islands by Order in Council. It is the practice to consult the Islands before any United Kingdom legislation is extended to them.'

4.58   By contrast, it would be both inappropriate, and serve no purpose, for Parliament to seek to legislate for territories it has no power to govern, and so it is taken not to intend to do so.[137]

The Presumption against Extraterritorial Application

4.59   'Whether an English statute applies extraterritorially depends on its construction. There is, however, a presumption against extraterritorial application which is more or less strong depending on the subject matter.'[138] The 'presumption against extraterritoriality'[139] has been expressed by the Supreme Court in the following terms:

> Unless the contrary intention appears ... an enactment applies to all persons and matters within the territory to which it extends, but not to any other persons and matters.[140]

4.60   The presumption has particular force in relation to the acts of foreigners located outside the UK. This is because the presumption is 'underpinned by considerations of international comity and law',[141] and '[t]he near universal rule of international law is that sovereignty ... is territorial, that is to say it may be exercised only in relation to persons and things within the territory of the state concerned or in respect of its own nationals'.[142] Accordingly, it would usually be 'contrary to ordinary principles of international law governing the jurisdiction of states'[143] and 'objectionable in terms of international comity ... for Parliament to assert its authority over the subjects of another sovereign who are not within the

---

[137] See *R (Carson) v Secretary of State for Work and Pensions* [2002] EWHC 978 (Admin) [19] (Stanley Burnton J): 'The comity of nations is doubtless one basis for this presumption: one state should not be taken to interfere with the sovereignty of another state by enacting legislation extending to its territory. Another is practicality: most legislation cannot practically be applied to those present in another state.' But although this is undoubtedly correct, it appears—with respect—that the learned judge was actually concerned with questions of application rather than extent. This point was not considered on appeal (see [2003] EWCA Civ 797, [2003] 3 All ER 577 [15] (Laws LJ)).

[138] *Cox v Ergo Versicherung AG* [2014] UKSC 22, [2014] AC 1379 [27] (Lord Sumption).

[139] *Masri v Consolidated Contractors International (UK) Ltd (No 4)* [2009] UKHL 43, [2010] 1 AC 90 [16] ('*Masri (No 4) (SC)*') (Lord Mance).

[140] ibid [10] (Lord Mance), citing Bennion, *Statutory Interpretation* (2002) (n 133) section 128, 306 (in Jones, *Statutory Interpretation* (2013) (n 130), see at section 128, 339). Lord Mance caveated this, however, stating that: 'The principle may not apply, at any rate with the same force, to English subjects', as to which see the discussion below at paragraph 4.61. See also *Lawson* (n 131) [6] (Lord Hoffmann): 'The general principle of construction is, of course, that legislation is prima facie territorial'; and *King v Director of Serious Fraud Office* [2009] UKHL 17, [2009] 1 WLR 718 [32] (Lord Phillips), referring to 'the well-established canon of construction that requires clear language if an Act is to be given extra-territorial effect'.

[141] *Masri (No 4) (SC)* (n 139) [16] (Lord Mance).

[142] *Société Eram Shipping Co Ltd v Cie Internationale de Navigation* [2003] UKHL 30, [2004] 1 AC 260 [80] (Lord Millett).

[143] *Cox* (n 138) [27] (Lord Sumption), citing as exceptions to this general rule the application of legislation to acts of a state's 'own citizens abroad and certain crimes of universal jurisdiction such as torture and genocide'.

United Kingdom', as well as being 'futile in practice'. Accordingly, 'in the absence of any indication to the contrary, a court will interpret legislation as not being intended to affect such people'.[144] In line with these principles, the presumption against extraterritoriality is often more narrowly—though also more forcefully— framed in terms only of avoiding exorbitant jurisdiction over foreigners abroad. Lord Scarman expressed the presumption as follows:

[U]nless the contrary is expressly enacted or so plainly implied that the courts must give effect to it, United Kingdom legislation is applicable only to British subjects or to foreigners who by coming to the United Kingdom, whether for a short or a long time, have made themselves subject to British jurisdiction.[145]

4.61 In view of these conceptual underpinnings, the presumption against extraterritoriality may carry less force in relation to the applicability of legislation to British persons abroad, since 'there can be no objection in principle to Parliament legislating for British citizens outside the United Kingdom, provided that the particular legislation does not offend against the sovereignty of other states'.[146] Nevertheless, Parliament will usually not seek to legislate for the conduct of British citizens or companies abroad, so as not to interfere with the territorial sovereignty of other states and because legislation of this kind 'would usually be unnecessary and would often be, in any event, ineffective'. However, sometimes it will have a 'legitimate interest' in doing so and will intend to do so.[147] Whether it will be taken to intend this result will depend on whether this appears from the express words of the statute or an inference from its 'language ... object ... subject-matter or history'.[148] Where an Act is ambiguous, the court will consider the 'overall nature and purpose' of the legislation,[149] and will ask:

[W]hether, on a fair interpretation the statute in question is intended to apply to [British persons] only in the United Kingdom or also, to some extent at least, beyond the territorial limits of the United Kingdom.[150]

---

[144] *Al-Skeini* (n 131) [45] (Lord Rodger). See to similar effect *Lawson* (n 131) [6] (Lord Hoffmann): 'The United Kingdom rarely purports to legislate for the whole world. Some international crimes, like torture, are an exception. But usually such an exorbitant exercise of legislative power would be both ineffectual and contrary to the comity of nations.'

[145] *Clark (Inspector of Taxes) v Oceanic Contractors Inc* [1983] 2 AC 130 (HL) 145D–E, citing *Ex p Blain* (1879) 12 Ch D 522 (CA) 526 (James LJ) and 531–32 (Cotton LJ). This statement by Lord Scarman was cited with approval in *Cox* (n 138) [27] (Lord Sumption) and *Al-Skeini* (n 131) [46] (Lord Rodger). Note that at 145E–F, Lord Scarman clarified that for UK legislation to apply to a person within the jurisdiction: 'Presence, not residence, is the test.' See also *Office of Fair Trading v Lloyds TSB Bank plc* [2007] UKHL 48, [2008] 1 AC 316 [4] (Lord Hoffmann): 'extraterritorial effect means seeking to regulate the conduct or affect the liabilities of people over whom the United Kingdom has no jurisdiction'.

[146] *Al-Skeini* (n 131) [46] (Lord Rodger).

[147] ibid [49] (Lord Rodger).

[148] ibid [46] (Lord Rodger), citing P St J Langan, *Maxwell on the Interpretation of Statutes*, 12th edn (London, Sweet & Maxwell, 1969) 171.

[149] *Al-Skeini* (n 131) [49] and [52] (Lord Rodger), citing Langan (n 148) 169.

[150] *Al-Skeini* (n 131) [47] (Lord Rodger).

4.62 It is important, however, not to overstate the force of the general presumption against extraterritoriality, even in relation to acts of foreigners located abroad.[151] Although the presumption will provide 'the starting point',[152] in every case (as always), the question of an enactment's intended application is ultimately a question of the construction of that enactment.[153] As Lord Scarman emphasised, his statement of the presumption (cited at paragraph 4.60 above) was intended as 'a rule of construction only'.[154] And in the same case, Lord Wilberforce stated that:

> [T]he 'territorial principle' … is really a rule of construction of statutes expressed in general terms … which as … a 'broad principle', requires an inquiry to be made as to the person with respect to whom Parliament is presumed, in the particular case, to be legislating. Who, it is to be asked, is within the legislative grasp, or intendment, of the statute under consideration?[155]

4.63 The context will be particularly important in determining whether extraterritorial effect is intended; as Lord Sumption has stated, the presumption is 'more or less strong depending on the subject matter'.[156] In the modern world, the acceptability of exercising jurisdiction over those abroad can be expected to depend on the overall degree of connection of a person or matter with the UK (and particularly with matters in relation to which the UK's jurisdiction is already readily accepted) and not simply on where a person is located at a given moment.[157] Where it is clear overall from the statutory wording and context that

---

[151] Though also not to understate it: see *Masri (No 4) (SC)* (n 139) in the Court of Appeal [2008] EWCA Civ 876, [2010] 1 AC 90 ('*Masri (No 4) (CA)*') [16] (Sir Anthony Clarke MR) and [80] (Lawrence Collins LJ), both stating that Lawrence Collins LJ 'may have understated the current relevance of the presumption against extraterritoriality' in *Masri v Consolidated Contractors International (UK) Ltd (No 2)* [2008] EWCA Civ 303, [2009] QB 450 when he stated at [31] that: 'nowadays the presumption has little force and it is simply a matter of construction'.

[152] *Masri (No 4) (CA)* (n 151) [16] (Sir Anthony Clarke MR).

[153] ibid. See also *Bilta (UK) Ltd (in Liquidation) v Nazir* [2015] UKSC 23, [2016] AC 1 [212] (Lord Toulson and Lord Hodge): 'In the past it was held as a universal principle that a United Kingdom statute applied only to United Kingdom subjects or foreigners present in and thus subjecting themselves to a United Kingdom jurisdiction unless the Act expressly or by necessary implication provided to the contrary … That principle has evolved into a question of interpreting the particular statute' (citations omitted). The cases cited show that this statement is not to be understood as denying the existence of any presumption, but rather as emphasising that in every case the question is one of 'the construction of the relevant statute'.

[154] *Clark* (n 145) 145E (Lord Scarman).

[155] ibid 152C–D (Lord Wilberforce), citing *Blain* (n 145) 526 (James LJ). This passage in *Clark* was cited with approval in *Lawson* (n 131) [6] (Lord Hoffmann), stating: 'In principle … the question is always one of the construction of [the relevant enactment]'; and in *Masri (No 4) (SC)* (n 139) [10] (Lord Mance), who also used the language of 'intendment' at [19] and [26]. See also *Agassi v Robinson (Inspector of Taxes)* [2006] UKHL 23, [2006] 1 WLR 1380 [16]–[17] (Lord Scott), citing with approval both Lord Scarman's rule of construction (emphasising the need to understand it as such) and this statement of Lord Wilberforce.

[156] *Cox* (n 138) [27] (Lord Sumption).

[157] See *Masri (No 4) (SC)* (n 139) [19] (Lord Mance), though ultimately he held that the 'presumption of territoriality' had not been displaced in that case: see at [26]. See also *Office of Fair Trading*

it is appropriate to do so, the presumption will not prevent the courts from construing statutes to encompass persons, conduct, matters or transactions outside the UK.[158]

4.64 Even where legislation is construed to apply extraterritorially, its application in a given case may also be discretionary, and it may be appropriate for the courts to take into account the degree of connection a matter has with the UK as a highly material factor in the exercise of its discretion.[159]

The Presumption against Extraterritoriality in Statutory Criminal Offences

4.65 One aspect of the presumption against extraterritorial effect is the particular 'well-established presumption' applicable in the context of construing

(n 145), where Lord Hope held that a 'transaction' in s 75(1) of the Consumer Credit Act 1974 could include a transaction which took place abroad and was governed by foreign law, in particular because there was no contrary indication in the language of the subsection and because this accorded with the policy behind the legislation of consumer protection. In this context, at [11]–[12] he stated: 'As there is no indication to the contrary, the ordinary territorial limitation applies. [Section 75(1)] states what the law is in regard to transactions which have a sufficient nexus with the United Kingdom for them to be subject to its laws ... The answer to the question ... is to be found in the words of the statute, not in any presumption either way as to its application extraterritoriality'; and see also, eg, *Lawson* (n 131) [36]–[40] (Lord Hoffmann), who appeared to accept in broad terms that the strength of an employment relationship's connection with the UK was the key underlying principle in determining whether Employment Tribunals were intended to have jurisdiction in unfair dismissal claims brought by employees working outside Great Britain.

[158] See, eg, *Office of Fair Trading* (n 145) and *Lawson* (n 131), discussed in the previous note. See also, eg, *Re Paramount Airways Ltd* [1993] Ch 223 (CA), in particular at 235F–239F (Sir Donald Nicholls VC), holding that the words 'any person' in s 238(2) of the Insolvency Act 1986 (in relation to court orders to set aside transactions at an undervalue) were intended to be given their 'literal, and natural, meaning' and not to be restricted to persons with any particular kind of connection with England and Wales. As such, the court had jurisdiction under that section to make an order against a bank registered abroad which had no place of business in the UK. The reasoning in this case was followed in *Bilta* (n 153) in relation to s 213 of the same Act: see at [110] (Lord Sumption) and [214] (Lord Toulson and Lord Hodge). Compare *Re Tucker (A Bankrupt)* [1990] Ch 148 (CA), where it was held that the courts' power to summon 'any person' under s 25(1) of the Bankruptcy Act 1914 did not apply extraterritorially, even to British subjects. See also, eg, *Agassi* (n 155), in particular at [17] (Lord Scott) and [30]–[35] (Lord Mance), where the House of Lords held that foreign sportspeople and entertainers were liable to pay tax on payments received in connection with their UK commercial activities; *Dar Al Arkan Real Estate Development Co v Al Refai* [2014] EWCA Civ 715, [2015] 1 WLR 135, where the Court held that committal proceedings could be brought against the director of a company in respect of the company's contempt in proceedings before the English court, even though the director was domiciled and resident abroad; and *Al-Skeini* (n 131), where the House of Lords held that s 6 of the Human Rights Act 1998 applied to certain acts of UK public authorities carried out abroad.

[159] See *Paramount Airways* (n 158) 239F–240F (Sir Donald Nicholls VC). By contrast, in some cases there will be no scope for any discretion to be exercised on the basis of considerations of extraterritoriality: see *Lawson* (n 131) [24] (Lord Hoffmann).

statutory criminal offences that 'in the absence of clear and specific words to the contrary', an enactment is 'not intended to make conduct taking place outside the territorial jurisdiction of the Crown an offence triable in an English criminal court'.[160] In view of the rules of international law,[161] '[t]he presumption against a parliamentary intention to make acts *done by foreigners abroad* offences triable by English criminal courts is even stronger'.[162]

4.66   It is important to note, however, that these are not technical and inflexible rules, but merely presumptions designed to respect the interests of international comity. Accordingly, particularly when dealing with crimes that may have a multinational dimension, the courts have espoused a 'modern approach to jurisdiction, involving an adjustment to the circumstances of international criminality'.[163] This means that:

> [W]here a substantial measure of the activities constituting a crime takes place within the jurisdiction, then the courts of England and Wales have jurisdiction to try the crime, save only where it can seriously be argued on a reasonable view that these activities should, on the basis of international comity, be dealt with by another country.[164]

4.67   In all cases, as with other instances of the presumption against extraterritoriality (discussed above), the question of territorial limitation is ultimately a matter of construction in the context of each particular enactment.[165]

---

[160] *Air-India v Wiggins* [1980] 1 WLR 815 (HL) 819A–C (Lord Diplock), continuing by citing *Cox v Army Council* [1963] AC 48 (HL) 67 (Viscount Simonds): 'apart from those exceptional cases in which specific provision is made in regard to acts committed abroad, the whole body of the criminal law of England deals only with acts committed in England'. For an application of the presumption in the slightly broader context of the scope of evidence gathering powers under the Police and Criminal Evidence Act 1984, see *Rottman* (n 26) [67]–[68] (Lord Hutton).

[161] See *Serious Organised Crime Agency v Perry* [2012] UKSC 35, [2013] 1 AC 182 [94] (Lord Phillips): 'Subject to limited exceptions, it is contrary to international law for country A to purport to make criminal conduct in country B committed by persons who are not citizens of country A'; and see generally the discussion above at paragraphs 4.60–4.61.

[162] *Air-India* (n 160) 819C (Lord Diplock).

[163] *R v Rogers* [2014] EWCA Crim 1680, [2015] 1 WLR 1017 [54] (Treacy LJ, giving the judgment of the Court), having cited at [53] the judgment of Lord Woolf CJ in *R v Smith (Wallace Duncan) (No 4)* [2004] EWCA Crim 631, [2004] QB 1418 [55].

[164] *R v Rogers* (n 163) [39] (Treacy LJ, giving the judgment of the Court), summarising Lord Woolf CJ's conclusions in *Smith* (n 163).

[165] See, eg, *R v Sissen* [2001] 1 WLR 902 (CA), in particular at [37]–[39] (Ouseley J, giving the judgment of the Court), in the context of an offence relating to a breach of EU Regulations.

The Presumption of Regularity

4.68 Finally, it is worth noting an *evidential* presumption followed by the courts in applying legislation, sometimes referred to as the 'presumption of regularity'[166] or the 'presumption of validity'.[167]

4.69 'The presumption of regularity is the principle that public law acts stand and are to be regarded and relied upon as lawful unless and until quashed as being unlawful by the court'.[168] The presumption applies to 'both administrative and subordinate legislative acts'.[169]

4.70 The courts have stressed that the presumption is an 'evidential matter at the interlocutory stage' rather than a '*rule* that lends validity to invalid acts. In a practical world, however, a court will usually assume that subordinate legislation, and administrative acts, are valid unless it is persuaded otherwise'.[170]

---

[166] See, eg, *McEldowney v Forde* [1971] AC 632 (HL) 655F–G (Lord Pearson): 'When the Minister has made a regulation, and purports to have made it under section 1 (3) of the Act, the presumption of regularity (omnia praesumuntur rite esse acta) applies and the regulation is assumed prima facie to be intra vires. But if the validity of the regulation is challenged, and it is contended that the regulation was made otherwise than for the specified purposes, the courts will have to decide this issue, however difficult the task may be for them in some circumstances.' The Latin words used by Lord Pearson translate as: 'all things are presumed to be properly done'.

[167] See, eg, *R v Budimir* [2010] EWCA Crim 1486, [2011] QB 744 [37]–[38] (Lord Judge CJ, giving the judgment of the Court), citing *Smith* (n 99) 769–70 (Lord Radcliffe).

[168] *R (Archway Sheet Metal Works Josif Family Trustees) v Secretary of State for Communities and Local Government* [2015] EWHC 794 (Admin) [44] (Dove J), also citing (at [45]) *Smith* (n 99) 769–70 (Lord Radcliffe).

[169] *Budimir* (n 167) [37]–[38] (Lord Judge CJ, giving the judgment of the Court).

[170] *Boddington* (n 88) 174B (Lord Steyn), citing with approval the speech of Lord Hoffmann in *R v Wicks* [1998] AC 92 (HL). In that case, at 115E–H, referring to the speech of Lord Diplock in *F Hoffmann-La Roche & Co AG v Secretary of State for Trade and Industry* [1975] AC 295 (HL), Lord Hoffmann stated: 'The presumption of validity to which Lord Diplock referred was in my view an evidential matter at the interlocutory stage and the presumption existed pending a final decision by the court. Lord Diplock was not putting forward the sweeping proposition that subordinate legislation must be treated for all purposes as valid until set aside.'

5

Interaction of Legislation

5.1 This chapter addresses the general ways in which one piece of legislation may interact with another, by expressly or impliedly changing its content, form or effect, or by affecting its interpretation. The specific and far-reaching effects of three particular statutes on the interpretation and application of other legislation are discussed in Chapter 8 (the Interpretation Act 1978), Chapter 10 (the Human Rights Act 1998) and Chapter 12 (the European Communities Act 1972).

5.2 In summary, the following principles apply in this area:

5.2.1 Parliament has the power to legislate to alter existing legislation. This exercise of this power is known as 'amendment'. When it uses this power (expressly or impliedly) to abolish existing legislation, this is known as 'repeal'. When it repeals legislative provisions while also re-enacting them in the same or similar form in order to tidy up the statute book, this is known as 'consolidation'.

5.2.2 Secondary legislation may also be used to amend existing legislation where the parent Act grants a power that allows this. However, such powers are usually restrictively construed.

5.2.3 It is generally permissible, as an aid to its interpretation, to refer to earlier law as part of the *context* in which legislation is made. Otherwise, earlier legislation cannot generally be used to interpret later legislation, as a piece of legislation is generally intended to be interpreted as a standalone instrument.

5.2.4 It is generally not permissible *at all* to construe earlier legislation by reference to later legislation.

5.2.5 Exceptions to the general rules in paragraphs 5.2.3 and 5.2.4 apply: (i) where there is express reference in one Act to another; (ii) where consolidation and amendment occur; (iii) where Acts are *in pari materia*;[1] and (iv) in relation to the interactions between secondary legislation and the parent Act under which it was made.

---

[1] As to when statutes are to be considered *in pari materia*, see paragraph 5.31 below.

Amendment, Repeal and Consolidation

Amendment

5.3   Many Acts contain provisions which are intended to amend existing legislation. Where a substantial part of an Act's purpose is to make amendments to specific statutes, its long title may state this expressly.[2] Amendments may be classified
into two forms:[3]

5.3.1   *Textual amendment*: that is, where an Act provides that stated text
(whether words, phrases or whole provisions) is to be inserted into, substituted for
or removed from the text of specified earlier statutes.[4] Given the clarity that this
approach to amendment provides, this is the usual practice for making amendments in modern times.

5.3.2   *Non-textual amendment*: that is, where an Act evinces an intention to alter
existing statute law, but does not expressly identify the statutory provisions to be
amended and/or any specific textual alteration of the earlier Act. This intention
may be express[5] or it may be implied.[6] However, the scope for implied amendment

---

[2] See, eg, the long title of the Digital Economy Act 2010: 'An Act … to amend the Video Recordings
Act 1984.' However, caution must be exercised in using a statement of this kind in a long title as an aid
to the interpretation of any particular section of an Act: see *R v G* [2003] UKHL 50, [2004] 1 AC 1034
[48]–[49] (Lord Steyn).

[3] For further discussion of amendments generally, including other ways in which they may be classified, see, eg, Helen Xanthaki, *Drafting Legislation* (Oxford, Hart Publishing, 2014) ch 12, 223–41; and
Oliver Jones, *Bennion on Statutory Interpretation*, 6th edn (London, LexisNexis, 2013) sections 77–80,
261–68.

[4] See *R v Brown (Northern Ireland)* [2013] UKSC 43, [2013] 4 All ER 860 [33]–[36] (Lord Kerr),
referring to the concept of 'textual amendment' by reference to Francis Bennion, *Bennion on Statutory
Interpretation*, 5th edn (London, LexisNexis, 2008) 290. For the relevant passage in Jones,
Statutory Interpretation (2013) (n 3) see at section 78, 263–66.

[5] Jones, *Statutory Interpretation* (2013) (n 3) refers to this concept, where the intention to amend
is express, as 'indirect express amendment' (see section 79, 266–67), a term that was used in *Kennedy
v Information Commissioner* [2012] EWCA Civ 317, [2012] 1 WLR 3524 [40]–[43] (Ward LJ) to
describe the way in which it was considered that a later Act had amended an earlier one. On appeal
to the Supreme Court ([2014] UKSC 2, [2015] AC 455 ('*Kennedy (SC)*')), the Court did not expressly
consider this concept, but the majority did reject the idea that the later Act could be used to construe
the earlier (which in substance is what Ward LJ had done): see at [33] (Lord Mance), with whom
Lord Neuberger and Lord Clarke agreed, and [152] (Lord Sumption), agreeing with Lord Mance.
See further the discussion of 'indirect referential amendment' in Xanthaki, *Drafting Legislation* (2014)
(n 3) 236–37.

[6] An implied amendment may occur either by way of 'implied repeal' (as discussed at paragraphs
5.15–5.16 below) or by way of an 'enactment by implication' (see *IRC v Dowdall, O'Mahoney & Co
Ltd* [1952] AC 401 (HL) 420–21 (Lord Reid), discussed in *Kirkness v John Hudson & Co Ltd* [1955] AC
696 (HL) 736 (Lord Reid) as follows: 'There … the later Act could only have effect if it could be held
to enact an amendment. But it was held that it could not be so interpreted'). Implied enactment can
arise out of an assumption by Parliament as to the meaning of existing law. Such assumptions do not

is very limited,[7] and it will certainly not be found to have occurred where its effect would be 'to alter the law retrospectively'.[8]

5.4 Note that where an enactment is referred to in other enactments, the reference is to the enactment as amended (unless the contrary intention appears).[9]

5.5 *Construction of amended legislation*: the starting point is that 'amended legislation is to be construed as a whole in its revised form',[10] and the court should look first to construe the 'amended statute itself as if it were a free-standing piece of legislation'.[11] However, it is permissible, and indeed 'may be necessary', to refer to the history of any amendments as an aid to the construction of the amended legislation.[12]

---

generally change the law (although they may give rise to an implied interpretive directive about existing legislation in appropriate cases: see paragraphs 5.39–5.42 below), and the courts are not precluded '[i]n the ordinary course … from ruling that the parliamentary understanding was mistaken' (*R (Jackson) v Attorney General* [2005] UKHL 56, [2006] 1 AC 262 [68] (Lord Nicholls), and see also *R v H* [2007] UKHL 7, [2007] 2 AC 270 [93] (Lord Mance), both citing *West Midland Baptist (Trust) Association Inc v Birmingham Corporation* [1970] AC 874 (HL) 898F–G (Lord Reid)). However, it may be that in an exceptional case a parliamentary assumption inherent in an enactment will alter the law 'if the provisions of the enactment were such that they would only be workable if the law was as Parliament supposed it to be' (*West Midland* 898G–H (Lord Reid), applied in *Jackson* [68] (Lord Nicholls): 'the later legislation … simply could not have had effect if the earlier legislation was not validly enacted'). See generally the discussion of implied enactment in *R (W) v Lambeth London Borough Council* [2002] EWCA Civ 613, [2002] 2 All ER 901 [35]–[41] (Brooke LJ).

[7] It is clear that implied amendment will only be found to have occurred very rarely, since: (i) it will entail either (or both) implied enactment (discussed in the previous note) or implied repeal (as to which see paragraphs 5.15–5.16 below), both of which are themselves rare occurrences; (ii) given the existence of presumptions against implied repeal and implied change in the common law (see Chapter 4.13–4.16), it would be surprising if any other form of implied change in the law would be readily found to have occurred; and (iii) as a matter of practice, the skill of modern legislative draftsmen suggests that such a finding will rarely be appropriate, as intended amendment will usually be effected textually and expressly (as with repeal—see paragraph 5.14 below); drafting errors are rare and, as stated in Xanthaki, *Drafting Legislation* (2014) (n 3) 225: 'Implied amendment presupposes a drafting error.' In this regard, see, eg, *R (Kaziu) v Secretary of State for the Home Department* [2015] EWCA 1195, [2016] 1 WLR 673 [56] (Sales LJ): 'It would require a very clear indication indeed from the way in which section 40 of the Act was amended and section 40A was added before it could be inferred that Parliament also intended impliedly to amend section 6, which it left untouched. There is no such indication. As Mr Moffett points out, generally an amendment does not affect the construction of the unamended parts of a statute as originally enacted', citing in support of this final sentence *R (Brown) v Secretary of State for the Home Department* [2015] UKSC 8, [2015] 1 WLR 1060 [24] (Lord Toulson) and [33] (Lord Hughes), which case is discussed below at n 14.

[8] *Kirkness* (n 6) 713 (Viscount Simonds).

[9] Interpretation Act 1978, s 20(2).

[10] *R v Brown* (n 4) [36] (Lord Kerr), cited with approval in *R (Brown)* (n 7) [24] (Lord Toulson), but see the discussion below at n 14. This takes account of the legislative decision to amend existing legislation, rather than create entirely new legislation (as to which see n 16 below and the text to that note).

[11] *Inco Europe Ltd v First Choice Distribution* [1999] 1 WLR 270 (CA) ('*Inco (CA)*') 272H–273A (Hobhouse LJ). This decision was affirmed on appeal ([2000] 1 WLR 586 (HL) ('*Inco (HL)*')), although no reference was made to this proposition.

[12] *Inco (CA)* (n 11) 273A–B (Hobhouse LJ): 'in certain circumstances it may be necessary to look at the amending statute as well. This involves no infringement of the principles of statutory

5.6 This history may obviously be relevant in ascertaining the origins and in 'considering the purpose of an amendment'.[13] It may also be important to understand how an Act has been amended when considering the meaning of its *unamended* provisions, as the general rule is that an amendment to one provision of an Act *does not* change the meaning of its other provisions.[14] However, this general rule will not apply where it is apparent that Parliament intended for an amendment to have a wider effect, such as where a statutory definition is amended.[15]

5.7 Beyond referring to the legislative history to identify the existence, origins and intended purpose of amendments, the amending legislation cannot be used more generally to construe the amended Act—*including* the amended provisions, since these are intended to form part of the amended Act (although there is an exception to this rule in some circumstances where the two Acts are *in pari materia*).[16] It has been said that the courts may take into account, as 'persuasive

interpretation: indeed it is an affirmation of them. The expression of the relevant parliamentary intention is the *amending* Act'. See also *R v Brown* (n 4) [36] (Lord Kerr): 'while the amended legislation is to be construed as a whole in its revised form, it does not follow that its antecedent history be left entirely out of account'. In each case, the history of the amendment was considered as a key part of the court's reasoning. Note that the court can—and indeed should in appropriate cases—consider the meaning of legislation prior to amendment, as in, eg, *Inco (HL)* (n 11). This approach is open to the court even where the relevant amendment involved a repeal of part of the original enactment: see *R (English Bridge Union Ltd) v English Sports Council* [2015] EWHC 2875 (Admin), [2016] 1 WLR 957 [36]–[37] (Dove J).

[13] *R (Brown)* (n 7) [24] (Lord Toulson).

[14] See *Boss Holdings Ltd v Grosvenor West End Properties* [2008] UKHL 5, [2008] 1 WLR 289 [23] (Lord Neuberger): 'In my opinion, the legislature cannot have intended the meaning of a subsection to change as a result of amendments to other provisions of the same statute, when no amendments were made to that subsection, unless, of course, the effect of one of the amendments was, for instance, to change the definition of an expression used in the subsection.' This passage was cited with approval in *R (Brown)* (n 7) [24] (Lord Toulson), who rejected a submission that it contradicted Lord Kerr's statement in *R v Brown* (n 4) [36] (as cited at the text to n 10 above), stating: 'There is no inconsistency between what was said in the two cases. In construing any legislation it is relevant to consider its purpose and that may include considering the purpose of an amendment. Parliament may sometimes amend legislation in order to correct a previous interpretation by the court. That said, and with the qualification that we have not heard full argument, I am content for present purposes to accept that generally speaking an amendment cannot affect the construction of an Act as originally enacted.' This rule that 'generally an amendment does not affect the construction of the unamended parts of a statute as originally enacted' was endorsed by the Court of Appeal in *Kaziu* (n 7) [56] (Sales LJ). See also *Bloomsbury International Ltd v Department for Environment, Food and Rural Affairs* [2011] UKSC 25, [2011] 1 WLR 1546 [66] (Lord Phillips), stating that an amendment that was 'peripheral to the Act as a whole' ought not to affect the Act's construction more generally, as it was not 'right to allow the tail (the amendment) to wag the dog (the Act)'. For an example of a case where amendments were considered to have wider interpretive relevance, see *41–60 Albert Palace Mansions (Freehold) Ltd v Craftrule Ltd* [2011] EWCA Civ 185, [2011] 1 WLR 2425 [20] (Smith LJ).

[15] See *Boss Holdings* (n 14), as cited in that note.

[16] See *Brown v Bennett (No 2)* [2002] 1 WLR 713 (Ch) [39]–[42] (Neuberger J). At [40] he set out the general rule that 'one cannot normally construe a provision of one Act … by reference to the provisions of another Act', citing with approval the following passage in Francis Bennion, *Statutory Interpretation*, 3rd edn (London, LexisNexis, 1997) section 78, 213: 'the function of the amending Act is to serve as an instrument for altering the text of the earlier Act, subject only to the need for commencement

authority', Parliament's view as to the meaning of the unamended provisions of an Act if this is evidenced by the amendments it has made to that Act.[17] However, save insofar as this falls within the strictures of the rules discussed at paragraphs 5.39–5.43 below (relating to Acts *in pari materia*), it is difficult to see why this should be permissible, given the general rule that later legislation cannot be used to construe earlier legislation.[18]

5.8 *Powers to amend subordinate legislation*: where an Act confers a power on a person to make subordinate legislation, it will by implication (unless the contrary intention appears) also confer 'a power, exercisable in the same manner and subject to the same conditions or limitations, to revoke, amend or re-enact any instrument made under the power'.[19]

5.9 *Powers to amend primary legislation by subordinate legislation ('Henry VIII clauses')*: some statutes contain provisions expressly conferring on someone a power to amend primary legislation—whether that statute itself or others, past or future—by subordinate legislation.[20] Such provisions are commonly termed 'Henry VIII clauses'.[21]

---

and transitional provisions. Unless the contrary intention appears, the other provisions of the amending Act should not affect the construction of words inserted by it into the earlier Act' (the equivalent passage in Jones, *Statutory Interpretation* (2013) (n 3) is at section 78, 265). At [41]–[42], he explained (again by reference to Bennion) 'that there is an exception to this general rule' where the later Act and the earlier Act are *in pari materia*, which they were not in that case (as to when Acts may be considered *in pari materia*, see paragraph 5.31 below). This exception was applied in *John Mander Pension Trustees Ltd v Revenue and Customs Commissioners* [2015] UKSC 56, [2015] 1 WLR 3857 [33] (Lord Neuberger), stating: 'it is clearly permissible, indeed appropriate, when interpreting new sections inserted into an Act, to take into account transitional provisions contained in the section of the later Act which introduced the new sections. The transitional provisions are plainly in pari materia with the new sections'. The limited nature of the scope for using later legislation *in pari materia* to construe earlier legislation is addressed at paragraphs 5.39–5.43 below. However, provided that this exception extends only to allowing the *amended text* to be construed by reference to the amending Act (as in *John Mander*), it is unobjectionable, since it does not strictly involve using a later Act to interpret an earlier Act: the amended text was enacted by means of the amending Act (and therefore *contemporaneously* with its other provisions).

[17] See, eg, *British Pregnancy Advisory Service v Secretary of State for Health* [2011] EWHC 235 (Admin), [2012] 1 WLR 580 [31] (Supperstone J); *Bloomsbury* (n 14) [10] (Lord Mance): 'it is not lightly to be concluded that Parliament, when making the amendment, misunderstood the general scheme of the original legislation, with the effect of creating a palpable anomaly'.

[18] See paragraph 5.27 below.

[19] Interpretation Act 1978, s 14.

[20] See, eg, Civil Procedure Act 1997, s 4, considered in *A Local Authority v A Mother and Child* [2001] 1 Costs LR 136 (CA), in particular at [20] (Hale LJ).

[21] See *Thoburn v Sunderland City Council* [2002] EWHC 195 (Admin), [2003] QB 151 [13] (Laws LJ). See also *Public Law Project v Lord Chancellor* [2016] UKSC 39, [2016] AC 1531 [25] (Lord Neuberger), using the phrase 'Henry VIII power' to refer to the power given by provisions of this kind to amend primary legislation by way of subordinate legislation. For a lecture dated 12 April 2016 by the former Lord Chief Justice, Lord Judge, discussing the association of these provisions with Henry VIII and their impact on parliamentary sovereignty, see www.kcl.ac.uk/law/newsevents/newsrecords/2015-16/Ceding-Power-to-the-Executive---Lord-Judge---130416.pdf.

5.10   The general rule is that where there is 'genuine doubt' about the scope of a provision delegating such power, that provision should be 'narrowly and strictly construed'. This is in '[r]ecognition of Parliament's primary law-making role' under our constitution, which makes such a delegation exceptional,[22] and means that 'Parliament should be told, in clear terms, if the executive intends to amend primary legislation'.[23] In assessing the scope of Henry VIII clauses, therefore, the touchstone is whether the statutory words have 'sufficient clarity' to confer the power in question.[24] What is sufficient will depend on the context.[25]

5.11   The general rule does not apply in respect of section 2(2) of the European Communities Act 1972, which grants power to the government to pass legislation to give effect to the UK's international obligations under the EU treaties. It has been said that this provision is not a Henry VIII clause which must be construed narrowly, but rather it confers a *sui generis* power which is to be interpreted in its own particular context.[26]

Repeal

5.12   'Repeal' is the term for an amendment which causes all or part of an Act to cease to have effect. 'Revocation' is the equivalent term in relation to amendments causing the cessation of effect of subordinate legislation.

---

[22] *R v Secretary of State for the Environment, Transport and the Regions ex p Spath Holme Ltd* [2001] 2 AC 349 (HL) 382E–H (Lord Bingham), citing the judgment of Lord Donaldson MR in *McKiernon v Secretary of State for Social Security* (1989–90) 2 Admin LR 133 (CA), and its endorsement in *R v Secretary of State for Social Security ex p Britnell* [1991] 1 WLR 198 (HL) 204F (Lord Keith), who stated: 'a power to modify the provisions of a statute should be narrowly and strictly construed'. These passages were all cited with approval in *Public Law Project* (n 21) [27]–[28] (Lord Neuberger).

[23] See *R (To Tel Ltd) v First-tier Tribunal (Tax Chamber)* [2012] EWCA Civ 1401, [2013] QB 860 [17]–[18] (Moses LJ), explaining that otherwise 'the full implication and width of the power may pass unnoticed in the democratic process'.

[24] ibid [19] (Moses LJ). See also *Public Law Project* (n 21) [26] and [36] (Lord Neuberger), making clear that for a particular purported exercise of a Henry VIII power to be authorised, it may not be sufficient that it falls within the literal meaning of a widely framed Henry VIII clause. By contrast, see at [30], where he stated that 'the natural meaning of the words in question is an important factor in an issue of statutory interpretation, *particularly* when they suggest that a so-called Henry VIII power *does not extend* to authorise the subordinate legislation in question' (emphasis added).

[25] For instance, it is particularly unlikely that Parliament will have intended to confer a power to interfere with fundamental rights: see Chapter 4.17–4.22, discussing the principle of legality. Particular clarity may also be required to authorise cutting down statutory rights created under another Act: see *R v Secretary of State for Social Security ex p Joint Council for the Welfare of Immigrants* [1997] 1 WLR 275 (CA) 290A–B (Simon Brown LJ), 293E (Waite LJ), considered in *To Tel* (n 23) [28]–[31] (Moses LJ) and *R (UNISON) v Lord Chancellor* [2017] UKSC 51, [2017] 3 WLR 409 [104]–[105] (Lord Reed).

[26] See *Oakley Inc v Animal Ltd* [2005] EWCA Civ 1191, [2006] Ch 337 [18]–[19] (Waller LJ) and [70] (Jacob LJ). As to the scope of the power conferred by this section, see Chapter 12.7. See also *Ahmed v HM Treasury* [2010] UKSC 2, [2010] 2 AC 534 [212] (Lord Mance), agreeing with this aspect of the Court of Appeal's decision in *Oakley* and stating: 'The same applies to the power conferred by section 1(1) [of the United Nations Act 1946] to give effect to Security Council Resolutions under article 41 [of the United Nations Charter].'

5.13 The effect of repeals is the subject of specific provision in sections 15–17 of the Interpretation Act 1978. The general effect of these sections is to prevent repeals from causing undesirable side-effects, such as the revival of laws that had been repealed by an enactment that is now itself being repealed.

5.14 Repeal or revocation is 'usually effected expressly'.[27] This may be carried out by provisions in the body of the legislation being used for this purpose,[28] but where a number of repeals are enacted, a schedule is often used for convenience.[29]

5.15 However, repeal can occur without the use of express words directing a repeal. Where a later enactment is inescapably inconsistent with an earlier enactment that it has the power to repeal, it may be considered to have effected an *implied repeal* of the earlier enactment to the extent it is inconsistent.[30]

5.16 *Principles governing implied repeal*: the following principles apply to ascertaining whether Parliament intends an implied repeal in any particular case:[31]

5.16.1 The test for whether an implied repeal has occurred is: 'Are the provisions of a later Act so inconsistent with, or repugnant to, the provisions of an earlier Act that the two cannot stand together?'[32] The existence of an 'anomaly' caused by 'the combined effect of the two statutes' is not a sufficient basis for inferring implied repeal.[33]

---

[27] *Hamnett v Essex County Council* [2017] EWCA Civ 6, [2017] 1 WLR 1155 [26] (Gross LJ).

[28] See, eg, Video Recordings Act 2010, s 1(a); Armed Forces Act 2016, s 14.

[29] See, eg, Digital Economy Act 2010, s 45, giving effect to sch 2 to that Act.

[30] See *Thoburn* (n 21) [37] (Laws LJ): 'The rule is that if Parliament has enacted successive statutes which on the true construction of each of them make irreducibly inconsistent provisions, the earlier statute is impliedly repealed by the later. The importance of the rule is, on the traditional view, that if it were otherwise the earlier Parliament might bind the later, and this would be repugnant to the principle of parliamentary sovereignty.' For the principle that the repeal or 'disapplication' takes effect only to the extent necessary (ie, 'pro tanto'), see *Thoburn* [43] (Laws LJ) and *R (O'Byrne) v Secretary of State for the Environment, Transport and the Regions* [2002] UKHL 45, [2002] 1 WLR 3250 [59] (Lord Scott). Of course, as is clear from Laws LJ's discussion of this point, implied repeal may operate as a complete repeal in appropriate cases, depending on the nature of the relevant inconsistency.

[31] See generally the principles set out in *Henry Boot Construction (UK) Ltd v Malmaison Hotel (Manchester) Ltd* [2001] QB 388 (CA) 401H–403C (Waller LJ), holding that s 55 of the Access to Justice Act 1999 did not impliedly repeal s 69(8) of the Arbitration Act 1996. Those principles were endorsed and applied in *Smith International Inc v Specialised Petroleum Services Group Ltd* [2005] EWCA Civ 1357, [2006] 1 WLR 252 [19] (Mummery LJ).

[32] *Churchwardens and Overseers of West Ham v Fourth City Mutual Building Society* [1892] 1 QB 654 (QB) 658 (AL Smith J), cited with approval in *Henry Boot* (n 31) 401H–402A (Waller LJ). See also *Thoburn* (n 21) [37] (Laws LJ), in the passage cited at n 30 above, asking whether the later Act is 'irreducibly inconsistent' with the earlier.

[33] *R (O'Byrne) v Secretary of State for the Environment, Transport and the Regions* [2001] EWCA Civ 499, [2002] HLR 30 ('*O'Byrne (CA)*') [65] (Laws LJ), although he considered that an 'absurdity', in the sense of 'a more deeply unreasonable result', might suffice; see also at [26] (Buxton LJ, dissenting). The Court of Appeal's decision was affirmed on different grounds by the House of Lords on appeal: see the citation at n 30 above.

5.16.2 In assessing whether that test is met, there is a general presumption 'that Parliament does not intend an implied repeal'.[34] That presumption is a 'strong' one in 'modern times, when standards of parliamentary draftsmanship are high' (and when, therefore, statutes may be expected to make express provision for intended repeals),[35] and is especially strong where important interests are at stake.[36]

5.16.3 This presumption against implied repeal 'is even stronger the more weighty the enactment that is said to have been impliedly repealed'.[37] Indeed, statutes of a 'constitutional nature' will almost certainly require express provision to be amended (although the scope of that class is not entirely clear).[38]

5.16.4 Accordingly, it has been said that the potential inconsistency must be 'inescapable', the result of giving the relevant legislation its 'only rational interpretation'.[39]

5.16.5 There is also a more specific presumption against implied repeal where a later, more general enactment covers (amongst other things) a set of circumstances that is already provided for by a more specific provision in an earlier enactment. In these circumstances, it is presumed that—unless a particular contrary intention can be discerned—the earlier, more specific provision is to continue to apply

---

[34] *H v Lord Advocate* [2012] UKSC 24, [2013] 1 AC 413 [30] (Lord Hope), citing *Henry Boot* (n 31) 405D–E (Arden J).

[35] *H* (n 34) [30] (Lord Hope), citing *Nwogbe v Nwogbe* [2000] 2 FLR 744 (CA) [19] (Robert Walker LJ). Specifically in this regard, where a statute makes express provision for repeals, this may be an indication that Parliament did not intend that statute impliedly to make any further repeal in a similar context to the express repeals: see *Henry Boot* (n 31) 403B (Waller LJ). Further, the presumption against implied repeal will be stronger where the later legislation is *in pari materia* with the legislation said to have been impliedly repealed, especially where it is 'promoted or promulgated by the same government department': see *R (ZA (Nigeria)) v Secretary of State for the Home Department* [2010] EWCA Civ 926, [2011] QB 722 [19] (Lord Neuberger MR). As to statutes *in pari materia*, see paragraph 5.31 below.

[36] See *Nwogbe* (n 35) [19] (Robert Walker LJ), holding that there was no sufficiently strong indication in the relevant Act of an implied repeal in that case 'especially as this is an area of the law in which liberty of the subject is at stake'.

[37] *H* (n 34) [30] (Lord Hope), citing Bennion, *Statutory Interpretation* (2008) (n 3) 305. The equivalent passage in Jones, *Statutory Interpretation* (2013) (n 3) is at section 87, 280.

[38] *H* (n 34) [30] (Lord Hope), with respect to the Scotland Act 1998. See also *Thoburn* (n 21) [63] Laws LJ: 'Ordinary statutes may be impliedly repealed. Constitutional statutes may not.' To repeal constitutional statutes (of which he set out a list of examples at [62]), he considered that express words or an 'irresistible' inference showing Parliament's 'actual' intention would be needed. See also *Earl of Antrim's Petition* [1967] 1 AC 691 (HL) 724D–E (Lord Wilberforce), doubting that 'an Act of such constitutional significance as the Union with Ireland Act is subject to the doctrine of implied repeal or of obsolescence'; and *Re Parliamentary Privilege Act, 1770* [1958] AC 331 (PC) 350 (Viscount Simonds): 'The conclusion that this privilege, solemnly reasserted in the Bill of Rights, was within a few years abrogated or at least vitally impaired cannot lightly be reached.' As to which Acts may be constitutional statutes, see the list of 'constitutional instruments' identified in *R (Buckinghamshire County Council) v Secretary of State for Transport* [2014] UKSC 3, [2014] 1 WLR 324 [207] (Lord Neuberger and Lord Mance); and see *Jackson* (n 6) [102] (Lord Steyn), discussing enactments having constitutional effect, referring in particular to the Human Rights Act 1998 and the Scotland Act 1998.

[39] *O'Byrne (CA)* (n 33) [68] (Laws LJ).

within its scope and is not repealed by the more general enactment.[40] This is an instance of a wider principle of construction that 'general words do not derogate from specific words', so that '[w]here there is an unqualified specific provision, a general provision is not to be taken to override that specific provision'.[41]

5.16.6 Conversely, the application of this principle where the later Act is more specific may indicate that it is intended to prevail over a more general earlier provision.[42]

5.16.7 Ultimately, whether or not a general or specific provision should prevail where there may be a conflict is 'a matter of legislative intention, which the courts endeavour to extract from all available indications'.[43]

Consolidation

5.17 As its name implies, 'consolidation' is the legislative process of tidying up the form of existing legislation on a particular subject matter by simultaneously repealing provisions scattered throughout the statute book and re-enacting them in a single piece of legislation for ease of use.[44] The courts have identified three types of consolidation:[45]

5.17.1 *'Pure' consolidation*, that is, re-enactment, where no amendment to the text is made.[46]

---

[40] See *Henry Boot* (n 31) 402C–H (Waller LJ) and the cases there cited; and *McE v Prison Service of Northern Ireland* [2009] UKHL 15, [2009] 1 AC 908 [98] (Lord Carswell) and the cases there cited (and setting out a passage from *Halsbury's Laws of England*, 4th edn, vol 44(1) (Reissue) (London, Butterworths, 1995) para 1300).

[41] See, eg, *Vinos v Marks & Spencer plc* [2001] 3 All ER 784 (CA) [27] (Peter Gibson LJ), in the context of two provisions in a single set of rules. As discussed in *McE* (n 40), in the passage cited in that note, this principle is sometimes known by the Latin maxim '*generalia specialibus non derogant*', which may be translated as 'general things do not derogate from specific things'. As to this principle, see further Chapter 3.21.

[42] See *R v Director of Serious Fraud Office ex p Smith* [1993] AC 1 (HL) 43H–44A (Lord Mustill).

[43] *Associated Minerals Consolidated Ltd v Wyong Shire Council* [1975] AC 538 (PC) 553H–554B (Lord Wilberforce), cited with approval in *McE* (n 40) [98] (Lord Carswell). For a case where it was clear that the more general later statute should apply despite a more specific earlier regime (so that appeal rights were expanded), see, eg, *Walker v Hemmant* [1943] KB 604.

[44] See *Farrell v Alexander* [1977] AC 59 (HL) 82B–C (Lord Simon): 'All consolidation Acts are designed to bring together in a more convenient, lucid and economical form a number of enactments related in subject matter (and often by cross-reference) previously scattered over the statute book.' See also *IRC v Joiner* [1975] 1 WLR 1701 (HL) 1711A–D (Lord Diplock): 'The purpose of a consolidation Act is to … [bring] together in a single statute all the existing statute law dealing with the same subject matter which forms the general context in which the particular provisions of the Act fall to be construed, so that it will be no longer necessary to seek that context in a whole series of amended and re-amended provisions appearing piecemeal in earlier statutes. This is the only purpose of a consolidation Act; this is the only "mischief" it is designed to cure.'

[45] *Farrell* (n 44) 82D–F (Lord Simon), noting that these three kinds of consolidation involve 'a short-circuiting of the normal parliamentary procedures'. See also *R v Heron* [1982] 1 WLR 451 (HL) 460C (Lord Scarman), adopting this analysis.

[46] Although not every example of repeal and re-enactment is consolidation: see, eg, Video Recordings Act 2010, s 1.

5.17.2 *Consolidation with 'corrections and minor improvements'*, under the procedure laid down by section 1 of the Consolidation of Enactments (Procedure) Act 1949. This allows limited improvements to be made without altering the 'essential character' of the exercise as one of re-enactment.[47]

5.17.3 *Consolidation with Law Commission amendments*, where the Law Commission has recommended consolidation along with certain specific (potentially more substantial) amendments to improve the law.[48]

5.18 In addition, certain Acts may seek in part to *consolidate* and in part to *amend* existing legislation.[49]

5.19 Where any provision is repealed and then re-enacted (with or without modification), references to the repealed provision in other legislation are to be construed as references to the re-enacted provision (unless the contrary intention appears).[50]

5.20 *Construction of consolidation Acts*: as discussed above, the main purpose of consolidation is convenience, enhancing the clarity and accessibility of the provisions consolidated. Accordingly, so as not to defeat this purpose, the general rule is that a 'self-contained' statute intended to consolidate the law (whether with or without amendments) should be construed on its own terms 'if reasonably possible'.[51] This means it is normally 'not legitimate' to construe a consolidation statute by reference to the repealed provisions it has consolidated,[52] and 'courts should not routinely investigate the statutory predecessors of provisions in

---

[47] See *R v Heron* (n 45) 460C–D (Lord Scarman). The term 'corrections and minor improvements' is defined in s 2 of the Consolidation of Enactments (Procedure) Act 1949 as: 'amendments of which the effect is confined to resolving ambiguities, removing doubts, bringing obsolete provisions into conformity with modern practice, or removing unnecessary provisions or anomalies which are not of substantial importance, and amendments designed to facilitate improvement in the form or manner in which the law is stated, and includes any transitional provisions which may be necessary in consequence of such amendments'.

[48] See, eg, Highways Act 1980, where the long title states: 'An Act to consolidate the Highways Acts 1959 to 1971 and related enactments, with amendments to give effect to recommendations of the Law Commission.'

[49] See, eg, Equality Act 2010, where the long title states: 'An Act ... to *reform and harmonise* equality law and *restate* the greater part of the enactments relating to discrimination and harassment related to certain personal characteristics' (emphasis added). See the contrast drawn between Acts of this kind and the three types of consolidation Act in *Farrell* (n 44) 82E–H (Lord Simon).

[50] Interpretation Act 1978, s 17(2)(a).

[51] *Farrell* (n 44) 73B–C (Lord Wilberforce).

[52] ibid 82D (Lord Simon); and see also at 83E–F (Lord Simon): 'it is the consolidation Act itself which falls for interpretation. The initial judicial approach is the same as with the interpretation of any other statute', going on to state that in interpreting the legislation, regard should be had (among other things) to the facts that would have been known to the draftsmen of the repealed provisions; and 72H–73C (Lord Wilberforce). See also *Bentine v Bentine* [2015] EWCA Civ 1168, [2016] Ch 489 [42]–[44] (Sales LJ), citing *Farrell*: 'Where Parliament passes a consolidation Act, especially where (as here) it sets out a self-contained code for dealing with a particular topic in one place and keeps the code up to date as appropriate for the context, the inference is that Parliament intends the Act to be construed according to its natural linguistic meaning, without the need for reference back to the prior

a consolidation statute, particularly where … the issue concerns the construction of a single word or expression'.[53]

5.21 This is not an absolute rule. In certain cases it is permissible, and indeed necessary, to have recourse to legislative antecedents to interpret a consolidation Act. Ascertaining the meaning of the previous legislation may assist because there is a 'very strong presumption' that Parliament does not intend by a consolidation Act 'to make any substantial alteration of the existing law',[54] except to the extent that the same Act also purposely effects amendments.[55] However, this presumption is rebuttable and 'must yield to plain words to the contrary'[56] or to contextual indications that a change in meaning was intended.[57]

5.22 Recourse to legislative antecedents to interpret consolidating legislation (whether or not that legislation also effects amendments)[58] is appropriate where:

5.22.1 in the provision in question, 'there is a real and substantial difficulty or ambiguity which classical methods of construction cannot resolve'.[59] In such cases, 'the courts should not hesitate to refer to the legislative history';[60]

---

legislative history or previous authority unless there is an ambiguity or real doubt about its meaning. The presumption is that a consolidation Act is intended to be a reliable statement of the law on which citizens can rely according to its ordinary meaning, as read as it stands at the date it falls to be applied.' But note the disagreement between the members of the Court in *Bentine* over whether and when reference to authoritative case law on the repealed legislation is appropriate: see at [43]–[44] and [57] (Sales LJ), [78]–[80] (Sir Bernard Rix), [102]–[107] (Arden LJ). See also in this regard Chapter 3.53–3.55, and in particular at n 144, with regard to the *Barras* principle and its doubtful application to consolidation Acts, at least as a matter of course (but note the specific scenario envisaged by Sales LJ in *Bentine* at [43], where he considered it may apply).

[53] *Spath Holme* (n 22) 388C (Lord Bingham).

[54] *Maunsell v Olins* [1975] AC 373 (HL) 382C (Lord Reid). Lord Simon described this presumption as a 'secondary canon of construction' in *Farrell* (n 44) at 84E, applicable only where there is a 'failure of the primary aids to construction', and see to similar effect at 73B–C (Lord Wilberforce) and *Bentine* (n 52) [45] (Sales LJ), referring to this as a 'subordinate presumption'. See also *Joiner* (n 44) 1711D–G (Lord Diplock); *Beswick v Beswick* [1968] AC 58 (HL) 79F–G (Lord Hodson), 84F–G (Lord Guest) and 104G (Lord Upjohn); and *Grey v IRC* [1960] AC 1 (HL) 13 (Viscount Simonds).

[55] *Spath Holme* (n 22) 388E (Lord Bingham).

[56] *Grey* (n 54) 13 (Viscount Simonds). See also *Beswick* (n 54) 79F–G (Lord Hodson), 84F–G (Lord Guest) and 105D–G (Lord Upjohn).

[57] *Canterbury City Council v Colley* [1993] AC 401 (HL) 408G (Lord Oliver). However, Lord Oliver also stated (at 408E–H) that where a 'later statute expressly incorporates and applies' a provision from another statute by reference, it will be 'impossible' to give that provision a different meaning in the later statute as compared with the earlier.

[58] *Farrell* (n 44) 73B–C (Lord Wilberforce); *R v Heron* (n 45) 460B–E (Lord Scarman).

[59] *Farrell* (n 44) 73B–C (Lord Wilberforce), cited with approval in *R v Heron* (n 45) 460E–F (Lord Scarman), and applied in, eg, *Sheldon v RHM Outhwaite (Underwriting Agencies) Ltd* [1996] AC 102 (HL) 140E–F (Lord Keith) and 144E–G (Lord Browne-Wilkinson), Lord Nicholls agreeing with both, with the Court declining in that case to look at predecessor provisions as an aid to interpretation. See also *Farrell* 97B–C (Lord Edmund-Davies), regarding a consolidation Act: 'only if its wording is ambiguous and its ambit obscure is one permitted to consider its legislative ancestry'.

[60] *R v Heron* (n 45) 460F (Lord Scarman), continuing: 'In some cases, as in the present, it will still doubt and resolve difficulty.'

5.22.2   even when a provision is not ambiguous, the court is otherwise unable to 'interpret the provision in the social and factual context which originally led to its enactment'. In such a case it is 'incumbent' on the court to examine any antecedent provision in its relevant context 'for such help as it may give'.[61]

5.23   Such recourse may also be necessary insofar as the doctrine of precedent requires an authoritative judicial ruling on the antecedent legislation to be followed in respect of the interpretation of the consolidating legislation.[62]

5.24   Even where legislative history may permissibly be investigated, it may be only 'rarely' that it resolves the issue in question,[63] particularly since the historical provisions may themselves be ambiguous.[64] In some cases, though, it will hold the key to reaching the correct interpretation.[65]

Construction by Reference
to Other Legislation: General Rules

5.25   *Using existing legislation as an aid to interpretation*: 'Parliament must be presumed to have been aware of the relevant pre-existing law' when it passed an Act (both pre-existing statute law and case law).[66] Accordingly, the corpus

---

[61]   *Spath Holme* (n 22) 388D–E (Lord Bingham), citing with approval (among other passages) *Farrell* (n 44) 84A–C (Lord Simon). See also *Johnson v Moreton* [1980] AC 37 (HL) 57B–E (Lord Hailsham), citing the same passage in *Farrell*. This exception may be especially applicable where recourse to antecedents is required to understand the *purpose* of a provision: see *Farrell* 84A–C (Lord Simon) and *Johnson* 62H–63A (Lord Simon).

[62]   Whether this is required was the subject of discussion and disagreement, but no decision, in *Bentine* (n 52), in the passages cited in that note.

[63]   *Farrell* (n 44) 84H (Lord Simon).

[64]   See *Maunsell* (n 54) 393A–B (Lord Simon and Lord Diplock, dissenting), considering that antecedent provisions can *only* be an aid to construction if they are themselves unambiguous (and that unambiguous meaning is one 'which the words in the consolidation Act can fairly bear'). While in practice antecedent provisions may give little assistance if they are unclear, this statement of principle is probably overly restrictive given the seemingly more permissive statements in *R v Heron* (n 45) 459H–460F (Lord Scarman) and *Spath Holme* (n 22) 388C–F (Lord Bingham).

[65]   See, eg, *Goodes v East Sussex County Council* [2000] 1 WLR 1356 (HL) 1361B–F (Lord Hoffmann), where the legislative history of a particular duty of a highway authority was traced back through various consolidation Acts to the common law. See also, eg, *Epping Forest District Council v Essex Rendering Ltd* [1983] 1 WLR 158 (HL) 162C–E (Lord Templeman), relying on legislative history to construe a requirement to obtain written consent as 'mandatory' rather than 'directory' (but note *R v Soneji* [2005] UKHL 49, [2006] 1 AC 340 [14]–[23] (Lord Steyn), explaining the 'rigid' distinction historically drawn between so-called 'mandatory' and 'directory' provisions, and holding that it has 'outlived [its] usefulness' and should no longer be applied).

[66]   See *R v G* (n 24) [46] (Lord Steyn). See also, eg, *R v Secretary of State for the Home Department ex p H* [1995] QB 43 (CA) 56D (Rose LJ), in relation to provisions regarding review of detention under the Criminal Justice Act 1991 and the Mental Health Act 1983: 'when Parliament passed the Act of 1991 it knew of the Act of 1983 scheme generally and of its section 50 provisions for discharge dependent on medical opinion specifically'.

of existing legislation at the time an enactment is passed provides part of the *contextual background* against which an enactment is to be construed.[67] The importance of this background will vary depending on the circumstances, but particular assistance may be derived from looking at earlier legislation on the same or a related subject matter, especially where it can be discerned that the draftsman was seeking to follow or depart from the meaning of that earlier legislation,[68] and especially where the subject matter of the earlier legislation is so closely connected to that of the legislation under consideration that the two instruments can be considered '*in para materia*'.[69] The potentially important role of earlier legislation in the interpretation of amended and consolidated legislation was discussed above (see respectively at paragraphs 5.5–5.7 and 5.20–5.24).

5.26   Beyond that, save where the contrary is stipulated and in certain other specific instances (discussed below), enactments are intended to be construed on their own terms and not by reference to other enactments.[70]

---

[67] See *Attorney General v Prince Ernest Augustus of Hanover* [1957] AC 436 (HL) 461 (Viscount Simonds), referring to the 'context' to be taken into account in interpreting legislation as including both 'the existing state of the law' generally, and 'other statutes in pari materia' specifically (as to which see paragraphs 5.31–5.38 below). See also, eg, *H* (n 66), in the passage cited in that note, and the discussion (of that case and another) in n 69 below.

[68] See *Wickland (Holdings) Ltd v Telchadder* [2014] UKSC 57, [2014] 1 WLR 4004 [62] (Lord Toulson): 'it is a matter of judgment what weight should be given to the legislative history in a given case. Sometimes it may throw considerable light on the proper interpretation of a later statute; in other cases the court may be left uncertain about the reason for a change of wording, in which event a comparative study will not help the court in its task of giving to the current statute the meaning which appears to fit best with its purpose'; and see at [16]–[20] (Lord Wilson) and [82] (Lord Carnwath, dissenting). For an example of an approach to construction 'in the light of the prior legislation', see *Mitsui Sumitomo Insurance Co (Europe) Ltd v Mayor's Office for Policing and Crime* [2016] UKSC 18, [2016] AC 1488 ('*Mitsui (SC)*') [18]–[34] (Lord Hodge).

[69] See n 67 above; and see also *Pennine Raceway Ltd v Kirklees Metropolitan Borough Council* [1983] QB 382 (CA) 388A–B (Eveleigh LJ), referring to the ability to refer as an aid to construction to 'an earlier statute dealing with the same subject matter' and commenting 'we are unlikely to find much help unless the statute is in pari materia'; but see *H* (n 66) for an example of a case where consideration of a more distantly related statute was central to the court's decision. See generally at paragraphs 5.31–5.38 below regarding statutes *in pari materia* and the use of earlier statutes *in pari materia* as aids to construction.

[70] See, eg, *Pennine Raceway* (n 69) 387G–H (Eveleigh LJ). See also, to similar effect, *R v Commissioners of Customs and Excise ex p Nissan (UK)* (CA, 19 November 1987) (Purchas LJ). We note that these passages might be taken to suggest that one ought first to construe the words in a statute without reference to other Acts even as context, but such an approach would not accord with the contextual approach to construction espoused by (among others) Viscount Simonds in *Prince Ernest Augustus* (n 67) 461, and more generally explained and advocated in this book—as to which, see in particular Chapter 3.43–3.44 and Chapter 7.43.1, and the paragraphs, notes and cases cited in the notes to those paragraphs. See also, eg, *Brown v Bennett* (n 16) [40] (Neuberger J), as cited in that note, in the context of a later Act which amends an earlier Act, but speaking in broad terms. Note that this is the same approach as the courts have held ought to be applied, in the first instance, to the interpretation of amended and consolidation Acts (see paragraphs 5.5 and 5.20 above), the intention being that the *ordinary rules of interpretation* ought (as a starting point, and subject to context-specific principles) to be applied in those contexts (see in particular *Farrell* (n 44) 83E–F (Lord Simon), as cited in n 52). Accordingly, the courts' statements in those contexts that Acts are generally to be interpreted as freestanding instruments can be read as being of general application.

5.27   *Using later legislation as an aid to interpretation*: as a general rule, the terms of a later enactment cannot be used as an aid to the construction of an earlier enactment, since they cannot have been in the contemplation of the legislator in passing or making that earlier enactment.[71]

Construction by Reference
to Other Legislation: Specific Instances

5.28   There are certain circumstances in which, going beyond the general rules above, it may be a legitimate exercise to use one enactment—even, exceptionally, a later one—to inform the interpretation of another. The principal instances[72] (discussed in turn below) are:

5.28.1   where one Act expressly refers to another;

5.28.2   where consolidation or amendment has occurred;

---

[71]   *R v Barnet London Borough Council ex p Shah* [1983] 2 AC 309 (HL) 348H–349A (Lord Scarman): 'It cannot be permissible in the absence of a reference (express or necessarily to be implied) by one statute to the other to interpret an earlier Act by reference to a later Act'; *Miller v Secretary of State for Exiting the European Union* [2017] UKSC 5, [2017] 2 WLR 583 [113] (Joint majority judgment): 'A statute cannot normally be interpreted by reference to a later statute, save in so far as the later statute intends to amend the earlier statute or the two statutes are *in pari materia*'; *Kennedy (SC)* (n 26) [33] (Lord Mance); *R (ZYN) v Walsall Metropolitan Borough Council* [2014] EWHC 1918 (Admin), [2015] 1 All ER 165 [52] (Leggatt J): 'the meaning of legislation must be ascertained by reference only to circumstances existing at the time of its enactment and cannot be affected by later events … This follows, as I see it, from the nature of the interpretation and the constitutional principle of parliamentary sovereignty'.

[72]   There may be others. As stated in *McCarthy & Stone (Developments) Ltd v Richmond upon Thames London Borough Council* [1992] 2 AC 48 (HL) 72G (Lord Lowry): 'The circumstances in which resort can be had to later legislation for the purpose of statutory interpretation are not entirely clear.' A possible further exception to the general rule that later legislation cannot be used to interpret earlier legislation may be the approach the courts have taken to the construction of certain key pieces of discrimination legislation—see, eg, *Anyanwu v South Bank Student Union* [2001] UKHL 14, [2001] 1 WLR 638 [2] (Lord Bingham), regarding the construction of the Race Relations Act 1976: 'Since the 1976 Act is one of a trio of Acts (with the Sex Discrimination Act 1975 and the Disability Discrimination Act 1995) which contain similar statutory provisions although directed to different forms of discrimination, it is legitimate if necessary to consider those Acts in resolving any issue of interpretation which may arise on this Act.' These Acts are probably not strictly *in pari materia*, given that they address different (albeit closely related) subject matter, each forms a self-contained code, and this approach to interpretation does not fit within the restrictions the courts have explained elsewhere regarding the limits on using later Acts to influence the interpretation of earlier Acts *in pari materia* (see the discussion of Acts *in pari materia* below at paragraphs 5.31–5.42). Instead, the rationale for this passage in *Anyanwu* appears to be a broader acknowledgement that, where the general context and overarching purposes of two or more Acts are closely aligned, how Parliament worded one Act to achieve certain aims may be instructive in ascertaining the degree to which—bearing in mind any commonality of purpose—identical, similar or divergent language in another Act is intended to have an identical, similar or divergent effect. This is broadly the way this passage in *Anyanwu* was understood and explained in *Oyarce v Cheshire County Council* [2008] EWCA Civ 434, [2008] 4 All ER 907 [37]–[38] (Buxton LJ). See further the discussion of this passage in *Anyanwu*, and the history of the discrimination Acts referred to in that passage, in *Rhys-Harper v Relaxion Group plc* [2003] UKHL 33, [2003] 4 All ER 1113 [73]–[88] (Lord Hope), especially at [74].

5.28.3 where two Acts are *in pari materia*;

5.28.4 the use of parent legislation to inform the meaning of subordinate legislation;

5.28.5 in certain cases, the use of subordinate legislation to inform the meaning of its parent legislation.

Express Reference

5.29 Where one Act expressly refers to a second Act, or does so by necessary implication, the second Act may be referred to in order to construe the first Act.[73] Further, if Parliament makes what is sometimes called a 'declaratory enactment', providing that certain words or provisions in another enactment are to be given a particular meaning, the declaratory enactment can be used to construe that other enactment.[74]

Amendment and Consolidation

5.30 The ability to refer to other legislation in construing amended Acts and consolidated Acts is addressed above at paragraphs 5.5–5.7 and 5.21–5.24 respectively.

Statutes *in Pari Materia*

5.31 One Act may be used to inform the interpretation of another, in accordance with the principles discussed below, where (and to the extent that) it can properly be said to be '*in pari materia*' with the other Act. This Latin phrase (which roughly translates as 'upon the same subject') is used by the courts to denote the circumstances where the connection between two Acts is sufficiently strong that it is considered appropriate to allow one Act to inform the meaning of the other to a greater extent than would ordinarily be appropriate. There is a degree of uncertainty as to the precise circumstances in which Acts (or certain of their

---

[73] See, eg, *R v Thames Metropolitan Stipendiary Magistrate ex p Horgan* [1998] QB 719 (QB) 724H (Pill LJ), construing s 731(2) of the Companies Act 1985 by reference to s 127 of the Magistrates' Courts Act 1980, to which it referred. See also *Shah* (n 71), in the passage cited in that note, and the cases cited in n 78 below.

[74] See, eg, *Wood v Gossage* [1921] P 194 (CA) 203 (Younger LJ) and the example there cited; *ZYN* (n 71) [53] (Leggatt J) and the example there cited; and *Kirkness* (n 6) 735 (Lord Reid).

provisions) will be considered to be *in pari materia*, but these have been said to include when:[75]

5.31.1   they share a collective title[76] or have the same or similar long or short titles;[77]

5.31.2   it is stated in the later statute that they are to be construed as one;[78] and/or

5.31.3   they deal with the same subject matter on the same or similar lines.[79]

---

[75] See the cases cited at nn 76–79 below, and see more generally *Miller* (n 71) [113] (Joint majority judgment), referring to when 'two statutes are *in pari materia*, ie they are given a collective title, are required to be construed as one, have identical short titles, or "deal with the same subject matter on similar lines"', citing Jones, *Statutory Interpretation* (2013) (n 3), section 28(13), 154 (and see further in the same work section 210 at 553–54, and the similar citation from an earlier edition in *Brown v Bennett* (n 16) [41] (Neuberger J)). A similar list is set out in *Augean plc v Commissioners of HM Revenue & Customs* [2008] EWHC 2026, [2009] Env LR 6 [34] (David Richards J), citing *Halsbury's Laws*, 4th edn, vol 44(1) (Reissue) (n 40) para 1220 (for the relevant reference in the most recent edition, see *Halsbury's Laws of England*, 5th edn, vol 96 (London, LexisNexis, 2012) para 633). Notwithstanding the listing of these broad categories by the courts, there remains considerable uncertainty as to when legislation should properly be considered *in pari materia*, since it is not clear exactly how close a connection is envisaged by phrases such as 'same subject matter' and 'on similar lines'. It is therefore helpful, and important, to have regard to judicial statements which illuminate the underlying rationale for using statutes (or other legislation) *in pari materia* as an aid to construction, as to which see *R (Innovia Cellophane Ltd) v Infrastructure Planning Commission* [2011] EWHC 2883 (Admin), [2012] PTSR 1132 [27] (Cranston J): 'Construing statutes in pari materia is probably no more than a recognition of the reality that the drafter of a later statute, obviously related to an earlier one, will have employed a word or concept in the sense that has become accepted in the interpretation of the earlier', referring to the 'well understood' meaning of a phrase used in previous primary and secondary legislation in the same field; and *Walker v Leeds City Council* [1978] AC 403 (HL) 421B–D (Lord Simon, dissenting): 'The Public Health Act 1961 and the Gaming Act 1968 are not in pari materia; that is to say, they are not so far related as to form a system or code of legislation', noting that where Parliament's intention is to incorporate parts of an earlier Act into a later Act 'the drafting technique nowadays is to provide a cross-reference' (although Lord Simon considered that, in the context of that case, the earlier Act could nevertheless be used 'to get a general impression of what is meant' by a term also used in the later Act). See also the doubts expressed about using the 1961 Act to construe the 1968 Act by Lord Wilberforce (at 418B–C) and Lord Salmon (at 425D–F).

[76] A collective title is in effect a short title that refers to multiple Acts, sometimes with a date range and sometimes without. See, eg, 'The Income Tax Acts', defined by s 5 of and sch 1 to the Interpretation Act 1978 as meaning 'all enactments relating to income tax, including any provisions of the Corporation Tax Acts which relate to income tax'.

[77] See *R v Wheatley* [1979] 1 WLR 144 (CA) 147D–E (Bridge LJ), considering the Explosives Act 1875 and the Explosive Substances Act 1883 to be *in pari materia* on the basis of their short titles, long titles and the nature of their provisions. See also, eg, *Chief Adjudication Officer v Foster* [1993] AC 754 (HL) 769E–F (Lord Bridge), referring to the 'social security legislation as a whole' and confirming his construction of s 22 of the Social Security Act 1986 by reference to the design of various provisions of the Social Security Act 1975.

[78] See, eg, *Phillips v Parnaby* [1934] 2 KB 299 (KB) 302–03 (Lord Hewart CJ), citing with approval a passage in *Canada Southern Railway Co v International Bridge Co* (1883) 8 App Cas 723 (PC) 727 (Lord Selbourne LC), and noting the existence of an exception where there is 'some manifest discrepancy, making it necessary to hold that the later Act has to some extent modified something found in the earlier Act'.

[79] See, eg, *R v Wheatley* (n 77), as cited in that note; and *Palm Developments Ltd v Secretary of State for Communities and Local Government* [2009] EWHC 220 (Admin), [2009] 2 P&CR 16 [40]

5.32   This principle is of long standing and was frequently applied in older cases. Lord Mansfield expressed it in the following terms: 'Where there are different statutes in pari materia though made at different times, or even expired, and not referring to each other, they shall be taken and construed together, as one system, and as explanatory of each other.'[80]

5.33   However, in more recent times the courts have questioned the scope of the principle, stating that it 'is a principle which can easily be pressed too far',[81] which should (at least in certain contexts) be taken 'with a pinch of salt'[82] and 'applied with caution'.[83] If a general rule now can be stated, it is that 'statutes in pari materia should be construed consistently if possible'.[84] How far consistent interpretation is possible will depend on the circumstances.

5.34   For all the broad statements that have been made about statutes *in pari materia*, in substance the courts draw a clear distinction between the principles that apply to using earlier Acts to construe later Acts, and those that apply to using later Acts to construe earlier Acts. These different approaches are considered in turn below.

5.35   *Using an earlier Act* in pari materia *to construe a later Act*: it is uncontroversial that, in general, earlier Acts can and should be used to inform the meaning of later Acts *in pari materia* as a contextual aid,[85] and that it can be assumed that Parliament generally intends for later legislation to be construed in the light of and

(Cranston J): 'In my judgment the felling licence provision in the Forestry Act 1967 is *in pari materia* with the tree preservation order provision of the [Town and Country Planning Act 1990]. Both are directed at preserving the amenity provided by trees, woodlands or forests. The one can therefore be used to interpret the other.' See also, eg, *John Mander* (n 16) [33] (Lord Neuberger), as cited in that note, finding that provisions inserted into an Act by way of amendment could be construed by reference to closely connected transitional provisions in the amending Act.

[80] *R v Loxdale* (1758) 1 Burr 445, 447; 97 ER 394, 395.

[81] *Fendoch Investment Trust Co v IRC* [1945] 2 All ER 140 (HL) 144D–F (Lord Simonds), having acknowledged the general principle 'that in construing the latest of a series of Acts dealing with a specific subject matter, particularly where all such Acts are to be read as one, great weight should be attached to any scheme which can be seen in clear outline and amendments in later Acts should if possible be construed consistently with that scheme'.

[82] *Littlewoods Mail Order Stores Ltd v IRC* [1961] Ch 597 (CA) 632–33 (Harman LJ), in relation to 'a long series of Acts' in the taxation context, citing both *R v Loxdale* (n 80) and *Fendoch* (n 81).

[83] *Norman v Cheshire Fire & Rescue Service* [2011] EWHC 3305 (QB) [83] (Andrew Smith J). This is because the full force of the principle places an unrealistic expectation on the skill of the legislative draftsman. In support, the judge cited Bennion, *Statutory Interpretation* (2008) (n 3) 604. The equivalent passage in Jones, *Statutory Interpretation* (2013) (n 3) is at section 210, 554.

[84] *R (George) v Secretary of State for the Home Department* [2014] UKSC 28, [2014] 1 WLR 1831 [30] (Lord Hughes), and see also at [15] (Lord Hughes).

[85] See *Prince Ernest Augustus* (n 67) 467 (Lord Normand): 'In order to discover the intention of Parliament it is proper that the court should ... inform itself of the legal context of the Act, including Acts so related to it that they may throw light upon its meaning'; and see in similar vein at 461 (Viscount Simonds) and 473 (Lord Somervell), both referencing 'statutes in pari materia' as admissible context.

consistently with existing laws *in pari materia*.[86] This principle has particular force where a general scheme can be discerned across a series of enactments and where legislation states that two (or more) Acts should be construed as one. Conversely, it will be weaker where no such scheme can be discerned.[87]

5.36   However, since the interpreter is always searching for Parliament's intention, this presumptive approach must give way, when appropriate, to other indications of that intention, for instance when 'this is necessary to give ... proper effect to the object of the statute'[88] or where it is clear (for example, from a 'manifest discrepancy' between two Acts) that Parliament intended for a later Act to modify an earlier one, rather than for the two to be construed as one.[89]

5.37   Although on occasion it has been said that there must be an ambiguity in the later Act before the earlier Act can be considered as an aid to its interpretation,[90] such statements are arguably unsound. Not only must context (which includes related Acts) be looked at to discern if there is any ambiguity to begin with,[91] but high authority suggests that statutes *in pari materia* can in principle be used to give language in a later statute a 'meaning which it does not naturally bear'.[92]

5.38   It should also be noted that, in some instances, case law authoritatively interpreting an earlier Act may be taken to have been endorsed by Parliament when adopting the same language in a later Act *in pari materia*: see the discussion of the *Barras* principle in Chapter 3.53–3.56.[93]

5.39   *Using a later Act* in pari materia *to construe an earlier Act*: the scope for using a later Act *in pari materia* to construe an earlier Act is very limited.[94]

---

[86]   *George* (n 84), as cited in the text to that note; and see, eg, *R v Wheatley* and *Foster* (n 77), in the passages cited in that note.

[87]   *Fendoch* (n 81), in the passage cited in that note.

[88]   *Littlewoods* (n 82) 633 (Harman LJ).

[89]   *Phillips* (n 78), in the passage cited in that note.

[90]   See, eg, *Pennine Raceway* (n 69) 388A (Eveleigh LJ): 'I appreciate that light may be thrown on the meaning of a phrase in a statute by reference to a specific phrase in an earlier statute dealing with the same subject matter, and such an aid to construction is permissible where there is an ambiguity'; and *Farrell* (n 44) 94D (Lord Edmund-Davies), citing *R v Titterton* [1895] 2 QB 61, 67 (Lord Russell of Killowen CJ).

[91]   See *Prince Ernest Augustus* (n 67) 461 (Viscount Simonds), on the use of context generally, and 467 (Lord Normand), on the particular importance of related Acts; and see further on the role of context in interpretation Chapter 3.43–3.44 and Chapter 7.43.1, and the paragraphs, notes and cases cited in the notes to those paragraphs.

[92]   *Fendoch* (n 81) 144F (Lord Simonds).

[93]   And see in particular Chapter 3, n 139. See also the discussion in n 52 above regarding the uncertain application of the *Barras* principle in relation to consolidation Acts.

[94]   As to the principle that later statutes *in pari materia* provide an exception to the general rule that later statutes cannot be used to help construe earlier ones, see *Miller* (n 71), as cited in that note (although the nature of the exception was not discussed in that case).

No doubt this is because this practice is difficult to justify as a matter of principle in the light of the general rule identified in paragraph 5.27 above.[95] The only situation in which this is clearly allowed is where the earlier Act is ambiguous, and the later legislation can be treated as giving an implied interpretive directive concerning the earlier Act.

5.40   The requirement for there to be an ambiguity is stringent, applying even where legislation states that two statutes are to be construed as one, and even where the effect of the two statutes together is to create an injustice or anomaly.[96] Further, to be ambiguous in the relevant sense, a provision must be 'open to two perfectly clear and plain constructions' or 'fairly and equally open to divers meanings'.[97] This means that 'it is not enough to show simply that there are two arguable constructions. One has to go further and show that they are both equally tenable, and that there are no indications in the Act under construction favouring one rather than the other'.[98]

5.41   Where an ambiguity is present, subsequent legislation, if it is *in pari materia*,[99] may be used to interpret earlier legislation where it 'can properly be regarded as providing a legislative interpretation' of that legislation.[100] In a recent survey of the law in this area, Leggatt J concluded that the applicable principle and its underlying rationale are as follows:

> If Parliament has proceeded on the basis that an existing law has a particular meaning at a time when, if Parliament had understood the law to have a different meaning, it is

---

[95] Indeed, even the well-established instance of this practice discussed in paragraphs 5.39–5.42 is somewhat difficult to justify: see *Kirkness* (n 6) 736 (Lord Reid), stating 'that the canon of construction established by the *Ormond* case may not be entirely logical, but on a broader view I think that there are very good grounds for it', referring to *Ormond Investment Co Ltd v Betts* [1928] AC 143 (HL), which is discussed at n 97 below.

[96] See *W Devis & Sons Ltd v Atkins* [1977] AC 931 (HL) 960F–H (Lord Simon), citing *Kirkness* (n 6) 735 (Lord Reid) in support of the first of these two propositions, the second being said to follow 'a fortiori'.

[97] *Ormond* (n 95) 154 and 156 (Lord Buckmaster), endorsing, and explaining the meaning of 'any ambiguity' in, the oft-cited statement of Lord Sterndale MR in *Cape Brandy Syndicate v IRC* [1921] 2 KB 403 (CA) 414 that 'subsequent legislation on the same subject may be looked to in order to see what is the proper construction to be put upon an earlier Act where that earlier Act is ambiguous. I quite agree that subsequent legislation, if it proceed upon an erroneous construction of previous legislation, cannot alter that previous legislation; but if there be any ambiguity in the earlier legislation then the subsequent legislation may fix the proper interpretation which is to be put upon the earlier'.

[98] See *Finch v IRC* [1985] Ch 1 (CA) 15C–G (Oliver LJ), citing *Kirkness* (n 6) and *Ormond* (n 95).

[99] *IRC v Butterley* [1955] Ch 453 (CA) 475 (Evershed MR). This decision was affirmed on appeal ([1957] AC 32 (HL)), but without reference to this point. See also *Re MacManaway* [1951] AC 161 (PC) 177 (Lord Radcliffe): 'The conditions under which a later Act may be resorted to for the interpretation of an earlier Act are therefore strict: both must be laws on the same subject', citing the passage in *Cape Brandy* (n 97) cited in that note.

[100] *Camille and Henry Dreyfus Foundation v IRC* [1954] Ch 672 (CA) 700 (Jenkins LJ), and see also to similar effect at 711 (Hodson LJ). This decision was affirmed on appeal ([1956] AC 39 (HL)).

reasonable to infer that it would have acted differently, that may properly be treated as an implied directive as to how a previously ambiguous law should be interpreted.[101]

5.42   In determining whether Parliament has given such an 'implied directive', it is assumed that Parliament is 'a rational and informed body pursuing the identifiable purposes of the legislation it enacts in a coherent and principled manner', so that it is not to be lightly concluded that Parliament has acted on the basis of 'an error or oversight' concerning the meaning of earlier legislation.[102] It is also important to take account of the area of law in which Parliament is legislating, and in particular the speed of legislative change in that sphere, in assessing whether any 'legislative assumption' can properly be inferred in a given case.[103]

5.43   In view of the 'strict' limitations expressly placed by the courts on the use of later legislation to interpret earlier legislation,[104] it must be at least highly doubtful that there exists any wider principle (sometimes referred to as the doctrine of 'statutory exposition') whereby one can rely more generally, as 'persuasive authority', on a view imputed to Parliament from the content of later legislation as to the meaning of earlier legislation.[105]

Using Parent Acts to Interpret Subordinate Legislation

5.44   Subordinate legislation derives its authority from its parent Act, and so falls to be construed by reference to that Act.[106] In particular, pursuant to section 11 of the Interpretation Act 1978, expressions used in subordinate legislation have the same meaning as in the parent Act, unless the contrary intention appears.

---

[101] *ZYN* (n 71) [59] (Leggatt J), having cited at [57] *Cape Brandy* (n 97), *Ormond* (n 95) and *MacManaway* (n 99). See generally Leggatt J's discussion of this area at [52]–[59], and his application of the relevant principles to the facts of that case at [60]–[66].

[102] *ZYN* (n 71) [65] (Leggatt J). See also *Bloomsbury* (n 14) [10] (Lord Mance), in the passage cited in n 17.

[103] *George* (n 84) [30] (Lord Hughes): 'a later statute is not a reliable guide to the meaning of an earlier one, especially in a field such as immigration where social and political pressures have led to fast-moving changes in the legislation'.

[104] See *MacManaway* (n 99), in the passage cited in that note.

[105] But for an apparent example of the courts taking such an approach, see *British Pregnancy Advice Service* (n 17).

[106] See, eg, *Mac Fisheries (Wholesale & Retail) Ltd v Coventry Corporation* [1957] 1 WLR 1066 (QB) 1071 (Lord Goddard CJ), having read the relevant provision in both the parent Act and the subordinate regulations: 'It is quite obvious to my mind that the object of the Act of 1955, and therefore the object of the regulations, is to procure the protection of the public health. Those words must be kept in mind when one is construing the regulations.' Subordinate legislation is also presumptively to be interpreted on the basis that it was intended to be within the legislative powers conferred by the parent Act: see *Raymond v Honey* [1983] 1 AC 1 (HL) 13A–B (Lord Wilberforce), discussing the scope of a statutory power under which certain regulations were made and stating: 'The regulations themselves must be interpreted accordingly, otherwise they would be ultra vires.'

Using Subordinate Legislation to Interpret Parent Acts

5.45   In certain circumstances, subordinate legislation may be referred to as an aid to the construction of its parent legislation (provided it is in fact valid legislation and not ultra vires). Lord Lowry provided guidance on when this is permissible in the following terms:

(1) Subordinate legislation may be used in order to construe the parent Act, but only where power is given to amend the Act by regulations or where the meaning of the Act is ambiguous.

(2) Regulations made under the Act provide a Parliamentary or administrative contemporanea expositio of the Act but do not decide or control its meaning: to allow this would be to substitute the rule-making authority for the judges as interpreter and would disregard the possibility that the regulation relied on was misconceived or ultra vires.

(3) Regulations which are consistent with a certain interpretation of the Act tend to confirm that interpretation.

(4) Where the Act provides a framework built on by contemporaneously prepared regulations, the latter may be a reliable guide to the meaning of the former.

(5) The regulations are a clear guide, and may be decisive, when they are made in pursuance of a power to modify the Act, particularly if they come into operation on the same day as the Act which they modify.

(6) Clear guidance may also be obtained from regulations which are to have effect as if enacted in the parent Act.[107]

5.46   While this guidance remains authoritative,[108] in more recent years it has sometimes been applied restrictively, with the courts being concerned to find a principled basis for using subordinate legislation to interpret parent Acts, given the general illegitimacy of allowing the views of the Executive (expressed in this instance through subsequent subordinate legislation) to influence the meaning of an existing Act of Parliament.[109]

---

[107] *Hanlon v The Law Society* [1981] AC 124 (HL) 193H–194C, explained further at 194C–G. For a case applying these guidelines, see, eg, *R v Lord Chancellor ex p Lightfoot* [2000] QB 597 (CA) 625F–627C (Simon Brown LJ), interpreting the scope of enabling provisions in the Insolvency Act 1986 by reference to secondary legislation enacted under that Act.

[108] *Mitsui (SC)* (n 68) [38] (Lord Hodge), citing Lord Lowry's guidance with approval, although not having recourse to the relevant regulations as an interpretive aid in that case. Lord Hodge seems to suggest in this paragraph, but without explanation, a link between the use of secondary legislation as an aid to interpretation and reliance upon evidence of settled practice to this end (as to which see Chapter 3.58–3.60). See also, eg, *R (National Aids Trust) v National Health Service Commissioning Board (NHS England)* [2016] EWCA Civ 1100, [2017] 1 WLR 1477 [32] (Longmore LJ), citing Lord Lowry's speech in *Hanlon* and stating that accordingly 'it is not only permissible but right … to have regard to the ambit of regulations intended to be made pursuant to the Act in relation to the commissioning of services and, in fact, made shortly after it was passed. Those regulations will be the best guide to the ambit of NHS England's responsibilities since it can hardly have been intended to authorise the commissioning by regulations of services which NHS England had no power to commission in the first place'.

[109] See, eg, the discussion of *Hanlon* (n 107) in *Legal Services Commission v Loomba* [2012] EWHC 29 (QB), [2012] 1 WLR 2461 [51] (Cranston J): 'The Hanlon case is binding authority: regulations are

5.47   Recent decisions (although not fully dissecting Lord Lowry's propositions) have emphasised the need for there to be (i) sufficient contemporaneity between the passage of the parent Act and the making of the subordinate legislation, and (ii) ambiguity in the parent Act before reliance is placed on subordinate legislation for interpretive purposes. They have also stressed the limitations of the assistance to be derived from subordinate legislation, stating that 'regulations do not decide or control the meaning of the statute under which they are made'.[110]

5.48   Overall, the authorities suggest that the case for having recourse to subordinate legislation to interpret its parent Act may be at its strongest in the following circumstances:

5.48.1   Where its text was before Parliament, or Parliament was aware of its intended immediate enactment, during the passage of the parent Act.[111] Note that

an aid to the construction of an Act if "contemporaneously prepared". That accords with constitutional principle. If Parliament, in passing a Bill, knows of the putative regulations to be made under it when enacted, the parliamentary intention behind the Bill is formed with that background knowledge. The regulations are thus a reliable guide to the meaning of the Act. Later regulations made under the Act will be formulated by the executive. If Parliament has a role in relation to them it will be to approve or reject them as a whole. By exercising the power delegated by Parliament to make such regulations, the executive can in no way alter the intention behind the enabling Act. Those regulations made by the executive can have no bearing on what an Act means', and see at [51]–[54] more generally. See also *Mitsui (SC)* (n 68) in the Court of Appeal: [2014] EWCA Civ 682, [2015] QB 180 ('*Mitsui (CA)*') [112]–[113] (Lord Dyson MR), doubting that much, if any, weight could be given to regulations that were not laid before Parliament, since they would then represent only the view of the Executive. The Court of Appeal's decision was overturned on other grounds on appeal, but the Supreme Court considered *Hanlon* and confirmed that, as a matter of principle, regulations not laid before Parliament can be used to interpret their parent Act. However, they would be given less weight: see at [38] (Lord Hodge): 'The Regulations were not laid before Parliament. But that of itself, while affecting their weight, would not exclude them from consideration as a guide to statutory meaning in accordance with Lord Lowry's guidance in *Hanlon*.'

[110]   See *MS (Palestinian Territories) v Secretary of State for the Home Department* [2010] UKSC 25, [2010] 1 WLR 1639 [35]–[36] (Dyson JSC), paraphrasing part of Lord Lowry's second proposition in *Hanlon* (n 107) and declining to construe s 82 of the Nationality, Immigration and Asylum Act 2002 by reference to the Immigration (Notices) Regulations 2003, which were made 'some months after the 2002 Act was enacted', stating: 'the meaning of section 82(2)(h) is clear and unambiguous and there is no need to seek "confirmation" or "light" from the 2003 Regulations as an aid to construction, even if it is a legitimate exercise to do so'. As to the importance of contemporaneity, see also, eg, *Loomba* (n 109), in the passage cited in that note, and *Forde and McHugh Ltd* [2014] UKSC 14, [2014] 1 WLR 810 [13] (Lord Hodge): 'It is not appropriate to interpret an Act of Parliament by reference to subordinate legislation which was made years after the primary legislation', citing Lord Lowry's speech in *Hanlon* and *Deposit Protection Board v Barclays Bank plc* [1994] 2 AC 367 (HL) 397E–F (Lord Browne-Wilkinson), who had referred to the need for the relevant regulations to be 'roughly contemporaneous with the Act being construed'. As to the need for ambiguity, see also, eg, *Mitsui (CA)* (n 109) [110] (Lord Dyson MR): 'we do not consider that the meaning of the subsection is ambiguous. That is fatal to any reliance on the Regulations'. On appeal in *Mitsui (SC)* (n 68), the Supreme Court overturned the Court of Appeal's decision on other grounds and, although briefly considering *Hanlon*, did not consider the point of principle in this statement specifically.

[111]   See *Mitsui (SC)* (n 68) [38] (Lord Hodge), as cited in n 109; Lord Lowry's fifth proposition in *Hanlon* (n 107), cited in paragraph 5.45; and *Loomba* (n 109), in the passage cited in that note, which

it is not necessary for subordinate legislation to have been laid before Parliament in order for it to be admissible as an aid to construction, but if it has not been, it will carry less weight in the interpretive exercise.[112]

5.48.2   Where Parliament can be said to have intended that the subordinate legislation should be considered as part of 'the same legislative exercise' as the parent statute.[113] This intention may be expressly stated in the parent statute[114] or it may be implied, in particular from the fact of contemporaneous or at least 'roughly contemporaneous' enactment of the relevant subordinate legislation.[115]

suggests that the rationale for recourse to subordinate legislation in such cases is that it may be taken to have formed part of Parliament's 'background knowledge'.

[112] See *Mitsui (SC)* (n 68) [38] (Lord Hodge), as cited in n 109.

[113] See *R(A) v Director of Establishments of the Security Service* [2009] UKSC 12, [2010] 2 AC 1 [42] (Lord Hope), stating of a parent Act and subordinate legislation made two months later: 'The interval was so short that, taken together, they can be regarded as all part of same legislative exercise'; Lord Lowry's fourth proposition in *Hanlon* (n 107), cited in paragraph 5.45; *Loomba* (n 109) [52] (Cranston J): 'the Act and the regulations must be part of the same legislative cloth'; and *R v Secretary of State for the Home Department ex p Mehari* [1994] QB 474 (QB) 483 (Laws J): 'a statutory instrument ... may be prayed in aid to construe main legislation, where it is clear that the two are intended to form an overall code'.

[114] See Lord Lowry's sixth proposition in *Hanlon* (n 107), as cited in paragraph 5.45. Indeed, Lord Lowry's fourth, fifth and sixth propositions in *Hanlon* (all cited in the same paragraph) suggest that greater, and potentially decisive, weight can be given to subordinate legislation referred to in order to interpret its parent Act where it is clear from the parent Act itself that Parliament intended for such reference to be made.

[115] See *R(A)* (n 113) [40]–[42] (Lord Hope), citing *Deposit Protection Board* (n 110) as authority for the need for the regulations to be 'roughly contemporaneous'. This passage in *R (A)* suggests that this means the regulations need to be made within a period of months rather than years after the enactment of the parent Act, but see *MS* (n 110) [36] (Dyson JSC), considering that even four months may have been too long in that case.

6

Internal Aids to Interpretation

6.1   This chapter considers what are sometimes called 'internal' or 'intrinsic' aids to interpretation of domestic legislation: that is, those features and parts of an enactment that may be used to help ascertain the meaning of its operative provisions, including certain commonly occurring types of operative provision which can be expected to provide particular interpretive assistance.[1] Within that term we include: (i) all of the ancillary components of the legislation which may influence the interpretation of its operative provisions;[2] (ii) the legislation's punctuation, format and structure; (iii) interpretation provisions (that is, operative components of legislation designed to provide particular assistance in interpreting the remainder of the legislation); (iv) deeming provisions; and (v) provisos and savings.

Interpretive Effect of Ancillary Components

6.2   The interpretation of the operative components of an enactment may be influenced by certain of the enactment's ancillary (ie, non-operative) components.[3] The interpretive relevance of different types of ancillary components is discussed below.

6.3   In general, the courts will take account of all ancillary components that are able to elucidate the operative parts of an Act or statutory instrument (SI). However,

---

[1] See *R v Secretary of State for the Environment, Transport and the Regions ex p Spath Holme Ltd* [2001] 2 AC 349 (HL) 397C (Lord Nicholls): 'the courts employ ... internal aids. Other provisions in the same statute may shed light on the meaning of the words under consideration'. On one reading, this may appear to say no more than that an Act must be construed as a whole. While that is true, it is also trite and unenlightening, and unlikely to have been what was meant. As such, we consider the concept of internal aids to construction is more useful when defined as set out in paragraph 6.1. The use of 'external' or 'extrinsic' aids to construction—ie, those found outside the boundaries of an enactment—is considered in Chapter 7.

[2] As to the meaning of 'operative' and 'ancillary' components, see Chapter 2.12.

[3] As to the meaning of 'operative' and 'ancillary' components, see Chapter 2.12. The particular ancillary components referred to in this part of this chapter are discussed (among others) in Chapter 2.

as discussed further below at paragraph 6.8, a distinction is drawn between the use of ancillary components whose content the legislator can affect[4] and those whose content it cannot.[5] In practical terms this means that, since Parliament cannot amend them, headings in Acts fall to be treated as *external* rather than *internal* aids to construction, with less weight being accorded to them than to amendable ancillary components (other things being equal).[6]

6.4   Subject to this caveat, it is submitted that the following principles can be derived from the cases as a whole regarding the use of ancillary components as internal aids to construction:

6.4.1   The courts will be willing to look at ancillary components as internal aids to determine the context and purpose of an enactment, which they will take into account in construing all its provisions, 'ambiguous' or otherwise.[7]

6.4.2   However, since they are not operative components (that is, they are not intended to create law in themselves), their interpretive import is limited. There are limits on the extent to which contextual and purposive factors can be allowed to interfere with the apparent meaning of the operative statutory wording.[8] Ultimately, while ancillary components may be referred to for context, they 'cannot override the clear provisions of the statute'.[9]

6.4.3   Accordingly, apart from generally illuminating the context and purpose of an enactment, they may be taken into account in determining the meaning of

---

[4] Such as the preamble, long title and short title of an Act, and all ancillary components of an SI (other than those that simply give dates when matters occurred).

[5] Such as headings or chapter numbers of Acts.

[6] *R v Montila* [2004] UKHL 50, [2004] 1 WLR 3141 [34]–[36] (Lord Hope), as cited at paragraph 6.8 below.

[7] See *Attorney General v Prince Ernest Augustus of Hanover* [1957] AC 436 (HL) 460–61 (Viscount Simonds) and at 463: 'it must often be difficult to say that any terms are clear and unambiguous until they have been studied in their context'. See also at 474 (Lord Somervell): 'The word "unambiguous" must mean unambiguous in their context.' See also the discussion in paragraph 6.15 below, especially at n 14 (in the context of the use of the long title of an Act as an internal aid).

[8] ibid 463 (Viscount Simonds): 'the context of the preamble is not to influence the meaning otherwise ascribable to the enacting part unless there is a compelling reason for it', which will not be the case where the preamble's 'own meaning is in doubt'. See also to similar effect at 467 (Lord Normand), 471 (Lord Morton) and 474–75 (Lord Somervell). On the role of context in interpretation, and the primacy of the text, see Chapter 3.13.

[9] *Matthew v Trinidad and Tobago* [2004] UKPC 33, [2005] 1 AC 433 [46] (Lord Bingham, Lord Nicholls, Lord Steyn and Lord Walker, in a joint dissenting opinion). *Matthew* was overruled generally in *Hunte v Trinidad and Tobago* [2015] UKPC 33 on the basis that the Board had not had jurisdiction in that case to commute a lawfully passed sentence on the grounds of unconstitutionality, but without commenting on this proposition (or the issue to which it related).

operative statutory wording only when (after context and purpose have been duly considered) that wording is unclear, ambiguous or leads to absurdity.[10]

6.4.4 The interpretive weight to be given to an ancillary component as an internal aid will always depend on the context.[11]

Ancillary Components in Acts

6.5 *Long titles*: the long title is a legitimate point of reference when construing a statute. During the passage of a Bill, a long title's function is to define the Bill's scope to place boundaries on parliamentary debates regarding the Bill. As such, long titles are particularly useful for identifying the purpose of an enactment and they are routinely referred to by the courts to this end.[12] Although the Court of Appeal has stated that long titles cannot be used to interpret an Act unless the Act is ambiguous,[13] it is submitted that this cannot have been intended to disallow reference to the long title to help determine an Act's context and purpose, and whether there is an ambiguity in its terms to begin with.[14]

---

[10] *Prince Ernest Augustus* (n 7) 463 (Viscount Simonds), 474–75 (Lord Somervell). These passages refer only to legislation's being 'clear and unambiguous' as standing in the way of relying upon a preamble in construing a statute, making no reference to absurdity. However, in formulating a general rule it is probably better to refer to lack of clarity, ambiguity *and absurdity* as the courts have in the context of reliance upon external aids to interpretation, since a fortiori the same principle must apply to internal aids: see *Spath Holme* (n 1) 397F–398E (Lord Nicholls), and more generally Chapter 7 on external aids. As for the relevance of ambiguity to the interpretive import of ancillary components, see further the cases cited at nn 13, 14 and 17 below, and the text to those notes.

[11] *Prince Ernest Augustus* (n 7) 474–75 (Lord Somervell).

[12] See, eg, *R (Quintavalle) v Secretary of State for Health* [2003] UKHL 13, [2003] 2 AC 687 [26] (Lord Steyn): 'The long title of the [Human Fertilisation and Embryology Act 1990] makes clear, and it is in any event self-evident, that Parliament intended the protective regulatory system in connection with human embryos to be comprehensive. This protective purpose was plainly not intended to be tied to the particular way in which an embryo might be created'; and [41] (Lord Millett). See also, eg, *R (Miller) v Secretary of State for Exiting the European Union* [2017] UKSC 5, [2017] 2 WLR 583 [88] (Joint majority judgment), referring to the long title of the European Communities Act 1972; *Manchester Ship Canal Co Ltd v United Utilities Water plc* [2014] UKSC 40; [2014] 1 WLR 2576 [51]–[52] (Lord Neuberger), regarding the purposes of the Water Industry Act 1991 and a related Act; and *Wilson v First County Trust Ltd (No 2)* [2003] UKHL 40, [2004] 1 AC 816, [99] (Lord Hope), regarding the purpose of the Human Rights Act 1998.

[13] See *R v Galvin* [1987] QB 862 (CA) 869B–C (Lord Lane CJ): 'One can have regard to the title of a statute to help solve an ambiguity in the body of it, but it is not, we consider, open to a court to use the title to restrict what is otherwise the plain meaning of the words of the statute simply because they seem to be unduly wide.' See also *Watkinson v Hollington* [1944] KB 16 (CA) 20 (Scott LJ): 'Where ambiguous language is used in an Act one is entitled to look at the long title'; and *Manuel v Attorney General* [1983] Ch 77 (CA) 108B–C (Slade LJ).

[14] The need to always interpret words in context is made clear in *Prince Ernest Augustus* (n 7) (see the references cited at that note), and there is no difference of principle between referring to preambles and long titles as part of that context. Further, this approach appears to be taken to external aids, so a fortiori it should also apply to internal aids: see the passage in *Spath Holme* (n 1) cited at n 10 above, and see generally Chapter 7 on external aids. This approach is also supported by *Watkinson v Hollington*

6.6   *Short titles*: in principle, short titles can also be considered in interpreting an Act. However, given their brevity, they may be of more limited utility as aids to interpretation.[15]

6.7   *Preambles*: where a statute has a preamble (although these are rare nowadays in public Acts), it may be referred to as an aid to interpretation for understanding the Act's provisions in the light of the Act's purpose and context, and more widely where there is an ambiguity.[16] As a number of distinguished Law Lords have said:

> Of course, the preamble to a statute cannot override the clear provisions of the statute. But it is legitimate to have regard to it when seeking to interpret those provisions ... and any interpretation which conflicts with the preamble must be suspect.[17]

6.8   *Headings*: individual statutory provisions, or groups of provisions, are often set out under headings.[18] Headings of all kinds may be referred to as aids to construction.[19] However, they have a lesser status than other ancillary components.

(n 13) 22–23 (Goddard LJ), who referred to the need to construe an Act in context, which he clearly took to include the long title. See also *Black-Clawson International Ltd v Papierwerke Waldhof-Aschaffenburg AG* [1975] AC 591 (HL) 647F (Lord Simon), stating that ambiguity is not needed before referring to a long title, which 'can be amended in both Houses' and 'is the plainest of all the guides to the general objectives of a statute. But it will not always help as to particular provisions'.

[15] Note that both long and short titles can be amended during a Bill's passage through Parliament, and in principle both ought therefore to be relevant as an aid to interpretation. As to the use of short titles in this regard, see *Re Boaler* [1915] 1 KB 21 (CA) 40–41 (Scrutton J): 'the Court should give less importance to the title than to the enacting part, and less to the short title than to the full title, for the short title being a label, accuracy may be sacrificed to brevity; but I do not understand on what principle of construction I am not to look at the words of the Act itself, to help me to understand its scope in order to interpret the words Parliament has used by the circumstances in respect of which they were legislating'. See also, eg, *R v Galvin* (n 13), where the unsuccessful argument that a document or information needed to be of an 'official' sort to come within the Official Secrets Act 1911 appears to have been made on the basis of both the Act's long title and its short title. Although the judgment focuses on the long title, the reasoning applies to both. For an instance where a title in the style of a short title was considered relevant in the context of a statutory instrument, see n 52 below.

[16] See *Prince Ernest Augustus* (n 7) at the references cited there and at nn 8, 10 and 11 above, and the text to those notes. See also *Director of Public Prosecutions v Schildkamp* [1971] AC 1 (HL) 19F (Viscount Dilhorne, dissenting): 'The preamble to a Bill can be amended during the Bill's passage through Parliament. A preamble to an Act can, therefore, be assumed to have had the approval of Parliament.'

[17] *Matthew* (n 9) [46] (Lord Bingham, Lord Nicholls, Lord Steyn and Lord Walker, in a joint dissenting opinion), a decision now overruled as explained in that note. In the text omitted from the quotation, they cite Francis Bennion, *Bennion on Statutory Interpretation*, 4th edn (London, LexisNexis, 2002) section 246. The equivalent reference in Oliver Jones, *Bennion on Statutory Interpretation*, 6th edn (London, LexisNexis, 2013) is in section 246, 682. See also *R (Jackson) v Attorney General* [2005] UKHL 56, [2006] 1 AC 262 [89] (Lord Steyn): 'arguments based on the Preamble cannot possibly prevail against the clear language of the substantive provisions'.

[18] Prior to 2001, there would be side-notes or marginal notes to individual sections, rather than headings: see *Montila* (n 6) [31] (Lord Hope), citing Bennion, *Statutory Interpretation* (2002) (n 17) 636. The equivalent passage in Jones, *Statutory Interpretation* (2013) (n 17) is at section 256, 696–97.

[19] See, eg, *Bulmer v IRC* [1967] Ch 145 (Ch) 165E–F, per Pennycuick J: 'Chapter headings ... are admissible upon the construction of a statute'; *Montila* (n 6) [31]–[36] (Lord Hope), permitting reference to 'headings to each group of sections' and section headings (or, in older legislation, equivalent marginal notes or side notes: see n 18 above); *Schildkamp* (n 16) 10 (Lord Reid), making clear that cross-headings and side-notes (now section headings) can be referred to.

Since (unlike long and short titles and any preamble) they are 'included in the Bill not for debate but for ease of reference … less weight can be attached to them than to the parts of the Act that are open for consideration and debate in Parliament'.[20] Accordingly, they fall to be treated in the same way as external aids to construction such as Explanatory Notes, as 'there is no logical reason why they should be treated differently'.[21]

6.9   Further, the courts have indicated that caution must be exercised in referring to headings, since they can only ever give a broad guide to what follows them and because amendments to provisions may have rendered their phrasing less apt.[22]

Ancillary Components in Statutory Instruments

6.10   *Titles*: as with an Act, a title may be referred to as an aid to interpretation, for such assistance as it may give.[23]

6.11   *Preambles*: reference may be had to the preamble of an SI as an aid to its interpretation. In particular, 'the narrative accompanying the identification of any specified enabling power may provide an indication as to the aims of the statutory instrument, and the preamble may thus have effect in the sense of being a legitimate aid to interpretation'.[24]

6.12   *Headings*: headings of various kinds may be taken into account in interpreting SIs.[25] With Acts, a lesser interpretive status is given to headings since these

---

[20] *Montila* (n 6) [34] (Lord Hope), continuing: 'But it is another matter to be required by a rule of law to disregard them altogether. One cannot ignore the fact that the headings and sidenotes are included on the face of the Bill throughout its passage through the legislature. They are there for guidance. They provide the context for an examination of those parts of the Bill that are open for debate. Subject, of course, to the fact that they are unamendable, they ought to be open to consideration as part of the enactment when it reaches the statute book.' It is clear from the passage at [31]–[37] that this statement was made in the context of both section headings and headings to groups of sections, and was intended to apply to all forms of headings. See to similar effect *Schildkamp* (n 16) 20E–G (Viscount Dilhorne, dissenting).

[21] *Montila* (n 6) [36] (Lord Hope). This seems right as a matter of principle: in a statutory construction exercise, although both are relevant, the words that the legislator may have influenced ought to be given more weight than words that may have influenced the legislator.

[22] See *Schildkamp* (n 16) 10E–F (Lord Reid), applied, eg, in *R v Okedare (No 2)* [2014] EWCA Crim 1173, [2014] 1 WLR 4088 [21]–[23] (Jeremy Baker J).

[23] See, eg, *McDonald v National Grid Electricity Transmission plc* [2014] UKSC 53, [2015] AC 1128 [143] and [158] (Lord Reed, dissenting), referring to the Asbestos Industry Regulations 1931, SR & O 1931/1140, stating: 'That title suggests that the Regulations are concerned with something identifiable as the asbestos industry, rather than with the use of the products of that industry in the work of other industries.'

[24] *Vibixa Ltd v Komori UK Ltd* [2006] EWCA Civ 536, [2006] 1 WLR 2472 [26] (Arden LJ).

[25] *Brown v Innovatorone* [2009] EWHC 1376 (Comm), [2010] 2 All ER (Comm) 80 [17] (Andrew Smith J): 'headings are relevant when interpreting delegated legislation'.

cannot be debated. However, the same reasoning does not apply to SIs, and so it may not be appropriate to give headings any lesser status than other ancillary components used as internal aids.[26]

Structure, Format and Punctuation

6.13   It is also relevant to consider legislation's structure, format and punctuation as internal aids to construction, albeit that it is inapt to speak of these as 'components' in themselves: structure and format relate to how other components are set out, while punctuation forms an integral part of an Act or SI's other components. Although these elements cannot (in the case of an Act) be amended by Parliament (or at least are not amended in practice),[27] they still carry some weight when interpreting Acts and SIs, as discussed below.

6.14   *Structure and format*: as Lord Hope has stated, 'the format or layout is part of an Act',[28] and it can therefore be taken into account as part of the interpretive exercise. An Act's operative provisions 'need to be understood in the context of the structure of the Act as a whole'.[29] The structure and format of legislation are discussed further in Chapter 2.

6.15   *Use of punctuation*: 'Punctuation can be of some assistance in construction',[30] and it is unrealistic to ignore it.[31] While it may not form a strong basis on which to base a particular construction of statutory provisions, courts are nevertheless astute to recognise that the placing of commas

---

[26] ibid [17] (Andrew Smith J), noting this distinction and its potential import, but not deciding the point. See also *Cawley v Secretary of State for the Environment* (1990) 60 P&CR 492 (QB) 495 (Lionel Read QC sitting as a deputy High Court judge), recognising the difference between headings in Acts and SIs: 'A heading in a statutory instrument must necessarily have a somewhat different status because the instrument is not enacted by Parliament. It is made by the Minister ... Hence in that sense the heading is part of the language used by the maker of the Order, although it does not run grammatically with the text.'
[27] See *Schildkamp* (n 16) 10B–C (Lord Reid).
[28] *Montila* (n 6) [33] (Lord Hope), citing Bennion, *Statutory Interpretation* (2002) (n 17) 638. The equivalent passage in Jones, *Statutory Interpretation* (2013) (n 17) is at section 257, 697.
[29] *Rowstock Ltd v Jessemey* [2014] EWCA Civ 185, [2014] 1 WLR 3615 [12] (Underhill LJ). See also, eg, *Director of the Serious Fraud Office v O'Brien* [2014] UKSC 18, [2014] AC 1246 [18] (Lord Toulson): 'for a proper understanding of its purpose and construction it is necessary to see how the section fits into the structure of the Act'.
[30] *Schildkamp* (n 16) 10E (Lord Reid).
[31] *Hanlon v Law Society* [1981] AC 124 (HL) 198B–C (Lord Lowry): 'I consider that not to take account of punctuation disregards the reality that literate people, such as Parliamentary draftsmen, punctuate what they write, if not identically, at least in accordance with grammatical principles. Why should not other literate people, such as judges, look at the punctuation in order to interpret the meaning of the legislation as accepted by Parliament?'

(and other punctuation marks) in a statute is not 'accidental' or something that one can simply 'ignore'.[32]

Interpretation Provisions

6.16   When seeking to ascertain the meaning or scope of a statutory provision, the issue may well turn on the signification of a particular word or phrase. Enactments often contain *interpretation provisions*, which are intended to control the meaning of the terms (whether words or phrases) defined within them to the extent stated.[33] These are one of the first things that should be considered when construing any legislation.

Scope and Location of Interpretation Provisions

6.17   The scope of interpretation provisions varies, and their location within legislation normally depends on their intended scope:

6.17.1   Where an interpretation provision seeks to define terms for the whole of an enactment,[34] it will usually be found at the beginning or end of that enactment.

6.17.2   Where an interpretation provision seeks only to define terms for part of an enactment (such as a Chapter or Part),[35] it will likely be found towards the beginning or end of that part.

---

[32] See, eg, *Kennedy v Information Commissioner* [2011] EWCA Civ 367, [2012] 1 WLR 3524 [20] (Ward LJ): 'Punctuation may be used as a guide to interpretation but the presence of a comma may often be a slender thread on which to hang the answer to a disputed point of construction', but considering that in that case a difference in punctuation between two subsections 'cannot be assumed to be accidental'. In affirming the Court of Appeal's decision on appeal, the Supreme Court likewise analysed the significance of the punctuation in these subsections: [2014] UKSC 20, [2015] AC 455 [28] (Lord Mance). See also *Dingmar v Dingmar* [2006] EWCA Civ 942, [2007] Ch 109 [88] (Ward LJ): 'Punctuation may not be the strongest tool for statutory interpretation but in a troublesome section … it cannot be ignored', going on to note that commas in a particular section had the significant effect of putting a phrase in parenthesis.

[33] See *Wyre Forest District Council v Secretary of State for the Environment* [1990] 2 AC 357 (HL) 365E–F (Lord Lowry): 'if Parliament in a statutory enactment defines its terms (whether by enlarging or by restricting the ordinary meaning of a word or expression), it must intend that, in the absence of a clear indication to the contrary, those terms as defined shall govern what is proposed, authorised or done under or by reference to that enactment'.

[34] See, eg, Freedom of Information Act 2000, s 84: 'In this Act, unless the context otherwise requires– …', followed by various definitions.

[35] See, eg, Communications Act 2003, s 151, headed: 'Interpretation of Chapter 1'; see also, eg, Antarctic Act 2013, s 13, contained in Part 1 of that Act (not yet in force), which gives interpretive guidance for certain words 'In *this Part*', but also in certain cases 'For the purposes of *this Act*' (emphasis added).

6.17.3 Where an interpretation provision is intended only to govern an individual section, it will often be found within that section.[36]

6.18 *Limitations on scope*: certain interpretation provisions may deploy a form of words (often at their outset), such as '*except where*' or '*unless the context otherwise requires*', to indicate that they will not apply to define a term if in certain instances the surrounding context requires that the words of that term should be read differently.[37] Words of this kind should alert the interpreter to the possibility that different contexts may give rise to different constructions of statutory wording.[38] At the same time, such words may well have been included on a purely precautionary basis and do not necessarily signify that the relevant term does have different meanings in different parts of the relevant enactment.[39]

Language and Effect of Interpretation Provisions

6.19 Various forms of wording may be used in interpretation provisions to define terms depending on the effect intended to be achieved by the relevant provision. For example, an interpretation provision may be intended to:

6.19.1 *fix* the meaning of a term by providing an exhaustive and comprehensive definition for it;[40]

6.19.2 *include* a particular meaning within the scope of a term, which may have the effect of *enlarging* or *expanding* the meaning a term would otherwise have,[41] or simply *clarifying* its meaning, for the avoidance of doubt;[42]

---

[36] See, eg, Defamation Act 2013, s 10(2).

[37] See, eg, Limitation Act 1980, s 38(1), using the latter phrase.

[38] See, eg, *Wathan v Neath and Port Talbot County Borough Council* [2002] EWHC 1634 (Admin) [13]–[16] (Sir Edwin Jowitt), finding that the context required that a definition should not apply to a term in a particular section.

[39] See *M v Secretary of State for Work and Pensions* [2004] EWCA Civ 1343, [2006] QB 380 [84] (Sedley LJ): 'The saving for context in a definition section is a standard device to spare the drafter the embarrassment of having overlooked a differential usage somewhere in his text.' This decision was overturned on appeal, but without commenting on this point: [2006] UKHL 11, [2006] 2 AC 91.

[40] See, eg, *Coltman v Bibby Tankers Ltd* [1988] AC 276 (HL) 298F–G (Lord Oliver), finding that in relation to the terms '"employee" and "fault" … the Act makes it clear that there is to be a single exclusive meaning for the purposes of the Act'.

[41] See, eg, *Thomas v Marshall (Inspector of Taxes)* [1953] AC 543 (HL) 556 (Lord Morton), finding that the object of an interpretation provision which stated '"settlement" includes any disposition, trust, covenant, agreement, arrangement or transfer of assets' was 'to make it plain that in section 21 the word "settlement" is to be enlarged to include other transactions which would not be regarded as "settlements" within the meaning which that word ordinarily bears'. See also, eg, *Phillips v News Group Newspapers* [2012] UKSC 28, [2013] 1 AC 1 [19]–[20] (Lord Walker).

[42] See, eg, *Coltman* (n 40) 298G–H and 299E (Lord Oliver), considering whether a ship fell within the meaning of the word 'equipment', where an interpretation provision stated: '"equipment" includes any plant and machinery, vehicle, aircraft and clothing'. He found that it did, rejecting an argument that ships had been deliberately omitted from the definition (unlike vehicles and aircraft) and that the word

6.19.3   *exclude* a particular meaning from the scope of a term, which may have the effect of *narrowing* or *restricting* the meaning a term would otherwise have, or of *clarifying* its meaning, for the avoidance of doubt;[43]

6.19.4   *incorporate* the meaning given to a term in another enactment into the enactment in which the interpretation provision appears.[44]

6.20   The following wording is commonly employed to achieve these effects:

6.20.1   '*Means*': if a definition states that a term '*means*' something in particular, the definition is usually intended exhaustively to fix the meaning of a term, to the exclusion of matters not mentioned,[45] although very rarely it may operate only to include a particular matter without thereby excluding others.[46] However, where the definition of what a term 'means' is in the form of a list, and the final item of the list refers to the term itself (for example, W means X, Y, Z or any other type of W), then this usually means that the provision is intended to act as an *inclusive* definition. That is, the legislator is specifying (whether by way of expansion or clarification of the ordinary meaning of W) that X, Y and Z are included in—but are not exhaustive of—the meaning of W. At the same time, the definition should be read as a whole, and the meaning of W 'may be of assistance in determining' the intended meaning of X, Y and Z in that context.[47]

'equipment' must therefore be read narrowly as excluding them. He considered that the interpretation provision was a 'clarifying and not an enlarging one', included 'for clarification and the avoidance of doubt', to make plain that a wide definition of the word 'equipment' was meant. See also *IRC v Parker* [1966] AC 141 (HL) 161E (Viscount Dilhorne): 'It is a familiar device of a draftsman to state expressly that certain matters are to be treated as coming within a definition to avoid argument on whether they did or not', cited in *Trustees of the Sema Group Pension Scheme v IRC* [2002] EWCA Civ 1857, [2003] Pens LR 29 [86] (Jonathan Parker LJ).

[43]   See, eg, s 81(5) of the Regulation of Investigatory Powers Act 2000, which provides: 'For the purposes of this Act detecting crime shall be taken to include [certain matters]; and any reference in this Act to preventing or detecting serious crime shall be construed accordingly, *except that, in Chapter I of Part I, it shall not include a reference to gathering evidence for use in any legal proceedings*' (emphasis added). As for specifying matters for the avoidance of doubt, see the previous note.

[44]   See, eg, s 105(1) of the Children Act 1989, which provides that '"care home" has the same meaning as in the Care Standards Act 2000'. See also, eg, Defamation Act 2013, s 10(2).

[45]   *R (Sisangia) v Director of Legal Aid Casework* [2016] EWCA Civ 24, [2016] 1 WLR 1373 [22] (Lewison LJ): 'There are well recognised techniques of drafting definition clauses. Thus a clause might say that "X means Y" in which case the definition is likely to be an exclusive one. Or it might say "X includes Y" in which case things within the natural meaning of X will be included in the definition.' These were contrasted with an 'exclusionary definition' in the form '"X does not constitute Y" unless two conditions are satisfied'. See also the cases cited in n 50 below.

[46]   See, eg, the divergent views taken of the definition of the phrase 'personal care' in the Registered Homes Act 1984 in *Joy Margaret Harrison v Cornwall County Council* (1991) 90 LGR 81 (CA), where the definition provided that the phrase 'means care which includes assistance with bodily functions where such assistance is required'. Dillon and McCowan LJJ considered the definition to be inclusive, while Nolan LJ agreed with Kennedy J at first instance that it was 'an exhaustive definition'.

[47]   *Phillips* (n 41) [19]–[21] (Lord Walker), finding that: 'for present purposes the essential point is that the definition in section 72(5) [of the Senior Courts Act 1981] contains the words "technical or commercial information". Parliament has made plain that information within that description is, for

6.20.2 '*Includes*': if a definition states that a term '*includes*' subsequently stated matters, this usually means it is 'what may be termed an inclusive definition' and 'is normally intended to widen the ordinary natural meaning of the word defined or at least to remove doubts as to the extent of that meaning', rather than to restrict or limit the meaning of the term defined.[48] However, depending on the context, it can also be used to *restrict*[49] or even exhaustively *fix* the meaning of a term.[50]

6.20.3 '*Any*': likewise, the use of the word '*any*' in relation to a category or type of thing may (especially if used in conjunction with 'includes') indicate a generally

the purposes of section 72, to be regarded as intellectual property, whether or not it would otherwise be so regarded'.

[48] *Whitsbury Farm and Stud Ltd v Hemens (Valuation Officer)* [1988] AC 601 (HL) 613G (Lord Keith). See also *Sisangia* (n 45), in the passage cited in that note; *St John's College School Cambridge v Secretary of State for Social Security* [2001] ELR 103 (QB) [32]–[33] (Munby J), noting that that draftsman had tellingly chosen not to use the word 'means' instead of 'includes'; and similarly *Coltman* (n 40) 298F–G (Lord Oliver), contrasting inclusively drafted definitions within the relevant Act with those 'where the Act makes it clear that there is to be a single exhaustive meaning for the purposes of the Act'. See also, eg, *R v Wheatley* [1979] 1 WLR 144 (CA) 147B–D (Bridge LJ), considering a provision which stated: 'the expression "explosive substance" shall be deemed to include any materials for making an explosive substance' (and other matters which appeared to go beyond the obvious meaning of that phrase). He described this as 'an expansive definition. Whatever an explosive substance means, that definition extends the meaning to materials which would otherwise not be within the primary connotation of the phrase'. In view of the nature of this interpretation provision, he commented that it (by contrast with another interpretation provision also being considered) 'provides no indication of the primary meaning of what is meant by an "explosive substance"'.

[49] See, eg, *Whitsbury* (n 48) 614A–B (Lord Keith): 'I think there can be no doubt that in some cases the language of an "inclusive" definition, considered with the general context, can have the effect that the ordinary natural meaning of a word or expression is to some extent cut down.' Compare *Parker* (n 42) 161E (Viscount Dilhorne), where the context indicated that words had been included for the avoidance of doubt: 'Nor do I think that it is right to seek to interpret the general words in the light of the particular instances given in the section. It is a familiar device of the draftsman to state expressly that certain matters are to be treated as coming within a definition to avoid argument on whether they did or not.'

[50] See, eg, *Secretary of State for Defence v Guardian Newspapers Ltd* [1985] AC 339 (HL) 348E (Lord Diplock): 'Although ... this definition is introduced by the words "includes" rather than "means", the context in which it appears ... makes it clear that it is intended as a complete and comprehensive definition of the term.' See also, eg, *National Dock Labour Board v John Bland & Co Ltd* [1972] AC 222 (HL) 232F–233B (Viscount Dilhorne), citing the speech of Lord Watson in *Dilworth v Commissioner of Stamps* [1899] AC 99 (PC) at 105–106 in support of his conclusion that the word 'include' had in that instance been 'intended to ... exhaustively define the areas ... covered by the Scheme'. In *Dilworth*, Lord Watson opined that the word 'include' could have two meanings: 'The word "include" is very generally used in interpretation clauses in order to enlarge the meaning of words or phrases', but 'where the context of the Act is sufficient to shew' such an intention, it can also 'be equivalent to "mean and include", and in that case it may afford an exhaustive explanation of the meaning' of a relevant term 'for the purposes of the Act'. Lord Watson's dictum was also cited with approval in, eg, *Whitsbury* (n 48) 613G–H (Lord Keith) and *St John's College School* (n 48) [32] (Munby J) (in the former, a restrictive but not exhaustive, meaning was found to have been intended in the particular context; in the latter, it was held (at [33]) that the 'normal meaning of the word "includes"' should apply, as the context did not indicate that a restrictive meaning was intended). See also *Coltman* (n 40) 298E–F (Lord Oliver): 'there may be circumstances in which an inclusive definition of this sort can have a restrictive effect'.

wide or enlarged breadth of scope, in accordance with 'its colloquial, and also dictionary, sense of "no matter which, or what".[51]

6.20.4 *'Does not include'*: a definition may state that a term does *not* include a particular matter. The extent to which any inference can be drawn from such an exclusion as to the ordinary meaning of the relevant term may well be limited, particularly since, as with an inclusive definition, a matter may have been excluded only for the avoidance of doubt.[52]

6.20.5 *'Except'*: interpretation provisions may also contain explicitly stated 'exceptions' which may either serve to enlarge (for example, '... except that X includes ...')[53] or narrow (for example, '... except X does *not* include ...')[54] the effect of the preceding words of definition in the provisions. (See further the discussion of 'provisos' and 'savings' at paragraphs 6.29–6.35 below).

6.21 *Lists*: sometimes a provision stating what a term includes, excludes or means will take the form of a list. One form of list sometimes used was discussed in paragraph 6.20.1 above. Another form of list which may be used is one phrased such that the final item is more general than the preceding words (for example, 'hats, scarves, gloves or other clothes', or 'cows, pigs, goats, or any other type of animal'). In these cases, the meaning of the final term may be restricted by the preceding, more specific, items in the list if those items are all of the same kind. This is an example of a principle of construction of general application

---

[51] *Jackson* (n 17) [29] (Lord Bingham), continuing: '"Any" is an expression used to indicate that the user does not intend to discriminate, or does not intend to discriminate save to such extent as is indicated.' See also *Coltman* (n 40) 299A–B (Lord Oliver); and *Whitsbury* (n 48) 614C–D (Lord Keith).

[52] See (by analogy) *Ealing London Borough Council v Race Relations Board* [1972] AC 342 (HL) 363E (Lord Simon), in relation to the construction of a general statutory provision by reference to a saving clause: 'considerable caution is needed in construing a general statutory provision by reference to its statutory exceptions. "Saving clauses" are often included by way of reassurance, for avoidance of doubt or from abundance of caution' (as to saving provisions, see paragraphs 6.33–6.35 below). See also (though in a contractual context and not in relation to interpreting a definition) the doubts expressed about inferring inclusion from an expression of exclusion in *Thorn v The Mayor and Commonalty of London* (1876) 1 App Cas 120 (HL) 131–32 (Lord Chelmsford); and similarly *Prestcold (Central) Ltd v Minister of Labour* [1969] 1 WLR 89 (CA) 98H (Lord Diplock): 'This is to stand the rule on its head: "exclusio unius inclusio alterius", and even statisticians do not do that' (although again this was not in the context of construing a definition clause, and Lord Diplock accepted that where an exclusion was included in one provision, an inference could be drawn from the absence of such an exclusion in another). However, in some cases it may be legitimate to draw an inference of inclusion from the specific exclusion of certain matters from the scope of a term: see, eg, *Jackson* (n 17) [138] (Lord Rodger), as cited in Chapter 3, n 93. For an example of an 'exclusionary definition' in a different form, see *Sisangia* (n 45), in the passage cited in that note.

[53] See, eg, Public Health (Control of Disease) Act 1984, s 74: '"vessel" has the same meaning as in the Merchant Shipping Act 1894 *except that it includes* a hovercraft within the meaning of the Hovercraft Act 1968' (emphasis added).

[54] See, eg, Charities Act 2011, s 248(2): '"Benefit" means a direct or indirect benefit of any nature, *except that it does not include* any remuneration (within the meaning of section 185) whose receipt may be authorised under that section' (emphasis added).

sometimes known as the '*ejusdem generis*' principle, which is discussed further at Chapter 3.36–3.39.

6.22   Overall, particular weight should be given to the words of an interpretation provision, since it can be expected to have been drafted with care for its intended purpose. The courts have accordingly expressed reluctance at attempts to cut down 'general and unambiguous words' in a definition by reference to a provision's intended purpose[55] and have been resistant to attempts at restricting a term's defined meaning by reference to its ordinary meaning.[56] However, like any other provision (and as many of the examples cited show), an interpretation provision must always be considered in its context.[57]

6.23   Further, as Lord Hoffmann has said, the fact that a term is defined 'does not mean that the choice of words adopted by Parliament must be wholly ignored. If the terms of the definition are ambiguous, the choice of term to be defined may throw some light on what they mean'.[58]

6.24   However, other judicial statements (including by Lord Hoffmann) have not referred to the need for there to be ambiguity before the choice of term can be taken into account in construing a definition.[59] It may be that the true principle

---

[55] See *Parker* (n 42) 161D–E (Viscount Dilhorne): 'I do not think that one should restrict the general and unambiguous words of the definition in the statute by regard to the mischief which it is thought that the section is aimed at.' Note, however, that the context in that case also demanded a wide interpretation of the relevant provision, as later cases held: see the discussion in *Sema Group* (n 42) [84]–[89] (Jonathan Parker LJ).

[56] See *Yates v Starkey* [1951] Ch 465 (CA) 476 (Jenkins LJ), who stated he must apply statutory definitions according to 'their true construction, however remote from the ordinary conceptions of [the defined term] the content of the definitions may in any given instance appear to be' (cited with approval in *Thomas* (n 41) 555 (Lord Morton), and see generally at 555–56 on the purpose and effect of the interpretation provision in question). See also *Phillips* (n 41) [19]–[21] (Lord Walker), although he accepted that in principle the choice of the term being defined 'may be of assistance' in construing part of its definition.

[57] See, eg, *Bulmer* (n 19), in which Pennycuick J distinguished *Thomas* (n 41), discussed in that note, in finding that the same definition imported an implied restriction that it did not extend to bona fide commercial transactions, stating (at 165D–E): 'there is no doubt that, where the context so requires, the court may imply some restriction upon the scope of general words in a statute'. See also, eg, the passage in *Whitsbury* (n 48) cited at n 49 above, and *Phillips* (n 41) as cited at n 56 above; and see generally n 59 below.

[58] *MacDonald v Dextra Accessories Ltd* [2005] UKHL 47, [2005] 4 All ER 107 [18]. This passage was cited in *Aspinalls Club Ltd v Revenue and Customs Commissioners* [2013] EWCA Civ 1464, [2015] Ch 79 [10]–[11] (Moses LJ), emphasising the need for ambiguity. Of course, in some cases, the chosen term may itself provide little assistance: see, eg, *Phillips* (n 41) [19]–[20] (Lord Walker). See further the discussion in *Sisangia* (n 45) [11]–[21] (Lewison LJ), citing *MacDonald* and other cases, and finding that 'the judge's error was to ignore what it was that was being defined'.

[59] See *Birmingham City Council v Walker* [2007] UKHL 22, [2007] 2 AC 262 [11] (Lord Hoffmann): 'Although successor is a defined expression, the ordinary meaning of the word is part of the material which can be used to construe the definition.' And to similar effect, see *Oxfordshire County Council v Oxford City Council* [2006] UKHL 25, [2006] 2 AC 674 [38] (Lord Hoffmann): 'in construing a definition, one does not ignore the ordinary meaning of the word which Parliament has chosen to define.'

is that the courts will always construe words used in definitions in their context, which includes Parliament's choice of words regarding the term being defined, but where the meaning of a definition, viewed in that context, is clear, they will be very slow to depart from it, even where it is not in keeping with the ordinary meaning of the term being defined.[60]

Deeming Provisions

6.25   What are commonly termed 'deeming provisions' are legislative provisions that lay down a hypothesis on the basis of which those applying the legislation, and those to whom it applies, must proceed. These hypothetical stipulations may or may not reflect reality, and they are therefore sometimes referred to as 'statutory fictions'.

6.26   Deeming provisions take a variety of forms and have a variety functions. For example, they may: (i) appear in the interpretation sections of a statute to modify a definition;[61] (ii) relate to the legal, jurisdictional or geographical status of particular persons;[62] (iii) be used to regulate contractual terms;[63] (iv) be used to affect the basis for the calculation of payments such as tax[64] or compensation;[65] or (v) stipulate when something has been done,[66] or regulate whether it has been done in time.[67]

It is all part of the material available for use in the interpretative process', though in that case (for reasons set out at [39]) he declined to allow the ordinary meaning to restrict the relevant definition. Lord Scott dissented on this point, emphasising at [81]–[83] the importance in the interpretation exercise of the ordinary meaning of the defined word.

[60]   See n 7 above on the need to consider terms in their context in order to assess whether or not they are ambiguous.

[61]   See, eg, s 38(2) of the Limitation Act 1980, which provides that: 'For the purposes of this Act a person shall be treated as under a disability' when certain circumstances apply.

[62]   See, eg, s 11(1) of the Immigration Act 1971, which for the purposes of the Act deems persons not to have entered the UK in certain circumstances despite their physical presence in the country. This section was considered in, eg, *R (ST) v Secretary of State for the Home Department* [2012] UKSC 12, [2012] 2 AC 135.

[63]   See, eg, Equality Act 2010, s 66(1): 'If the terms of A's work do not (by whatever means) include a sex equality clause, *they are to be treated as* including one' (emphasis added). The following subsection then defines the term 'sex equality clause'.

[64]   See, eg, s 80 of the Taxation of Chargeable Gains Act 1992, which provides that certain persons ceasing to be resident in the UK shall be deemed to have sold and reacquired certain assets at the time of ceasing to be resident, at their market value at that time.

[65]   See, eg, s 5(4) of the Banking (Special Provisions) Act 2008, setting out assumptions on the basis of which compensation had to be calculated for the transfer of securities under the Act. This section was considered, in the context of the Northern Rock plc Compensation Scheme Order 2008, SI 2008/718, by the Court of Appeal in *R (SRM Global Master Fund LP) v Commissioners of HM Treasury* [2009] EWCA Civ 788, [2010] BCC 558.

[66]   See, eg, CPR 6.26 on when documents will be deemed to have been served.

[67]   See, eg, Taxes Management Act 1970, s 118(2).

6.27   The Supreme Court has given guidance as to how courts should approach the construction of deeming provisions (endorsing a number of earlier cases), which can be summarised as follows:[68]

(1)   One should start by ascertaining, so far as possible, the purpose of a deeming provision's enactment, and specifically 'for what purposes and between what persons the statutory fiction is to be resorted to'.

(2)   The words of deeming provisions should then generally be given 'their ordinary and natural meaning, consistent as far as possible with the policy of the Act and the purposes of the provisions so far as such policy and purposes can be ascertained'.

(3)   However, where applying this approach leads to 'an unjust, anomalous or absurd result', then 'the application of the statutory fiction should be limited to the extent needed to avoid such injustice or absurdity, unless such application would clearly be within the purposes of the fiction'.

(4)   In deciding how far it is permissible to depart from the ordinary meaning of the words of a deeming provision, one must 'take into account the fact that one is construing a deeming provision'. This is not to disapply normal rules of construction (which would be contrary to principle), but rather to accept that it is unrealistic to expect the legislature precisely to delimit when and how far 'artificial assumptions' should be made.

(5)   In applying deeming provisions, one must also 'treat as real the consequences and incidents inevitably flowing from or accompanying that deemed state of affairs, unless prohibited from doing so'.

6.28   The Supreme Court also endorsed the frequently cited principle that one should not take a deeming provision's 'hypothesis further than [is] warranted'.[69] In this regard, it is important to note that the Court of Appeal has stated that the principle that '[t]he hypothetical must not be allowed to oust the real further than obedience to the statute compels'[70] should not be treated as laying down a 'special rule which requires a statutory hypothesis to be narrowly and literally construed'. Rather, each deeming provision must be construed on its own terms applying the usual rules of construction. 'A statutory hypothesis, no doubt, must not be carried further than the legislative purpose requires, but the extent to which it must be

---

[68] See *DCC Holdings (UK) Ltd v Revenue and Customs Commissioners* [2010] UKSC 58, [2011] 1 WLR 44 [36]–[40] (Lord Walker), and the cases there cited.

[69] ibid [40].

[70] *Polydor Ltd v Harlequin Record Shops Ltd* [1980] 1 CMLR 669 (Ch) [11] (Sir Robert Megarry V-C). Although the case was overturned on appeal ([1980] 2 CMLR 413), this statement has subsequently been cited with approval in *Shanks v Unilever plc* [2010] EWCA Civ 1283, [2011] RPC 12 [33] (Jacob LJ), who also cited other cases to similar effect.

carried depends upon ascertaining what the purpose is.'[71] Thus, working out the legislative purpose will often be the central element in the interpretation of deeming provisions (in accordance with the Supreme Court's guidance in this area, as discussed in the previous paragraph).

Provisos and Savings

6.29   Legislation may contain 'provisos' or 'savings', whose purpose is to qualify the effect of all or part of the legislation. The term 'proviso' is usually applied to wording designed to limit the scope or effect of the particular provision in which it is contained, whereas 'saving' is used to describe wording (often in its own separate section) designed to enact a more far-reaching restriction on the scope or effect of the entire piece of legislation or certain of its provisions. In some cases, provisos and savings can be used to assist in the interpretation of the provision, or piece of legislation, in which they appear.

6.30   *Provisos* are generally drafted in a form commencing with words such as 'provided that'[72] or 'unless'.[73] The function of a proviso—at least in the case of a 'true proviso'[74]—'as the word implies' is 'to qualify, override, cut down or derogate from that which goes before'.[75] Consequently, a true proviso will normally appear at the end of the provision which it qualifies and can be expected to 'be limited in its operation to the ambit' of that provision.[76]

6.31   Interpreters must be alive to the possibility that what appears from its form to be a proviso is not in fact 'a true proviso limiting or qualifying what preceded it'. In every case 'it is the substance and content of the enactment, not its form, which has to be considered, and that which is expressed to be a proviso may itself add to

[71] See *Bricom Holdings Ltd v Commissioners of Inland Revenue* [1997] STC 1179 (CA), where Millet LJ considered the dictum of Sir Robert Megarry V-C in *Polydor* (n 70) cited in the text to that note.

[72] See, eg, Maritime Conventions Act 1911, ss 1(1), 2 and 3(1) (now repealed), considered in *Owners of the Ship 'Anangel Horizon' v Owners of the Ship 'Forest Duke'* (CA, 2 July 1997).

[73] See, eg, Highways Act 1980, s 31(1), considered in *R (Godmanchester Town Council) v Secretary of State for the Environment, Food and Rural Affairs* [2007] UKHL 28, [2008] 1 AC 221.

[74] See further paragraph 6.31 below.

[75] *Anangel Horizon* (n 72) (Staughton LJ), adopting the description of a proviso in *Goulandris Bros Ltd v B Goldman & Sons Ltd* [1958] 1 QB 74 (QB) 93 (Pearson J).

[76] *Lloyds and Scottish Finance Ltd v Modern Cars and Caravans (Kingston) Ltd* [1966] 1 QB 764 (QB) 780G (Edmund Davies J). See also *Re Memco Engineering Ltd* [1986] Ch 86 (Ch) 98D (Mervyn Davies J): 'a proviso is usually construed as operating to qualify that which precedes it'; and *Thompson v Dibdin* [1912] AC 533 (HL) 541 (Earl Loreburn LC): 'the proviso must be limited to the subject-matter of the enacting clause'.

and not merely limit or qualify that which precedes it'.[77] Thus, in some cases the words 'provided that' are effectively to be read as 'and' or 'in which case'.[78]

6.32　As with other provisions, provisos ('true' or otherwise) are to be interpreted as part of the legislation as a whole.[79] But true provisos, given their purpose, will have particular import for the construction of the provision in which they are contained,[80] and vice versa.[81] That said, a degree of caution needs to be exercised in construing a section by reference to a proviso that qualifies it, as '[p]rovisos are often inserted ex abundanti cautela' (that is, out of an abundance of caution).[82]

6.33　*Savings* often appear in a self-contained provision with a dedicated heading in a statute.[83] There is no universal drafting form, but they commonly begin with the words: 'nothing in this Act'. Whereas provisos are generally framed as qualifications of particular provisions, savings are often framed by reference to what is intended to remain undisturbed by the legislation in question, such as an existing area of law,[84] the law applicable to certain past events or transactions[85] or the validity of things that have been done under previously existing law.[86]

---

[77] *Commissioner of Stamp Duties v Atwill* [1973] AC 558 (PC) 561G–H (Viscount Dilhorne), and see generally at 561G–563G.

[78] ibid 563C–G.

[79] *Jennings v Kelly* [1940] AC 206 (HL) 229 (Lord Wright): 'The proper course is to apply the broad general rule of construction, which is that a section or enactment must be construed as a whole, each portion throwing light, if need be, on the rest. I do not think that there is any other rule even in the case of a proviso in the strictest or narrowest sense.' This passage was cited with approval in *Atwill* (n 77) 563A–C (Viscount Dilhorne).

[80] See, eg, *McDonald* (n 23), where the Supreme Court derived assistance from a proviso in the preamble to the Asbestos Injury Regulations 1931 (n 23) in interpreting the opening words of the preamble. See especially in the judgment of Lord Kerr at [11]–[12]: 'Although this proviso cut down the scope of the Regulations, it gives some insight into the width of their intended ambit', and at [42], with Lord Clarke agreeing at [113].

[81] See, eg, *Godmanchester Town Council* (n 73) [34] (Lord Hoffmann), construing the proviso in s 31(1) of the Highways Act 1980 in the context of the section as a whole. See also *Thompson* (n 76) 544 (Lord Ashbourne), referring to 'the settled rule of construction that a proviso must prima facie be read and considered in relation to the principal matter to which it is a proviso … The words are dependent on the principal enacting words, to which they are tacked as a proviso. They cannot be read as divorced from their context'.

[82] *Taylor v Provan* [1975] AC 194 (HL) 219F (Lord Simon, dissenting). See also, eg, *Mohammed v Ministry of Defence* [2017] UKSC 1, [2017] 2 WLR 287 [41] (Lady Hale), discussing the effect of the proviso in section 2(1) of the Crown Proceedings Act 1947, but stating: 'It may be that the proviso was unnecessary.' And see, by parity of reasoning, the statements in relation to savings in *Ealing London Borough Council* (n 52), as cited in that note.

[83] See, eg, Misrepresentation Act 1967, s 5, headed 'Saving for past transactions'.

[84] See, eg, Trade Marks Act 1994, s 2(2): 'No proceedings lie to prevent or recover damages for the infringement of an unregistered trade mark as such; but nothing in this Act affects the law relating to passing off', considered in *Inter Lotto (UK) Ltd v Camelot Group plc* [2003] EWCA Civ 1132, [2003] 4 All ER 575 [34]–[38] (Carnwath LJ).

[85] See, eg, Misrepresentation Act 1967, s 5: 'Nothing in this Act shall apply in relation to any misrepresentation or contract of sale which is made before the commencement of this Act.'

[86] See, eg, the raft of 'General savings' enacted by s 16(1) of the Interpretation Act 1978, stating various effects that repeals are intended not to have ('unless the contrary intention appears').

6.34 Given their ordinary function of preserving the status quo in some way, what is in substance a saving provision should not be treated as expanding existing law[87] or as codifying it and limiting its further development.[88]

6.35 As with provisos, savings are to be construed as part of the legislation as a whole, and in appropriate cases may inform the meaning and effect of other parts of that legislation.[89] Again, though, as with provisos, caution must be exercised in using savings to interpret other parts of an Act, as they 'are often included by way of reassurance, for avoidance of doubt or from abundance of caution'.[90]

---

[87] *Arnold v The Mayor, Aldermen and Burgesses of the Borough of Gravesend* (1856) 2 Kay & J 574, 590–91; 69 ER 911, 918 (Sir William Page Wood V-C): 'But I ask, when the statute only "saves" rights, why should we say it "gives" them? ... I should have thought it impossible successfully to contend that a saving would give any further right than the party already had.'

[88] *Attorney General v Times Newspapers Ltd* [1992] 1 AC 191 (HL) 215E–F (Lord Ackner).

[89] See the citation from *Jennings* (n 79) in that note, which is expressed in general terms, and by parity of reasoning must apply to savings in the same way as to provisos. For a specific example, see *Inter Lotto* (n 84) [34]–[38] (Carnwath LJ), where an argument that the Trade Marks Act 1994 conferred exclusive rights, including to the exclusion of rights under the law of passing off, was rejected as being inconsistent with the broad saving in section 2(2) (set out at n 84 above).

[90] *Ealing London Borough Council* (n 52) 363E (Lord Simon), and see the more extensive citation in that note.

7

External Aids to Interpretation

7.1 The courts can sometimes derive assistance in construing an enactment from a variety of sources *outside* the enactment itself, which have been termed 'external aids' to interpretation.[1]

7.2 This chapter explores first the rationale for recourse to 'external aids' in interpreting legislation. It then addresses how various specific types of aid have been used by the courts, focusing on the principal external aids connected with the legislative process that brought the relevant enactment into being, such as Hansard reports of parliamentary debates, Explanatory Notes, White Papers and Law Commission reports. The chapter then concludes with a brief statement of the general principles which, it is submitted, can be derived from the case law in relation to the use of external aids generally.

The Rationale for Recourse to External Aids

7.3 The rationale for having regard to external aids to construction is the reality that '[n]o legislation is enacted in a vacuum'[2] and that, to be properly understood, it must be understood in *context*. Understanding that context may help shed light on the issue (or 'mischief') at which a measure was directed or the purpose it was intended to achieve.[3] Looking at an enactment in isolation, even with the

---

[1] See, eg, *R v Secretary of State for the Environment, Transport and the Regions ex p Spath Holme Ltd* [2001] 2 AC 349 (HL) 397E (Lord Nicholls). They have also been termed 'extrinsic aids' to interpretation: see, eg, *R v T* [2009] UKHL 20, [2009] 1 AC 1310 [7] (Lord Phillips).

[2] *Spath Holme* (n 1) 398C (Lord Nicholls).

[3] See *R (Westminster City Council) v National Asylum Support Service* [2002] UKHL 38, [2002] 1 WLR 2956 ('*NASS*') [5]–[6] (Lord Steyn), in the context of the use of Explanatory Notes to an Act as an external aid (as to which see paragraphs 7.26–7.32 below), stating in particular at [5]: 'language in all legal texts conveys meaning according to the circumstances in which it was used. It follows that the context must always be identified and considered before the process of construction or during it'. Lord Steyn then went on to cite the speech of Lord Blackburn in *River Wear Commissioners v Adamson* (1877) 2 App Cas 743 at 763 in relation to statutory construction: 'In all cases the object is to see what is the intention expressed by the words used. But, from the imperfection of language, it is impossible to know what that intention is without inquiring farther, and seeing what the circumstances were with reference to which the words were used, and what was the object, appearing from those

help of all relevant internal aids to construction, will not always be sufficient to ascertain clearly the legislator's intention as expressed in the words used, understood in their context, which is the aim of any statutory interpretation exercise: see Chapter 3.2–3.3. Indeed, in certain cases, the legislator's intention may be clearly and appropriately ascertainable from an external source, while, unfortunately, the wording of the legislation itself is unclear, ambiguous or productive of absurdity.[4]

7.4 However, as set out below, the nature of external aids means that there are limits as to how far they can legitimately be allowed to inform the interpretation of an enactment. These limits reflect important constitutional principles: that it is the legislation alone which represents the law, and which the court is required to interpret;[5] and that the law must be accessible to those expected to comply with it.[6]

7.5 These constitutional considerations also circumscribe the materials which can be legitimately referred to as external aids. This category comprises a wide range of materials, and the list is not closed. But it has been said that, as a matter of principle, the only material which should be referred to as an external aid is that 'which is in the public domain and of clear potential relevance to the issue of interpretation of a legislative instrument', rather than simply anything which may speak to the 'subjective policy intent' of the promoter of the legislation.[7]

circumstances, which the person using them had in view; for the meaning of words varies according to the circumstances with respect to which they were used.' See also the discussion of external aids to construction in *Spath Holme* (n 1) 397C–398E (Lord Nicholls), in particular at 397E: 'Nowadays the courts look at external aids for more than merely identifying the mischief the statute is intended to cure. In adopting a purposive approach to the interpretation of statutory language, courts seek to identify and give effect to the purpose of the legislation. To the extent that extraneous material assists in identifying the purpose of the legislation, it is a useful tool.'

[4] See, eg, *Pepper (Inspector of Taxes) v Hart* [1993] AC 593 (HL) 620B–D (Lord Oliver), 634F–635B (Lord Browne-Wilkinson).

[5] *Williams v Central Bank of Nigeria* [2014] UKSC 10, [2014] AC 1189 [104] (Lord Neuberger): 'First, the court's constitutional role in any exercise of statutory interpretation is to give effect to Parliament's intention by deciding what the words of the relevant provision mean in their context. Secondly, it follows that, in so far as any extraneous material can be brought into account, it is only as part of that context.' See further paragraph 7.43.3.1 below.

[6] See *Bogdanic v Secretary of State for the Home Department* [2014] EWHC 2872 (QB) [13] (Sales J) [13] (as discussed in the following note); and *Spath Holme* (n 1) 397F–398B (Lord Nicholls).

[7] *Bogdanic* (n 6) [13] (Sales J), explaining that 'it is a basic constitutional principle that the citizen or person subject to the relevant law should have the means of access to any material which is said to provide an aid to construction of that instrument'. See also the cases cited in that paragraph, in particular *Black-Clawson International Ltd v Papierwerke Waldof-Aschaffenberg* [1975] AC 591 (HL) 614A–B (Lord Reid): 'it would seem wrong to take into account anything that was not public knowledge at the time. That may be common knowledge at the time or it may be some published information which Parliament can be presumed to have had in mind'. See also the apparent concern expressed in *Evans v Amicus Healthcare* [2004] EWCA Civ 727, [2005] Fam 1 [45] (Thorpe and Sedley LJJ) that the court should refer only to a limited class of 'antecedent public documents'.

Specific Kinds of External Aids and their Use

7.6 In our discussion of specific external aids below, we address first those which record, or are produced as part of, the legislative process itself: reports of parliamentary debates; Explanatory Notes; and Explanatory Memoranda. We then discuss those sources which pre-date that process, which are principally those sources which inspire or initiate the legislative process: Green and White Papers; Law Commission reports; and the like.[8]

7.7 We then comment on the different approach taken to the use of materials produced *after* the legislative process has concluded, such as subsequent statements of government departments or bodies administering legislation. By their nature, these cannot have informed the context in which legislation was passed and, accordingly, they are best not categorised as true 'external aids' at all. However, it is convenient to address them here.

Parliamentary Statements

7.8 Until 1992, there was a 'self-imposed judicial rule that forbade any reference to the [parliamentary] legislative history of an enactment as an aid to its interpretation',[9] sometimes referred to as the 'exclusionary rule' (although it was not always scrupulously followed).[10] As discussed below, the rule was relaxed, to a certain degree, by the House of Lords in *Pepper v Hart*.[11] Since then, it has been relaxed further still.[12]

Hansard

7.9 The 'Official Report' of what is said in Parliament—both on the floors of the House of Commons and the House of Lords, and in committees—is known as '*Hansard*' after the printer to the House of Commons who produced the report from 1811 onwards. It is not strictly a verbatim record of everything said, as minor

---

[8] In *Spath Holme* (n 1) 397D (Lord Nicholls), a list of examples of external aids to interpretation included 'a statute's legislative antecedents'. The particular principles that apply to the role of previous legislation in an interpretation exercise are addressed separately in Chapter 5 (see that chapter generally, and especially at 5.25–5.26 and 5.29–5.38), and consequently previous legislation is not treated as an 'external aid' for the purposes of this chapter.

[9] *Pepper v Hart* (n 4) 617D–E (Lord Griffiths).

[10] ibid 630D–631D (Lord Browne-Wilkinson), expressing this as 'a general rule that references to Parliamentary material as an aid to statutory construction is not permissible'.

[11] *Pepper v Hart* (n 4), as discussed at paragraphs 7.10–7.16 below.

[12] See paragraph 7.17 below.

errors are corrected and minor redundancies left out. But for all practical purposes it provides a full, official and substantially verbatim record of the principal proceedings in Parliament. Accordingly, when parliamentary legislative history is admissible as an aid to construction, the courts will recognise Hansard as an authoritative account of the relevant proceedings.

The Rule in *Pepper v Hart*

7.10   Under what is commonly known as 'the rule in *Pepper v Hart*', reference by the courts to parliamentary material is permissible to assist in construing an Act of Parliament when the following three conditions (set out by Lord Browne-Wilkinson in that case) are met:

    (a)   legislation is ambiguous or obscure, or leads to an absurdity;

    (b)   the material relied upon consists of one or more statements by a Minister or other promoter of the Bill together if necessary with such other Parliamentary material as is necessary to understand such statements and their effect;

    (c)   the statements relied upon are clear.[13]

7.11   Parliamentary materials may be used to aid the construction of statutory instruments (SIs) as well as Acts of Parliament.[14] It was said in *Pepper v Hart* that the use of parliamentary materials in that context is 'logically indistinguishable' from their use in aid of interpreting Acts of Parliament, which suggests that the same rules on admissibility will apply in both contexts.[15]

7.12   The *Pepper v Hart* criteria have been repeatedly reaffirmed at the highest level, with Lord Bingham stating in *Spath Holme* that they 'should be strictly insisted upon'.[16] As he explained, the first criterion avoids burdening both courts

---

[13] *Pepper v Hart* (n 4) 640C (Lord Browne-Wilkinson). As to the third condition, Lord Browne-Wilkinson considered (at 634D–E) that 'references in court to Parliamentary material should only be permitted where such material clearly discloses the mischief aimed at or the legislative intention lying behind the ambiguous or obscure words'. See also *Melluish (Inspector of Taxes) v BMI (No 3) Ltd* [1996] AC 454 (HL) 481F–H (Lord Browne-Wilkinson), emphasising that the statements relied upon must be 'directed to the very point in question in the litigation'.

[14] *Pickstone v Freemans plc* [1989] AC 66, 112B–C (Lord Keith).

[15] See *Pepper v Hart* (n 4) 635F (Lord Browne-Wilkinson). But see *Re Recovery of Medical Costs for Asbestos Diseases (Wales) Bill* [2015] UKSC 3, [2015] AC 1016 [56] (Lord Mance), stating that there may be a distinction between the scope for reliance upon such materials in connection with 'primary legislation by the UK Parliament', on the one hand, and 'other legislative and executive decisions', on the other, on the basis that Art 9 of the Bill of Rights 1689 did not apply to the latter, but declining 'to go further into this difficult area' in that case. Note, however, that this comment was made in the context of referring to parliamentary materials to assess the proportionality of legislation for the purposes of the Human Rights Act 1998 (as to which see paragraphs 7.18–7.20 below), rather than under the rule in *Pepper v Hart*.

[16] *Spath Holme* (n 1) 392D–E, with the agreement of Lord Hope (at 408C–D) and Lord Hutton (at 413G–H). See also, eg, *Gopaul v Baksh* [2012] UKPC 1 [3] (Lord Walker); and *Ministry of Justice, Lithuania v Bucnys* [2013] UKSC 71, [2014] AC 480 [32] (Lord Mance). It has been said, in particular by Lord Steyn on a number of occasions (see, eg, *McDonnell v Congregation of Christian Brothers*

and lawyers with having to trawl through parliamentary history 'in practically every case', when this will often be a futile and wasteful task.[17] The second criterion helps ensure that the statement in Parliament to which reference is made is one that can usefully be relied upon to elucidate the legislative meaning (at least where the relevant clause in the Bill is not amended after the statement is made).[18] The third criterion avoids the risk that the court may appraise or criticise parliamentary material and stray into the constitutionally impermissible territory of breaching parliamentary privilege (protected by Article 9 of the Bill of Rights);[19] it also recognises that, if an aid is not itself 'clear and unequivocal', it will be 'of little or no value'.[20]

Trustees [2003] UKHL 63, [2004] 1 AC 1101 [29]; *Jackson v Attorney General* [2005] UKHL 56, [2006] 1 AC 262 [97]; and *NASS* (n 3) [6]) that the rule in *Pepper v Hart* (n 4) should be understood more narrowly as a form of estoppel, applying only to constrain the Executive from relying on an interpretation of legislation when it is has given an assurance to Parliament that the true interpretation was otherwise. However, the three cases cited at the start of this note show that the orthodox view involves a wider reading of *Pepper v Hart*, which (when the relevant criteria are met) generally permits recourse to be had to parliamentary materials to assist in ascertaining the meaning of statutory language. Accordingly, it now appears to be clear that the 'statement of Lord Steyn does no more than create a category of case where statements made prior to legislation become admissible': see *Solar Century Holdings Ltd v Secretary of State for Energy and Climate Change* [2014] EWHC 3677 (Admin) [66] (Green J).

[17] *Spath Holme* (n 1) 391E–F and 392D–F (Lord Bingham). See also, eg, *Wilson v First County Trust (No 2)* [2003] UKHL 40, [2004] 1 AC 816 [140] (Lord Hobhouse); and *Robinson v Secretary of State for Northern Ireland* [2002] UKHL 32 [39]–[40] (Lord Hoffmann), stating that Lord Mackay was right to predict in *Pepper v Hart* (n 4) that permitting reference to Hansard 'would increase the expense of litigation without contributing very much of value to the quality of decision-making', remarking that '[r]eferences to Hansard are now fairly frequently included in argument and beneath those references there must lie a large spoil heap of material which has been mined in the course of research without yielding anything worthy even of a submission'.

[18] *Spath Holme* (n 1) 391G (Lord Bingham). Note that the relevant statement by the minister or other promoter must be directed to the 'very point in question in the litigation': see *Melluish* (n 13), as cited in that note. See also in relation to the second criterion *Hone v Going Places Leisure Travel Ltd* [2001] EWCA Civ 947 [20] (Longmore LJ), stressing the importance of reading admissible ministerial statements in context. It is clear that the relevant statement may be one made in debate on the floor of either House or in committee: see, eg, *Spath Holme* 400H (Lord Nicholls): 'In considering whether a ministerial statement is clear and unequivocal, regard must be had to the circumstances in which it was made. Extempore answers given in the course of vigorous debate in the House or in committee cannot be expected to be as comprehensive and precise as more formal statements'; *Pepper v Hart* (n 4) 625F–629H (Lord Browne-Wilkinson), referring to numerous ministerial statements in committee; and *R (Minton Morrill Solicitors) v Lord Chancellor* [2017] EWHC 612 (Admin) [35] and [51] (Kerr J), referring to statements at the committee and report stages. But see *R (Hillingdon London Borough Council) v Secretary of State for Transport* [2017] EWHC 121 (Admin), [2017] 1 WLR 2166 [69] (Cranston J), stating (without any further explanation or any citation of authority) that 'statements in committee, made in response to points raised in debate and often without considered thought, can have no role in a *Pepper v Hart* exercise'. In the light of the other cases cited above, this statement is perhaps best read as simply emphasising the importance of understanding parliamentary statements in context.

[19] *Spath Holme* (n 1) 391H–392A (Lord Bingham). Article 9 of the Bill of Rights (passed in 1689) states: 'the freedom of speech and debates or proceedings in Parliament ought not to be impeached or questioned in any court or place out of Parliament'. On the issue of parliamentary privilege more generally, see *Office of Government Commerce v Information Commissioner* [2008] EWHC 774 (Admin), [2010] QB 98 [46]–[50] (Stanley Burnton J).

[20] *Spath Holme* (n 1) 398H–399C (Lord Nicholls), and see also at 400H (Lord Nicholls), as cited in n 18 above, with regard to the task of assessing whether parliamentary statements are sufficiently clear

7.13　Lord Bingham also considered that the nature of these criteria meant it would be 'most unlikely' that parliamentary materials could be used as an aid to construction where the issue is 'the scope of a statutory power' rather than 'the meaning of a statutory expression'.[21]

7.14　Further, as with any external aid, it must always be remembered that statements of ministers or others, however made or however explicit, 'cannot control the meaning of an Act of Parliament';[22] it is the enactment itself which represents the law. Accordingly, in the interests of legal certainty and fairness for the citizen, the courts have indicated that certain specific situations may make recourse to Hansard inappropriate as an aid to interpretation:

7.14.1　It has been doubted whether parliamentary materials can be used to overturn a previous decision of the House of Lords that was decided before such materials became admissible as an external aid, save perhaps in exceptional circumstances.[23]

7.14.2　It has been said that Hansard should not be used to give a broader meaning to an ambiguous statute so as to make someone criminally liable.[24]

---

and unequivocal for the purposes of the rule in *Pepper v Hart* (n 4). See also *Melluish* (n 13), as cited in that note; and, eg, *R (Brown) v Secretary of State for the Home Department* [2015] UKSC 8, [2015] 1 WLR 1060 [27] (Lord Toulson): 'ministerial answers to questions should only be admitted under *Pepper v Hart* ... in the plainest of cases'.

[21] *Spath Holme* (n 1) 392B–D (Lord Bingham), Lord Hope (407E–408F) and Lord Hutton (414G–414F) agreeing on this point. This is because it is readily conceivable that a minister might have explained clearly the meaning of a particular expression, but he would be unlikely to have sought to give a definitive statement as to a provision's legal effect, or all the ways in which a power might be used. Lord Bingham continued: 'Only if a minister were, improbably, to give a categorical assurance to Parliament that a power would not be used in a given situation, such that Parliament could be taken to have legislated on that basis, does it seem to me that a parliamentary statement on the scope of a power would be properly admissible.' Contrast Lord Nicholls in the minority on this point at 398F–H. See further, eg, *R (H-S) v Secretary of State for Justice* [2017] EWHC 1948 (Admin) [58]–[60] (Lang J), applying the statements of Lord Bingham and Lord Hope in this regard.

[22] *Wilson* (n 17) [58] (Lord Nicholls); and see also at [139] (Lord Hobhouse): 'it is a fundamental error of principle to confuse what a minister or a parliamentarian may have said (or said he intended) with the will and intention of Parliament itself'. See also *Public Law Project v Lord Chancellor* [2015] EWCA Civ 1193, [2016] AC 1531 [20] (Laws LJ), considering reference to both the views of parliamentary committees and ministerial statements: 'The opinions of Members of either House as to the import or merits of provisions contained in LASPO (or the Order) are, with great respect, not relevant to the fulfilment of this court's duty to construe the statute.' This decision was overturned in part on appeal to the Supreme Court, but without consideration of this point (see [2016] UKSC 39, [2016] AC 1531).

[23] *McDonnell* (n 16) [20] (Lord Bingham): 'I would need much persuasion that it would, save possibly in exceptional circumstances, be proper for the House to depart, in reliance on material derived from Hansard, from an authoritative ruling on a point of statutory construction reached at a time when such material was not regarded as a permissible aid to construction.'

[24] See *R v Tilley* [2009] EWCA Crim 1426, [2010] 1 WLR 605 [40]–[41] (Scott Baker LJ); *Thet v Director of Public Prosecutions* [2006] EWHC 2701 (Admin), [2007] 1 WLR 2022 [15] (Lord Phillips CJ). This is supported by the principles expressed in *R v Rimmington* [2005] UKHL 63, [2006] 1 AC 459 [33] (Lord Bingham). But note that broadening criminal liability by reference to Hansard was the effect of *R v T* (n 1) (discussed at paragraph 7.16 below).

7.15   It is also impermissible to use statements in Parliament to interpret legislation that had already been enacted at the time those statements were made, since they cannot have formed part of the context in which that legislation was passed.[25]

7.16   Accordingly, the courts have emphasised that it will be a 'rare' case where it is 'legitimate and helpful to consider ministerial statements in Parliament under the principle in *Pepper v Hart*'.[26] However, such cases do arise from time to time. For example, in *R v T*, Lord Phillips relied on various external aids, including Hansard, to determine that an ambiguous section of the Crime and Disorder Act 1998 had been intended to abolish the defence of *doli incapax* for 10–14 year olds[27] and not merely reverse the presumption that it applied.[28] Lord Carswell and Lord Brown[29] emphasised the particular assistance to be derived from Parliament's rejection of a draft amendment whose purpose had been to make the relevant section alter the presumption rather than abolish the defence. Lord Carswell considered this 'very cogent evidence of intention, stronger even than the statements of ministers'.[30]

Reference for Context and to Ascertain Mischief

7.17   Despite the strictness with which the rule in *Pepper v Hart* continues to be applied on questions of detailed interpretation as to the meaning of particular

---

[25] See *Williams* (n 5) [53] (Lord Neuberger): 'What a committee recommended in 1936, or what was said in Parliament in 1939, cannot, as I see it, possibly affect the meaning of a definition in a statute enacted in 1925'; and *R (H) v Inland Revenue Commissioners* [2002] EWHC 2164 (Admin) [27] (Stanley Burnton J): 'The beliefs or assumptions of Parliament are not an admissible aid to the interpretation of previous legislation.' See also *Hillsdown Holdings plc v Pensions Ombudsman* [1997] 1 All ER 862 (QB), 899A–C (Knox J), declining to consider statements in Parliament regarding the meaning of a provision of earlier legislation that was effectively being re-enacted with amendments by the legislation then passing through Parliament, stating that citations from Hansard can only be used to shed light on the meaning of 'legislation then going through Parliament on the way to the statute book'. But see *Brown* (n 20) [26] (Lord Toulson), declining to 'lay down a firm rule that the Hansard record of a ministerial statement in a debate on predecessor legislation can never be admissible in circumstances where the wording of the later Act is materially identical'.

[26] *R v T* (n 1) [35] (Lord Phillips). See also, eg, *Robinson v Secretary of State for Northern Ireland* [2002] UKHL 32 [40] (Lord Hoffmann), emphasising that such cases will be 'very rare indeed'; and *R (Minton Morrill Solicitors) v Lord Chancellor* [2017] EWHC 612 (Admin) [54] (Kerr J), stating that that case was 'one of those relatively rare cases where the statements of the minister responsible for promoting legislation in Parliament conclusively resolve an ambiguity as to its true meaning'.

[27] Historically, this defence had raised a rebuttable presumption that children aged 10–14 did not have the capacity for criminal intent.

[28] *R v T* (n 1) [29]–[35] (Lord Phillips). Lord Rodger ([37]) and Lord Carswell ([39]–[40]) doubted whether resort to Hansard was required, but agreed that it helped put the matter 'beyond doubt'. Lord Brown ([42]) expressly endorsed the use of Hansard. Lord Mance ([44]) agreed with all judgments.

[29] *R v T* (n 1) [40] and [42], respectively.

[30] This may suggest some flexibility in the second limb of the rule in *Pepper v Hart* (n 4), as set out at paragraph 7.10 above; note, however, that Lord Phillips cited and relied upon the statements of the minister opposing the draft amendments (at [31] and [32]), as well as the fact of their rejection. See, in a similar vein, the reliance placed upon changes made to a draft Bill in *R (Evans) v Attorney General* [2015] UKSC 21, [2015] AC 1787 [170] (Lord Wilson, dissenting) and [156] (Lord Hughes, also dissenting), but compare [92] (Lord Neuberger, in the majority).

legislative language, it now appears to be clear that parliamentary materials can be relied upon as a matter of course as part of an exercise of statutory construction 'to identify the mischief at which legislation was directed and its objective setting'. This is a distinct principle from the rule in *Pepper v Hart*.[31]

Human Rights and EU Law Cases

7.18   The courts have stated that in the specific contexts of assessing the compatibility of legislation with Convention rights for the purposes of the Human Rights Act 1998 (HRA 1998) or with EU law, they will take a broadly permissive approach to the use of parliamentary materials.[32] Since it is now clear that parliamentary materials can always be referred to on questions of general context and mischief when interpreting legislation (see the previous paragraph), the statements made in relation to these specific areas may be of rather less significance than in the past, but they are still important to note.

7.19   *Convention Rights under the HRA 1998*: 'For the strictly limited purpose of considering whether legislation is compatible with Convention rights' (for the purposes of the HRA 1998), the courts can have regard to whatever information can be gleaned from the records of proceedings in Parliament that may be of assistance.[33] This may include statements by any 'member of either House in the course of a debate on a Bill',[34] written questions and answers, or proceedings in select committees.[35] The entitlement to consider parliamentary materials in this context arises 'under a rule quite distinct from that in *Pepper v Hart*'.[36]

---

[31] *Jackson* (n 16) [97] (Lord Steyn), approved in *Presidential Insurance Co Ltd v Resha St Hill* [2012] UKPC 33 [23]–[24] (Lord Mance), approved in turn in *Williams* (n 5) [105] (Lord Neuberger). See also *Gopaul* (n 16) [3] (Lord Walker) (also approved by Lord Mance in *Presidential Insurance* at [23]); *Kennedy v Information Commissioner* [2014] UKSC 20, [2015] AC 455 [118]–[119] (Lord Toulson); *Solar Century* (n 16) [51] (Green J), citing *R (Bradley) v Secretary of State for Work and Pensions* [2008] EWCA Civ 36, [2009] QB 114 [43] (Chadwick LJ); and, eg, *SJ & J Monk v Newbigin* [2017] UKSC 56, [2017] 1 WLR 851 [21] (Lord Hodge). This wider approach permitting recourse to Hansard for ascertaining context and mischief may have been what Lord Hope had in mind in *Gow v Grant* [2012] UKSC 29, 2012 SLT 829 when he stated (at [29]) that 'the rather strict rules that were laid down in [*Pepper v Hart*] have become gradually more relaxed'. See also the discussion of some of this case law in *H-S* (n 21) [60]–[65] (Lang J), stating that the ability to refer to Hansard to ascertain the mischief at which a statute was directed cannot be used to get around the limits the courts have placed on the use of Hansard to 'identify the scope of a discretionary power conferred by statute', discussed at paragraph 7.13 above.
[32] Strictly, the use of parliamentary materials in these contexts may not always involve their use as an aid to interpretation as such. But given the treatment in this book of ss 3 and 4 of the HRA 1998 (see Chapter 10) and the duty to interpret legislation compatibly with rules of EU law (see Chapter 12.21–12.29), it is convenient to address generally here the use of parliamentary materials in these contexts.
[33] *Wilson* (n 17) [118] (Lord Hope).
[34] ibid [64] (Lord Nicholls).
[35] ibid [118] (Lord Hope).
[36] *Re Asbestos* (n 15) [55] (Lord Mance).

7.20 As always, when referring to and considering parliamentary proceedings in this connection, parliamentary privilege (under Article 9 of the Bill of Rights) must be respected. But so long as the courts look to such materials only for 'background information', or information as to the 'practical impact' or 'rationale underlying' legislation, their reference to parliamentary debates should not involve any infringement of that privilege.[37]

7.21 *Rights under EU law*: in a similar vein, the courts have held that the exclusionary rule does not prevent reference to Hansard for the purposes of determining whether domestic legislation implementing an EU law obligation is compatible with that obligation, including determining whether that legislation can be construed consistently with that obligation.[38] Again, this is distinct from the rule in *Pepper v Hart*, but the courts must still be alive to the need to observe parliamentary privilege.[39]

The Practicalities of Using Hansard

7.22 As the courts have repeatedly recognised, reference to Hansard can be extremely time-consuming and a poor use of resources for both courts and legal advisors alike.[40] Nevertheless, when a practitioner is called upon to argue about or advise upon the meaning of an (arguably) unclear piece of legislation, the potential for debate about the permissibility or usefulness of referring to parliamentary materials means that work will often be required to research the parliamentary record to see what can be gleaned. When it comes to deciding whether and how the fruits of these endeavours should be used in argument before the court, those presenting the case should then take a considered and responsible view as to the benefit that can truly be derived by the court from these materials.[41] Adverse costs orders may be made where Hansard material is cited inappropriately.[42]

7.23 Where practitioners do decide to cite Hansard before a court, there is a Practice Direction requiring them to notify the other parties and the court of this

---

[37] *Wilson* (n 17) [63]–[64] (Lord Nicholls). As to parliamentary privilege, see n 19 above. See further the citation from *Re Asbestos* (n 15) in that note, which suggests that there may be a distinction between the extent to which parliamentary materials may be used in assessing the proportionality of Acts of Parliament as opposed to secondary legislation.

[38] See *R (Amicus) v Secretary of State for Trade and Industry* [2004] EWHC 860 (Admin), [2007] ICR 1176 [61]–[65] and [115] (Richards J), and the cases cited there.

[39] See *R (Buckinghamshire County Council) v Secretary of State for Transport* [2014] UKSC 3; [2014] 1 WLR 324 [78]–[79] (Lord Reed), stating that if and insofar as EU law may seem to require the courts to go beyond what would otherwise be considered permissible under Art 9 of the Bill of Rights, this would raise a question of high constitutional importance requiring consideration.

[40] See n 17 above.

[41] See, eg, *Spath Holme* (n 1) 399A (Lord Nicholls), hoping that counsel would in future be 'more realistic and more sparing in their references to such material', given its limitations.

[42] See *Melluish* (n 13) 481F–482B (Lord Browne-Wilkinson).

intention at least five clear working days in advance of the hearing, with the court empowered to make such order as it considers appropriate if this is not done, including with regard to costs.[43]

7.24 Hansard research may be conducted by reference to paper and online resources:

7.24.1 Hansard is published daily in hard copy and electronic copy. Annual bound hard copies are produced and can often be found in law libraries.

7.24.2 The Parliament website has Hansard records of more recent proceedings in the House of Commons dating back to November 1988[44] and in the House of Lords dating back to November 1995.[45] The records are searchable not only by date, but also (in relation to certain more recent proceedings) by member and other categories (for example, by Bill). For proceedings occurring since May 2010, a free text search can also be performed.[46]

7.24.3 Historic Hansard records from 1803 to 2005 are also searchable online.[47]

7.24.4 Acts can be looked up in the relevant volume of *Current Law Statutes Annotated* (again, often available in law libraries), which contains a helpful list of the occasions on which the relevant Bill that became the Act was debated, whether on the floor of either House or in Committee. Those references can be followed up in Hansard (whether in hard copy or online).

Explanatory Notes

7.25 As discussed in more detail below, Explanatory Notes may accompany both Acts of Parliament and SIs. In each case, they can be taken into account as external aids. They are distinct from Explanatory Memoranda, which are discussed below at paragraphs 7.35–7.37.

---

[43] Practice Direction (Hansard: Citation) (Sup Ct) [1995] 1 WLR 192. Where Hansard material is cited in circumstances where the Practice Direction has not been complied with, it is open to the court to 'waive the irregularity', and it has been said that it would have 'a strong reason to do so if the material were necessary to resolve a question of statutory construction': see *Ivey v Genting Casinos UK Ltd* [2016] EWCA Civ 1093, [2017] 1 WLR 679 [61] (Arden LJ).

[44] See the archive at www.parliament.uk/business/publications/hansard/commons for proceedings between November 1998 and March 2016, and see hansard.parliament.uk for proceedings from May 2010 to the present day.

[45] See the archive at www.parliament.uk/business/publications/hansard/lords for proceedings between November 1995 and March 2016, and see hansard.parliament.uk for proceedings from May 2010 to the present day.

[46] At hansard.parliament.uk.

[47] At hansard.millbanksystems.com.

Explanatory Notes to Acts

7.26   With respect to Acts, the production and publication of Explanatory Notes is now standard practice for most government Bills, although this is a relatively recent phenomenon, having begun in 1999.[48] As Lord Steyn has explained, they are drafted by the government department responsible for the Bill in question and will accompany the Bill upon its introduction to Parliament, being amended as the Bill itself is amended (although they are not subject to amendment by Parliament itself). If the Bill is passed, a finalised copy will be published along with the Act. The Explanatory Notes are not themselves endorsed by Parliament in any way, although the practice of producing them is.[49]

7.27   The purpose of Explanatory Notes is 'to explain what the Act sets out to achieve and to make the Act accessible to readers who are not legally qualified'.[50] They often take the format of a brief statement of the background to the Act, followed by an overview of its structure, and then a concise section-by-section commentary.

7.28   Explanatory Notes to Acts are readily accessible online. They can be found at www.legislation.gov.uk by finding the relevant Act and then clicking on the 'Explanatory Notes' or 'More Resources' tabs. Explanatory Notes accompanying Bills going through Parliament may also be available on the www.parliament.uk website via the 'Bill documents' page for the relevant Bill.

7.29   Explanatory Notes to Acts are 'always admissible aids to construction' insofar as they 'cast light on the objective setting or contextual scene of the statute, and the mischief at which it is aimed'. That is so whether or not the legislation itself is ambiguous, since 'language in all legal texts conveys meaning according to the circumstances in which it was used'.[51] However, there appears to have been a degree

---

[48]   Before 1999, 'Notes on Clauses' were produced, initially only for ministers but later also for all Members of Parliament. For an explanation of the history and nature of Explanatory Notes and Notes on Clauses (encompassing this point among others), see *NASS* (n 3) [3]–[4] (Lord Steyn). In accordance with the applicable principles (as to which see paragraph 7.5 above), Notes on Clauses will only be admissible as an aid to interpretation when they have been published so as to make them 'available to the public at large', which is not normally the case: see *R (Public and Commercial Services Union) v Minister for the Civil Service* [2010] EWHC 1027 (Admin), [2011] 3 All ER 54 [53]–[55] (Sales J), refusing to take into account Notes on Clauses as an interpretive aid in that case. For a recent case where Notes on Clauses have been referred to, see, eg, *R (Eastenders Cash & Carry plc) v Revenue and Customs Commissioners* [2014] UKSC 34, [2015] AC 1101 [45] (Lord Sumption and Lord Reed), where the Notes had been appended to the report of a committee reporting on the relevant Bill.

[49]   See *NASS* (n 3) [4] (Lord Steyn).

[50]   See the helpful glossary at www.legislation.gov.uk/help. See also *NASS* (n 3) [4] (Lord Steyn): 'The purpose is to help the reader to get his bearings and to ease the task of assimilating the law.'

[51]   *NASS* (n 3) [5] (Lord Steyn), as cited in that note, and see also to like effect *R (S) v Chief Constable of South Yorkshire Police* [2004] UKHL 39, [2004] 1 WLR 2196 [4] (Lord Steyn). This part of Lord Steyn's speech in *NASS* was cited with approval in *R v Montila* [2004] UKHL 50, [2004] 1 WLR 3141 [35]–[36] (Lord Hope, giving the opinion of the Committee), but see further the discussion in the following note.

of debate in the case law as to whether and how far the 'contextual scene' provided by external aids should be allowed to influence the interpretation of legislative provisions whose meaning otherwise appears to be clear and unambiguous.[52] Whatever the precise limits of the role of context and mischief in interpretation, what is clear beyond doubt is that it is the statutory language itself which the courts must ultimately interpret, and context and mischief do not give them a licence to take a 'free-wheeling view of the intention of Parliament' which does not give proper respect to the actual words Parliament has chosen.[53]

7.30 While the use of Explanatory Notes to illuminate the 'context and purpose' of an Act is well-accepted, it has been said that they 'cannot be taken into

---

[52] In *NASS* (n 3) [5], Lord Steyn emphasised that statutory language can only be properly understood in its context, while also making clear that it is ultimately that language itself which must be interpreted. This part of Lord Steyn's speech was cited with approval in *Montila* (n 51) [35]–[36] (Lord Hope, giving the opinion of the Committee), and *Flora v Wakom (Heathrow) Ltd* [2006] EWCA Civ 1103, [2007] 1 WLR 482 [15]–[16] (Brooke LJ). Similarly, in *Spath Holme* (n 1) at 398B–C, Lord Nicholls stated that context provided by external aids could be used to help decide 'whether statutory language is clear and unambiguous and not productive of absurdity', although he stressed that the courts should be 'slow to permit external aids to displace meanings which are otherwise clear and unambiguous and not productive of absurdity'. See also *Solar Century* (n 16) [52] (Green J), stating that 'if there is a collision between a literal interpretation of an enactment and the contextual material with the consequence that the literal interpretation *"is manifestly contrary to the intention which one may readily impute to Parliament, when having regard to the historical context and the mischief …"*, then the enactment should be construed in the light of the purpose as evident from the historical context and mischief', citing *R v Z (Attorney General for Northern Ireland's Reference)* [2005] UKHL 35, [2005] 2 AC 645 [49] (Lord Carswell). (This passage in *Solar Century* was cited with approval in *Director of Legal Aid Casework v Briggs* [2017] EWCA Civ 1169 [82] (King LJ).) But compare *R (D) v Secretary of State for Work and Pensions* [2010] EWCA Civ 18, [2010] 1 WLR 1782 [45]–[47] (Carnwath LJ), discussing the interpretive assistance provided by Explanatory Notes and Explanatory Memoranda in relation to SIs, and stating that where statutory language is 'unambiguous', the court is not 'free to rewrite it by reference to the explanatory notes' (at least in the context of domestic law, and where the plain meaning does not lead to absurdity). Carnwath LJ noted that Lord Steyn's views in *NASS* were not approved by the other members of the House and that his speech relied upon case law in the contractual context. He stated that the 'orthodox position' was as expressed by Lord Hope in *Coventry and Solihull Waste Disposal Co Ltd v Russell* [1999] 1 WLR 2093 (HL) 2103E: 'an explanatory note may be referred to as an aid to construction where the statutory instrument to which it is attached is ambiguous', but not otherwise (as to this passage in *Coventry*, see n 63 below). However, it is notable that Lord Hope's speech in *Montila* was not cited to the Court in *R (D)*. In a similar vein to *R (D)*, see *The PNPF Trust Co Ltd v Taylor* [2010] EWHC 1573 (Ch), [2010] Pens LR 261 [479] (Warren J): 'The note cannot be used, in my view, to create an ambiguity where none exists' (but again, *Montila* does not appear to have been cited to the Court in that case). As to the courts' approach generally to contextual factors when interpreting legislation, including when these are in conflict with the apparent meaning of the text, see Chapter 3.43–3.44 and the paragraphs, notes and cases cited in the notes to those paragraphs.

[53] *Williams* (n 5) [72] (Lord Neuberger): 'When interpreting a statute, the court's function is to determine the meaning of the words used in the statute. The fact that context and mischief are factors which must be taken into account does not mean that, when performing its interpretive role, the court can take a free-wheeling view of the intention of Parliament looking at all admissible material, and treating the wording of the statute as merely one item. Context and mischief do not represent a licence to judges to ignore the plain meaning of the words that Parliament has used.' See also *NASS* (n 3) and *R (D)* (n 52), as cited in n 52 above.

account in the detailed interpretation' of an Act.[54] However, although that is probably true as a general rule, the courts have also said that they can be used as external aids:

7.30.1   in the same way as Explanatory Notes to SIs (as to which, see below at paragraphs 7.32–7.34);[55] and

7.30.2   where the rule in *Pepper v Hart* can be applied (at least on a narrow reading of that rule).[56]

7.31   The courts have recognised that Explanatory Notes may be particularly helpful aids to construction, explaining that they 'will sometimes be more informative and valuable … than pre-parliamentary aids' because of their closer connection 'with the shape of the proposed legislation'.[57] (As to pre-parliamentary aids, see paragraphs 7.38–7.40 below.)

Explanatory Notes to Statutory Instruments

7.32   Explanatory Notes to SIs have been drafted by government and published along with SIs ever since the introduction of SIs under the Statutory Instruments Act 1948. They are principally designed to give the reader of an SI 'a concise and clear statement of the substance and purpose of the instrument', and may also contain supplemental information (for example, in relation to the authority under which the instrument is made where this is not set out in the instrument's preamble).[58] They can be found online at www.legislation.gov.uk by finding the relevant SI and clicking on 'Explanatory Note' as listed in the 'Table of Contents' tab.

---

[54] *MS (Uganda) v Secretary of State for the Home Department* [2014] EWCA Civ 50, [2014] 1 WLR 2766 [31] (Elias LJ), finding that the Notes in that case gave a confirmatory indication as to the purpose of the relevant provision, but that this amounted to 'something of a make-weight argument'.

[55] *R v A (No 2)* [2001] UKHL 25, [2002] 1 AC 45 [82] (Lord Hope).

[56] See *NASS* (n 3) [6] (Lord Steyn), stating that a clear assurance by the executive in Explanatory Notes 'may in principle be admitted against the executive in proceedings in which the executive places a contrary contention before a court. This reflects the actual decision in *Pepper v Hart*' (n 4). Lord Steyn thus sought to apply the rule in *Pepper v Hart* to the use of Explanatory Notes as an external aid, whilst also seeking to endorse a narrow view of that rule. However, his view of *Pepper v Hart* has not been generally adopted (as to which, see n 16 above, and as to the rule in *Pepper v Hart*, see generally paragraphs 7.10–7.16 above). It may therefore be appropriate instead to permit the use of Explanatory Notes in this context in accordance with the orthodox (wider) view of the application of the rule in *Pepper v Hart* (adapted as necessary). That would be in keeping with the circumstances in which it has been said that Explanatory Notes to SIs and Explanatory Memoranda can be used as external aids, as discussed below at paragraphs 7.34 and 7.37, respectively. And see further n 60 below, and the general principles in relation to the use of external aids set out at paragraph 7.43 below.

[57] *NASS* (n 3) [5] (Lord Steyn), citing Rupert Cross, John Bell and George Engle, *Statutory Interpretation*, 3rd edn (Oxford, Oxford University Press, 1995) 160–161. Lord Steyn's statement was endorsed on this point in *Director of Assets Recovery Agency v David Green* [2005] EWHC 3168 (Admin) [11] (Sullivan J).

[58] *Statutory Instrument Practice*, 4th edn (London, Her Majesty's Stationery Office, 2006) 29–30, paras 2.13.2–2.13.4.

7.33 It is important to emphasise that, although Explanatory Notes are published together with SIs and are attached to them, they do not form part of those SIs (and their text will often say so in terms).[59]

7.34 It has been said that Explanatory Notes to SIs may be used as external aids:[60]

7.34.1 'to ascertain the context of the provision and the mischief which it addresses as aids to purposive interpretation';[61]

7.34.2 to determine the purpose of an SI, in particular to decide whether any mistakes have been made with its drafting, and if so what mistakes;[62]

7.34.3 when 'the statutory instrument to which it is attached is ambiguous';[63]

7.34.4 when they (alone or in conjunction with other external aids) are 'clear and unequivocal'.[64]

---

[59] *Pickstone* (n 14) 127A–B (Lord Oliver): 'the explanatory note ... is not, of course, part of the Regulations'.

[60] More generally, as a matter of principle, it should be possible to use Explanatory Notes to Acts, Explanatory Notes to SIs and Explanatory Memoranda as external aids in the same broad ways as one another, given the reasons of principle for allowing the use of these materials in these ways, and given that these materials all similarly provide contemporaneous insight into the contextual scene and the promoter's intentions regarding the relevant legislation. Thus, regardless of whether legislation is ambiguous, these sources should always be admissible to 'cast light on the objective setting or contextual scene of the statute, and the mischief at which it is aimed' (see *NASS* (n 3) [5] (Lord Steyn), in relation to Explanatory Notes to Acts), and they may be used to provide further interpretive assistance where the *Pepper v Hart* (n 4) criteria are met. See further paragraph 7.30.1 above, n 63 below and the general principles for using external aids at paragraph 7.43 below.

[61] *McDonald v Newton* [2017] UKSC 52, 2017 SLT 87 [30] (Lord Hodge), citing *Spath Holme* (n 1) 397–98 (Lord Nicholls). See also *Pickstone* (n 14) 127A–B (Lord Oliver), stating that an Explanatory Note to an SI could be referred to for 'identifying the mischief the Regulations were attempting to remedy'.

[62] *R (Confederation of Passenger Transport UK) v Humber Bridge Board* [2003] EWCA Civ 842, [2004] QB 310 ('*CPTUK*') [49] (Clarke LJ), in the context of determining whether it was permissible for the Court, by means of interpretation, to correct a clear error in legislative drafting (as to which see Chapter 3.49–3.51).

[63] *Coventry* (n 52) 2103E (Lord Hope). This was said to represent 'the orthodox position' in *R (D)* (n 52) [48] (Carnwath LJ). But see *Montila* (n 51) [35]–[36] (Lord Hope), approving both his statement in *Coventry* and Lord Steyn's statement in *NASS* (n 3) at [5] (as cited in the text to n 51 above) that Explanatory Notes to an Act can 'always' be looked at to cast light on a statute's context and the mischief at which it is aimed. Accordingly, the requirement for ambiguity in *Coventry* may best be understood as a prerequisite for allowing an external aid to have a greater bearing on the meaning of legislation than it can have when referred to simply as part of the general contextual scene. This is supported by the Court of Appeal's express endorsement of applying the *Pepper v Hart* (n 4) criteria to the use of Explanatory Memoranda as external aids, since these similarly provide an official statement by the government as to the intended purpose and effect of an SI: see paragraph 7.37.1 below.

[64] *CPTUK* (n 62) [52] (Clarke LJ), applying *Pepper v Hart* (n 4) and *Spath Holme* (n 1).

Explanatory Memoranda

7.35 Since 1999, some SIs laid before Parliament have been accompanied by an Explanatory Memorandum drafted by the government department responsible for the SI. The production of these Memoranda has become standard practice for SIs laid before Parliament since around 2005. Their purpose is to set out for the benefit of Parliament's committees and members, in language accessible to those who are not legally qualified, information about the 'policy objective and policy implications' of the relevant SI.[65]

7.36 Unlike Explanatory Notes, Explanatory Memoranda are not published directly alongside the SI itself (having been produced principally for the benefit of Parliament rather than the public at large). However, they are publicly available documents, and can be sourced at www.legislation.gov.uk by finding the relevant SI and then clicking on the 'Explanatory Memorandum' or 'More Resources' tab.

7.37 In relation to the use of Explanatory Memoranda as external aids, the courts have stated that:[66]

7.37.1 they may be relied upon where the *Pepper v Hart* criteria are met;[67]

7.37.2 they may be used as an external aid where an SI is ambiguous or productive of absurdity;[68]

7.37.3 the help to be derived from Explanatory Memoranda (and Explanatory Notes) 'may be even stronger in relation to an SI than a statute, at least where the explanatory material emanates from the Secretary of State who is directly responsible for making the instrument', since they will represent a formal statement of the author's intention and because Parliament only has an approval and not an amending function in connection with SIs.[69]

---

[65] See the glossary at www.legislation.gov.uk/help (which suggests that the production of Explanatory Memoranda became standard practice in June 2004) and *R (D)* (n 52) [50] (Carnwath LJ), setting out the note regarding Explanatory Memoranda provided to the Court by Counsel (which suggests their production became standard practice in 2005).

[66] More generally, the principles which apply to the use of Explanatory Memoranda should be the same as those applying to the use of Explanatory Notes to Acts and SIs: see n 60 above.

[67] *Broadhurst v Tan* [2016] EWCA Civ 94, [2016] 1 WLR 1928 [28] (Lord Dyson MR), stating that, had there been any doubt as to the meaning of the SI under consideration, it would have been 'legitimate to use the Explanatory Memorandum as an aid to construction ... because the three conditions specified by Lord Browne-Wilkinson in *Pepper v Hart* ... would be satisfied'. As to the rule in *Pepper v Hart* (n 4), see paragraphs 7.10–7.16 above.

[68] *R (D)* (n 52) [47]–[48] (Carnwath LJ) and see generally the discussion at [44]–[51].

[69] ibid [49] (Carnwath LJ).

Pre-legislative Materials

7.38 A variety of pre-legislative materials (that is, materials produced prior to the beginning of the relevant legislative process) are also admissible as external aids,[70] although in some cases they may be less valuable than the sources considered above since they may be more remote from the content of the legislation itself.[71] Materials to which the courts have referred include:

7.38.1 *Green and White Papers*: these pre-legislative materials were discussed in Chapter 1.[72] Many can be found online.[73] In *R v T*, Lord Phillips made reference to a government consultation document (which are sometimes called 'Green Papers') and a government White Paper (a policy document)—as well as to Hansard—in order to ascertain the intended purpose and effect of an ambiguous statutory provision in a criminal law context.[74]

7.38.2 *Government responses to consultations*: a government response to consultation on proposed legislation has been said to have a 'similar status to a White Paper as a legitimate aid to interpretation', where 'in substance it fulfilled the same role of explaining the background to a legislative proposal introduced by the Government'.[75]

---

[70] See generally *Pepper v Hart* (n 4) 633E (Lord Browne-Wilkinson), referring to 'white papers, reports of official committees and Law Commission reports to which the courts already have regard' to ascertain mischief; *Spath Holme* (n 1) 397D (Lord Nicholls), identifying 'reports of Royal Commissions and advisory committees, reports of the Law Commission (with or without a draft Bill attached), and a statute's legislative antecedents' as examples of external aids (but see n 8 above with regard to the way in which the interpretive assistance to be derived from legislative antecedents is addressed in this book); and *Wilson* (n 17) [56] (Lord Nicholls), stating: 'Reports of the Law Commission or advisory committees, and government white papers, are everyday examples of background material which may assist in understanding the purpose and scope of legislation'.

[71] See paragraph 7.31 above.

[72] See Chapter 1.17.

[73] See www.gov.uk/government/publications.

[74] *R v T* (n 1) [29], [30] and [35]. The Court of Appeal in that case ([2008] EWCA Crim 815, [2009] 1 AC 1310), whose decision was affirmed on appeal, additionally referred to a Labour Party pre-governmental consultation paper at [19] (but the House of Lords did not refer to this). See also, eg, *Melville Dundas v George Wimpey (UK) Ltd* [2007] UKHL 18, [2007] 1 WLR 1136 [65] (Lord Neuberger), referring to a government consultation paper as being 'consistent' with his conclusion. This was cited in *PNPF* (n 52) [516] (Warren J), stating: 'However, it is rare that such papers, being after all only consultations, will point conclusively to a particular interpretation'. See also *R (Sisangia) v Director of Legal Aid Casework* [2016] EWCA Civ 24, [2016] 1 WLR 1373 [31] (Lewison LJ), stating that the meaning of the consultation paper must itself be clear before it can 'provide real support for a disputed interpretation' (see the fuller quotation at n 92 below); and see to similar effect with regard to a White Paper *Dyson Ltd v Qualtex (UK) Ltd* [2006] EWCA Civ 166, [2006] RPC 31 [11] (Jacob LJ).

[75] *R (Best) v Chief Land Registrar* [2015] EWCA Civ 17, [2016] QB 23 [72] (Sales LJ).

7.38.3 *Reports of the Law Commission and its predecessors*: the Law Commission was established in 1965 with the mandate of reviewing the law and making recommendations for its improvement. It publishes reports from time to time which Parliament will sometimes consider in making new laws. The reports can be found online.⁷⁶ Other similar bodies have performed this function in the past.⁷⁷ In *R v Secretary of State for Transport ex p Factortame Ltd (No 1)*,⁷⁸ Lord Bridge considered the Law Commission's Report on Remedies in Administrative Law (1976), and its proposed draft Bill, in interpreting section 31 of the Supreme Court Act 1981 (now the Senior Courts Act 1981). He drew an inference as to the meaning of the Act from Parliament's decision not to enact a section to reflect one of the clauses proposed in the Law Commission's draft Bill.⁷⁹

7.38.4 *Reports of advisory committees*: sometimes a pre-legislative report from a body such as a Royal Commission, an official committee or a parliamentary committee provides the impetus for an Act or influences its content, in which case that report may be referred to as an external aid.⁸⁰

---

⁷⁶ Reports dating back to 1965 are available at www.bailii.org/ew/other/EWLC. Reports (particularly those since 1995) can also be found at www.lawcom.gov.uk/document.

⁷⁷ The Law Revision Committee reported between 1934 and 1939 on a number of topics. The Law Reform Committee has existed since 1952, and the Criminal Law Revision Committee since 1959, to give ad hoc reports at the Lord Chancellor's request. However, both are now effectively defunct in view of the work of the Law Commission.

⁷⁸ *R v Secretary of State for Transport ex p Factortame Ltd (No 1)* [1990] 2 AC 85 (HL).

⁷⁹ ibid 148C–149H (Lord Bridge) and in particular at 149G–H. As noted in *Pepper v Hart* (n 4) 630H–631A (Lord Browne-Wilkinson), this approach went beyond simply using the report to ascertain the mischief at which the legislation was aimed. See also *I v Director of Public Prosecutions* [2001] UKHL 10, [2002] 1 AC 285 [22]–[24] (Lord Hutton), interpreting a criminal statute by reference to a Law Commission report and a statement in a White Paper that the government intended to follow the Law Commission's recommendation; and *Williams* (n 5) [103]–[105] (Lord Neuberger), stating that a Law Revision Committee report to which an Act gave effect could be referred to as an external aid if the *Pepper v Hart* criteria were met or to ascertain the general legislative background and the mischief at which the legislation was aimed. The remarks of Lord Sumption at [25] and Lord Neuberger at [112] suggest that where Parliament enacts legislation following a Law Commission report, the Law Commission's views may be more readily attributed to Parliament if Parliament seeks to enact a Law Commission draft Bill or draft clauses.

⁸⁰ See *Fothergill v Monarch Airlines Ltd* [1981] AC 251 (HL) 281B–C (Lord Diplock): 'Where the Act has been preceded by a report of some official commission or committee that has been laid before Parliament and the legislation is introduced in consequence of that report, the report itself may be looked at by the court for the limited purpose of identifying the "mischief" that the Act was intended to remedy, and for such assistance as is derivable from this knowledge in giving the right purposive construction to the Act'; *Cooke v MGN Ltd* [2014] EWHC 2831 (QB), [2015] 1 WLR 895 [34]–[35] (Bean J): 'I consider that it is proper to refer … to the Joint Committee's Report on the draft Bill to identify the mischief at which it was aimed.' See also *Eastenders* (n 48) [45] (Lord Sumption and Lord Reed), referring to the report of a committee reporting on a draft Bill, on the question of whether Parliament intended certain legislation to change the existing powers of customs officers; and *Director of Public Prosecutions v Bull* [1995] QB 88 (CA) 94C–H, applying *Fothergill*.

7.39   Courts have also referred to other kinds of pre-legislative materials as external aids, such as reports of inspectors following public inquiries and decision letters of the Secretary of State.[81]

7.40   The precise limits on what pre-legislative materials may be referred to are not clear. But it is clear that, as a matter of principle, there are limits on the type of material to which regard may be had: see paragraphs 7.4 and 7.5 above.[82]

7.41   Pre-legislative materials, like the other aids discussed above, can be referred to in order to understand the general context of enactments and the mischief at which they are aimed.[83] As for their use with regard to more detailed questions of construction, it is submitted that they can be used in the same way as other aids (as to which see below at paragraph 7.43).

Post-legislative Materials

7.42   What may be termed 'post-legislative materials' (that is, documents produced *after* legislation has been passed) cannot be used to inform the interpretation of an enactment in the same way as materials produced during and prior to the legislative process (considered above), since they do not form part of an enactment's contextual background. Accordingly, the courts have held that while 'official statements by government departments administering an Act, or by any other authority concerned with an Act, may be taken into account as persuasive authority', they do not 'enjoy any particular legal status' and do not differ in their influence 'from a statement by an academic author in a textbook or an article'.[84]

---

[81]   *CPTUK* (n 62) [48] (Clarke LJ). See also, eg, *R (English Bridge Union Ltd) v The English Sports Council* [2015] EWHC 2875 (Admin) [35] (Dove J), allowing reference to a Memorandum which was effectively 'an amalgam of what would in current parlance be an Explanatory Memorandum and a White Paper'.

[82]   In relation to the interpretation of Acts of Parliament, in addition to the well-recognised types of aids discussed above at paragraph 7.38, it may be that reference could most easily be justified to the following types of document as a matter of principle, where they are publicly accessible and relate directly to the relevant legislation: (1) documents analogous to those materials (see, eg, *Best* (n 75) and *English Bridge Union* (n 81), as cited in those notes); and (2) any other document formally presented to Parliament by the government, such documents being known as 'Command Papers'. For information regarding Command Papers, see www.parliament.uk/documents/commons-information-office/p13.pdf. For subordinate legislation, it is less easy to identify in advance the further types of materials which are likely to be admissible as external aids, but again it is likely to be helpful to reason by analogy where possible from the types of aid which are already well-recognised.

[83]   See *Wilson* (n 17) [56] (Lord Nicholls); and *NASS* (n 3) [5] (Lord Steyn); and the other cases cited in n 86 below.

[84]   *Chief Constable of Cumbria v Wright* [2006] EWHC 3574 (Admin), [2007] 1 WLR 1407 [17] (Lloyd Jones J). This was cited with approval in *Grays Timber Products Ltd v Revenue and Customs Commissioners* [2010] UKSC 4, [2010] 1 WLR 497 [54]–[55] (Lord Hope), who emphasised the need for the relevant statement to be 'sufficiently precisely framed to amount to an official statement on the particular issue' before the court before it could be treated as having 'persuasive authority'.

In other words, their force is derived from the persuasiveness of their reasoning and they cannot 'directly affect the true construction' of legislation.[85] Accordingly, although such sources may assist a court, it is submitted that they are better not considered as a species of external aid properly so called.

General Principles for the Use of External Aids

7.43   The statements discussed above that have been made by the courts concerning the use of many different kinds of external aid reflect the varied circumstances in which they have had cause to refer to the specific aids in question in the cases before them. We have attempted to summarise below the general principles that emerge from the relevant case law in relation to the use of external aids generally:

7.43.1   External aids of all kinds can always be referred to for assistance in interpreting a piece of legislation through the elucidation of the general *context* in which it was enacted and the *mischief* at which it was aimed.[86]

7.43.2   In addition, in some instances, the courts can give greater weight to the guidance provided by external aids, allowing them to have very significant and even 'determinative' influence in resolving detailed questions of construction.[87] In the case of recourse to parliamentary material in Hansard in this regard, the circumstances in which this is permissible are narrowly circumscribed by the *Pepper v Hart* criteria.[88] In relation to other external aids, it appears that, in practice, the same or similar criteria are also applied.[89] Thus, before relying upon other external

---

[85] *Yemshaw v Hounslow London Borough Council* [2011] UKSC 3, [2011] 1 WLR 433 [56] (Lord Brown).

[86] See *NASS* (n 3) [5]–[6] (Lord Steyn), as cited in that note (this part of Lord Steyn's speech was cited with approval in *Montila* (n 51) [35]–[36] (Lord Hope, giving the opinion of the Committee)); *Spath Holme* (n 1) 397C–398E (Lord Nicholls), in particular at 397E, as cited in n 3 above; *Wilson* (n 17) [56] (Lord Nicholls); and *Williams* (n 5) [104]–[105] (Lord Neuberger). As to referring to parliamentary materials to ascertain context and mischief, see paragraph 7.17 above. With regard to other external aids, see the discussion in relation to Explanatory Notes at paragraph 7.29 above. As for the extent to which context can influence the meaning of apparently unambiguous legislation, see the discussion in that paragraph and nn 52–53 above.

[87] *Gopaul* (n 16) [3] (Lord Walker). Even in these cases, though, the role of the external aid necessarily remains limited to explaining the context and purpose of legislation: see *Williams* (n 5) [104]–[105] (Lord Neuberger), as cited in that note.

[88] See paragraphs 7.10–7.16 regarding the rule in *Pepper v Hart* (n 4).

[89] See in particular *Broadhurst* (n 67) [28] (Lord Dyson MR), as cited in that note, applying the *Pepper v Hart* (n 4) criteria to the use of Explanatory Memoranda (as to which see paragraphs 7.35–7.37 above); and *CPTUK* (n 62) [34]–[36] and [47]–[52] (Clarke LJ), referring to the *Pepper v Hart* criteria in deciding whether external aids could be used to construe an SI to determine if something had gone wrong with its language, and whether that error could be corrected by the Court. Given the nature of, and justification for, the *Pepper v Hart* criteria (as to which see paragraph 7.12 above), it is unsurprising that similar considerations are taken into account in relation to the use of other aids.

aids in relation to detailed questions of construction, the courts have often been concerned to establish that: (i) the legislation being interpreted is ambiguous, unclear or productive of absurdity;[90] (ii) the relevant external aid can fairly be expected to provide an authoritative statement of the intended meaning of the legislative provision in question;[91] and (iii) the meaning of the external aid on the relevant issue of interpretation is itself clear.[92]

7.43.3   At the same time, the courts have made clear that there are important constitutional limits on the extent to which external aids can be allowed to influence the meaning of legislation, and have emphasised the need for caution in their use:

7.43.3.1   It is the legislation itself, and not the external aid, that represents the law, and there is a consequent need to ensure that external aids are not permitted to 'control the meaning' of legislation.[93] Courts must not lose sight of the fact that their 'essential task is to construe the language of the legislation, not that of the explanatory material', and reference to external aids must not 'supplant' that task.[94]

7.43.3.2   Further, citizens 'should be able to rely upon what they read in an Act of Parliament', and the greater the extent to which resort may be had to extraneous materials in construing enactments, the more the principle of legal certainty may be undermined. Courts need, therefore, to 'approach the use of external aids with circumspection', and may have to 'strike a balance' to resolve the inherent 'tension between the need for legal certainty, which is one of the fundamental elements

---

[90] See *Coventry* (n 52) 2103D–E (Lord Hope), as cited and discussed above in paragraph 7.34.3 and n 63; *R (D)* (n 52) [45], [48] and [51] (Carnwath LJ); and *Broadhurst* (n 67) [28] (Lord Dyson MR).

[91] See *Broadhurst* (n 67) [28] (Lord Dyson MR); and *Williams* (n 5) [111] (Lord Neuberger).

[92] See *Sisangia* (n 74) [31] (Lewison LJ): 'In order for a consultation paper or other preliminary material to provide real support for a disputed interpretation, it is necessary to find some clear and definite statement. As Lord Steyn put it in relation to analogous travaux préparatoires in *Effort Shipping Co Ltd v Linden Management SA (The Giannis NK)* [1998] AC 605, 623: "Only a bull's-eye counts. Nothing less will do."' See to similar effect, with regard to the use of a White Paper specifically, *Dyson* (n 74) [11] (Jacob LJ), also citing *Effort Shipping*.

[93] *Spath Holme* (n 1) 399C–E (Lord Nicholls), emphasising that external aids are only ever 'a factor the court will take into account in construing legislation'. See also *Williams* (n 5) [104]–[105] (Lord Neuberger), and in particular the passage cited in that note; *NASS* (n 3) [6] (Lord Steyn): 'What is impermissible is to treat the wishes and desires of the Government about the scope of the statutory language as reflecting the will of Parliament ... the object is to see what is the intention expressed by the words enacted'; and *Wilson* (n 17) [139] (Lord Hobhouse): 'Once one departs from the text of the statute construed as a whole and looks for expressions of intention to be found elsewhere, one is not looking for the intention of the legislature but that of some other source with no constitutional power to make law.' See further paragraph 7.29 above.

[94] *R (D)* (n 52) [47] and [51] (Carnwath LJ), referring to external aids to construction generally (in the particular context of Explanatory Notes and Explanatory Memoranda). See also *Williams* (n 5) [105] (Lord Neuberger), as cited in that note.

of the rule of law, and the need to give effect to the intention of Parliament, from whatever source that (objectively assessed) intention can be gleaned'.[95]

7.43.4   The value of a given aid in a particular case will vary depending on the aid and the circumstances. An aid's value may depend in particular on how closely connected it is with the terms of the relevant legislation[96] and how well it can be expected to reveal the (objectively ascertainable) intention of the legislator in relation to the matter in issue.[97] Ultimately, the weight to be given to an aid in a particular case is a matter for the court.[98]

[95] *Spath Holme* (n 1) 397F–398E (Lord Nicholls); and see to similar effect *Pepper v Hart* (n 4) 620A–B (Lord Oliver). It should be noted that whether and to what extent external aids can be used to displace a clear, literal meaning has been the subject of some judicial debate: see paragraph 7.29 above.

[96] See *NASS* (n 3) [5] (Lord Steyn), as cited in paragraph 7.31 above; and *Solar Century* (n 16) [52] (Green J), citing Lord Steyn's speech in *NASS* and stating: 'not all … admissible sources are of equal weight'.

[97] See *Spath Holme* (n 1) 397F–398E (Lord Nicholls), as cited in paragraph 7.43.3.2 above; *R (D)* (n 52) [49] (Carnwath LJ); and the final sentence of n 79 above. See also *NASS* (n 3) [5] (Lord Steyn), commenting that external aids 'may be admitted for what logical value they have'.

[98] *Spath Holme* (n 1) 399D–E (Lord Nicholls).

8

The Interpretation Act 1978

8.1 A number of important and widely applicable rules of statutory construction are specifically enacted and set out in the Interpretation Act 1978 (hereinafter the 1978 Act). The 1978 Act generally provides that these rules are to apply 'unless the contrary intention appears' in the enactment being construed.

Scope of Application of the 1978 Act

8.2 *Commencement*: the 1978 Act came into force on 1 January 1979,[1] replacing its predecessor the Interpretation Act 1889.[2] As set out below, the 1978 Act has general application to legislation passed after its commencement date, but more limited application to legislation passed before that date. Accordingly, when dealing with older Acts, particular care will need to be taken to ascertain whether the 1978 Act is applicable.

8.3 *Application to Acts*:[3] pursuant to section 22, the 1978 Act applies to: (i) itself; (ii) any other Act passed after its commencement;[4] and (iii) Acts passed *before* its commencement, to the extent specified in Part I of Schedule 2. This Part, as well as addressing certain points on changes in definitions over time, provides that certain sections of the 1978 Act apply variously to: (i) all Acts whenever passed; (ii) Acts passed after 1850; and (iii) Acts passed after 1889.

8.4 *Application to subordinate legislation*:[5] pursuant to section 23, the 1978 Act also applies (apart from sections 1–3 and 4(b)) to almost all subordinate legislation made after its commencement 'so far as applicable and unless the contrary intention appears'. It applies only to a very limited extent (as specified in Part II of Schedule 2) to subordinate legislation made before its commencement.

---

[1] Pursuant to s 26 of the 1978 Act.
[2] Repealed almost entirely by s 25(1) of and sch 3 to the 1978 Act.
[3] 'Act' is defined in s 21(1) of the 1978 Act.
[4] Apart from s 20A of the 1978 Act, which relates to references to EU instruments and which (as stated in the section itself) applies only to Acts passed after 8 January 2007.
[5] 'Subordinate legislation' is defined in s 21(1) of the 1978 Act.

Key Provisions

8.5   In the following paragraphs we consider briefly a number of the provisions of the 1978 Act that are particularly worthy of note.

8.6   *Section 4 ('Time of commencement')*: section 4(b) provides that an Act comes into force on the day it receives Royal Assent, if it does not otherwise make provision for its commencement.

8.7   *Section 5 ('Definitions') and Schedule 1*: section 5 provides that the list of definitions set out in Schedule 1 should be used in construing any Act to which the 1978 Act applies 'unless the contrary intention appears'. These definitions include many commonly occurring statutory words and expressions such as: (i) 'person' (which 'includes a body of persons corporate or unincorporate'); (ii) 'writing' (which 'includes typing, printing, lithography, photography and other modes of representing or reproducing words in a visible form'); (iii) certain geographical words (eg, 'England'); and (iv) the short names by which various courts are known.

8.8   *Section 6 ('Gender and number')*: section 6 provides:

In any Act, unless the contrary intention appears,–

(a)   words importing the masculine gender include the feminine;
(b)   words importing the feminine gender include the masculine;
(c)   words in the singular include the plural and words in the plural include the singular.

This section exists for drafting convenience (rather than, say, to ensure gender or other equality).[6] Accordingly, in an appropriate case, the courts will find a contrary intention.[7]

8.9   *Section 11 ('Construction of subordinate legislation')*: section 11 provides: 'Where an Act confers power to make subordinate legislation, expressions used in that legislation have, unless the contrary intention appears, the meaning which they bear in the Act.'

---

[6]   *R (Wilkinson) v Inland Revenue Commissioners* [2005] UKHL 30, [2005] 1 WLR 1718 [15] (Lord Hoffmann): 'The purpose of section 6 is to save the parliamentary draftsman from having to say "he or she" or to find awkward gender-neutral terms.'
[7]   See, eg, ibid [14]–[19] (Lord Hoffmann), rejecting an argument that s 6 of the 1978 Act—when combined, if necessary, with s 3 of the Human Rights Act 1998—meant that the term 'widow' in a certain Act should be construed to include 'widower'. It was clear that the use of 'widow' was a deliberate, gender-specific choice as the relevant Part of the Act in question had 'no difficulty in finding a gender-neutral term' when desired.

8.10 *Section 12(1) ('Continuity of powers and duties')*: Section 12(1) provides: 'Where an Act confers a power or imposes a duty it is implied, unless the contrary intention appears, that the power may be exercised, or the duty is to be performed, from time to time as occasion requires.'[8]

8.11 *Section 14 ('Implied power to amend')*: section 14 broadly provides that, 'unless the contrary intention appears', a power to make subordinate legislation implies 'a power to revoke, amend or re-enact any instrument made under the power' (subject to the same constraints and procedures as the original power to make the subordinate legislation).

8.12 *Sections 15–17 ('Repealing enactments')*: these sections make provision to reduce the disruption caused by repeals, preventing various undesirable consequences that might otherwise obtain when legislation is repealed (or repealed and re-enacted).

8.13 *Sections 20 ('References to other enactments') and 20A ('References to EU instruments')*: these sections provide that references to enactments and EU instruments are, 'unless the contrary intention appears', to be read as references to those enactments or instruments as amended, extended or applied by another enactment or instrument.

---

[8] For an example of this section in operation, see *Re Wilson* [1985] AC 750 (HL).

9

The Effect of International Law
on Domestic Legislation

9.1 This chapter deals with the general principles governing the effect of international law on the interpretation of domestic legislation. The next three chapters consider the particularly significant impact on domestic law of certain rules of international law, specifically the European Convention on Human Rights (through the Human Rights Act 1998) and EU law (through the European Communities Act 1972).

Sources of International Law

9.2 Article 38(1) of the Statute of the International Court of Justice (hereinafter 'ICJ Statute') succinctly sets out the sources of public international law as follows:[1]

The Court, whose function is to decide in accordance with international law such disputes as are submitted to it, shall apply:

a. *international conventions*, whether general or particular, establishing rules expressly recognized by the contesting states;

b. *international custom*, as evidence of a general practice accepted as law;

c. the *general principles* of law recognized by civilized nations;

d. subject to the provisions of Article 59, *judicial decisions and the teachings of the most highly qualified publicists* of the various nations, as subsidiary means for the determination of rules of law. (Emphasis added)

9.3 A detailed consideration of all these sources is beyond the scope of this book, but we provide an outline of each below. Since by far the most important source (in domestic terms at least) is *treaty* law, followed by *customary* law, we focus in this chapter on the effect of those sources on the interpretation of domestic law. In view of the lesser role played by general principles, judicial decisions and

---

[1] This Article was cited in *Mutua v The Foreign and Commonwealth Office* [2011] EWHC 1913 (QB) [87] (McCombe J), stating: 'It is generally accepted that the sources of public international law are those appearing in Article 38 of the Statute of the International Court of Justice.'

academic writings, we do not provide any separate treatment of their effect on interpreting domestic law.[2]

International Conventions or 'Treaties'

9.4   Various terms such as 'treaty', 'charter', 'convention', 'declaration' and 'statute' are used to designate international agreements. But for the sake of consistency and simplicity in this book, we adopt the single term 'treaty' to refer to all written agreements (whether set out in one or multiple instruments) that are governed by international law and made between states, or between states and international organisations.

9.5   Treaties may be made between any number of parties agreeing to enter into them and to be bound by them by mutual consent. They may be (for example) bilateral,[3] regional[4] or worldwide[5] in their purview.

9.6   As set out in Articles 11–16 of the Vienna Convention on the Law of Treaties[6] (itself a treaty codifying customary international law in relation to treaties generally), states may provide their consent to be bound by treaties by various means, depending on the terms of the treaty and the way in which negotiations are conducted.[7] Mere signature is sometimes sufficient, but often a treaty will require 'ratification' before a state will be bound by it. This entails some form of further notification of acceptance of the treaty (often following a domestic approval procedure).

9.7   When giving its consent to be bound by a treaty, a state may make a unilateral statement known as a 'reservation' by which it expresses its wish *not* to be bound by particular provisions of the treaty, or to be bound instead in a different way.[8]

---

[2] For further discussion on the sources of international law, see Shaheed Fatima, *Using International Law in Domestic Courts* (Oxford, Hart Publishing, 2005); and James Crawford, *Brownlie's Principles of Public International Law*, 8th edn (Oxford, Oxford University Press, 2012).

[3] See, eg, Agreement between the United Kingdom of Great Britain and Northern Ireland and the Kingdom of the Netherlands Relating to the Exploitation of the Orca Field (adopted 27 November 2013, entered into force 27 November 2013) UKTS 12/2014 (Cm 8802, 2014).

[4] See, eg, Convention for the Protection of Human Rights and Fundamental Freedoms (European Convention on Human Rights, as amended) (ECHR).

[5] See, eg, Charter of the United Nations (adopted 26 June 1945, entered into force 24 October 1945) 1 UNTS XVI.

[6] Vienna Convention on the Law of Treaties (adopted 23 May 1969, entered into force 27 January 1980) 1155 UNTS 331.

[7] Article 11 of the Vienna Convention (n 6) states: 'The consent of a State to be bound by a treaty may be expressed by signature, exchange of instruments constituting a treaty, ratification, acceptance, approval or accession, or by any other means if so agreed.' Articles 12–16 then set out when each of these specified methods of giving consent will be taken to apply.

[8] See Art 2(1)(d) of the Vienna Convention (n 6) for the formal definition of a reservation. The procedure for making and objecting to reservations, and provisions regarding their effect, are set out in Arts 19–23.

A state may also seek, from time to time and in accordance with a treaty's terms, to derogate from certain of its provisions.

9.8   In the UK, the power to make treaties (by whatever means) is a function of the Crown (in practice, the government) exercising the Royal prerogative, and express parliamentary consent is not normally required to allow the government to ratify a treaty.[9] However, since 11 November 2010, in all but exceptional cases or those for which a different procedure is elsewhere prescribed, the government is not permitted to ratify a treaty unless Parliament has been given (and has not taken) an opportunity to resolve that it should not be ratified.[10]

9.9   The 'corollary'[11] of the fact that treaty making is an executive rather than legislative function is that 'a treaty is not part of English law unless and until it has been incorporated into the law by legislation'.[12] As long as it remains unincorporated, it will be 'non-justiciable' by the English courts; that is, they will 'have no jurisdiction to construe or apply' it directly.[13] It will also have no direct effect in English law; that is, it will of itself have 'no effect upon the rights and duties of citizens in common or statute law'.[14] This does not mean that the courts will never look at or seek to interpret unincorporated treaties, or that they can never influence the meaning of domestic law.[15] However, their effect will only ever be 'indirect',[16] where there is a 'sufficient foothold' in domestic law.[17]

---

[9] See *Miller v Secretary of State for Exiting the European Union* [2017] UKSC 5, [2017] 2 WLR 583 [55] (Joint majority judgment): 'Subject to any restrictions imposed by primary legislation, the general rule is that the power to make or unmake treaties is exercisable without legislative authority'; *JH Rayner (Mincing Lane) Ltd v Department of Trade and Industry* [1990] 2 AC 418 (HL) 499H (Lord Oliver); and *Higgs v Minister of National Security* [2000] 2 AC 228 (PC) 241A–C (Lord Hoffmann). For an example of where Parliament's consent is required to ratify a treaty, see s 2 of the European Union Act 2011.

[10] Under the procedure laid down by pt 2 (ss 20–25) of the Constitutional Reform and Governance Act 2010. Prior to this, since the 1920s, the government ordinarily followed a similar procedure under what was known as the 'Ponsonby Rule'.

[11] See *Higgs* (n 9) 241B–C (Lord Hoffmann): 'The Crown may impose obligations in international law upon the state without any participation on the part of the democratically elected organs of government. But the corollary of this unrestricted treaty-making power is that treaties form no part of domestic law unless enacted by the legislature.' This passage was cited with approval in *Miller* (n 9) [56] (Joint majority judgment).

[12] *JH Rayner* (n 9) 499F–500D (Lord Oliver). See also *Higgs* (n 9) 241A–242A (Lord Hoffmann). Note that this is not the case in every jurisdiction: in what are known as 'monist' legal systems (to be contrasted with 'dualist' systems like the UK), treaties entered into by the state will form part of domestic law without the need for any separate act of incorporation (as to which see paragraph 9.10 below).

[13] *Higgs* (n 9) 241C (Lord Hoffmann).

[14] ibid 241D–E (Lord Hoffmann).

[15] As explained in *JH Rayner* (n 9) 500D–501B (Lord Oliver).

[16] See *Higgs* (n 9) 241D–F (Lord Hoffmann).

[17] *Republic of Ecuador v Occidental Exploration and Production Co* [2005] EWCA Civ 1116, [2006] QB 432 [30]–[31] (Mance LJ): 'English courts are not therefore wholly precluded from interpreting or having regard to the provisions of unincorporated treaties. Context is always important.' The court held it was permissible to interpret a bilateral investment treaty to determine the scope of an arbitral tribunal's jurisdiction under an arbitration agreement. This case and specifically the concept of a 'domestic foothold' allowing the courts to interpret international law were cited with approval in *Mohammed v Ministry of Defence* [2017] UKSC 1, [2017] 2 WLR 287 ('*Mohammed (SC)*') [58]

9.10   The term '*incorporation*' is used to denote the process by which some part of international law (whether a treaty or customary rule) effectively becomes part of English law.[18] Incorporation of treaties must be *express and formal*, sufficient to give a treaty 'the force of statute under our law' to some extent,[19] although it need not take any specific form.[20] In practice, treaties are often incorporated by a statute expressing that the treaty, or certain of its provisions, shall have the 'force of law', with the treaty or the relevant provisions (or a translation)[21] often, but not always,[22] being scheduled to the statute.[23]

9.11   Often, however, Parliament will legislate to '*give effect*' to a treaty (or certain of its provisions) otherwise than by 'incorporating' it. This entails in some way and to some extent giving the force of law to its *substance* without expressly and directly giving the treaty itself (or certain of its provisions) force of law.[24] Parliament may or may not state in the legislation that this is what it is doing. But this practice is undoubtedly sufficient to allow the courts to refer to and consider the treaty that is being given effect.[25]

9.12   It is important to recognise that the differences between the wide range of methods available to reflect international law obligations in domestic law are a

(Lord Mance). See also *JH Rayner* (n 9) 500D–501B (Lord Oliver). As to the relevance of unincorporated treaties in interpreting domestic legislation, see below at paragraphs 9.25–9.29 (in relation to the presumption of conformity), paragraphs 9.32–9.36 (in relation to the presumption of compatibility) and paragraph 9.37 (in relation to their relevance to context).

[18] We adopt this term for convenience only, acknowledging that some consider other terminology more appropriate in this connection. Strictly speaking, as stated at paragraph 9.20 below, what is sometimes called 'incorporation' in fact involves domestic law adopting rules which *mirror* certain rules of international law, rather than those rules of international law becoming *part of* domestic law as such.

[19] See *EN (Serbia) v Secretary of State for the Home Department* [2009] EWCA Civ 630, [2010] QB 633 [58]–[59] (Stanley Burnton LJ): 'I doubt that there can be such a thing as informal incorporation', and [119] (Laws LJ): 'A treaty may only be incorporated into the domestic law of the UK by legislation, and therefore expressly ... there must be a distinct legislative act.'

[20] *R (European Roma Rights) v Prague Immigration Officer* [2004] UKHL 55, [2005] 2 AC 1 [42] (Lord Steyn): 'there is no rule specifying the precise legislative method of incorporation' (although his obiter finding that the Refugee Convention has been wholly and generally incorporated into English law has not been followed: see *R v Asfaw* [2008] UKHL 31, [2008] 1 AC 1061 [29] (Lord Bingham); and *EN (Serbia)* (n 19), especially at [56]–[60] (Stanley Burnton LJ)).

[21] See *James Buchanan & Co Ltd v Babco Forwarding & Shipping (UK) Ltd* [1978] AC 141 (HL) 152A–C (Lord Wilberforce).

[22] See, eg, European Communities Act 1972, ss 1 and 2.

[23] See, eg, Merchant Shipping Act 1995, s 224 and sch 11, pt I.

[24] Incorporation, of course, is itself a (strong) form of 'giving effect' to a treaty in domestic law. However, given the particular way in which the courts approach the interpretation of statutes which incorporate treaties (see paragraph 9.24 below), it is important to give particular consideration to the concept of incorporation.

[25] Whether as part of the legislative context or in order to consider the application of the presumptions discussed below: see paragraphs 9.20–9.37; and see *Salomon v Customs and Excise Commissioners* [1967] 2 QB 116 (CA) 141F–G (Lord Denning MR): 'Our statute does not in terms incorporate the convention, nor refer to it. But that does not matter. We can look at it.' See also, eg, *R (Mullen) v Secretary of State for the Home Department* [2004] UKHL 18, [2005] 1 AC 1 [5] (Lord Bingham). As to how Parliament's intention to give effect to a treaty may be discerned, see paragraph 9.25 below.

matter of degree rather than kind. It may ultimately make little difference, therefore, whether a treaty has been directly 'incorporated' or otherwise 'given effect'.
In both cases, as a matter of fundamental principle, '[i]t is not the treaty but the
statute which forms part of English law',[26] and it is the latter that the courts will
interpret and apply, in each case doing so, as far as appropriate, by reference to
international law (as considered below). Nevertheless, it is essential to consider
carefully in every case the precise means by which a treaty is incorporated or given
effect, as this may affect the application or force of the interpretive presumptions
discussed below.[27]

Customary International Law

9.13 'Customary international law results from a general and consistent practice
of states followed by them from a sense of legal obligation.'[28] As will be apparent,
this encompasses an objective and a subjective element.

9.14 The objective element is the requirement for a general state practice. This
requires 'a uniform, or virtually uniform practice of states conforming to the proposed rule, reflected in their acts and/or their public statements'.[29] The subjective element is that states follow the relevant practice out of a 'conviction that

---

[26] *R v Lyons* [2002] UKHL 44, [2003] 1 AC 976 [27] (Lord Hoffmann).

[27] In particular, the legislative words and method chosen may affect whether the relevant treaty
provisions should be taken as intended to apply in domestic law subject to some form of modification
or limitation. See paragraphs 9.27–9.28 below. And see generally *James Buchanan* (n 21) 152A–C (Lord
Wilberforce), stating that the legislative method of incorporating or giving effect to a treaty may affect
the interpretive principles that should be applied.

[28] *European Roma Rights* (n 20) [23] (Lord Bingham), adopting the formulation in the American
Law Institute's Restatement of the Foreign Relations Law of the United States (3d), s 102(2), as accurately reflecting the test applied by English courts to identify rules of customary international law. He
also approved the passage at s 102(3) regarding the interplay between treaties and customary rules:
'(3) International agreements create law for the states parties thereto and may lead to the creation
of customary international law when such agreements are intended for adherence by states generally
and are in fact widely accepted.' On the role of treaties in establishing customary international law, see
also *Mohammed v Ministry of Defence* [2015] EWCA Civ 843, [2016] 2 WLR 247 ('*Mohammed (CA)*')
[221] (Lord Thomas CJ). While an appeal against this decision was allowed in part in *Mohammed (SC)*
(n 17), the majority of the Supreme Court did not consider it necessary to decide the question whether
the alleged customary international law rule relied upon existed, and no doubt was cast on the statements of principle about the creation of customary international law made by the Court of Appeal or
the High Court ([2014] EWHC 1369 (QB) ('*Mohammed (HC)*')). On this issue in the Supreme Court,
see [14]–[16] (Lord Sumption), [147]–[151] (Lord Mance), [256]–[257] and [271]–[276] (Lord Reed,
dissenting).

[29] *Mohammed (SC)* (n 17) [14] (Lord Sumption). See also *Mohammed (HC)* (n 28) [255]–[256]
(Leggatt J), stating that the practice 'need not be of any particular duration but it must be extensive and
representative and virtually uniform', citing *North Sea Continental Shelf (Federal Republic of Germany/
Denmark; Federal Republic of Germany/Netherlands)*, Judgment, ICJ Rep 1969 (20 February), 3, paras 74
and 77. This aspect of Leggatt J's decision was affirmed on appeal to the Court of Appeal (*Mohammed
(CA)* (n 28)), and on this point in the Court of Appeal, see [220]–[221] (Lord Thomas CJ) (as for the
consideration of customary international law in this case on further appeal to the Supreme Court, see
n 28 above). See also *European Roma Rights* (n 20) [23] (Lord Bingham).

such practice reflects or amounts to law (opinio juris) or is required by social, economic, or political exigencies (opinio necessitatis).'[30] This need not be shown from direct evidence, but can be inferred from the 'acts or omissions' of states,[31] and in particular from the acts constituting the relevant practice and the way in which they have been carried out.[32]

9.15   Certain rules of customary international law have the status of peremptory norms or '*jus cogens*'. These are obligations of a particularly fundamental character, owed '*erga omnes*' (that is, to the international community as a whole), and from which no derogation is permitted.[33] Rules which have been recognised as *jus cogens* include the prohibition on torture[34] and 'the prohibition on genocide, slavery and the acquisition of territory by force'.[35] Lady Hale has suggested that prohibitions on race discrimination and cruel, inhuman and degrading treatment may also be or become such norms.[36] Articles 53 and 64 of the Vienna Convention provide that if a treaty conflicts with a peremptory norm, the treaty will be void—either from the time of its conclusion, if the norm existed then, or otherwise, if the norm emerges later, from the time it emerges.[37]

9.16   It has been said that the 'issue of the incorporation of customary international law into domestic law is not susceptible to a simple or general answer'.[38]

---

[30] *Mohammed (CA)* (n 28) [220] (Lord Thomas CJ) (as for the consideration of customary international law in this case on further appeal to the Supreme Court, see n 28 above). This subjective element is often referred to simply as '*opinio juris*' or '*opinio juris sive necessitatis*': see, eg, *European Roma Rights* (n 20) [23] (Lord Bingham), citing with approval the American Law Institute's Restatement (n 28); and *Mohammed (HC)* (n 28) [256] (Leggatt J).

[31] *European Roma Rights* (n 20) [23] (Lord Bingham), citing with approval the American Law Institute's Restatement (n 28).

[32] See *Mohammed (HC)* (n 28) [256] (Leggatt J) and *Mohammed (CA)* (n 28) [220] (Lord Thomas CJ), both citing *North Sea Continental Shelf* (n 29) (as for the consideration of customary international law in this case on further appeal to the Supreme Court, see n 28 above). For a discussion on how domestic courts determine the content of customary international law, see Fatima, *Using International Law* (2005) (n 2) para 13.8, 414–17.

[33] As to *jus cogens* rules, see generally *Belhaj v Straw* [2017] UKSC 3, [2017] 2 WLR 456 [107] (Lord Mance).

[34] *R v Bow Street Magistrate ex p Pinochet (No 3)* [2000] 1 AC 147 (HL) 198B–G (Lord Browne-Wilkinson), 261B–C (Lord Hutton), 278B (Lord Millett), and 290A–B (Lord Phillips); *A v Secretary of State for the Home Department (No 2)* [2005] UKHL 71, [2006] 2 AC 221 [33] (Lord Bingham); *Belhaj* (n 33) [258] (Lord Sumption).

[35] *R (Mohamed) v Secretary of State for Foreign and Commonwealth Affairs (No 1)* [2008] EWHC 2048 (Admin), [2009] 1 WLR 2579 [142] (Thomas LJ).

[36] *Stott v Thomas Cook Tour Operators Ltd* [2014] UKSC 15, [2014] AC 1347 [68]–[69] (Lady Hale).

[37] Vienna Convention on the Law of Treaties (n 6). These Articles are briefly considered in *Stott* (n 36) [68] (Lady Hale). See also, eg, *Ahmed v HM Treasury* [2010] UKSC 2, [2010] 2 AC 534 [11] (Lord Hope): 'Treaty provisions that are incompatible with ius cogens are void.'

[38] *R (Al-Haq) v Secretary of State for Foreign and Commonwealth Affairs* [2009] EWHC 1910 (Admin) [40] (Pill LJ). See generally on this issue *R (Keyu) v Secretary of State for Foreign and Commonwealth Affairs* [2015] UKSC 69, [2016] AC 1355 [144]–[150] (Lord Mance), who, having cautioned that the court had not heard argument on the point, concluded at [150]: 'Speaking generally, in my opinion, the presumption … is that [customary international law], once established, can and should shape the

Certain older dicta suggest that rules of customary international law 'are incorporated into English law automatically and considered to be part of English law unless they are in conflict with an Act of Parliament'.[39] However, in more recent cases, this broad and unqualified statement has been doubted by the courts, with support being expressed for the view that customary international law 'is not a part, but is one of the sources, of English law',[40] which can be drawn upon in appropriate circumstances to 'shape the common law'.[41]

9.17 At the very least, it is now clear that greater strictures exist on the domestic incorporation or application of customary international law rules than simply considering whether those rules directly conflict with an Act of Parliament. A broader limitation applies, which provides that such rules can be applicable 'only where the constitution permits'.[42] Accordingly, the courts have held that:

9.17.1 customary international law will not apply where legislation is inconsistent with its incorporation;[43]

common law, whenever it can do so consistently with domestic constitutional principles, statutory law and common law rules which the courts can themselves sensibly adapt without it being, for example, necessary to invite Parliamentary intervention or consideration.'

[39] *Trendtex Trading Corp v Central Bank of Nigeria* [1977] QB 529 (CA) 553B–C (Lord Denning MR), concluding at 554G–H: 'the rules of international law, as existing from time to time, do form part of our English law'; and see generally his discussion of this issue at 553–54, and the cases cited in *R v Jones* [2006] UKHL 16, [2007] 1 AC 136 [11] (Lord Bingham). Note Lord Mance's comments on *Trendtex* in the passage in *Keyu* (n 38) cited in that note.

[40] *R v Jones* (n 39) [11] (Lord Bingham), citing JL Brierly, 'International Law in England' (1935) 51 LQR 24, 31; and *Belhaj* (n 33) [252] (Lord Sumption), citing this statement with approval. See also the discussion in *R (Freedom and Justice Party) v Secretary of State for Foreign and Commonwealth Affairs* [2016] EWHC 2010 (Admin) [166] (Lloyd Jones LJ, giving the judgment of the Court); and *Al-Haq* (n 38) [60] (Cranston J). See also *R (Al-Saadoon) v Secretary of State for Defence* [2009] EWCA Civ 7, [2010] QB 486 [59] (Laws LJ), stating that the 'proposition that [a] customary rule may be sued on as a cause of action in the English courts is perhaps not so clear cut'. He considered that for this to be possible, the rule would have to not conflict with any provision of domestic law, and also amount to *jus cogens.*

[41] *Keyu* (n 38) [150] (Lord Mance), as cited in that note. See also *Belhaj* (n 33) [252] (Lord Sumption), stating that customary international law can 'affect the interpretation of ambiguous statutory provisions, guide the exercise of judicial or executive discretions and influence the development of the common law'. See paragraphs 9.62–9.65 below regarding the interpretation of domestic legislation in the light of customary international law.

[42] *R v Jones* (n 39) [23] (Lord Bingham), citing R O'Keefe, 'Customary International Crimes in English Courts' (2001) *British Yearbook of International Law* 293, 335, and at [26]–[31]. At [29], Lord Bingham stated that 'very compelling reasons' would be needed to depart from the principle that it was for Parliament, not the Executive or the courts, to make new criminal offences. See also *Keyu* (n 38), as cited in that note; and *Al-Haq* (n 38) [60] (Cranston J).

[43] *Keyu* (n 38) [117]–[122] (Lord Neuberger) and [151] (Lord Mance), stating that 'Parliament has effectively pre-empted the whole area of investigations into historic deaths', such that customary international law in this area could or should not be applied by domestic courts so as to extend the scope of when such investigations are required.

9.17.2   judges will be extremely unlikely to recognise a new crime arising solely out of customary international law;[44] and

9.17.3   customary norms that are ancillary to unincorporated treaties are likewise not incorporated.[45]

General Principles of International Law

9.18   This category consists of broad rules and principles that are well-recognised internationally and of general application, which can be drawn upon by courts in adjudicating questions of international law. In themselves, they have 'only marginal value as a source of rights and duties'.[46] Examples of general principles that have been recognised include the principle of good faith;[47] the principle that full restitution should be made for wrongs;[48] the principle of *res judicata*;[49] and the principle that 'no one is arbitrarily to be deprived of his nationality'.[50]

Judicial Decisions and Academic Writings

9.19   By their nature, and as the ICJ Statute says, these are *subsidiary* sources of law. Where international law obligations created by the sources considered above are otherwise in play, English courts may look to these subsidiary sources for assistance in their interpretive task:

9.19.1   As to judicial decisions, the role of international tribunals should be to expound existing law rather than create new law.[51] In any event, although decisions

---

[44]   *R v Jones* (n 39) [29] (Lord Bingham), as cited in n 42 above. Note the distinction drawn between customary international law affecting 'the substance of the criminal law' and 'a procedural bar to criminal proceedings' in *Freedom and Justice Party* (n 40) [171]–[172] (Lloyd Jones LJ, giving the judgment of the Court).

[45]   *R v Lyons* (n 26) [39] (Lord Hoffmann).

[46]   *R (ST) v Secretary of State for the Home Department* [2012] UKSC 12, [2012] 2 AC 135 [31] (Lord Hope), recognising the principle of good faith (and its application to treaty interpretation), but stating that it 'is not to be taken to be a source of obligation where none exists', citing *European Roma Rights* (n 20) [62] (Lord Hope). See further paragraph 9.46 below.

[47]   *ST* (n 46) [31] (Lord Hope), citing a number of ICJ cases. See further the discussion in the previous note.

[48]   *Chorzow Factory Case* (1928), Merits, PCIJ Series A, No 17, 47.

[49]   *Effect of Awards of Compensation Made by the United Nations Administrative Tribunal*, Advisory Opinion, ICJ Rep 1954 (13 July), 47, 53. *Res judicata* is a doctrine which applies to preclude parties from relitigating against one another points which have already been finally determined between them by a competent court.

[50]   Case C-135/08 *Rottmann v Freistaat Bayern* [2010] ECR I–1449, para 53; this statement was cited with apparent approval in *G1 v Secretary of State for the Home Department* [2012] EWCA Civ 867, [2013] QB 1008 [42] (Laws LJ).

[51]   Indeed, the ICJ Statute does not purport to make ICJ decisions binding precedents, although the Court does seek consistency in its decision making. Article 59 of the ICJ Statute (to which Art 38(1)

of international tribunals are often cited and may be persuasive authority, English courts will not be bound to follow them on matters of interpretation unless this is required by domestic legislation.[52]

9.19.2   As to academic writings, while these are a useful point of reference and often cited,[53] it is a long-standing principle of English law that:

> [W]riters on international law, however valuable their labours may be in elucidating and ascertaining the principles and rules of law, cannot make the law. To be binding, the law must have received the assent of the nations who are to be bound by it.[54]

Interpretation of Domestic Legislation in the Light of Treaties

9.20   It is important to note that, even when treaty provisions have by legislation been incorporated into or otherwise given effect in English law, *it is not the treaty provisions themselves which form part of domestic law, only the domestic legislation*.[55] Ultimately, therefore, in every case concerning the interpretation of domestic legislation where the rules of international law may be relevant, the courts' task will always be to give effect to the intention of Parliament as expressed in the words used in the *domestic legislation*.

9.21   Nevertheless, rules of international law can have a very significant effect on the interpretation of domestic legislation. As discussed below, they have effect in particular through: (i) the *presumption of conformity*; (ii) the *presumption of compatibility*; and (iii) contributing more generally to the *context* in which legislation falls to be interpreted.

(d) is expressly subject) provides: 'The decision of the Court has no binding force except between the parties and in respect of that particular case.'

   [52]   See *R v Lyons* (n 26) [27] (Lord Hoffmann), in the context of treaty interpretation: 'English courts will not (unless the statute expressly so provides) be bound to give effect to interpretations of the treaty by an international court, even though the United Kingdom is bound by international law to do so.' Domestic courts are required to follow decisions of the CJEU on matters of EU law under s 3(1) of the European Communities Act 1972 (see the discussion of this section at Chapter 12.9–12.14) and to 'take into account' decisions of the European Court of Human Rights under s 2(1) of the Human Rights Act 1998 (HRA 1998).

   [53]   See, eg, the citations from *R v Jones* (n 39) at nn 40 and 42 above.

   [54]   *R v Keyn* (1876) 2 Ex D 63, 202 (Cockburn CJ), cited with approval in *European Roma Rights* (n 20) [27] (Lord Bingham).

   [55]   See *R v Lyons* (n 26) [27] (Lord Hoffmann).

The Presumption of Conformity

9.22   Where legislation is passed to some extent to incorporate or otherwise give effect to a treaty (or refers to legislation passed for that reason),[56] it may be presumed that Parliament intends to that extent for the legislation to be interpreted in accordance with the relevant treaty's interpretation under international law.[57] We call this the *presumption of conformity*. How clear it is that this presumption should apply, and the strength of the presumption, will depend on the relevant legislative context.

9.23   This presumption was described by Lord Phillips as 'a presumption that, where a statute is passed in order to give effect to the obligations of the United Kingdom under an international Convention, the statute should be given a meaning that conforms to that of the Convention'.[58] However, the courts have made clear that this imperative to construe domestic legislation 'in the same sense' as the relevant treaty applies only insofar as 'the words of the statute are reasonably capable of bearing that meaning'.[59] If the legislative language has such a 'clear and unambiguous' meaning that it cannot be interpreted to conform with the treaty, it must ultimately be given that plain meaning.[60]

---

[56] See, eg, the definitions in s 9(2) of the Criminal Law Act 1977 by reference to certain treaty articles as they have 'effect in the United Kingdom by virtue of' certain incorporating legislation.

[57] The principles applied by the courts in interpreting treaties themselves are discussed below at paragraphs 9.38–9.61.

[58] *R (Adams) v Secretary of State for Justice* [2011] UKSC 18, [2012] 1 AC 48 [14] (Lord Phillips), citing in support *Salomon* (n 25) 141 (Lord Denning MR). See also the citations in the following note.

[59] *SerVaas Inc v Rafidain Bank* [2010] EWHC 3287 (Ch) [39] (Arnold J), endorsing 'the ordinary rule of statutory construction that domestic legislation which has been enacted in order to give effect to the UK's obligations under an international convention or treaty should be construed in the same sense as the convention or treaty if the words of the statute are reasonably capable of bearing that meaning', citing *Owners of Cargo Lately Laden on Board the MV Erkowit v Owners of the Eschersheim (The Eschersheim)* [1976] 1 WLR 430 (see below in this note). (This decision was appealed, but no appeal was heard on the issue in relation to which this point arose: see [2011] EWCA Civ 1256, [2012] 1 All ER (Comm) 527; and [2012] UKSC 40, [2013] 1 AC 595, both affirming another part of Arnold J's decision). Note also in *SerVaas* at [39] that Arnold J rejected the submission that this presumption was as powerful as the *Marleasing* principle, which is a 'strong duty of interpretation' requiring domestic courts to construe domestic law 'as far as possible' in conformity with EU law (as to which see Chapter 12.21–12.29). See also *The Eschersheim* 436B–D (Lord Diplock): 'As the Act was passed to enable Her Majesty's Government to give effect to the obligations in international law which it would assume on ratifying the Convention to which it was a signatory, the rule of statutory construction laid down in *Salomon* [(n 25)] … is applicable. If there be any difference between the language of the statutory provision and that of the corresponding provision of the Convention, the statutory language should be construed in the same sense as that of the Convention if the words of the statute are reasonably capable of bearing that meaning' (also citing *Post Office v Estuary Radio Ltd* [1968] 2 QB 740); and *JH Rayner* (n 9) 500E–F (Lord Oliver): 'it is well established that where a statute is enacted in order to give effect to the United Kingdom's obligations under a treaty, the terms of the treaty may have to be considered and, if necessary, construed in order to resolve any ambiguity or obscurity as to the meaning or scope of the statute'.

[60] See *Salomon* (n 25) 143E–F (Diplock LJ), as discussed further below at n 76. See also the discussion at paragraphs 9.34–9.36.

9.24   In practice, the presumption is most obviously applicable, and likely to be at its strongest, in cases where (all or part of) a treaty has been directly incorporated into domestic law (see paragraph 9.10 above). This practice provides a particularly strong indication of Parliament's desire for domestic law to conform to international law. And, in such cases, domestic law should be straightforwardly capable of being given a conforming construction, since its terms will mirror those of the relevant treaty.[61] Accordingly, the courts have held that where a 'Convention is in its own words incorporated into English law, the task of the court is to construe the Convention as it stands', as an international instrument (as to which, see paragraphs 9.38–9.61 below).[62] The terms of the incorporating legislation are likely to have little or no relevance to this task, apart from provisions that address the extent of incorporation or how the court should approach issues of interpretation.[63]

9.25   In cases not involving incorporation, Parliament's intention to give effect to a treaty may be expressly stated in the relevant legislation, but need not be. It may be discerned from cogent extrinsic evidence,[64] such as the close similarity between the subject matter or wording of the legislation and the treaty,[65] or from external aids to construction.[66] However, it is important to identify an intention

---

[61] See *JH Rayner* (n 9) 500D–F (Lord Oliver): 'Where ... a treaty is directly incorporated into English law by Act of the legislature, its terms become subject to the interpretative jurisdiction of the court in the same way as any other Act of the legislature.'

[62] *Gard Marine and Energy Ltd v China National Chartering Co Ltd* [2017] UKSC 35, [2017] 1 WLR 1793 [72] (Lord Clarke), citing with approval *CMA CGM SA v Classica Shipping Co Ltd* [2004] EWCA Civ 114, [2004] 1 All ER (Comm) 865; and see also the other cases cited in that paragraph, especially *James Buchanan* (n 21) and *Fothergill v Monarch Airlines Ltd* [1981] AC 251 (HL).

[63] See *Sidhu v British Airways plc* [1997] AC 430, 441H–442B (Lord Hope), in relation to the Carriage by Air Act 1961, which incorporated the Warsaw Convention into domestic law: 'Mr. Webb took us through various provisions in the statute which he said could be relied on as indicating that the intention was that the Convention should provide the exclusive remedy. Similar arguments were considered in the courts below. For my part I do not think that the wording of the statute can assist us one way or the other. What we are concerned with in this case is the meaning to be given to the Convention. This must depend upon the wording and structure of the Convention itself. All that need be taken from the Act for present purposes is that, in terms of section 1(1), the Convention as set out in Schedule 1 to the Act has the force of law in the United Kingdom in relation to any carriage by air to which the Convention applies; and that, in terms of section 1(2), if there is any inconsistency between the text in English in Part I of Schedule 1 and the text in French in Part II of that Schedule, the text in French shall prevail.' However, since the court is ultimately giving effect to *domestic law*, it is possible, in a clear enough case, that the application or interpretation of the relevant treaty will be affected by the particular context of the incorporating statute or other rules of domestic law. See, eg, *R (Buckinghamshire County Council) v Secretary of State for Transport* [2014] UKSC 3, [2014] 1 WLR 324 [207]–[208] (Lord Neuberger and Lord Mance): 'It is, putting the point at its lowest, certainly arguable ... that there may be fundamental principles, whether contained in other constitutional instruments or recognised at common law, of which Parliament when it enacted the European Communities Act 1972 did not either contemplate or authorise the abrogation.'

[64] *Salomon* (n 25) 144E–F (Diplock LJ).

[65] ibid 144F–G (Diplock LJ). See also *Mullen* (n 25) [35] (Lord Steyn), relying on the fact that the statutory wording 'closely tracks the provisions' of the relevant treaty.

[66] *Adams* (n 58) [14] (Lord Phillips), referring to parliamentary history. As to external aids to construction, see generally Chapter 7.

to give effect to specifically identifiable obligations: the presumption may be inapplicable, or at least very easily displaced, where legislation simply gives effect to international obligations generally.[67]

9.26   Where it can be discerned that Parliament intends for legislation to give effect, otherwise than by incorporation, to certain treaty obligations, there may be little difference in practical terms between the courts' approach in such cases from their approach in cases involving incorporation. In many cases, the effect of the presumption of conformity will be to make the interpretation of the treaty 'the key' to the interpretation of the domestic legislation, with the courts focusing on the meaning of the treaty itself in determining questions of construction.[68]

9.27   What is critical in every case is to ask not only *whether* legislation incorporates or gives effect to a treaty, but also 'for what purposes and to what extent'.[69] It may be that only certain provisions are incorporated,[70] or only a single definition.[71] Parliament may have intended to give force of law to a treaty only in particular contexts.[72] Or in certain cases, treaty provisions may be incorporated or given effect subject to a specific mechanism,[73] or by providing for a general

---

[67]   See *Boake Allen Ltd v Revenue and Customs Commissioners* [2007] UKHL 25, [2007] 1 WLR 1386 [51] (Lord Neuberger).

[68]   *Mullen* (n 25) [5] (Lord Bingham). See also, eg, *Adams* (n 58), in the context of the same statutory provision and treaty as were considered in *Mullen*, where Lord Phillips, after articulating the presumption of conformity at [14] (see the text to n 58), proceeded directly to interpret the treaty in question. See also *Samick Lines Co Ltd v Owners of the Antonis P Lemos* [1985] AC 711 (HL) 731 (Lord Brandon): 'a domestic statute designed to given [sic] effect to an international convention should, in general, be given a broad and liberal construction'. As to the interpretation of treaties themselves, see paragraphs 9.38–9.61 below.

[69]   *EN (Serbia)* (n 19) [58] (Stanley Burnton LJ).

[70]   *European Roma Rights* (n 20) [42] (Lord Steyn), referring to the exclusion of Art 13 ECHR from the Convention rights given effect under the HRA 1998 (but note that his conclusion in this paragraph regarding the general incorporation of the Refugee Convention has not been followed, as discussed in n 20 above).

[71]   See, eg, s 23 of the Antarctic Act 1994, defining 'Convention official' by reference to Article XXIV of the Convention on the Conservation of Antarctic Marine Living Resources (adopted 20 May 1980, entered into force 7 April 1982) UKTS (1982) 48 (Cmnd 8714, 1982).

[72]   *EN (Serbia)* (n 19) [58] (Stanley Burnton LJ): 'Parliament … expressly limited the force given to the Refugee Convention to the Immigration Rules.'

[73]   As, for example, with ECHR rights in UK law, which are not 'enforceable directly by individuals (otherwise than through the mechanism of the Human Rights Act 1998)': *R v Lyons* (n 26) [104] (Lord Millett). See also *Wilson v First County Trust Ltd (No 2)* [2003] UKHL 40, [2004] 1 AC 816 [126] (Lord Hobhouse), describing the approach of the HRA 1998 as 'more subtle' than other Acts which simply state that provisions of a treaty 'shall have the force of law'. The interposition of this mechanism doubtless lies behind doubts that have been expressed as to whether the HRA 1998 has strictly speaking *incorporated* the ECHR into domestic law (see, eg, *R v Lambert* [2001] UKHL 37, [2002] 2 AC 545 [135] (Lord Clyde)), although it is often said to have done so (see, eg, *Wilson* [154] (Lord Scott), [218] (Lord Rodger) and *EN (Serbia)* (n 19) [52] (Stanley Burnton LJ)). Considering various statements on this issue in *R (Minton Morrill Solicitors) v Lord Chancellor* [2017] EWHC 612 (Admin), [2017] HRLR 5 [24]–[27] (Kerr J), the court considered that Lord Clyde was correct to say in *Lambert* that the HRA 1998 has not strictly *incorporated* rights under the ECHR into domestic law.

domestic 'framework' through which they can operate.[74] Determining the extent (and limits) of legislation's intended conformity with a treaty is a matter of interpretation in every case.[75]

9.28   In some cases (especially those not involving incorporation) it may be apparent that, although it has legislated to give effect to a treaty, Parliament intends for all or part of the relevant legislation *not* to be given a conforming interpretation.[76] In particular, it may be discerned in some cases that Parliament intends for legislation to be broader[77] or narrower[78] in some way than the terms of the relevant treaty. An intention to depart from the meaning of the treaty as a matter of international law might be indicated by deliberate and significant departures in the domestic legislation from the language of the treaty, especially if external aids indicate that the purpose of this was to ensure that domestic law would have its own particular, non-conforming interpretation.[79] As stated above, 'clear and unambiguous' statutory language must ultimately be given effect, even

---

[74] See *R (Al-Fawwaz) v Governor of Brixton Prison* [2001] UKHL 69, [2002] 1 AC 556 [148] (Lord Rodger): 'Extradition arrangements are made by treaty ... What the 1870 and 1989 Acts do is to give the framework within which the extradition arrangements made by the treaties are given effect under our domestic law.' It is presumably that particular context that led Lord Rodger to state at [146]: 'The terms of an extradition treaty cannot be used to construe the Act of Parliament under which the treaty is given effect in our domestic law.'

[75] *Assange v Swedish Prosecution Authority* [2012] UKSC 22, [2012] 2 AC 471 [201] (Lord Mance).

[76] See, eg, *Ellerman Lines v Murray* [1931] AC 126 (HL), where the House of Lords interpreted legislation considered to be unambiguous on its own terms, without reference to the treaty to which it was intended to give effect. This case was cited in *Salomon* (n 25) 143E–F (Diplock LJ) as authority for the proposition that: 'If the terms of the legislation are clear and unambiguous, they must be given effect to, whether or not they carry out Her Majesty's treaty obligations, for the sovereign power of the Queen in Parliament extends to breaking treaties.' Note that *Ellerman* was distinguished in *Corocraft Ltd v Pan American Airways Inc* [1969] 1 QB 616 (CA) 657F–658B (Widgery LJ), and doubted in *James Buchanan* (n 21) 153D–E (Lord Wilberforce). However, whatever may be said about the court's approach to interpretation on the facts of that case, given the frequency with which Diplock LJ's judgment in *Salomon* is cited, there is no reason to doubt *Ellerman's* authority for the proposition Diplock LJ identified in that case. See also the summary of the applicable interpretive principles set out in *Assuranceforeningen Gard Gjensidig v International Oil Pollution Compensation Fund* [2014] EWHC 1394 (Comm), [2014] 2 Lloyd's Rep 219 [32] (Hamblen J), although it is submitted that this statement may be overly rigid and that, wherever legislation is enacted to give effect to a treaty, it is legitimate and indeed essential to look at the treaty as an aid to construction from the outset since it will form a key part of the statutory context.

[77] An approach accepted as theoretically possible, but not applicable in that case, in *Mullen* (n 25) [35]–[36] (Lord Steyn).

[78] See, eg, *R (Pepushi) v CPS* [2004] EWHC 798 (Admin) [27] and [33] (Thomas LJ), in relation to Parliament's enactment of s 31(2) of the Immigration and Asylum Act 1999, which was inconsistent with a previous Court of Appeal decision as to the meaning of Art 31 of the Refugee Convention: 'Parliament did not incorporate the terms of the Article but chose to use the language set out in s.31 which is narrower in scope than the meaning of Article 31 ... Parliament has decided to give effect to the international obligations of the UK in a narrower way.' See also to similar effect, in relation to the same subsection, *R v Asfaw* (n 20) [25] (Lord Bingham), [65] (Lord Hope) (but note that Lord Bingham preferred to leave open the question of the meaning of the Convention in this regard).

[79] *Pepushi* (n 78) [30]–[31] (Thomas LJ), focusing on the statutory language and continuing at [34] to refer to legislative history which further supported the court's conclusion that the legislation was narrower than the relevant treaty.

if its meaning differs from that of the treaty to which the legislation was intended to give effect.[80]

9.29 It may also be apparent from the particular method used to give effect to a treaty that Parliament does not intend for domestic law to be interpreted in conformity with it (such as where domestic legislation is designed to establish a general 'framework' through which a number of treaties are to have effect).[81]

9.30 Further, it should be noted that, where it is clear that Parliament does *not* intend for the meaning of legislation to conform to that of a treaty, this may similarly defeat the presumption of compatibility (discussed below).[82]

The Presumption of Compatibility

9.31 More generally, it is presumed that Parliament does not intend to legislate contrary to the UK's international obligations. Therefore, where statutory language permits, it should be given an interpretation consistent with those obligations. We call this the *presumption of compatibility.*

9.32 This presumption has been expressed in a variety of ways, for instance as 'the presumption that Parliament does not intend to pass legislation which would put the Crown in breach of its international obligations'[83] and as the 'principle that the courts will so far as possible construe domestic law so as to avoid creating a breach of the State's international obligations'.[84] By virtue of this presumption, a treaty—even an unincorporated treaty—may potentially impact upon questions of interpretation concerning *any* legislation, not just legislation intended to give it effect, although the 'principle is obviously at its strongest when it appears that the domestic law was passed to give effect to an international obligation or may otherwise be assumed to have been drafted with the treaty in mind'.[85] It is clear that the principle applies in respect of treaties made before legislation is passed, and it may also apply in relation to treaties made afterwards.[86]

---

[80] *Salomon* (n 25), as cited in n 76; and see the other cases cited in that note. See also paragraphs 9.34–9.36 below.

[81] See *Al-Fawwaz* (n 74), as cited and discussed in that note, in the context of extradition.

[82] *Pepushi* (n 78) [30] (Thomas LJ).

[83] *Higgs* (n 9) 241E (Lord Hoffmann).

[84] *Boyce v The Queen* [2004] UKPC 32, [2005] 1 AC 400 [25] (Lord Hoffmann). See also, eg, *R v Lyons* (n 26) [27] (Lord Hoffmann): 'there is a strong presumption in favour of interpreting English law (whether common law or statute) in a way which does not place the United Kingdom in breach of an international obligation'.

[85] *Boyce* (n 84) [26] (Lord Hoffmann). See also *Boake Allen* (n 67) [51] (Lord Neuberger). The general application of this presumption is also apparent from, eg, *R v Lyons* (n 26) [27] (Lord Hoffmann), as cited in n 84.

[86] *Boyce* (n 84) [26] (Lord Hoffmann), stating that the principle's 'application to laws which existed before the treaty is more difficult to justify as an exercise in construction', but that the majority was

9.33 It is important to note the distinction between this wider presumption and the overlapping, but narrower, presumption of conformity (discussed above at paragraphs 9.22–9.29).[87] Although in some cases it will make no difference to the result whichever presumption is applied, there is a potentially very material difference between a parliamentary intention that certain domestic legislation be given a *conforming* construction that *matches* that of a particular treaty and an intention that, whatever interpretation is given to certain domestic legislation, it should simply *not conflict*, and therefore be *compatible*, with a particular treaty.[88]

9.34 While the presumption of compatibility has been described as a 'strong presumption', it is important to recognise its limits, since Parliament is free to legislate contrary to a treaty if it so desires.[89] In this regard, it is instructive to consider Lord Hoffmann's expression of the relevant principle as being that 'if the legislation is *ambiguous* ... the court will, *other things being equal*, choose the meaning which accords with the obligations imposed by the treaty' (emphasis added).[90]

9.35 As for legislation needing to be '*ambiguous*', Lord Hoffmann explained that this means the legislation must be 'capable of a meaning which either conforms to or conflicts with' a treaty.[91] Elsewhere, the courts have said legislation will be

---

willing to 'proceed on the hypothesis' that it did so apply (although, given his conclusion, he did not need to decide the point). The minority were similarly willing to proceed on this basis.

[87] Particularly since they do overlap and since certain judicial statements of principle not focused on this distinction can potentially be read as eliding the two ideas: see, eg, *Salomon* (n 25) 143C–145B (Diplock LJ). The presumption of compatibility is wider, since it applies to all treaties and all domestic legislation, while the presumption of conformity applies only where particular legislation is intended to give effect to a particular treaty.

[88] For a good illustration of the practical effect of this distinction, see the argument in *Mullen* (n 25) referenced at n 77 above, and the text to that note. In that case, the presumption of compatibility would not have distinguished between giving domestic law a construction which strictly conformed to the terms of the relevant treaty, and one which was wider, but nevertheless compatible with, the terms of that treaty. By contrast, the presumption of conformity, which was effectively applied in *Mullen*, required a particular construction be given to the relevant domestic legislation and precluded the wider interpretation. See also *Adams* (n 58) [14] (Lord Phillips), expressly applying the principle of conformity to give legislation a meaning matching that of the treaty to which it gave effect (although he disagreed with the House of Lords' interpretation of the same treaty in *Mullen*). The difference between ensuring conformity and avoiding incompatibility is also apparent, eg, in the 'twin assumptions' referred to in *Office of the King's Prosecutor, Brussels v Cando Armas* [2005] UKHL 67, [2006] 2 AC 1 [8] (Lord Bingham), which appear to have been aimed at ensuring the latter result: 'Part 1 of the [Extradition Act 2003] did not effect a simple or straightforward transposition, and it did not on the whole use the language of the Framework Decision. But its interpretation must be approached on the twin assumptions that Parliament did not intend the provisions of Part 1 to be inconsistent with the Framework Decision and that, while Parliament might properly provide for a greater measure of cooperation by the United Kingdom than the Decision required, it did not intend to provide for less.' (Note that this case and this particular legislative scheme were discussed in detail in *Assange* (n 75).)

[89] *R v Lyons* (n 26) [27]–[28] (Lord Hoffmann). See also the passage in *Salomon* (n 25) cited in n 76 above.

[90] *Boyce* (n 84) [25] (Lord Hoffmann).

[91] ibid, citing *R v Secretary of State for the Home Department ex p Brind* [1991] AC 696 (HL) 747H (Lord Bridge).

ambiguous if it is 'reasonably capable of more than one meaning'.[92] In practice, the courts may be particularly willing to 'strive' to find the necessary ambiguity and give legislation a 'generous' interpretation where important rights are at stake, but even then there are limits.[93]

9.36   As for '*other things being equal*', it is important as ever to consider all other factors relevant to the construction of the legislation. In some cases, these may point towards the conflicting interpretation and, if strong enough, displace the presumption.[94] A key factor in this overall assessment may be the presence and strength of any indication that Parliament intended for the relevant legisla- tion to be compatible with *particular* treaty obligations, since (as noted above) the presumption is at its strongest where a specific intention of this kind can be discerned.[95]

Contribution to Context

9.37   More broadly still, both incorporated and unincorporated treaties, and Parliament's decisions in connection with them, may provide *context* for the inter- pretation of domestic legislation (whether or not it incorporates or gives effect to a treaty).[96]

Interpretation of Treaties

9.38   When the English courts construe a treaty itself (to assist in the interpreta- tion of domestic law or when this is otherwise permissible), they will adopt 'the

---

[92]   *Salomon* (n 25) 143F–G (Diplock LJ).

[93]   *Pepushi* (n 78) [30] (Thomas LJ), in a case concerning the Refugee Convention, ultimately find- ing a sufficiently generous construction impossible. See also *R v Asfaw* (n 20) [29] (Lord Bingham), also in a case concerning the Refugee Convention: 'While, therefore, one would expect any government intending to legislate inconsistently with an obligation binding on the UK to make its intention very clear, there can on well known authority be no ground in domestic law for failing to give effect to an enactment in terms unambiguously inconsistent with such an obligation.'

[94]   *Assange* (n 75) [201] (Lord Mance, dissenting but not on this point): 'The presumption is a canon of construction which must yield to contrary parliamentary intent and does not exclude other canons or admissible aids.' While this statement may strictly have been made in the context of the presumption of conformity, as a matter of principle it must apply equally to the presumption of compatibility. On discerning a contrary parliamentary intention, see generally paragraphs 9.27–9.29 above.

[95]   See the text to n 85 above.

[96]   See, eg, *R (Carson) v Secretary of State for Work and Pensions* [2005] UKHL 37, [2006] 1 AC 173 [18] (Lord Hoffmann), referring to treaties on social security to give context to domestic social security legislation; *Lambert* (n 73) [97] (Lord Hope), construing s 22 of the HRA 1998 against the background of the UK's decision *not* to incorporate Art 13 ECHR; *Republic of India v India Steamship Co Ltd (No 2)* [1998] AC 878 (HL) 910E–F (Lord Steyn), construing 'a provision of domestic origin designed to address a problem of domestic law' by reference to a treaty provision (applicable in a similar context)

same techniques of construction and interpretation as would an international tribunal'.[97]

9.39 The key principles in this regard are to be found in the Vienna Convention on the Law of Treaties,[98] and in particular Articles 31 and 32 (set out below), which the courts routinely apply.[99] Articles 31 and 32 should be applied whether or not the treaty being construed was concluded after the Vienna Convention came into force on 27 January 1980, since these Articles merely codify pre-existing customary international law.[100]

The General Rule

9.40 Article 31 of the Vienna Convention provides:

General rule of interpretation

1. A treaty shall be interpreted in good faith in accordance with the ordinary meaning to be given to the terms of the treaty in their context and in the light of its object and purpose.
2. The context for the purpose of the interpretation of a treaty shall comprise, in addition to the text, including its preamble and annexes:
    (a) Any agreement relating to the treaty which was made between all the parties in connexion with the conclusion of the treaty;
    (b) Any instrument which was made by one or more parties in connexion with the conclusion of the treaty and accepted by the other parties as an instrument related to the treaty.
3. There shall be taken into account, together with the context:
    (a) Any subsequent agreement between the parties regarding the interpretation of the treaty or the application of its provisions;
    (b) Any subsequent practice in the application of the treaty which establishes the agreement of the parties regarding its interpretation;
    (c) Any relevant rules of international law applicable in the relations between the parties.
4. A special meaning shall be given to a term if it is established that the parties so intended.

on which it had plainly been modelled; and at 912G–H (Lord Steyn), finding reinforcement for his construction of the word 'brought' in the same domestic legislative provision by reference to the Court of Appeal's interpretation of the same word in the 'analogous context' of a provision in another treaty.

[97] *R v Secretary of State for the Home Department ex p Adan* [2001] 2 AC 477 (HL) 529B–C (Lord Hobhouse), citing *Fothergill* (n 62), particularly at 281–83 (Lord Diplock).

[98] Vienna Convention on the Law of Treaties (n 6).

[99] See *Fothergill* (n 62) 290B–C (Lord Scarman): 'Faced with an international treaty which has been incorporated into our law, British courts should now follow broadly the guidelines declared by the Vienna Convention.' For a detailed account of the meaning of these Articles, see Richard Gardiner, *Treaty Interpretation*, 2nd edn (Oxford, Oxford University Press, 2015) chs 5–8.

[100] *Fothergill* (n 62) 282D (Lord Diplock), applying these Articles to a treaty from 1955. This passage was cited with approval in *Adan* (n 97) at 516D–E (Lord Steyn) and (in approving a much longer passage) at 529C (Lord Hobhouse).

9.41   Article 31(1) neatly expresses the core elements of treaty interpretation, which must all be considered together. Just as with interpreting domestic legislation, the court must consider the *text* in *context*, having regard to its *purpose*. This task must be approached in *good faith*. We first consider these elements, before addressing the effect of subsequent agreement and practice, and then how the international context of treaties informs the appropriate interpretive approach.

Core Elements

9.42   *The primacy of the text*: in every case 'the starting point of the construction exercise should be the text of the Convention itself', as ultimately the task of the court is 'one of interpreting the document to which the contracting parties have committed themselves by their agreement'.[101] In approaching this task, 'it is generally to be assumed that the parties have included the terms which they wished to include and on which they were able to agree, omitting other terms which they did not wish to include or on which they were not able to agree'.[102]

9.43   Accordingly, the scope for the implication of terms is very limited. It may occur when it is 'necessary or plainly right to do so. But the process of implication is one to be carried out with caution' to avoid imposing an obligation in the absence of agreement.[103] Any alleged implied term must therefore be 'clear by necessary implication from the text or from uniform acceptance by states that they would have agreed or have subsequently done so'.[104]

9.44   *Importance of context*: a treaty's terms must, and indeed can only, be understood in context. As Article 31(2) makes clear, this requires 'taking into account the text as a whole',[105] as well as any other connected agreements or instruments (such as unilateral interpretive 'declarations' formally put forward by a party with regard to treaty interpretation).[106] Reference to context has also been said to encompass

---

[101] *ST* (n 46) [31] (Lord Hope); and see also at [54] (Lord Dyson): 'The starting point is the language.' See also *Morris v KLM Royal Dutch Airlines* [2002] 2 AC 628 [147] (Lord Hobhouse): 'the relevant point for decision always remains: what do the actual words used mean?', cited with approval in *Feest v South West Strategic Health Authority* [2015] EWCA Civ 708, [2016] QB 503 [31] and [44] (Tomlinson LJ).

[102] *Brown v Stott* [2003] 1 AC 681 (PC) 703E (Lord Bingham), cited with approval in *ST* (n 46) [41] (Lord Hope).

[103] *Brown* (n 102) 703F–G (Lord Bingham).

[104] *Januzi v Secretary of State for the Home Department* [2006] UKHL 5, [2006] 2 AC 426 [4] (Lord Bingham), cited with approval in *ST* (n 46) [41] (Lord Hope).

[105] *Re Deep Vein Thrombosis and Air Travel Group Litigation* [2005] UKHL 72, [2006] 1 AC 495 [54] (Lord Mance); and see also *Januzi* (n 104) [4] (Lord Bingham). This will include reference to any unincorporated parts of the treaty: see, eg, *Re S (A Minor)* [1998] AC 750 (HL) 766C–E (Lord Slynn), referring for context to unincorporated parts of the relevant treaty.

[106] Context may also include, eg, a commentary adopted by a negotiating conference at the same time as the treaty: see *R (Corner House Research) v Director of the Serious Fraud Office* [2008]

consideration of the 'historical setting' of the treaty,[107] part of which is 'the legal position preceding its conclusion', as a matter both of international law[108] and of the domestic law of the contracting states.[109] Context has also been said to include 'subsequent treaty law' in similar fields and 'developments in customary international law'.[110]

9.45 *Purposive construction*: a treaty 'must be construed in the light of its object and purpose'.[111] The object and purpose of treaty provisions may be ascertained from the text of those provisions themselves,[112] from express statements of purpose in a treaty's preamble or certain of its terms,[113] or from a broader consideration of what a treaty seeks to achieve by reference to its full terms and history.[114] In practice this means that a commercial treaty may need to be given a sensible commercial construction.[115] And a human rights treaty 'should not be given a narrow or restricted interpretation',[116] but rather a 'generous and purposive' one,[117]

EWHC 714 (Admin), [2009] 1 AC 756 [130] (Moses LJ), although context was only listed as one of three possible ways in which the commentary might be admissible under the Vienna Convention (the others being as a 'supplementary means of interpretation' under Art 32 or as a declaration constituting state practice under Art 31(3)(b)). The House of Lords reversed the High Court's decision on appeal ([2008] UKHL 60, [2009] 1 AC 756), but did not consider this point.

[107] *Januzi* (n 104) [4] (Lord Bingham).

[108] *Revenue and Customs Commissioners v Anson* [2015] UKSC 44, [2015] 4 All ER 288 [58] (Lord Reed): 'The contemporary background of a treaty, including the legal position preceding its conclusion, can legitimately be taken into account as part of the context relevant to the interpretation of its terms', going on to consider earlier treaties as part of the relevant context for interpreting a treaty. But see *CMA* (n 62) [10] (Longmore LJ), considering that an existing treaty should be seen not as 'context', but as a 'supplementary means' falling within Art 32 of the Vienna Convention, to which recourse could only be had 'once the ordinary meaning has been ascertained' and which could only determine the meaning of the treaty 'when the ordinary meaning makes the convention ambiguous or obscure or when such ordinary meaning leads to a manifestly absurd or unreasonable result'. This paragraph in *CMA* was cited with approval in *Gard* (n 62) [74] (Lord Clarke), although *Anson* was not cited or considered in that case. As to the role of supplementary means in treaty interpretation generally, see paragraphs 9.57–9.61 below.

[109] See *Anson* (n 108), as cited in that note, and the two cases cited by Lord Reed in support of that passage: *Riverstone Meat Co Pty Ltd v Lancashire Shipping Co Ltd* [1961] AC 807 (HL) 836 (Viscount Simonds), construing the Hague Rules by reference to national legislation used by the treaty draftsmen as precedents; and *Effort Shipping Co Ltd v Linden Management SA* [1998] AC 605 (HL) 624F–G (Lord Steyn): 'It is permissible to take into account the legal position in the United Kingdom and in the United States regarding the shipment of dangerous cargo before the Hague Rules were approved. It is relevant as part of the contextual scene of the Hague Rules.'

[110] *R (Hussein) v Secretary of State for Defence* [2014] EWCA Civ 1087 [42] (Lloyd Jones LJ). Strictly, this may more aptly fall under Art 31(3)(c) of the Vienna Convention.

[111] *HJ (Iran) v Secretary of State for the Home Department* [2010] UKSC 31, [2011] 1 AC 596 [110] (Dyson JSC), with regard to the Refugee Convention.

[112] See *R (Bancoult) v Secretary of State for Foreign and Commonwealth Affairs (No 3)* [2014] EWCA Civ 708, [2014] 1 WLR 2921 [20] (Lord Dyson MR).

[113] See, eg, *Anson* (n 108) [57] (Lord Reed); *Bancoult* (ibid); and *S (A Minor)* (n 105), in the passage cited in that note.

[114] See, eg, *CMA* (n 62) [11] (Longmore LJ), cited with approval in *Gard* (n 62) [76] (Lord Clarke).

[115] *Corocraft* (n 76) 654D–E (Lord Denning MR), stating that ambiguous text in a treaty 'should be interpreted so as to make good sense amongst commercial men'.

[116] *Januzi* (n 104) [4] (Lord Bingham).

[117] *European Roma Rights* (n 20) [18] (Lord Bingham).

being understood as a 'living instrument in the sense that while its meaning does not change over time its application will'.[118] However, the courts have made clear that the need to give a generous and purposive construction to such instruments does not give the court a 'warrant to give effect to what [contracting states] might, or in an ideal world would, have agreed'.[119]

9.46 *Good faith*: the duty to interpret treaties in good faith 'is not to be taken to be a source of obligation where none exists' and imposes no duty to find a treaty to mean other than 'what it says'.[120] Its effect is relatively limited, being designed to ensure treaty rights are used responsibly, rather than abusively, arbitrarily or capriciously.[121]

Subsequent Agreement and Practice

9.47 Pursuant to Article 31(3)(a) and (b) of the Vienna Convention, subsequent agreement by parties to a treaty as to its meaning, either made expressly (Article 31(3)(a)) or evidenced by their subsequent practice in the application of the treaty (Article 31(3)(b)), can provide a guide to its interpretation. For Article 31(1)(b) to apply, there must be evidence of 'a sufficiently widespread and uncontroversial practice'.[122] However, even if the evidence of subsequent practice falls short of this, it can still be of 'some probative value' in the interpretation exercise.[123]

Treaties as International Instruments

9.48 A treaty 'must be interpreted as an international instrument, not a domestic statute'.[124] This general rule encompasses three more specific principles, discussed below, namely that a treaty must be understood as (i) a *multilateral agreement*, which is (ii) intended for *multinational application*, and which may have (iii) a *multilingual articulation*.

9.49 *Multilateral agreement*: unlike domestic legislation, whose formulation is often (at least largely) carefully devised by parliamentary counsel, treaties are

---

[118] *Sepet v Secretary of State for the Home Department* [2003] UKHL 15, [2003] 1 WLR 856 [6] (Lord Bingham). As to the concept of interpretation of legislation as a living instrument in the domestic context, see the discussion of the presumption that legislation is 'always speaking' in Chapter 3.26–3.33.

[119] *European Roma Rights* (n 20) [18] (Lord Bingham).

[120] *ST* (n 46) [31] (Lord Hope).

[121] See the analysis of the duty in *European Roma Rights* (n 20) [57]–[64] (Lord Hope).

[122] *Assange* (n 75) [108] (Lord Kerr). See also at [67]–[71] (Lord Phillips) and [130]–[131] (Lord Dyson). Lady Hale dissented on the application of Art 31(3)(b), stating at [191]: 'Failure to address minds to an issue is not the same as acquiescence in a particular state of affairs.' It is clear from these passages that the relevant practice need not be one engaged in by all of the contracting states.

[123] *Assange* (n 75) [109] (Lord Kerr) and [242] (Lord Mance), citing Ian Brownlie, *Principles of Public International Law*, 7th edn (Oxford, Oxford University Press, 2008).

[124] *ST* (n 46) [30] (Lord Hope).

'the product of ... negotiation and compromise' and so may not possess 'the same precision of language as ... an Act of Parliament'. Accordingly, although the starting point for interpretation is the language of a treaty, 'concentrating exclusively on the language' is inappropriate, and the court should take a broad and purposive approach to treaty construction 'rather than a narrow linguistic approach'.[125]

9.50 *Multinational application*: subject to what is said in the next paragraph, treaties are generally intended to be given a uniform interpretation by all states parties.[126] As international instruments intended for a 'varied judicial audience',[127] they should not be interpreted by reference to concepts and technical rules of English law unlikely to have been in the contemplation of those framing the treaty.[128] Rather, the court 'must search, untrammelled by notions of its national legal culture, for the true autonomous and international meaning of the treaty',[129] applying 'broad principles of general acceptation'.[130]

9.51 Accordingly, treaty provisions will often 'have an autonomous meaning, a meaning independent of that which they would be given in the domestic laws of any of the states parties'.[131] However, in certain cases a treaty's provisions may be intended to be interpreted by each state party by reference to its own national law. Such an intention may be apparent, for example, in relation to matters generally reserved to sovereign states and where there is 'no international standard by reference to which' such a matter could be determined.[132]

9.52 The fact that a provision should bear a single autonomous meaning does not entail that decisions of foreign courts on the meaning of that term must be followed if the English court does not agree with them, although they can be considered.[133]

---

[125] *R v Secretary of State for the Home Department ex p Adan* [1999] 1 AC 293 (HL) 305C–D (Lord Lloyd). See also *James Buchanan* (n 21) 157D–E (Viscount Dilhorne): 'In construing the terms of a convention it is proper and indeed right, in my opinion, to have regard to the fact that conventions are apt to be more loosely worded than Acts of Parliament.'

[126] See *Re H (Minors)* [1998] AC 72 (HL) 87F (Lord Browne-Wilkinson): 'An international Convention, expressed in different languages and intended to apply to a wide range of differing legal systems, cannot be construed differently in different jurisdictions. The Convention must have the same meaning and effect under the laws of all contracting states.' See also *Adan* (n 97) 517B (Lord Steyn): 'there can only be one true meaning'.

[127] *Fothergill* (n 62) 282A–B (Lord Diplock).

[128] See *Sarrio SA v Kuwait Investment Authority* [1999] 1 AC 32 (HL) 40E–G (Lord Saville); and *James Buchanan* (n 21) 152E (Lord Wilberforce). See also *Re H (Minors)* (n 126) 87E–G (Lord Browne-Wilkinson).

[129] *Adan* (n 97) 517B (Lord Steyn).

[130] *James Buchanan* (n 21) 152E (Lord Wilberforce).

[131] *Re K (A Child)* [2014] UKSC 29, [2014] AC 1401 [52] (Lady Hale).

[132] See, eg, *ST* (n 46) [55] (Lord Dyson), holding that the phrase 'lawfully in their territory' under the Refugee Convention was to be construed by reference to national law. See also at [32]–[40] (Lord Hope) to similar effect.

[133] See *Adan* (n 97) 518C–D (Lord Steyn); *Fothergill* (n 62) 295B–C (Lord Scarman); and *Morris* (n 101) [147] (Lord Hobhouse), cited with approval in *Feest* (n 101) [31] (Tomlinson LJ).

9.53   *Multilingual articulation*: treaties may not be drafted, or solely drafted, in English. Authoritative (or 'authentic') versions may exist in multiple languages. Sometimes, but not always, one of these versions may be expressly stated to prevail where there is a conflict between them. Sometimes the only authoritative text may be in a language other than English. To add to the complexity, Parliament may have chosen a variety of methods to incorporate or otherwise give effect to a treaty, including by providing a translation of an authoritative version. Differing interpretive principles may apply depending on the terms of the treaty, on which versions are designated as authentic and on the terms of the legislation incorporating or otherwise giving effect to the treaty.[134]

9.54   In summary, the practice adopted by the English courts when interpreting treaties is to look to construe a foreign language text where the domestic legislation incorporating or otherwise giving effect to a treaty sets out another language version or states that it is to prevail in the event of a difference,[135] or where the treaty itself indicates that a foreign language version is the authoritative version[136] (or, by parity of reasoning, where the treaty provides that the foreign text is to prevail in the event of a difference). Otherwise, the courts will start by construing the English text, but may refer to other authenticated language versions as 'a legitimate aid to the interpretation' of the English text,[137] whether or not the English text is ambiguous.[138]

9.55   This approach is in line with the terms of Article 33 of the Vienna Convention,[139] to which the courts expressly have regard in this context.[140] This provides:

Interpretation of treaties authenticated in two or more languages

1.   When a treaty has been authenticated in two or more languages, the text is equally authoritative in each language, unless the treaty provides or the parties agree that, in case of divergence, a particular text shall prevail.

2.   A version of the treaty in a language other than one of those in which the text was authenticated shall be considered an authentic text only if the treaty so provides or the parties so agree.

---

[134]   See *James Buchanan* (n 21) 152A–C (Lord Wilberforce).

[135]   See *Fothergill* (n 62) 293E–294A (Lord Scarman), holding that where the relevant Act provided that the French version of the Warsaw Convention prevailed over the English in the event of inconsistency, the court must 'take judicial notice of the French. We have to form a view as to its meaning'. He then discussed the practicalities of this exercise (which included using the English text as an aid to interpretation).

[136]   See *Corocraft* (n 76) 652B–653A (Lord Denning MR).

[137]   See *Adams* (n 58) [15]–[16] (Lord Phillips). See also, eg, *Assange* (n 75) [16]–[20] (Lord Phillips), considering the equally authoritative French text of a Framework Decision as well as the English, noting that as a matter of fact the French text was prepared before the English, and stating at [56]: 'The French version was the original and is to be preferred' (and see also his comments to similar effect at [58]).

[138]   See *James Buchanan* (n 21) 152C–G (Lord Wilberforce).

[139]   Vienna Convention on the Law of Treaties (n 6).

[140]   See *Adams* (n 58) [15] (Lord Phillips).

3. The terms of the treaty are presumed to have the same meaning in each authentic text.
4. Except where a particular text prevails in accordance with paragraph 1, when a comparison of the authentic texts discloses a difference of meaning which the application of articles 31 and 32 does not remove, the meaning which best reconciles the texts, having regard to the object and purpose of the treaty, shall be adopted.

9.56 As a practical matter, where a court considers the foreign language text of a treaty, it may rely upon its own knowledge of that language, on interpretive aids such as dictionaries, or on expert translation evidence, as appropriate in the circumstances.[141]

Supplementary Means of Interpretation

9.57 Article 32 of the Vienna Convention provides:[142]

Supplementary means of interpretation

Recourse may be had to supplementary means of interpretation, including the preparatory work of the treaty and the circumstances of its conclusion, in order to confirm the meaning resulting from the application of article 31, or to determine the meaning when the interpretation according to article 31:

(a) Leaves the meaning ambiguous or obscure; or
(b) Leads to a result which is manifestly absurd or unreasonable.

9.58 Article 32 is, on one level, broadly framed, permitting the courts, in their discretion, to have regard to a wide range of supplementary materials. At the same time, its drafting is restrictive, only permitting such recourse (for something beyond the limited purpose of confirming a meaning) where the conditions specified by Article 32(a) and (b) apply. However, since the courts have a reasonably wide ambit for determining that ambiguity or obscurity exists in a given case after applying Article 31, it may be that these conditions should not be seen as particularly constraining.[143]

9.59 In practice, English courts will have regard to a wide variety of materials in construing treaties: *travaux préparatoires* (documents evidencing preparatory

---

[141] See *Fothergill* (n 62) 273G–274B (Lord Wilberforce); and 293E–294A (Lord Scarman).

[142] Vienna Convention on the Law of Treaties (n 6).

[143] See Gardiner, *Treaty Interpretation* (2015) (n 99) ch 8, section 4.3, 377–82. But see *Effort Shipping* (n 109) 623E–F (Lord Steyn), which suggests that the court would need to be faced with 'truly feasible alternative interpretations' of a treaty for supplementary means to be relied upon as 'determinative' of an issue of construction.

work leading to the adoption of a treaty),[144] the content of negotiations concerning a treaty,[145] commentaries on a treaty[146] and, more generally, all the sources of international law referred to in paragraph 9.2 above.[147]

9.60   As to the use of *travaux préparatoires* and evidence of negotiations in particular (when using them for more than simply confirming an interpretation that is already apparent),[148] the courts have generally taken a narrow view of when these may be used, following the speech of Lord Wilberforce in *Fothergill v Monarch* in preference to broader statements by other judges in the same case condoning their use.[149] Lord Wilberforce stipulated two conditions for relying upon these materials: 'first, that the material involved is public and accessible, and secondly, that the travaux préparatoires clearly and indisputably point to a definite legislative intention'. As Lord Steyn paraphrased the second condition: 'Only a bull's-eye counts. Nothing less will do.'[150]

9.61   The use of supplementary means to assist treaty interpretation is perhaps, therefore, the area in which the practice of English courts most significantly diverges from the rules set out in the Vienna Convention. On the one hand, the courts are ready to refer to a wide range of sources, without necessarily identifying a particular ambiguity or obscurity or making clear that their purpose in doing so is simply to confirm the ordinary meaning of the text construed in context and in the light of its object and purpose. On the other hand, the courts may be

---

[144] See, eg, *Black-Clawson International Ltd v Papierwerke Waldhof-Aschaffenburg AG* [1975] AC 591 (HL) 640G–H (Lord Diplock). As to the definition of this term, see Gardiner, *Treaty Interpretation* (2015) (n 99) ch 1, section 3.4, 25–26.

[145] See, eg, *Agnew v Länsförsäkringsbolagens AB* [2001] 1 AC 223 (HL) 261D–E (Lord Millett, dissenting, but not on this point).

[146] See, eg, *Fothergill* (n 62) 284A–B (Lord Diplock), stating that commentaries produced after the conclusion of a treaty 'can have persuasive value only' and that their 'persuasive effect … will depend upon the cogency of their reasoning'. In some cases, the courts are specifically empowered by legislation to consider a particular commentary as an aid to interpretation: see, eg, Contracts (Applicable Law) Act 1990, s 3(3).

[147] See, eg, *Fothergill* (n 62) 294E–F (Lord Scarman), referring, among other potential aids, to 'international case law' and 'the writings of jurists'. For a detailed account of the way in which the courts take account of supplementary means of interpretation, see Fatima, *Using International Law* (2005) (n 2) ch 5; and Gardiner, *Treaty Interpretation* (2015) (n 99) ch 8.

[148] In accordance with Art 32 of the Vienna Convention, the courts will readily 'have recourse to what may be called the travaux preparatoires and the circumstances of the conclusion of the convention' in order simply to *confirm* the ordinary meaning as ascertained from applying Art 31: see *CMA* (n 62) [10] (Longmore LJ), cited with approval in *Gard* (n 62) [74] (Lord Clarke).

[149] *Fothergill* (n 62) 278A–C (Lord Wilberforce), in the context of *travaux préparatoires*. Contrast the speeches of Lord Diplock at 283A–D and Lord Scarman at 294B–295C. Lord Wilberforce's statement was followed in, eg, *Effort Shipping* (n 109) 623F–G (Lord Steyn), in the context of *travaux préparatoires*; *Jindal Iron and Steel Co Ltd v Islamic Solidarity Shipping Co Jordan Inc* [2005] UKHL 49, [2005] 1 WLR 1363 [20] (Lord Steyn), again in the context of *travaux préparatoires*; and *Fortis Bank SA/NV v Indian Overseas Bank* [2011] EWCA Civ 58, [2012] Bus LR 141 [51] (Thomas LJ), in the context of documents providing 'evidence in relation to the negotiation of international conventions'.

[150] *Effort Shipping* (n 109) 623F–G (Lord Steyn); but see the discussion of this case in *Gardiner* (n 99) 383–85.

overly restrictive in their approach by allowing reference to *travaux préparatoires* to assist in the interpretation of ambiguous or obscure treaties only when they give a definitive 'bull's-eye' of an answer.

Interpretation of Domestic Legislation in the Light of Customary International Law

9.62　The nature of customary international law means that its rules are not normally so easy to ascertain as those set out in treaties.[151] However, provided those rules can be established with clarity, they can influence the interpretation of domestic legislation in the same broad ways as treaty rules can—through the presumptions of conformity and compatibility, and by generally informing the context in which legislation may fall be to be interpreted.

The Presumption of Conformity

9.63　In some cases (although this may occur only rarely), it will be apparent that Parliament intends for its legislation to give effect to certain rules of customary international law. Where this is so, the courts have held that they should seek to give effect to that intention and read legislation so far as possible in a way that conforms with the relevant rules of customary international law (although ultimately the question will always be one of statutory construction).[152]

The Presumption of Compatibility

9.64　More generally, there is a presumption that legislation is to be read compatibly with international law, which applies to customary norms as well as to treaty norms.[153] The presumption may be particularly strong in relation to

---

[151] See the discussion at paragraphs 9.13–9.14 above on the nature of customary international law.
[152] This was the approach taken in *Pinochet (No 3)* (n 34), in relation to the construction of s 20 of the State Immunity Act 1978, especially at 210B–C (Lord Goff, dissenting, but not on this point). The key passages in this regard were identified and summarised in *Harb v Aziz* [2015] EWCA Civ 481, [2016] Ch 308 [31] (Aikens LJ): 'It is clear from statements of Lord Browne-Wilkinson, Lord Goff of Chieveley, Lord Hope of Craighead, Lord Hutton, Lord Saville of Newdigate, Lord Millett and Lord Phillips of Worth Matravers in *Pinochet No 3* that, in their view, Parliament cannot have intended to give heads of state or former heads of state any greater rights than they already enjoyed under customary international law, so that the immunity granted to a head of state and a former head of state by section 20 must reflect customary international law: see pp 203E, 210C, 240H, 251A, 265H, 268H–269A, 270C, 287H and 291G.'
[153] See *Salomon* (n 25) 143F–G (Diplock LJ): 'there is a prima facie presumption that Parliament does not intend to act in breach of international law, including therein specific treaty obligations'.

legislation giving effect to, or passed against the background of, certain rules of customary international law.[154] However, it will be displaced by clear and unambiguous language, or where it is otherwise clear that Parliament does not intend for domestic law to be compatible with customary international law.[155]

Contribution to Context

9.65   At the most general level, customary international law may be referred to in relevant cases as part of the general 'background' or context in the light of which any given piece of legislation falls to be interpreted.[156]

Although made in the specific context of treaty law, this classic statement of the presumption of compatibility is expressed in general terms applicable to *all* rules of international law. See also, eg, *Serious Organised Crime Agency v Perry* [2012] UKSC 35, [2013] 1 AC 182 [94] (Lord Phillips); and *Belhaj* (n 33) [252] (Lord Sumption): 'international law, whether customary or Treaty-based ... may ... affect the interpretation of ambiguous statutory provisions', citing *R v Lyons* (n 26) [13] (Lord Bingham).

[154] See *Alcom Ltd v Republic of Colombia* [1984] AC 580 (HL) 600A–B (Lord Diplock), considering that, in the context of interpreting the State Immunity Act 1978, the effect of certain rules of international law 'makes it highly unlikely that Parliament intended to require United Kingdom courts to act contrary to international law unless the clear language of the statute compels such a conclusion; but it does no more than this'. And see, in the context of the effect of treaty norms on the interpretation of domestic legislation, *Boyce* (n 84) [26] (Lord Hoffmann), as cited in the text to n 85 above.

[155] *Salomon* (n 25), as cited in n 76 above. See also the discussion of the limitations on the domestic incorporation or application of customary international law at paragraphs 9.16–9.17 above. As a matter of principle, the restrictions on customary international law being incorporated into or otherwise applied in domestic law where this would be inconsistent with the constitution or the will of Parliament as expressed in domestic legislation must also apply to prevent those unincorporated rules from being used to alter the meaning of domestic legislation through interpretation.

[156] *Alcom* (n 154) 597G–H (Lord Diplock); this passage was cited in *Harb* (n 152) [28] (Aikens LJ), stating: 'customary international law remains the background against which the [State Immunity Act 1978] is set'.

10

Impact of the Human Rights Act 1998: Sections 3 and 4

10.1 The introduction of the Human Rights Act 1998 (HRA 1998), which came into force on 2 October 2000, has had an important and extensive impact on the interpretation of domestic legislation.

10.2 That is because section 3 of the HRA 1998 creates a powerful rule that requires legislation to be interpreted and given effect, where necessary and so far as possible, compatibly with certain rights under the European Convention on Human Rights (ECHR). This provision has far-reaching consequences for the courts' reading of certain legislative provisions, empowering them to do far more than they could through the application of 'ordinary' principles of statutory construction alone.

10.3 However, even applying section 3, it may still not be possible for all legislation to be read compatibly with the relevant Convention rights. In those cases, depending on the nature of the relevant legislation, section 4 may permit the higher courts to make a *'declaration of incompatibility'* in respect of the incompatible legislation, which will then allow Parliament to address the incompatibility as it sees fit.

Section 3

The Interpretive Obligation in Section 3

10.4 Section 3(1) of the HRA 1998 (headed 'Interpretation of legislation') provides that: 'So far as it is possible to do so, primary legislation and subordinate legislation must be read and given effect in a way which is compatible with the

Convention rights.'[1] The term 'the Convention rights' comprises certain of the rights under the ECHR as specified in section 1 of the HRA 1998.[2]

10.5 As is immediately apparent from the statutory language, section 3(1) imposes a *mandatory* but *qualified* duty to *read* (that is, interpret) legislation compatibly with the Convention rights:[3]

10.5.1 The use of the word 'must' indicates that section 3 imposes a non-discretionary *duty*,[4] which is commonly referred to as an 'interpretative obligation'.[5]

10.5.2 The words '[s]o far as it is possible to do so' (particularly when read together with the rest of sections 3 and 4) indicate that 'Parliament expressly envisaged that not all legislation would be capable of being made Convention-compliant by application of section 3'.[6] Accordingly, '[t]he obligation, powerful though it is, is not to be performed without regard to its limitations'.[7]

10.6 It must also be noted that, as an *interpretive* duty, section 3(1) expressly does not affect 'the validity, continuing operation or enforcement of any incompatible primary legislation' or 'subordinate legislation if (disregarding any possibility of revocation) primary legislation prevents removal of the incompatibility'.[8]

---

[1] For a more detailed discussion of the interpretive obligation under section 3, see Jack Beatson et al, *Human Rights: Judicial Protection in the United Kingdom* (London, Sweet & Maxwell, 2008) paras 5-64–5-127, 486–510. See also Richard Clayton and Hugh Tomlinson, *The Law of Human Rights*, 2nd edn, vol 1 (Oxford, Oxford University Press, 2009) paras 4.29–4.45, 187–201; and Lord Lester, Lord Pannick and Javan Herberg, *Human Rights Law and Practice*, 3rd edn (London, LexisNexis, 2009) para 2.3, 41–48.

[2] Namely Arts 2–12 and 14 of the ECHR, and Arts 1–3 of the First Protocol and Art 1 of the Thirteenth Protocol to the ECHR, all as read with Arts 16–18 of the ECHR. These Articles are set out in sch 1 to the HRA 1998.

[3] In fact, 'the content of the section actually goes beyond interpretation to cover the way that legislation is given effect'. The section 'contains not one, but two, obligations' which are 'complementary' but 'distinct', requiring legislation not only to be *read* but also *given effect* compatibly with the Convention rights: *Ghaidan v Godin-Mendoza* [2004] UKHL 30, [2004] 2 AC 557 [107] (Lord Rodger). See also *R (GC) v Commissioner of Police of the Metropolis* [2011] UKSC 21, [2011] 1 WLR 1230 [71] (Lady Hale). However, our focus in this chapter is on the effect of s 3 on the interpretation of legislation.

[4] See *Ghaidan* (n 3) [59] (Lord Millett): 'It is a command … There is no residual discretion to disobey the obligation which the section imposes.' See also *Re S (Care Order: Implementation of Care Plan)* [2002] UKHL 10, [2002] 2 AC 291, [37] (Lord Nicholls), describing s 3 as 'a powerful tool whose use is obligatory. It is not an optional canon of construction. Nor is its use dependent on the existence of ambiguity'.

[5] See, eg, *Wilson v First County Trust Ltd (No 2)* [2003] UKHL 40, [2004] 1 AC 816 [14] (Lord Nicholls); Beatson et al, *Human Rights: Judicial Protection* (2008) (n 1) para 5-04, 459–60.

[6] *Ghaidan* (n 3) [27] (Lord Nicholls).

[7] *R v Lambert* [2001] UKHL 37, [2002] 2 AC 545 [79] (Lord Hope). These limitations are discussed further below at paragraphs 10.20–10.22.

[8] HRA 1998, s 3(2)(b) and (c). Note that 'primary legislation' and 'subordinate legislation' are defined terms under the HRA 1998: see s 22(1).

Scope of the Application of Section 3

10.7 *General application*: section 3 is of 'general application', imposing a duty not only on the courts but also on 'everyone else who may have to interpret and give effect to legislation', most obviously 'public authorities of all kinds' (such as 'organs of central and local government').[9]

10.8 *All legislation*: as stated in section 3(2)(a), the duty under section 3(1) applies to both 'primary legislation and subordinate legislation whenever enacted'.[10] It is thus 'retrospective in the sense that ... it ... may have the effect of changing the interpretation and effect of legislation already in force' prior to the date that the HRA 1998 came into force.[11]

10.9 *Not retrospective in effect*: however, the courts have repeatedly held that (except as provided by section 22(4))[12] the provisions of the HRA 1998, including section 3, are generally not to be applied with retrospective effect so as to affect or interfere with events[13] or transactions[14] which occurred, or rights which

---

[9] *Ghaidan* (n 3) [106] (Lord Rodger). See also *GC* (n 3) [55] (Lord Phillips), stating that s 3 applies to the police, and at [66] (Lady Hale): 'This obligation is laid upon everyone, not just upon the courts.'

[10] See also *Re S* (n 4), in the passage cited in that note, confirming that there is no threshold requirement, such as a need for ambiguity, before the interpretive duty applies (although the duty will only apply where necessary to avoid a breach of a Convention right: see paragraphs 10.10 and 10.12 below).

[11] *Wilson* (n 5) [17] (Lord Nicholls).

[12] Section 22(4) of the HRA 1998 provides a limited exception to the Act's general non-retrospectivity, allowing a victim of a breach by a public authority of a Convention right to rely on that right in legal proceedings 'brought by or at the instigation of a public authority whenever the act in question took place'.

[13] Accordingly, by way of example, the HRA 1998 cannot be used to impugn on appeal the fairness of a trial that occurred before it came into force: see *Lambert* (n 7) and *R v Kansal (No 2)* [2001] UKHL 62, [2002] 2 AC 69. Nor does the HRA 1998 require an inquest or investigation into a death occurring before it came into force: see *R (Hurst) v London Northern District Coroner* [2007] UKHL 13, [2007] 2 AC 189; and *Re McKerr* [2004] UKHL 12, [2004] 1 WLR 807. However, following *Re McCaughey* [2011] UKSC 20, [2012] 1 AC 725, the HRA 1998 does require certain investigations or inquests occurring *after* it came into force—including those concerning deaths occurring *before* it came into force—to comply with the procedural obligations under Art 2 ECHR. But this conclusion was said not to entail the retrospective operation of the HRA 1998, which was generally inappropriate: see at [76] (Lord Hope), [90] (Lady Hale), [110] (Lord Kerr) and [134] (Lord Dyson). See further in relation to the relevance of the HRA 1998 to investigations into deaths *R (Keyu) v Secretary of State for Foreign and Commonwealth Affairs* [2015] UKSC 69, [2016] AC 1355 [92]–[98] (Lord Neuberger); and *Al-Saadoon v Secretary of State for Defence* [2016] EWHC 773 (Admin), [2016] 1 WLR 3625 [168]–[174] (Leggatt J).

[14] Accordingly, by way of example, s 3(1) was not used to construe the Consumer Credit Act 1974 in relation to that Act's application to a loan agreement entered into before the HRA 1998 came into force: *Wilson* (n 5). With ongoing agreements, the application of the HRA 1998 may depend on whether its application would interfere with rights that 'vested' prior to its coming into force: see n 15 below.

vested,[15] or causes of action which accrued,[16] before the HRA 1998 came into force.

10.10 *Only when necessary*: the interpretive duty under section 3 only applies where the otherwise appropriate interpretation of a provision would entail a breach of a Convention right in the case before the court, so that the application of the duty becomes necessary in order to avoid such a breach (see further paragraph 10.12 below).[17] This means that a particular legislative provision may fall to be given *different interpretations* in different contexts, depending on whether recourse to section 3 is required on the facts of a given case.[18]

Performing the Interpretive Obligation under Section 3

10.11 The interpretive obligation in section 3 'is more radical' and 'goes much further' than 'ordinary methods of interpretation'.[19] Its enactment has effected an 'important change in the process of interpretation'[20] and the section has therefore been recognised as having 'a role of constitutional significance'.[21] It creates a 'very strong and far reaching' duty, intended to be 'the primary remedial measure' for curing incompatibility of statutory provisions with the Convention rights, although ultimately it is limited by what is 'possible'[22] (as to which, see paragraphs 10.13–10.22 below).

---

[15] See, eg, *PW & Co v Milton Gate Investments Ltd* [2003] EWHC 1994 (Ch), [2004] Ch 142, where Neuberger J, applying *Wilson* (n 5), held that although the head lease in that case had been entered into well *before* the HRA 1998 came into force, s 3 nevertheless did apply (through its impact on the interpretation and effect of provisions in the Law of Property Act 1925) so as to affect the consequences of a determination of that head lease by notice given just *after* the HRA 1998 came into force. This was because the earliest that the relevant rights could be said to have 'vested' was the date when notice was given, and there was therefore no question of the HRA 1998 interfering with rights vested prior to its coming into force.

[16] *Wilson* (n 5) [20] (Lord Nicholls), citing with approval *Wainwright v Home Office* [2001] EWCA Civ 2081, [2002] QB 1334 [61] (Mummery LJ). The general rule against retrospectivity in this context was said to be based on the need to avoid unfairness.

[17] *Hurst* (n 13) [44] (Lord Brown); and see Lester, Pannick and Herberg, *Human Rights Law and Practice* (2009) (n 1) para 2.3.4, 47. See also *Ghaidan* (n 3) [60] (Lord Millett), considering that the presumption that legislation is to be read compatibly with international law (see Chapter 9.31–9.36) would 'often be sufficient' to ensure compatibility with the Convention rights 'without recourse to section 3.'

[18] *Hurst* (n 13) [52] (Lord Brown), drawing an analogy with the effect of the '*Marleasing* principle', which requires domestic legislation to be construed so as to comply with EU law: 'In cases where no European Community rights would be infringed, the domestic legislation is to be construed and applied in the ordinary way.' See also at [12] (Lord Rodger). As to the *Marleasing* principle, see Chapter 12.21–12.29.

[19] *R v A (No 2)* [2001] UKHL 25, [2002] 1 AC 45 [44] (Lord Steyn).

[20] *R (Wilkinson) v IRC* [2005] UKHL 30, [2005] 1 WLR 1718 [17] (Lord Hoffmann).

[21] *HM Treasury v Ahmed* [2010] UKSC 2, [2010] 2 AC 534 [115] (Lord Phillips).

[22] *Sheldrake v Director of Public Prosecutions* [2004] UKHL 43, [2005] 1 AC 264 [28] (Lord Bingham).

10.12 *Preliminary question: is the legislation incompatible with the Convention rights?* As explained above, before having recourse to section 3, 'courts should always first ascertain whether, absent section 3, there would be any breach of the Convention'.[23] This task is to be carried out in the first instance by interpreting the allegedly incompatible legislation according to ordinary principles of construction,[24] but may also require the court to take account of the effect of *other* legislation, which may mean there is no breach.[25] If, following this approach, a breach is discerned, section 3 will come into play.

10.13 *Section 3 is not limited by the 'mere language' of a provision:* legislation need not be ambiguous for section 3 to apply[26] and accordingly, in interpreting a provision, '[s]ection 3 may require a court to depart from the unambiguous meaning the legislation would otherwise bear'.[27] Once this is recognised:

> [I]t becomes impossible to suppose Parliament intended that the operation of section 3 should depend critically upon the particular form of words adopted by the parliamentary draftsman in the statutory provision under consideration. That would make the application of section 3 something of a semantic lottery ... From this the conclusion which seems inescapable is that the mere fact the language under consideration is inconsistent with a Convention-compliant meaning does not of itself make a Convention-compliant interpretation under section 3 impossible.[28]

10.14 It is therefore clear that, although concerned with interpretation, section 3 allows the courts to look beyond the 'particular phraseology' or 'mere language' of legislation, to focus instead 'on matters of substance'.[29] Its proper application involves avoiding 'an excessive concentration on linguistic features of the particular statute' being construed and taking 'a broad approach concentrating, amongst other things, in a purposive way on the importance of the fundamental right involved'.[30]

---

[23] *Poplar Housing and Regeneration Community Association Ltd v Donoghue* [2001] EWCA Civ 595, [2002] QB 48 [75] (Lord Woolf CJ).

[24] See, eg, *Ghiadan* (n 3) [60] (Lord Millett), as cited in n 17.

[25] *Kennedy v Information Commissioner* [2014] UKSC 20, [2015] AC 455 [35] (Lord Mance).

[26] *Ghiadan* (n 3) [29] (Lord Nicholls): 'It is now generally accepted that the application of section 3 does not depend upon the presence of ambiguity in the legislation being interpreted. Even if, construed according to the ordinary principles of interpretation, the meaning of the legislation admits of no doubt, section 3 may none the less require the legislation to be given a different meaning'; and see at [44] (Lord Steyn). See also *R v A* (n 19) [44] (Lord Steyn), stating that the interpretive obligation under section 3 'applies even if there is no ambiguity in the language in the sense of the language being capable of two different meanings'; and *Ahmed* (n 21) [115] (Lord Phillips).

[27] *Ghiadan* (n 3) [30] (Lord Nicholls).

[28] ibid [31]–[32] (Lord Nicholls).

[29] ibid [123] (Lord Rodger).

[30] ibid [41] (Lord Steyn).

10.15   This approach to interpretation, which allows for a provision not to be given its plain meaning, has been described as permitting the courts to 'depart from the legislative intention of Parliament' in enacting that provision.[31]

10.16   *Section 3 may require the modification of language and meaning:* in view of the broad and substance-focused approach it mandates, section 3 allows the court not only to interpret legislation 'restrictively or expansively' but also to 'modify the meaning, and hence the effect, of … legislation'.[32] The court 'can do considerable violence to the language and stretch it almost (but not quite) to breaking point',[33] as '[i]t is "possible" to do a great deal with words'.[34]

10.17   The precise way in which this power should be exercised (where available) will vary from case to case:

> Sometimes it may be possible to isolate a particular phrase which causes the difficulty and to *read in* words that modify it so as to remove the incompatibility. Or else the court may read in words that qualify the provision as a whole. At other times the appropriate solution may be to *read down* the provision so that it falls to be given effect in a way that is compatible with the Convention rights in question. In other cases the easiest solution may be to *put the offending part of the provision into different words* which convey the meaning that will be compatible with those rights. The preferred technique will depend on the particular provision and also, in reality, on the person doing the interpreting. This does not matter since they are simply different means of achieving the same substantive result.[35] (Emphasis added)

10.18   Ultimately, '[t]he precise form of wording required to give effect to the claimant's rights is not critical … The court is not required to redraft the statute with the precision of a parliamentary draftsman, nor to solve all the problems which it may create in other factual situations'.[36] That said, the court should nonetheless make sure it identifies clearly any provision or provisions whose meaning or effect it considers ought to be modified in the case before it through the use of its power under section 3.[37]

---

[31] *Sheldrake* (n 22) [28] (Lord Bingham); and see in similar terms *Ghaidan* (n 3) [30] (Lord Nicholls).

[32] *Ghaidan* (n 3) [32] (Lord Nicholls).

[33] ibid [67] (Lord Millett).

[34] *McDonald v McDonald* [2016] UKSC 28, [2017] AC 273 [68] (Lord Neuberger and Lady Hale).

[35] *Ghaidan* (n 3) [124] (Lord Rodger).

[36] *Thomas v Bridgend County Borough Council* [2011] EWCA Civ 862, [2012] QB 512 [68] (Carnwath LJ), citing *Ghaidan* (n 3) [35] (Lord Nicholls).

[37] *Re S* (n 4) [41] (Lord Nicholls): 'When a court, called upon to construe legislation, ascribes a meaning and effect to the legislation pursuant to its obligation under section 3, it is important the court should identify clearly the particular statutory provision or provisions whose interpretation leads to that result. Apart from all else, this should assist in ensuring the court does not inadvertently stray outside its interpretation jurisdiction.'

10.19 In practice, the application of section 3 has seen the courts variously: read provisions more broadly;[38] read them down (that is, more restrictively);[39] read qualifications into them;[40] or read words into them.[41]

The Limits of Section 3

10.20 The courts have held that 'there is a limit beyond which a Convention-compliant interpretation is not possible',[42] since the court must not cross the 'boundary between interpretation and amendment' of legislation.[43] In assessing the limits of section 3, the courts will consider not only the legislation in question,

---

[38] See, eg, *Ghaidan* (n 3), reading 'living with the original tenant as his or her wife or husband' to include homosexual couples; *R (Middleton) v West Somerset Coroner* [2004] UKHL 10, [2004] 2 AC 182, holding that, in the context of considering for the purposes of an inquest 'how' someone died, the word 'how' meant not just 'by what means', but also 'in what circumstances'; and *Manchester City Council v Pinnock* [2010] UKSC 45, [2011] 2 AC 104 and *Hounslow London Borough Council v Powell* [2011] UKSC 8, [2011] 2 AC 186, reading widely a court's power to review a local authority's decision to seek an order for possession so as to enable a proportionality assessment under Art 8 ECHR (but note that *Pinnock* and *Powell* were described in *McDonald* (n 34) [61]–[62] (Lord Neuberger and Lady Hale) as involving the *reading down* of the mandatory nature of the requirement in the relevant provisions to make a possession order save in limited circumstances).

[39] See, eg, *Cachia v Faluyi* [2001] EWCA Civ 998, [2001] WLR 1966, reading the word 'action' as requiring a writ to have been served and not just issued; *Lambert* (n 7) and *Sheldrake* (n 22), holding that a requirement on a defendant to prove a matter only placed on him an *evidential* rather than a *legal* burden of proof; and *Connolly v Director of Public Prosecutions* [2007] EWHC 237 (Admin), [2008] 1 WLR 276, holding that s 3 could be used to protect the right under Art 10 ECHR to freedom of expression *either* by giving a 'heightened meaning' to the words 'indecent' and 'grossly offensive' in an offence of malicious communication *or* by reading in a qualification to the offence so as not to cover cases where the existence of an offence would entail an infringement of that right. See also, eg, *Pinnock* (n 38) and *Powell* (n 38), as discussed in *McDonald* (n 34) in the passage cited in n 38.

[40] See, eg, *Connolly* (n 39), as discussed in that note; *Pomiechowski v District Court of Legnica, Poland* [2012] UKSC 20, [2012] 1 WLR 1604, qualifying a strict time limit for appeals to allow for a discretion to extend time in exceptional cases; and *R v Waya* [2012] UKSC 51, [2013] 1 AC 294, qualifying the court's duty to make a confiscation order in certain circumstances so that it did not apply where it would be disproportionate and thus in breach of Art 1 of Protocol 1 to the ECHR to make such an order.

[41] See, eg, *R v A* (n 19), especially at [45] (Lord Steyn), reading in an 'implied provision' that evidence required to make a trial fair is not inadmissible; and *Principal Reporter v K* [2010] UKSC 56, [2011] 1 WLR 18, expanding the definition of 'relevant person' to prevent a breach of Art 8 ECHR and allow unmarried fathers to take part in certain children's hearings.

[42] *Sheldrake* (n 22) [28] (Lord Bingham), and see paragraph 10.5.2 above. Cases illustrating the limits of s 3 include: *R (Anderson) v Secretary of State for the Home Department* [2002] UKHL 46, [2003] 1 AC 837; *Bellinger v Bellinger* [2003] UKHL 21, [2003] 2 AC 467; *Wilkinson* (n 20); *R (Wright) v Secretary of State for Health* [2009] UKHL 3, [2009] 1 AC 739; and *McDonald* (n 34).

[43] *Re S* (n 4) [40] (Lord Nicholls). See also *McDonald* (n 34) [69] (Lord Neuberger and Lady Hale): 'there is a difference between interpretation, which is a matter for the courts and others who have to read and give effect to legislation, and amendment, which is a matter for Parliament'; and *Ghaidan* (n 3) [121] (Lord Rodger).

but also, where relevant, Parliament's intention as discerned from its enactment of, or decision not to enact, other legislation.[44] Conscious of their judicial role, the courts will also be mindful that the section does not 'require courts to make decisions for which they are not equipped', such as where it is apparent that 'legislative deliberation' is appropriate[45] or where a proposed interpretation would have 'important practical repercussions which the court is not equipped to evaluate'.[46] The courts have declined to 'formulate precise rules' about when the limits of section 3 will be reached, but have stated that those cases will be exceptional and should 'in practice be fairly easy to identify'.[47]

10.21   Nevertheless, judges have used a variety of phrases to describe those cases where section 3 cannot be applied, such as where a proposed Convention-compliant interpretation 'departs substantially from a fundamental feature'[48] or 'cardinal principle'[49] of the legislation, is incompatible with its 'underlying thrust',[50] would not 'go with the grain of the legislation,'[51] would 'change the substance of a provision completely'[52] or 'would remove the very core and essence, the "pith and substance" of the measure that Parliament had enacted'.[53] However, while this judicial guidance may be of great assistance, it has been said that none of these 'insights ... should be allowed to supplant the simple test enacted in the Act', that is, the test of what is 'possible'.[54]

10.22   There may also be further limits applicable in cases where it is argued that section 3 requires legislation to be interpreted so as to give effect to the UK's *positive* obligations under the Convention rights.[55] As Lady Hale has observed, it is 'difficult to assess whether and when [the application of section 3] is necessary

---

[44] See, eg, *R (Nicklinson) v Ministry of Justice* [2014] UKSC 38, [2015] AC 657 [130] (Lord Neuberger), stating that if there had been a breach of Art 8 ECHR in that case, s 3 of the HRA 1998 could not have been used to read any exception into a statutory offence of assisting suicide, since 'in 1961, Parliament decided, through section 2(1) [of the Suicide Act 1961], to create a statutory offence of assisting a suicide in a provision which admitted of no exceptions, and it confirmed that decision as recently as 2009 (when section 2(1) was repealed and re-enacted in more detailed terms) following a debate in which the possibility of relaxing the law on the topic was specifically debated'.

[45] *Ghaidan* (n 3) [33] (Lord Nicholls).

[46] *Re S* (n 4) [40] (Lord Nicholls).

[47] *Sheldrake* (n 22) [28] (Lord Bingham); however, of course, it 'may not always be easy to discern' where the boundary between interpretation and amendment lies: see *McDonald* (n 34) [69] (Lord Neuberger and Lady Hale).

[48] *Re S* (n 4) [40] (Lord Nicholls).

[49] *Ghaidan* (n 3) [116] (Lord Rodger), citing Lord Nicholls' language in *Re S* (n 4).

[50] *Ghaidan* (n 3) [33] (Lord Nicholls).

[51] ibid [121] (Lord Rodger).

[52] ibid [110] (Lord Rodger).

[53] ibid [111] (Lord Rodger).

[54] *Sheldrake* (n 22) [28] (Lord Bingham).

[55] That is, broadly, those obligations imposed by the Convention rights on the state to take *positive steps* to secure the protection of those rights, as opposed to the *negative* aspects of those rights, which simply *prohibit* the state from violating those rights.

in order to give effect to the positive obligations of the state and thus to afford one person a remedy against another person which she would not otherwise have had'.[56]

Section 4: Declarations of Incompatibility

10.23 Section 4 of the HRA 1998 creates a more limited jurisdiction than that provided by section 3, reserved to the higher courts alone,[57] providing that they *may* make a 'declaration of incompatibility' if they are 'satisfied that [a] provision is incompatible with a Convention right' to which the HRA 1998 gives effect in domestic law.[58]

10.24 *Applying section 3 is a prerequisite*: section 4 can only be applied where the court has first attempted the 'essential preliminary step' of interpreting the relevant provision in a Convention-compliant way using section 3.[59]

10.25 *Section 4 applies to both primary and subordinate legislation*: section 4(2) enables a declaration of incompatibility to be made with respect to incompatible *primary* legislation.[60] Where *subordinate* legislation is incompatible with a Convention right, the courts will often be able (through the exercise of their well-established powers to determine the legality of secondary legislation and their duty under section 6 of the HRA 1998 to act compatibly with the Convention rights) to declare the legislation invalid or to disapply it so far as is necessary.[61] This means

---

[56] *Bates van Winkelhof v Clyde & Co LLP* [2014] UKSC 32, [2014] 1 WLR 2047 [44] (Lady Hale).

[57] See s 4(5), defining 'court' for the purposes of s 4. The definition includes (among others) the Supreme Court, Privy Council, Court of Appeal and High Court, but does not include, eg, County Courts or any tribunals (such as the Upper Tribunal or the Employment Appeal Tribunal).

[58] The phrase 'the Convention rights' is a defined term for the purposes of the HRA 1998: see n 2 above as to the rights which are included.

[59] *Wilson* (n 5) [23] (Lord Nicholls).

[60] See HRA 1998, s 4(1) and s 4(2). Note that 'primary legislation' and 'subordinate legislation' are defined terms under the HRA 1998: see s 22(1). Under this definition, primary legislation includes, but is not limited to, Acts of Parliament.

[61] As to the courts' general power to declare subordinate legislation to be invalid, contrasting the position with primary legislation, see *R (Public Law Project) v Lord Chancellor* [2016] UKSC 39, [2016] AC 1531 [20]–[23] (Lord Neuberger). In relation specifically to this power in the context of subordinate legislation that is incompatible with the Convention rights, see, eg, *Re G (Adoption: Unmarried Couple)* [2008] UKHL 38, [2009] 1 AC 173 [3] (Lord Hoffmann), explaining that as a result of the courts' duty to act compatibly with the Convention rights under s 6(1) of the HRA 1998, incompatible subordinate legislation is 'overridden by Convention rights' (unless the courts are required to apply it regardless of that incompatibility under s 6(2)); and at [46] (Lord Hope), explaining that s 6 of the HRA 1998 makes it unlawful for public authorities to enact subordinate legislation which is incompatible with the Convention rights—but note that this only applies in relation to legislation made since the HRA 1998 came into force: see *R (T) v Chief Constable for Greater Manchester* [2014] UKSC 35, [2015] AC 49 [147] (Lord Reed). However, it will not always be appropriate for the courts to declare a

that no *general* power to make a declaration of incompatibility was needed in or provided by the HRA 1998 to address the majority of instances of incompatibility occurring in measures of subordinate legislation.[62] However, where the primary legislation under which a provision of subordinate legislation was made *prevents* the removal of the incompatibility (other than by revocation), section 4(4) allows for a declaration to be made.[63]

10.26 *Resort to section 4 is 'exceptional'*: since section 3 will ordinarily be able, when necessary, to render a provision compatible with the Convention rights, 'resort to section 4 must always be an exceptional course'.[64]

10.27 *Section 4 and the UK's 'margin of appreciation'*: a declaration may be made where the UK courts determine legislation to be incompatible with the Convention rights, even though the European Court of Human Rights would consider the alleged breach resulting from that incompatibility to be within the 'margin of appreciation' that that Court affords to the UK.[65]

10.28 *Discretionary*: where section 3 imposes a duty, section 4 grants a *discretion*. However, the courts have said that it would be 'unusual' *not* to make a declaration in circumstances where section 4 gives the court the power to do so,[66] provided that the relevant incompatibility adversely affects a litigant in the case before the court.[67]

10.29 *Effect of a declaration*: section 4(6) of the HRA 1998 provides that a declaration under section 4 'does not affect the validity, continuing operation or enforcement of the provision in respect of which it is given' and 'is not binding on the parties to the proceedings in which it is made'. Rather, its effect is to alert the government and Parliament to the existence of the incompatibility, and it is for

---

provision or piece of subordinate legislation to be ultra vires whenever it is found to be incompatible with the Convention rights: see the discussion in *R (T)* [54]–[66] (Lord Wilson, dissenting, but not on this point) and [144]–[157] (Lord Reed).

[62] *R (T)* (n 61) [54] (Lord Wilson, dissenting, but not on this point) and [150]–[151] (Lord Reed).

[63] See HRA 1998, s 4(3) and s 4(4).

[64] *Ghaidan* (n 3) [50] (Lord Steyn); see also *Sheldrake* (n 22) [28] (Lord Bingham).

[65] *Nicklinson* (n 44) [74] (Lord Neuberger), [295] (Lord Reed, dissenting, but not on this point), [299] (Lady Hale, dissenting, but not on this point).

[66] *Nicklinson* (n 44) [114]–[115] (Lord Neuberger), considering that the case before him would have been an example of just such an unusual case (had the conditions for making a declaration otherwise been met); see also *R (Chester) v Secretary of State for Justice* [2013] UKSC 63, [2014] AC 271 [39] (Lord Mance), declining to make a declaration.

[67] See *Secretary of State for Defence v Nicholas* [2015] EWCA Civ 53, [2015] 1 WLR 2116 [17]–[24] (Lewison LJ), and the cases there cited, which include the following passage in *Chester* (n 66) [102] (Lady Hale): 'the court should be extremely slow to make a declaration of incompatibility at the instance of an individual litigant with whose own rights the provision in question is not incompatible. Any other approach is to invite a multitude of unmeritorious claims'.

them to decide what (if anything) to do with the incompatible legislation in order to render it compatible with the Convention rights.[68]

10.30 This is an important provision, which respects and upholds the sovereignty of Parliament by not providing the court with any new power to declare invalid or disapply inescapably incompatible legislation.[69] Nevertheless, the jurisdiction gives the court an 'opportunity to collaborate to some extent with Parliament', and the 'court will be of maximum assistance to Parliament in this regard if it not only identifies the factors which precipitate the infringement but articulates options for its elimination'.[70]

---

[68] Potentially using the remedial powers in s 10 of and sch 2 to the HRA 1998, which enable the government to amend legislation by order to remove an incompatibility which has been declared under s 4.

[69] See, eg, *Anderson* (n 42) [63] (Lord Hutton): 'Parliament … remains supreme and … if a statute cannot be read so as to be compatible with the Convention, a court has no power to override or set aside the statute. All that the court may do, pursuant to section 4 of the 1998 Act, is to declare that the statute is incompatible with the Convention. It will then be for Parliament itself to decide whether it will amend the statute so that it will be compatible with the Convention.' See also *Public Law Project* (n 61) [20]–[23] (Lord Neuberger), discussing the ordinary limits of the courts' powers to declare primary and subordinate legislation invalid or to refuse to apply it.

[70] *Nicklinson* (n 44) [204] (Lord Wilson).

11

Sources of EU Law and the Nature, Anatomy and Structure of EU Legislation

11.1 The UK acceded to the European Economic Community on 1 January 1973. In consequence, a very large part of the legislation applicable in England and Wales now derives not from Westminster or Whitehall, but from Brussels and Strasbourg, where the legislative institutions of the European Union (EU) have their home.[1]

11.2 An explanation of the basis on which EU law falls to be applied in the UK is set out in Chapter 12, along with the relevant interpretive rules for construing EU legislation and construing and applying domestic legislation in the light of EU law. This chapter addresses the different types of EU legislation (and the sources of EU law more generally), as well as its origins, anatomy and structure. But before looking at these matters, we briefly describe the nature and development of (what is now) the EU.[2]

History and Development of the EU Treaties

11.3 The EU has been the subject of periodic and dramatic evolution in its constitution ever since its inception, and when considering any piece of EU legislation, a grasp of the developmental stage which the EU had reached at the time of its enactment may assist in working out how it should be interpreted.[3]

---

[1] See the Introduction for certain of the facts and figures regarding the volume of applicable EU legislation. The UK gave formal notice of its intention to withdraw from membership of the EU on 31 March 2017, following the result of a national referendum on continued EU membership on 23 June 2016. However, at the time of writing the UK remains a Member State, and we describe the law as it presently stands. We do not speculate in this book as to the possible nature of any future relationship between the UK and the EU.

[2] For ease of reference, save where otherwise clear from the context, the term 'EU' is used below to refer to both what is now called the European Union and also its predecessor organisations, the European Economic Community and European Community.

[3] A full treatment of these matters is beyond the scope of this book, the focus here being on the Treaties which have governed the EU from time to time.

11.4   The EU finds its basis in treaties entered into by its Member States. These treaties define the competence of the EU as a whole and of the institutions which govern it. The history of the major treaties underpinning the EU is set out below.[4]

The Treaty Establishing the European Economic Community 1957 (TEC)

11.5   Also known as the Treaty of Rome, the TEC was signed by the six founder members[5] of the European Economic Community (EEC) on 25 March 1957. It came into force on 1 January 1958. The EEC became one of three 'European Communities' along with the European Coal and Steel Community and the European Atomic Energy Community (generally known as Euratom). The TEC was and is incorporated[6] into English law by section 1(2) of the European Communities Act 1972 (ECA 1972), read together with Part 1 of Schedule 1 and section 2, and each of the subsequent Treaties was and is similarly incorporated by way of an amendment to section 1(2).[7]

The Single European Act 1986 (SEA)

11.6   The SEA was the first major revision of the TEC, signed at Luxembourg on 17 February 1986 and at The Hague on 28 February 1986. It came into effect on 1 July 1987.[8]

The Treaty on European Union 1992 (TEU)

11.7   The TEU is widely known as the Maastricht Treaty, after the city where it was signed on 7 February 1992. It came into force on 1 November 1993. The Treaty amended the TEC and established the EU. The EEC was renamed the European Community (EC) and became part of the first of three pillars which together formed the newly established EU. The second pillar related to forming a Common Foreign and Security Policy, and the third concerned cooperation in justice and home affairs.[9]

---

[4] See europa.eu/european-union/law/treaties_en for more information regarding the EU Treaties.

[5] Belgium, France, Germany, Italy, Luxembourg and the Netherlands.

[6] On the basis set out in the European Communities Act 1972.

[7] As to the effect of the ECA 1972, see Chapter 12.2–12.29.

[8] Section 1 of the European Communities (Amendment) Act 1986 amended s 1(2) of the ECA 1972 to incorporate the SEA into English law.

[9] Section 1(1) of the European Communities (Amendment) Act 1993 amended s 1(2) of the ECA 1972 to incorporate the TEU into English law.

The Treaty of Amsterdam 1997

11.8   This Treaty amended both the TEC and the TEU. Signed on 2 October 1997, it came into force on 1 May 1999.[10]

The Treaty of Nice 2001

11.9   As with the Treaty of Amsterdam, the Treaty of Nice made revisions to both the TEC and the TEU. It was signed on 26 February 2001 and came into force on 1 February 2003.[11]

The Treaty of Lisbon 2007

11.10   Signed on 13 December 2007, the Lisbon Treaty came into force on 1 December 2009. It made further amendments to the TEU[12] and the TEC, the latter being renamed the Treaty on the Functioning of the European Union (TFEU).[13] As Article 1(2) of each Treaty now states, the TEU and the TFEU 'have the same legal value'. The three-pillar structure was abolished, all three areas becoming subsumed within the newly consolidated entity of the EU.[14]

Practical Consequences of Treaty Revisions

11.11   These various Treaty revisions have entailed not only a significant reworking of the content of the Treaties, but in many cases also a considerable amount of renumbering of those provisions whose substance has endured. It is important to remember this when examining EU legislation and case law, which will often refer to Treaty articles. Given the inherent delays in bringing cases before the Court of Justice of the European Union (CJEU), its judgments often refer to Treaty articles by their former numbering.

11.12   In addition, the changes brought about by each Treaty have often brought with them a change in the EU's legislative procedures. An understanding of the relevant procedure applicable to any given enactment may assist in the process of

---

[10] Section 1 of the European Communities (Amendment) Act 1998 amended s 1(2) of the ECA 1972 to incorporate the Amsterdam Treaty into English law.

[11] Section 1(1) of the European Communities (Amendment) Act 2002 amended s 1(2) of the ECA 1972 to incorporate the Nice Treaty into English law.

[12] A consolidated version of the TEU as amended by the Lisbon Treaty is at [2008] OJ C115/13.

[13] A consolidated version of the TFEU as amended by the Lisbon Treaty is at [2008] OJ C115/47.

[14] Section 2 of the European Union (Amendment) Act 2008 amended s 1(2) of the ECA 1972 to incorporate the Lisbon Treaty into English law.

interpretation by reference to the working documents (*travaux préparatoires*) of the institutions involved in passing the relevant legislation.[15]

Sources of EU Law

11.13   As with domestic or international law, the starting point for interpreting EU legislation and interpreting domestic legislation in the light of EU law is to understand the relevant sources of EU law which the courts will take into account. Under EU Law since the Lisbon Treaty, the following 'hierarchy of norms' can be discerned (in descending order of precedence), each aspect of which is considered briefly below:[16]

(1)   (a) the Treaties, (b) the Charter of Fundamental Rights and (c) the general principles of EU law;
(2)   relevant international law;
(3)   EU legislation;
(4)   delegated acts;
(5)   implementing legislation.

(1)(a) The Treaties

11.14   The TEU and the TFEU are the EU's foundational documents[17] and form the EU's 'basic constitutional charter'.[18] These Treaties, together with the Charter of Fundamental Rights and the general principles of EU law, form the EU's *primary law* to which all other EU measures are necessarily subject.[19]

---

[15]   Construction with the aid of *travaux préparatoires* is addressed in Chapter 12.50–12.55.

[16]   This is not an exhaustive list of all EU measures that may be relevant, but covers the principal ones. The concept of the 'hierarchy of norms' is referred to in various EU cases: see, eg, Cases C-402/05 P and C-415/05 P *Kadi and Al Barakaat International Foundation* [2008] ECR I-6351, para 305. However, a complete formal statement of this hierarchy is not set out anywhere in the Treaties or any one case, and instead it must be discerned from an analysis of EU law as a whole (and it may therefore be subject to evolution or argument). For a fuller exposition of the hierarchy of norms, see Allan Rosas and Lorna Armati, *EU Constitutional Law: An Introduction*, 2nd revised edn (Oxford, Hart Publishing, 2012) Chapter 4; and Paul Craig and Gráinne de Búrca, *EU Law: Text Cases and Materials*, 6th edn (Oxford, Oxford University Press, 2015) Chapter 5.

[17]   See Art 1(2) TFEU: 'This Treaty and the [TEU] constitute the Treaties on which the Union is founded.'

[18]   Case 294/83 *Parti Ecologiste 'Les Verts' v European Parliament* [1986] ECR 1339, para 23.

[19]   See Case C-362/14 *Schrems v Data Protection Commissioner* [2016] QB 257, para 60: 'the European Union is a union based on the rule of law in which all acts of its institutions are subject to a review of their compatibility with, in particular, the Treaties, general principles of law and fundamental rights'.

11.15 Since the primary law—and most explicitly the Treaties—define and delimit the competence of the EU as a whole to take action, including by way of passing legislation, the validity of that legislation will depend on whether there was power to pass it and power to pass it in the way it has been passed.[20] More importantly for the purposes of this work, the treaties themselves are a source of EU law and, through the ECA 1972, are incorporated into UK law as well. In certain cases they will have 'direct effect' such that it will be possible for individuals to rely on them in UK courts without the need for any specific implementing legislation beyond the ECA 1972 (as amended).[21] This may work by imposing obligations only on the Member State, so that (for example) it is unable to enforce certain national laws against individuals, such as customs tariffs prohibited by the EU.[22] In other cases, this may work by conferring rights or obligations directly on individuals or other private persons.[23]

11.16 Whether a Treaty article (or another provision of EU law) has direct effect and, if so, who can enforce it and against whom will be an interpretive question in each case depending on the relevant provision. For a provision to be capable of having direct effect, the court will need to determine both that its terms are 'sufficiently precise' (that is, setting out an obligation in 'unequivocal terms') and 'unconditional' (that is, 'not qualified by any condition, or subject, in its implementation or effects, to the taking of any measure either by the institutions of the

---

[20] See previous note, and *Les Verts* (n 18) para 23. Note that UK courts do not have the power to declare EU legislation invalid: see Case C-344/04 *IATA and ELFAA v Department for Transport* [2006] ECR I-403, para 27, citing Case 314/85 *Foto-Frost v Hauptzollamt Lübeck-Ost* [1987] ECR 4199, para 15. However, they may grant interim relief suspending national measures adopted to implement EU law: see *Foto-Frost*, para 19 and Case C-465/93 *Atlanta Fruchthandelsgesellschaft mbH v Bundesamt für Ernährung und Forstwirtschaft* [1995] ECR I-3761, para 30. Note that since 'acts of the Community institutions are presumed to be lawful ... they produce legal effects until such time as they are withdrawn, annulled ... or declared invalid': see Case C-199/06 *CELF v SIDE* [2008] ECR I-469, para 60. See further Chapter 12.14 (regarding references to the CJEU on questions of validity).

[21] See *Miller v Secretary of State for Exiting the European Union* [2017] UKSC 5, [2017] 2 WLR 583 [63] (Joint majority judgment): 'the EU Treaties themselves are directly applicable by virtue of section 2(1) [of the ECA 1972]. Some of the provisions of those Treaties create rights (and duties) which are directly applicable in the sense that they are enforceable in UK courts' (using the phrase 'directly applicable' rather than 'directly effective'); and see the decision of the CJEU in Case 26/62 *Van Gend en Loos v Nederlandse Administratie der Belastingen* [1963] ECR 1: 'the Community constitutes a new legal order of international law for the benefit of which the states have limited their sovereign rights, albeit within limited fields, and the subjects of which comprise not only Member States but also their nationals. *Independently of the legislation of Member States*, Community law therefore not only imposes obligations on individuals but is also intended to confer upon them rights which become part of their legal heritage. These rights arise not only where they are expressly granted by the Treaty, but also by reason of obligations which the Treaty imposes in a clearly defined way upon individuals as well as the Member States and upon the institutions of the Community' (emphasis added).

[22] See, eg, *Van Gend en Loos* (n 21).

[23] See, eg, Case 43/75 *Defrenne v Sabena* [1976] ECR 455, para 39: 'since Article 119 is mandatory in nature, the prohibition on discrimination between men and women applies not only to the action of public authorities, but also extends to all agreements which are intended to regulate paid labour collectively, as well as to contracts between individuals'. See generally Derrick Wyatt, Alan Dashwood et al, *Wyatt and Dashwood's European Union Law*, 6th edn (Oxford, Hart Publishing, 2011) 253–54.

European Union or by the Member States').[24] Once this is established, the court must then consider whether the provision confers rights upon anyone and, if so, against whom.[25]

(1)(b) The Charter of Fundamental Rights

11.17   Article 6(1) TEU gives effect to the Charter in EU law and accords it a status commensurate with the Treaties:

> The Union recognises the rights, freedoms and principles set out in the Charter of Fundamental Rights of the European Union of 7 December 2000, as adapted at Strasbourg, on 12 December 2007, which shall have the same legal value as the Treaties.
>
> The provisions of the Charter shall not extend in any way the competences of the Union as defined in the Treaties.
>
> The rights, freedoms and principles in the Charter shall be interpreted in accordance with the general provisions in Title VII of the Charter governing its interpretation and application and with due regard to the explanations referred to in the Charter, that set out the sources of those provisions.

11.18   The Supreme Court considered the scope and effect of the Charter in domestic law in *Viagogo*.[26] Lord Kerr (with whom all other members agreed), having cited Article 6(1), stated:

> Although the Charter thus has direct effect in national law, it only binds member states when they are implementing EU law—article 51(1). But the rubric, 'implementing EU law' is to be interpreted broadly and, in effect, means whenever a member state is acting 'within the material scope of EU law': see eg *R (Zagorski) v Secretary of State for Business, Innovation and Skills* [2011] HRLR 140, paras 66–71, per Lloyd Jones J. Moreover, article 6(1)EU of the EU Treaty requires that the Charter must be interpreted with 'due regard' to the explanations that it contains.

---

[24] See, eg, Case C-194/08 *Gassmayr v Bundesminister für Wissenschaft und Forschung* [2010] ECR I-6281, paras 44–45. See to similar effect the statement in Case C-108/01 *Consorzio del Prosciutto di Parma v Asda Stores Ltd* [2003] 2 CMLR 31, para 85, that to create rights (ie, to have direct effect), a measure must be 'sufficiently clear, precise and unconditional'.

[25] A detailed treatment of direct effect is beyond the scope of this book. A helpful analysis of when various kinds of rules of EU law will have direct effect can be found in Wyatt, Dashwood et al, *European Union Law* (2011) (n 23) 244–70.

[26] *Rugby Football Union v Consolidated Information Services Ltd (Formerly Viagogo Ltd) (in Liquidation)* [2012] UKSC 55, [2012] 1 WLR 3333 [28] (Lord Kerr). For a discussion of when the Charter applies, see Daniel Denman, 'The EU Charter of Fundamental Rights: How Sharp are its Teeth?' [2014] *Judicial Review* 160, who concludes that there must be 'something more than a tenuous and indirect link with EU law' and that it is 'not enough that the national measure in question is within an area that is in some way regulated by EU law' (at para 19).

11.19   The relevant 'explanations' to which the courts must have due regard are contained in the document 'Explanations relating to the Charter of Fundamental Rights'.[27]

11.20   It should be noted that certain of the Charter's provisions, particularly the provisions on social and economic matters in Title IV, do not create directly effective *rights* in themselves, but are merely *principles* which may be relevant to the interpretation of other measures.[28] Indeed, the extent to which various Charter provisions have direct effect (whether alone or read together with EU legislation) is an open question in many cases.[29]

11.21   It should also be noted that Charter rights are not necessarily absolute. Article 52(1) of the Charter provides:

> Any limitation on the exercise of the rights and freedoms recognised by this Charter must be provided for by law and respect the essence of those rights and freedoms. Subject to the principle of proportionality, limitations may be made only if they are necessary and genuinely meet objectives of general interest recognised by the Union or the need to protect the rights and freedoms of others.

(1)(c) The General Principles of EU Law

11.22   The CJEU has declared that '[t]he general principles of Community law have constitutional status'.[30] These principles express values of high legal importance which possess a 'general, comprehensive character' such that they pervade EU law as a whole.[31] There is no comprehensive codification of these principles, which have been declared and developed by the courts of the EU over time.

---

[27] [2007] OJ C303/17.
[28] See Art 52(5) of the Charter, and its Explanation which provides a non-exhaustive list of examples; and see Denman, 'The EU Charter' (n 26) paras 20-43 regarding this distinction.
[29] See the discussion of the key CJEU cases in *Benkharbouche v Embassy of the Republic of Sudan* [2015] EWCA Civ 33, [2016] QB 347 [76]–[81] (Lord Dyson MR, giving the judgment of the Court), considering this question in the context of the horizontal direct effect of Art 47 of the Charter. The Court noted (at [80]) that the CJEU has not made 'clear which rights and principles contained in the Charter might be capable of having horizontal direct effect', but concluded that 'EU Charter provisions which reflect general principles of EU law will do so', following Case C-555/07 *Kücükdeveci* [2010] ECR I-365 (but see *United States v Nolan* [2015] UKSC 63, [2016] AC 463 [43] (Lord Mance), stating, though not required to decide the point in that case: 'It is not clear in European law how far and when the principles in … Kücükdeveci … apply in cases not involving age discrimination'). By contrast, the Court noted that, where a Charter provision 'required specific expression in Union or national law … to take effect', it will not have direct effect: see at [79], citing Case C-176/12 *Association de médiation sociale v Union locale des syndicats CGT* [2014] ICR 411. As to the distinction between horizontal and vertical direct effect, see below at paragraph 11.31.
[30] Case C-101/08 *Audiolux SA v Groupe Bruxelles Lambert SA* [2009] ECR I-9823, para 63.
[31] ibid para 42.

However, certain of these principles are now enshrined in the Treaties. Article 2 TEU provides:

> The Union is founded on the values of respect for human dignity, freedom, democracy, equality, the rule of law and respect for human rights, including the rights of persons belonging to minorities. These values are common to the Member States in a society in which pluralism, non-discrimination, tolerance, justice, solidarity and equality between women and men prevail.

And Article 6(3) provides:

> Fundamental rights, as guaranteed by the European Convention for the Protection of Human Rights and Fundamental Freedoms and as they result from the constitutional traditions common to the Member States, shall constitute general principles of the Union's law.

11.23 This constitutional status—recognised by the reference to these principles in Article 6(3) TEU—places the general principles at least on a par with the Treaties and the Charter.[32] Indeed, in certain cases, a prima facie obligation under one of the Treaties may give way to one of the general principles. In *Omega*,[33] the CJEU affirmed that ensuring respect for human dignity[34] and the protection of fundamental rights (with the ECHR having 'special significance in that respect')[35] were both general principles of EU law. Accordingly, it was compatible with EU law for the German authorities to ban a game which involved the simulation of 'acts of homicide', even though this interfered with the free movement of services (a fundamental EU law freedom enshrined in the Treaties),[36] since the restriction imposed was proportionate to the aim pursued.[37] Just like the Treaties and the Charter, general principles are also capable of having direct effect.[38]

(2) Relevant International Law

11.24 The EU is empowered by Article 216(1) TFEU (read together with other more specific Treaty provisions or EU legislation) to conclude treaties in certain

---

[32] See the recognition of this status in, eg, *Schrems* (n 19), in the passage cited in that note. Rosas and Armati suggest that certain principles might constitute 'super-primary' law, to which even the Treaties are subject, citing *Kadi* (n 16): see Rosas and Armati, *EU Constitutional Law* (2012) (n 16) 54–55 and 59.

[33] Case C-36/02 *Omega Spielhallen v Bonn* [2004] ECR I-9609.

[34] ibid para 34.

[35] ibid para 33.

[36] Protected by Art 56 TFEU.

[37] *Omega* (n 33) paras 39–41. See to similar effect Case C-112/00 *Schmidberger v Austria* [2003] ECR I-5659, paras 73–74, finding that the need to respect fundamental human rights could justify 'a restriction of the obligations imposed by Community law, even under a fundamental freedom guaranteed by the Treaty such as the free movement of goods'.

[38] See, eg, *Kücückdevici* (n 29) para 43; and the discussion in Wyatt, Dashwood et al, *European Union Law* (2011) (n 23) 254–56.

areas relevant to its competences. Under Article 216(2), any treaties concluded by the EU are binding on its institutions and on its Member States. The procedure by which such treaties can be made is set out in Article 218 TFEU.[39]

11.25 These treaties have a status below the primary law of the EU,[40] but have primacy over its secondary law.[41] Accordingly, EU legislation may be held invalid in the light of the terms of a treaty, subject to three conditions:[42]

(1)   the relevant treaty provisions must be binding on the EU;
(2)   the content of those provisions must be unconditional and sufficiently precise; and
(3)   the 'nature and broad logic of the [treaty] do not preclude this'.

11.26 Customary international law is also 'binding upon the institutions of the European Union'.[43] It can similarly be relied upon to challenge the validity of acts of the EU, where:[44]

(1)   customary law calls into question the competence of the EU to act in a certain way;
(2)   'the act in question is liable to affect rights which the individual derives from [EU] law or to create obligations under [EU] law in this regard'; and
(3)   the EU institution 'made manifest errors of assessment concerning the conditions for applying those principles'. (The scope of review is limited in this way because customary international law is less precise than treaty law.)

11.27 Further, given the status of international law in EU law, the courts have an obligation to interpret EU legislation *so far as possible* in the light of certain rules

---

[39]   This procedure is subject, in the case of treaties in the context of the common commercial policy, to certain special rules set out in Art 207 TFEU. The validity of such treaties can be challenged before the CJEU, including on the grounds of their compatibility with other norms of international law: see, eg, *R (Western Sahara Campaign UK) v Commissioners for HM Revenue and Customs* [2015] EWHC 2898 (Admin), where Blake J agreed to make a preliminary reference to the CJEU to consider the validity of acts of the EU in making agreements with Morocco that did not distinguish between its own territory and the occupied territory of Western Sahara. These agreements were challenged on the basis of their incompatibility with the UN Charter and customary international law. The challenge regarding compatibility with the UN Charter was based on Art 3(5) TEU, which obliges the EU in 'its relations with the wider world' to 'contribute to ... the strict observance and the development of international law, including respect for the principles of the United Nations Charter'. Challenges on the basis of customary international law are considered below at paragraph 11.26.

[40]   See *Kadi* (n 16) paras 307–08.

[41]   See Case C-308/06 *R v Intertanko* [2008] ECR I-4057, para 43: 'agreements concluded by the Community ... have primacy over secondary Community legislation'.

[42]   ibid paras 43–45. Those paragraphs describe these as 'two conditions', combining what are called conditions (2) and (3) above. We follow Case C-366/10 *Air Transport Association of America v Secretary of State for Energy and Climate Change* [2011] ECR I–13755 ('*ATAA*'), paras 52–54 (citing *Intertanko*) in describing these as three conditions.

[43]   *ATAA* (n 42) para 101.

[44]   ibid paras 107–10.

of international law, and this interpretation may limit its scope. This duty certainly applies to treaties entered into by the EU,[45] and by the same logic ought to apply to rules of customary international law (where these are sufficiently clear and precise to permit this).[46]

(3) EU Legislation

11.28   The three principal types of instrument by which the EU institutions can make laws are *Regulations, Directives* and *Decisions*. Article 288 TFEU defines the nature of each:

> A regulation shall have general application. It shall be binding in its entirety and directly applicable in all Member States.

> A directive shall be binding, as to the result to be achieved, upon each Member State to which it is addressed, but shall leave to the national authorities the choice of form and methods.

> A decision shall be binding in its entirety. A decision which specifies those to whom it is addressed shall be binding only on them.

11.29   *Regulations*: upon enactment, from the time stipulated in the Regulation, a Regulation forms part of the law of England, without the need for any intermediary implementing legislation; that is to say, it is 'directly applicable' in accordance with Art 288 TFEU.[47] That does not mean, however, that it will necessarily have *direct effect*, for which it must meet the relevant conditions (as to which see paragraph 11.16 above).[48] An example of a Regulation is considered below at paragraphs 11.44–11.56, where its anatomy and structure are discussed.

---

[45] See Case C-61/94 *Commission v Germany* [1996] ECR I-3989, para 52: 'the primacy of international agreements concluded by the Community over provisions of secondary Community legislation means that such provisions must, so far as is possible, be interpreted in a manner that is consistent with those agreements'.

[46] This could fall within the slightly broader formulation of the relevant principle in, eg, *SGAE v Rafael Hoteles SA* [2006] ECR I–11519, para 35: 'Community legislation must, so far as possible, be interpreted in a manner that is consistent with international law, in particular where its provisions are intended specifically to give effect to an international agreement concluded by the Community'.

[47] Case 34/73 *Fratelli Variola SpA v Amministrazione italiana delle Finanze* [1973] ECR 981, para 10. Indeed, paras 10–11 go on to state that Member States must not pass implementing legislation which would 'obstruct' the direct applicability of Regulations, for example by concealing their nature as EU rules. See also Case 93/71 *Leonesio v Ministero dell'Agricoltura e Foreste* [1972] ECR I-287, paras 22–23. In *Leonesio* at paras 5–6, the CJEU stated that implementing legislation should only be passed where it is required by a Regulation itself. Where that is required, the Member State must not do so 'in an incomplete or selective manner': Case 128/78 *Commission v UK* [1979] ECR I-419, para 9.

[48] These principles were applied with respect to a Regulation in, eg, *Consorzio* (n 24) para 85. The Court also held that a measure must be published (and specifically in the language of the relevant Member State) before it can impose an obligation on an individual.

11.30 *Directives*: unlike Regulations, Directives are not 'directly applicable'. Instead, Member States are obliged to put in place implementing legislation to give effect to Directives within the timeframe stipulated by the relevant Directive. In the UK the Secretary of State is given a general power to enact implementing legislation for this purpose under section 2(2) of the ECA 1972.[49] An example of a Directive is Directive 2000/31/EC, known as the 'Directive on electronic commerce',[50] implemented in the UK by way of the Electronic Commerce (EC Directive) Regulations 2002.[51]

11.31 Notwithstanding that Directives are not 'directly applicable', after the cut-off date for the implementation of a particular Directive, its provisions may nevertheless have a limited degree of direct effect provided they meet the relevant criteria.[52] This is principally in the form of 'vertical direct effect', so called since it only permits the Directive to be relied upon as against the Member State required to implement it (including various bodies considered to be emanations of the State). In exceptional cases, some unimplemented Directives may also be relied upon to create 'horizontal' effects against private persons.[53]

11.32 Whether or not and however the UK chooses to implement a measure, from the cut-off date for implementation the obligation of the UK to correctly implement the Directive remains binding upon it, including upon its courts. As a result, after this date the courts will have an interpretive obligation to read all legislation (including but not limited to implementing legislation), subject to certain limitations and so far as possible, in a way which is compatible with the Directive.[54] Before the cut-off date, but after a Directive has entered into force, the duty of Member States is limited to refraining from any action which would 'seriously compromise' the achievement of the aim of the Directive in the period after the cut-off date. This includes a duty on the courts, 'so far as possible', to interpret legislation to avoid such a result.[55] These interpretive obligations are discussed at Chapter 12.21–12.29.

11.33 A 'Framework Directive' is not a different type of legislative instrument, but rather a name given to a Directive which takes a particular form, that is, one

---

[49] See Chapter 12.26–12.27.

[50] Directive 2000/31/EC of the European Parliament and of the Council of 8 June 2000 on certain legal aspects of information society services, in particular electronic commerce, in the Internal Market (Directive on electronic commerce) [2000] OJ L178/1.

[51] Electronic Commerce (EC Directive) Regulations 2002, SI 2002/2013.

[52] See above at paragraph 11.16.

[53] For a discussion of the direct effect of Directives, see Wyatt, Dashwood et al, *European Union Law* (2011) (n 23) 258–67, and also 278–84, where the authors consider further the potential horizontal effects of unimplemented Directives.

[54] See Case C-106/89 *Marleasing SA v La Comercial Internacional de Alimentacion SA* [1990] ECR I-4135, as discussed in *R (IDT Card Services Ireland Ltd) v Commissioners for HMRC* [2006] EWCA Civ 29 [73]–[92] (Arden LJ); and see more generally Chapter 12.21–12.29.

[55] See Case C-212/04 *Adeneler v Ellinikos Organismos Galaktos* [2006] ECR I-6057, paras 121–123; and see Chapter 12.23.4.

which sets out the broad framework of goals to be achieved but which contemplates (and will be subject to the detail contained within) future instruments designed to give greater definition and specificity as to the measures to be taken to achieve those goals.

11.34   *Decisions*: in many cases, Decisions are instruments which will be addressed only to specific persons, although they may be more general in scope. Depending on their terms, they are capable of having direct effect.[56] An example of a Decision is the Decision of the Commission to fine Microsoft Corporation for breach of competition law rules.[57]

(4) Delegated Acts

11.35   Article 290 TFEU empowers EU lawmakers to delegate powers to the Commission 'to adopt non-legislative acts of general application to supplement or amend certain non-essential elements of the legislative act'. In reality, this is a small-scale legislative power, and is exercised by way of Regulations, Directives and Decisions which must be labelled as 'delegated'.[58] Where the Commission then makes a delegated act, this will have the effect of altering EU law as it applies in the UK, with the precise effect of this depending on the nature of the legislative instrument that the act modifies.

(5) Implementing Acts

11.36   Article 291 TFEU allows provision to be made in any legally binding EU act for 'implementing powers' to be given to the Commission (or the Council in certain cases) when there is a need for 'uniform conditions for implementing' those acts. This power will be exercised by way of Regulations, Directives and Decisions, labelled as 'implementing'.[59] The distinction between delegated and implementing acts is that the former entail amendment or supplementation of existing legislation, while the latter do not.

11.37   It should be noted that, prior to the Lisbon Treaty, there was no divide between delegated legislation and implementing measures, these being grouped together as secondary legal measures under Article 202 EC.

---

[56] See Case 9/70 *Franz Grad v Finanzamt Traunstein* [1970] ECR I-825, paras 5–6. Where addressed to a Member State rather than a private party, their direct effect will be limited in the same way as with a Directive: see Case C-80/06 *Carp v Ecorad* [2007] ECR I-4473, paras 20–21.

[57] Available at ec.europa.eu/competition/antitrust/cases/dec_docs/39530/39530_3162_3.pdf (summary published at [2013] OJ C120/15).

[58] Article 290(3) TFEU.

[59] Article 291(4) TFEU.

Framework Decisions

11.38   Following the Nice Treaty, and until Lisbon, Article 34 EC enabled the making of a further kind of instrument known as 'Framework Decisions' in respect of the EU's third pillar, that is, police and judicial cooperation in criminal justice matters.[60] Their purpose was the 'approximation of the laws and regulations of Member States' in this area. As with Directives, they were binding on Member States as to the result to be achieved, with implementing measures required for their application in the laws of Member States. However, Article 34 EC provided for Framework Decisions *not* to entail direct effect.

11.39   As part of the Lisbon Treaty negotiations, the UK government obtained the right to opt out of existing measures on police and judicial cooperation in criminal justice matters. It notified the European Council in July 2013 that it wished to exercise this block opt-out right, with effect from 1 December 2014.[61] However, it then proceeded to opt back in to 35 of these measures.[62] Until the UK opted back in to these measures, there was no interpretive obligation upon the UK as a matter of EU law in respect of Framework Decisions,[63] although there was as a matter of international law more generally.[64] Now, following the opt-in, EU law requires the UK to interpret its domestic law in conformity with the relevant measures so far as possible.[65]

Legislative Procedure

11.40   Given the variety of legislative procedures that are and have been used by the EU during its history, we limit ourselves here to outlining the principal way in which legislation is now enacted under the Treaties.

11.41   The principal executive and legislative institutions of the EU are, and historically have been: (i) the Commission (the body that usually proposes

---

[60] These measures are preserved under the Lisbon Treaty, until repealed, annulled or amended, by Art 9 of the Protocol on Transitional Provisions.

[61] Available at http://data.consilium.europa.eu/doc/document/ST-12750-2013-INIT/en/pdf.

[62] The UK's request to opt in to certain measures is at http://data.consilium.europa.eu/doc/document/ST-15398-2014-INIT/en/pdf. The Council and Commission Decisions permitting this opt-in are at [2014] OJ L345/1 and L345/6. For more information, see generally the EU press release at www.consilium.europa.eu/uedocs/cms_data/docs/pressdata/en/jha/145981.pdf.

[63] *Assange v The Swedish Prosecution Authority* [2012] UKSC 22, [2012] 2 AC 471 [202]–[217] (Lord Mance) considering Case C-105/03 *Pupino* [2005] ECR I-5285.

[64] *Assange* (n 63) [217] (Lord Mance); and as to the interpretation of domestic legislation in the light of international law generally, see Chapter 9.20–9.37.

[65] *Cretu v Local Court of Suceava, Romania* [2016] EWHC 353 (Admin), [2016] 1 WLR 3344 [14]–[17] (Burnett LJ). This decision was cited with approval in *Goluchowski v District Court in Elblag, Poland* [2016] UKSC 36, [2016] 1 WLR 2665 [46] (Lord Mance).

legislation); (ii) the Council of Ministers (representatives of the governments of the Member States); and (iii) the European Parliament (a body whose members are directly elected by EU citizens). Over time there has been a trend towards greater involvement of the European Parliament in the making of legislation.

11.42   Following Lisbon, in the vast majority of cases the legislative procedure stipulated by the Treaties is the so-called 'ordinary legislative procedure' set out in Article 294 TFEU. This entails a proposal for a Regulation, Directive or Decision from the Commission being considered and adopted jointly by the Council of Ministers and the European Parliament.

11.43   Article 294 TFEU lays down the following steps which will usually apply in full when the ordinary legislative procedure is to be followed[66] (although the later stages may not be required where agreement is reached earlier in the process):

Proposal:

(1)   The Commission submits a proposal to the Parliament and Council.

First reading:

(2)   The Parliament will adopt a position on the proposal.
(3)   The Council then considers the proposal and the Parliament's position. If it agrees, the measure will be adopted in those terms. If it disagrees, it must communicate its position, and reasons for that position, to the Parliament.

Second reading:

(4)   The Parliament then has three months (or four months if it or the Council chooses to extend the period) to, by a majority of its members: (i) agree with the Council's position, in which case the measure will be adopted; (ii) disagree, in which case the measure will not be adopted; or (iii) propose amendments, in which case the measure is sent back to the Council. The Commission will in this case deliver an opinion on the amendments to the Council.
(5)   The Council then has three months (or four, if it or the Parliament chooses to extend the period) to approve or reject the amendments. It will usually act by qualified majority, but must act unanimously where the Commission has expressed a negative opinion on a particular amendment.[67] If all amendments are approved, the measure will be adopted. Otherwise, the President of the Council must convene a meeting of the Conciliation Committee in agreement with the President of the Parliament.

---

[66] An abridged form of this procedure applies in the limited circumstances identified in Art 294(15) TFEU, specifically where (in cases provided for in the Treaties) legislation is initiated not by the Commission, but by the Member States, the European Central Bank or the CJEU.

[67] 'Qualified majority' is a defined term requiring votes in favour to meet certain quorum and proportional requirements: see Art 16 TEU.

Conciliation:

(6)   An equal number of members of the Council and the Parliament will form a Conciliation Committee, which has six weeks (or eight, if the Council or the Parliament chooses to extend the period) to reach agreement on a joint text. Agreement must be by a majority of the Parliament members and a qualified majority of the Council members, on the basis of the second reading positions of the Parliament and the Council. The Commission will take part to assist the process. If no agreement is reached, no measure will be adopted.

Third reading:

(7)   For the Conciliation Committee's approved joint text to become law, it must be approved within six weeks (or eight, if the Council or Parliament chooses to extend the period) by: (i) the Parliament, on a majority of votes cast; and (ii) the Council, acting by qualified majority. Otherwise, the measure will not be adopted.

The Anatomy and Structure of EU Legislation

11.44   A helpful guide to the anatomy and structure of EU legislation can be found in the Joint Practical Guide of the European Parliament, the Council and the Commission for persons involved in the drafting of European Union legislation (hereinafter the 'Guide').[68] While it may be that not every EU act will have been drafted entirely in line with this guidance, the Guide nevertheless provides a good starting point for understanding the anatomy and structure of most EU acts.

11.45   Guideline 7 provides that: 'All Acts of general application shall be drafted according to a standard structure (Title—Preamble—Enacting Terms—Annexes, where necessary).' We consider each of these sections in turn below, by reference specifically to Regulation 593/2008 (EC), known as 'Rome I'.[69]

11.46   *Title:*[70] this is the heading of the act, which contains the key information by which it can be identified. This will normally include: (i) stipulation of the type of act it is (Regulation, Directive etc); (ii) the legal order which is making the act (the EEC, the EC, the EU etc); (iii) the unique number of the act, and its year (for example, 593/2008); (iv) which institutions adopted the act (the European Parliament, the Council etc); (v) its date of signature or adoption; and

---

[68]   Available at www.eur-lex.europa.eu/content/techleg/KB0213228ENN.pdf.
[69]   Regulation (EC) No 593/2008 of the European Parliament and of the Council of 17 June 2008 on the law applicable to contractual obligations (Rome I) [2008] OJ L177/6.
[70]   See generally Guidelines 7.1 and 8 of the Guide.

(vi) a unique title[71] which is intended to state concisely the purpose of the measure. Acts amending other acts must refer to those other acts in their titles.[72] In addition to these items, the title may also include, where appropriate, a short title for ease of reference (for example, 'Rome I'). The title may be followed by certain other technical information.[73]

11.47   By way of example, the full title of Rome I reads:

REGULATION (EC) No 593/2008 OF THE EUROPEAN PARLIAMENT
AND OF THE COUNCIL

of 17 June 2008

on the law applicable to contractual obligations (Rome I)

11.48   *The Preamble:*[74] this comprises everything between the title (and any following technical information) and the enacting terms, including the solemn forms which begin and end the preamble. In the case of Rome I, the solemn forms declare that 'THE EUROPEAN PARLIAMENT AND THE COUNCIL OF THE EUROPEAN UNION … HAVE ADOPTED THIS REGULATION'. Between the opening and closing parts of the solemn forms, the preamble contains first *citations* and then *recitals*, which are included to comply with Article 296 TFEU, which provides that: 'Legal acts shall state the reasons on which they are based and shall refer to any proposals, initiatives, recommendations, requests or opinions required by the Treaties.' This is to allow parties to defend their interests and to allow the CJEU properly to exercise its powers of review.[75]

11.49   *Citations:*[76] these state the *legal basis* of the act and outline the *principal procedural steps* taken in its adoption. In particular, the citations should state which Treaty and which provision(s) of that Treaty or of secondary legislation empower those adopting the act to do so. Citations will often begin with the words 'Having regard to'.

11.50   *Recitals:*[77] the role of the recitals is to state concisely the *reasons* for the adoption of the act. How extensive a statement of reasons needs to be will depend

---

[71] Or 'title proper', as the word title can be used to refer both to the act's unique and descriptive name, and the totality of the information in the heading used to identify an act: see Guideline 8.1 of the Guide and, more generally, Guidelines 7 and 8.

[72] Guideline 8.3 of the Guide.

[73] For example, the authentic language version of the act, or its relevance to the EEA: see Guideline 7.1 of the Guide.

[74] See generally Guidelines 7.2 and 9 to 11 of the Guide.

[75] See Case 24/62 *Germany v Commission* [1963] ECR 63.

[76] See generally Guideline 9 of the Guide.

[77] See generally Guideline 10 of the Guide.

on the nature of the measure in question and the circumstances of each case.[78] But in a strong enough case, an act may be annulled if the reasons given for it are inadequate, vague or inconsistent.[79] In practice, recitals will need to address the reasons for all of the main enacting terms, and it may be appropriate to explain why certain matters have not been included within the act, and to set the act in its broader historical context, including by reference to previous acts. In many cases, the recitals will be extensive. The statement of the recitals will commence with the word 'Whereas' and the following recitals will then be numbered in sequence (unless there is only one). Although recitals are not themselves part of the enacting terms (and therefore do not themselves create binding obligations), they can be used as an aid to interpretation of those terms since they can help explain their purpose.[80]

11.51   In the case of Rome I, the preamble extends to around four pages and has 46 recitals. A portion is set out below[81] to give a flavour of the kind of matters that are commonly covered in recitals (such as the legislation's broader purpose, how the act achieves that purpose, the history of EU action in an area, the reasons for specific provisions, the reasons for excluding certain matters, any governing principles and the scope of application):

THE EUROPEAN PARLIAMENT AND THE COUNCIL OF THE

EUROPEAN UNION,

Having regard to the Treaty establishing the European Community, and in particular Article 61(c) and the second indent of Article 67(5) thereof,

Having regard to the proposal from the Commission,

Having regard to the opinion of the European Economic and Social Committee ...

Acting in accordance with the procedure laid down in Article 251of the Treaty,

Whereas:

(1)   The Community has set itself the objective of maintaining and developing an area of freedom, security and justice. For the progressive establishment of such an area, the Community is to adopt measures relating to judicial cooperation in civil matters with a cross-border impact to the extent necessary for the proper functioning of the internal market.

(2)   According to Article 65, point (b) of the Treaty, these measures are to include those promoting the compatibility of the rules applicable in the Member States concerning the conflict of laws and of jurisdiction.

---

[78] See Case C-265/97 P *Coöperatieve Vereniging De Verenigde Bloemenveilingen Aalsmeer BA (VBA) v Florimex BV* [2000] ECR I-2061, para 93.

[79] See *Germany v Commission* (n 75).

[80] See Chapter 12.46–12.47.

[81] Excluding internal footnotes, which generally give references for where other publications may be found in the EU's Official Journal.

(3)   The European Council meeting in Tampere on 15 and 16 October 1999 endorsed the principle of mutual recognition of judgments and other decisions of judicial authorities as the cornerstone of judicial cooperation in civil matters and invited the Council and the Commission to adopt a programme of measures to implement that principle.

...

(9)   Obligations under bills of exchange, cheques and promissory notes and other negotiable instruments should also cover bills of lading to the extent that the obligations under the bill of lading arise out of its negotiable character.

(10)   Obligations arising out of dealings prior to the conclusion of the contract are covered by Article 12 of Regulation (EC) No 864/2007. Such obligations should therefore be excluded from the scope of this Regulation.

(11)   The parties' freedom to choose the applicable law should be one of the cornerstones of the system of conflict-of-law rules in matters of contractual obligations.

...

(46)   In accordance with Articles 1 and 2 of the Protocol on the position of Denmark, annexed to the Treaty on European Union and to the Treaty establishing the European Community, Denmark is not taking part in the adoption of this Regulation and is not bound by it or subject to its application,

HAVE ADOPTED THIS REGULATION:

11.52   *Enacting terms:*[82] these are the operative, legislative part of the act. The basic unit is the article, and articles may be grouped or subdivided as required, as set out in Guideline 15 of the Guide and as summarised below.

11.53   Articles may be grouped into *Chapters* (which may be subdivided into *Sections*), which may in turn be grouped into *Titles* and then into *Parts*. Rome I, for example, is grouped into Chapters (but does not use other groupings).

11.54   Articles may be subdivided into (in descending order): (i) *paragraphs*, which may be *numbered* (where the divided elements of the article are independent) or *unnumbered* (where the divided elements of the article are not independent); (ii) *subparagraphs* of numbered paragraphs (these are unnumbered); (iii) *points* (usually preceded by an introductory phrase); (iv) *indents*; and (v) *sentences*.[83]

11.55   Acts will usually be structured to address matters in the following order:[84]

(1)   *Subject matter and scope*: the act may begin with an article setting out its subject matter (that is, what it deals with) and its scope (that is, to which situations and persons it applies).[85]

---

[82] See Guidelines 7.3 and 12–15 of the Guide.
[83] A helpful reference to subdivisions of EU acts can be found in the Guide at p 45.
[84] See Guideline 15 of the Guide.
[85] See Guideline 13 of the Guide.

(2) *Definitions*: next will come any article used to provide definitions for certain terms used in the act.[86]

(3) *Rights and obligations*: those articles conferring rights and imposing obligations will usually comprise the main part of the act, since they are the principal operative provisions of the legislation (or 'normative provisions' as the Guide calls them).

(4) *Provisions delegating powers and conferring implementing powers*: where required, these logically follow the articles which contain the obligations or rights in respect of which delegated or implementing powers are being conferred.

(5) *Procedural provisions*: in some cases, certain procedural steps will be mandated as part of an act's operative provisions. For example, an act may require Member States to report on certain matters at certain times or may require European institutions to carry out a review of the legislation within a particular time period.

(6) *Measures relating to implementation*: these are the detailed provisions regarding the implementation of measures in a Member State, such as by when a Directive must be transposed, or the forms of remedies to be applicable in certain cases.

(7) *Transitional and final provisions*: these cover repeals, amendments of earlier acts, regimes governing transition from the former system to that established by the act, and the timeframe during which the act will apply.

(8) *Annexes*: these are sometimes used as a matter of drafting convenience, where the material which needs to be presented 'is voluminous or technical or both'. They form part of the enacting terms, but will follow the other elements of those enacting terms set out above and those elements discussed in the following paragraphs.

11.56 Following the various enacting terms (apart from any Annexes) will be a statement of the date and place of enactment, and signatures of the heads of the enacting institutions. This may be immediately preceded (depending on the type of act being adopted) by a statement of the identity of those to whom it is addressed. Thus, the final part of Rome I, above the relevant signatures, reads:

> This Regulation shall be binding in its entirety and directly applicable in the Member States in accordance with the Treaty establishing the European Community.

> Done at Strasbourg, 17 June 2008.

11.57 A Directive, by contrast, will usually state in its final Article: 'This Directive is addressed to the Member States', before setting out the date and place of enactment and signatures.

---

[86] See Guideline 14 of the Guide.

12

Interpretation of EU Law and its Effect on Domestic Legislation

12.1 The various sources of EU law (or 'Community law', as much of it was formerly known) have been discussed above in Chapter 11. The focus of this chapter is on: (i) the basis on which, as a matter of domestic law, these sources have legal effect in the UK; (ii) the effect of EU law on the application and interpretation of domestic law; and (iii) the interpretation of EU law. We also address in this chapter the role of the Court of Justice of the European Union (CJEU) as the ultimate interpreter of EU law, and the use of *travaux préparatoires* as an aid to interpretation of EU law.

The Legal Basis for Application of EU Law in the UK

12.2 Rights and obligations under EU law are given effect in domestic law by the European Communities Act 1972 (ECA 1972), as amended from time to time. Such is its profound effect on the UK legal order that the ECA 1972 Act has been described as having a special status as a 'constitutional statute'.[1] The terms of the Act, and its interpretation by the courts, mean that for most practical purposes, EU law has a status in the UK as a superior form of law.[2] The nature and effect of that status are discussed later in this chapter. The purpose of this section is to outline the basic scheme of the ECA 1972.

---

[1] See *Thoburn v Sunderland City Council* [2002] EWHC 195 (Admin), [2003] QB 151 [62]–[63] (Laws LJ). This description was adopted in *R (Buckinghamshire County Council) v Secretary of State for Transport* [2014] UKSC 3, [2014] 1 WLR 324 [206]–[208] (Lord Neuberger and Lord Mance); see also *Miller v Secretary of State for Exiting the European Union* [2017] UKSC 5, [2017] 2 WLR 583 [65]–[68] (Joint majority judgment).

[2] See *Miller* (n 1) [65] (Joint majority judgment): 'So long as the 1972 Act remains in force, its effect is to constitute EU law an independent and overriding source of domestic law.'

Section 2(1) of the ECA 1972: Effect Given Generally to 'Directly Enforceable' Provisions of EU Law

12.3   Section 2(1) of the ECA 1972 provides:

All such rights, powers, liabilities, obligations and restrictions from time to time created or arising by or under the Treaties, and all such remedies and procedures from time to time provided for by or under the Treaties, as in accordance with the Treaties are without further enactment to be given legal effect or used in the United Kingdom shall be recognised and available in law, and be enforced, allowed and followed accordingly; and the expression 'enforceable EU right' and similar expressions shall be read as referring to one to which this subsection applies.

12.4   The broad effect of this provision[3] is to give legal effect to the various sources of EU law within the UK to the extent that the EU Treaties require those sources, or any part of them, to be recognised or applied by Member States directly, that is, without the need for any specific implementing measures in their national laws. For practical purposes, what this means is that provisions of EU law can be relied upon before UK courts as having legal effect to the extent that they have what is known in EU law as 'direct effect'.[4] Those provisions of EU law having direct effect

---

[3] Especially when read together with s 2(4), which requires primacy to be given to enforceable EU rights in the event of any conflict with domestic law (as to which see below at paragraph 12.8).

[4] See, eg, *Oakley Inc v Animal Ltd* [2005] EWCA Civ 1191, [2006] Ch 337 [20] (Waller LJ), describing s 2(1) as bringing into force 'laws of the European Union to which direct effect must be given'. Section 2(1) also has the effect of making so-called 'directly applicable' provisions of EU law such as Regulations part of English law, since (by definition) EU law requires such measures to become part of national law without implementation measures: see Chapter 11.28–11.29 and, eg, *Miller* (n 1) [63] (Joint majority judgment): 'where the effect of the EU Treaties is that EU legislation is directly applicable in domestic law, section 2(1) provides that it is to have direct effect in the United Kingdom without the need for further domestic legislation. This applies to EU Regulations (which are directly applicable by virtue of article 288FEU of the FEU Treaty)'; and *Oakley* [61] (Jacob LJ): 'Section 2(1) operates to make regulations automatically part of United Kingdom law.' That s 2(1) gives effect to directly applicable rules of EU law also appears to have been recognised in s 18 of the European Union Act 2011, a declaratory enactment affirming that EU law forms part of UK law only as long as there is a statutory basis for this (and see also the Explanatory Notes to that Act at [118]–[124]). But not all directly applicable legislation is directly effective, and when it is not, it may have little practical import: see, eg, *R (Jaspers (Treburley) Ltd) v Food Standards Agency* [2013] EWHC 1788 (Admin) [31] (Singh J). Note that the terms 'directly effective' and 'directly applicable' are often used interchangeably (as indeed they appear to have been in the citation from *Miller* above, but see at [190] (Lord Reed, dissenting), acknowledging that there may be a distinction). However, although many measures may be both, these terms refer to distinct concepts. As to the distinction between these concepts (and the fact that both directly effective and directly applicable measures are incorporated into UK law by s 2(1) of the ECA 1972), see *Consorzio del Prosciutto di Parma v Asda Stores Ltd* [1998] 2 CMLR 215 (Ch) [48] (Lawrence Collins QC). On appeal to the House of Lords [2001] UKHL 7, [2001] 1 CMLR 43 ('*Consorzio (HL)*'), that decision was overturned (but see the decision of the CJEU on a reference from the House of Lords in Case C-108/01 *Consorzio del Prosciutto di Parma v Asda Stores Ltd* [2003] ECR I-5121 ('*Consorzio (CJEU)*')). However, the House of Lords affirmed the distinction between directly applicable and directly effective legislation at [21] (Lord Hoffmann): 'Of course the fact that it is directly applicable does not necessarily mean that it creates rights and duties enforceable in the courts ... One would normally assume, however, that unless the Regulation contemplated that it

and consequently caught by section 2(1) are often referred to by the English courts as 'directly enforceable' rules of EU law, a term adopted in the discussion below.[5]

12.5   The extent to which any given provision has direct effect is a matter of EU law. In general, a provision will have direct effect where its terms are 'sufficiently precise' (that is, setting out an obligation in 'unequivocal terms') and 'unconditional' (that is, 'not qualified by any condition, or subject, in its implementation or effects, to the taking of any measure either by the institutions of the European Union or by the Member States').[6] The scope of the doctrine of direct effect has been addressed in outline in relation to various sources of EU law in Chapter 11 (although a full treatment of this topic is beyond the scope of this book).[7]

Section 2(2) of the ECA 1972: Power to Implement EU Law by Delegated Legislation

12.6   Section 2(2)(a) of the ECA 1972 empowers the government to make delegated legislation[8] (by order, rules, regulations or scheme) for the purpose of giving effect to EU law rights and obligations in the UK. Section 2(2)(b) permits the making of delegated legislation to address matters 'arising out of or related to any such obligation or rights'. The powers in section 2(2) are not limited to giving effect to, or legislating in relation to, rules of EU law falling within section 2(1) (that is, principally, directly enforceable provisions)[9] and accordingly they have particular application to the implementation of Directives in domestic law.[10]

---

would have to be fleshed out by domestic or Community legislation, it was intended to be effective to create rights or duties or both.'

[5]   See, eg, *R v Secretary of State for Transport ex p Factortame Ltd* [1990] 2 AC 85 (HL) 134H–135A (Lord Bridge); *Consorzio (HL)* (n 4) [20] (Lord Hoffmann).

[6]   See, eg, Case C-194/08 *Gassmayr v Bundesminister für Wissenschaft und Forschung* [2010] ECR I-6281, paras 44–45. See to similar effect the statement in *Consorzio (CJEU)* (n 4) para 85, that to create rights (ie, to have direct effect), a measure must be 'sufficiently clear, precise and unconditional'.

[7]   See the discussion of the sources of EU law at Chapter 11.13–11.39. For a fuller analysis of when various kinds of rules of EU law will have direct effect, see Derrick Wyatt, Alan Dashwood et al, *Wyatt and Dashwood's European Union Law*, 6th edn (Oxford, Hart Publishing, 2011) 244–70.

[8]   Specifically, it empowers Her Majesty to make Orders in Council and designated government ministers and departments to make other forms of delegated legislation. As to Orders in Council and other forms of delegated legislation generally, see Chapter 1.22.

[9]   Although they do extend to such rules: see the definition of the term 'EU Obligation', used in s 2(1)(a), in sch 1, pt 2, para 1 of the ECA 1972 ('any obligation created or arising by or under the Treaties, whether an enforceable EU obligation or not'); see also, eg, *AB v JJB* [2015] EWHC 192 (Fam) [50] (Sir Peter Singer). Note, however, that it will sometimes be unlawful for Member States to use implementing measures to give effect to EU law instruments, such as Regulations, that are directly applicable: see Case C-34/73 *Fratelli Variola SpA v Amministrazione italiana delle Finanze* [1973] ECR 981, paras 10–11; and see further Chapter 11, n 47.

[10]   See *Miller* (n 1) [63] (Joint majority judgment): 'section 2(2) ... applies mainly to EU Directives'; *Oakley* (n 4) [61] (Jacob LJ): 'Section 2(2) ... is clearly designed with directives in mind'; and *United States v Nolan* [2015] UKSC 63, [2016] AC 463 [52] (Lord Mance): 'A right or obligation under a Directive is the classic instance' of what section 2(2) is concerned with.

12.7 Section 2(4) provides that the powers under section 2(2) permit the making of 'any such provision (of any such extent) as might be made by Act of Parliament', subject only to limited exceptions prescribed in Schedule 2 to the Act.[11] Despite the breadth of the powers under section 2(2), that section is not to be treated as a Henry VIII clause and interpreted narrowly,[12] but instead is to be treated as a *sui generis* provision requiring a broader interpretation consistent with its purpose of enabling the UK to comply with its obligations under the EU Treaties.[13]

Section 2(4) of the ECA 1972: Primacy of Directly Enforceable EU Law Rules

12.8 Section 2(4) also provides that 'any enactment passed or to be passed ... shall be construed and have effect subject to the foregoing provisions' of section 2. The effect of this is to give primacy to directly enforceable rules of EU law over any conflicting provision in any UK legislation, including subsequent Acts of Parliament, just as if a provision were included in all other legislation stating that its provisions are 'without prejudice' to such rules.[14] Ultimately, however, it may be that the scope of the primacy generally accorded to certain rules of EU law by section 2(4) is limited by other constitutional principles.[15]

[11] Schedule 2, para 1 provides broadly that the power conferred by s 2(2) does not include power to raise taxes, pass retroactive legislation, delegate legislative authority (except for making 'rules of procedure for any court or tribunal') or create criminal offences to which serious punishments apply.

[12] As to Henry VIII clauses, see Chapter 5.9–5.11.

[13] As to the nature and proper construction of s 2(2), see *Oakley* (n 4), especially [18]–[39] (Waller LJ), [46]–[47] (May LJ), and [64]–[80] (Jacob LJ). As discussed at length in that case, the scope of the powers under s 2(2)(a) and 2(2)(b) are different, with the latter designed (in the words of Waller LJ at [39]) to 'enable further measures to be taken which naturally arise from or closely relate to the primary purpose being achieved'. Lord Mance described *Oakley* as the 'leading authority' on the meaning of s 2(2) in *Nolan* (n 10) at [53], and see further the other cases cited in that paragraph. Having cited substantial passages from *Oakley*, Lord Mance considered the ambit of s 2(2), and s 2(2)(b) in particular, at [59]–[72].

[14] See *Factortame* (n 5) 140C (Lord Bridge), cited with approval in, eg, *Fleming v Revenue and Customs Commissioners* [2008] UKHL 2, [2008] 1 WLR 195 [24] (Lord Walker), *Autologic Holdings plc v IRC* [2005] UKHL 54, [2006] 1 AC 118 [16] (Lord Nicholls) and *Imperial Chemical Industries plc v Colmer (No 2)* [1999] 1 WLR 2035 (HL) 2041C–G (Lord Nolan). See also *R v Budimir* [2010] EWCA Crim 1486, [2011] QB 744 [3] (Lord Judge CJ), stating that 'section 2(4) of the European Communities Act 1972 prohibits the application domestically of statutory provisions which are inconsistent with directly applicable EU law. It is therefore not open to us to ignore EU law. Parliament has obliged us to apply it, even if the effect may be to render an Act of Parliament unenforceable'.

[15] See *Buckinghamshire County Council* (n 1) [79] (Lord Reed), referring to this possibility in the context of a potential conflict with Art 9 of the Bill of Rights 1689, but not needing to resolve the issue in that case. See also to similar effect at [207]–[208] (Lord Neuberger and Lord Mance), referring to the potential insights to be gained in this regard from the 'penetrating discussion' of connected issues in *Thoburn* (n 1) [58]–[70] (Laws LJ).

Section 3 of the ECA 1972: Resolution of Questions of EU Law

12.9   Section 3(1) of the ECA 1972 provides:

> For the purposes of all legal proceedings any question as to the meaning or effect of any of the Treaties, or as to the validity, meaning or effect of any EU instrument, shall be treated as a question of law (and, if not referred to the European Court, be for determination as such in accordance with the principles laid down by and any relevant decision of the European Court).[16]

12.10   This section directs the UK courts to treat questions of EU law as questions of law to be resolved either by the UK courts themselves, in line with the case law of the CJEU, or by the CJEU on a reference from the UK judicial system.[17] A full discussion of the power and obligation under EU law to refer questions of EU law to the CJEU is beyond the scope of this book. But the following brief outline may help place the role of the UK courts as interpreters of EU law in context.[18]

12.11   As a matter of EU law (applied in the UK by section 3(1) of the ECA 1972), the CJEU has ultimate authority to decide upon the interpretation of the EU Treaties and other EU instruments.[19] It also has sole authority to declare EU instruments (or other acts of EU entities) invalid.[20] Accordingly, Article 267 of the Treaty on the Functioning of the European Union (TFEU) provides for legal questions on these issues to be referred to the CJEU by 'any court or tribunal of a Member State'. It does so in two ways:

12.11.1   It confers a general *discretion* on national courts and tribunals, providing that they 'may' refer a question to the CJEU if the national court 'considers that a decision on the question is necessary to enable it to give judgment'.

12.11.2   In certain circumstances, it *requires* a reference to be made to the CJEU where the relevant question of EU law arises before a court or tribunal in respect

---

[16] The 'European Court' is defined in sch 1, pt 2, para 1 of the ECA 1972 as the CJEU. Section 3 goes on to provide for judicial notice to be taken of the EU Treaties and decisions and opinions of the CJEU. It also sets out how EU instruments may be evidenced.

[17] The effect of s 3 is that decisions of the CJEU on points of law are 'not open to question' in the domestic courts, though it is for domestic courts to apply those decisions to the facts as they find them: see *HM Revenue and Customs v Aimia Coalition Loyalty UK Ltd* [2013] UKSC 15, [2013] 2 All ER 719 [56] (Lord Reed); and see *R (Newby Foods Ltd) v Food Standards Agency* [2017] EWCA Civ 400 [49] (Lloyd Jones LJ).

[18] For a detailed discussion of this topic, see Wyatt, Dashwood et al, *European Union Law* (2011) (n 7) 209–31; and Richard Gordon and Rowena Moffatt, *European Law in Judicial Review*, 2nd edn (Oxford, Oxford University Press, 2014) 114–45.

[19] Although this does not preclude dialogue between domestic courts and the CJEU: see, eg, *Buckinghamshire County Council* (n 1) [187]–[189] (Lord Neuberger and Lord Mance).

[20] See Case C-344/04 *IATA and ELFAA v Department for Transport* [2006] ECR I-403, para 27; and see further paragraph 12.14 below and Chapter 11, n 20.

of whose decisions there is 'no judicial remedy under national law' (such as courts of final appeal).

12.12   Article 267 TFEU has been interpreted so that in practice it gives a considerable degree of autonomy and flexibility to national courts to determine whether to make a reference, and it is rare for the CJEU to refuse to hear a case referred to it.[21] It has been said that the practice of the English courts, in the exercise of their discretion, should generally be to make a reference if an EU law issue is 'critical' to its decision and there is a 'real doubt' as to the answer.[22] However, all the circumstances will be taken into account, and the courts have made clear that making a reference is less likely to be considered appropriate if the relevant issue is not one of 'wider significance' and if CJEU case law has already established principles which the English court can apply in the case at hand.[23] When a reference is made, the national court should assist the CJEU by setting out the reasons why it considers the reference is necessary.[24]

12.13   There are two main exceptions to the CJEU's permissive approach to references from national courts. The first (deriving directly from the wording of Article 267 TFEU) is where the national court is in effect finally determining a

---

[21] See Case C-439/01 *Cipra v Bezirkshauptmannschaft Mistelbach* [2003] ECR I-745, para 18, which also discusses the 'exceptional circumstances' in which the CJEU may refuse to accept a reference at para 19: 'The Court may refuse to rule on a question referred for a preliminary ruling by a national court only where it is quite obvious that the interpretation of Community law that is sought bears no relation to the actual facts of the main action or its purpose, where the problem is hypothetical, or where the Court does not have before it the factual or legal material necessary to give a useful answer to the questions submitted to it.'

[22] See *R v International Stock Exchange ex p Else (1982) Ltd* [1993] QB 534 (CA) 545D–F (Sir Thomas Bingham MR): 'if the facts have been found and the Community law issue is critical to the court's final decision, the appropriate course is ordinarily to refer the issue to the Court of Justice unless the national court can with complete confidence resolve the issue itself', discussing in the course of this passage factors to consider when deciding whether such confidence is warranted, before summarising: 'If the national court has any real doubt, it should ordinarily refer.' See also *R (ZO (Somalia)) v Secretary of State for the Home Department* [2010] UKSC 36, [2010] 1 WLR 1948 [51] (Lord Kerr, giving the judgment of the Court): 'what is required is for the national court to conduct a careful examination of the reasoning underlying any contrary argument ranged against the view that it has formed. If, having done so, the court is of the opinion that such an argument, on any conventional basis of reasoning, could not be accepted, a reference should not be made'.

[23] See *Trinity Mirror plc v Commissioners of Customs and Excise* [2001] EWCA Civ 65, [2001] 2 CMLR 33 [51]–[53] (Chadwick LJ), citing the passage in *Else* (n 22) set out in that note, but considering that there was a need for 'a greater measure of self-restraint' in making references, particularly where the question in issue does not have wider importance beyond the case at hand, and where there is 'an established body of [CJEU] case law which could relevantly be transposed to the facts of the instant case'. See also *Professional Contractors Group Ltd v Commissioners of Inland Revenue* [2001] EWCA Civ 1945, [2002] 1 CMLR 46 [91] (Robert Walker LJ), confirming that 'the principles stated [in *Else*] still hold good. But in applying them the court must also take account of the guidance given by the Court (following European authority) in *Trinity Mirror*'; and *R (Gibraltar Betting & Gaming Association Ltd) v Commissioners for HM Revenue and Customs* [2015] EWHC 1863 (Admin) [8]–[15] (Charles J).

[24] *IATA* (n 20) para 31.

question of EU law, with no prospect of an appeal to or review of its decision by a higher court. In those circumstances, there will generally (subject to the exceptions identified below) be a duty to refer that question of EU law to the CJEU.[25] However, without prejudice to the court's *discretion* to make a reference (where applicable and appropriate), there is no *duty* to refer a question of EU law:

12.13.1   that is irrelevant to the outcome of the case;[26]

12.13.2   'where previous decisions of the [CJEU] have already dealt with the point of law in question'.[27] Matters already resolved by previous CJEU decisions are sometimes referred to as being 'acte éclairé';[28]

12.13.3   where the 'correct application' of EU law is 'so obvious as to leave no scope for any reasonable doubt as to the manner in which the question raised is to be resolved'. To be satisfied of this, the national court must decide that the answer would be 'equally obvious to the courts of the other Member States and to the [CJEU]'.[29] Questions admitting of an obvious answer in this way are sometimes referred to as being 'acte clair'.[30] Where a number of judges are considering a case and disagree as to a question of interpretation, this is generally considered to indicate that the issue is not acte clair.[31]

---

[25] This means that a court of final appeal will have to consider whether a reference is required as part of any application to it for leave to appeal: see Case C-99/00 *Lyckeskog* [2002] ECR I-4839, para 18. See in the UK context *Chiron Corp v Murex Diagnostics Ltd (No 8)* [1995] All ER (EC) 88 (CA).

[26] See Case 283/81 *CILFIT v Ministero della Sanità* [1982] ECR 3415, para 10.

[27] ibid para 14, going on to explain that this applies even where 'the questions at issue are not strictly identical'. As to this exception, and the following one, see *Buckinghamshire County Council* (n 1) [127] (Lord Sumption), discussing 'formal recommendations' issued in 2012 by the CJEU regarding references from national courts of last resort.

[28] See, eg, *Mirga v Secretary of State for Work and Pensions* [2016] UKSC 1, [2016] 1 WLR 481 [3] (Lord Neuberger); and *Magmatic Ltd v PMS International Group plc* [2016] UKSC 12, [2016] 4 All ER 1027 [28] (Lord Neuberger).

[29] *CILFIT* (n 26) para 16. The CJEU gave guidance as to what the national court must bear in mind in considering if this test is met at paras 16–20. See also *Buckinghamshire County Council* (n 1) [127] (Lord Sumption), as discussed in n 27 above.

[30] See, eg, *Magmatic* (n 28) [28] (Lord Neuberger); and *R (Countryside Alliance) v Attorney General* [2007] UKHL 52, [2008] 1 AC 719 [31], [35] (Lord Bingham), [66] and [70]–[72] (Lord Hope).

[31] See, eg, *Test Claimants in the FII Group Litigation v Revenue and Customs Commissioners* [2012] UKSC 19, [2012] 2 AC 337 ('*FII Group (SC)*') [1] (Lord Hope), [120] (Lord Walker), [140] (Lord Dyson), [208] (Lord Sumption), [246] (Lord Reed). Strictly, however, a majority could decide that a point was acte clair and refuse to make a reference notwithstanding dissenting judgments. See also, eg, *Office of Communications v Information Commissioner* [2010] UKSC 3, [2010] Env LR 20 [3], [12]–[14] (Lord Mance), where the Court gave a single judgment unanimously holding that the answer to the critical question of EU law was 'not obvious', and referring the question to the CJEU. However, it also recorded and outlined in its judgment the differences of view taken by an unidentified majority and minority of the Supreme Court. And see further *HM Revenue and Customs v Aimia Coalition Loyalty UK Ltd* [2013] UKSC 42, where the Supreme Court acknowledged the power to make a *further* reference to clarify an issue if necessary, but (unanimously) declined to do so notwithstanding the Court's 3:2 split (see the citation at n 17 above) on how to address the case in the light of the CJEU's judgment on an earlier reference.

12.14   The second exception to the CJEU's permissive approach applies where there is a real question, which is relevant to the outcome of the case, as to the *validity* (rather than interpretation) of an act of an EU institution (including an EU instrument). Since the CJEU has sole authority to declare such an act invalid, if there is a 'well founded' argument that it is (whether raised by a party or the national court itself), the national court must make a reference to the CJEU on that issue. By contrast, if national courts consider that the arguments that an act is invalid are 'unfounded, they may reject them, concluding that the act is completely valid', and they are not required to make a reference to the CJEU in those circumstances.[32]

The Effect of EU Law on Domestic Law: Duties of Disapplication and Conforming Interpretation

12.15   The English courts' approach to the interaction of domestic and EU law involves two key duties: (i) the *duty to disapply domestic law* insofar as it conflicts with directly enforceable EU law; and (ii) the *duty to construe domestic law in conformity with EU law* so far as possible so that such conflicts do not arise. This was neatly summarised by Lord Walker in the following terms:

> [I]t is a fundamental principle of the law of the European Union, recognised in section 2(1) of the European Communities Act 1972, that if national legislation infringes directly enforceable Community rights, the national court is obliged to disapply the offending provision. The provision is not made void but it must be treated as being ... 'without prejudice to the directly enforceable Community rights of nationals of any member state of the [EU]' ...[33]

> Disapplication is called for only if there is an inconsistency between national law and EU law. In an attempt to avoid an inconsistency the national court will, if at all possible, interpret the national legislation so as to make it conform to the superior order of EU law ...[34] Sometimes, however, a conforming construction is not possible, and disapplication cannot be avoided.[35]

---

[32] See *IATA* (n 20) paras 29–30 and 32, applied in, eg, *R (Telefonica O2 Europe plc) v Office of Communications* [2007] EWHC 3018 (Admin) [3] (Mitting J): 'If I am satisfied that the challenge to the validity of the Roaming Regulation is unfounded, I can and should so declare ... If I consider the issue to be arguable, I cannot determine it myself but may refer it for decision to the [CJEU] ... The European Court alone is competent to make such a decision' (and see at [4], observing that 'not unfounded' meant the same as 'reasonably arguable'). See also Case C-461/03 *Gaston Schul Douane-expediteur BV v Minister van Landbouw, Natuur en Voedselkwaliteit* [2005] ECR I-10513, para 25, confirming that a reference must be made even if the CJEU has previously declared analogous provisions in a comparable measure to be invalid.

[33] Citing *Factortame* (n 5) 140C (Lord Bridge).

[34] Citing *Pickstone v Freemans plc* [1989] AC 66 (HL) and *Litster v Forth Dry Dock & Engineering Co Ltd* [1990] 1 AC 546 (HL).

[35] *Fleming* (n 14) [24]–[25] (Lord Walker).

12.16 In practice, what this means is that in approaching domestic legislation whose scope overlaps with provisions of EU law, the court will first engage in an exercise of interpretation and will only then turn to consider disapplication if necessary. The interpretation exercise involves a two-stage approach:[36]

12.16.1 The court will interpret the relevant rules of EU law in accordance with the applicable principles.

12.16.2 It will then interpret the relevant domestic legislation in the light of those rules of EU law and see if a compatible construction is possible.

12.17 If a compatible construction of the domestic legislation is not possible, then, depending on the nature of the rules of EU law in question, the court will need to consider whether it is required to disapply the domestic legislation.

12.18 We consider first the duty of disapplication before turning to questions of interpretation—both the scope of the duty to interpret domestic law in conformity with EU law and how to interpret EU law itself (whether as a precursor to seeking a conforming interpretation of domestic law, or as a freestanding exercise).

The Duty of Disapplication

12.19 'Disapplication of national legislation is an essentially different process from its interpretation so as to conform with EU law.' It can only properly be described as a 'process of construction' at all because the duty arises out of section 2(4), whose effect was described above.[37] As our focus is on interpretive questions, we do not consider here the potentially complex consequences for the Member State where disapplication is required.

12.20 For our purposes, it is sufficient to note the following points:

12.20.1 The duty of disapplication applies only where the relevant rule of EU law is directly enforceable.[38] As to the extent to which rules of EU law are directly enforceable, see paragraphs 12.4–12.5 above and the references there to Chapter 3.

---

[36] See *Commissioners for HM Revenue and Customs v IDT Card Services Ireland Ltd* [2006] EWCA Civ 29 [68] (Arden LJ), referring to the 'two different levels' at which interpretation must be performed. The need for a 'two-stage' approach was endorsed in *Lehman Bros International (Europe) v CRC Credit Fund Ltd* [2012] UKSC 6, [2012] 3 All ER 1 [131] (Lord Dyson).

[37] *Fleming* (n 14) [25] (Lord Walker); and paragraph 12.8 above.

[38] As recognised by Lord Walker in the passage cited from *Fleming* (n 14) at paragraph 12.15 above. See generally above at paragraph 12.8 on the primacy of directly enforceable (ie, directly effective) rules of EU law. There is some debate about the need for EU law to be directly effective before it must be given primacy in national law, at to which see Wyatt, Dashwood et al, *European Union Law* (2011) (n 7) 278–84. The debate is largely theoretical, turning essentially on whether certain case law is properly

12.20.2   Disapplication of a provision of domestic law is not an 'all-or-nothing' matter: it must only be disapplied *insofar as* it conflicts with EU law. The effect of the duty of disapplication under section 2(4) of the ECA 1972 is exactly the same as if wording were read into the relevant statute to say that its provisions are without prejudice to directly enforceable EU law rights.[39] Accordingly, a national measure whose application in certain circumstances would be incompatible with EU law might still be applicable in other circumstances, where its application would cause no interference with directly enforceable provisions of EU law. This may be the case, for example, in relation to its application to persons outside the EU[40] or in relation to what are called 'purely internal situations'.[41] In every case, therefore, the court must assess the precise *extent* of any incompatibility by interpreting both the relevant EU and domestic law.

12.20.3   In certain limited circumstances, where domestic law is incompatible with EU law but a policy judgement by Parliament or the government is required to determine how it should be rendered compatible, it may not be possible to disapply the incompatible domestic law, but only to grant a declaration regarding the incompatibility.[42]

12.20.4   The duty of disapplication may not apply if the courts were to be faced with a rule of EU law which conflicted with other constitutional principles of UK law in such a way that that rule should not to be given primacy over national law.[43]

The Duty of Conforming Interpretation

12.21   The UK courts have a 'well-established duty to interpret domestic legislation so far as possible in a manner conforming with any obligations imposed by a

---

characterised as involving direct effect. We follow Wyatt, Dashwood et al in understanding direct effect more broadly and considering it to be a prerequisite for disapplication of conflicting national law. Note that, in practical terms, a claimant need not necessarily possess himself the relevant directly enforceable EU law right in order to bring a claim to give effect to its primacy, although the identity, rights and interest of the claimant will be relevant to what relief should be granted: see *R (Gibraltar Betting & Gaming Association Ltd) v Secretary of State for Culture, Media and Sport* [2014] EWHC 3236 (Admin), [2015] 1 CMLR 28 [201]–[220] (Green J); and *Gibraltar* (n 23) [102]–[104] (Charles J).

[39] See the cases and passages cited in the first sentence of n 14 above.

[40] *Colmer* (n 14) 2041E–G (Lord Nolan).

[41] Where the application of the provision in question does not affect the EU's internal market, such that it does not fall within the scope of EU law. See, eg, Joined Cases C-35 and 36/82 *Morson and Jhanjan v Netherlands* [1982] ECR 3723; and *R (Gibraltar Betting and Gaming Association) v Commissioners for HM Revenue and Customs* (CJEU, 13 June 2017), especially at para 43, referring to 'a situation confined in all respects within a single Member State'.

[42] See, eg, *R (Chester) v Secretary of State for Justice* [2013] UKSC 63, [2014] AC 271 [72]–[74] (Lord Mance).

[43] Such a situation has not yet arisen, but as to the theoretical possibility, see paragraph 12.8 above, especially at n 15.

Directive' or other rules of EU law.[44] More specifically, the CJEU has expressed the duty in the following terms (again in the context of a Directive):

> [W]hen it applies domestic law, and in particular legislative provisions specifically adopted for the purpose of implementing the requirements of a directive, the national court is bound to interpret national law, so far as possible, in the light of the wording and purpose of the directive concerned in order to achieve the result sought by the directive.[45]

12.22　This duty is sometimes referred to as the *Marleasing principle*, after one of the leading CJEU cases on this issue.[46] As explained in that case,[47] the duty arises as a matter of EU law principally from the duty of Member States under:

12.22.1　Article 249 TFEU (and the terms of the relevant Directive, which will direct its own implementation) to 'achieve the result envisaged by the Directive'; and

12.22.2　Article 4(3) of the Treaty on European Union (TEU) requiring their sincere cooperation, including through their courts, and specifically requiring them to 'take any appropriate measure, general or particular, to ensure fulfilment of the obligations arising out of the Treaties or resulting from the acts of the institutions of the Union'.[48]

---

[44] *British Airways plc v Williams* [2012] UKSC 43, [2013] 1 All ER 443 [17] (Lord Mance), citing Case C-106/89 *Marleasing SA v La Comercial Internacional de Alimentación SA* [1990] ECR I-4135 and Joined Cases C-397–403/01 *Pfeiffer v Deutsches Rotes Kreuz, Kreisverband Waldshut eV* [2004] ECR I-8835, paras 109–20.

[45] See *Pfeiffer* (n 44) para 113.

[46] *Marleasing* (n 44). However, although known by this name, the principle was first recognised in Case C-14/83 *Von Colson v Land Nordrhein-Westfalen* [1984] ECR 1891, paras 26–28.

[47] *Marleasing* (n 44) para 8. See also *Pfeiffer* (n 44) para 110.

[48] As to the source of the obligation, see also, eg, Case C-212/04 *Adeneler v Ellinikos Organismos Galaktos* [2006] ECR I-6057, para 113. The precise basis upon which this duty applies in its full extent in *domestic* law is somewhat unclear—although the fact it applies is not in any doubt. It has been said that, as a matter of domestic law, the duty arises because there is a strong presumption that the UK intends to comply with its treaty obligations: see *Test Claimants in the FII Group Litigation v IRC* [2010] EWCA Civ 103 ('*FII Group (CA)*') [108] and [261] (Arden LJ) (on appeal against the finding at [261] to the Supreme Court, this statement of principle was not considered, and while both Courts applied the *Marleasing* principle to achieve a conforming interpretation, the Supreme Court did so in a different way: see *FII Group (SC)* (n 31) [118]–[119] (Lord Walker)). However, if this is correct, it can only be because for some reason that presumption carries particular force in the context of obligations under the EU Treaties: see *Assange v Swedish Prosecution Authority* [2012] UKSC 22, [2012] 2 AC 471 [203] and [215] (Lord Mance, dissenting, but not on this point), making clear that the *Marleasing* principle goes significantly further than the general presumption of compatibility with international law. From Lord Mance's judgment at [201]–[217], it appears that he considered the duty of conforming interpretation to arise out of s 2 of the ECA 1972, although he does not explain precisely how (and see to similar effect *IDT* (n 36) [73]–[74] (Arden LJ)). Lord Mance also appears to have doubted that it arises out of the duty of cooperation in Article 4(3) TEU, which he said was a duty on the state and not its courts, and 'is not a principle of domestic interpretation'. Note that, since December 2014, the duty of conforming interpretation does apply to Framework Decisions of the kind considered in *Assange*: see Chapter 11.38–11.39, especially at n 65.

12.23   *Scope of the duty's application*: the circumstances in which the *Marleasing* principle applies are wide-ranging, and have been expounded by the CJEU and UK courts as follows:

12.23.1   The principle is often expressed (as it is often applied) solely in terms of its application to legislation designed to implement particular rules of EU law,[49] and it plainly has particular force in that context.[50] However, the CJEU has made clear that its application extends to the interpretation of all domestic legislation potentially in conflict with EU law, and that courts should consider how they can apply 'national law as a whole' so as to achieve a compliant result.[51] In particular, it should be noted that the principle extends to provisions of domestic law enacted before the relevant rule of EU law arose.[52]

12.23.2   Although often invoked in the context of Directives, the principle also applies with regard to other sources of EU law,[53] or at least those that are directly effective.[54]

---

[49] See, eg, the formulations in *Swift v Robertson* [2014] UKSC 50, [2014] 1 WLR 3438 [20] (Lord Kerr); and *Parkwood Leisure Ltd v Alemo-Herron* [2011] UKSC 26, [2011] 4 All ER 800 [20] (Lord Hope).

[50] See *Pfeiffer* (n 44) para 112, stating that the principle applies 'a fortiori' when the national court is interpreting legislation 'specifically enacted for the purpose of transposing a directive intended to confer rights on individuals'. See also *Lock v British Gas Trading Ltd* [2016] EWCA Civ 983, [2017] 1 CMLR 25 [81] (Sir Colin Rimer).

[51] See, eg, *Pfeiffer* (n 44) para 115. The need to construe all provisions of national law compatibly with EU law, and not just specific implementing measures, is clear from the result of *Marleasing* (n 44) as well. In *IDT* (n 36) Arden LJ appears to have suggested (at [91]) that it was 'an open question' whether the English courts would follow *Pfeiffer* in applying the interpretive obligation to the whole body of domestic legislation and not just implementing legislation. However, in *Webb v Emo Air Cargo Ltd* [1993] 1 WLR 49 (HL), Lord Keith seemed to accept (at 59F–G) the wider application of the *Marleasing* principle, at least to all legislation 'in any field covered by a Community Directive'. Further, Arden LJ herself appeared to accept the need to interpret all national law compatibly with EU law, in the context of an obligation arising under the general principles of EU law to ensure that a right exists to reclaim tax paid in breach of EU law, in *FII Group (CA)* (n 48) [256]–[264]. On appeal, the Supreme Court similarly held that a conforming interpretation should be applied to domestic law to ensure compatibility with EU law, but (overruling the Court of Appeal on this point) considered this should be achieved by way of a different interpretive route: see *FII Group (SC)* (n 31) [118]–[119] (Lord Walker). See also *Twentieth Century Fox Film Corp v British Telecommunications plc* [2011] EWHC 2714 (Ch), [2012] Bus LR 1461 [93] (Arnold J), citing *Pfeiffer* with approval (though also citing *IDT* [91]).

[52] *Marleasing* (n 44) para 8; *Webb* (n 51) 59G (Lord Keith), citing *Marleasing*.

[53] See, eg, Case C-262/97 *Rijksdienst voor Pensioenen v Engelbrecht* [2000] ECR I-7321, paras 37–39 in the context of Treaty articles, citing *Marleasing* (n 44) para 8, and Case C-165/91 *Van Munster v Rijksdienst voor Pensioenen* [1994] ECR I-4661, para 34.

[54] See *FII Group (SC)* (n 31) [176] (Lord Sumption): '*Marleasing*, at any rate as it has been applied in England, is authority for a highly muscular approach to the construction of national legislation so as to bring it into conformity with the directly effective Treaty obligations of the United Kingdom'; and see the application of the principle in relation to a Treaty article at [118]–[119] (Lord Walker). See also *Re Digital Satellite Warranty Cover Ltd* [2013] UKSC 7, [2013] 1 WLR 605 [20] (Lord Sumption), stating that *Marleasing* 'requires English legislation to be construed as far as possible so as to conform with *mandatory* requirements of EU law'. In view of his judgment in *FII Group*, this is presumably meant as a reference to directly effective EU law provisions.

12.23.3 While the principle applies generally to provisions of EU law that have direct effect,[55] it also applies, in relation to Directives requiring implementation in national law, to provisions that do not.[56] Where applicable, the principle may be relied upon regardless of who the parties to the case are or who is affected as a consequence of the principle's invocation.[57] Consequently, it is sometimes referred to as the principle of 'indirect effect', since in practice it gives effect to rules of EU law in the national laws of Member States even though those rules may not have direct effect.

12.23.4 The principle applies not only to Directives which the Member State has sought to implement,[58] but also to *unimplemented* Directives,[59] provided the time permitted for implementation has expired.[60] Prior to this time expiring, a less stringent interpretive duty applies in relation to unimplemented Directives, requiring national courts not to interpret national law in a way that would 'seriously compromise' their effective implementation after the deadline has passed.[61]

12.24 So the duty of conforming interpretation is broad in its scope. However, in accordance with the general principles of legal certainty and non-retroactivity in EU law, the duty does *not* apply where its effect would be, independently of any implementing legislation, to create a new criminal liability for a person or aggravate a person's criminal liability.[62]

12.25 Further, it should be noted that, just like the duty of disapplication, the duty of conforming interpretation only applies in circumstances where recourse to it is necessary to avoid an outcome contrary to EU law. This means that, perhaps counter-intuitively, the same domestic enactment may be interpreted differently in different cases depending on whether, in a given case, the ordinary construction

---

[55] See, eg, Case 157/86 *Murphy v Bord Telecom Eireann* [1988] ECR 673, para 11.

[56] See, eg, *Von Colson* (n 46) paras 27–28; and *Adeneler* (n 48) para 113.

[57] See, eg, *Marleasing* (n 44), where the principle was applied in litigation so as to affect the situation between private parties. But note that the principle is subject to the limitations discussed at paragraph 12.24 below.

[58] As in, eg, *Von Colson* (n 46).

[59] As in, eg, *Marleasing* (n 44).

[60] See *Adeneler* (n 48) paras 114–15.

[61] ibid para 123.

[62] See Case C-80/86 *Kolpinghuis Nijmegen* [1987] ECR 3969, paras 13–14. Case C-168/95 *Arcaro* [1996] ECR I-4075, para 42 might be read as suggesting that this qualification extends more generally to prevent unimplemented Directives from imposing obligations on individuals. However, it is submitted that that passage should not be seen as intending to extend the qualification beyond the sphere of criminal law. The importance of the criminal law context to this qualification has been emphasised in subsequent judgments: see, eg, Case C-7/11 *Caronna* (CJEU, 28 June 2012) paras 51–56, where the CJEU stated that the 'obligation to interpret national law in conformity with European Union law is subject to certain limits *in criminal matters*' (emphasis added). That this qualification is limited to the criminal context was also the view taken by AG Jacobs in his Opinion in Case C-456/98 *Centrosteel Srl v Adipol GmbH* [2000] ECR I-6007, paras 31–35.

of the enactment would lead to a result incompatible with EU law. If it would not, the enactment should be construed and applied in the ordinary way.[63]

12.26   This also means that the duty does not prevent domestic courts from finding that domestic law goes *beyond* what is required by EU law, unless such a course is precluded by EU law.[64] However, where domestic legislation has been enacted to give effect to certain provisions of EU law, it may well be that the domestic legislator has intended to do no more than give effect to those provisions.[65] How far domestic law is intended to mirror EU law is a question of construction in every case.

12.27   *Nature and limits of the duty*: as a matter of EU law, the extent of the duty to construe domestic legislation in conformity with EU law 'so far as possible' depends on the flexibility of (and limitations on) what can be done by 'applying the interpretative methods recognised by domestic law'.[66] In practice, the English courts have determined that the domestic tools of construction available for performing this duty are powerful, enabling a 'highly muscular approach' to interpretation.[67] Indeed, it has been said that the duty is 'broad and far-reaching [and] not constrained by conventional rules of construction'.[68] Its extent is essentially

---

[63] *Gingi v Secretary of State for Work and Pensions* [2001] EWCA Civ 1685, [2002] 1 CMLR 20 [44]–[47] (Arden LJ), cited with approval (in the analogous context of the effect of s 3 of the Human Rights Act 1998) in *R (Hurst) v London Northern District Coroner* [2007] UKHL 13, [2007] 2 AC 189 [52] (Lord Brown). See above at paragraph 12.20.2 in relation to the operation of the same principle in connection with the duty of disapplication.

[64] See *Energy Solutions (EU) Ltd v Nuclear Decommissioning Authority* [2017] UKSC 34, [2017] 1 WLR 1373 [30] (Lord Mance); and see *Parkwood* (n 49) [32] (Lord Hope), where the question of what EU law would permit in this regard was referred to the CJEU: see Case C-426/11 *Alemo-Herron v Parkwood* [2014] 1 CMLR 21. See also *Nolan* (n 10) [14] (Lord Mance): 'Where a Directive offers a member state a choice, there can be no imperative to construe domestic legislation as having any particular effect, so long as it lies within the scope of the permitted. Where a Directive allows a member state to go further than the Directive requires, there is again no imperative to achieve a "conforming" interpretation.'

[65] See *Parkwood* (n 49) [27]–[30] (Lord Hope); *Energy Solutions* (n 64) [39] (Lord Mance); *Nolan* (n 10) [14] (Lord Mance): 'It may in a particular case be possible to infer that the domestic legislature did not, by a domestic formulation or reformulation, intend to go further in substance than the European requirement or minimum'; and *Howe v Motor Insurers' Bureau (No 1)* [2016] EWHC 640 (QB), [2016] 1 WLR 2707 [27] (Stewart J): 'Unless there is something in domestic legislation which suggests that it was intended to be more generous than that found in a Directive, the domestic legislation is to be construed first to conform with the Directive.' In the light of Lord Mance's judgment in *Nolan*, it may be that the use of a 'domestic formulation or reformulation' in transposing a Directive is sufficient to require a more case-specific, and less presumptive, approach to interpretation in this context.

[66] *Adeneler* (n 48) paras 108–111. As stated in that passage, the 'obligation cannot serve as the basis for an interpretation of national law *contra legem*' and only 'requires national courts to do whatever lies within their jurisdiction'. Given the liberal approach to ensuring a conforming interpretation adopted by domestic courts, detailed discussion of what the CJEU means by '*contra legem*' is likely to be unprofitable: see *Lock* (n 50) [100]–[104] (Sir Colin Rimer).

[67] *FII Group (SC)* (n 31) [176] (Lord Sumption), as cited in n 54 above.

[68] *Vodafone 2 v Revenue and Customs Commissioners* [2009] EWCA Civ 446, [2010] Ch 77 [37]–[38] (Sir Andrew Morritt C).

the same as that of the interpretive duty under section 3 of the Human Rights Act 1998, which is likewise circumscribed by what is 'possible'.[69] That duty is considered in Chapter 10.

12.28   In a passage that has been endorsed by the Supreme Court,[70] the Court of Appeal has authoritatively described the nature and extent of the duty of conforming interpretation as follows:

> [T]he obligation on the English courts to construe domestic legislation consistently with Community law obligations is both broad and far-reaching. In particular: (a) it is not constrained by conventional rules of construction; (b) it does not require ambiguity in the legislative language; (c) it is not an exercise in semantics or linguistics; (d) it permits departure from the strict and literal application of the words which the legislature has elected to use; (e) it permits the implication of words necessary to comply with Community law obligations; and (f) the precise form of the words to be implied does not matter.
>
> … The only constraints on the broad and far-reaching nature of the interpretative obligation are that: (a) the meaning should 'go with the grain of the legislation' and be 'compatible with the underlying thrust of the legislation being construed'. An interpretation should not be adopted which is inconsistent with a fundamental or cardinal feature of the legislation since this would cross the boundary between interpretation and amendment; and (b) the exercise of the interpretative obligation cannot require the courts to make decisions for which they are not equipped or give rise to important practical repercussions which the court is not equipped to evaluate.[71]

12.29   It should also be noted that, in appropriate cases, the interpretive obligation permits not only the reading *in* of words to legislation,[72] but also permits

---

[69] As recognised in *Rowstock v Jessemey* [2014] EWCA Civ 185, [2014] 1 WLR 3615 [40] (Underhill LJ), the approach taken by the courts to the duty of conforming interpretation has been 'assimilated' by the House of Lords to that taken when applying the interpretive duty in s 3 of the Human Rights Act 1998: see *Ghaidan v Godin-Mendoza* [2004] UKHL 30, [2004] 2 AC 557 [48] (Lord Steyn) and [118] (Lord Rodger). See also, eg, *IDT* (n 36) [85] (Arden LJ), stating that *Ghaidan* is 'authority as to what is "possible" as a matter of statutory interpretation' and that 'the guidance given by the House of Lords in that case as to the limits of interpretation can also in general be applied to when the limits of interpretation under the Marleasing principle arise for consideration'; *Blackwood v Birmingham and Solihull Mental Health NHS Foundation Trust* [2016] EWCA Civ 607, [2016] ICR 903 [48] (Underhill LJ); *Hurst* (n 62) [52] (Lord Brown); and the repeated references to *Ghaidan* in the passage from *Vodafone 2* (n 68) set out (with citations omitted) at paragraph 12.28 below.

[70] See *Swift* (n 49) [21] (Lord Kerr); and *Nolan* (n 10) [14] (Lord Mance). See also, in the Court of Appeal, eg, *Lock* (n 50) [103] (Sir Colin Rimer); and *Rowstock* (n 69) [41] (Underhill LJ).

[71] *Vodafone 2* (n 68) [37]–[38] (Sir Andrew Morritt C), citations omitted. The citations are principally from *Ghaidan* (n 69), *Pickstone* (n 34), *Litster* (n 34) and *IDT* (n 36).

[72] For examples of the courts reading in words to ensure compatibility, see, eg, *Pickstone* (n 34) 120H–121A (Lord Templeman) and *Litster* (n 34) 554G–H (Lord Keith), 558E–H (Lord Templeman), both citing *Pickstone*. In *IDT* (n 36), Arden LJ suggested (at [91]) that the *Marleasing* principle may require the courts, if there is a choice, to prefer the interpretive route that 'involves least change from the domestic legislation given its normal meaning', though she left this open. Some support may be gained for this from *FII Group Litigation* (n 31) [119] (Lord Walker), who considered it preferable to follow the 'simpler and more natural way' to achieving a compatible interpretation on the case before him; see also at [205] (Lord Sumption).

'reading it down (ie to narrow its potential field of application)' and also (but more rarely) 'disapplying or striking down part of it in order to make it compatible'.[73] As the Court of Appeal has emphasised, 'there is no significance in the interpretative tool that is used': the fundamental question is always whether the proposed interpretive course goes beyond what is *possible* in view of the constraints which apply to the *Marleasing* principle (discussed in the passage above).[74]

Interpretation of EU Law

12.30   This section addresses the interpretation of rules of EU law as such. As stated above, this will be the first stage of a domestic court's inquiry in determining whether and how to interpret or disapply national law to ensure conformity with EU law. As section 3 of the ECA 1972 states, in interpreting EU law, domestic courts are to apply the same rules of interpretation as the CJEU.

Hierarchy of Norms

12.31   The starting point is to understand the nature of the provision of EU law to be interpreted. The various sources of EU law were discussed in Chapter 11, and that discussion addressed where each source fits within the 'hierarchy of norms' recognised by EU law.[75] As a general rule, the sources of EU law are to be interpreted in accordance with that hierarchy of norms. Thus, EU legislation, as *secondary* law, is to be interpreted, so far as possible, so as to be consistent with those sources superior in the hierarchy such as the Treaties and the 'general principles' of EU law.[76] Where EU legislation cannot be interpreted compatibly with higher norms, it may be liable to be set aside as invalid.[77]

---

[73] See *Vidal-Hall v Google Inc* [2015] EWCA Civ 311, [2016] QB 1003 [89]–[90] (Lord Dyson MR and Sharp LJ), although they considered that disapplication under the *Marleasing* principle was not possible in that case: see at [92]–[93].

[74] ibid [90].

[75] See Chapter 11.13–11.37, especially at n 16.

[76] See Case 314/89 *Rauh v Hauptzollamt Nürnberg-Fürth* [1991] ECR I-1647, para 17: 'where it is necessary to interpret a provision of secondary Community law, preference should as far as possible be given to the interpretation which renders the provision consistent with the Treaty and the general principles of Community law'; and see Case C-61/94 *Commission v Germany* [1996] ECR I-3989, para 52, with regard to the duty to interpret EU legislation, so far as possible, in accordance with treaties binding on the EU (and see further Chapter 11.24–11.27 in this regard).

[77] See Case C-362/14 *Schrems v Data Protection Commissioner* [2016] QB 257, para 60: 'the European Union is a union based on the rule of law in which all acts of its institutions are subject to a review of their compatibility with, in particular, the Treaties, general principles of law and fundamental rights'; and Case C-308/06 *R v Intertanko* [2008] ECR I-4057, paras 43–45, in relation to the CJEU's power to review the validity of EU legislation in the light of treaties binding on the EU. See further Chapter 11.15 and 11.25–11.26.

12.32   Further, as discussed in Chapter 11, the general principles of EU law as laid down by the CJEU over the years (and as in part now codified in the EU Charter of Fundamental Rights) have been used to guide the interpretation of not only EU legislation, but also the Treaties themselves.[78]

The General Principles of EU Law

12.33   Given the importance of the general principles to questions of interpretation of EU law and the frequency with which they are invoked by the CJEU, we discuss here briefly a number of the key principles which have been established by the CJEU:[79]

12.33.1   *Equality of treatment or non-discrimination*: the principle of equal treatment is 'one of the fundamental principles' of EU law.[80] 'According to settled case law, that principle requires that comparable situations must not be treated differently and that different situations must not be treated in the same way unless such treatment is objectively justified.'[81] Note, however, that it is not permissible to rely 'on an unlawful act committed in favour of another' to support a claim for equal treatment.[82]

12.33.2   *Legal certainty*: the principle of legal certainty requires 'that rules must enable those concerned to know precisely the extent of the obligations which they impose on them'[83] and 'in particular that rules involving negative consequences for individuals should be clear and precise and their application predictable for those subject to them',[84] so that they 'may take steps accordingly'.[85] Its purpose

---

[78] See Chapter 11.23.

[79] For a detailed treatment of the general principles of EU law, see Takis Tridimas, *The General Principles of EU Law*, 2nd edn (Oxford, Oxford University Press, 2007).

[80] Joined Cases 117/76 and 16/77 *Albert Ruckdeschel & Co v Hauptzollamt Hamburg-St Annen* [1977] ECR 1753, para 7.

[81] Case C-550/07 P *Akzo Nobel Chemicals Ltd v Commission* [2010] ECR I-8301, paras 54–55.

[82] See Case 134/84 *Williams v Court of Auditors* [1985] ECR 2225, para 14. As the court explained, this is because the 'principle of equality of treatment ... must be reconciled with the principle of legality'. See also to similar effect, eg, Joined Cases C-259 and 260/10 *Commissioners for HM Revenue and Customs v The Rank Group plc* [2011] ECR I-10947, paras 59–65.

[83] Case C-209/96 *United Kingdom v Commission* [1998] ECR I-5655, para 35. See also, eg, *Consorzio (CJEU)* (n 4) para 89, and at para 85 referring also to the 'principle of transparency', with both principles said to require EU law to be reasonably accessible through publication in the language of the relevant Member State before it can impose obligations on individuals there.

[84] *Akzo* (n 81) para 100.

[85] Case C-110/03 *Belgium v Commission* [2005] ECR I-2801, para 30: 'the principle of legal certainty is a fundamental principle of Community law which requires, in particular, that rules should be clear and precise, so that individuals may be able to ascertain unequivocally what their rights and obligations are and may take steps accordingly'. See also *Buckinghamshire County Council* (n 1) [165] (Lord Neuberger and Lord Mance), also describing the principle as fundamental and stating 'Union citizens and others need to know and are entitled to expect that the legislation enacted by their European legislator will be given its intended effect'.

is 'to ensure that situations and legal relationships governed by Community law remain foreseeable'.[86] The CJEU has made clear that the 'requirement of legal certainty must be observed all the more strictly in the case of rules liable to entail financial consequences'[87] and specifically 'that a penalty, even of a non-criminal nature, cannot be imposed unless it rests on a clear and unambiguous legal basis'.[88] However, it must be borne in mind that 'the existence of possible ambiguity in a provision can only be established by reference to the context of that provision'.[89] Note that, as well as applying to the interpretation of EU legislation, this principle also applies to Member States when transposing EU legislation into domestic law, requiring them to adopt provisions with sufficient clarity to ensure that EU rights and obligations will be observed.[90]

12.33.3 *Effective judicial protection (equivalence and effectiveness)*: 'the principle of effective judicial protection is a general principle of Community law'.[91] As a general rule, 'in the absence of Community rules governing the matter, it is for the domestic legal system of each Member State to designate the courts and tribunals having jurisdiction and to lay down the detailed procedural rules governing actions for safeguarding rights which individuals derive from Community law'. In other words, EU law generally gives procedural autonomy to the Member States. However, as the Member States 'are responsible for ensuring that those rights are effectively protected', the designation of courts and the detailed procedural rules laid down 'must be no less favourable than those governing similar domestic actions (*principle of equivalence*) and must not render practically impossible or excessively difficult the exercise of rights conferred by Community law (*principle of effectiveness*)' (emphasis added). These two requirements 'embody the general obligation on the Member States to ensure judicial protection of an individual's rights under Community law'.[92]

---

[86] Case C-63/93 *Duff v Minister for Agriculture and Food* [1996] ECR I-569, para 20.

[87] Case C-255/02 *Halifax plc v Commissioners of Customs and Excise* [2006] ECR I-1609, para 72. This was considered, eg, in *Milk Supplies Ltd v Department for the Environment, Food and Rural Affairs* [2010] EWCA Civ 19, [2010] 2 CMLR 40 [42]–[49] (Aikens LJ), with the court holding that the provisions in question were 'clear and unambiguous' in imposing a penalty.

[88] Case 117/83 *Karl Könecke GmbH & Co KG v BALM* [1984] ECR 3291, para 11. See also, eg, Case C-274/04 *ED & F Man Sugar Ltd v Hauptzollamt Hamburg-Jonas* [2006] ECR I-3269, paras 14–19, where a Regulation was interpreted in the light of this principle. See also the passage from *Milk Supplies* (n 87) cited in that note, where this principle was considered.

[89] See Case C-296/95 *R v Customs and Excise Commissioners ex p EMU Tabac SARL* [1998] ECR I-1605, para 39 (and more generally the discussion at paras 37–40).

[90] See Case 120/88 *Commission v Italy* [1991] ECR I-621, para 11; and Case 361/88 *Commission v Germany* [1991] ECR I-2567, para 30.

[91] See, eg, Case C-268/06 *Impact v Minister for Agriculture and Food* [2008] ECR I-2483, para 43, and generally the discussion at paras 43–47. See also generally the discussion of the principle in Case C-432/05 *Unibet (London) Ltd v Justitiekanslern* [2007] ECR I-2271, paras 37–44; and see also *Berlioz Investment Fund SA v Directeur de l'administration des contributions directes* (CJEU, 16 May 2017), para 54, noting that this principle is 'now set out in Article 47 of the Charter [which] secures in EU law the protection afforded by Article 6(1) and Article 13 of the ECHR'.

[92] *Impact* (n 91) paras 44–47. These principles were cited in *Budimir* (n 14) [52] (Lord Judge CJ), going on to discuss the principle of effectiveness at [54]–[72]. See also, eg, Joined Cases C-222–225/05

12.33.4 *Proportionality*: 'the principle of proportionality is a general principle of Community law that … requires that measures adopted by Community institutions should not exceed the limits of what is appropriate and necessary in order to attain the objectives legitimately pursued by the legislation in question; when there is a choice between several appropriate measures, recourse must be had to the least onerous, and the disadvantages caused must not be disproportionate to the aims pursued'.[93] Note that in areas where the relevant EU institution enjoys a broad discretion due to the nature of the measure in question, the standard for a review of legality on the grounds of proportionality will be whether the measure is 'manifestly inappropriate having regard to the objective which the competent institution is seeking to pursue'.[94] The proportionality principle applies to national measures within the scope of EU law as well as acts of EU institutions.[95]

12.33.5 *Fundamental rights*: 'fundamental rights form an integral part of the general principles of law' applied by the CJEU. These derive from 'the constitutional traditions common to the Member States' and various human rights treaties, especially the European Convention on Human Rights.[96] Of course, many of these rights recognised as general principles will now overlap with rights under the Charter.[97]

General Rules of Interpretation of EU Instruments

12.34 *The basic rule—words, context and purpose*: the 'basic rule' applicable to the interpretation of a provision of EU law is that 'it is necessary to consider not only its wording, but also the context in which it occurs and the objectives pursued by the rules of which it is part'.[98]

Van der Weerd v Minister van Landbouw, Natuur en Voedselkwaliteit [2007] ECR I-4233, paras 28–42, where the CJEU held that the principles of equivalence and effectiveness did not require the national court to raise a point of EU law of its own motion in that case. In general, the principle of effectiveness does not require this provided that 'the parties are given a genuine opportunity to raise a plea based on Community law before a national court': see at para 41. Specific exceptions are discussed at paras 39–40. The principle of equivalence will require a national court to raise a point of EU law of its own motion if it would do so in relation to equivalent provisions of domestic law: see at paras 29–31; and Case C-564/15 *Farkas v Nemzeti Adó- és Vámhivatal Dél-alföldi Regionális Adó Főigazgatósága* (CJEU, 26 April 2017), para 35.

[93] Case C-170/08 *Nijemeisland v Minister van Landbouw, NatuurenVoedselkwaliteit* [2009] ECR I-5127, para 41, where the principle was considered in the context of interpreting a Regulation.

[94] See, eg, Case C-58/08 *Vodafone Ltd v Secretary of State for Business, Enterprise and Regulatory Reform* [2010] ECR I-4999, para 52.

[95] See Case C-210/91 *Commission v Greece* [1992] ECR I-6735, para 19; and *R (Lumsdon) v Legal Services Board* [2015] UKSC 41, [2016] AC 697 [24]–[25] (Lord Reed and Lord Toulson).

[96] Case C-36/02 *Omega Spielhallen v Bonn* [2004] I-9609, para 33. See further the discussion of *Omega* at Chapter 11.23.

[97] See, eg, *Berlioz* (n 91), as cited in that note.

[98] Case C-306/05 *SGAE v Rafael Hotels SA* [2006] ECR I-11519, para 34. In *Twentieth Century Fox* (n 51) [94] (Arnold J), this passage was cited and described as '[t]he basic rule of interpretation, which has been frequently reiterated by the European Court of Justice'.

12.35   *Interpreting the wording of the text*: the wording of the text to be construed provides an obvious starting point for any interpretation exercise. As a general rule, the 'meaning and scope of terms for which European Union law provides no definition must be determined by considering their usual meaning in everyday language, while also taking into account the context in which they occur and the purposes of the rules of which they are part'.[99] However (as discussed immediately below), when approaching the text to discern its meaning, account must be taken of the fact that EU law texts are officially published in multiple different language versions, which are all 'equally authoritative for the purpose of the texts' interpretation'[100] and 'must be given a uniform interpretation'.[101] This uniform interpretation will generally be an 'autonomous' one, that is, one that does not depend on the meaning of the national law of (any of) the Member States.[102]

12.36   *Different language versions*: the CJEU has stated that 'it must be borne in mind that Community legislation is drafted in several languages and that the different language versions are all equally authentic. An interpretation of a provision of Community law thus involves a comparison of the different language versions'.[103] The basis of this requirement is the principle that, as well as being equally authentic, 'the different language versions of a Community text must be given a uniform interpretation'.[104] For obvious reasons, consideration of context and purpose will be particularly important where the ordinary meaning of the text differs between language versions. Thus, as the CJEU has stated, where there is a 'divergence between the language versions, the provision in question must be interpreted by reference to the purpose and general scheme of the rules of which it forms a part'.[105]

12.37   In accordance with these principles, the Supreme Court has stated that, in relation to EU legislation, '[t]he starting point in interpretation is ... the different language versions of the text, to understand their purpose and scheme'.[106]

---

[99]   C-482/09 *Budějovický Budvar, národní podnik v Anheuser-Busch Inc* [2011] ECR I-8701, para 39.
[100]   *R (Khatun) v Newham London Borough Council* [2004] EWCA Civ 55, [2005] QB 37 [68] (Laws LJ). See also *CILFIT* (n 26) para 18. See further paragraphs 12.36–12.39 below.
[101]   Case C-372/88 *Milk Marketing Board of England and Wales v Cricket St Thomas Estate* [1990] ECR I-1345, para 19. See further paragraphs 12.36–12.40 below.
[102]   See further paragraph 12.40 below.
[103]   *CILFIT* (n 26) para 18.
[104]   *Milk Marketing Board* (n 101) para 19.
[105]   ibid. This was a case where a divergence between different language versions needed to be resolved: see the discussion at paras 13–25, where the CJEU rejected the contention that the fact the legislation had been devised to address a UK situation meant the English version of the text should be preferred. See also *EMU* (n 89) paras 33–36, where the CJEU rejected the contention that certain language versions should be 'disregarded' because they differed from the text of the majority of different language versions and because they were in the languages of small Member States which were not well known outside of those countries. For a further example of resolving divergent meanings, see, eg, Case 9/79 *Koschniske v Raad van Arbeid* [1979] ECR 2717.
[106]   *Buckinghamshire County Council* (n 1) [169] (Lord Neuberger and Lord Mance), having cited at [167] the CJEU's general guidance in *CILFIT* (n 26).

12.38   As a matter of practice, however, the English courts do not always look beyond the English version of the text—whether because they are not addressed on other language versions or because they consider that the answer is clear enough without the need to have recourse to them.[107] This focus on the English version reflects the fact that, while the courts are 'becoming more accustomed to looking at a few of the different language versions' of EU legislation, the CJEU's guidance 'is not always easy to apply', since realistically 'the number of different language versions that the court can examine is limited'.[108] It also reflects the reality that, unless the parties present arguments regarding different language versions, the court may be unlikely to take those texts into account, and that there will be limits to the research that all but the best-funded and most diligent parties can or will conduct.[109]

12.39   In recognition of these practical difficulties, the Court of Appeal has given guidance as to the steps a party should take if it wishes to rely on a foreign-language version of an EU instrument. The guidance advises that the appropriate course for a party wishing to rely on a foreign-language text should generally be 'to alert the other side to this fact and to seek to agree a translation of that version', which the court will then be likely (though not bound) to accept. The Court also advised as to the approach to take where agreement on a translation cannot be reached.[110]

12.40   *Autonomous interpretation*: 'the need for uniform application of Community law', as well as 'the principle of equality', mean that:

> [T]he terms of a Community law provision which makes no express reference to the law of the Member States for the purpose of determining its meaning and scope must

---

[107] Of course, as the CJEU cases on divergent language versions show, an exclusive focus on the English version—however clear it seems—may not lead to the correct result.

[108] *IDT* (n 36) [70] (Arden LJ).

[109] But see *R (Condron) v Merthyr Tydfil County Borough Council* [2010] EWCA Civ 534, [2010] 3 CMLR 32 [41] (Arden LJ), where, although the parties had not taken the Court to any other language version, Arden LJ conducted her own review of the French version, remarking that it did 'not suggest any material difference in the text'.

[110] See *R v Commissioners of Customs and Excise ex p EMU Tabac Sarl* [1997] Eu LR 153 (CA) 160B–E (Schiemann LJ): 'It seems to us that an appropriate way of approaching the problems posed by differing authentic versions is for any party which proposes to rely on a version in a foreign tongue to alert the other side to this fact and to seek to agree a translation of that version. If there is agreement it is improbable that the court will wish to disagree. Certainly if it does then it should indicate its views so that the parties can comment on them. If there is no agreement between the parties then the appropriate course is for the parties' legal advisers first to consider whether it is really likely to be productive in the national court to pursue submissions based on disputed translations of texts expressed in foreign languages. That will seldom be the case. If, however, the conclusion of one or more parties is that it is likely to be productive then evidence by translators should be filed on each side. That will usually suffice for the judge to be prepared to come to a decision on the point. Cross examination is an option but not one which we would generally wish to encourage. In a case where the difference in meaning attributed to the authentic versions is crucial to the decision and the point is irresolvable on the affidavits then the appropriate course may well be to refer the matter to the [CJEU] which is linguistically better placed than any national court to resolve the matter.'

normally be given an *autonomous* and *uniform* interpretation throughout the Community, having regard to the context of the provision and the objective pursued by the legislation in question.[111] (Emphasis added)

Accordingly, one must always 'bear in mind that words may have autonomous meanings in EU law'.[112] Further, since EU law represents a separate legal order from the laws of its constituent Member States, the relevant autonomous meanings may embody autonomous legal concepts that 'do not necessarily have the same meaning in Community law and in the law of the various Member States'.[113]

12.41   *Construction to support the effectiveness of important principles of EU law*: provisions which seek to derogate from important principles of EU law (such as consumer protection) will be interpreted 'strictly'.[114] Conversely, exceptions to such derogations will be construed 'broadly'.[115] Further, terms appearing in provisions designed to ensure the effectiveness of important principles should not be interpreted strictly.[116]

12.42   *The role of context and purpose*: account must be taken both of the relevant provision's particular context and also of the wider context 'of the provisions of Community law as a whole, regard being had to the objectives thereof and to its state of evolution at the date on which the provision in question is to be applied'.[117] Other legislation in the same field, or earlier versions of the same legislation, may have particular relevance.[118]

---

[111] Case C-195/06 *KommAustria v ORF* [2007] ECR I-8817, para 24.

[112] *Condron* (n 109) [41] (Arden LJ), though finding in that case that '[t]he relevant expressions do not have autonomous EU law meanings'.

[113] *CILFIT* (n 26) para 19. For examples of the CJEU considering certain matters to be autonomous concepts, see, eg, Case C-256/01 *Allonby v Accrington & Rossendale College* [2004] ECR I-873, paras 62–72 (concept of 'worker' in a Treaty article, also making clear that there is no single definition of 'worker' consistent throughout EU law); and Case C-201/13 *Deckmyn v Vandersteen* (CJEU, 3 September 2014), paras 14–17 (concept of 'parody' in a Directive).

[114] See Case C-336/03 *easyCar (UK) Ltd v Office of Fair Trading* [2005] ECR I-1947, para 21: 'When … terms appear … in a provision which constitutes a derogation from a principle or, more specifically, from Community rules for the protection of consumers, they must, in addition, be interpreted strictly'; and Case C-175/09 *Commissioners for HM Revenue and Customs v AXA UK plc* [2010] ECR I-10701, para 25: 'the terms used to specify the exemptions set out in Article 13 of the Sixth Directive are to be interpreted strictly, since they constitute exceptions to the general principle that VAT is to be levied on all goods and services supplied for consideration by a taxable person. Nevertheless, the interpretation of those terms must not deprive the exemption in question of its intended effect'. See also *Office of Communications* (n 31) [11] (Lord Mance), in the context of disclosure of information: 'The restrictive interpretation of exceptions is a general Community law principle.'

[115] See, eg, *AXA* (n 114) para 30.

[116] See, eg, *Allonby* (n 113) paras 64–66.

[117] *CILFIT* (n 26) para 20.

[118] See Case C-197/13 P *Spain v Commission* (CJEU, 4 September 2014), paras 77–80; and *Digital Satellite* (n 54) [13] (Lord Sumption).

12.43   The *purpose* of a measure is also generally an important factor in its interpretation.[119] In this regard, the CJEU has laid down a specific rule of construction
that when a provision is open to more than one interpretation, and one interpretation will allow it to 'achieve its purpose' and 'ensure that [it] retains its effectiveness', the court should prefer that interpretation over others that do not.[120]

12.44   However, the courts must bear in mind that, whether because EU legislation can be a product of compromise or otherwise, proposed objectives may not
always be fully achieved by a measure. If the legislative intent is 'clearly expressed'
in the text, therefore, it should usually be followed, as 'it is not for courts to rewrite
the legislation' by reference to its perceived purpose.[121] As a general rule, as with
the interpretation of domestic law, the clearer the wording of a provision, the
more that will be required before the courts will permit its clear language to give
way to other factors 'demanding an interpretation which goes beyond the actual
wording of the provision'.[122]

12.45   *Lex specialis*: when faced with an apparent conflict between two provisions
in a measure, one of which is general in scope and the other more specific, the
more specific measure will usually be regarded as a '*lex specialis*' such that it 'takes
precedence over' the more general provision 'in the situations which it is intended
specifically to govern'.[123]

12.46   *Reference to recitals*: when construing the language of an EU instrument,
reference may be (and commonly is) made to the numbered introductory recitals
in its preamble in order to assist in identifying the purpose of the measure and
determining the correct interpretation to be given to its provisions. As explained
at Chapter 11.50, the purpose of recitals is to explain the reasons for the adoption
of an EU act. Accordingly, it is well established that 'the preamble of a European
Union measure may explain its content'.[124]

12.47   However, recitals are not themselves operative, legislative parts of EU
acts, and their ability to influence the interpretation of those operative parts is

[119] See paragraph 12.34 above. See also *IDT* (n 36) [71] (Arden LJ): 'the objectives of a measure have
a greater normative force under Community law than they would under English law'.
[120] Case 187/87 *Land de Sarre v Ministre de L'Industrie* [1988] ECR 5013, para 19.
[121] *Buckinghamshire County Council* (n 1) [170]–[171] (Lord Neuberger and Lord Mance).
[122] See Case 107/84 *Commission v Germany* [1985] ECR 2655, para 12, which appears to be underpinned by this proposition. In that case, the provision was considered to be 'such a clear provision' that
other factors would have to be 'conclusive' to permit a departure from the natural meaning.
[123] See *Belgium v Commission* (n 85) para 39.
[124] *Budvar* (n 99) para 40. See also, eg, *Re Digital Satellite Warranty Cover Ltd* [2011] EWCA Civ
1413, [2012] Bus LR 990 [40] (Patten LJ): 'Difficulties of language may (and often do) exist in relation
to the Directives themselves but the conventional use of extensive recitals often provides a useful guide
to what the Directive was intended to do.' On appeal (citation at n 54 above), upholding the Court of
Appeal's decision, the Supreme Court likewise referred to the recitals to determine the object of the
relevant Directive: see at [13] (Lord Sumption).

accordingly limited. The preamble 'has no binding legal force and cannot be relied upon either as a ground for derogating from the actual provisions of the act in question or for interpreting those provisions in a manner clearly contrary to their wording'.[125] In practice, therefore, recitals are often relied upon to support[126] or confirm[127] a construction which arises from the actual wording of a substantive provision.

12.48   *Reference to title*: like recitals, the title of a measure (which is also not an operative part of the legislation) can be referred to as an aid to its interpretation, and it may be of particular assistance in determining a measure's intended purpose.[128]

12.49   *Reference to explanatory notes*: where official explanatory notes have been produced by the European Commission, the CJEU has held[129] that they 'may be an important aid' to interpretation, but it has also emphasised that they 'do not have legally binding force'.[130] Accordingly, they cannot be used to alter the meaning of the actual legislative provisions.[131]

External Aids to the Interpretation of EU Legislation: *Travaux Préparatoires*

12.50   Just as certain documents that shed light on the legislative history of domestic legislation can be used as external aids to assist in its interpretation, in construing EU legislation, reliance can be placed on certain documents which reveal the legislative history of the relevant EU act. These documents are sometimes called 'preparatory acts' or '*travaux préparatoires*' (or simply '*travaux*').

12.51   *Travaux* encompass a range of materials that shed light on the process by which an EU act became law. They can be accessed through the 'Preparatory acts' page of the EUR-Lex website.[132] What sort of *travaux* exist for a particular

---

[125] Case C-136/04 *Deutsches Milch-Kontor GmbH v Hauptzollamt Hamburg-Jonas* [2005] ECR I-10095, para 32. See also Case 215/88 *Casa Fleischhandels-GmbH v BALM* [1989] ECR 2789, para 31: 'Whilst a recital in the preamble to a regulation may cast light on the interpretation to be given to a legal rule, it cannot in itself constitute such a rule.'

[126] See, eg, *Budvar* (n 99) paras 46–47.

[127] See, eg, Case C-280/99 *Moccia Irme SpA v Commission* [2001] ECR I-4717, paras 41–43.

[128] See, eg, Case C-55/02 *Commission v Portugal* [2004] ECR I-9387, para 47.

[129] At least in the context of the Combined Nomenclature of the Common Customs Tariff.

[130] Case C-143/96 *Leonard Knubben Speditions GmbH v Hauptzollamt Mannheim* [1997] ECR I-7039, para 14. The position will be different where what are termed 'Explanatory Notes' are in fact an integral part of a piece of legislation, in which case they are to be taken into account in the same way as any other provision: see, eg, Case 143/86 *Margetts and Addenbrooke v Cuddy* [1988] ECR 625, paras 11–13.

[131] Case C-35/93 *Develop Dr Eisbein GmbH & Co v Hauptzollamt Stuttgart-West* [1994] ECR I-2655, paras 20–22.

[132] Available at www.eur-lex.europa.eu/collection/eu-law/pre-acts.html.

measure will depend on its specific legislative history. In this regard, reference may need to be had to the Treaties in force as at the time of passage of the relevant legislation, so as to ascertain the precise legislative procedure which applied to its passage and set the available *travaux* in their proper context.[133] The sort of documents cited as *travaux* include original and revised legislative proposals,[134] and explanatory memoranda from the European Commission,[135] among many others.[136]

12.52 Although *travaux* may take many forms, it is nevertheless important to ensure that a document truly forms part of a measure's legislative history before seeking to rely upon it as an authoritative aid to interpretation. The courts have deprecated reference to statements which do not actually form 'part of the relevant *travaux préparatoires*, and are made by bodies or institutions whose word is not an authoritative source of the legislation's true construction'.[137]

12.53 The Supreme Court has recognised that 'recourse to the travaux préparatoires may be an important aid to identification of the correct meaning' of EU legislation, and perhaps more so than in the interpretation of domestic law.[138] European and domestic case law show that, in appropriate cases, *travaux* can be used both as a direct aid to ascertaining the meaning and purpose of particular provisions,[139] and as a means of identifying the intended scope and purpose of a measure as a whole (which will inform the meaning of its individual provisions).[140]

[133] See Chapter 11.42–11.43, where the most common current legislative procedure is described (which involves proposals from the Commission being considered and approved by the Parliament and the Council), and Chapter 11.5–11.10, which explains which Treaties were in force from time to time.

[134] See, eg, Case C-178/97 *Banks v Théâtre Royal de la Monnaie* [2000] ECR I-2005, para 23; and *Office of Fair Trading v Abbey National* [2009] UKSC 6, [2010] 1 AC 696 [6], [44] (Lord Walker).

[135] See, eg, Case C-275/96 *Kuusijärvi v Riksförsäkringsverket* [1998] ECR I-3419, paras 45–46; and *Khatun* (n 100) [61]–[63] (Laws LJ).

[136] See, eg, the range of sources cited in *Khatun* (n 100) at [58]–[64] (Laws LJ); and Case C-133/00 *Bowden v Tuffnells Parcels Express Ltd* [2001] ECR I-7031, paras 35 and 42.

[137] *R (Marchiori) v Environment Agency* [2002] EWCA Civ 3, [2002] Eu LR 225 [56] (Laws LJ).

[138] *Buckinghamshire County Council* (n 1) [169] (Lord Neuberger and Lord Mance), having cited with apparent approval at [168] a passage from Sir David Edward and Robert Lane, *Edward & Lane on European Union Law* 3rd edn (Cheltenham, Edward Elgar Publishing, 2013) para 6.24, which states that in the EU law context, recourse will be had to *travaux* 'to a much greater extent than is normally the case in national law'. But see *Sanneh v Secretary of State for Work and Pensions* [2015] EWCA Civ 49, [2016] QB 455 [77] (Arden LJ), suggesting that it was unusual for the CJEU to examine *travaux* to assist it in reaching its conclusions.

[139] See, eg, *Banks* (n 134) para 23; *Kuusijärvi* (n 135) paras 44–46; *Debt Collect London Ltd v SK Slavia Praha-Fotbal AS* [2010] EWCA Civ 1250, [2011] 1 WLR 866 [40]–[42] (Lloyd LJ); *R (Infant and Dietetic Foods Association Ltd) v Secretary of State for Health* [2008] EWHC 575 (Admin), [2009] Eu LR 1 [38]–[43] (Mitting J).

[140] *Marchiori* (n 137) [56] (Laws LJ): 'European legislative measures must be interpreted purposively; and a measure's *travaux preparatoires* are to be taken into account, for they may greatly illuminate its purpose. So much is well known and well accepted.' For examples of cases where *travaux* were used to identify the overall purpose or scope of measures, see, eg, *Bowden* (n 136) paras 34–35 and 42; Case C-578/08 *Chakroun v Minister van Buitenlandse Zaken* [2010] ECR I-1839, paras 55 and 61–62; *Khatun* (n 100) [57]–[64], where Laws LJ reviewed various *travaux* (outlining his conclusions at [80]); *Blackland Park Exploration Ltd v Environment Agency* [2003] EWCA Civ 1795, [2004] Env LR

12.54   However, for *travaux* to be able to assist in the interpretive exercise, or at least for them to do so otherwise than by simply supporting or confirming a construction that is already apparent, they must clearly demonstrate the intended meaning of the legislation in question.[141] The Court of Appeal has cautioned in strong terms against having recourse to *travaux* where they lack the necessary degree of clarity:

> I would add generally that travaux préparatoires, if not bang on the point, seldom help. If the meaning of the ultimate document is ambiguous, or obscure, then, even if the travaux préparatoires are admissible, *there is no point in trawling through them unless they are clear as to what was intended and meant.* Constructing arguments around unexplained changes, passages in themselves ambiguous, or mere possible hints as to what would have been intended if the actual point in issue had actually been addressed, is just a waste of time … 'Only a bull's-eye counts'[142] … There is no point in relying upon travaux préparatoires which are not directly in point—you just substitute the puzzle posed by the actual language to be construed by another puzzle about other language at first or even second remove.[143] (Emphasis added)

12.55   A clear legislative intention may well not be demonstrated, for example, where the *travaux* referred to indicate merely that a certain proposed provision or amendment was not adopted, since the inferences that can legitimately be drawn

---

33 [32]–[33] (Scott Baker LJ); and *Abbey National* (n 134) [6], [44] (Lord Walker), referring to the 'complex message' to be derived from the *travaux* of a certain Directive 'reflecting not only a compromise between the opposing aims of consumer protection and freedom of contract, but also the contrast between consumer protection and consumer choice'.

[141] Joined Cases C-68/94 and 30/95 *France v Commission* [1998] ECR I-1375, para 167: 'with respect to the *travaux préparatoires*, it appears from the documents in the case that they cannot be regarded as expressing clearly the intention of the authors of the Regulation as to the scope of the term "dominant position". In those circumstances, the *travaux préparatoires* provide no assistance for the interpretation of the disputed concept'. This was cited and apparently accepted as authority for the need for *travaux* to show a 'clear intent' to be useful as an aid to construction in *Infant and Dietetic Foods Association* (n 139) [38]–[43] (Mitting J).

[142] Citing Lord Steyn's speech in *Effort Shipping Co Ltd v Linden Management SA* [1988] AC 605 (HL). In that case, speaking in the context of using *travaux* to interpret international treaties generally, Lord Steyn stated at 623F–G: 'I would be quite prepared, in an appropriate case involving truly feasible alternative interpretations of a convention, to allow the evidence contained in the travaux préparatoires to be determinative of the question of construction. But that is only possible where the court is satisfied that the travaux préparatoires clearly and indisputably point to a definite legal intention … Only a bull's-eye counts. Nothing less will do.'

[143] *Nova Productions Ltd v Mazooma Games Ltd* [2007] EWCA Civ 219, [2007] Bus LR 1032 [42] (Jacob LJ). See also *Green Lane Products Ltd v PMS International Group Ltd* [2008] EWCA Civ 358, [2008] Bus LR 1468 [74] (Jacob LJ), as to the need for a 'bull's eye' when referring to *travaux*; and in a similar vein *T-Mobile (UK) Ltd v Office of Communications* [2008] EWCA Civ 1373, [2009] 1 WLR 1565 [10] and [34] (Jacob LJ), regarding the lack of assistance provided by references made to *travaux* in that case; and *Kupeli v Atlasjet Havacilik Anonim Sirketi* [2017] EWCA Civ 1037, [2017] 4 Costs LO 517 [13]–[14] (Lewison LJ), citing *Effort Shipping* (n 142), as cited in that note, and stating that, there being no 'bull's eye' in the *travaux* cited to the Court in that case, 'I prefer, therefore, to concentrate on the Directive'.

from this may be limited.[144] By contrast, where the legislative history shows that a particular proposed approach was deliberately rejected in favour of another, this can provide a strong indication of legislative intent.[145] Likewise, *travaux* may provide clear support for an interpretation where they show that a provision was adopted to address a gap in legislation identified in a specific judicial decision[146] or where they plainly reveal an intention behind earlier drafts of legislation that has become somewhat obscured in the version finally adopted.[147]

---

[144] See, eg, Case C-216/98 *Commission v Greece* [2000] ECR I-8921, paras 17 and 22, where a failure to adopt a proposal made by the Economic and Social Committee to remove a word from a Directive was found not to assist in the interpretation of the final wording, as the CJEU considered that the proposed amendment would have been 'pointless'. See also, eg, *R (British Telecommunications plc) v Secretary of State for Culture, Olympics, Media and Sport* [2012] EWCA Civ 232, [2012] Bus LR 1766 [56] (Richards LJ), rejecting recourse to an argument from *travaux* that involved attributing 'to the Commission a speculative and improbable reason for its rejection of the proposal' in question.

[145] See *Banks* (n 134); *Bowden* (n 136); and see also *Buckinghamshire County Council* (n 1) [175]–[178] and [187]–[189] (Lord Neuberger and Lord Mance).

[146] See *Kuusijärvi* (n 135), and *Debt Collect* (n 139).

[147] See *Infant and Dietetic Foods Association* (n 139).

13

Research Tools and Works of Reference

13.1 Various research tools and works of reference are available for obtaining assistance in interpreting legislation. Our focus in this chapter is on using these resources to: (i) find legislation and related commentaries and materials; and (ii) ascertain the meaning of particular words or phrases in legislation.

Finding Legislation and Related Commentaries and Materials

13.2 The following are examples of sources that can be used to find the text of legislation (together, in some cases, with related commentaries and materials). As some sources may be better for certain tasks than others, we have also provided a brief description of the particular features of each source.

Printed Sources

13.3 *Current Law Statutes Annotated:*[1] this is a series of yearly volumes which contain the text of Acts made that year, as originally enacted. They also provide commentary on individual provisions, the overall schemes of Acts, the context of their enactment, and the objectives of the legislation (and specific provisions), along with references to relevant parliamentary debates (useful for Hansard research). This commentary has been referred to by the courts from time to time as a helpful source of guidance on questions of interpretation.[2]

---

[1] Published under the name '*Current Law Statutes*' between 1994 and 2004.

[2] See, eg, *R (GC) v Commissioner of Police of the Metropolis* [2011] UKSC 21, [2011] 1 WLR 1230 [66] (Lady Hale), regarding the purpose of s 6 of the Human Rights Act 1998; *Grays Timber Products Ltd v Revenue and Customs Commissioners* [2010] UKSC 4, [2010] 1 WLR 497 [56] (Lord Hope), regarding the 'theme' of the Finance Act 2003; and *Hounslow London Borough Council v Powell* [2011] UKSC 8, [2011] 2 AC 186 [64] (Lord Hope), regarding the factual background to a section of an Act, but see also at [58], where a suggestion in the commentary was not followed.

13.4   *Halsbury's Statutes of England and Wales*: this work in many volumes, currently in its fourth edition, sets out the up-to-date (that is, as amended) text of all UK public general Acts. It is kept updated through periodic loose-leaf updates, annual cumulative supplements and reissued volumes as required. The Acts are annotated to provide commentary on matters such as legislative purpose, amendments and repeals, defined terms, and relevant case law, along with references to relevant parliamentary debates (useful for Hansard research). As with *Current Law Statutes Annotated*, this commentary has been cited from time to time by the courts as a source of guidance on issues of statutory construction.[3]

Electronic Sources: Free to Access

13.5   *Legislation.gov.uk*: the National Archives provide access to a vast amount of both primary and delegated UK legislation, available free of charge at www.legislation.gov.uk. The website allows users to view both original (that is, as enacted) legislation (sometimes in original print pdf format) and a revised version incorporating amendments, although not all revised versions are fully up-to-date as the large task of fully updating all legislation is an ongoing one.[4] Legislation can be browsed by date or searched for by title, date or keyword, but a search for text within legislation is not possible. This service is particularly useful for finding historical original versions of legislation that may not be available (or available so easily) through subscription-only services. It can also be used to find materials such as Explanatory Notes and Explanatory Memoranda (as to which see Chapter 7.25–7.37).

13.6   *BAILII*: the British and Irish Legal Information Institute website allows the user to browse and search (including for text within legislation)[5] UK Acts from 1988 onwards in original (that is, as enacted) form and Acts before that date largely in revised (that is, updated) form.[6] UK statutory instruments (SIs) enacted since 1947 can also be searched[7] and browsed[8] in original form.[9]

---

[3] See, eg, *Al-Jedda v Secretary of State for the Home Department* [2013] UKSC 62, [2014] AC 253 [18] (Lord Wilson), regarding the purpose of an Act; *R v Meeking* [2012] EWCA Crim 641, [2012] 1 WLR 3349 [7] (Toulson LJ), regarding the provenance of a provision in an amendment and the purpose of that amendment.

[4] Available at www.legislation.gov.uk/changes indicates that at present all changes up to 2002 have been fully incorporated into the revised versions of legislation available on the site. That page allows users to check what other changes have been made since that date, and revised versions of legislation on the site will be often be marked to indicate that there are revisions yet to be incorporated, or where further changes may occur in future when certain provisions are brought into force.

[5] Available at www.bailii.org/form/search_legis.html.

[6] A description of the versions of primary and delegated legislation on BAILII, and access to primary legislation to browse, can be found at www.bailii.org/uk/legis/num_act.

[7] See the link at n 5 above.

[8] Available at www.bailii.org/uk/legis/num_reg.

[9] See the link at n 6 above.

13.7   *EUR-Lex*: EU legislation is available on the EUR-Lex website.[10] The search engine allows the user to search for text within legislation as well as for individual pieces of legislation by year and number. The website also provides a directory in which users can search by subject matter for legislation in force.[11] *Travaux préparatoires* for EU legislation can be accessed through the 'Preparatory acts' page of the website.[12]

Electronic Sources: Subscription-Only Services

13.8   *LexisLibrary*: this subscription-based service allows searches for up-to-date legislation by name and date, as well as searches for text within legislation. In addition, users are able to search within 'historical' versions of legislation as in force at any date back to 1 January 1998. Legislation can also be browsed by name.[13]

13.9   *Westlaw UK*: this subscription-based service also allows searches for up-to-date legislation by title, date and text. Keyword searches are also possible. The 'Advanced Search' option permits searches within 'historical' versions of legislation as in force at a date entered by the user back to 1991 for Acts and 1948 for SIs. Acts and SIs can be browsed from within the legislation tab by year and title. When looking at a particular provision as in force at a given date, the user can also select to view versions as in force at other dates (where these are available).

13.10   *Lawtel*: this subscription-based service does not provide up-to-date versions of legislation. But for legislation from 1984 onwards, it provides the original full text of Acts (which can be browsed by title and date, and searched by title, year, subject or text within the legislation) and SIs (which can be searched in the same ways, and also by reference to an enabling Act, or by reference to legislation which an SI has amended or by which it has been amended). The text of Acts is accompanied by a 'Statutory Status Table' which will explain when and how any provisions have been amended or repealed, with a similar feature used to indicate when changes have been made to SIs. Lawtel also provides copies of, or links to, numerous resources relating to the legislative history of an Act such as the original Bill and Explanatory Notes presented to Parliament, and various amended further versions of these created during the Bill's passage. In addition, it allows searches to be made for government 'Command Papers' (such as White Papers and Law Commission reports).

---

[10] Available at www.eur-lex.europa.eu/homepage.html; for an advanced search, see www.eur-lex.europa.eu/advanced-search-form.html.

[11] Available at www.eur-lex.europa.eu/browse/directories/legislation.html.

[12] Available at www.eur-lex.europa.eu/collection/eu-law/pre-acts.html. For further discussion of *travaux préparatoires*, see generally Chapter 12.50–12.55.

[13] In particular under the headings 'UK Parliament Acts' and 'UK Parliament SIs'.

Finding the Meaning of Words and Phrases

13.11   Sometimes one may wish to ascertain whether a particular word or phrase occurring in legislation has been previously considered by the courts, either in the context of that legislation or in a different context. Note, however, that since the role of the courts is to make decisions in fact-specific instances, the courts are unlikely to have sought to provide a general definition of a term where Parliament has not, as this would normally be 'inappropriate'.[14]

13.12   The courts will sometimes find it helpful to refer to decisions on the meaning of certain words in other statutory contexts, either to help ascertain their 'natural and ordinary meaning'[15] or as part of a process of reasoning by analogy.[16] However, real caution must be exercised in seeking to interpret terms in this way, because the meaning of words is always to be determined in the specific statutory context in which they appear.[17]

Electronic Case Law and Commentary Searches

13.13   One potentially useful research avenue to find cases which consider a particular word or phrase may be to enter the relevant word or phrase into the 'free text' search function of electronic case law databases. Some of these are subscription-only services such as LexisLibrary, Westlaw UK and Lawtel (discussed above), while others are free to use. The free services include:

—   *BAILII*:[18] this website contains a database of UK case law which allows free text searching.

---

[14]   See *R (Ghai) v Newcastle City Council* [2010] EWCA Civ 59, [2011] QB 591 [33] (Lord Neuberger MR). See also *RFC 2012 plc v Advocate General for Scotland* [2017] UKSC 45, [2017] 1 WLR 2767 [11] (Lord Hodge): 'the courts at the highest level have repeatedly warned of the need to focus on the words of the statute and not on judicial glosses, which may clarify or illustrate in a particular case but do not replace the statutory words'.

[15]   See, eg, *R v Barnet London Borough Council ex p Shah* [1983] 2 AC 309 (HL) 341C–344F (Lord Scarman), considering the natural meaning of 'ordinarily resident' in the Education Acts of 1962 and 1980 by reference to previous cases considering the same term when used in taxation legislation.

[16]   See, eg, *R v Unah* [2011] EWCA Crim 1837, [2012] 1 WLR 545 [8] (Elias LJ).

[17]   See, eg, *Knowles v Liverpool City Council* [1993] 1 WLR 1428 (HL) 1432F–G (Lord Jauncey): 'I do not find it helpful to look at the same words occurring in other statutes passed for different purposes as an aid to the construction of those words in this Act whose purpose is very clear.' See also, eg, *Unah* (n 16) [8]–[11] (Elias LJ), referring to decisions on the Terrorism Act 2000 to help construe the words 'reasonable excuse' in s 25(5) of the Identity Cards Act 2006, but stating: 'It is only with caution that one should seek to draw analogies with other statutory contexts where the concept of reasonable excuse is employed.'

[18]   Available at www.bailii.org; and see paragraph 13.6 above.

— *CURIA*:[19] this website allows the user to search the case law of the Court of Justice of the European Union.
— *HUDOC*:[20] this website allows the user to search the case law of the European Court of Human Rights.

13.14 As well as allowing free text searches of cases, the subscription-only services also provide other tools which may assist in finding cases relating to specific statutory terms:

— *LexisLibrary*: after locating the relevant statutory provision, the user can then (where these are available) click on 'Cases', 'Commentary' or 'Journals' in the 'Find out more' box. These links should bring up cases or commentary that consider the provision in question and potentially a particular word or phrase within in it.
— *Westlaw UK*: As with LexisLibrary, when looking at a particular provision, the user can (where available) click on 'Key Cases Citing', 'All Cases Citing', 'Journal Articles' or 'Books' to help find cases or commentary considering that provision. Westlaw also allows users to search for cases considering the meaning of specific words or phrases by entering the relevant term in the 'Term Defined' box on the Cases search tab. Further, users can search specifically for provisions defining particular terms by entering the relevant term in the 'Statutory Definition' box in the Legislation search tab.
— *Lawtel*: Lawtel's case search allows users to search for cases considering specific legislation by searching within the 'Legislation' box on the case search form.

Printed Sources

13.15 *Stroud's Judicial Dictionary of Words and Phrases*:[21] this is a work of reference in which one can search for a particular legislative word or phrase whose meaning has been considered by the courts in one or more contexts.

13.16 It is a work to which the courts may refer or be referred to indicate how words and phrases under consideration have been used in other legislative regimes. However, given the caution that must be employed in reading across a term's meaning from one statutory regime to another (see paragraph 13.12

---

[19] Available at curia.europa.eu/juris.
[20] Available at hudoc.echr.coe.int/eng#.
[21] Daniel Greenberg, *Stroud's Judicial Dictionary of Words and Phrases*, 9th edn (London, Sweet & Maxwell, 2016).

above), *Stroud's* may be most useful when seeking to demonstrate that a term has been held to have various meanings depending upon its context.[22]

13.17   *Dictionaries*: courts will often refer to dictionaries (and in particular a version of the *Oxford English Dictionary*) to help ascertain the meaning of words.[23] Although this is particularly useful with regard to words not defined in the legislation, even where terms are defined, their dictionary definition may still have some bearing on their meaning.[24]

---

[22] See, eg, *Maunsell v Olins* [1975] AC 373 (HL) 383G–H (Viscount Dilhorne) citing *Stroud's* as illustrating that: '"Premises" is an ordinary word of the English language which takes colour and content from the context in which it is used.' See also, eg, *R v Wood* [2000] 1 WLR 1687 (CA) 1693E (Roch LJ): 'the only assistance we derive from *Stroud's Judicial Dictionary* is that "convicted" can mean many different things depending upon the context in which the word appears'.

[23] See, eg, the references to the *Oxford English Dictionary* in *Shah* (n 15) 342C–D (Lord Scarman), as to the definitions of 'ordinarily' and 'resident'; and *BBC v Sugar (No 2)* [2012] UKSC 4, [2012] 1 WLR 439 [70] (Lord Walker), as to the definition of 'journalism'.

[24] See Chapter 6.23–6.24.

14

Checklist: Practical Considerations

14.1 The following is a practical checklist of some useful questions to consider when setting about a specific task of statutory interpretation under English law, which aims in large part to consolidate key elements of the exposition in the preceding chapters. It is not intended to be exhaustive, and specific situations may require further issues to be explored.

Application of Legislation

14.2 *Is the relevant statutory provision in force (or was it in force at the relevant date)?* It may seem obvious, but it is vital at the outset to check whether the provision in question is yet, or still, in force, or (as the case may be) was in force at the relevant date. That requires ascertaining: (1) if and when the relevant provision was brought into effect; (2) if and when it has been subject to repeal; and (if relevant as a result of amendment to the legislation) (3) what version applied at the relevant time. This is particularly important in the case of legislation which is old, very recent, or governs areas of rapidly developing social, scientific or technological change. The legislation services of various online professional legal resources[1] will usually state in the notes at the top or bottom of the page the date when a statutory provision came into force and whether it is still in force. Bear in mind that different provisions of a single piece of legislation may come into force at different times.

14.3 *Does the provision extend to the relevant jurisdiction?* Parliament will generally be taken to legislate for the whole of the UK unless it states otherwise. However, it is not uncommon for legislation to be intended to become part of the law only in certain parts of the UK. On occasion, Parliament may even legislate for other territories for which it has competence to do so. Accordingly, it is important to consider in which jurisdictions an enactment is intended to be law.[2]

---

[1] Such as LexisLibrary and Westlaw UK, discussed in Chapter 13.8–13.9.
[2] See Chapter 4.57–4.58.

14.4 *Did Parliament intend the legislation to apply to persons located and/or events occurring outside the UK?* Since Parliament's principal role is to act as the supreme legislature only for the UK, it generally does not seek to legislate in respect of persons located or events occurring abroad (although it may more readily seek to do so with respect to the conduct of British citizens located in other countries). However, in every case, whether and to what extent Parliament intends to legislate in respect of such persons and matters will be a question of construction, and in relevant cases that question will need to be considered.[3]

Relevance of Other Legislation and Aids to Interpretation

14.5 *Are Convention rights and/or EU law in play?* Ordinary principles of interpretation may be substantially affected by whether a piece of domestic legislation: (1) interferes with rights under the European Convention on Human Rights as given effect in English law by the Human Rights Act 1998 (HRA 1998) (thereby potentially engaging sections 3 or 4 of the HRA 1998);[4] and/or (2) gives effect to, or is affected by, the rules of EU law (thereby potentially engaging the '*Marleasing* principle' or the duty to disapply conflicting domestic law).[5] It is important to have these issues in mind at an early stage when construing domestic legislation.

14.6 *Are any international law obligations in play?* Similarly, although not to the same extent as where the HRA 1998 or EU law is in play, the interpretation of a measure may be affected by rules of international law which bind the UK. This may be the case where: (1) legislation is passed to give effect to certain obligations arising under international law; and/or (2) where a particular interpretation of legislation would place the UK in breach of its international law obligations.[6]

14.7 *Does any other legislation bear on the construction of the relevant provision?* The Interpretation Act 1978 applies to many enactments and may provide assistance as to the meaning of certain words or on other issues.[7] Further, as a general rule, the state of the law as at the date of an enactment's passage will be a relevant contextual factor in its construction.[8]

---

[3] See Chapter 4.59–4.67.
[4] See Chapter 10.
[5] See Chapter 12.15–12.29.
[6] See Chapter 9.22–9.36.
[7] See Chapter 8.
[8] See Chapter 3.52 and Chapter 5.25.

14.8   In addition, in some cases other legislation may have a particular bearing on the meaning of an enactment. This may be the case, for example, where legislation amends, repeals or consolidates existing legislation; where one piece of legislation refers to another; where Acts are *in pari materia*; or where secondary legislation has been made under its parent statute.[9]

14.9   *Can any guidance be derived from internal aids to interpretation?* Legislation often contains interpretation provisions, deeming provisions or other supplementary provisions which can assist the interpreter in ascertaining the meaning of its main contents. In addition, an enactment's title and preamble, and the various kinds of headings used in an enactment, can help inform its meaning.[10]

14.10   *Can any guidance be derived from external aids to interpretation?* Recourse can generally be had to materials produced as part of the legislative history of a measure to help elucidate its context and purpose. Additionally, although to a more limited extent, reference can be made to external aids to construction to help answer more detailed questions of interpretation that may arise in relation to a particular measure.[11]

Interpretive Considerations

14.11   *Where does the relevant provision appear in the overall structure of the legislation?* Although interpreters are often concerned with the meaning and operation of a particular provision (or provisions) within a piece of legislation, it is important to look at the general scheme, layout and structure of the whole enactment to place a provision in its immediate context. To gain an overview, it may be helpful to refer to the 'Arrangement of sections' or 'Arrangement of regulations' that usually appears at the beginning of a piece of legislation as published (whether in hard copy or online) and which serves in effect as a *table of contents* for the legislation. These can be found in the volume of *Current Law Statutes Annotated* that contains the relevant enactment and can also be viewed on the www.legislation. gov.uk website by clicking on the 'Table of Contents' for the relevant enactment.

14.12   *What is the purpose of the legislation and/or the relevant provisions within it?* As discussed at Chapter 3.45–3.48, one of the key factors to take into account in interpretation is the intended purpose of a provision or piece of legislation.

---

[9] See Chapter 5.
[10] See Chapter 6.
[11] See Chapter 7.

So, in construing the statutory language, one should seek to identify and bear in mind the purpose or purposes both of the particular provision in question and the legislation in which it is found.

14.13 The legislative purpose may be apparent from the terms of the Act itself. It may also be gleaned by reference to the wider context, such as earlier legislation in the same field, or the legislative history of a measure.

14.14 The determination of statutory purpose may have particular relevance in public law cases, in view of what is sometimes known as the '*Padfield* principle'— that powers conferred by statute must be used 'to promote the policy and objects of the Act', and not to 'frustrate the legislation's objectives'.[12]

14.15 *Does the provision confer a power or impose a duty?* Legislation often achieves its aims by conferring powers or imposing duties on persons—such as government ministers, public authorities, companies or individuals. The question may arise whether a particular provision grants a power or prescribes a duty. In such cases, it is crucial to consider whether the provision states that the relevant person 'may' do something (indicating that they are being given the *power* to do it) or 'shall'/'must'/'will' do something (indicating that they owe a *duty* to do it).[13]

14.16 Whenever a power or duty is conferred on a person, one should check to see whether the legislation has provided that its exercise is subject to any express conditions. Even in the absence of express conditions, the exercise of the relevant power or duty may still be subject to implied constraints. These may include, particularly where the power has been given to a public authority, the requirements of procedural fairness or the public law duties to act lawfully and reasonably.[14]

---

[12] See *Padfield v Minister of Agriculture, Fisheries and Food* [1968] AC 997 (HL) 1030B–D (Lord Reid): 'Parliament must have conferred the discretion with the intention that it should be used to promote the policy and objects of the Act; the policy and objects of the Act must be determined by construing the Act as a whole and construction is always a matter of law for the court.' See also *R (GC) v Commissioner of Police of the Metropolis* [2011] UKSC 21, [2011] 1 WLR 1230 [83] (Lord Kerr), referring to 'the principle for which *Padfield* ... is the seminal authority: that a discretion conferred with the intention that it should be used to promote the policy and objects of the Act can only be validly exercised in a manner that will advance that policy and those objects. More pertinently, the discretion may not be exercised in a way that would frustrate the legislation's objectives'. See further on the *Padfield* principle Michael Fordham, *Judicial Review Handbook*, 6th edn (Oxford, Hart Publishing, 2012) 534–36.

[13] As to the contrast between the meaning of 'may' and 'shall', see, eg, *Greenweb v Wandsworth London Borough Council* [2008] EWCA Civ 910, [2009] 1 WLR 612 [32] (Stanley Burnton LJ).

[14] As to the implication of duties of procedural fairness, see Chapter 4.23–4.26.

14.17 *Are listed items cumulative/conjunctive or alternative/disjunctive?* Statutory provisions often contain lists of matters, with separate items set out, for example, as (a), (b), (c) or (i), (ii), (iii) etc. These lists may be used to stipulate, for example, when or to whom a provision applies, or to place conditions on its use. In such cases, it is important to determine whether these listed items are *cumulative/ conjunctive* or *alternative/disjunctive*. Normally, cumulative conditions are denoted by the use of the word '*and*' before the final condition, with alternative conditions denoted by the word '*or*'.[15]

14.18 *Is there any reason to suppose that Parliament did not intend the words of the legislation to bear the meaning that is otherwise the most natural in the relevant context?* Parliament is presumed to act reasonably. Accordingly, where a proposed construction of legislation leads to absurd or otherwise highly unreasonable results that it is hard to believe Parliament could have intended, the courts will seek if possible to give the legislation a different construction which avoids that result. As a general rule, the more unreasonable the result of a proposed construction, the clearer the language that Parliament will need to have used before the courts will accept that this result was truly intended.[16] An even stronger principle (sometimes called the *principle of legality*) applies in the realm of fundamental precepts of the common law and human rights: the courts will presume that Parliament does not intend these to be removed or infringed unless legislation uses clear language to that effect, or it is a *necessary* implication of the legislation.[17]

14.19 *Could something have gone wrong with the legislative language?* In rare cases, the courts consider it permissible to correct mistakes in legislation where it is clear that something has gone wrong with the legislative language, and it is clear what was in fact intended and how the error should be fixed.[18]

---

[15] However, in exceptional cases, it may be appropriate to read one of these words as if it had the meaning of the other. In this regard, see *Federal Steam Navigation Co Ltd v Department of Trade and Industry* [1974] 1 WLR 505 (HL), where a majority of the House of Lords accepted that the reference in s 1(1) of the Oil in Navigable Waters Act 1955 to the 'owner or master' of a ship being criminally liable for the discharge of oil from that ship had to be read conjunctively as meaning, in effect, 'the owner and the master shall each be guilty': see at 522C–F (Lord Wilberforce). See also at 524 (Lord Salmon): 'There is certainly no doubt that generally it is assumed that "or" is intended to be used disjunctively and the word "and" conjunctively. Nevertheless, it is equally well settled that if so to construe those words leads to an unintelligible or absurd result, the courts will read the word "or" conjunctively and "and" disjunctively, as the case may be; or, to put it another way, substitute the one word for the other.' Lord Simon considered (see at 523C–E) that the case involved an error on the part of the draftsman, with the result that 'and' should be substituted for 'or' in the relevant provision. As to the courts' power to correct clear legislative errors, see Chapter 3.49–3.51.

[16] See Chapter 4.3–4.7.

[17] See Chapter 4.17–4.22.

[18] See Chapter 3.49–3.51.

14.20   *Could the drafting of an enactment have used alternative language to convey a particular meaning or effect?* If a statutory provision appears open to a particular interpretation, but it nevertheless remains questionable that that meaning was in fact intended, a useful way of testing if it was is to consider whether Parliament could easily have adopted a specific, alternative form of words which would have made this clear. While not usually conclusive, this can be a useful test exercise to carry out, as it is not uncommon for courts to state as part of their reasoning that if Parliament had intended a provision to have a certain effect, it would or could easily have said so expressly in the statutory language.[19] This consideration may have particular force where Parliament has used different language in different provisions of a single enactment, apparently opting not to adopt wording in one place that it had used elsewhere.[20]

14.21   *Does a provision impose a statutory threshold test?* Certain statutory provisions set threshold tests for the exercise of a power or imposition of a duty. Many forms of wording used in these tests are used in multiple contexts, and some common examples are considered below. However, it is important to note that the same words may bear different meanings in different legislative contexts and that many of these tests are intended to have a highly fact-sensitive application. Examples of wording frequently used in statutory threshold tests include the following:

— *Likely*: the word 'likely' in a statutory provision *may* mean 'probable' or 'more likely than not', but not necessarily. See, for example, Lord Nicholls' discussion of the meaning of this word in section 12(3) of the HRA 1998, determining that, depending on the factual circumstances of the case before the court, it could entail a lower threshold than 'more likely than not'.[21]

— *Reasonably practicable*: some statutory tests are defined by reference to what is (or is not) 'reasonably practicable'.[22] This has been said in one context to

---

[19] See, eg, *R (Forge Care Homes Ltd) v Cardiff and Vale University Health Board* [2017] UKSC 56, [2017] PTSR 1140 [36]–[37] (Lady Hale); *Austin v Southwark London Borough Council* [2010] UKSC 28, [2011] 1 AC 355 [38] (Lord Hope); *R (Buckinghamshire County Council) v Kingston upon Thames Royal London Borough Council* [2011] EWCA Civ 457, [2012] PTSR 854 [36] (Pill LJ); and *Feakins v Department for Environment, Food and Rural Affairs* [2005] EWCA Civ 1513, [2006] Env LR 44 [169] (Moses LJ).

[20] See, eg, *R v G* [2009] UKHL 13, [2010] 1 AC 43 [73] (Lord Rodger): 'Had Parliament intended to provide substantially the same defence to both sections, nothing would have been easier than to use the same language.' See further Chapter 3.22–3.25.

[21] See *Cream Holdings Ltd v Banerjee* [2004] UKHL 44, [2005] 1 AC 253 [20]–[22] (Lord Nicholls), and the cases there cited.

[22] See, eg, s 11(1) of the Freedom of Information Act 2000, requiring public authorities, where an 'applicant expresses a preference for communication' by certain means, to give effect to that preference 'so far as reasonably practicable', with s 11(2) providing: 'In determining for the purposes of this section whether it is reasonably practicable to communicate information by particular means, the public authority may have regard to all the circumstances, including the cost of doing so.'

connote something more than what is merely 'reasonable'.[23] But its meaning will vary depending on the statutory context,[24] and a determination of when something is or is not 'reasonably practicable' is likely to be highly fact-sensitive.[25]

— *Frivolous/vexatious*: many statutory provisions impose a threshold condition to prevent the pursuit of claims, complaints, applications or proceedings that are 'frivolous' and/or 'vexatious'.[26] A 'frivolous' application has been held, in the context of an application for a case to be stated from a Magistrates' Court, to mean one which was 'futile, misconceived, hopeless or academic',[27] and in the context of a claim to an Employment Tribunal, a 'frivolous claim' has been said to be one which is 'utterly hopeless', has 'no substance' or is 'bound to fail'.[28] In a similar vein, the 'hallmark of a vexatious proceeding' has been described as being:

[T]hat it has little or no basis in law (or at least no discernible basis); that whatever the intention of the proceeding may be, its effect is to subject the defendant to inconvenience, harassment and expense out of all proportion to any gain likely to accrue to the claimant; and that it involves an abuse of the process of the court, meaning by that a use of the court process for a purpose or in a way which is significantly different from the ordinary and proper use of the court process.[29]

---

[23] See *Palmer v Southend-on-Sea Borough Council* [1984] 1 WLR 1129 (CA) 1141D–E (May LJ), considering the scope of an exception to the time limit for bringing an employment claim which applied where it was 'not reasonably practicable' to bring the claim within the time limit: 'to construe the words "reasonably practicable" as the equivalent of "reasonable" is to take a view too favourable to the employee. On the other hand "reasonably practicable" means more than merely what is reasonably capable physically of being done'.

[24] ibid 1141E (May LJ), contrasting the meaning of 'reasonably practicable' in that context (see previous note) with 'its construction in the context of the legislation relating to factories'. See also, eg, *R (Friends of the Earth) v Secretary of State for Energy and Climate Change* [2009] EWCA Civ 810, [2010] Env LR 11 [24] (Maurice Kay LJ), considering that it was 'not appropriate to read across from previous legislation' in other contexts to determine the meaning of the phrase 'so far as reasonably practicable' in the legislation under consideration in that case.

[25] *Palmer* (n 23) 1141G (May LJ): 'the answer to the relevant question is pre-eminently an issue of fact for the industrial tribunal'.

[26] See, eg, Freedom of Information Act 2000, s 50(2)(c); Broadcasting Act 1996, s 114(2)(c).

[27] *R v North West Suffolk (Mildenhall) Magistrates' Court ex p Forest Heath District Council* [1998] Env LR 9 (CA) 16 (Lord Bingham CJ), stating that he considered it 'very unfortunate that the expression "frivolous" ever entered the lexicon of procedural jargon', given that its ordinary meaning was 'suggestive of light-heartedness or a propensity to humour'.

[28] *Balamoody v United Kingdom Central Council for Nursing, Midwifery and Health Visiting* [2001] EWCA Civ 2097, [2002] ICR 646 [45]–[46] (Ward LJ). See also at [77] (Sir Christopher Slade), considering that 'any application which has no chance whatever of success, whether because of the facts or the law or both, is capable of being regarded as "frivolous" and/or "vexatious"'.

[29] *Attorney General v Barker* [2000] 1 FLR 759 (CA) [19] (Lord Bingham CJ). See also *Balamoody* (n 28) [77] (Sir Christopher Slade), as cited in that note.

While the precise meaning of these terms may vary depending on their context, it seems clear that they are intended to impose a high threshold which is not 'lightly' to be considered to have been met.[30]

— *Real/substantial/significant*: certain provisions adopt words such as 'real',[31] 'substantial'[32] and 'significant'[33] as part of threshold tests, the meanings of which vary, as ever, depending on their statutory context.

---

[30] *Mildenhall* (n 27) 16 (Lord Bingham CJ).

[31] See, eg, *Easyair Ltd v Opal Telecom Ltd* [2009] EWHC 339 (Ch) [15] (Lewison J), summarising the key case law in the context of the test for summary judgment under CPR 24.2(2)(a) that a party must have 'no real prospect' of success in relation to a claim or issue. The case law provided that, to have a 'real prospect' of success, a party must have 'a "realistic" as opposed to a "fanciful" prospect of success', with a 'realistic' claim being 'one that carries some degree of conviction. This means a claim that is more than merely arguable'.

[32] The word substantial is inherently 'protean', and its meaning will depend upon the statutory context: see *R v Monopolies and Mergers Commission ex p South Yorkshire Transport Ltd* [1993] 1 WLR 23 (HL) 29A–E (Lord Mustill), in the context of the phrase 'substantial part of the United Kingdom' in s 64(3) of the Fair Trading Act 1973 (now repealed), explaining that '"substantial" accommodates a wide range of meanings. At one extreme there is "not trifling". At the other, there is "nearly complete", as where someone says that he is in substantial agreement with what has just been said. In between, there exist many shades of meaning, drawing colour from their context'. He warned against the courts seeking to redefine such 'inherently imprecise' words, but sought to give a 'general indication' of where its meaning lay in that context, using the phrase 'worthy of consideration for the purpose of the Act'. See also, eg, s 2(2) of the Contempt of Court Act 1981, which provides for a 'strict liability rule' (only) for 'a publication which creates a *substantial risk* that the course of justice in the proceedings in question will be seriously impeded or prejudiced' (emphasis added). The meaning of 'substantial risk' in this provision was considered in, eg, *Attorney General v Associated Newspapers Ltd* [2011] EWHC 418 (Admin), [2011] 1 WLR 2097 [22] (Moses LJ), who held (by reference to earlier cases) that it denoted a risk that was 'more than remote or minimal'.

[33] See, eg, *R v Lang* [2006] EWCA Crim 2864, [2006] 1 WLR 2509 [17] (Rose LJ), considering that, in the phrase 'significant risk' in ss 225(1) and 226(1) of the Criminal Justice Act 2003, 'significant' entailed 'a higher threshold than mere possibility of occurrence and in our view can be taken to mean (as in the Concise Oxford Dictionary) "noteworthy, of considerable amount … or importance"'. See also the discussion of this decision in *R v Stephens* [2007] EWCA Crim 1249, [2007] 2 Cr App R 26 [26]–[31] (Moore-Bick LJ), in the context of s 5 of the Domestic Violence, Crime and Victims Act 2004, the Court considering that the phrase 'significant risk' ought to bear its ordinary meaning and that the judge 'should not have sought to define it' in his direction to the jury.

INDEX

Academic writings (international law)
  effect on interpreting domestic law 9.3
  source of international law 9.19.2
Acts of Parliament *see* **Statutes**
Affirmative Resolution Procedure 1.25.3
Aids to interpretation
  ancillary components of statutes
    general rule 6.2–6.4
    headings 6.8–6.9
    preambles 6.7
    titles 6.5–6.6
  ancillary components of SIs as aids to
    interpretation
    general rule 6.2–6.4
    headings 6.12
    preambles 6.11
    titles 6.10
  external aids
    contextual factor 3.44.6
    explanatory memoranda 7.32–7.34
    explanatory notes 7.26–7.34
    general principles for use 7.43
    interpretation of treaties by English
      courts 9.57–9.61
    parliamentary statements
      (Hansard) 7.8–7.24
    post-legislative materials 7.42
    pre-legislative materials 7.38–7.41
    practical checklist 14.10
    travaux préparatoires
      (EU law) 12.50–12.55
    underlying rationale 7.3–7.5
  Human Rights Act 1998 7.18–7.19
  internal aids
    ancillary components of SIs 6.10–6.12
    ancillary components of statutes 6.2–6.9
    deeming provisions 6.25–6.28
    important part of context 3.44.2
    interpretation provisions 6.16–6.24
    practical checklist 14.9
    provisos 6.29–6.32
    punctuation 6.15
    saving provisions 6.33–6.35
    structure and format 6.13–6.14
  using other legislation as an aid to
    interpretation
    amended legislation 5.5–5.7

    consolidated legislation 5.20–5.24
    express references 5.29
    general rule 5.25–5.27
    interpretation of parent Acts 5.45–5.48
    interpretation of subordinate
      legislation 5.44
    overview of specific instances 5.28
    statutes *'in pari materia'* 5.31–5.43
'Always speaking' presumption 3.26–3.33
Amendments
  classification 5.3
  consolidating legislation 5.18
  construction of amended legislation 5.5–5.7
  effect on other legislation
  indication of amendments 2.17
  Interpretation Act 1978 8.11
  overview 1.18
  power to amend primary legislation
    using subordinate legislation,
    'Henry VIII clauses' 5.9–5.11
  power to amend to subordinate
    legislation 5.8
  powers under European Communities
    Act 1972 5.11
  references in other enactments
    effect on other legislation 5.4
  statutory instruments 1.21, 1.26, 5.8
  strict construction of certain powers to
    amend 5.10
Anatomy and structure *see* **Constituent**
  components of legislation
Ancillary components of legislation *see under*
  Constituent components of legislation
'And' 4.17
'Any' 6.20.3
Autonomous interpretation of EU law 12.40
Autonomous interpretation of
  treaties 9.50–9.52

BAILII 13.6, 13.13
***Barras* principle** 3.53–3.56, 5.38
Bills
  debate and scrutiny 1.11
  five-stage procedure 1.12
  introduction to Parliament 1.9
  role of House of Lords 1.13–1.14
  types of Bills 1.10

Charter of Fundamental Rights
  (EU law)   11.17–11.21
Checklist *see* **Practical checklist**
Commencement
  Interpretation Act 1978   8.2
  presumption against retroactivity   4.47
  provisions of IA 1978   8.6
  statutes   2.18.4, 2.9
  statutory instruments   2.29
Commencement Orders   1.22.4, 2.25
Committee stage for Bills   1.12
Committees scrutinising SIs   1.27
Common law
  legislation affecting basic tenets (legality
    principle)
    necessary implication or express
      language   4.21–4.22
    presumption against contrary
      legislation   4.17–4.20
  presumption against changes
    generally   4.13–4.16
Common sense approach   4.2
Compatibility
  with Convention rights under s 3 HRA 1998
    assessing compatibility   10.12
    obligation to interpret
      compatibly   10.4–10.22
  with customary international law   9.64
  declarations of incompatibility under
    HRA 1998
    applicability   10.25
    discretionary power   10.28
    effect of declaration   10.29
    importance   10.30
    last resort provision   10.26
    limited jurisdiction under s 4   10.23
    s 3 as an 'essential preliminary step'   10.24
    UK's margin of appreciation   10.27
  with EU law   11.25, 12.20.2, 12.20.3
  external aids and the Human Rights Act
    1998   7.18–7.19
  with international law generally   4.54
  presumption of compatibility with
    treaties   9.31–9.36
Components of legislation *see* **Constituent
  components of legislation**
Conformity
  presumption of conformity with customary
    international law   9.63
  duty of conforming interpretation with EU
    law   12.21–12.29
  presumption of conformity with
    treaties   9.22–9.30
  with international law generally   4.54
Conjunctive language *see* '**And**'
Consolidation
  amendments   5.18
  construction   5.20–5.24

  effect on other statutes   1.18
  meaning and scope   5.17
  repeals   5.19
  types   5.17
Constituent components of legislation
  ancillary components of SIs as aids to
    interpretation
    general rule   6.2–6.4
    headings   6.12
    preambles   6.11
    titles   6.10
  ancillary components of statutes as aids to
    interpretation
    general rule   6.2–6.4
    headings   6.8–6.9
    preambles   6.7
    titles   6.5–6.6
  EU law
    citations   11.49
    Joint Practical Guide   11.44–11.45
    preambles   11.48
    recitals   11.50–11.54
    structure and format   11.52–11.57
    titles   11.46–11.47
  statutes
    headings and divisions   2.19–2.20
    introductory components   2.2–2.11
    operative components   2.12–2.18
    titles   2.8
  statutory instruments
    headings and divisions   2.36
    introductory components   2.21–2.32
    operative components   2.33–2.35
    signature   2.37
    titles   2.28
Construction *see* **Interpretation and
  construction**
Consultation responses   7.38.2
Context
  Barras principle   3.53–3.57
  centrality to interpretation   3.43–3.44
  customary international law as context   9.65
  treaties as context   9.37
  interpretation of EU law   12.34,
    12.42–12.44
  interpretation of treaties in context   9.44
  Presumption that Parliament knows the
    law   3.52–3.57
  relevant contextual factors   3.44
Conventions *see* **Treaties**
Criminal statutes
  mens rea presumption   4.27–4.30
  need for clear penal provisions   4.8–4.12
  presumption against extraterritorial
    application   4.65–4.67
Crown
  see also **Royal Assent**
  making of treaties   9.8

presumption that legislation does not
bind   4.41
CURIA   13.13
Current Law Statutes Annotated   13.3
Customary international law
incorporation into/application in national
law   9.16–9.17
interpretation of domestic legislation
contextual role   9.65
presumption of compatibility   9.64
presumption of conformity   9.63
jus cogens   9.15
key elements   9.13–9.14

Decisions
Framework Decisions   11.38–11.39
type of EU legislation   11.34
**Declarations of incompatibility under
HRA 1998**
applicability   10.25
discretionary power   10.28
effect of declaration   10.29
importance   10.30
last resort provision   10.26
limited jurisdiction under s 4   10.23
s 3 as an 'essential preliminary step'   10.24
UK's margin of appreciation   10.27
Deeming provisions
aids to interpretation   6.25–6.28
contextual factor   3.44.2
ouster clauses   4.37.4
Definitions *see* **Meaning of words and
definitions**
Delegated acts (EU law)   11.35
Dictionaries   13.17
Directives
duty of conforming
interpretation   12.21–12.29
structure and format   11.57
type of EU legislation   11.30–11.33
Divisions
see also **Headings**
statutes   2.19–2.20
statutory instruments   2.36
'Does not include'   6.20.4

Effect of legislation *see* **Intended effect of
legislation**
**Effective judicial protection principle
(EU law)**   12.33.3
Ejusdem generis **principle**   3.36–3.39, 6.21
Electronic sources see **Internet tools and
references**
Equality (EU law)
autonomous interpretation   12.40
general principle of EU law   12.33.1
**Equivalence and effectiveness
(EU law)**   12.33.3

Errors in legislation
correction by consolidating statute   5.17.2
correction by courts   3.49–3.51
practical checklist   14.19
EU law
see also **Human Rights Act 1998;
International law**
constituent components of EU legislation
citations   11.49
Joint Practical guide   11.44–11.45
preambles   11.48
recitals   11.50–11.54
structure and format   11.52–11.57
titles   11.46–11.47
contextual factor   3.44.5
duty of conforming
interpretation   12.21–12.29
duty to disapply domestic law   12.15–12.20
Hansard as aid to interpretation   7.21
hierarchy of norms   11.13–11.37,
12.31–12.32
history and development of treaties
consequences of treaty
revisions   11.11–11.12
overview   11.3–11.4
Single European Act 1986 (SEA)   11.6
Treaty Establishing the EEC 1957
(TEC)   11.5
Treaty of Amsterdam 1997   11.8
Treaty of European Union 1992
(TEU)   11.7
Treaty of Lisbon 2007   11.10
Treaty of Nice 2001   11.9
Interpretation Act 1978   8.13
interpretation and construction
generally   12.33–12.55
general principles of EU law   11.22–11.23,
12.33
general rules of
interpretation   12.34–12.49
place within hierarchy of
norms   12.31–12.32
travaux préparatoires   12.50–12.55
interpretation of and effect on UK legislation
European Communities Act
1972   12.2–12.14
legal basis for application in UK
delegated legislation   12.6–12.7
'directly enforceable' provisions   12.3–12.5
primacy of directly enforceable rules   12.8
resolution of questions of EU
law   12.9–12.14
legislative procedure
overview   11.40–11.42
steps laid down by TFEU   11.43
overview   11.1–11.2
practical checklist   14.5
reference to the CJEU   12.9–12.14

sources
   Charter of Fundamental
      Rights   11.17–11.21
   Decisions   11.34
   delegated acts   11.35
   Directives   11.30–11.33
   Framework Decisions   11.38–11.39
   general principles   11.22–11.23
   hierarchy of norms   11.13–11.37
   implementing acts   11.36–11.37
   international law   11.24–11.27
   Regulations   11.29
   Treaties   11.14–11.16
   types of legislation   11.28
   travaux préparatoires   12.50–12.55
European Communities Act 1972
   amending powers   5.11
   legal basis for application of EU law
      delegated legislation   12.6–12.7
      'directly enforceable' provisions
         12.3–12.5
      primacy of directly enforceable rules   12.8
      resolution of questions of EU
         law   12.9–12.14
'Except'   6.20.5
Explanatory memoranda   1.28–1.29, 1.16,
7.35–7.37
Explanatory notes
   aids to interpretation
      statutes   7.26–7.31
      statutory instruments   7.32–7.34
   EU law   12.49
Expressio unius **principle**   3.40–3.42
Extent *see* **Territoriality**
External aids to interpretation
   see also **Internal aids to interpretation**
   contextual factor   3.44.6
   explanatory memoranda   7.32–7.34
   explanatory notes
      statutes   7.26–7.31
      statutory instruments   7.32–7.34
   general principles for use   7.43
   interpretation of treaties by English
      courts   9.57–9.61
   parliamentary statements
      Hansard   7.9, 7.21, 7.22–7.24
      historical exclusionary rule   7.8
      Human Rights Act 1998   7.18–7.19
      identification of context and mischief to
         which legislation is directed   7.17
      parliamentary privilege   7.12, 7.20
      Pepper v Hart, rule in   7.10–7.16
   post-legislative materials   7.42
   practical checklist   14.10
   pre-legislative materials   7.38–7.41
   travaux préparatoires   12.50–12.55
   underlying rationale   7.3–7.5
Extraterritoriality *see* **Territoriality**

Fairness presumption
   implicit requirement   4.23–4.25
   notice of decisions   4.26
Foreign languages
   interpretation of EU law   12.36, 12.39
   interpretation of treaties   9.53–9.56
Format
   aid to interpretation   6.13–6.14
   EU law   11.52–11.57
   practical checklist   14.11
Framework Decisions   11.38–11.39
Fundamental rights
   see also **Human Rights Act 1998**
   Charter of Fundamental Rights (EU
      law)   11.17–11.21
   customary international law (*jus
      cogens*)   9.15
   general principle of EU law   12.33.5
   legality principle
      necessary implication or express
         language   4.21–4.22
      presumption against contrary
         legislation   4.17–4.20

General principles
   EU law
      equality   12.33.1
      fundamental rights   12.33.5
      legal certainty   12.33.2
      non-discrimination   12.33.1
      source of law   11.22–11.23
   source of international law   9.18
'Golden rule'   3.11–3.15
Good faith
   general principle of international
      law   9.18
   interpretation of treaties   9.46
   Vienna Convention on the Law of
      Treaties   9.40–9.41
Green Papers   1.17.1, 7.38.1

*Halsbury's Statutes of England and
   Wales*   13.4
Hansard
   aid to interpretation   7.9
   EU law rights   7.21
   parliamentary statements as external
      aid   7.8–7.24
   practicalities of using   7.22–7.24
Headings
   see also **Divisions**
   aids to interpretation
      statutes   6.8–6.9
      statutory instruments   6.12
   statutes   2.19–2.20
   statutory instruments   2.36
'Henry VIII clauses'   5.9–5.11
HUDOC   13.13

Human Rights Act 1998
see also **EU law; Fundamental rights;
  International law**
aids to interpretation 7.18–7.19
declarations of incompatibility
  (s 4 HRA 1998)
  applicability 10.25
  discretionary power 10.28
  effect of declaration 10.29
  importance 10.30
  last resort provision 10.26
  limited jurisdiction under s 4 10.23
  requirement for 'essential preliminary
    step' 10.24
  UKs margin of appreciation 10.27
overview 10.1–10.3
practical checklist 14.5
section 3 interpretive obligations
  defined 10.4–10.6
  limits of 10.20–10.22
  performance of obligation 10.11–10.19
  scope of application 10.7–10.10
Hybrid Bills 1.10.3

ICJ statute 9.2
Implementing acts (EU law) 11.36–11.37
Implied repeal 5.15–5.16
'in pari materia' **statutes** 5.31–5.43, 14.8
'Includes' 6.20.2
**Intended effect of legislation, presumptions
  as to**
changes to common law 4.13–4.16
common sense approach 4.2
conformity or compatibility with
  international law 4.54
Crown not bound 4.41
evidential presumption of
  regularity 4.68–4.70
fairness presumption 4.23–4.26
legality principle 4.17–4.22
mens rea for statutory offences 4.27–4.30
no authorisation of tortious conduct 4.40
no exclusion of judicial review 4.31–4.39
penal provisions to be strictly
  construed 4.8–4.12
practical checklist 14.18
reasonableness 4.3–4.7
retrospectivity 4.42–4.53
territoriality 4.55–4.67
Interaction of legislation
amendments
  classification 5.3
  construction of amended
    legislation 5.5–5.7
  European Communities Act 1972 5.11
  power to amend primary legislation using
    subordinate legislation, '*Henry VIII*
    clauses' 5.9–5.11

  power to amend to subordinate
    legislation 5.8
  references in other enactments 5.4
  strict construction of certain powers to
    amend 5.10
consolidation
  amendments 5.18
  construction 5.20–5.24
  meaning and scope 5.17
  precedent 5.23
  repeals 5.19
overview 5.1–5.2
repeal/revocation
  defined 5.12
  implied repeal 5.15–5.16
  Interpretation Act 1978 5.13
using other legislation as an aid to
  interpretation
  amended legislation 5.5–5.7
  consolidated legislation 5.20–5.24
  express references 5.29
  general rule 5.25–5.27
  interpretation of parent Acts
    5.45–5.48
  interpretation of subordinate
    legislation 5.44
  overview of specific instances 5.28
  statutes '*in pari materia*' 5.31–5.43
Internal aids to interpretation
see also **External aids to interpretation**
ancillary components of SIs
  headings 6.12
  preambles 6.11
  titles 6.10
ancillary components of statutes
  general rule 6.2–6.4
  headings 6.8–6.9
  preambles 6.7
  titles 6.5–6.6
contextual factor 3.44.2
deeming provisions 6.25–6.28
interpretation provisions
  importance 6.16
  language and effect 6.19–6.24
  scope and location 6.17–6.18
practical checklist 14.9
provisos 6.29–6.32
punctuation 6.15
saving provisions 6.33–6.35
structure and format 6.13–6.14
International law
see also **EU law; Human Rights Act 1998**
contextual factor 3.44.5
customary international law
  interpretation of domestic
    legislation 9.62–9.65
  contextual role 9.65
  presumption of compatibility 9.64

presumption of conformity   9.63
source of law   9.13–9.17
practical checklist   14.6
presumption of conformity or compatibility
  with   4.54
source of EU law   11.24–11.27
sources
  academic writings   9.19.2
  customary international law   9.13–9.17
  general principles   9.18
  ICJ statute   9.2
  judicial decisions   9.19.1
treaties
  context for interpretation   9.37
  interpretation of domestic
    legislation   9.20–9.37
  presumption of compatibility
    9.31–9.36
  presumption of conformity   9.22–9.30
  source of law   9.4–9.12
Internet tools and references
  BAILII   13.6
  case law databases   13.13–13.14
  legislation.gov.uk   13.5
  subscription only services
    Lawtel   13.10
    LexisLibrary   13.8
    Westlaw UK   13.9
Interpretation Act 1978
  application
    statutes   8.3
    subordinate legislation   8.4
  commencement   8.2
  key provisions
    amendments   8.11
    commencement   8.6
    definitions   8.7
    EU law   8.13
    gender and number   8.8
    powers and duties   8.10
    repeals   8.12
    subordinate legislation   8.9
  practical checklist   14.7
  repeals   5.13
Interpretation and construction
  see also **Interaction of legislation**
  Barras principle   3.53–3.57
  centrality of context   3.43–3.44
  correction of errors by courts   3.49–3.51
  determining objective intention of
    legislator   3.2–3.8
  effect of EU law on domestic law
    duty of conforming
      interpretation   12.21–12.29
    duty to disapply domestic
      law   12.15–12.20
  EU law
    generally   12.33–12.55

general principles   11.22–11.23, 12.33
general rules   12.34–12.49
place within hierarchy of
  norms   12.31–12.32
travaux préparatoires   12.50–12.55
place within hierarchy of
  norms   12.31–12.32
external aids to interpretation *see* **External
  aids to interpretation**
impact of customary international law
  contextual role   9.65
  presumption of compatibility   9.64
  presumption of conformity   9.63
impact of HRA   1998
  declarations of
    incompatibility   10.23–10.30
  limits of s 3   10.20–10.22
  obligation under s 3   10.4–10.6
  overview   10.1–10.3
  performance of obligation under
    s 3   10.11–10.19
  scope of s 3   10.7–10.10
importance of purpose   3.45–3.48
impact of treaties
  context for interpretation   9.37
  presumption of compatibility   9.31–9.36
  presumption of conformity   9.22–9.30
intended effect of legislation *see* **Intended
  effect of legislation, presumptions as to**
internal aids to interpretation *see* **Internal
  aids to interpretation**
interpretation of treaties
  core elements   9.42–9.46
  general rule   9.40–9.41
  as international instruments
    9.48–9.56
  international tribunal rules   9.38
  subsequent practice   9.47
  supplementary means (external
    aids)   9.57–9.61
  Vienna Convention on the Law of
    Treaties   9.39, 9.40, 9.55, 9.57
language presumptions
  consistency of meaning   3.22–3.24
  different words have different
    meanings   3.25
  general provisions do not override specific
    provisions (*generalia specialibus non
    derogant*)   3.21
  language must be given some effective
    meaning   3.18–3.20
  language used correctly and
    exactly   3.16–3.17
  as understood in current
    circumstances ('always speaking'
    presumption)   3.26–3.33
  words given ordinary or natural
    meaning   3.11–3.15

language principles
ejusdem generis principle 3.36–3.39
expressio unius principle 3.40–3.42
noscitur a sociis principle 3.34–3.35
legal basis for application of EU law
delegated legislation 12.6–12.7
'directly enforceable' provisions
12.3–12.5
primacy of directly enforceable rules 12.8
resolution of questions of EU
law 12.9–12.14
practical checklist
aids to interpretation 14.5–14.10
extraterritoriality 14.4
interpretive considerations 14.11–14.21
is the statutory provision in force? 14.2
territorial extent and
application 14.3–14.4
presumption that Parliament knows the
law 3.52–3.57
reading statutory language
appropriate starting point 3.9
role of 'rules' of interpretation 3.10
role of subsequent practice 3.58–3.60
Interpretation provisions
importance 6.16
language and effect
'any' 6.20.3
defined terms 6.23–6.24
'does not include' 6.20.4
'except' 6.20.5
forms of wording 6.19
'includes' 6.20.2
lists 6.21
'means' 6.20.1
weight to be attached 6.22
operative component of statute 2.18.1
scope and location 6.17–6.18

**Joint Committee on Statutory Instruments
(JCSI)** 1.27.1
Judicial decisions
Barras principle 3.53–3.56
contextual factor 3.44.4, 12.55
presumed endorsement by
Parliament 3.53–3.57
presumption Parliament knows the
law 3.52–3.57
source of international law 9.19.1
Judicial review
implied limitations on availability 4.39
ouster clauses
applicability of strict interpretation
presumption 4.33–4.35
presumption of strict interpretation
4.31–4.32, 4.36–38
Jurisdiction see **Territoriality**
Jus cogens 9.15

Languages see **Foreign languages**
treaties 9.53–9.56
Law Commission
recommended consolidation and
amendments 5.17.3
reports as external aids 7.38.3
Lawtel 13.10, 13.14
Legal certainty
EU law
duty of conforming interpretation 12.24
general principle of EU law 12.33.2
external aids to interpretation 7.43.3.2
purposive interpretation 3.47–3.48
presumption against retroactivity 4.42
recourse to *Hansard* 7.14
reliance on subsequent practice 3.59
Legal professional privilege
legality principle 4.20
Legality principle
instances
generally 4.20
presumption of fairness 4.23–4.26
presumption of *mens rea* 4.27–4.39
presumption of notice 4.26
presumption of judicial oversight of
executive decisions 4.31–4
necessary implication or express
language 4.21–4.22
presumption against contrary
legislation 4.17–4.22
Legislation.gov.uk 13.5
Legislative procedure
Bills
debate and scrutiny 1.11
five-stage procedure 1.12
introduced to Parliament 1.9
role of House of Lords 1.13–1.14
types of Bills 1.10
effect on other statutes 1.18
EU law
overview 11.40–11.42
steps laid down by TFEU 11.43
pre and post-legislative materials 1.14
statutory instruments
Affirmative Resolution Procedure
1.25.3
amendments 1.26
committee scrutiny 1.27
enabling powers 1.19
laying before Parliament 1.25.1
Negative Resolution Procedure 1.25.2
Super-Affirmative Procedure 1.25.4
Lex specialis (EU law) 12.45
LexisLibrary 13.8, 13.14
Lists of matters
language and effect 14.17
practical checklist 14.17
Local Acts and personal Acts 1.8.2

Margin of appreciation 10.27
Marleasing **principle** 12.21–12.29
Meaning of words and definitions
  deeming provisions 6.25–6.28
  Interpretation Act 1978 8.7
  interpretation provisions
    'any' 6.20.3
    defined terms 6.23–6.24
    'does not include' 6.20.4
    'exceptions' 6.20.5
    forms of wording 6.19
    'includes' 6.20.2
    'lists' 6.21
    'means' 6.20.1
    weight to be attached 6.22
  language presumptions
    consistency of meaning 3.22–3.24
    different words have different
      meanings 3.25
    language must be given some effective
      meaning 3.18–3.20
  lists of matters 14.17
  practical checklist 14.20
  primacy of the text 3.13
  reading statutory language
    appropriate starting point 3.9
    consistency of meaning 3.22–3.24
    different words have different
      meanings 3.25
    ejusdem generis principle 3.36–3.39
    expressio unius principle 3.40–3.42
    general provisions do not override specific
      provisions (*generalia specialibus non*
      derogant) 3.21
    language must be given some effective
      meaning 3.18–3.20
    language used correctly and
      exactly 3.16–3.17
    noscitur a sociis principle 3.34–3.35
    'rules' of interpretation 3.10
    as understood in current
      circumstances ('always speaking'
      presumption) 3.26–3.33
    words given ordinary or natural
      meaning 3.11–3.15
  research tools and reference works
    internet case law databases 13.13–13.14
    overview 13.11–13.12
    technical meanings 3.15
'Means' 6.20.1
Mens rea **presumption** 4.27–4.30
Mischief rule 3.46
Money Bills 1.14
Multiple languages *see* **Foreign languages**

Necessary implication
  generally 4.21–4.22
  legal powers deriving from the Royal
    prerogative 1.5

  legislation contrary to fundamental
    norms 4.17, 4.21–4.22
  presumption as to extent 4.57
  presumption of *mens rea* 4.27, 4.30
  presumption of notice 4.26
  presumption that legislation does not bind
    the Crown 4.41
  presumption that tortious conduct not
    authorised 4.40
  removal of rights of appeal in criminal
    cases 4.33
Negative Resolution Procedure 1.25.2
Non-discrimination (EU law)
  autonomous interpretation 12.40
  general principle of EU law 12.33.1
  TEU Art 2 11.23
Non-retroactivity *see* **Retrospectivity**
Noscitur a sociis **principle** 3.34–3.35

Object and purpose
  core principles 3.2–3.8
  identification
    generally 3.45
    use of external aids 7.43
    use of internal aids 6.4.1
  importance to interpretation 3.45–3.48
  interpretation of EU law 12.34, 12.42–12.44
  'mischief rule' 3.46
  practical checklist 14.12–14.14
Orders in Council 1.7, 1.22.2
Orders of Council
Ouster clauses
  application of strict interpretation
    presumption 4.33–4.35
  presumption of strict interpretation
    4.31–4.32, 4.36–4.38
Oxford English Dictionary 13.17

Parent Acts
  enabling powers 1.19–1.21
  interaction with subordinate legislation
    interpretation of parent Acts 5.45–5.48
    interpretation of subordinate
      legislation 5.44
  parliamentary scrutiny of SIs 1.23–1.26
Parliamentary privilege 5.16.3, 7.12,
  7.20–7.21
Parliamentary statements
  external aid to interpretation 7.8–7.24
  Hansard
    aid to interpretation 7.9
    EU law rights 7.21
    practicalities of using 7.22–7.24
  historical 'exclusionary' rule 7.8
  Human Rights Act 1998 7.18–7.19
  identification of context and mischief to
    which legislation is directed 7.17
  parliamentary privilege 7.12, 7.20–7.21
  Pepper v Hart, rule in 7.10–7.16

Penal provisions
legal certainty (EU law)   12.33.2
maximum sentences   4.30.3
need for clear law   4.8–4.12
procedural changes   4.52
strict interpretation   3.51, 4.8–4.12
Pending proceedings *see* **Retrospectivity**
Pepper v Hart, **rule in**   7.10–7.16
Plain meaning *see* **Primacy of the text**
Post-legislative materials
see also **Pre-legislative materials**
role in interpretation   7.42
Practical checklist
aids to interpretation
EU law   14.5
external aids to interpretation   14.10
Human Rights Act 1998   14.5
internal aids to interpretation   14.9
international law   14.6
Interpretation Act 1978   14.7
legislation *in pari materia*   14.8
application of legislation
extraterritoriality   14.4
is the statutory provision in force?   14.2
territorial extent and
application   14.3–14.4
interpretive considerations
could Parliament have used different
language?   14.20
errors in drafting   14.19
imposition of power or duty
14.15–14.16
intended effect of legislation   14.18
lists of matters   14.17
purpose   14.12–14.14
statutory threshold tests   14.21
structure and format   14.11
Pre-legislative materials
see also **Post-legislative materials**
aids to interpretation   7.38–7.41
relationship with of legislative
process   1.15–1.17
Preambles
aids to interpretation
statutes   6.7
statutory instruments   6.11
EU law   11.48
statutes   2.10
statutory instruments   2.31–2.32
Precedent
'rules' of construction   3.10
construction of consolidating
legislation   5.20, 5.23
ICJ decisions   9.19.1
Presumptions
Barras principle   3.53–3.56
compatibility
with customary international law   9.64
with treaties   9.31–9.36

conformity
with customary international law   9.63
with treaties   9.22–9.30
implied repeal   5.16
intended effect of legislation
changes to common law   4.13–4.16
common sense approach   4.2
conformity or compatibility with
international law   4.54
Crown not bound   4.41
evidential presumption of
regularity   4.68–4.70
fairness presumption   4.23–4.26
legality principle   4.17–4.22
mens rea for statutory offences   4.27–4.30
no authorisation of tortious conduct   4.40
no exclusion of judicial review   4.31–4.39
penal provisions to be strictly
construed   4.8–4.12
reasonableness   4.3–4.7
retrospectivity   4.42–4.53
territoriality   4.55–4.67
presumption that Parliament knows the
law   3.52–3.57
reading statutory language
consistency of meaning   3.22–3.24
different words have different
meanings   3.25
general provisions do not override specific
provisions   3.21
language must be given some effective
meaning   3.18–3.20
language used correctly and
exactly   3.16–3.17
as understood in current
circumstances ('always speaking'
presumption)   3.26–3.33
words given ordinary or natural
meaning   3.11–3.15
territoriality presumptions
as to extent   4.57–4.58
against extraterritorial
application   4.59–4.64
application of criminal statutes   4.65–4.67
Primacy of the text
interpretation of treaties by English
courts   9.42
'plain meanings'   3.13
Primary legislation
status of Orders in Council and Royal
Charters   1.7
statutes
legislative procedure   1.9
status as law   1.5–1.6
statutory instruments
distinguished   1.1–1.4
types of statute   1.8
Principles *see* **General principles**
Private Bills   1.10.2

Privilege
   against self-incrimination   4.3, 4.52
   legal professional privilege (legality
      principle)   4.20
   parliamentary privilege   5.16.3, 7.12, 7.20,
      7.20–7.21
Procedural changes *see* **Retrospectivity**
Proportionality (EU law)   12.33.4
Provisos
   contextual factor   3.44.2
   interpretation of and role as internal
      aid   6.29–6.32
Public Bills   1.10.1
Public general Acts   1.8.1
Punctuation   6.15
Purpose *see* **Object and purpose**
Purposive construction
   criminal law statutes   3.48, 3.51
   generally   3.45–3.51
   interpretation of treaties by English
      courts   9.45
   shift towards   3.47

Reasonableness presumption   4.3–4.7
Recitals (EU law)
   aid to interpretation   12.46–12.47
   component of EU legislation   11.50–11.54
Reference works *see* **Research tools and
   reference works**
Regularity presumption   4.68–4.70
Regulations
   domestic legislation   1.22.1
   EU law
      structure and format   11.56
      type of EU legislation   11.29
Repeals/revocation
   consolidating legislation   5.19
   defined   5.12
   effect on other statutes   1.18
   implied repeal   5.15–5.16
   Interpretation Act 1978   5.13, 8.12
   statutory instruments   1.21
Research tools and reference works
   electronic sources
      BAILII   13.6
      legislation.gov.uk   13.5
   finding the meaning of words
      internet case law databases   13.13–13.14
      overview   13.11–13.12
      printed sources   13.15–13.17
   printed sources
      Current Law Statutes Annotated   13.3
      *Halsbury's Statutes of England and
         Wales*   13.4
   subscription only services
      Lawtel   13.10
      LexisLibrary   13.8
      Westlaw UK   13.9

Retroactivity *see* **Retrospectivity**
Retrospectivity
   duty of conforming interpretation with EU
      law   12.24
   general presumption against   4.42–4.46
   Human Rights Act 1998   10.9
   specific presumptions
      against 'retroactive' legislation   4.47–4.48
      against interference with 'vested
         rights'   4.49–4.50
      that pending proceedings not
         affected   4.51
      that procedural changes apply
         generally   4.52–4.53
Revocation   5.12
Rights *see* **Fundamental rights; Human Rights
   Act 1998**
Royal Assent
   Interpretation Act 1978   8.6
   legislative process   1.6, 1.12–1.14
Royal Charters   1.7
Rules   1.22.3

Saving provisions
   contextual factor   3.44.2
   interpretation of and role as internal
      aid   6.33–6.35
**Secondary Legislation Scrutiny Committee
   (SLSC)**   1.27.3
**Select Committee on Statutory Instruments
   (SCSI)**   1.27.2
Self-incrimination *see* **Privilege**
Signature
   EU legislation
      Directives   11.57
      Joint Practical Guide   11.46
      Regulations   11.56
   statutory instruments   2.37
   treaties   9.6
Single European Act 1986 (SEA)   11.7
Sources of law
   EU law
      Charter of Fundamental
         Rights   11.17–11.21
      Decisions   11.34
      delegated acts   11.35
      Directives   11.30–11.33
      Framework Decisions   11.38–11.39
      general principles   11.22–11.23, 12.33
      implementing acts   11.36–11.37
      international law   11.24–11.27
      Regulations   11.29
      Treaties   11.14–11.16
      types of legislation   11.28
   international law
      academic writings   9.19.2
      customary international law   9.13–9.17
      general principles   9.18

ICJ statute 9.2
judicial decisions 9.19.1
treaties 9.4–9.12
Statutes
see also **Statutory instruments**
application of Interpretation Act 1978 8.3
constituent components
headings and divisions 2.19–2.20
introductory components 2.2–2.11
operative components 2.12–2.18
titles 2.8
explanatory notes 7.26–7.31
HRA 1998
applicability of 10.8
declarations of incompatibility 10.25
'*in pari materia*' 5.31–5.43, 14.8
legislative procedure
Bills 1.9–1.14
effect on other statutes 1.18
pre-parliamentary and parliamentary
materials 1.15–1.17
status as primary legislation 1.5–1.7
statutory instruments distinguished 1.1–1.4
types of statute 1.8
Statutory instruments
see also **Statutes**
power to amend other legislation 1.21,
5.9–5.11
application of Interpretation Act 1978 8.4
constituent components
headings and divisions 2.36
introductory components 2.21–2.32
operative components 2.33–2.35
signature 2.37
titles 2.28
explanatory notes 1.28–1.29, 7.32–7.34
interaction with other legislation
interpretation of parent Acts 5.45–5.48
interpretation using parent Act 5.44
legislative procedure
Affirmative Resolution Procedure 1.25.3
amendments 1.26
committee scrutiny 1.27
enabling powers 1.19
laying before Parliament 1.25.1
Negative Resolution Procedure 1.25.2
Super-Affirmative Procedure 1.25.4
parliamentary scrutiny and
control 1.23–1.27
status in law 1.20
statutes distinguished 1.1–1.4
types of statutory instrument 1.22
ultra vires 1.20, 10.25
Statutory interpretation *see* **Interpretation and
construction**
Statutory language
appropriate starting point 3.9
consistency of meaning 3.22–3.24

different words have different meanings 3.25
ejusdem generis principle 3.36–3.39
expressio unius principle 3.40–3.42
general provisions do not override specific
provisions (*generalia specialibus non
derogant*) 3.21
language must be given some effective
meaning 3.18–3.20
language used correctly and
exactly 3.16–3.17
noscitur a sociis principle 3.34–3.35
'rules' of interpretation 3.10
language must be given some effective
meaning 3.18–3.20
technical meanings 3.15
as understood in current
circumstances ('always speaking'
presumption) 3.26–3.33
words given ordinary or natural
meaning 3.11–3.15
Statutory threshold test 14.21
***Stroud's Judicial Dictionary of Words and
Phrases*** 13.15–13.16
Structure and format
aids to interpretation 6.13–6.14
EU law 11.52–11.57
practical checklist 14.11
Subordinate legislation
commencement orders 1.22.4
delegated acts (EU law) 11.35
delegated powers in statute 2.18.3
European Communities Act 1972
12.6–12.7
HRA 1998
applicability of 10.8
declarations of incompatibility 10.25
interaction with other legislation
interpretation of parent Acts 5.45–5.48
interpretation using parent Act 5.44
Interpretation Act 1978
applicability 8.4
construction of 8.9
Orders in Council 1.22.2
power to amend primary legislation using
subordinate legislation, '*Henry VIII*
clauses' 5.9–5.11
power to amend subordinate legislation 5.8
power to make subordinate
legislation 1.19–1.20
regulations 1.22.1
rules 1.22.3
status in law 1.19–1.20
statutory instruments
explanatory notes 1.28–1.29, 7.32–7.34
legislative procedure 1.23–1.27
parliamentary scrutiny and
control 1.23–1.27
revocation 5.12

statutes distinguished 1.1–1.4
   types of statutory instrument 1.22
ultra vires 1.20, 10.25
Subsequent practice
   interpretation of treaties by English
     courts 9.47
   role in interpretation 3.58–3.60
Super-Affirmative Procedure 1.25.4
Supplementary means 9.57–9.61
Surplusage, presumption against 3.18

Technical meanings 3.15
Territoriality
   extent and application
     distinguished 4.55–4.58
   practical checklist 14.4
   presumptions
     as to extent 4.57–4.58
     against extraterritorial
       application 4.59–4.64
     application of criminal statutes 4.65–4.67
Threshold tests 14.21
Titles
   aids to interpretation
     statutes 6.5–6.6
     statutory instruments 6.10
   EU law
     aid to interpretation 11.48
     constituent components of
       legislation 11.46–11.47
   statutes 2.8
   statutory instruments 2.28
**Tortious conduct not authorised, presumption
   that** 4.40
Travaux préparatoires
   EU law 12.50–12.55
   interpretation of treaties by English
     courts 9.57–9.61
Treaties
   binding effect 9.5–9.17

Crown function in UK 9.8
different methods of adoption 9.12
'giving effect to' 9.11
history and development of EU treaties
   consequences of treaty
     revisions 11.11–11.12
   overview 11.3–11.4
   Single European Act 1986 (SEA) 11.6
   Treaty Establishing the EEC 1957
     (TEC) 11.5
   Treaty of Amsterdam 1997 11.8
   Treaty of European Union 1992
     (TEU) 11.7
   Treaty of Lisbon 2007 11.10
   Treaty of Nice 2001 11.9
incorporation into national law 9.9–9.10
interpretation by English courts
   core elements 9.42–9.46
   general rule 9.40–9.41
   as international instruments 9.48–9.56
   international tribunal rules 9.38
   subsequent practice 9.47
   supplementary means (external
     aids) 9.57–9.61
   Vienna Convention on the Law of
     Treaties 9.39, 9.40, 9.55, 9.57
interpretation of domestic legislation
   context for interpretation 9.37
   key considerations 9.20–9.21
   presumption of compatibility
     9.31–9.36
   presumption of conformity 9.22–9.30
source of EU law 11.14–11.16
terminology 9.4

Vested rights *see* **Retrospectivity**

Westlaw UK 13.9, 13.14
White Papers 1.17.2
Words *see* **Meaning of words and definitions**